THE LIMITED ELITE

Donald B. Rosenthal

THE LIMITED ELITE:
Politics and
Government in
Two Indian Cities

The University of Chicago Press
Chicago and London

International Standard Book Number: 0-226-72810-2
Library of Congress Catalog Card Number: 70-121818

The University of Chicago Press: Chicago 60637
The University of Chicago Press, Ltd., London W.C.1

Contents

Preface   vii

1. The Context of Local Politics   1

2. Politicians and Political Groups   26

3. Electoral Behavior in Agra   59

4. The Poona Electoral Process in 1962   79

5. Corporator Participation in Agra and Poona   104

6. Contests for Municipal Office   133

7. Sources of Conflict in Municipal Government   153

8. Administrative Politics   180

9. Local Politics Outside the Municipal Arenas   210

10. Municipal Politics in 1968   246

11. Municipal Politics and the Indian Political System   282

Appendix: Political Identifications in the Two Cities   295

Notes   306

List of Abbreviations   348

Glossary   350

Index of Persons Mentioned   353

Subject and Author Index   356

Preface

After submitting cheerfully to a long interview and generously providing me with a substantial dinner, the man who served as mayor of Poona in early 1964 felt it was his turn to ask a few questions. He began with the usual inquiries into the American character: Was there really a conspiracy of the Right behind the Kennedy assassination, as some of the Indian papers were insisting? Why were race relations in the United States so bad? Not having formulated pat answers to these questions, I fumbled as best I could to come up with responses which would do more than simply turn aside his earnest interest from questions which were obviously painful for an American to answer. Perhaps bored with my excessively cautious responses, he turned to a new subject: "You have been in Poona for some months now studying the working of local self-government. You are a professor of political science in the United States. What do you think we can do to make our municipal corporations work better?"

If I had some trouble answering his previous questions, I found this last inquiry both strangely poignant coming from a man who was highly skilled in the ways of local politics, and challenging to me as a political scientist. Although the mayor pressed me for specific recommendations and admitted to a variety of very specific frustrations with his position, I believe that my responses under fire were rather poor. Even today, I am not certain that political scientists are or can be *trained* to play meaningful policy roles either here or in other nations. If policy recommendations flow from the work of some political scientists, they come usually as afterthoughts or as outgrowths of personal preferences. Academic preparation in political science of any quality should normally make one cautious about attempting to bridge the gap between the world of practical men and the limited sphere of activity of the intellectual.

In the case of national politics, at least, a study of leading politicians may have important policy implications even if these are not directly verbalized; when one comes to research on Indian urban politics, however, the justifications are less readily translated into policy terms. At a time when demands for "relevant" research are growing, a study of politics in two Indian cities which merely attempts to describe and understand the situation as it is may appear to be of limited value. However, as previous studies of Indian politics have suggested, a proper understanding of what happens at the national or state levels in India depends upon adequate consideration of the economic, social and political arrangements which prevail at the local level. The success of Indian democracy in penetrating into the lower status groups of the city and countryside has made such an emphasis important; a reciprocal tendency toward localism in the larger political system has made it a subject of central concern to anyone interested in trying to think about the future course of Indian political development. Therefore, while this study tends to view the Indian political system from the bottom looking upward, much of what follows should also be viewed as the stuff of which the larger political order and its political fate are made.

Research plans for the study described in this volume were formulated in the spring of 1963 as I was completing work on a comparative study of decision making in American cities, with reference to the controversial issue of fluoridating local water supplies. My original intention was to undertake research in two Indian cities which would draw heavily upon the concepts and methods of American studies of local government and politics in order to develop a framework for the comparative study of urban politics. For reasons detailed in Chapter 1, any expectations I had of doing an inter-nation comparison of decision-making styles at the urban level disintegrated fairly soon after my field research got underway in the fall of 1963. Consequently, the study reported here is rather different in orientation from the one originally intended. Instead of focusing on the "outputs" of local political systems in urban India (including the manner in which political and administrative decision making redistributes available societal resources), my interviews ultimately led me toward a greater concern with other aspects of urban politics—the roles of political parties and social groupings in political life; how individuals are recruited and socialized into municipal government; what kinds of activities actors in municipal politics undertake as part of their larger community responsibilities; how the interactions of elected and administrative officials promote or manage conflict in local government.

Unfortunately, systematic explanations for observed behaviors are not always readily available. While some social scientists might prefer direct specification of a few explanatory variables and an emphasis on these variables through formal survey techniques, my own experience in India made me rather cautious about trying to quantify or weight the many variables introduced in the following text. Indeed, the intervening years between the initiation of this research and its conclusion—years which included a second visit to the two cities in the summer of 1968—left me with considerable "hard" data, particularly in the realm of electoral statistics, but with a decreasing certainty that anyone has yet developed a vocabulary (either verbal or statistical) adequate to the task of explaining the political behaviors found in Indian urban politics. Failing the development of such a vocabulary, I have attempted simply to present a fairly detailed account of local political events in the cities of Agra and Poona between 1959 and 1969. Naturally in the organization of these materials, I have had to make certain judgments about the importance of the behaviors being discussed and the motives or goals suggested by certain courses of action on the part of particular political actors. Fortunately, a recent growth of interest in urban politics in India promises to yield a number of studies in the next few years which employ a variety of techniques to get at some of the questions raised here. The present study will have served its purpose if later works make use of some of its data to develop a more adequate approach to urban politics both in India and from a general comparative perspective.

What understanding I had of politics and social organization in India at the time I first visited that nation was derived from the work of several persons active at the University of Chicago while I was completing my graduate education there. Though my formal training in Indian studies was rather limited before my initial field work, the Committee on Southern Asian Studies at Chicago provided me with intellectual and financial support (both then and later) of enormous importance in bringing the present volume into being. I wish to thank Professors McKim Marriott, Lloyd Rudolph, and Milton Singer for the encouragement they have given me over the years. Professor Rudolph has been particularly helpful as the present manuscript reached its final form. This study also owes a considerable debt to the pioneering work of Professors Myron Weiner and Paul Brass, some of which I encountered in the form of unpublished materials before entering the field. Most of all, I have had the privilege of learning a great deal on an informal basis from Professor Maureen Patterson, who has greatly stimulated studies in the Maharashtra region. Finally, I owe personal obligations to Miss Judy Aronson of a kind which a formal acknowledgment can hardly hope to repay.

While I was prepared, therefore, to withstand some of the more common sources of cultural shock encountered in India, I was not entirely ready for what might better be called research shock—the difficulties of conducting research in rather large Indian cities marked by enormous internal variations in economic, social, and cultural modes of political articulation. Under the circumstances, I was peculiarly fortunate to choose cities where other scholars were conducting studies complementary to mine: Owen M. Lynch in Agra and Eleanor Zelliot in Poona. Both of them contributed enormously to enriching my understanding of India during that period and in the years which have followed. I owe each a great debt as scholar and friend.

My first visit to India was sponsored by the American Institute of Indian Studies. Professor Richard Lambert, then serving as Director in Poona, and Dr. D. D. Karve, Executive Officer of the Institute, both contributed considerably to my orientation to Indian life. Professor Lambert, in subsequent years, has continued to assist me in ways which are far above the call of normal academic duty. My second visit to India took place in the summer of 1968 under a grant from the Research Foundation of the State University of New York. This additional period in India permitted me to add a time dimension to the narrative and to fill in some of the blanks left behind by my analysis of the data from the first trip.

Along the way I have had to depend upon many other persons. My research assistants have included Peter Gluck, Dale Posgate, and Frank Dishaw. Among the typists who have labored on all or parts of various drafts, I should single out for special notice Cindy Breuckman, Dorothy Driscoll and Eileen Graber. During the long period of germination, the Department of Political Science and the Council on International Studies and World Affairs of the State University of New York at Buffalo provided financial support. I want to thank Professors Fred Burke and James A. Moss for their particular aid.

Roderick Church, Rodney Jones, Peter Mayer and Ralph Meyer have all contributed important elements through their valuable criticisms of the first draft of this study. They have done what they could to improve the study. In recent years, Philip Oldenburg has played a most prominent role in my formulation of the argument and he has been kind enough to allow me to incorporate some of the materials he gathered for his MA thesis into the present manuscript.

My greatest debts, of course, are to the many Indians who participated in making this book possible. The more than three hundred interviewees (local politicians, administrators, and informed citizens) who displayed good humor and enormous hospitality in the face of what must sometimes have been perceived as hostile questioning deserve individual thanks. Many of the names are mentioned in the text; where persons are not specified by name it is because of the confidentiality which was promised as part of the interview. It is my hope that any comments which may seem to place certain political actors in an unfavorable light will be accepted as one very tentative interpretation of events as they were culled from many conflicting sources. Much in the way of "reality" would be missing from this attempt to isolate some of the strands of local politics in India if such materials were removed.

In addition to the many local politicians and municipal administrators who made my task so enjoyable, I wish to thank the staff of the All-India Congress Committee office in New Delhi for allowing me to use their newspaper files for background materials for this study. The libraries of Agra and Poona Universities and the Gokhale Institute of Politics and Economics in Poona were also most kind in making their facilities available to me, as were the editors of newspapers in the two cities: *Sakal, Kesari,* and the *Poona Herald* in Poona; *Sainik* and *Amar-ujala* in Agra. The district election offices in both cities and the municipal election office in Poona were most accommodating in permitting me to draw freely upon the electoral materials available from the recent elections discussed in this volume.

Opportunities to meet with Indian scholars like Professors Yogesh Atal and Rajeshwar Prasad in Agra and V. M. Sirsikar and M. P. Mangudkar in Poona enhanced my understanding of local political life considerably. My research assistants in India—Harish Johri and Raghu Nath Vashishta in Agra; M. M. Palod and P. K. Gaikwad in Poona—helped make the process of doing research in India meaningful on a personal level.

Several articles based on the materials gathered in Agra and Poona have been published at various stages of development of the overall argument. These include "Administrative Politics in Two Indian Cities," *Asian Survey,* April 1966; "Factions and Alliances in Indian City Politics," *Midwest Journal of Political Science,* August 1966; "Deference and Friendship Patterns in Two Indian Municipal Councils," *Social Forces,* December 1966; and "Functions of Urban Political Systems," in *Community Structure and Decision-Making,* edited by Terry N. Clark (San Francisco, 1968). While some of the same materials are employed in the present text, their use differs at vital points from these articles.

Among these acknowledgments should be listed an overarching debt to Professor James Q. Wilson. Although he never guided any of my work on India, his interest in urban politics and the perspective on that field of study which he and Edward C. Banfield formulated inform the spirit of the present work despite the very different political systems within which American and Indian urban politics take place. I hope that this study does justice to what I think I began to learn from Professor Wilson nearly a decade ago.

1

THE CONTEXT
OF LOCAL POLITICS

When this study was organized in 1963, analyses of those patterns of behavior which account for the configuration of political power and the exercise of influence in *particular* communities had largely displaced older institutional treatments of city government in the United States. A heated dialogue over the appropriate methods and models to be employed in describing the findings of these newer studies of "community power" was being carried on.[1] Research then in preparation was already beginning to emphasize the need to move forward from such debates to more rigorous comparative treatments of participation and decision making in different American contexts;[2] unfortunately, the few studies of urban government done outside the United States up to that time either continued to tread traditional paths with their excessively legal-administrative perspectives or else they formed part of the cannon fodder for the warfare being conducted over theories and methods.[3]

Once I was in the cities selected for study, it soon became evident to me that strict dedication either to the "power structure" methodology or to municipal decision-making would direct my attention away from a large part of what Indian urban politics was all about. If the American literature tends to favor a highly instrumental vision of the nature of politics—to borrow from one recent formulation, "who governs, where, when and with what effects?"[4]—there was a range of politically relevant activities observed in the two Indian cities which did not fall within that view. Decision making of a kind took place, but the instrumentalities of decision making were largely controlled by state-appointed and local bureaucrats who were, in turn, subject to extensive state oversight. Areas of municipal autonomy were restricted. In practice, administrative behaviors were frequently influenced on a particularistic basis by the assiduous efforts of political groups and elected public representatives, but usually without these elements' having made any concerted attempt to effect long-range shifts in the "scopes" of municipal government.[5] Indeed, even in those areas where elected members of the two municipal bodies might readily have controlled decisional outcomes, they were often reluctant to assume responsibility or preferred to accept administrative leadership.

In contrast with a decision-making process which was often consensual in character when it was not openly bureaucratic, a politics of party and personality found free rein in the two cities. Electoral participation was fairly high—a turnout of well over 50 percent in municipal elections as compared with about 60 percent in elections for the two state assemblies and for the national parliament; even more impressive were the great number of party-supported and independent candidates

1

who competed for municipal office. It is tempting though possibly misleading to characterize this participation as growing largely out of expressive needs—the desire, in particular, to establish or affirm one's personal standing or the status of one's political group in the nature of things. Still, a great deal of time, money, and energy was expended in promoting electoral outcomes whose immediate rewards were of a limited substantive nature. Even those material benefits which *were* available were frequently intermingled with elements which met expressive or symbolic group needs; rarely were they material-based public or private goods of the kind generally considered when the "outputs" or "decisions" of a political system are discussed.[6]

Thus, while the remainder of this chapter and the ones which follow include much material describing the formal institutions of local government in two Indian cities and the political and nonpolitical environments in which these institutions operate, one of our major concerns is the identification of those subtler personal and group values which are maximized through participation in local politics in India. Hopefully, political scientists have sufficiently re-learned a lesson which makes this enterprise worthwhile in structural terms: that political structures are the product of certain societal values (what, to follow the current fashion, may be designated as the dominant "political culture"[7]) and, in turn, have certain consequences for political behavior.[8]

By political structure, however, I mean much more than the formal mechanisms of government; equally important are the components of the political infrastructure: in particular, the electoral system and the configuration of partisan and political interest groups which operate in that system. These are examined in some detail in the chapters which follow. Also explored are the behaviors of a particular set of political actors—those politicians and bureaucrats whose activities impinge either directly or indirectly upon the political lives of the two *municipal arenas.*[9] In particular, we will be concerned with the character (backgrounds, behaviors, and ambitions) of those men who constitute the representative element within the councils of the two municipal bodies.

If this study does not draw heavily upon the theory and terminology of comparative politics, that may reflect the condition of the field in the mid-1960s and the apparent failure, even more recently, of comparative politics to come fully to grips with cross-polity studies at a subsystem level.[10] With one notable exception, which only serves to point up the many theoretical and methodological hazards which lie in wait for comparative studies of local politics,[11] a recent growth in interest in the field of comparative urban politics has yielded rich results in terms of our knowledge of particular nations but rather meager foundations upon which to base propositions about local political life which are generalizable from one nation to another.[12] For the most part, therefore, the present study is framed as an attempt to understand the Indian political system by an examination of some of its component elements. Thus, while examining local politics in two Indian cities, we shall be looking not only at political subsystems (municipal arenas, local political systems) within a single national political society and at two regional subsystems with differing social structures, histories, economies, and political experiences, but at the way in which these subsystems are woven into the fabric of a national political system.

THE APPROACH OF THIS STUDY

At the time that my research was undertaken, scholarship on urban government and politics in India was restricted largely to one major historical survey,[13] several legal-administrative treatments of particular regions or problems,[14] and two collections of published papers.[15] Under the circumstances, it was necessary to "experiment" with a broad range of ideas about the ways in which political life is organized in Indian cities.[16]

The two cities finally selected for study—Agra in the state of Uttar Pradesh and Poona in Maharashtra—are among the largest fifteen in the country but in no sense are they intended to be "representative" of a particular universe of Indian cities. Considering the spatial separation involved—Agra and Poona are more than six hundred miles apart—and the distinct linguistic, cultural, historical, and political traditions which identify the regions in which they are located, the only things they might seem at first glance to hold in common are their nationality and a form of government now found among India's largest cities—the municipal corporation system. However, these two facts of political life loom large in the municipally relevant political behaviors of the citizens of Agra and Poona. Despite many situational differences attributable in part to differences in social and economic structures, common institutions and a similar historical experience are immediately apparent. Moving back and forth between the two cities requires very little change in an understanding of the *range* of governmental problems and the kinds of goals which participants in the system characteristically seek through politics. Indeed, one of the threads which runs throughout this report is the existence of a sense of national identity on the part of almost all those interviewed in the two cities—a finding which could be lightly dismissed if fears of national dismemberment were not so commonly expressed by observers of Indian society.

Data for the study were gathered in India during 1963-64 and, again, for three months in 1968. The emphasis on municipal politics is reflected in the fact that all but a handful of the 125 members of the two corporations—sixty in Agra, sixty-five in Poona—were interviewed on the first visit and about half that number of council members were interviewed or reinterviewed on the revisit. These interviews were all conducted personally by the author for periods ranging from thirty minutes to upwards of eight hours (in multiple sittings). In some instances, it was not possible to complete interviews, with the result that some of the quantitative data presented in later chapters does not include all of the corporators. In almost every instance, however, interviewees were extremely cooperative.

Interviews included certain items in common: matters of personal and political biography; several sociometric, historical and personality-identification items which attempted to test interpersonal relations within the two municipal bodies and the extent of intergroup sharing of values.[17] Otherwise, the interviewing situation was left open for the collection of information and opinions relevant to the particular respondent. In addition to being interviewed, members of the two municipal bodies were observed in the course of their interactions with other members of the municipal government—at corporation meetings and in administrative offices—and with the general public.

The corporators constituted only a portion of the total number of persons interviewed. Approximately 250 other interviews were held with members of the two municipal bureaucracies (principally at the higher or middle levels of the local administration) and with district and state politicians, nonlocal administrators, and reputedly knowledgeable observers of the local political scene (journalists, educators, and organizational leaders).

On the basis of these interviews, along with the analysis of national, state, and municipal voting data and census materials, and the inspection of documents, newspaper reports, and unpublished correspondence, it was possible to develop a sense of the configuration of political groups and leading political participants in the two cities. It is difficult to attribute motives to particular political actors in one's own society, let alone to those in an unfamiliar one. But it is possible to categorize certain classes of observed behavior and to draw some conclusions about the kinds of incentives available to participants in local politics. To a considerable extent, dimensions of *system inducements* and *actor-perceived opportunities* constitute the major axes of this study. They are particularly interesting to examine given the limited capabilities of these local political systems in generating substantive material benefits for participants.

THE NATURE OF THE TWO CITIES

What makes the politics of Agra different from the politics of Poona? At least three analytically distinct dimensions may be used to distinguish between the two cities in political behavior:

1. The *environments* of the two local political systems. Nonpolitical environmental factors of interest include the geographical, historical, and economic circumstances which affect the nature of intergroup relations in the two cities, and, ultimately, influence the character of local political behavior. These environmental factors are not fed "raw" into politics. Thus, in the case of "caste" or "community," which reveal themselves in Indian politics in various ways, only certain aspects of such identifications are mobilized for political purposes. Ultimately, however, our universe of special interest is composed of political men coming to their roles from a variety of origins and with a considerably divergent set of motivations but operating within an environment which places certain kinds of constraints upon their behaviors.

2. The nature of the *political arenas* in which intergroup and interpersonal conflicts are played out. We have already pointed to the importance of political structures in setting the rules for political behavior. Municipal governments in India, as elsewhere, are circumscribed by the larger political systems in which they are embedded. It might well be argued that the same social pressures which operate at the level of a municipality are operative for other levels of the political order, but the *effects* of these pressures are limited by the particular nature of the political structures through which they operate and the consequent expectations which are built around those structures. Awareness of the capacities of the municipal arenas is, therefore, essential.

3. The kinds of *political actors* who make use of the available arenas as opportunity structures. Our principal concern throughout this volume is less with a

systematic description of existing political structures than with attempting to understand the behaviors of those individuals and groups which participate actively in urban politics.

In the remainder of this chapter, therefore, some of the more important features of the nonpolitical environments of Agra and Poona will be briefly introduced; a concluding section will describe some of the formal outlines of governmental institutions relevant to the study. Chapter 2 sets the stage for the appearance of the political actors who have taken the leading roles in recent municipal politics by describing the political arenas which help to shape political behavior in the two cities.

Geohistorical Considerations

Some cities in India (Varanasi, Gaya, Madurai) are prominent because of their special religious character; others (Calcutta, Bombay, Madras) are principally the product of Western commercial expansion. Agra and Poona, in turn, are significant historically as the capitals of relatively late Indian political powers in the subcontinent. The periods of their greatest luster as imperial centers were contemporaneous with the arrival of Europeans in India; with the decline of these indigenous ruling houses, both cities experienced periods of stagnation—Agra for a period somewhat longer than Poona. They both proved of value to the British as administrative centers in the nineteenth century, however, and the logic of their physical locations prevented their further decline. Today, if one includes immediately adjacent populations, Poona ranks ninth and Agra thirteenth in population among Indian cities.

The city of Agra lies on the western bank of the Jumna River as the latter flows southeastward from Delhi, which is 124 miles away. Agra was apparently a minor fort and outpost for local kingdoms in 1504 when it was selected as a new capital for the Delhi Sultanate.[18] The Mughal Empire, which succeeded the Sultanate in 1526, maintained Agra as its capital.[19] Among its more favorable physical features were its location on a major river system, its access to the Gangetic plain on the east and its viability as a military base for operations into the south and west, since the city bordered on the princely territories which have become part of contemporary Rajasthan and Madhya Pradesh.

Agra flourished under the early Mughal emperors. They left behind them an impressive series of monuments including Agra Fort, the royal palaces at nearby Fatehpur Sikri, and the most important symbol of Agra's connections with the past (and its current claim to world attention as a tourist center), the Taj Mahal. Begun in 1632 and completed in 1652, the construction of the Taj Mahal coincided with the apex of the Mughal presence in Agra and their power in India.

In 1666 the seat of empire was removed to Delhi, and Agra became a secondary city. The next century saw the disruption of the empire, and, by the last half of the eighteenth century, Agra was a regular victim of invading political forces. From 1757 to 1803, when Lord Lake captured the city for the British, Agra changed hands seven times, with the Marathas—part of whose forces were associated with the political authority centered in the Poona area—holding the city during three separate periods including the years from 1785 to 1803.

The use of Agra Fort as a garrison provided some continuing importance to the city under the British. For a time, Agra served as the capital of a province, but the Indian revolt in 1857 convinced the British of the need for administrative reorganization and relocation of the provincial capital to Allahabad, which was closer to the principal areas of British-Indian conflict.

During the nineteenth century, the city experienced the growth of Western-style colleges and hospitals; railway lines were laid, which helped to reaffirm the city's earlier importance as a transportation center lying now on the important national routes from Delhi to Bombay and Delhi to Calcutta. Minor industrialization occurred in Agra in the latter part of the century in the form of spinning factories and edible oil mills, but most of Agra's industry was (and remains) on a small scale.

A relatively low rate of economic modernization in Agra is reflected in the pattern of the city's population growth over the past century. As against a figure which might have been as high as 200,000 during the period of Mughal greatness, one survey suggests that there were only 35,000 residents in 1838[20] and 125,262 in 1852. As late as 1901, the total population of the municipality and its urbanized fringe was only 188,022. It reached 229,764 in 1931, an increase during these thirty years of 22.2 percent. Between 1931 and 1961, however, the rate of growth accelerated, as the figures in table 1.1 indicate.

TABLE 1.1

Population and Growth Rate, Agra City
1931-1961

Year	Population	Rate of Increase
1931	229,764	22%
1941	284,149	24
1951	375,665	32
1961	509,108	36

These figures include the municipality and its immediate environs designated in the 1961 census as the "Agra Town Group." Source: Census of India, 1961.

A substantial part of Agra's recent growth is due simply to the rapid rate of natural increase in India (21.5 percent between 1951 and 1961), as well as to gradual migration from the Punjab and Sind after the disruption created by the Partition of 1947. No doubt, the "push" from overburdened landholdings accounts for part of the population increase, but the actual influence of this factor is difficult to estimate.[21]

Poona, like Agra, is a rather late urban center by Indian standards. While it may have been on a significant trading and migration route in prehistoric times,[22] there is no indication of major urban settlement at the present site until the seventeenth century. Lying at a major point on the northern access route to the Deccan and the South from the western coast of India, Poona is 119 miles southeast of Bombay. It is at the confluence of two rivers, the Mula and the Mutha.

Of considerable geohistorical significance is the location of the city at 1,850 feet above sea level among the Western Ghats. While the city itself is located on a gently rolling plain, hilly areas nearby provided important protection to the Bhonsale family and its retainers as they laid the groundwork for what became the Maratha Empire in the period after 1635.

The myth-surrounded figure of Shivaji Bhonsale is still prominent in the lore and symbology of Poona and in the political life of the state of Maharashtra. Coming from the regionally dominant peasant community of Marathas,[23] Shivaji challenged the authority of the Mughal Empire and by 1662 held a substantial area along the western coast stretching inland as much as 160 miles. By the time of his death in 1680, the Marathas had become a considerable force in Indian politics.

Shivaji's actual exploits are less important to us than the symbolic importance attributed to them. As one study of Indian history puts it:

> Some modern writers have seen him as the expression, almost as much as the leader, of a great popular movement, which they regard as a renaissance of the Hindu power; others have regarded him merely as a successful freebooter; others, again, as a military and political genius, whose mental horizon widened as he went forward—originally a freebooter who was also a dreamer, but later a soldier, statesman and administrator of unquestioned eminence.[24]

After Shivaji's death, his hereditary successors resided at places other than Poona, but the *Peshwa* (Prime Minister) in the employ of Shivaji's grandson began the tradition of carrying on the administration of the empire from Poona. Drawn from the small Chitpavan Brahmin community, a familial succession of six Peshwas worked skillfully at consolidating and expanding the empire. For much of the eighteenth century, Poona was the effective capital of the Maratha holdings, but dissensions developed within the empire, and by 1797 conflicting factions were clashing in the streets of the city.[25] In 1802, enemies of the Peshwa attacked the city and only the intervention of the British kept him in office. In November 1817, however, British forces directly engaged the Peshwa's army at Kirkee, now a suburb of the city, with the result that the city came under direct British rule.

British administrators, led by Mountstuart Elphinstone, spent the next several years winning over the previously powerful Brahmin community. Colleges were established both in traditional and Western subjects and the socially dominant Brahmins flocked to these new institutions and into the service of the British administration.[26] The numerically superior Maratha peasantry remained aloof from educational institutions, although they did supply manpower to the British army. As late as 1881, it is estimated that over 90 percent of the college students in the Poona area were Brahmins, even though they constituted less than 10 percent of the population of the region.[27]

As in the case of Agra, Poona's population decreased temporarily with the decline in the power of the empire. From a supposed population of several hundred thousand in 1802, the city shrank to about a hundred thousand in 1808,[28] and to eighty thousand in 1823.[29] Symbolic of this decline in importance as a political center, the Peshwa's palace was by then being used as a combined jail, madhouse, and hospital. It burned to the ground in February 1827.

The pleasant weather of the city as well as its strategic access to the Deccan led the Government of Bombay to employ Poona as a monsoon capital for the Bombay Presidency and to establish a major military encampment or "cantonment" there for the British army in the Deccan. Poona served as the home of the forces organized under the Southern Command. It has continued to do so since India became independent.[30]

From the end of the nineteenth century until Gandhi's assumption of leadership of the Indian National Congress in 1920, Poona was a major center for those educational and intellectual activities which foreshadowed and encouraged the development of the nationalist movement. Quasi-political organizations, like the Poona Sarvajanik Sabha (People's Service Society) organized in 1867, provided platforms for the first stirrings of national consciousness. In the following fifty years members of the Chitpavan Brahmin community based in Poona were particularly prominent in the Congress: G. K. Gokhale, for example, operated in the style of the English Liberals by seeking reforms within the system; B. G. Tilak, in contrast, appealed for greater self-government by making skillful use of traditional Hindu symbols as well as the Shivaji legend. Associated with both men in a network of educational institutions, service organizations, and newspapers were an impressive array of dedicated social reformers and political propagandists.[31]

In the days of its intellectual leadership, Poona was still best known as a college town and resort area. As late as 1863, nearly fifty years after the Peshwa's defeat, there were only about 80,000 persons in the city; even in 1931, the city had not overtaken Agra in size. In that year, 198,078 people were counted as living within the then municipal boundaries.[32]

Since 1931, however, both the city and its metropolitan area have expanded considerably. If one includes the two large cantonments, which contain substantial civilian populations, the metropolitan population of Poona has grown from 186,515 in 1911 to 722,896 in 1961.[33] The pattern of expansion is indicated in table 1.2.[34]

The great influx of population between 1941 and 1951 is particularly noteworthy. It reflects, at least in part, the establishment of important military industries in the Poona area during the period and the expansion of nonmilitary industries out from Bombay after World War II. Indeed, the road from Poona to Bombay is now one of the major industrial arteries in India. Much of this industry is located on the outer edges of the city or in its suburbs.

TABLE 1.2

Population and Growth Rate, Poona and Poona "Town Group," 1911-1961

Year	City Population	Rate of Increase	Area Population	Rate of Increase
1911	140,261	—	186,515	—
1921	180,098	28	231,181	24
1931	213,680	19	265,789	15
1941	278,165	30	345,897	30
1951	480,982	73	588,545	70
1961	597,562	24	722,896	23

Source: Census of India, 1961.

These recent economic changes in the base of the city have obscured the earlier image of Poona as a quiet educational and institutional center. It is now an economically heterogeneous industrial city with the added historical advantage of a substantial middle class composed of articulate and educated citizens. Even so, traditional conflicts find a place in the style and appeals of its political life; they mix with the politics of a modern city suffering many of the physical ills of rapid urbanization in a country where governmental investment in urban development is restricted.

Economic Development

Agra is located in the Hindi-speaking heartland of India in the western part of Uttar Pradesh. It is connected by a few hours' bus travel to Delhi and the Punjab and has benefited from commercial traffic with this relatively prosperous hinterland; culturally, however, its high-status citizens are still heavily influenced by the traditionalism more characteristic of the regions to its south and west, Rajasthan and Madhya Pradesh.

Agra's immediate rural marketing area is not as economically backward as much of the territory elsewhere in Uttar Pradesh. To the observer, however, the nontourist part of Agra gives the impression of an overgrown market town. Indeed, its leading community consists of merchants, both by profession and by caste. Many of these continue to traffic in agricultural produce, although a good number have gone into small-scale industries or the professions in recent decades.

While tourism provides some employment, the major "industrial" supports for the economy are small shoe factories, grain mills, oil presses, and a complex of spinning and weaving mills which have been in receivership for nearly twenty years. One estimate of employment suggests that 50,000 workers were engaged in the city's shoe businesses and allied industries in 1963, ranking Agra second behind the more heavily industrialized city of Kanpur in the production of shoes for the Indian market and for export to Eastern Europe and the Soviet Union. Indicative of the small size of shoe "factories" is the estimate that the 50,000 shoe workers were distributed among 3,100 shoe-producing units. In addition to the leather trades, about thirty-five oil mills employed 1,500 workers and another 1,400 workers were in service to the spinning and weaving mills.[35]

In contrast to only eleven establishments in all of Agra employing over 100 workers,[36] there were eighty-five manufacturing units in the Poona labor market in 1964 employing over 100 persons each. Indeed, twenty-four of these units employed over 500 workers.[37] This striking contrast reflects the economic imbalance which exists not only between the two cities but also between the two regions in which Agra and Poona are located.[38]

The greater economic development of Poona is associated with a higher literacy rate and a higher status for women in Maharashtrian society. In 1961, there was a national literacy rate of 24 percent. Agra City recorded a rate of 36 percent, whereas Poona's was 55 percent. Equally important, only a quarter of the women in Agra—where traditions of female seclusion remain strong even among Hindus— are nominally literate; the women of Poona are 45 percent literate. The latter rate prevails among *men* in Agra.

Thus, in terms of accepted indices of modernization like income and education, Poona is in advance of Agra. To the extent that these differences are directly exhibited in politics, they may appear as part of what might be termed a more "middle-class" style of political behavior in Poona, but such a style also reflects the peculiar social structural differences between the two cities.

Social Structure and Ecology

The traditional social structure of India—the caste system—has aroused the interest of Western scholars to such an extent that it would be tempting to fall prey to a "casteist interpretation" of Indian politics. While certain aspects of this traditional social stratification system have been converted into important political identifications for some contemporary political groups, the overall social product of the last century of economic and political change is so much an innovation in Indian history and a deviation from the original conceptions associated with caste that we must treat political behaviors supposedly reflecting caste identifications gingerly. Unfortunately, reliable measures of class composition are not readily available. For example, the occupational categories employed by the Census conceal considerable differences in income ranges. In this section, therefore, we merely introduce the subject of social stratification by providing some of the grosser details of caste structure in the two cities; in later chapters, materials will be introduced to specify further the political relevance of these caste distributions. A correspondence between traditional caste position and economic rank is still assumed to exist, but the evidence on this point is limited.[39]

Despite the overlay of Islamic culture in Agra, the Partition of India and the recent migration of Hindus to the city has left the city predominantly Hindu in composition. In census terms, about 78 percent of the residents of the municipality are Hindus, 16 percent are Muslims and there are small representations of Jains, Sikhs, Buddhists, and Christians.[40]

These data do not take into account the existence of important cleavages among those listed as Hindus by the Census of Religions. In particular, Agra's 1961 Hindu population included 88,317 members of the Scheduled Castes.[41] About 80 percent of these "ex-untouchables" belong to one community, the Jatavs; their presence accounts, in large part, for the level of development of the shoe industry in Agra. Enumeration of the Jatav community is complicated slightly by the conversion of some Jatavs to Buddhism in the past fifteen years. While many did not identify themselves as recent converts to Buddhism for the Census of 1961, about 2,500 indicated their antipathy to traditional Hinduism by declaring themselves Buddhist even though such a declaration threatened the loss of places in education and employment. For some Jatavs, however, being a Buddhist or Scheduled Caste is a situational matter.

The traditional merchant stratum of Agra society consists of several subcommunities ("castes" or *jatis*) with the Agarwals constituting the largest single *jati*. For the purposes of simplicity, these several "castes" will be collectively referred to by the generic Bania term commonly employed in Agra, although this usage may be at variance with a strict anthropological definition. As a collectivity, Banias constitute in the vicinity of 22 percent of the population of the municipality, but they are rarely united on any social or political question. From what could be learned on this point, political cleavages within the broad Bania category rarely took place along *jati* lines.[42] Closely related to this broad category of distinct social units are the Jains, who are religiously separate from the Hindu Banias, but are a constituent element of the Bania stratum.[43]

While members of the other "twice-born" castes (Brahmins, Thakurs) are present in the population in appreciable numbers, neither of these communities has acted as an independent group in political life. Individual Brahmins and Thakurs, as well as the ritually middle-status (but economically and educationally upper-status) Kayasthas, are quite active in local politics but they have worked within political groups which are multicaste in character.

In table 1.3, we present an *approximation* of Agra's population by traditional caste categories—categories which we shall term "primordial" since they are associated with ties of birth and blood. It should be emphasized, again, that these are social classifications rather than readily mobilizable "real" units. Indeed, groups we have listed together under rubrics like "Intermediate" and "Backward Class" include some uncomfortable political bedfellows. For the purpose of the present study, however, it was neither possible nor necessary to determine the nature of those subdivisions more precisely. In all instances where "caste" Hindus are listed, the percentages are based on interview materials and are rather suspect. Precise figures on Hindu castes have not been collected officially in India since 1931.

Poona has a larger proportion of educated and westernized citizens, but for certain purposes traditional social and religious identifications remain salient. Thus, many educated Poona Brahmins hold strong attachments to conservative Hindu organizations and political groups. The large Maratha community, on the other hand, harbors some resentment against earlier Brahmin domination, which appears

TABLE 1.3

Primordial Groups in Agra

Primordial Group	Estimated Proportion of Population (percent)	
Hindus:	78	
Brahmins-Thakurs		12
Banias		22
Intermediate*		13
Backward Classes		13
Scheduled Castes		18
Muslims	16	
Jains	3	
Buddhists†	1	
Christians	1	
Sikhs	1	
Total	100	

* Includes Kayasthas, Khatris, Sonars, and Hindus of nonlocal origin like the "Punjabis" and "Sindhis."

† Exclusively recent converts to Buddhism from among the ex-untouchables.

in political behaviors. A strong undercurrent of anti-Muslim sentiment also runs through the population of Poona despite the comparatively small Muslim population in the city, the most recent outburst of violent anti-Muslim feeling having occurred in 1965.

On the whole, Poona is a more heterogeneous city than Agra. While 72.6 percent of the population give Marathi as their primary language, a quarter of the population claim other mother tongues: Urdu, Telugu, Hindi, and Gujarati. (Few persons in Agra are non-Hindustani speakers.)

Despite this heterogeneity, two major caste categories predominate: the Brahmins, who constitute about 20 percent of the population; the Marathas, who are slightly more numerous.[44] This balance is very different from the situation which prevails in nearby sections of rural Maharashtra, where the Marathas are nearly in an absolute majority while the Brahmins are now less than 10 percent of the population. Table 1.4 offers an outline of the chief primordial groups in urban Poona.[45]

Following the pattern of many Western cities prior to the twentieth century, both Agra and Poona grew up about highly concentrated central cores. Multistoried buildings are still common in the congested areas where many of the merchant communities reside in Agra. Since World War II, however, there has been a considerable movement outward from core areas—first by the more prosperous professionals and government officials, and more recently by members of the merchant communities. In the process, the poor have either been pushed further out or been bypassed in undesirable portions of the city.[46]

In practice, residential segregation by caste and community exists in Agra and Poona much as it has traditionally done in Indian towns and villages. Despite some

TABLE 1.4

Primordial Groups in Poona

Primordial Group	Proportion of Population (percent)	
Hindus:	79	
Brahmins		20
Marathas		22
Intermediate*		18
Backward Classes		12
Scheduled Castes†		7
Muslims	8	
Christians	4	
Jains	2	
Buddhists	6	
Others (Parsis, Jews, Sikhs)	1	
Total	100	

* Includes CKPs, Malis, Pardeshis, Kachis, Lingayats, and certain non-Maharashtrians like non-Jain Gujaratis and Marwaris.
† This figure should be considered in relation to the one for Buddhists.

movement to the urban fringe, many Agra Banias continue to live in their traditional areas near the Fort; the Gujaratis and Marwaris who perform mercantile functions in Poona[47] reside in the older business sections of that city. Other castes are similarly located in particular parts of each city although newer neighborhoods contain more of a mixture drawn along class lines. In both cities, the ex-untouchables and Muslims tend to live somewhat apart from the "caste" Hindus in their own *mohallas* (neighborhoods). One of the results of these patterns of residential concentration is to aggregate the numbers needed to produce electoral outcomes reflecting social arrangements in the cities. Indeed, one of the niceties of the municipal electoral systems in the two cities is the production of representative municipal bodies based as much on intragroup as on intergroup conflicts, a phenomenon not unfamiliar to Americans experienced in the ways of ethnic politics and ward elections.

Overview

On any universal continuum of urban development, Agra and Poona are not very far apart. Despite its link with a national network of transportation and communication, Agra's dominant culture is more traditional than Poona's measured by such indices as their relative economic and educational patterns. Some of the characteristics distinguishing the two cities might be summed up better by an example familiar to the visitor: Agra's image is that of the bicycle ricksha driver (his ricksha generally owned by a wealthy Punjabi or Sindhi entrepreneur) straining to ascend one of the steep inclines which make up major sections of the main roads of the city or painfully attempting to negotiate his ricksha's passage through the narrow lanes of the central bazaars congested with their human and animal traffic.[48] This image contrasts rather sharply with the brisk self-assurance of a Poona driver rapidly, though bumpily, weaving his way through a congestion of bicycles, taxis, and automobiles on Poona's broad streets in one of the motorized rickshas (frequently owned by the driver) characteristic of that city.

This does not mean that Poona has escaped the many other ills associated with modern urbanism. Poona's slums are as unpleasant as those of Agra, but they are probably more distinctly *urban* in their oppressiveness. Still, both cities contain some areas of relative luxury and other wards which are essentially transplants of village life into the city, if they are not the original villages themselves.

THE MUNICIPAL GOVERNMENTS

The Governmental Environments

Despite their size, the cities of Agra and Poona are dwarfed governmentally and politically by their rural hinterlands. The Indian political system, as it has developed over the past twenty years, has shifted considerable power and influence from urban to rural areas. The organization of rural populations by urban political elites during the nationalist movement has gradually given way to the self-assertions of autonomous rural political elites increasingly in control not only of their own recently democratized rural governments but of their state governments as well.[49]

Whether justified or not, there is a feeling common among politicians in the two cities that their problems receive less attention from their respective state governments than do the needs of the rural areas. This sense of relative deprivation reflects the considerable resources which have been expended recently on behalf of district (rural) governments through the system of *panchayati raj.*[50] These new three-tiered (from village to district) patterns of government provide a major vehicle for rural demands to be heard in matters bearing on the distribution of state resources. They also offer important new opportunity structures for those attracted into political life.[51]

Indian districts vary considerably in territory and population, but rarely do urban elements constitute as much as half the population of such districts.[52] For a variety of reasons, both programmatic and partisan in nature, neither Agra nor Poona City is represented in its respective district government, nor are the smaller municipalities in either district. Admittedly, one of the major purposes of contemporary district government is to encourage rural participation in more rapid economic and social development of the countryside, but the exclusion of urban populations from district government has also probably had the effect of slowing the growth of opposition political organization in the countryside, at least until recently. Thus, in 1964, 56 of the 66 members of the Agra *zilla parishad* (district committee)—the highest unit of the Uttar Pradesh system—were associated with the Congress Party. Congress dominance in rural Poona was equally pronounced.[53]

The transition to rural political autonomy is fairly advanced in the rest of Maharashtra and Uttar Pradesh, but there is still considerable overlap between urban-based politicians and government in rural Agra. These politicians have been eager to make use of the resources available through the new political arenas. It should be noted, however, that such urban-rural political relationships are rather complex because individuals who play linkage roles occasionally have equally strong urban and rural bases of strength; a man may maintain a residence or occupation in the city but own considerable hereditary property in a village in the same district. In many cases he may choose to work in rural or urban politics purely on the basis of the immediate opportunities he sees for himself.

As presently constituted, district governments have considerable autonomy. The president of the *zilla parishad*, an important Congress figure in both Agra and Poona Districts in 1964, combined legislative and executive authority in his position, although the day-to-day administration was directed by an appointed Chief Executive Officer. In addition to its oversight of certain developmental activities in which the state and national governments have made investments, the *parishad* is an important source of employment in the districts since there are at least 2,500 people including public school teachers directly under it in a district the size of Agra. To the extent that politicians can influence such appointments—an influence varying with the state and the nature of the appointment—the political rewards attached to office in a *zilla parishad* are bound to be perceived as high in an underemployed society like India's.

Most of the activities of rural government and politics do not impinge directly on the urban political systems of Agra and Poona, except through those few individuals who participate in both. At the same time, certain functions are performed for the residents of the two cities by officials who are district-based but not directly under the control of either the rural or the municipal governments. Most important is the District Magistrate—also called the Collector or the Deputy Commissioner—who is responsible for the administration of criminal justice and certain aspects of civil administration in both urban and rural parts of the district and for revenue collection in the rural area.[54] He, in turn, is technically a subordinate of the Divisional Commissioner, who oversees the work of several districts. Other state-appointed officials serve under these officers or cooperate in the administration of the district. Although the Commissioner and the District Magistrate both maintain their headquarters in the principal urban centers of their administrative domains—in both cases, Agra and Poona Cities—their major formal contact with the municipality is through their responsibility for maintaining law and order and administering justice in the city. Other functions may also be performed for the city through coordinated district services. Firefighting, for example, is subsumed under the police organization in Agra.

The municipal corporation has not been granted the power to run its own court system in either city, but must rely upon the district courts to carry out their legal orders. The city of Agra does maintain a link with the courts through a City Magistrate, an associate of the District Magistrate, who handles cases arising in the city. In practice, this system works reasonably well because the District Magistrate (DM) and the Municipal Commissioner or Chief Executive Officer (CEO) of the corporation are likely to maintain close personal relations. One aide to the District Magistrate of Agra described this informal system as follows:

> The Commissioner of the Division, the District Magistrate, and the Chief Executive Officer of the municipal corporation come from a common pool of service and they simply do business over the telephone with each other. Under the corporation there is no power for the CEO to pass laws or issue orders. If the city wants to ban rotten fruit, for example, it has to go to the City Magistrate or the DM for such an order. Basically the corporation has no power to punish anyone for acts. For punishment they need the District Magistrate. They work well together. The corporation can levy taxes and where they cannot be collected they must seek the aid of the District Magistrate in his job as Collector.

In addition to the district governments which impinge on the two municipalities, each has military bases immediately bordering its territory. As organized by the British, these "cantonment" areas included not only barracks but residential areas for officers and civilian employees. Standards of health and safety maintained by the British also attracted members of westernized Indian elites to the areas. In Poona and Agra, where these military headquarters were important, the civilian populations of the cantonments became quite sizable.

The cantonments are governed by boards which are ultimately controlled by the military, although they do include representation of the civilian population. Thus, in Agra, elections are held for seven (of fourteen) seats on the board. The seven other seats are filled, however, by nominations from the military, and the president of the board is commander of the military base. An Executive Officer appointed by the central government, which maintains direct supervision over cantonments, is in charge of actual administration of the area.

For the most part, relations between the municipal corporations and their cantonment boards have been equable. Conflicts occasionally arise, as in Agra when the corporation, which supplies water to the cantonment, charged slightly higher rates to that body than it did to its own citizens. The resultant controversy extended over several years, during which the board refused to pay its water bill until a proper modification was reached.

The two units in Agra have also had disagreements over such matters as the licensing of bicycle rickshas, bicycles, and other conveyances. In September 1963 a conflict arising from the lowering of fee schedules by the cantonment led to a few days in which vehicles (particularly rickshas) registered in the cantonment were given tickets for operating in the city. The board responded in kind. This small war was finally resolved by negotiating a new registration system.[55]

The most important contacts of the corporations with their governmental environments come through their clear dependence upon their state governments for financial support and policy ratification. The nature of this dependence can best be understood through a brief discussion of the history and character of the municipal corporation system in India.

The Origins of the Corporation Form [56]

Governmental structures at the municipal level in India are essentially Western imports. Two sometimes antagonistic currents have been evident in the approaches of higher governmental authorities—both English and Indian—to municipal government over the past century. On the one hand, there is the *administrative tradition,* which conceives of municipal affairs as consisting largely of providing amenities like sanitation and water to the public at minimum cost. At least since the second half of the nineteenth century, however, a second purpose has been attributed to Indian local governments: to act as *training schools for democracy.* Despite the realization of Independence in 1947, these two modes of thought continue to operate in contemporary India and still come into occasional conflict.

While acts were passed as early as 1850 to regularize the growth of municipalities in India, systems of nomination carefully circumscribed local initiative. The elective principle was gradually introduced, but as late as 1880 only a few cities were not controlled mainly by servants of the British provincial governments.[57] One of the few exceptions was the city of Bombay. By 1872, ratepayers elected one-half of that corporation body and appointed the Health Officer and the Executive Engineer, subject to the approval of the Government of Bombay. The Municipal Commissioner—the chief administrative authority—remained a government appointee.[58]

In 1882, Lord Ripon in his capacity as Viceroy issued a declaration that it was the intention of the Government of India to promote local governments in rural areas, as well as in municipalities, as arenas of increasing local participation. "It is not primarily with a view to improvement in administration that this measure is put forward and supported. It is chiefly designed as an instrument of political and popular education." While the short-run goal may not have been of an administrative nature, the same document did argue that in the course of time "improved efficiency will in fact follow" the development of local knowledge and local interest.[59]

Members of the British bureaucracy in India were slow to follow Ripon's recommendations, and it was in the face of their obstruction that the Bombay Municipal Act of 1888 was framed and became a model for later municipal corporations. Hugh Tinker has summarized that act's central features in the following terms:

> The kernel of the system lay in the recognition of the Corporation as the supreme governing body of the city, and in the recognition of the Municipal Commissioner as responsible for carrying out the will of the Corporation with full authority over staff, installations, and all routine municipal activities. . . . Government control was almost completely abrogated; the Commissioner was appointed by Government, but might be removed by the Corporation; fiscal autonomy was complete, although loans could not be raised without government sanction.[60]

By American rather than European standards, even this degree of local autonomy might not appear to be very extensive.

As late as 1947 most of the larger cities still did not follow the corporation system. Instead, they shared a form of government, the municipal board or committee, with the smaller municipalities. This system concentrated legislative and administrative authority in a board of elected and nominated local people, who then appointed an Executive Officer to act as a subordinate of the board in administering the city. The arrangement permitted more direct authority to the members of the city's council than did the corporation form.

A major change which gradually did take place during the half-century before 1947 in many local governments was a shift in the nature of representation. The influence of officials and nominated members in these bodies was sharply reduced, and ex-officio or nominated chairmen were replaced by persons elected by the representatives. Examples of these changes over time in membership patterns are indicated in table 1.5 for Poona, a city which acted earlier than many others in reducing the influence of nominated members.[61]

The British were slower to enfranchise voters than to increase the number of elected representatives. In 1883, there were only 4,000 eligible voters in a total population of 100,000 living within the municipal boundaries of Poona. Furthermore, seats were distributed on the basis of certain occupational or status categories, such as lawyers, graduates, persons honored by the government, persons retired from government service, and ratepayers not included in other categories. By 1921, however, those enfranchised in Poona had increased to 42,700;[62] the potential electorate remained relatively stable until the first municipal elections after Independence in 1952, when all adults were given the right to vote.[63]

At the same time that the municipal franchise was being expanded after 1947, municipal boards were being abandoned in many of the largest cities in favor of the corporation system, thereby decreasing the direct control over administration available to elected representatives. *Civic Affairs,* an Indian journal devoted to

TABLE 1.5

Elected and Nominated Members of Poona Municipal Government by Year, 1873-1968

Years	Nominated by Government	Elected	Total
1858-73	7	—	7
1873-75	38	—	38
1883-85	28	—	28
1885-98	12	12	24
1898-1912	18	20	38
1912-21	13	26	39
1921-28	7	43	50
1928-38	5	45	50
1938-50	—	60	60
1952-67	—	65	65
1968 onward	—	73	73

Source: *Poona Herald,* 18 June 1968.

municipal administration and politics, in an editorial of September 1963, challenged the prevailing assumptions about the inherent conflict between efficiency and democracy which prompted state legislators to foster the corporation system of municipal government:

> While local bodies in India remain inferior or second class democratic institutions, that is, democracy in them remains very much diluted by the superior control of the State Government over them, the administrative efficiency of their working is not any better for that reason.
> This is the result of conflicting trends. Democracy is sacrificed in the name of administrative efficiency, and, no attempts are made to improve administrative efficiency on account of lip homage to Democracy.

Like most municipal governments, a fundamental source of these weaknesses of municipal administration in India is their financial situation. While some observers attribute these difficulties to the lack of an adequate financial base, others argue that Indian city officials (especially the elected representatives) are notably reluctant to levy even those taxes available to them and to strictly enforce their collection. The system of valuation of houses and other property has come in for particular criticism. Still, any consideration of the fiscal shortcomings of municipal governments in India must include, as one writer has noted, a recognition of "the general poverty of the people, the unfair distribution of resources between the Central, State and Local Governments . . . and restrictions placed on the powers of the municipality to levy taxes."[64]

The fiscal burden on urban bodies is compounded by administrative corruption—which is alleged to divert substantial amounts of municipal income—and overstaffing, an endemic feature of Indian government. State governments have also increased local responsibilities in recent years by mandating expenditures without augmenting the capacities of municipal governments to draw upon additional resources. Aside from determining the size of a municipality's grants-in-aid and sanctioning loans, state oversight continues to extend to the approval of specifics associated with taxation and other policies.[65]

By their natures, municipal governments are legally dependent on higher authorities for their existence. In the United States, where this is the formal relationship, it is rather rare (though not unknown) for a state government to go beyond supervision and assume the powers of the municipality by appointing an administrative official to run the city in place of its elected body. This power of *supersession* is a common feature of Indian political life. Such authority was available to the British but was not much used since most municipalities were responsive to the demands of higher government. In the 1920s, however, supersession was occasionally employed to counteract nationalist obstruction in the working of municipalities.

Since 1947, a variety of reasons have been provided in cases where supersession has been authorized. In one notable instance, where the municipality of Gorakhpur was superseded in 1956, "maladministration, persistent incompetence, abuse of powers and party factions" were the grounds provided by the state government of Uttar Pradesh.[66] As the result of such supersessions, Calcutta was under the rule of a state-appointed Administrator from 1948 to 1951; the city of Nagpur (in Maharashtra) was taken over for a three-year period beginning in 1965; and, Agra was without representative government twice: first from 1942 to 1959, and again from 1966 to 1968 when it and the other KAVAL[67] corporations were placed under Administrator rule. Indeed, of the eighteen municipal corporations set up in India before 1960, at least nine have experienced supersession at least once. The practice, as we have noted in the case of Gorakhpur, is by no means limited to the larger cities.

The decision to supersede is ultimately a political one and, occasionally, partisan. Thus, when the Nagpur corporation was superseded in October of 1965 on the grounds that the financial position of the corporation had deteriorated and the corporation was failing to provide adequate water supply, these factors did not seem sufficient grounds to some observers who felt such charges fit most corporations.[68] Equally important in this case, as in others, may have been the fact that the Nagpur corporation was operating with a solid non-Congress majority at a time when the state of Maharashtra was otherwise dominated by the Congress Party. Similarly, the decision to supersede the five corporations of Uttar Pradesh in 1966 (rather than hold new elections immediately or extend the lives of the existent bodies) may have been influenced by the shaky position of the Congress Party in the state.

The interplay of state politics and local government is a major dimension of municipal affairs in India and will be explored in considerable detail in the remainder of this volume. Before turning to these considerations, we must briefly specify some of the more salient aspects of municipal history in Agra and Poona leading to the creation of the corporations. In the last section of this chapter, the institutional framework of the corporations is described.

Local Self-Government in Agra and Poona

The corporation system existed in only three cities before 1947. Since Independence, however, the number of cities employing this form has risen to at least twenty-three, including most of the largest cities of the nation.[69]

Poona received corporation status in 1950 after nearly one hundred years as a municipality. Restrictions on the franchise had not prevented the previous municipality from including among its members some of the most prominent leaders in Poona's history including major figures in the early nationalist movement. As one might expect, these representatives came from upper-caste and upper-class elements in the community. Non-Brahmins were not very active in local politics before 1918. In that year, the "advanced castes"–principally Brahmins, Parsis, and high-status non-Maharashtrians–constituted 77 percent of the membership of the municipality. By 1928 they had been reduced to only 30 percent.

The modern Congress party entered the Poona municipality in 1932 when it won twelve seats (24 percent of the total). Its pre-Independence peak was reached in 1938 with thirty-two members in a body of sixty. With the onset of World War II in 1939, however, the Congress party withdrew from local and state governments. When it returned to participate in a local government election held in Poona in 1946, it won only twelve seats.[70]

The municipality performed many of the same functions for which the corporation is currently responsible. These include the establishment, regulation and maintenance of roads, streets, wells, drains, sewers, waterworks, and markets. One of the major functions assumed by the municipality in 1925 was primary education. In that year, a school board was created with twelve members drawn from the local body. Unfortunately, members of the school board showed a tendency to interfere more directly in educational matters (including promotions) than the state government felt to be proper; as a result, the first Congress government of Bombay in 1938 withdrew the municipality's authority over education.[71] Limited influence in this field was restored only when the corporation came into being in 1952.

After Independence, the Government of Bombay appointed a committee "to examine and report on measures to ensure the more efficient Municipal Government of the Greater Poona region."[72] It is symptomatic of the impact of the earlier alternative approaches to local government that the newly-established state government should have stressed an administrative perspective in its charge to this committee responsible for drawing up The Bombay Provincial Municipal Corporations Act of 1949. Intended principally for the cities of Poona and Ahmedabad–the latter was then part of Bombay State–the act represented an adaptation of the Bombay City system with its separation of administrative from "deliberative" (legislative) functions.

The Poona Municipal Corporation was formally inaugurated in February 1950 upon the amalgamation of the previous Poona municipality and a suburban municipality created in 1884. In August of 1950, seventeen adjoining villages were added to the corporation, thus bringing into municipal life a substantial rural area. In a few instances, traditional rural leaders simply shifted from being village headmen to being members of the municipal council. It was also relatively easy for a number of members serving in the old Poona municipality to transfer their services to the successor body. This was the result of a gap of less than three years between the two systems and a fairly representative system prior to 1946.

Such was not the case in Agra. As compared to Poona, Agra had developed neither a high level of participation in municipal government nor a government marked by much partisan organization prior to 1942. The municipality was constituted in 1863, but well into the twentieth century it consisted largely of British sympathizers from upper-class backgrounds. Indeed, it was not until the passage of the United Provinces Municipalities Act of 1916 that "official" chairmen (government officials) were replaced by nonofficial presidents elected by members of the municipal board; this change had taken place in Poona in 1884.

In 1941, the Agra Municipal Board was largely composed of supporters of the government. The President was a wealthy "rai bahadur," the latter being a title bestowed upon local notables for services rendered the British; the Vice-President was a titled Muslim notable. Among the twenty elected members and five government nominees were a few Congressmen including Seth Achal Singh, the man who was to become Agra's Member of Parliament (MP) after 1952. Even he was from one of the wealthiest and most influential families of the city.[73]

Because of the city's mounting debts, a Governmental Inquiry Committee was constituted in 1941 to look into the finances of Agra; that body recommended that the municipality be superseded. Administrators appointed by the state government then presided over the operations of the city administration until shortly after Independence. One of the two men who served in both the 1941 body and the corporation elected in 1959 conceded that the municipality probably deserved supersession because of its failure to meet its obligations, but he went on to place its democratic successor in an equally unfavorable light. This member's father had served on the municipal body prior to 1916 and he himself sat there continuously from 1929 until the supersession. From his perspective,

> Previously members were all respected people. They belonged to high families and were good speakers. They did not belong to parties. There was only Congress then and the people who were independents worked with Congress with no bad feelings.
>
> Back then we knew that the officials would not take money. Now that is not so. I used to like the job of being a member of the municipality. Previously I had the power to get jobs for people I liked; now in order to get anything out of the corporation, it is necessary to give money.

Even if we accept this statement at face value, it overlooks the implications of a certain element of democratization for the conversion of bases of influence in the matter of appointments from status to money resources. More important, it recognizes the inability of current corporation members to influence appointments in quite the manner previously characteristic of the municipality.

Under the Administrator regime which functioned from 1943 to 1947, popular participation in municipal administration was highly restricted. It was only partially restored in November 1947, when the Congress government of Uttar Pradesh appointed an eleven-member Municipal Committee, consisting almost entirely of Congress members, to preside over the municipal government. These nominees took the place of the state-appointed Administrator.[74]

This "temporary" body functioned for about four years as a municipal board or until its life was ended in the wake of intraparty conflicts between certain local Congress leaders and the state Congress. In particular, some of the members of the committee refused to support local candidates of the UP Congress nominated for seats in the state and national legislatures in the general elections of 1951-52. This impasse symbolized the emergence of party factionalism in Agra—factionalism which has plagued the Congress in Agra for most of the last seventeen years.

On the basis of a recommendation made by the last Administrator before his departure, a separate Improvement Trust was created for the city in 1950 to deal with city planning and housing problems. As we noted earlier, there was some reluctance, particularly on the part of the dominant merchant community, to build homes on the outskirts of the central city. Several factors lay behind this reluctance: uneasiness about the political consequences of Partition; the fear of *dacoits*—armed robbers active in the countryside near Agra; the failure of the city to provide amenities in these areas. The Improvement Trust set about developing land for housing colonies and providing basic facilities to attract citizens to the outskirts of the city. The trust was organized with its own Executive Officer and a separate nominated board during the period of the nominated Municipal Committee.

After the Municipal Committee was superseded, there was an expectation that a new system of democratic local government would be speedily intro- duced. Instead, the revived Administrator regime remained in operation in Agra until the passage of the Uttar Pradesh Nagar Mahapalika [Municipal Corpora- tion] Act in late 1958.

One of the factors which contributed to lengthening the legislative process was the factionalism which existed within the Uttar Pradesh Congress Party and its fear of unfavorable results in any election arising from the promulgation of the new act. Certainly, procrastination could hardly be attributed to the demands of innovation. The act which emerged was based largely on the Bombay Provincial Corporations Act with a rather limited number of modifications. Elections for the representative section of the new corporation were finally scheduled for October 1959, after some additional hesitation on the part of the Uttar Pradesh Government.

Corporation Organization

The corporation system operative in both Agra and Poona nominally subordinates the municipal commissioner—also called the Chief Executive Officer (CEO) or, in the Hindi version, *Mukhya Nagar Adhikari* (Chief City Officer)—to the legislative determinations of the elected council. In fact, he has considerable independence from them both because of the manner of his appointment and the inclusion in the act of areas of administrative authority which do not depend upon his receiving the support of the council.

In its formal attributes, the role of CEO resembles that of a European *prefect*, who is an agent of a higher authority and is not especially concerned with exhibiting loyalty or responsibility to the local body with which he is dealing.[75] The CEO, like the District Magistrate, is usually a member of the national administrative elite, the Indian Administrative Service; he is appointed to his local post for a term of three years by a state government. In practice, CEO's are subject to reassignment at any time, which generally means more rapid movement than the recommended term length would suggest. The appointment of CEO's involves little consultation with local politicians.

Because his orientations are toward the state government, any control over a CEO's actions exercised from the local level may actually be best achieved by working through the state capital. In Uttar Pradesh, for example, the CEO is appointed by the Chief Minister of the state—the leader of the majority group in the state assembly—in consultation with the Chief Secretary, who is at the apex of the state bureaucracy but is sensitive to the currents of political life in the state. Complaints to the Chief Minister have, on occasion, been more effective in influencing the behaviors of CEO's than local pressure directly applied.

The CEO is a channel for communication between the state and municipal governments. Only under extreme circumstances is he likely to be subject to the formal will of the elected corporation members. They can bring a vote of no confidence (requiring a five-eighths majority) against him, but in the normal course of events this is not an effective instrument of control, especially since municipal councils tend to be divided into numerous factions and a CEO should be able to keep them divided with a minimal investment of effort. Enough cases of successful or attempted votes of no confidence have occurred, however, to keep some pressure on the CEO to conform to strongly held local values.

The members of the municipal council ("corporators") are elected under slightly different arrangements in Agra and Poona. In Agra, there are sixty seats in the corporation: forty-four of these are now general seats open to all contestants, while ten are reserved for the election of members of the Scheduled Castes.[76] These fifty-four seats are distributed among twenty-seven two-member wards. In addition, the law provides that six aldermen be elected by members of the corporation. These aldermen were supposed to play the role of elder statesmen; they were to be drawn from among distinguished local notables and nonpolitical persons who might not be inclined to engage in political campaigns. In practice, the men elected to these positions are most commonly chosen on the basis of partisan attachments.[77] Despite discussion of possible alterations in the system after 1959, no changes were made for the 1968 elections.

In Poona, a major revision of electoral organization took place in 1968. Until that year, the city was divided into twenty wards from which sixty-five corporators were elected—fifty-nine from general seats and six from seats reserved to the Scheduled Castes. For the 1968 elections, the twenty wards were replaced by seventy-three single-member districts. (There are no aldermen in Poona.) Up to 1968, districts varied in size and number of representatives because of efforts to maintain the traditional *peths* (wards) of the city as meaningful political entities. Under the earlier system, the smallest *peths* received two seats while the largest one was allocated six.[78]

The bodies when fully constituted elect their own presiding officers: a mayor and deputy mayor. Both cities elect mayors annually; Poona does this for the deputy mayor as well, but the deputy mayor of Agra has additional stature. Not only is he the presiding officer at general meetings in the mayor's absence, but he is an ex-officio member and presiding officer of the two major committees of the corporation. The deputy mayor's position is enhanced by a provision in the act that makes his term coterminous with the life of the corporation. As we shall see, this fact has contributed to considerable political in-fighting in the Agra corporation.

A further difference between the procedures in the two cities is that the mayors and deputy mayors in Poona may be chosen only from among the membership of the corporation; this principle applies to the deputy mayor of Agra, but there is no such restriction in the case of the mayor.[79] And, in fact, Agra went outside the body for two of its four mayors during the period from 1959 to 1965.

Despite the conflicts which have arisen over the mayoral position in both cities, it is an office lacking in formal power. Political factors have tended to limit most mayors to one term (at least in Poona) with the result, as one suggested, that "you spend a few months going around from meeting to meeting being congratulated, and before you know it, the contest has already begun for the next year."[80] The mayors do have a limited appointive power for some minor positions, but the more important appointments to the bureaucracy are made in consultation with the Municipal Commissioner, who is often the dominant figure in these relationships, or upon the recommendation of the State Public Service Commission.

Each corporaton has committees which process much of the work of the corporation before it comes to the floor of the general body. Agra has two principal committees: an Executive Committee, which passes on budgetary and policy matters and sets the agenda for general meetings; a Development Committee, which is charged with setting up and maintaining a Master Plan and with reviewing major building and development schemes for the city. The latter body replaced the Improvement Trust, which was absorbed into the corporation under the act of 1959.

All twelve members of the Agra Executive Committee are elected from the general body of corporators and aldermen. In addition to ten corporators elected to the Development Committee, two persons are coopted from the general public. The two coopted members are supposed to contribute special skills to the work of the committee. In fact, like the aldermen, they are chosen on a partisan basis. Half of each committee retires every year with contests over these posts providing an additional occasion for partisan points to be registered.

There are a greater number of committees in Poona and almost any corporator with an interest in municipal work can achieve election to one of them. The most important within the corporation itself is the Standing Committee, which plays much the same role for Poona that the Executive Committee does in Agra. It processes recommendations for action from other committees and scrutinizes the budget before that document (which, as in Agra, is prepared by the CEO and his staff) is sent to the floor. Other important committees include two which are only partially under the corporation: the Transportation Committee, which is responsible for making policy for the municipally-owned but semi-autonomous Poona Municipal Transport (PMT) system; and the School Committee, which passes on matters affecting the publicly-operated primary schools of the city. Other corporation committees deal with such matters as public works, public health, law, and improvements. (The latter committee resembles Agra's Development Committee in its concern with planning). Committees vary in size from nine to twelve members with their chairmen being elected by members of each committee usually on an annual basis; a member's length of service on a particular committee also varies with the Transportation and School Committees involving longer terms than the others. Indeed, four-year staggered terms for members of the Transportation Committee occasionally result in defeated corporators continuing to sit on this corporation-related body for several years after their rejection by the voters. The term of the office of the School Board members is three years; the life of that body as a whole ends with the expiration of the term of the corporation which elected the School Board members.

Overview

If municipal corporations do not permit as much direct political authority to democratically elected members as is the case in the municipal board system, critics of the latter subject that form to what they consider to be a more serious set of charges: boards fall prey to internal warfare which disrupts municipal administration; the fragmentation which sometimes results from allowing various members of a board to supervise certain departments may create financial and political confusion; in some instances, it is difficult to hold anyone responsible for the failure of the city to perform the tasks set for it by higher units of government.

It was in this light that spokesmen for the corporation system argued that the largest cities of India required more than sporadic oversight by audit and inspection agencies. In effect, the corporation acts created the role of CEO as a check to the possible abuse of power by popularly-elected bodies.[81] But if he is the formal head of the local bureaucracy, the CEO is also an administrative transient. His subordinates may be local people or appointees of the corporation more readily "reached" by the public. When these local bureaucrats do not share a strong sense of dedication to their work, they are available to the pressures exerted by local politicians, especially the corporators. This is a reflection of the process by which democratization alters those institutional arrangements which are not in keeping with the political temper of a society, even when democratization is not posited as one of purposes which the system itself is expected to accentuate.

Whether desired or not, the municipal institutions introduced into Agra and Poona by their corporation acts have been significantly influenced by the political and social processes found in the two cities during the past twenty years. It is to a discussion of those processes that we turn next.

2

POLITICIANS AND POLITICAL GROUPS

Before examining the political and administrative behaviors observed within the municipal arenas of Agra and Poona, it is important to identify some of the mechanisms through which participants gain access to those arenas. In this chapter, we present an outline of the major political groups, key individuals, and pivotal events which have played a part in defining the character of local politics in the two cities since Independence.

For the purposes of this discussion, it should be made clear that political parties are being viewed as opportunity structures only slightly inferior to government itself. They are structures through which individuals or groups hope to advance status claims, accrue material benefits, or find platforms for the expression of ideas. Such political infrastructures are bound to be of particular importance in a society in which mobility along other dimensions tends to be restricted, as in the case of the economy, or where the status system is in considerable flux. In the latter instance, where a status structure based on ritual behavior is being subverted by an emerging conflict between class-based and egalitarian ethics, the importance of political organizations in recognizing and advancing demands for the registration of status claims on a society-wide basis becomes almost as important as the immediate distribution of specific benefits by government.

At the same time, the functions performed by political parties in India do not appear to assure particular parties a permanent capacity for organizational maintenance. A curious fact of contemporary Indian life is the rapid proliferation of political groups and the inability of existent organizations to absorb and retain group and individual loyalties. This may be the result of the highly instrumental character of many of these political organizations and of politics itself; it may also reflect the limited stock of material incentives available to maintain most political parties.

For nearly a generation after Independence, the Congress Party managed to retain an aura of "specialness" which made it distinct from other political organizations, but from the start this image barely cloaked highly divergent political factions. Deriving its post-1947 strength from an earlier period when the nationalist movement was a rival to the established government in attracting investments of energy and commitment by those drawn into political activity, the Congress continued after Independence as an arena where diverse groups sought to adjust their differences before referring to the larger political system.[1] When, in the late 1950s and early 1960s, the organization was no longer capable of aggregating newly emergent and older established interests with its earlier skill, the party's utility as an opportunity structure began to decay. Newer elements, as well as some of the party's older activists, began to withhold their support and to create rival political structures or to vitalize some of the minor parties which already existed.

In this respect, local politics in Agra and Poona can be understood fully only in relation to the successes and failures of the Congress organization nationally in adapting to change after 1947. The two cities chosen present a quite different image if viewed at the same point in time: in Agra, there was a marked decline in Congress strength between 1947 and 1967 as a younger generation of politicians found the party incapable of providing an adequate political outlet for them, and newly politicized lower-status groups sought their advancement through alternate outlets; like the Agra Congress, the party in Poona underwent a decline in the mid-1950s, but it emerged from this experience by 1962 with revitalized leadership and a new social base apparently capable of assuring it a large voice in local political affairs for many years to come.

A TYPOLOGY OF URBAN POLITICAL GROUPS

The individuals and political groups with which we are concerned in this volume are those which make demands upon political authority, participate actively in electoral campaigns—sometimes as candidates in their own right, sometimes working for candidates through political parties, sometimes as participants in ad hoc fronts or in independent political campaigns—and, most important, those who exercise influence in local political life because of the positions they hold in major political organizations or in government.

The heterogeneity of social structures in urban India and the unsteadiness of partisan political loyalties on the part of both the electorate and leading political activists makes it difficult to identify local party systems in a simple fashion. "Parties" are themselves often congeries of political groups; it is these smaller behavioral units and the nature of their distribution in larger political organizations which lends certain emphases to particular political parties. In behavioral rather than structural terms, four types of political groups are most readily identifiable as operating in the two local political systems: (1) personal followings; (2) ideational groupings; (3) political machines; and (4) primordially-based groups.[2]

The *personal following* grows out of the attachment which people have to a person or to his house "and not from regard for his political principles, loyalty to the party he represents, or in expectation of material rewards."[3] Followers attempt to enhance the political influence of the leader and, in turn, benefit from his advancement, but the prestige of the leader is a major interest pursued in their relations with other groups.

Ideational groupings hold a certain set of moral or social principles in common. These principles need not constitute a well-articulated or coherent social philosophy, but they are a significant force in holding membership in the group and differentiating it from other groups, even though in some cases it may be a matter of marginal differentiation. Thus, those persons holding ideational commitments to their political groups may perceive major differences even where analysis suggests that the groups are similar in many respects.

Political machines are groups for the collection and distribution of rewards to contributors of time and effort. Rewards are not exclusively material; they may include symbolic benefits like honorific offices, but most political machines persist on the basis of an ability to distribute relatively tangible prizes to their memberships and to provide services to the general public.

Primordial groups draw their support and part of their content from the ascriptive ties (blood, caste, religion, language) which members share, and from the nature of the demands which such groups make upon the political system. These demands may involve a desire for enhancement of the symbolic position of the group in the social order as well as in the political process. Where caste or religious interests are formally organized into associations, a political group may "represent" them in the governmental process, but there are instances in which such formal associations exist without being directly represented in politics. Conversely, individuals from a given social background may operate in politics without *speaking for* those social groups from which they spring.[4]

Despite fundamental disagreements in India over the nature of the proper political order, political actors at the local level demonstrate an ability and willingness to work within a system which is essentially "instrumental" in character. In the words of David Apter, "ultimate ends do not color every concrete act."[5] Almost every political group in India, no matter how fixed its ideational or primordial content, has found occasions on which it seemed worthwhile to reach agreements with groups which were hostile to some of the values it represented.

Political instrumentalism is reflected in two related features of the Indian political system. First, party loyalty is weak even among those persons most active in public life. With Independence, a number of leading figures in the dominant Indian National Congress left that organization to form their own political groups when their demands could not be met within the party. The Congress has continued to experience such defections on a regular basis. As other political organizations have grown since 1947, they have gone through some of the same difficulties in trying to maintain loyalties. As a result, national political organizations have had to carry on continuing bargaining relationships with various levels of their memberships and with autonomous regional and local political groupings to maintain or extend their support.[6]

A second, and closely connected, feature of Indian politics is the organization of most political parties on a relatively loose federal basis. Considerable autonomy is exercised by lower level organizational units in pursuing local or state gains even where party principle may be sacrificed in the process. Party identifications at various levels of the political order are, therefore, less a coherent set of interlocking cells of a single functioning organism than an unsteady series of arrangements among political groups bound together in a highly expedient fashion.[7]

As a result of this instrumentalism, it is not unusual to find all four types of political groups operating within the framework of a single "party" organization, although the nature of the "mix" may vary with the party. Indeed, Indian political parties are best seen as intermediate aggregative units lying somewhere between crystallized political groups[8] and expedient alliances. The more tightly integrated a political party is, the more it resembles a single political group, but for the reasons we have noted, this is a rare political phenomenon in India. For the most part, as in the case of the Congress, those loosely organized political "parties" characteristic of the system are themselves arenas in which more solidary political groups contest.

In that light, we may distinguish among four types of "alliances" operating in Agra and Poona during the period of the study:

1. The *pragmatic party* in which machine and other political groups come together for the achievement of limited material and symbolic ends. The Congress Party of Agra is the prototype of such an alliance. In 1964 it was composed of two major groups, one a personal following with machine overtones and the other essentially a machine. Both groups consisted of a variety of primordial elements. The kind of "groupism" evident in Agra was exacerbated at the local level throughout Uttar Pradesh (UP) by the bitter factionalism within the state Congress organization. In contrast, the Congress party in Maharashtra has been relatively unified since that state was created in 1960 under the leadership of Y. B. Chavan, now Central Home Minister. Chavan helped to construct a state organization which has been much closer to the model of a single political machine than any of the other groups observed in the two regions. The solidity of this machine owes much, as we shall see, to its identification with the interests of the single most important primordial group in Maharashtra.

2. A "purer" form of alliance is the *electoral agreement.* In multiparty systems, groups may retain their identities while forging a common ticket or refraining from supporting candidates of their own in certain contests as part of a larger bargain. Frequently, there is no commitment to postelection cooperation. Thus, the Republican party—almost exclusively composed of ex-untouchables—and prominent Muslims of Agra (both primordial groups) participated in an alliance for the 1962 MP (Member of Parliament) and MLA (Member of the [State] Legislative Assembly) elections. They achieved some notable electoral successes in Agra District, but this agreement was not institutionalized.

3. Cooperation may be extended for limited purposes to allow the formation of *governmental coalitions* where diverse political groups associate for the sake of temporary majorities. Thus, in Agra sixteen independents (including three Muslims) worked in coalition with the Republicans and the philosophically anti-Muslim, Hindu-conservative Jan Sangh. In coalition, they controlled the positions of mayor and deputy mayor in the corporation and the minor perquisites that went with those offices. Since the 1967 general elections, half the Indian states have experienced coalitions of a similar nature.

4. Finally, a *fusion organization* brings together a diversity of political groups to fight an election with the expectation that the organization will persist to participate in government. It attempts to obliterate the separate identities of the participating groups. Poona has had several such groups since 1947 including: the Samyukta Maharashtra Samiti (United Maharashtra Committee), which functioned as a party demanding a separate linguistic state of Maharashtra in the second half of the 1950s; and the Nagri Sanghatna (City Party), which has appealed to the voters of Poona as a "good government" front opposed to "party politics" in the municipal elections of 1952, 1962, and 1968. In practice, such fusion organizations have gained much of their electoral support *just because* they consisted of some persons with strong attachments to ongoing political groups. Supporters of these organizations included others who had broken with the Congress, as well as some few who joined a fusion party precisely because they favored its "nonpartisan" stance.

Thus, while group conflicts have been pervasive in the two cities, each system has developed devices for achieving cooperation and aggregating a range of political forces into a governmental majority. To a considerable extent, types 2, 3, and 4 of alliance have been employed by anti-Congress political organizations as a means of countering the strength which flowed to the Congress from its association with the wielders of power at the state and national levels. (The Congress was in the majority in both states before 1967.) The alliances formed against the faction-ridden Congress in Agra brought together a diverse set of political groups merely for the purposes of a governmental coalition. In Poona, the operation of the Congress (after 1960) as a well-integrated political machine dominated by the non-Brahmins of the state created a situation in the peculiar climate of Poona politics—with its balance between benefit-seeking Marathas and ideologically-inspired Brahmins—where primordial, ideational, and personalistic groups which did not fit into the Congress mold coalesced into opposition alliances. The remainder of this chapter details some of the leadership and group factors which contributed to the creation of these two related but distinct local political styles in the period leading up to the creation of the corporation in Agra in 1959 and to the first municipal elections in Poona following the creation of the Marathi-speaking state of Maharashtra in 1960.

POLITICS IN AGRA BEFORE THE CORPORATION

Paul Brass, drawing on his study of Congress organization in five districts of Uttar Pradesh, suggests that the factional politics characteristic of that state depend largely upon the formation of groups around particular political leaders at the local level. The resulting groups pursue material benefits as well as attempting to advance the relative political status of the group leader.[9] Not only is this basis of group formation evident in the Congress organization in Agra, but it is also characteristic of other political parties active in the city. Viewing the local political system as a whole, however, it is clear that personality and material benefits are not the only stimuli for the formation of political groups. Thus, primordial and ideational differences clearly separate organizations like the Republican Party of India and the Jan Sangh from each other. More subtle differences also separate the Congress from each of these opposition parties. These differences involve an ideational, and somewhat generational, dimension, which requires some specification in the following pages.

The Agra Congress

The Congress organization in Agra was dominated during the nationalist movement and for the next twenty years by men of upper-caste and upper middle-class backgrounds. One of the key persons in local politics who typified this stratum was Shri Krishan Dutt Paliwal (1894-1968), who came of a Brahmin landowning family in Agra district. He was educated at Agra and Aligarh Universities, receiving an MA and LLB from the latter in 1921. After becoming active in the Congress organization in Kanpur, he returned to Agra in 1924 and began his own Hindi newspaper, *Sainik*.[10]

Because of Paliwal's own political skills and the low level of institutionalization of the Congress organization at the time, it did not take long for him to
become a dominant figure in Congress politics in both the city and the district. At
various times, he held the presidency of the city and district Congress committees;
he was also prominent in state party affairs. As the leader of the local Congress, he
was automatically a member of the United Provinces Congress Committee (UPCC)
and he also became a member of the All-India Congress Committee (AICC)—the
governing assemblies for the state and national parties, respectively. (The United
Provinces were renamed "Uttar Pradesh" after Independence.) In 1927, Paliwal
served as a Secretary of the UPCC. He later became President of the state party
during the difficult period from 1940 to 1946.

In 1946, as Independence loomed, Paliwal was selected for the important
position of Minister for Finance and Information in the Uttar Pradesh Cabinet.
Despite an earlier affinity for the more aggressive elements of the party, he was now
associated with moderates in the party like Rafi Ahmed Kidwai and J. B. Kripalani.
Along with these leaders, Paliwal became engaged in a series of battles for control
of the Uttar Pradesh and All-India Congress organizations.[11] An offer made to
Paliwal of a seat in Parliament for the 1952 elections fell considerably short of his
desire for a nomination for MLA (and a possible ministerial post) with the result
that he quit the party and helped to organize the Kisan Mazdoor Praja Party
(KMPP; "Peasants', Workers', and People's Party") in Uttar Pradesh—an organization composed largely of disaffected Congressmen.[12]

There was no obvious successor to Paliwal in the Agra Congress. If, as Paul
Brass suggests, many political factions in Uttar Pradesh are based largely on
personal ties to a particular leader rather than on personal interests, resignations
from the Agra Congress should have been more numerous than they were following
Paliwal's departure. Instead, despite Paliwal's active opposition to the Congress in
1952, the party won easily in the contests for the twelve legislative seats (ten for
MLA and two for MP) in the district. For the MP seat from the area which included
Agra City, the Congress nominee—Seth Achal Singh—won with something over
fifty-seven thousand votes better than Paliwal, his nearest rival.[13]

Seth's political career paralleled that of Paliwal, although it was more heavily
concentrated in urban Agra. His family members were moneylenders and
substantial property owners in Agra and in nearby areas of Rajasthan. With four or
five other families in the city, they are said to have "run things" in Agra at the turn
of the century. Unlike Paliwal, Seth was scantily educated, having foregone part of
his education for the more exciting world of politics. From 1918 to 1930, he served
as vice-president of the Agra City Congress Committee and in 1930 became
president of that body. In 1937 and, again, in 1946, he was elected to the State
Assembly. When Paliwal withdrew from the Congress, Seth was an obvious choice
to replace him in the contest for MP.

Seth was much less involved than Paliwal in the factional battles within the
Uttar Pradesh Congress in the years immediately after Independence. Indeed, he
became a regular member of the AICC and UPCC only after 1948. There was no
question, however, that he was then and remains today a personally popular figure
in Agra City. He is a well-known philanthropist and is admired for his devotion to

his religious community, the Oswal Jains. For over thirty years he has held major positions in Jain organizations and for nearly a decade was President of the All-India Oswal Jain Association.[14]

While Seth inherited some of the Congress organization upon Paliwal's departure, there were other claimants to leadership. One group was led by the MLA for the northern part of the city—a person of Bania caste; another group was headed by a Brahmin lawyer, Bhogilal Misra. Smaller than the other two, Misra's group held a balance of power between them for a brief period.

In the years from 1952 to 1957, the anti-Seth forces seemed to weaken as the MLA withdrew from politics and Misra was appointed Government Counsel, which meant he had to give up an active role in politics. Those elements opposed to Seth—representing no coherent primordial, ideational, or personal groupings—came under the nominal leadership of Adiram Singhal, an Agarwal (Bania) businessman.

Informants suggest that Singhal became a group leader only by chance. As one summarized the situation, "he had a car and some time." Singhal did represent a better-educated group of activists than those associated with Seth, having been educated at Fergusson College in Poona, but the differences between the Singhal and Seth groups of the Congress were marginal as concerns social backgrounds and general attitudes. In terms of organizational activity, however, Singhal was much less a public man than Seth. He tended to work within the party and to draw heavily upon his influence with those who played important roles within the local and state Congress structures.

One of the men with whom the Singhal group maintained contact was J. P. Rawat. Like Paliwal, Rawat was born into a landholding Brahmin family based in rural Agra. He received an LLB from Agra College in 1929 and embarked upon a political career in Agra district. The MLA district which he has represented for a greater part of the past twenty years includes the village where he was born, and he claims kinship with persons in many of the other villages in the constituency. During the early 1930s, Rawat worked as Secretary of the District Congress and was elected to the United Provinces Assembly in 1937. He was Parliamentary Secretary to Kidwai when the latter served as Home Minister in the Uttar Pradesh government after the 1946 elections[15] and a Secretary of the Uttar Pradesh Congress from 1942 to 1946. Although Rawat joined Paliwal in his dissidence from the Congress organization after 1947, he remained with the party when Paliwal departed, and assumed a position of leadership in Agra district.

Rawat is representative of those urbanized political leaders in Agra who have strong support and influence in the rural parts of the district. The pattern of urban-rural relationships is by no means unidirectional. Thus, the first mayor under the Agra corporation elected in 1959 was a rural-based politician who had some minor property holdings in the city and was well known to the City Congress organization. Similarly, Rawat occasionally became involved in city politics because of his personal ties and organizational commitments at the state level.[16]

Before 1959, some informants claim, both the Singhal and Seth groups in the city and the Rawat group in rural Agra were associated with the wing of the state party led by C. B. Gupta. In the 1957 elections, for example, Rawat lost his MLA seat while C. B. Gupta was losing his own contest and both withdrew from legislative activity to concentrate on building up their organizational influence. Rawat served as General Secretary of the UPCC in 1958-59 while C. B. Gupta dominated that organization.

Subsequently, Rawat was appointed to a major patronage position as Chairman of the Provincial Mortgage Bank, a post which he held until his reelection to the Assembly in 1962. In the distribution of portfolios in the new State Cabinet led by Gupta as Chief Minister, Rawat was given only a Deputy Ministership, despite his seniority in the party. The result was a falling out with Gupta.[17] This disagreement was aggravated by the fact that the Gupta forces now had a more reliable base in Agra district, a base which they had acquired through marriage into a Bania family influential in both the city and district.

The family in question was headed politically by Ram Chand Gupta, one of five brothers born into a prosperous landowning family before the turn of the century. Ram Chand Gupta came to Agra City for his education and eventually established himself as a leading lawyer in the city, but the family's connections to their land were maintained. By the 1950s, Gupta was a senior advocate of the Supreme Court and had held various legislative positions in the state (MLA, 1937-52) and nationally (Constituent Assembly, 1946-50; Rajya Sabha, 1952-60), but he did not join the Congress until 1946. Prior to that time he was an independent.

Ram Chand Gupta's son, Shiv Prasad, was one of the few major figures under sixty in the Agra Congress in 1964. He was born in 1915 and earned an MA in 1938 from Agra College before entering private business. Only in 1952 did he become involved in political life when he was appointed President of the predemocratized District Board for Agra; he served in that position until 1957. In 1960, he was elected to the Uttar Pradesh *Vidhan Parishad* (the upper house of the Legislature) from a local bodies constituency.[18] He has since become a powerful figure in Agra district politics, a situation enhanced by his designation as a Deputy Minister in 1962 when C. B. Gupta became Chief Minister.

Certain central points emerge from this description of some of the leaders of the Agra City and District Congress organizations. Except for Shiv Prasad Gupta, the Congress Party's top leadership as late as 1959—and even in 1967—remained in the hands of men who were active in public life prior to 1947. As we shall see, this situation contrasts sharply with the generational turnover and social change which the Poona Congress has experienced in the last two decades.

In terms of traditional status, the Agra Congress has been controlled throughout this time by persons belonging to the old upper-status local elite or those fairly close to it. In primordial terms, this means middle- to upper-class Brahmins, Banias, Kayasthas, and Khatris with important leadership roles being played also by Thakurs and Jats in rural Agra. This is not a closed "ruling elite" by any Western sense of that term, since the groupism already mentioned encourages a considerable degree of recruitment and solicitation of support from middle- and lower-status groups in the city. As late as 1968, however, the impact of widespread recruitment efforts had only been felt sporadically within the Congress at the *leadership* level; it was increasingly reflected in the candidacies of the Congress for municipal, state, and national offices, but difficulties flowed from the generational facts of Agra political life where the "nationalists" still ran the Congress organization without permitting much access to younger elements anxious to advance their political ambitions.

This is not meant to denigrate the changes which have taken place in Agra politics over the past thirty years. Power passed in 1947 from the British and influence from a class of Indians sympathetic to them to a generation of dedicated nationalists—men who had participated in the struggle for freedom from British rule, served time in prison, helped in the work of the Congress and generally identified with the causes promoted by the Gandhian leadership. Once in power, however, the nationalists of Agra became political pragmatists and participants in the machine and group politics of Uttar Pradesh. Groups developed over division of the perquisites of power—offices, favors, public projects. Conflicts over personal status also became endemic. As a result, in Agra the Congress ceased to be an instrument for change; by 1962 it was in partial disarray and fairly restrictive in its approach to new political entrants.

Internal party divisions first began to take their toll on the Congress in the municipal elections of 1959. Until that time, there had been no viable organizational alternative to the Congress in Agra. An individual like Paliwal might occasionally capitalize upon particular events to win personal victories over the Congress. But such defeats were relatively insignificant organizationally, as, for example, Paliwal's victory over the wife of Bhogilal Misra (herself an active political worker) in a by-election for an MLA seat in 1956, or his even more impressive defeat of Rawat in the general elections of 1957, when Paliwal received the backing of a dissident leader of the Thakur caste in the district.[19] By 1957, growing dissidence within the Congress contributed to a substantial fall in the Congress vote throughout Uttar Pradesh, but the party managed to hold on to a large legislative majority.[20]

The Republican Party

Since 1956, members of the Jatav caste have emerged as a major political force in Agra politics. They were traditionally placed among the lowest untouchable status groups in the Hindu hierarchy. In North Indian villages, Jatavs performed such highly polluting tasks as the dehiding and disposal of the carcasses of dead cattle. In urban areas, they have turned their leatherworking tradition to the making of shoes. This occupation provided them with a significant economic foundation for the series of political and social changes which have characterized the community in the past fifty years.

For the first three decades of this century, Jatavs engaged in a self-improvement campaign which included efforts to raise the status position of the community within the traditional caste hierarchy. Like other mobility-seeking castes, they attempted to emulate higher status groups in social practices and to create a more favorable history of the caste which included a claim to higher traditional status.[21] At the same time, they pursued education and certain social reforms along Western lines.

In the 1920s, the community achieved limited symbolic successes through political appointments to certain legislative positions. These were backed up by the entry of Jatavs into educational institutions and minor bureaucratic positions as clerks in government and police officers. The Jatav effort at mobility by traditional means was slowed, however, by the very success of their shoe businesses. The making of shoes was too close to the Jatavs' traditional occupational position to permit the stigma of pollution to be abandoned readily, but it was too profitable for the Jatavs to abandon. Increased benefits extended by the Government to the Scheduled Castes in the 1930s also tended to weaken efforts at traditional forms of mobility.[22] Finally, in the 1930s, this Agra community was attracted to the westernizing influence of B. R. Ambedkar, a national leader for certain Scheduled Caste groups.[23]

Ambedkar was born in the province of Bombay and educated in the United States (a PhD in economics from Columbia University) and England (a law degree from the University of London). A member of the untouchable Mahar community of Maharashtra, he provided the intellectual leadership and symbolic identification point that certain aspiring outcaste communities rallied behind. After 1930, Ambedkar frequently acted as the spokesman of the Scheduled Castes at political negotiations and on public occasions. Ambedkar strongly opposed what he regarded to be Gandhian efforts to better integrate the outcastes into the traditional Hindu social order on terms of accepted inferiority. He pressed, instead, for political power and group separation from Hinduism. The latter effort was capped in 1956 with his own conversion to Buddhism. This conversion was emulated by a large number of Mahars in Bombay and Poona and by a lesser number, though still a politically significant element, of the Jatavs of western Uttar Pradesh.

Although Ambedkar was a recognized figure in national political life—he served as Law Minister in the first Nehru government after Independence and played a leading role in the formulation of the Indian Constitution—his efforts at turning the untouchables into a viable political force were not very successful. Following Ambedkar's lead, the Jatavs of Agra did organize local units of his Scheduled Caste Federation in 1944-45, as did the Mahars of Maharashtra. For many of them, this organization was a mark of their break with the dominant social and political order, but the party also raised a dilemma with which the Jatavs and Mahars are still struggling: Is partisan separatism feasible for a distinct primordial minority within a large and partially antagonistic social system?

One of the factors contributing to the weakness of the Scheduled Caste Federation (SCF), aside from problems of mobilizing a previously subjugated people, was the manner in which the system of reserved seats operated. As the result of a pact made between Gandhi and Ambedkar in 1932 in Poona—a pact which Gandhi forced upon Ambedkar by resort to a fast—reserved seats were to be filled by voters from all primordial backgrounds living in a given geographical area. As Ambedkar feared, this arrangement allowed the Congress to draw upon its large base of support among the general Hindu population to elect many of the Scheduled Caste candidates it put up rather than representatives of other political parties including the SCF. Furthermore, the practical political calculations growing out of this situation encouraged the bulk of the Scheduled Castes to continue their support of the Congress.

In 1946, when elections were held in Agra, a division clearly emerged in the Jatav community. Some of the more cautious businessmen and community leaders feared possible harm to the community or to their own economic interests if the

Jatavs were not loyal to the Congress;[24] the more "militant" Jatavs worked with the SCF. In return for their support, the "conservatives" within the Jatav community received nominations for reserved seats within the Uttar Pradesh Assembly and they were easily able to defeat the candidates of the SCF. Over the next ten years, however, the non-Congress Jatav politicians gradually improved their relative position within their own ranks, and the weakening hold of the Congress began to tell in their favor as the margin of defeat narrowed. Still, as late as 1957, the Jatavs were not capable of mounting a successful challenge to the Congress in elections for reserved legislative seats.[25]

By 1959, however, a growing part of the Jatav community appeared to be opting for the more difficult political alternative of opposition to the Congress and the larger Hindu public.[26] While some Jatavs continued working with the Congress and some of these were even supported by their own community in return for being useful channels for the presentation of group demands within the "enemy" camp, the anti-Congress militancy of Ambedkar's later years and the self-consciousness induced through its conversion to Buddhism made the community highly "available" for anti-Congress partisan identifications. When a new political organization, the Republican Party of India (RPI), was formed in 1958, the Jatavs of Agra quickly organized a local unit. The RPI was intended by Ambedkar (before his death in 1957) to be different from the SCF by directing its appeals not only at members of the Scheduled Castes but at all persons seeking the improvement of the position of the "downtrodden" communities of India.

The new party, with major bases in Maharashtra, western Uttar Pradesh, and the Punjab, has failed to achieve any considerable support outside the ranks of the Scheduled Castes and neo-Buddhists. Despite these built-in limitations, the Agra party was able to win some impressive victories in 1959 and 1962; more recently, divisions within the RPI itself have reduced the effectiveness of the party, but even in 1968 the Republican Party in Agra provided a major focus for the political activity of the sizable Jatav community and a potential ally for other political groups in the city.

The Jan Sangh

In 1959, the Jan Sangh stood clearly to the right of the Congress in terms of its antipathy to Muslims, its narrower high-status base of support centered in the more orthodox segments of the Hindu community, and its militancy on such issues as relationships with Pakistan, support for a total ban on cow slaughter, and policies which would maintain or reinvigorate a traditionalized social order.

Part of the weakness of the Jan Sangh in Agra was due to the ability of the local Congress to preempt some of its policy positions and to gain the group support that went with them. At the same time, Congress as a pragmatic party sought support as best it could from among Muslims and the Scheduled Castes.

The Jan Sangh is the latest expression of Hindu communalism, although it would be misleading to argue that it is simply that and no more. The organization of such sentiments in modern India began with groups like the Arya Samaj, which was active in northern India by the late 1870s.[27] Within the boundaries of a definite commitment to Hinduism, the Samaj attempted to effect certain changes in traditional practices and ways of thinking which would make Hinduism capable of responding to the challenges of Westernization. In 1915, the Hindu Mahasabha emerged as a more distinctly political group. The Mahasabha was geared particularly to fighting against the political demands of the Muslims. A decade later, the Rashtriya Swayamsevak Sangh (RSS; National Volunteers' Organization) originated as a "cultural" group which conducted prayer meetings and celebrated Hindu festivals, while providing a militant "strong arm" for the Mahasabha when the occasion warranted.

For some years, the RSS worked in conjunction with the Hindu Mahasabha, but differences arose over the extent of support the RSS was willing to provide to the Mahasabha in political matters. After the assassination of Mahatma Gandhi by a Poona Brahmin in 1948—an act in which the RSS was vaguely implicated—the leader of the RSS, Mahadev Golwalkar, spoke of the desirability of withdrawing the organization entirely from politics,[28] but other leaders favored the formation of a new political party which ultimately became the Bharatiya Jan Sangh (Indian Peoples' Party) in 1951.

Militant young activists of the RSS helped to form the Jan Sangh in western Uttar Pradesh. Recent national leaders of the party like Deen Dayal Upadhyaya and Atal Behari Vajpayee worked among those receiving their higher educations in Agra to form a cadre of young men from middle-class families of high caste backgrounds dedicated to building a strong Indian nation stamped with a reinvigorated Hindu culture. Not only was this perspective acceptable to many Brahmins and Banias in a city like Agra, but an additional base was provided to the party by the partition of the subcontinent. The migration to Agra of large numbers of refugees from the Punjab and Sind gave the Jan Sangh a political field which they were able to sow with their propaganda. By the 1950s, the physical activities and paramilitary style of the organization was exciting the imagination of a new generation of adolescents and college students in a way that the Congress no longer could.

Typical of the early leaders of the Agra Jan Sangh was Ram Babu Verma—a *Sonar* (Goldsmith) by caste. Born in Agra in 1923 of a wealthy business family, Verma attended an Arya Samaj College before becoming a "full-time worker" for the RSS in 1947; he was in charge of a city unit of the RSS at the age of twenty-four. The reluctance of leaders of the RSS to get directly involved in partisan politics caused Verma and others to leave active work in the organization in 1948-49. During this hiatus, Verma received his law degree from Agra College and began to practice, but he was drawn back to political activity when a Jan Sangh unit was set up for Agra. He became the District Organizing Secretary of the new party, a key position, but in the wake of the elections of 1952, internal party quarrels erupted and Verma withdrew to his legal practice.

Indeed, for the first six years of its life, the Agra Jan Sangh experienced a series of internal disputes over the nature of the party, its relationship to the RSS, and the role of particular leaders. After Verma departed, a claim to leadership was advanced by Bal Krishna (Baloji) Agarwal. Baloji was born into a spice merchant family and was attracted to the RSS through his classmates at Agra College. He became an organizer for the RSS and at the age of twenty-six (in 1950) he had organizational responsibility for the territory which included Agra and Etawah districts and the city of Meerut.

Like Verma, Baloji participated in the formation of the Agra Jan Sangh in 1951 and held a major directive position for the party in the five districts of Agra Division from 1954 to 1959. In 1957, he was the party's nominee for MLA in Agra City (North) because, according to Baloji himself, "there was no other suitable choice. I was well known among the party workers and could get their support." [29]

Coming into the municipal elections of 1959, however, the Jan Sangh was beset by new quarrels between Baloji and other leaders of the organization. The resultant disruption created enough instability in the party's appeal to weaken it for participation in the elections. As we shall see, the party did poorly. It took some time to recover from the subsequent open split in its leadership.

It is significant, nonetheless, that this generation of highly ambitious young politicians associated themselves with the Jan Sangh rather than the Congress, which might have accommodated some of them just as well. Furthermore, even when particular individuals and their followings withdrew from the Jan Sangh, they found little in the Congress to attract them. Instead, they joined a sizable "pool" of independents looking for an organizational base in Agra.

Other Political Groups

Although national political parties like the Praja [People's] Socialist Party (PSP) and Communist Party of India (CPI) were represented in Agra in 1959, they were small and ineffective political organizations. Agra provided an unfavorable climate for their leftist appeals. In 1957, in the MLA contest waged between Baloji for the Jan Sangh and Adiram Singhal for the Congress, the PSP managed to choose a candidate with some local appeal, but this was the high point of its electoral participation through 1967.

Factionalism within both the Congress and the Jan Sangh created a situation about the time of the first corporation elections which produced a large number of local political actors who were not immediately identified with any political party. A few, like Paliwal, had sufficient stature to stand without party backing for MP and MLA seats with some hope of success. Many were persons who had rejected their previous party connections, or had been rejected by parties for nominations, or were interested in politics but not in partisan terms.

Thus, in 1959 we find at least four major political groups and one "potential group" active in Agra: members of the two Congress factions—one more of a personal following, the other, a political machine; members of the Jan Sangh and Republican Parties; and a sizable number of non-affiliated individuals who at that time constituted a "group" only in the sense of potentiality. As we shall see in chapter 3, this potential was realized in 1959-60 with marked effect upon the course of municipal politics in Agra.

POLITICAL GROUPS IN POONA

The municipal body elected in Poona in 1962 was the third such body since the introduction of the corporation system in 1952. While the election of 1962 did not represent a turning point in terms of innovation in local political structures, it did follow upon more than a decade of major changes in the distribution of influence among participants in the local political arena and helped to further crystallize moves toward a new set of political arrangements in the city.

In Poona's relatively middle-class population, ideational phraseology is a regular feature in politics. Verbal darts are aimed from both the left and the right, primarily at the Congress, which stands pragmatically in the middle. While it would be a gross error to attempt to explain ideational and organizational differences simply in terms of caste, there does seem to be a tendency for the Brahmins of Poona to be more readily identifiable with ideational political groups—ranging from the extreme right to the extreme left—while the non-Brahmins (and here we refer especially to the Marathas) tend to dominate the non-ideological middle ground. In practice, this means that the people of Poona commonly speak of the Congress Party as a party controlled by Marathas—a generic term which sometimes includes both Marathas and other non-Brahmin groups. They also tend to see organizations like the Hindu Mahasabha and the Jan Sangh, on the right, as Brahmin in character. The Praja Socialist Party (and, since its birth in 1964, the Samyukta [United] Socialist Party) as well as the two Communist parties are more ambiguous in their social bases: non-Brahmin "interests" are represented in these parties, and some of their most active leaders are non-Brahmins, but there are also Brahmins in many prominent positions. As in Agra, however, the closest to a self-professed primordial political group is the Republican Party, which is dominated in Poona by Mahars.

Almost until Independence, the Congress organization in Poona tended to be heavily influenced by Brahmin leaders. Within the Brahmin community itself, the Chitpavan subcaste took the lead in nationalist politics much as it did in intellectual and administrative life in the region before the turn of the century.[30] With the advent of Gandhi, however, the more revolution-minded Brahmins became unhappy with the Congress and began to drift into other political organizations.

The Hindu Right

While B. G. Tilak, before his death in 1920, advocated a nonrevolutionary course for the nationalist movement, some of his Poona followers did not. The "Kesari group"—named for the newspaper which Tilak edited in Poona—opposed many of Gandhi's policies. After 1930, some of them were particularly upset by what they considered to be concessions being made by both the British and Congress to the Muslims. Many of these found a congenial home in the Hindu Mahasabha.

Particularly under the leadership of V. D. Sarvarkar, a Maharashtrian, the Mahasabha attracted a considerable following in Poona among high-caste Hindus; it managed to elect a plurality of the members of the pre-Independence Poona municipality. The Mahasabha and other Brahmin-led right-wing organizations were badly hurt by Gandhi's murder at the hands of a Poona Brahmin. As one local leader of the Mahasabha described the situation in February and March of 1948:

> There were riots for a month in Poona in which many Brahmin-owned houses and shops were destroyed. Many presses and the offices of the Hindu Mahasabha were attacked. Thirty people were killed. The murder of Gandhi gave the non-Brahmins an excuse to act against the Brahmins. The non-Brahmins in the Congress also saw their chance to avenge themselves on the Brahmins.

The Mahasabha emerged from these events much debilitated. After it resumed its political activity, it continued to champion a demand for "Hindu Rashtra" (Hindu Nation)—the creation of a "Hindu" state as opposed to the "secular" state favored by the Congress—but it failed to recruit new members, and many of its former members drifted out of the organization. Some of these continued to work within the RSS. They were a receptive audience when the Jan Sangh was formed in Poona in 1953-54—some time after the activation of Jan Sangh units in the north.

The social views of persons in the Jan Sangh and those few who remain in the Mahasabha are rather difficult to distinguish, but the comments of a Jan Sangh woman member of the corporation suggest her understanding of these rather narrow distinctions:

> I was sympathetic to the Mahasabha before the Jan Sangh was formed but since freedom the Mahasabha is a different question. Every man now has one vote in this country and we should work from as broad a base as possible. All persons with faith in Bharatiya [India] should be welcome here. I favor Bharatiya Rashtra [the Indian Nation] rather than Hindu Rashtra. Any man who serves the nation should be welcome. As long as the Hindus are the most powerful group and are in strong numbers, there is no danger from allowing other groups to take part.

As noted earlier, it is misleading to regard Jan Sangh members as merely traditionalists. Because of their overriding interest in building a strong Indian state, they have readily accepted those features of Western science and professional skills which they feel will contribute to that cause. It is not unusual to find doctors, lawyers, and those with technical expertise within their ranks. Members are able to think both in terms of cow protection and the development of nuclear weapons without any apparent shift in their cognitive structures. The woman quoted above, for example, was the wife of a geologist, and two of her three sons were doctors trained in Western-style medicine—activities hardly in keeping with traditional Brahmin roles.

The Leftist Parties

The Communist Party has never had a great following in Poona, but socialist appeals have received a responsive hearing in the city for over thirty years from among Brahmin and non-Brahmin intellectuals and from the industrial workers of the city. In some part, this is due to the personal popularity of two of the most prominent citizens of Poona—S. M. Joshi and N. G. Goray.

The backgrounds of the two men are strikingly similar. Both were born in the first decade of this century into lower middle-class Brahmin families. Joshi's father was a minor court official in a *taluka* (an intermediate rural administrative unit) near Poona; Goray's was a clerk in the Education Department of Bombay Province. Both men attended Fergusson College in Poona in the 1920s and then plunged into politics. They took part in the Congress movements of the 1930s, but they were less attracted to Gandhianism than to Western-bred ideas of socialism. While Joshi held important positions in the Poona Congress—he was Secretary of the District Congress in 1936 and a member of the AICC—he and Goray felt that Congress leadership was unresponsive to the economic realities of the time. For that reason, they participated in the formation of the Congress Socialist Party (CSP) as a sub-unit within the Congress in 1934. Goray has remarked on the development of the CSP:

> 1934 was the time of the Great Depression and the time when Russia was just beginning on its series of plans. We believed that only a socialist society could plan while a capitalist society is incapable of it. We started thinking of the needs of India after Independence and wanted to start organizing for it and spreading the ideology because the Congress was not suitable to such a program since it was a mass movement involving all sorts of people.[31]

Upon Independence, leaders of the CSP hoped to continue their work within the Congress, but the machinery of the party was in conservative hands. Sardar Vallabhbhai Patel, one of whose biographers concedes that he was not unsympathetic to the RSS,[32] was clearly opposed to socialism.[33] After Gandhi's death, Patel moved to end separatist groups within the Congress; a provision was added to the party constitution in 1948 which amounted to a virtual ultimatum to the CSP to disband.[34] Recognizing their weak position in the Congress, the Socialists chose to withdraw and set up their own party.

Like the KMPP, which consisted of Gandhian dissidents from the Congress, the Socialists hoped to emerge from the elections of 1951-52 with a clear-cut role as the major opposition party in India. Instead, they received only 10.6 percent of the national popular vote while the KMPP drew 5.8 percent. Despite the differences between the two groups, they merged in September 1952 to become the Praja Socialist Party (PSP). Shortly thereafter, the Congress began to make overtures to elements within the party. These efforts included the passage of a Congress resolution at a party meeting held at Avadi in 1954 which declared that henceforth the Congress was dedicated to the "establishment of a Socialistic pattern of society."

The effect of such Congress activities was to weaken the relationship between the moderate and militant wings of the PSP. In 1955, the more strongly anti-Congress forces under the leadership of Ram Manohar Lohia withdrew from the PSP and began the Socialist Party. In Poona, a small Lohia-ite group came into being, but leaders like Joshi and Goray remained with the PSP. In the years immediately preceding the 1957 elections, however, the elements associated with the PSP in Poona were less actively concerned with the propagation of socialism than with propagandizing a demand for the creation of a Marathi linguistic state—Maharashtra.

The Congress Party

While the Poona Congress did not exclude non-Brahmins from positions of leadership during the nationalist movement, prior to 1946 politically mobile non-Brahmins were not wholly comfortable in the organization. In the course of the first four decades of the present century, the non-Brahmins of Maharashtra had made important strides in education and in adaptation to the economic changes sweeping the society, but their political activities were relatively restricted. It was not until 1929 that an important group of non-Brahmins, led by K. M. Jedhe, joined the Congress.[35] Maratha leaders held positions of some consequence in government. S. S. More, for example, was President of the Poona District Board from 1935 to 1940, but he felt, in his own words, that he "remained an outsider in the organization."[36]

In 1932, Jedhe became Vice-President of the Maharashtra Pradesh Congress Committee (MPCC)—the organizational unit of the Congress set up for the Marathi-speaking region of Bombay State.[37] This did not constitute the first easy step to the takeover of the Maharashtra Congress by the non-Brahmins, however. While many non-Brahmins were nominated (and elected) by the party in the legislative elections of 1937, the President of the MPCC continued to be Shankarrao Deo, a Gandhian Brahmin, and the ministry formed as a result of the 1937 elections was led by B. G. Kher, a Brahmin, and composed essentially of non-Maharashtrians and Brahmins.

After the first postwar elections were held in 1946, the ministry was again formed by Kher, who followed much the same representational scheme as in 1937. The President of the MPCC then was N. V. Gadgil, a Poona Brahmin. In March, 1946, Gadgil was replaced by Jedhe as President, but this only exacerbated the conflict between the non-Brahmins in the party organization and the state ministry which refused to yield to non-Brahmin demands for ministerial recognition.

During the war, Jedhe had started a peasants' organization, and late in 1946 it was institutionalized as the Peasants and Workers League within the Congress. While intended as an instrument to increase non-Brahmin peasant support for the Congress, in Jedhe's hands it was also seen as a challenge to the Brahmin leadership of the Congress. When the national party moved in 1948 against the CSP, Shankarrao Deo, who was then serving as General Secretary of the All-India Congress Committee, pointed to that resolution as the basis for a demand that Jedhe's League be dissolved. Though Jedhe was still President of the MPCC, he chose to take some of his supporters out of the Congress and to form the Peasants and Workers Party in April 1948.[38] Proclaiming a distinctly leftist ideology, it made a strong bid for working-class support. In the context of the Maharashtrian economy and society, this meant its efforts were aimed principally at improving the position of the non-Brahmins.

Indeed, the caste bias of the PWP was a major stumbling-block to its association with an obvious ally, the PSP. Brahmins within the PSP resented the strong streak of anti-Brahminism which ran through the statements of some leaders of the PWP. By 1964, a leader like S. M. Joshi could look back on the problem with considerable compassion for the Marathas:

> From the time of the Peshwas, the rulers of Maharashtra were Brahmins. This resulted in the hatred of the non-Brahmins for the Brahmins. We were the elite and the trading community came from another place so that the non-Brahmins felt they had no place in policy-making. There was the sense after 1947 that though *swaraj* [self-government] had come, they were not getting their share. The PWP was one result of that feeling.[39]

The late S. S. More put the matter of relations between the PWP and PSP more personally: "There was a undercurrent against me because of my association with the non-Brahmins while most of the leaders of the Socialist Party were Brahmins." Thus, when Asoka Mehta, then one of the major leaders of the PSP, extended an invitation to Marathas to join the Socialist Party, he was rebuffed by both Marathas and elements within his own ranks.[40]

The PWP, running on its own, made some impact upon the Maharashtrian countryside in the elections of 1952 when it emerged as the chief opposition party to the Congress in the region. S. S. More himself was elected to Parliament from a seat in Sholapur District. But differences within the PWP soon appeared as More and some of his more socialist-inclined colleagues tried to press their ideas upon the peasant-proprietor Maratha community. As in the case of some of the members of the PSP, the Avadi resolution of 1954 provided an attractive opportunity for More and some of his associates to rejoin the Congress. A former aide of his explained the return to Congress in the following terms:

> More is an intellectual person but he gave up hope that any strong opposition party to Congress would be possible within his lifetime. He tried to form opposition to Congress around a socialist policy, but failed and decided it was better to join the party.

At the time that More rejoined, however, many Marathas continued to feel that they were not getting the kinds of benefits from the political system that their numbers in the population warranted. As electoral democracy became a more potent weapon in the hands of the larger communities, it soon was obvious that the remaining Brahmins would have to give way in the Maharashtra region. In the city of Poona, however, the situation was obviously more complex: the Marathas and Brahmins were evenly balanced; the city had a sizable non-Maharashtrian population which could vote either way; there existed a series of political groups based on appeals which cut across primordial loyalties. How the matter was resolved within the framework of democratic party politics is a central concern in our subsequent discussion of politics in Poona since 1952.

The Republican Party

Poona contains about 75,000 persons generally identifiable as ex-untouchables. Unlike Agra, a single group does not predominate. Most of the Scheduled Castes in the city—Chambhars, Mangs, Bhangis—accepted a minor position in the ranks of the Congress at least up to 1967. Only the Mahars, like the Jatavs, became politicized by operating within their own party organizations. The stages they went through in reaching this point resemble those described earlier for the Jatavs. On the whole, Ambedkar's influence penetrated deeper and had wider effects upon the aspirations of the Mahar community to which he belonged. In terms of local political power, however, the RPI and its SCF precursor had little impact in Poona up to 1960. Since 1960, the RPI has been additionally hampered by the existence of several factions. Indeed, it is probably better to describe the Republican Party as two political groups because two distinct political entities have functioned in Poona and elsewhere in Maharashtra since 1960, each claiming to be the true political heir of Ambedkar. We shall explore some of the sources of this division later in this chapter.

In the present section, we have identified some of the political groups operating on the Poona scene in the period leading up to 1952: the pragmatic Congress with its uneasy balance between increasingly politicized non-Brahmins and an embattled Brahmin leadership; the remnants of the Brahmin-based Hindu Mahasabha; Brahmin-led but non-Brahmin supported ideational groupings in the PSP and Socialists Parties; the Maratha-dominated, ideationally-tinged PWP; the Scheduled Caste Federation with its Mahar primordial base. As in Agra, many nonparty people functioned in Poona politics in the period prior to the general elections of 1952 and the corporation elections which immediately followed. After 1952, however, a number of these were absorbed, at least for municipal purposes, into a nonpartisan fusion organization, the Nagri Sanghatna (City Party), which served as an institutional haven for municipal opposition to the Congress.

ELECTORAL POLITICS IN POONA: 1952

Despite the numerous political groups which emerged in Poona after Independence, the Congress appeared much stronger than any other single political group or combination of groups after the MP and MLA elections of early 1952. One MP district and four MLA constituencies were then located substantially in metropolitan Poona, including one MLA district composed of the area within the Poona cantonment. In 1952, the Congress won all four seats for MLA, three by margins greater than 50 percent. The one seat where a Congress candidate failed to get 50 percent of the vote involved the most candidates—six. The winner there, a Maratha, received 48 percent with a non-Brahmin Socialist finishing second with 27 percent.[41]

The most revealing contest in the city was that for MP. The candidate of the Congress was N. V. Gadgil, a Brahmin. Gadgil was a long-time worker of the Congress and a man sympathetic to the Nehru wing of the national party. After holding positions at the local level for about a decade, Gadgil was elected to the Central Assembly in 1934 and remained prominently involved in national politics. He was Minister for Works, Mines, and Power in the first post-Independence Cabinet under Nehru. Thus, when he ran for office in 1952, he was an important Congress leader at both the national and state levels. Against this strong Congressman, the PWP countered with its own leader, K. M. Jedhe. The third major candidate was S. M. Joshi, who was supported by the Socialists. The field was completed by a candidate running on the ticket of a minor Hindu orthodox party. Despite the formidable opposition represented by the candidacies of Joshi and Jedhe, Gadgil received 53 percent of the vote against 22 percent for Jedhe and 17 percent for Joshi. If anything, Jedhe and Joshi probably succeeded only in hurting each other. Since Jedhe was the only Maratha candidate in the contest, the results also indicate—as will be apparent throughout this study—that primordial appeals are hardly reliable indices for predicting electoral outcomes.

In the wake of its easy victories in the general elections, the Congress might have been expected to be quite strong in the municipal elections which followed. In fact, the party's very successes made it more difficult for ambitious non-Brahmin aspirants working within the Congress structure to press their demands for more organizational influence. The outcome of the election also brought home to anti-Congress forces in the city the need for the creation of some semblance of a coalition to prevent Congress from winning too many seats on the basis of a divided opposition.

The lead in this matter was taken by N. B. Parulekar, the editor of the leading newspaper of Poona, the Marathi-language *Sakal,* with its claimed circulation of seventy thousand in the highly literate population of Poona and nearby districts of Maharashtra. Parulekar avowedly sought to remove the municipal arena from the "clutches" of political parties, particularly the Congress. While the organization which resulted, the Nagri Sanghatna, included some persons previously uninvolved in public affairs, the effort received substantial support from those sectors of the urban population which were already opposed to the Congress. The existent political parties did not formally participate in the Sanghatna, but some members of the Socialist Party and of the Hindu Mahasabha took part along with many non-Congress independents. The resultant organization strikingly resembled the "good government" middle-class fusion parties characteristic of the United States earlier in this century.

Such a party might have proved electorally inadequate if the dissatisfaction of an element of the non-Brahmin community with Congress leadership had not come to the aid of the Sanghatna. A major local leader of the Maratha community, B. N. Sanas, who was then aligned with the Congress, offered to work with the Sanghatna. In return, he and approximately thirteen of his followers were given Sanghatna tickets for the corporation.[42] Among the ironies of this alliance was that, prior to the agreement, one of the rationales behind the Sanghatna was the declared desire to build an organization which would exclude from the corporation those persons who had not performed in a manner consistent with the values the Sanghatna represented. Since Sanas had been President of the Poona Municipality for four years (1946-50) with Congress help, it is unlikely that he would have been included among the most desirable candidates if the Sanghatna had followed its own public precepts.

Sanas had had a checkered career in politics until this time, as was characteristic of other non-Brahmin leaders. He was a rich businessman and was noted (like Seth Achal Singh) for his charitable work and his willingness to come forward in behalf of those in need of intervention with administrators or to provide other aid and comfort when necessary. Many informants approvingly cited his efforts in helping to put down anti-Muslim riots in 1947 as a factor making him popular among Muslims. Before 1952 he was sometimes an independent, but in the 1952 general elections he worked with the Congress. Afterward, however, when he tried to exercise some influence over the selection of nominees of the Congress for the corporation elections, he was apparently rebuffed in at least one selection and turned his group toward cooperation with the Sanghatna. Sanas brought to that organization what it lacked—a following among a section of the Maratha masses.

Despite its divided nature, the Sanghatna emerged from the election looking very stong. Table 2.1 summarizes the outcome of these elections: the Nagri Sanghatna outpolled the Congress in popular votes and captured ten more seats than the Congress with two fewer candidates. Of the fifteen persons elected as independents, two were Hindu Mahasabha members who had withdrawn from the Sanghatna. The Sanghatna was able to command a corporation majority with the

TABLE 2.1

Outcome of Poona Municipal Elections, 1952 [43]

Party	Number of Candidates	Seats Won	Total Votes	Percentage
Nagri Sanghatna	62	30	106,213	36
Congress	64	20	97,635	33
Independents	84	15	90,377	31
Total	210	65	294,225	100

aid of independents. As a reward for his contribution to their victory, the Sanghatna made Sanas the first mayor under the new corporation system.

In tables 2.2 and 2.3 we look more closely at the candidates and the winners in this election. From these tables we can see the extent to which local political contests were more than simply primordial contests between Brahmins and Marathas. While their conflicts have contributed one dimension to Poona's political life, members of both communities worked within the frameworks of larger political organizations which appealed to almost all the major groups in the city for electoral support.

Thus, in table 2.2 [44] it is apparent that the Congress was bidding in 1952 for the support of the Marathas; Marathas greatly outnumbered Brahmins among Congress candidates. At the same time, members of the Sanas group represented only a part of the non-Brahmin element among Sanghatna candidacies. Aside from the Brahmin-Maratha dimension, it is notable that the Congress gave five tickets to Muslims in 1952, while the Nagri Sanghatna with its Hindu Mahasabha support gave only one. As one might expect, that was in a ward where the Muslim population was especially high. Finally, almost all of the nominations made by the Nagri Sanghatna for the six reserved seats went to the anti-Congress Mahar community— then organized in the Scheduled Caste Federation—while the Congress tried to win some support among the Mahars, but also felt a commitment to those Scheduled Caste communities which regularly gave their electoral support to the party.

If both the Congress and the Sanghatna appealed to a diversity of elements in the city, the consequences of those appeals differed. Despite the presence of Brahmins among the leaders of the Congress, that party was unable to elect a single one of its Brahmin candidates. Similarly, Mahars were not drawn to Congress nominees. For the most part, Congress met with the least "sales resistance" in 1952 among the Marathas and the Muslims, although Marathas were more strongly represented among the Sanghatna corporators.

The pattern of nominations and self-started candidacies may offer a very crude index of group "politicization" during this period. To the extent that primordial politics has a place in Poona, we have argued that Brahmins, Marathas, and Mahars were the most readily identifiable groups active in politics. In addition to participating in various political parties, however, a considerable number of individual Brahmins or Marathas stood on their own in politics. One measure of the degree to which persons belonging to a particular primordial group are generally integrated into organized political life might, then, be the extent to which persons of such backgrounds stand as independents. The assumption is that partisan

TABLE 2.2

Primordial Groups and Parties of Candidates in Corporation Elections–Poona, 1952

Primordial Group	Congress		Sanghatna		Independents	
	N	%	N	%	N	%
Brahmins*	9	14.0	13	21.0	29	34.6
Intermediate†	8	12.5	8	12.9	4	4.8
Marathas	19	29.7	14	22.6	21	25.0
Low Hindus‡	5	7.8	6	9.7	6	7.1
Mahars	3	4.7	6	9.7	6	7.1
Other Scheduled Caste§	3	4.7	1	1.6	5	5.9
Muslims	5	7.8	1	1.6	2	2.4
Non-Maharashtrians‖	11	17.2	12	19.4	4	4.8
Other #	–	–	–	–	1	1.2
Unidentified	1	1.6	1	1.6	6	7.1
Totals	64	100.0	62	100.1	84	100.0

* Includes three Brahmins who ran on non-Sanghatna Hindu Mahasabha tickets and one Brahmin who ran as a Socialist in the same ward.
† For the composition of this group and the make-up of the category designated "Low Hindu" see the scheme outlined in Richard Lambert, *Workers, Factories and Social Change in India* (Princeton: Princeton University Press, 1963) pp. 233-35. The present category includes eleven Malis and six CKP's along with Pardeshi, Kachi, and Dhangar representatives. This is a very broad status range, which would not represent a "real" grouping by any means.
‡ Groups which Lambert identifies as "artisan" and "servant" castes. The former include five Salis (Weavers) and two Shimpis (Tailors); the latter include four Kumbhars (Potters), two Telis (Oil Pressers), two Bhois (Fishermen) and single Nhavi (Barber) and Lonare candidates.
§ Includes Mangs, Chambhars and Bhangis.
‖ The larger component of this category consists of merchant communities from Gujarat, Rajasthan ("Marwaris") and Uttar Pradesh. In the present table, we have included with these northerners a very small contingent of candidates with origins in the south—Madras or Andhra.
One Christian ran for the corporation as an independent.

nominations normally represent the preferable route to advancement in the two cities; they are the product of efforts on the part of organizational leadership to draw upon the voting strength of particular groups in the community, and reflect, in turn, a willingness on the part of members of such groups to regard those organizational channels as meaningful opportunity structures. On the other hand, independent candidacies are the result of considerable enterprise on the part of the individual candidate and reflect dissatisfaction, on either an individual or a group basis, with existent political organizations.

Table 2.4 records the partisan and independent involvements of different primordial groups in Poona for the 1952 corporation elections. Among the major groups, the long politicized Brahmins were clearly the most willing to run as independents, a finding which argues against any simple notion of their politicization solely through partisan organizations. Candidates are not merely a product of resource availability, however, since independent candidacies also occurred with

TABLE 2.3

Primordial Groups and Parties of Winners, Poona Corporation in 1952

Primordial Group	Congress	Sanghatna	Others	Totals
Brahmins	—	7	8*	15
Intermediate†	2	3	2	7
Marathas	6	8	2	16
Low Hindus	3	1	2	6
Mahars	1	4	—	5
Other Scheduled Caste§	1	—	—	1
Muslims	4	1	1	6
Non-Maharashtrians‖	3	6	—	9
Totals	20	30	15	65

* Two members were elected on non-Sanghatna Hindu Mahasabha tickets.
† Four Malis (Congress 2; Nagri Sanghatna 2); two CKP (Nagri Sanghatna; Independent) and one Pardeshi (Independent).
‡ Weaver (Congress); Shimpi (Independent); two Kumbhars (Nagri Sanghatna; Congress); Koli (Congress); Bhoi (Independent).
§ Mang.
‖ Two southerners were elected on Nagri Sanghatna tickets; the others belonged to northern trading communities.

TABLE 2.4

Partisan Candidacies by Primordial Groups, Poona, 1952

Primordial Group	Total Candidates	Nonparty	Percentage Outside Party
Brahmins	51	27*	55
Intermediate	20	4	20
Marathas	54	21	39
Low Hindus	17	6	35
Mahars	15	6	40
Other Scheduled Caste	9	5	56
Muslims	8	2	25
Non-Maharashtrians	27	4	15

* Among the "non-partisan" candidates were the three Hindu Mahasabha rebels against the Sanghatna, since that "rebellion" indicates a degree of political autonomy on their part.

some frequency among members of the Scheduled Castes. Some from these groups were nominated by the major parties for reserved seats, but others were not extended an opportunity to contest in general seats. A demand for additional political rewards apparently existed among these groups—a demand which some persons resolved by putting themselves forward as independent candidates.[45]

In contrast to these high activity rates, potentially well-financed groups like the Gujaratis and the Marwaris (included among the non-Maharashtrians) were not politically active in 1952, except where recruited by one of the contending parties. Much the same appears to be true of the relatively well-off Hindu Maharashtrians identified here as "Intermediates." Presumably, either the demands of these groups for representation were adequately met through the existent party structures or individuals from these communities did not look upon political participation as an important outlet for personal ambition.

The result of these group and individual efforts was the creation in 1952 of a body which placed Marathas and Brahmins on an almost even par. The system also gave significant representation to Mahars and Muslims and extended recognition to other groups. Indeed, if any primordial group was markedly overrepresented in that year, it was the non-Maharashtrians, since they constituted about 7 percent of the city's population but won 14 percent of the seats.

With the election of B. N. Sanas as mayor, the latent cleavages within the Sanghatna began to come to the surface. The fusion party managed to remain together only until 1954 or until the selection of a new mayor became the subject of dispute between the Sanas group and the more consistently anti-Congress section of the Sanghatna. The entry of an increasing number of Poona non-Brahmins into the Congress after 1954 also encouraged the Sanas group to move closer to the Congress. Ultimately, Sanas and his followers were reconciled with the Congress, and a Congress majority was established in the corporation. For the last two years of the body, a Congress majority dominated elections for mayor and deputy mayor and the selection of members for the corporation committees.

THE SAMYUKTA MAHARASHTRA MOVEMENT

In the period 1952-58, many of the animosities of Poona politics were subordinated to promotion of the demand for a separate linguistic state. Before 1956, Marathi speakers were part of several different administrative units. Poona was in the Maharashtra region of Bombay State, a unit which brought together several linguistic areas. For the purposes of party organization, the Congress since the 1920s had recognized the demand for linguistic distinctiveness by setting up regional party organizations based on linguistic distinctions including a Maharashtra Pradesh (Provincial) Congress Committee (MPCC). After Independence, however, the national leadership of the Congress consigned the matter of linguistic reorganization of governments to a relatively low place in its list of priorities.[46] Only as a result of violent agitations in the Telugu-speaking areas of the south, which led to the creation of the state of Andhra Pradesh in 1953, did the government confront the larger issue of the demand for linguistic states by appointing a States Reorganization Commission (SRC). That commission issued a recommendation to the central government in 1955 that the nation be divided into sixteen states including a reconstituted Bombay State, which would be bilingual— combining the region of Gujarat with Maharashtra and the city of Bombay.

The chief stumbling block to the creation of a single linguistic state for speakers of Marathi was the fate of Bombay City. Bombay was the business capital of western India, but many of its economic leaders were non-Maharashtrians, who feared they would not have sufficient political leverage if the city was absorbed into a Maharashtra state. They brought pressure on the central government for a bilingual state in which a strong Gujarati contingent would provide them with the protection they desired.

After the SRC issued its report, the movement for a distinct Maharashtra which had been simmering for twenty years around Poona and western Maharashtra erupted in the form of a demand for Samyukta Maharashtra (United Maharashtra) including Bombay City. Agitations in late 1955 and early 1956 heightened a tense situation, and riots led to a number of deaths.

In Poona, where the demand had a strong base of support, almost all the opposition parties rallied behind the cause; indeed, many local Congressmen were openly opposed to the leadership of the national Congress on this issue. As the agitations increased, these Congressmen were placed in a politically embarrassing position. Protests against the central government took the form of resignations by opposition members of the Bombay legislature and, in Poona, members of the corporation resigned en masse in January 1956. Rather than hold new corporation elections under these circumstances, the state government turned the Poona Corporation over to an Administrator for a year.

Within the Congress organization, there was something of a public split on the Maharashtra issue; most non-Brahmins and some Brahmins (including N. V. Gadgil), were fully committed to the demand for Maharashtra, but certain Congressmen in leadership positions were hesitant. Caught between popular support for the Maharashtra demand at the local level and the temporizing of the national party, a Brahmin member of the Rajya Sabha from Poona—a prominent figure in the local and state Congress Party—has written of that period:

> The leadership of the movement had already passed into the hands of Communists and Praja Socialists who dominated in the United Maharashtra Samiti. They began to provoke people that nothing short of Samyukta Maharashtra with Bombay City will be accepted. The mass fury was growing. . . . The leaders of the Congress were therefore put in an awkward position. They could not pacify the masses, nor could they prevail on the Congress High Command to run to their help. . . . There was great rift among them. In their private meetings, they expressed it unequivocally that their demand for Samyukta Maharashtra was unassailable, that the High Command was prejudiced, and they should better resign and get out. It was the most uphill task to keep that element under control.[47]

Anti-Congress Brahmins and a few prominent non-Brahmin leaders from Poona took the lead in pressing the Maharashtra demand. Prominent among these were S. M. Joshi, N. G. Goray, K. M. Jedhe, and Tilak's grandson, J. S. Tilak. (Tilak continues to edit *Kesari* in Poona and has lent personal backing to various political movements in the last two decades including the Nagri Sanghatna.) The views of one local leader, a Hindu Mahasabha member, suggested the streak of populism which appealed to both the leftists and the regional chauvinists in the Maharashtra movement:

> We wanted to develop a socialist state in Maharashtra. All trade and commerce here is in the hands of the non-Maharashtrians, especially in the villages. The whole economic system of Maharashtra and of all India is in the hands of non-Maharashtrians with Bombay being a key point.

The Samiti organized demonstrations in Poona and Bombay in the first three months of 1956 which caused mounting alarm among local Congress leaders. Despite these activities, the central government insisted on going ahead with its plans for the creation of a bilingual state. Within the MPCC, there was also a struggle going on for ascendancy between two Marathas. Y. B. Chavan, till then a secondary figure in Bombay state politics, received the support of elements favorable to Morarji Desai, the Gujarati Chief Minister of Bombay State. B. S. Hiray, a well-known Maratha leader, got the backing of many Maharashtrian organizations including a large section of the Poona Congress.

The latter contest was joined in June 1956, when members of the MPCC led by Hiray determined to resign from the party in protest against central party policy on the Maharashtra demand. A smaller section of the organization led by Chavan argued that no purpose would be served by such an action. In a vote, Hiray's position won 66 to 56, and he went to Delhi to offer his resignation, but the national leadership talked him out of it. From that point, Chavan gained ground in the MPCC.

When the Center insisted upon pressing its plan for a bilingual Bombay State, violence occurred for the first time in Gujarat in mid-1956. These agitations were brought to a halt only when Morarji Desai, the dominant figure in the Gujarat Congress, went on a fast. In the face of a threat by Hiray to stand against him for Chief Minister of the new state and the evident divisions both in Gujarat and Maharashtra, Desai decided to step aside and throw his support behind Chavan for Chief Minister. Hiray received considerable support from Maharashtra in that intraparty contest, but Desai lined up sufficient Gujarati and Bombay City strength for Chavan to achieve the election of the latter.

Thus, Chavan came into office as Chief Minister of bilingual Bombay State in late 1956, presiding over a difficult situation from a shaky power base in his own home region. Yet, within four years Chavan was a folk hero in Maharashtra and the unquestioned leader of the government and the Congress Party in that state. Describing the situation as of 1 November, when Chavan assumed office, an Indian political scientist has written:

> Few in Maharashtra appreciated Chavan's stand or sympa-
> thized with him. Many considered him a traitor to the cause
> of Maharashtra. . . . People from the City of Bombay enter-
> tained apprehensions of this rustic peasant and his capacity
> to develop enough sophistication to give a proper lead to
> the cosmopolitan city of Bombay. The national leadership
> of Government and the Congress Party also were not sure
> of this newcomer.[48]

The general elections, coming in February of 1957, did nothing to raise the expectations of Congressmen. Perhaps Poona Congressmen did not fully appreciate the depth of feeling on the Maharashtra issue or its electoral explosiveness. Thus, when Sanas resigned from the corporation in early 1956, he did not sever his ties with the Congress. Chavan, seeking influence within local Congress organizations, helped Sanas to get a nomination for MLA in 1957 and supported a later bid by him to become the leader of the Poona Congress. The immediate consequence was that Sanas ran for MLA in a Poona constituency in 1957 where his chief rival was S. M. Joshi running on the ticket of the Samyukta Maharashtra Samiti (SMS).

The latter organization emerged for these elections as a full-fledged political party. In addition to Joshi, the Samiti formed a complete slate of candidates for election in the city and region drawn from a full range of parties; it proceeded to decimate the Congress in much of the Maharashtrian heartland. As compared with 116 seats won by the Congress in that region in 1952, only 33 were held by the party in 1957. In Poona City, every MLA seat and the MP seat changed from Congress to Samiti hands.[49]

In the contest for MP, for example, the incumbent (N. V. Gadgil) plummeted from 54 percent of the vote in the previous election to 41 percent against the SMS nominee, N. G. Goray. In the MLA races, J. S. Tilak defeated his Congress opponent in a Brahmin constituency by a proportion of 70 to 30; in a heavily non-Brahmin constituency, however, Joshi barely managed to defeat Sanas with 53 percent of the vote. The third major urban constituency found a Communist winning on the basis of Samiti support, but he received only 52 percent. In the fourth constituency, the cantonment, a member of the PSP backed by the Samiti was elected with the support of 47 percent of the electorate in the only three-man contest in the city. (The Congress incumbent in that race skidded from 62 percent in 1952 to 38 percent of the vote in 1957.)

This reversal of form in Poona was associated with a markedly higher turnout. In 1952, the four MLA constituencies ranged from 45 to 61 percent in turnout; in 1957, the figures were between 65 percent of the eligible voters and a remarkable 78 percent. The intensity of public feeling on the Samyukta Maharashtra demand was obvious.

Disheartened by this rout, the Congress Party was in no condition to contest the municipal elections held a short time later. Rather than go down to what promised to be a disastrous defeat, the Congress made no formal designations but permitted party members to stand as independents. In contrast, the buoyant Samiti fielded a complete slate of sixty-five candidates. These municipal elections were by no means conceded to the Samiti. At least 38 Congressmen ran as independents; another 96 persons ran with the support of groups not in the Samiti or without group affiliation. Compared to 1952, then, there were only 11 fewer candidates for the corporation. The outcome was predictable: the SMS won 48 seats and several of the independents elected were local notables sympathetic to their cause.

Table 2.5 indicates the slight shift in the nature of the elements composing the Samiti compared to its Nagri Sanghatna analogue of 1952.[50] The key difference, as one might expect, was in the relative lack of non-Maharashtrians—groups frequently represented as the "enemy" in the rhetoric of the movement. Some of them ran as Congress-associated candidates but very few as independents; the total number contesting fell sharply from 27 to 14 between the municipal elections of 1952 and 1957.

Hidden within the "Intermediate" category of the table is the activation of members of a major non-Brahmin caste: the Malis. The latter are a traditional agrarian community. In terms of status, the Malis are not much behind the Marathas and, on an aggregate basis, they are possibly better educated and more prosperous than the Marathas in Poona City. In 1952, there were eleven Mali

TABLE 2.5

*Primordial Groups and Parties of Candidates in Corporation Elections, Poona,
1957*

Primordial Group	Congress		Samiti		Others	
	N	%	N	%	N	%
Brahmins	7	18.4	15	23.0	28*	29.2
Intermediate†	6	15.8	13	20.0	8*	8.3
Marathas	8	21.0	20	30.8	23	24.0
Low Hindus‡	7	18.4	6	9.3	7	7.3
Mahars	1	2.6	5	7.7	7	7.3
Other Scheduled Caste§	1	2.6	1	1.5	8	8.3
Muslims	2	5.3	1	1.5	8	8.3
Non-Maharashtrians‖	6	15.8	4	6.2	4	4.2
Unidentified	—	—	—	—	3	3.1
	38	99.9	65	100.0	96	100.0

* Includes three Brahmins and two Malis running with Nagri Sanghatna backing.
† Nineteen were Malis. The remainder included four Pardeshis, two CKP's and
  one each of the following: Kachis, Dhangar.
‡ 5 Weavers; 4 Kumbhars; 3 Shimpis; 2 Bhois; 2 Dhobis; one each: Teli, Sonar,
  Koli.
§ Mang; Chambhar; Bhangi; Vadar.
‖ Marwaris; Gujaratis; "southerners."

candidates in the field for the corporation—four from the Sanghatna, five from the
Congress and two as independents. In 1957, the total number increased to
nineteen: five on Congress tickets; six as independents and eight for the Samiti.
Their large representation in the Samiti reflected the association of several
prominent Mali politicians with the PSP in Poona. The overall scatter of Malis
among different parties indicates, however, that the primordial group was not
directly activated as a partisan political organization.

Except for the non-Maharashtrians the Congress did badly in almost all social
categories (see table 2.6). These elections represented the nadir of Congress appeal
in Poona, but they gave (along with the results of the general elections) the state
Congress leadership the evidence of popular feeling it needed to press the national
Congress for creation of Maharashtra. Under the skillful direction of Chavan, the
Maharashtrian point of view was successfully presented and Chavan received much
of the political credit for it. There was also a waning of distrust on the part of
non-Maharashtrians in Bombay City as Chavan's government won the support of a
broad range of interests. The final result was the creation of the two new states of
Maharashtra and Gujarat in 1960.[51]

Despite the strong support given the movement by Brahmins, the emergence
of Maharashtra signalled the full realization of political dominance by Marathas in
the new state. Chavan attempted to ease the anxieties of the Brahmins and
Scheduled Castes, in particular, during the changeover. For example, he announced
that all claims for repayment of loans advanced to the Brahmin community
following destruction of their property in the riots of 1948 would be dropped.[52]
Although Brahmins continued to withdraw from or be replaced in positions of

TABLE 2.6

Primordial Groups and Parties of Winners, Poona, 1957

Primordial Group	Congress	Samiti	Others	Total
Brahmins	—	15	1	16
Intermediate*	2	6	—	8
Marathas	3	15	1	19
Low Hindus†	2	5	—	7
Mahars	1	3	—	4
Other SC‡	—	1	1	2
Muslims	1	—	1	2
Non-Mahar.§	4	3	—	7
Totals	13	48	4	65

* Six Malis (5 Samiti; 1 Congress), a Congress Pardeshi and Samiti Dhangar.
† Three Weavers (2 Congress; 1 Samiti); 2 Samiti Kumbhars; a Samiti Tambat and a Samiti Bhoi.
‡ A Samiti Mang and Independent Chambhar.
§ Includes one southerner (Samiti) and six from northern merchant castes.

leadership in the Congress, Chavan called upon intellectuals to increase their involvement in solving the problems of the new state for which they had fought so hard.[53] In the case of the Mahars, the Congress realized considerable goodwill by continuing benefits due the Scheduled Castes for those persons who had converted to Buddhism. Chavan also provided the community with symbolic benefits by making Ambedkar's birthday a public holiday and granting the community the plot of ground in Nagpur where Ambedkar had undergone his conversion.[54]

Equally important, Chavan pursued an active policy of recruiting to the Congress prominent figures from opposition parties. During the first three years after the creation of Maharashtra, a considerable number of "bright young men" from the PSP and many non-Brahmins from the PWP and other opposition groups were convinced of the desirability of joining the Congress. One result was the effective weakening of the Samiti in the Poona corporation by 1960. The local Congress organization did everything it could to encourage this decline by seeking an increasing base among the non-Brahmins of the city.

From 1938 to 1957, Brahmins had filled the office of President of the Poona City Congress Committee. The last Brahmin President withdrew in 1957 to work with Gandhian institutions. The formal transition was smooth as the out-going President (a non-Maharashtrian Brahmin) favored the choice of Sanas and was also able to get his own candidates elected treasurer and local representative to the MPCC.[55] In both of these instances, as in the case of Sanas, the winners were non-Brahmins.

Those Brahmins who had not already left the organization prior to Independence, at the departure of the Socialist Party or during the Samyukta Maharashtra movement, now withdrew. One of these, a former leader of the Congress, rather bitterly characterized the situation after 1957:

> Chavan came into power only because of the support of
> Morarji Desai and Gujarati votes. As Chief Minister he

thought he could dispense with the old Congressmen and bring in his own men. He did not say so openly but in his actions we could see that we were not wanted. Chavan got absolute control and the Brahmins were completely wiped out in the Congress.

This is something of an exaggeration since Brahmin attrition from the Maharashtra Congress had been going on at a moderate pace for over twenty years prior to Chavan's emergence. There have also been a few prominent Brahmins in the Congress since 1957 whose rapid rise in the organization indicates how the system can work in favor of a few really competent Brahmins. Nevertheless, such mobility is on an individual basis; in the primordial context of the post-1957 Congress organization, it is little more than Brahmin "tokenism." [56]

The Samiti's strength in the corporation was also undermined after 1960 by the withdrawal from the alliance of the PSP. Leaders of the latter party were uneasy about their cooperation with the Communist Party under the Samiti label. The Communists, they felt, were trying to turn the Samiti into a permanent organizational weapon to employ against the national government. The PSP wanted to dissolve the Samiti as soon as its immediate goal of Maharashtra had been achieved. For all practical purposes, the withdrawal of the PSP spelled the end of the effectiveness of the Samyukta Maharashtra Samiti in Poona, though not its total demise. [57]

POONA CORPORATION POLITICS: 1960-62

Of the original forty-eight Samiti members elected to the corporation in 1957, about sixteen were members of the PSP in national politics, another eight to ten were associated with lesser parties. The remainder were independents, many of whom were drawn into politics by the Maharashtra movement. Among the latter was Shivajirao Dhere, a twenty-seven-year-old Maratha, who was not active in politics before his election; his father had served for a period in the municipality many years earlier. With a group of about seven or eight nonparty men, Dhere wielded some influence during the last years of the corporation body elected in 1957.

One of the occasions for this was in the election of a mayor in 1960. For the first three years, a policy of rotation had been followed in the Samiti with candidates from the PWP, Hindu Mahasabha, and PSP succeeding each other in office. The PSP mayor, R. V. Telang, presided during the break-up of the Samiti. Telang, a prominent leader of the local and state PSP, came under attack from his own party men for carrying on normal administrative relationships with the Chief Minister in his capacity as mayor at the same time that the PSP was conducting its agitations against the state government. When Telang invited Chavan to visit the city on corporation business, the Samiti organized a public demonstration against their own mayor. Chavan tactfully indicated his concern for the delicacy of the mayor's position by offering to withdraw his acceptance of the mayor's invitation. The Chief Minister's responsiveness in the face of the Samiti's behavior was apparently influential in Telang's subsequent decision (in 1961) to quit the PSP and join the Congress.

After Telang stood down as mayor in 1960, a contest developed over his successor. PSP elements wanted another one of their members; nonparty people and some individuals in the Hindu Mahasabha wanted Dhere. Congress made it a three-man contest by naming its own candidate. Reflective of the occasional strategies of such political contests, the Congress and PSP backed the only two corporation members belonging to a tiny timber merchant (Kirad) community. In both instances, however, these were men who were already playing leading roles in their respective parties. The Congress nominee was a member of the MPCC and had served in the previous corporation; the Samiti nominee was active in the PSP. On the first ballot, Dhere was eliminated as the third candidate; on the second ballot, the Congress elected its nominee for mayor, thus bringing the Samiti's majority to a formal end in the Poona corporation.[58]

The accretion of new members to the Congress brought problems in its wake. Differences began to appear between some of the "old-timers" and the "new-comers." These conflicts reached their zenith at the time of election of the chairman of the major committee of the municipal corporation—the Standing Committee. The City Congress, which plays a major part in the designation of party candidates for mayor, deputy mayor, and chairmen of committees, set up a candidate disliked by some of the old-timers in the corporation. This group of Congressmen happened to have a majority on the Standing Committee which did the actual balloting. To counter the party's choice of a Congress Mali, the old Congressmen and the Dhere group of independents supported a Jan Sangh Mali[59] and defeated the official Congress nominee by a vote of 10 to 2, even though the Congress nominally held a 7-5 majority on the committee.[60]

Leaders of the City Congress were angered by this action, and, at the directive of the MPCC, the Congress Party in the corporation was declared dissolved. Members were only unofficially associated with the state and national Congress during the remaining life of the body. Before the dissolution of the sitting corporation scheduled for late 1961, however, Poona was hit by a great flood. Because of this flood, which dislocated over ten thousand families,[61] the Government of Maharashtra decided to extend the life of the corporation by one year. This permitted another contest for mayor in 1961.

In that election, a group of former Congressmen backed one nominee; the PSP continued its support to its previous candidate, and Dhere was favored by a group which included residues of the Samiti, a few "unofficial" Congressmen, and the tiny contingent of Jan Sangh members. Still, Dhere was elected on the second ballot over the PSP nominee by a vote of thirty-one to thirty and became the youngest mayor in Poona history.

OVERVIEW

Thus, at the time of the corporation elections of 1959 in Agra and the general elections of 1962 in Poona, there were a variety of political groups and individual political actors working through the two local political systems. These municipal arenas represented local extensions of activity for some groups with national and state orientations; at the same time, they functioned as opportunity structures for primordial, ideational, and personalistic groups and ambitious individuals who were receiving little hearing in state or national politics.

The great dependence of national parties like the Congress on their grass roots organizations to maintain or expand their power ultimately has meant that political activities which have gone on in substantial population centers like Poona or Agra receive prompt attention from concerned state party leaders. Particularly where there is a tendency toward partisan fragmentation at the state level, as in Uttar Pradesh, an incentive exists for party leaders to become locally involved. In Maharashtra, where a similar problem existed before 1962, experiences gathered from other states and from the struggles within the Congress before the creation of the new state have continued to prompt intervention by state party leaders as a preventative measure, but such intervention could have been subverted easily had local Congress leaders not found their connection with the state party beneficial.

In Agra in 1959, two groups recruited and divided most of the followers of the Congress. Each group (one a machine, the other combining personalistic and machine elements) had its own connections to the two major groups operating within the state. While certain individuals at both levels resisted being identified with either of the competing factions, the nature of rewards was so structured that the few persons "above the conflict" frequently lost out for positions of influence in the system or had to depend on the maximization of old services to the party as a protective "selling point" for sustaining their autonomy.

In contrast to the power exercised within the Agra Congress before 1959, opposition political groups were rather weak and divided. The Republican Party was homogeneous in primordial terms but was too narrow in its appeal to constitute a direct threat to the Congress. The Jan Sangh, at the time, faced the municipal elections from a position of weakness brought on by disruptions within its local leadership abetted by the discontent of state party leaders with that leadership. Along with these relatively new and unproven organizations, Agra politics was marked by the presence of a rather large group of party dissidents and nonparty people interested in finding places for themselves in local government but unable to come to satisfactory terms with the existing political infrastructure.

In the general elections of 1962 in Poona, the picture was marginally different. Under the leadership of Y. B. Chavan, the Congress in Maharashtra was being newly organized into a statewide pragmatic party machine capable of uniting various non-Brahmin primordial groups under members of the numerically dominant Maratha community. This organization reputedly traded heavily in services for its members, governmental posts and favors for those in its good graces. With statewide support, the Poona and Maharashtra organizations generated the capacity for action reflected in their willingness and ability to reprimand the Poona corporation party for defying party directives.[62] The Poona Congress was being carefully molded in the political style of the state organization. As a result of this close supervision, *self-defeating* group differences did not appear in the 1962 elections for MP and MLA. The setback in the corporation elections of 1962, as we shall see, reflected both the strengths and weaknesses of the new Congress organization, but it provided the basis for future organizational maintenance.

No single group in Poona was in a position to challenge the Congress in 1962. The PSP was badly hurt by defections to the Congress and by its own lack of ideational clarity; the Jan Sangh was a relatively new group in local politics and had played a rather reluctant role in the period of the Samyukta Maharashtra movement; the Hindu Mahasabha was losing much of its earlier support to the Jan

Sangh and, in response, was experimenting desperately with means to preserve itself including talk of "Hindu socialism" and coalitions with the Communist Party; the PWP, with its appeal greatest among peasants, found it difficult to vie with the Congress in Poona City for non-Brahmin votes; the two electoral groups which claimed to speak for the Republican Party in 1962 and contended over the inheritance of Ambedkar weakened the Mahar community for maximum impact upon the local political process. In addition to these widely divergent groups, Poona also had small units of the Lohia Socialist Party, the Communist Party, and certain persons with their own followings who operated outside the framework of party organizations.

The local political systems of Agra and Poona are somewhat different in character, if not in kind. Certainly, differences abound in terms of focal personalities, some of the economic and social ideas which have taken root in the two systems, and the regionally specific primordial factors at play within the local political systems. While the Congress Party is a common focus of political attention in both cities, local contexts make the problems of the two organizations rather distinct.

Yet, at the heart of political conflict in both Agra and Poona by the early sixties was the carrying forward of democratic political processes initiated upon the achievement of national Independence in 1947. Poona, from 1947 to 1960, engaged in a series of changes which displaced an old political elite—an elite which was, by its nature, predemocratic in character. At the same time, members of that old elite gradually regrouped to facilitate their operation within the framework of contemporary political alternatives. The resultant political organizations, as we shall see, continued to press the Congress closely for local political dominance and the support of the existing universe of interests in the city.

In a somewhat truncated fashion, the rise of the Republican Party and the generational and ideational challenge represented by the Jan Sangh to the Congress hegemony in Agra followed a similar line of development. Both raised alternatives to the political elite which had dominated local politics before 1959. As we shall see in later chapters, the political system in Agra by 1968 came much closer to resembling the Poona pattern of 1962 than it had in 1959 or even 1964.

3 ELECTORAL BEHAVIOR IN AGRA

Thus far, we have identified some of the leading political groups and personalities in Agra and Poona and some of the institutional and environmental constraints within which they operate. In this and the following chapter we shall begin to examine the processes by which particular individuals are recruited to roles in the municipal bodies and the patterns of interaction between these actors and their "publics," that is, corporator-constituency relations. We shall have occasion, in the course of this discussion, to examine further the influence of state politics on the municipal arena and the interplay among local political groups. In later chapters we shall deal with recruitment and constituency relations more directly from the perspective of the individual corporator.

THE NOMINATION PROCESS

For the Republican Party, the selection of party nominees for the Agra corporation elections in 1959 was largely resolved at the local level; the Jan Sangh reached its decisions locally with the assistance of the Organizing Secretary of the party for western Uttar Pradesh. In the case of the Congress, factional differences at the local level were exacerbated by interventions on the part of the State Congress.

Because of its position as the dominant political organization in the state, Congress Party tickets were highly coveted. At the same time, the State Congress recognized that its clear advantages in elections for MP and MLA—factors like superior organization and greater financial resources—were partially neutralized by the considerable personal influence non-Congress "notables" were able to exercise in the small constituencies created for the corporation. Divisions in the State Congress Party and many of the municipal parties were also expected to take some electoral toll in the elections for each of the five corporations of Uttar Pradesh. Thus, there was apparent hesitancy on the part of the Congress government of the state in setting a date for the elections. Originally scheduled for July, they were postponed to the last week of October on the claim that July was a bad time of the year for holding elections; the postponement was also said to be a response to requests from the Communist Party and Jan Sangh.[1]

The selection of candidates soon found the Congress (State) Election Committee—the body responsible for reviewing lists of nominees submitted to it by City Congress Committees—embroiled in factional disputes. The Minister for Finance in the Uttar Pradesh government, to cite the most prominent example, resigned from this electoral body over the handling of nominations for the city of Lucknow;[2] as a result of factional differences in Kanpur, according to the

Hindustan Times, "many" independents who stood for the corporation were Congressmen "supported surreptitiously by powerful Congress interests manoeuvering for the prize posts of Mayor and Deputy Mayor." [3]

In an effort to paper over some of the differences within the party and to get the help of local notables, the Uttar Pradesh Congress introduced a rule that one-third of all nominations should go to persons newly recruited into political life. Instead of promoting greater harmony, this "33 percent rule" made the factional situation worse. The point was spelled out in an electoral postmortem in the *National Herald* (Lucknow) on 4 November 1959:

> A cover of generosity is provided for this departure from the established policy, by saying that the Congress is as considerate to outsiders as to Congressmen. It should have been realized that this "generosity" is one of the principal causes of mounting indiscipline in the Congress organization. Most Congressmen who rebel just before elections are those against whom outsiders are preferred for Congress tickets. They defy Congress decisions, and put themselves up as independent candidates, and it is not seldom that they defeat the "outsiders." The "outsiders" do greater harm to the Congress, when, in their campaigns, they smash the Congress principles, and approach the voters in the name of caste or religion. The vicious circle expands, and even the Congressmen stoop to invoke methods to which the Congress has been hostile throughout its long life.

While it is rather questionable whether Congressmen are necessarily less likely to approach voters "in the name of caste or religion," certainly Agra witnessed the disruptive effects of the "33 percent rule" along with marked local factionalism.

The Agra Congress

The strength of the Congress in Agra was nominally based on its past nationalist services and its role as the ruling party in India. By 1959, however, it was not an effective mass organization in the city. The Agra Congress listed on the order of twenty-one thousand "four-anna" or *primary* members, but these were largely inactive. Fewer than four hundred persons belonged officially to the category of *active* members of the party. Even some of these, it is alleged, were bogus members put on the party rolls to bolster support for one or the other of the local factions, since only active members participated in organizational elections.

Formally, the City Congress consists of several tiers of organization from *mohallas* (neighborhoods) through twenty-two *mandals* (wards), each having its own executive committee. The President of each *mandal* is automatically a member of the City Congress Committee, which included forty-four members in 1964. In addition to *mandal* representatives, various ex officio members including the MP and MLA's for the city are represented on the City Committee as are persons coopted from certain social categories: young people; women, the Scheduled Castes and "social workers." The latter are persons involved in service organizations rather than politics. Members of the City Congress Committee choose an Executive Committee including a President, four Vice-Presidents, four Secretaries (one is designated General Secretary) and six additional members.

When municipal elections take place, a City Election Committee is designated from the City Congress to pass on candidates and submit a list to the State Election Committee. In 1959, the Agra list favored the group of Seth Achal Singh, which then had a majority in the City Executive. The President of the Congress was a close adherent of Seth and other key positions including that of General Secretary were held by the Seth group.

On the other hand, Agra City's representation to the UPCC was slightly tipped toward the Singhal faction. Agra had seven representatives to that central governing body of the Uttar Pradesh Congress: the MP (Seth); two MLA's (Adiram Singhal; and, a Seth supporter); the City Congress President; and three district representatives from the city. The latter positions were all held by men favorable to Singhal (and to Rawat). Thus, there was a four to three division in this top party body among persons most directly in a position to influence the decisions of the State Election Committee. As a result, the list which was actually returned to Agra was altered at the state level by the exclusion of several followers of Seth to achieve a greater balance between factions. In about a dozen instances, failure to get a Congress nomination was sufficient cause for men to run against the official party nominees as independents. Reports that some of the dissidents received the sub-rosa support of one faction against Congress nominees supported by the opposing faction were current during and after the elections.

Electoral defections are a common feature of political life in Agra, much as they are in the rest of India. One informant took the problem in stride by suggesting that "this is bound to happen in any election, but those who go against the Congress because they did not get a ticket are not true Congressmen." Even this assertion is open to some question given the weak boundary-maintenance characteristic of the Congress. An elderly Congressman, who had been a member of Congress since the 1920s, had the experience of seeing his name announced in the papers for the Congress ticket in his ward and then found a day later that another man had replaced him on the list. His reaction was indicative of some of the factors which inspire persons to take the dissident route:

> I was very angry with the Congress over this and took it as a personal insult. I decided to run as an independent. Many people in the area came to see me and asked me to run. While I ran as an independent, I did not join with any other independents.

Even while running against the two "official" party candidates, the speaker continued to regard himself as a good Congressman suffering from the wrongful effects of party factionalism; to some extent, he felt he was serving the true interests of the party by opposing its mistaken choices. Thus, when he was elected by an overwhelming margin, neither he nor the Congress leadership saw anything incongruous in the fact that he was approached by the Education Minister of Uttar Pradesh to rejoin the party, and he immediately did so as a member in good standing.[4]

Vexed by the proliferation of such conflict situations, a few Agra Congressmen suggested in interviews that the only real solution was for the Congress to refrain from contesting local elections, not because of any "good government" notion of taking partisan politics out of municipal affairs, but simply because they felt that such disputes over corporation tickets tended to weaken the party for participation in state and national politics. As we shall see in a later examination of the 1962 general elections in Agra, there was considerable ground for this concern.

Following the directives of the State Congress, Agra party leaders had recruited local notables interested in running on Congress party tickets. This was done on a factional basis, nonetheless, since each faction attempted to recruit persons with local prestige to its own group as well as to the party. The result was that some of the newcomers were soon as much tied into the factional network as were the older members of the Congress organization.

Still, there were many who favored the principle behind the "33 percent rule." One corporator offered the following defense of that practice:

> Sometimes decent people are unwilling to contest elections, but Congress feels it is important to seek them out and convince them to take part. Simply being a Congress worker is not a qualification for a ticket. Many people who are good workers really have no ties in the small local constituencies. The party does not want to put up men who cannot command influence in these smaller units. At that level there are no major issues and men who are right for MLA seats may not be strong personalities locally, where personality counts for so much.

Even though the Congress may have gained a few seats in the short run from this arrangement, subsequent events suggest that the notables added little to the long-term strength and stability of the party in Agra.

The Jan Sangh

As in the Congress, primary membership in the Jan Sangh involves only a four-anna membership fee and a pledge to support the principles of the party. The formal organization of the party in 1959 duplicated many of the features of the Congress, except that the City Jan Sangh participated as a major unit *within* the District Jan Sangh; in the Congress, the city and district units are coordinate but autonomous within their own spheres. Many positions on the party's Executive Committee were also filled by appointment rather than election.

At the time of the corporation elections, the membership of the party was rather small, and there were major parts of the city where the Jan Sangh could claim no real following. The leadership of the City Committee was largely responsible for designating the party's candidates in consultation with persons appointed by the State Jan Sangh. Apparently the party's prospects were not such as to inundate it with applications for nominations.

Baloji Agarwal, the party's candidate for MLA in 1957 and a leading figure in the City Jan Sangh, found himself at odds with another major leader of the party over several candidacies in those areas of the city where the party had some chance of winning. Their fundamental quarrel, however, was over leadership of the local organization. In fact, the Jan Sangh placed only thirty-four nominees in the field for the fifty-four seats available, and some of these were intended mainly to initiate the process of building up the party's public support at the ward level. Some candidates running as independents received nominations from the Jan Sangh with the understanding that they would be willing to join the party after the elections. As it turned out, none of them did.

It is alleged that, during the campaign, the dissident Baloji faction worked actively for nominees belonging to that group, but either withheld active support or worked *against* nominees supported by the majority element in the City Committee. The party's response to these actions, as we shall see, led to an open break within the Jan Sangh after the elections.

The Republican Party

The RPI was the least institutionalized of the three major political parties in Agra. As recently as the general elections of 1957 it had not been a fully operative political organization. The result was that it did not receive governmental recognition as a full-fledged party for the corporation elections. The party's elephant symbol was given to many of the candidates it supported in the corporation elections, but this was done on an "unofficial" basis which made it difficult for even some party leaders to be sure (when interviewed four years later) how many real adherents of the party stood for the corporation and how many were simply endorsed candidates. Some claims go as high as thirty-two candidates including endorsed nonparty people.

In 1959, the party was both financially weak and organizationally diffuse, but it had penetrated the thinking of a large proportion of the Jatavs of Agra. There existed a sixty-member City Executive Committee based on seven districts, but this was largely a paper organization. Not all the subordinate positions were filled, and many participants in leading party circles were self-selected. Almost anyone with real political interest could get some position of prominence in the Agra party.

The responsibility for choosing candidates for the corporation was left largely to the President of the RPI, a man who led the organization in a rather authoritarian manner. Some informants allege that he required candidates to offer Rs. 250 for each ticket. Whether this was a fee to cover party expenses or went into his own pocket later became a matter of considerable controversy within the party. Many Jatav candidates would not have been in a financial position to pay such a sum; a few wealthier men may have actually been asked to pay a fee to help defray the general campaign expenses of others,[5] but the evidence is contradictory.

In a few cases, however, it is clear that candidates paid for their endorsements even in instances where they did not perceive that endorsement as an enduring tie to the party. Thus, a Bania doctor with a highly successful practice, Dr. Prakash Narayan Gupta, originally entered the corporation elections as an independent; some of his Jatav clients suggested that a Republican endorsement might be made available to him. Knowing little about the party except its primordial overtones, he accepted the endorsement and helped defray both his own electoral expenses and those of his Jatav running mate (seeking a reserved seat) and contributed an additional amount to the party. Within a year, he was one of the leaders of the party in Agra and a major figure in municipal politics.

Where electoral units are multimember, as they were in Agra in 1959, parties may try to tailor their slates of candidates to several dimensions of the social climate in a particular ward. This kind of ticket balancing can become quite complex since one must take into account not only the size and influence of certain communities in a ward, but the number of candidates already standing or likely to stand from those communities. In some instances, therefore, a party may run a candidate from a medium-sized community on the expectation that contestants from the major communities will split their community's vote just enough to allow their own man to win. In a double-member constituency, they may also hope to pick up the second vote cast by members of the majority community.

Ticket balancing may also serve a tactical function on a citywide basis, as when the Jan Sangh runs a Muslim (usually in a Muslim ward) to demonstrate that it is not a communal party, or the RPI runs high-caste persons to weaken the image of the party as an exclusively Scheduled Caste organization. As we shall see below, however, successful election campaigns depend in Agra, as elsewhere in India, on many other factors besides the mobilization of primordial identifications.

THE CAMPAIGNS

The willingness of individuals to stand as independents and of parties like the Congress to seek out nonparty people or even opposition party members for party candidacies contributes to a highly fluid political situation in much of India. This is ultimately reflected in a city like Agra in the failure of party identifications to determine the outcome of municipal and other elections in any dependable fashion.

The organization of a campaign is a highly individualistic matter for most municipal candidates in a city like Agra. Personal workers are employed to perform the "manual labor" of a campaign—sticking up posters, publicizing meetings, and sometimes, it is charged, acting as goondas ("strong-arm men"). They also provide the continuing contact between the candidate and his electorate which is so vital for democratic politics. Adrian Mayer notes in his study of an election in a small municipality in Madhya Pradesh:

> . . . it seems that general campaign issues are not more im-
> portant than personal loyalties and interests, and that these
> latter must be tapped by approaches to each voter. This
> implies that the candidate with the most social strings to his
> bow has an advantage. The man who has caste fellows,
> employees, debtors and, of course, neighbors in his ward
> and who has taken the trouble to cement these ties with
> personal interest and involvement—if necessary going to
> marriages and funerals, helping with domestic problems—
> will be a strong candidate.[6]

Of course, the situation is not usually so clear cut since there are frequently competing ties; an employer may not be a caste fellow, nor may one's debtor be under political obligation; neighbors may speak a different language or belong to a different religion (although this is not generally the case). Even in a village, personal animosities may divide members of a family, caste, or neighborhood.

Delineating the ways in which various parties in Bombay City employed both traditional loyalties and modern political forms, Henry Hart writes of the 1957 municipal elections:

> Both Congress and the PSP are pluralistic in their solutions to the besetting urban problems of competing loyalties. The PSP made room for alternative solutions to the competing claims of trade union and language loyalties. Congress still had three members who appealed to Marathi speaking voters on the basis of traditional loyalties, despite having fought and lost power on the bilingual issue. . . . The Communists manipulated traditional loyalties (e.g., of sectarian Muslims, Marathi speakers, Malayalees or Andhras in Bombay). . . . The Republican Party politicians, with some exceptions, used every tactical opening in city government or the Samiti coalition to win places for their "community," usually more specifically for the Mahar caste.[7]

"Issues," to the extent that they appear at all, tend to take the familiar form of opposition to alleged corruption in office or insistence that it is "time for a change." Where immediate targets are not available, state or national issues may become salient. In such circumstances, the Congress is often forced to fight municipal elections through appeals to the contribution it has made in the past to India or in terms of current linkages to the state or national government. Thus, in Bombay City the Congress reacted to arguments that change in government is, in itself, a good thing—an argument advanced particularly by the PSP in the 1961 elections—by appealing for votes on the basis of "the vastness and greatness of the Congress organization, its long unbroken record of services to the citizens of Bombay and its ability and confidence to serve the people of Bombay better than other parties."[8]

Occasionally, opposition parties themselves foster the extension of issues from outside of the municipal arena into municipal politics by seeking votes on the basis of matters which cannot have direct municipal outcomes. The elections of 1957 in Poona, as we have already pointed out, were fought on the Samyukta Maharashtra issue; similarly, parties in municipal elections may complain about the high price of food or unemployment. Except in those rare cases where a single issue is overriding, however, issues do not appear to be determinative of municipal election outcomes. Basically, elections are won by particular individuals organizing personal and bloc support.

Even those candidates supported by political parties have to assume the burden of their own electoral organization and expenses; the party may provide a few centralized services like the printing and distribution of party literature and posters. It may also lend visibility to a candidate's campaign effort by bringing prominent government officials or party leaders into the city to speak on behalf of candidates for municipal office, but it is difficult to gauge the impact of such factors as compared to personal influence exercised by or on behalf of a candidate.

The campaigns themselves add a festive air to the city as processions are taken out, public meetings are held, and candidates tour their localities calling on citizens. Supporters canvass door to door for a candidate. Campaign posters are everywhere, and occasional fights may break out among zealous workers for opposing candidates. Wealthy candidates may spend lavishly on advertising, make "contributions" to local social and religious organizations,[9] and hold public dinners for important group leaders and campaign workers in their wards.

The Candidacies

In addition to approximately 115 candidates who ran with partisan affiliations in 1959, another 113 entered the Agra municipal elections as independents.[10] This meant that the two-man wards averaged more than eight candidates each. Since party nominations in common were no guarantee of intraparty cooperation in a ward, these contests were often free-for-alls.

Table 3.1 illustrates the candidacies by primordial groups and by Congress or Jan Sangh support. A majority of Republican Party nominations went to Jatavs,

TABLE 3.1

Primordial Groups and Parties of Candidates in Agra Corporation Elections, 1959

Primordial Group	Congress		Jan Sangh		Others	
	N	%	N	%	N	%
Bania/Jain	20	39	16	47	23	16
Brahmin	6	12	5	15	22	15
Other high*	8	16	3	9	11	8
Refugees†	1	2	2	6	6	4
Low castes‡	3	6	5	15	24	17
Jatavs	9	18	3	9	32	22
Muslims	4	8	—	—	25	17
Total	51	101	34	101	143	99

* Includes ten Kayasthas, seven Khatris, and five Thakurs.
† Six Hindus from the Punjab and Sind and three Sikhs.
‡ These are essentially traditional Hindu craft or service castes. They consisted of the following numbers belonging to the indicated communities: *five* Koris; *four* Herdsmen; *three* Ahirs and "Purobias"; *two* Goldsmiths, Potters, Khatiks, Kachis, Kahars; *one* Sweeper, Kumbhar, Milkman and Kurmi. Three other persons described as belonging to the Backward Classes could not be identified more specifically.

while Banias were prominently represented among the candidates for both the Congress and Jan Sangh. Muslims were underrepresented in these parties, although many Muslims were politically active enough to stand as independents in the elections; in contrast, the Brahmins were well represented in party nominations. Small, highly modernized communities like the Kayasthas have been disproportionately influential in Uttar Pradesh politics, and their level of participation is reflected in these figures. The Jains, as we indicated earlier, are a religiously defined subsection of the Agarwal-Mathur Vaish communities constituting the bulk of the Bania category.

If we employ the "party crystallization" measure introduced in the last chapter, which also suggests patterns of party recruitment, the Banias and "Other high castes" were relatively "satisfied" by the recruitment patterns of the Congress and Jan Sangh—only 39 percent of the Banias contesting (out of a total of 59 candidacies) did not stand for these two parties; this was true of 50 percent of those included among the other high castes (Khatris, Kayasthas, Thakurs). The Brahmins were markedly less "satisfied"—67 percent ran as independents. At the other end of the status hierarchy, 73 percent of the Jatavs who stood for the corporation were not sponsored by the Congress or Jan Sangh, but the recruitment of at least twenty into politics through the RPI actually made them the *most* "satisfied" group in the corporation elections by leaving only 27 percent outside the party system. The *least* satisfied group in these terms would be the Muslims; twenty-nine Muslims stood for the corporation but only six (21 percent) were supported by the three major parties.[11]

The pattern of candidacies was influenced, of course, by the fact that eight of the twenty-seven wards contained reserved seats. Almost all the nominees put up by the three parties for these reserved seats were Jatavs, but Jatav candidates did not confine themselves to contesting for these seats. Fifteen ran in general constituencies, and six of these—principally candidates who stood with RPI support in areas of high Jatav density—were elected.

A Survey of Contests

There are no "typical" wards in Agra. In some wards, primordial identifications make a difference in electoral outcomes; in other wards, such identifications are neutralized by the presence of many candidates of the same primordial background. While party may have played a part in a few wards, in most of them it was subordinated in 1959 to personal contacts. In lieu of a quantitative analysis, which was attempted but failed to produce reliable patterns, in this section we will simply suggest some of the factors at work in particular instances by presenting case studies from three wards of the city which portray the configuration of candidacies and outcomes under varying conditions.

Chhatta 2. Agra is divided into six traditional sections. In the area along the river is the Chhatta district where the main business areas are located. The four electoral units in this district varied considerably in population (from 12,795 to 29,167) and social structure. Chhatta 2, the largest ward in the city in terms of population, was at the same time the twelfth highest in Scheduled Caste population and the eleventh highest in literacy among the twenty-seven wards. This results from the fact that in addition to its high Scheduled Caste population (25 percent of the total), it also contains a sizable concentration of Brahmins and fairly large elements of the high-caste Refugee communities—Punjabis and Sindhis. Reflecting the differences in social structure, the ward consisted of two distinct areas: lower-class *mohallas* near a railway depot, where the Jatavs are congregated; and several middle-class *mohallas,* where merchants with substantial commercial interests, particularly in grains, reside.

There were fourteen candidates for the corporation from this ward in 1959: nine for the general seat and five for the reserved. As table 3.2 illustrates, four Brahmins contested for the former along with two Sikhs, a Bania, and a Kori; the Republican Party attempted to win both seats by running a Jatav in the general contest. All of the candidates for the reserved seat were Jatavs. The Congress supported two candidates in this ward, while the Jan Sangh backed only one. The

TABLE 3.2

Chhatta 2: Candidates and Votes in Corporation Elections, 1959

Candidate	Party	Primordial Group	Vote	Percentage*
1. ACG	Jan Sangh	Brahmin	1,917	15.3
2. BLB (R)	Independent	Jatav	1,410	11.3
3. JS	Congress	Sikh	1,304	10.4
4. RS (R)	Independent	Jatav	1,288	10.3
5. HS	Independent	Brahmin	1,018	8.1
6. IR (R)	Congress	Jatav	1,004	8.0
7. KCN	Independent	Brahmin	955	7.6
8. HC	Independent	Kori	905	7.2
9. PDP	Independent	Brahmin	627	5.0
10. PS	Republican	Jatav	553	4.4
11. KC (R)	Independent	Jatav	509	4.1
12. PSN	PSP	Sikh	470	3.8
13. TC (R)	Republican	Jatav	450	3.6
14. RR	Independent	Bania	119	0.9
Total			12,529	100.0

* Based on the total vote.   (R) Reserved seat candidate.

latter party made some effort to find a suitable Jatav candidate for the reserved seat, but the man they finally settled upon withdrew shortly before the election in favor of a Jatav running as an independent.

The Jan Sangh candidate was a young man (ACG) whose father had been active in the Congress in the 1920s, but ACG was not himself involved in partisan politics prior to 1959. While working for a major newspaper in the city, he also had been active as a union functionary in the Mill Workers Union. He agreed to run in 1959 for the Jan Sangh as a result of personal contacts with some party leaders, but he was willing to assert four years later that he did not like many of the principles of the party, "especially its views on segregation and casteism." [12]

The presence of four Brahmin candidates including ACG in the race should have made it difficult for any one of them to win the single available seat. In this case, being the candidate of the Jan Sangh may have made some difference, since the Refugee population was inclined to identify its interests with the Jan Sangh. In contrast to the Congress candidate, who did not live in the ward, the Jan Sangh nominee also had taken an active interest in local organizations. Thus, three of the upper-status *mohallas* in the ward had *samitis* (committees) which undertook local problem solving. According to the Jan Sangh nominee (in 1964),

> these samitis do all sorts of things in the mohalla like set-
> tling disputes about sanitation. I used to help in deciding
> these cases. I am no longer active in them, but I have men
> working in them. They meet regularly—at least once in two
> months—and all the inhabitants could be members. Since all
> the people living in that part of the ward are high caste,
> there are very few other persons. Even Jatavs could be
> members, but this does not happen very often. The *samiti*
> does not work for any party. People in the *samiti* go into
> their own parties.

While these *samitis* may not have been partisan appendages in a technical sense, activity in them obviously provided a potential candidate for municipal office with some benefits.

Another factor which may have worked in this candidate's favor was the presence of an RPI candidate in the general contest. The entry of a Jatav in the race for a general seat reportedly alarmed some of the high-status residents of the ward, who feared a divided high-caste vote might allow a Jatav to win. In appealing to this fear, the Jan Sangh may have shifted the balance in its candidate's favor. Finally, the Jan Sangh candidate is alleged to have received the help of the winner in the neighboring constituency—the elderly Congressman mentioned earlier who was denied his party's ticket and ran as an independent. The latter was interested in exhibiting his personal popularity and influence not only in his own ward but in places where he had personal connections. As a prominent figure in the area's Brahmin community, he may have been particularly effective in getting members of that caste to consolidate support behind the eventual winner.

Both men elected from Chhatta 2 were quite young. The Jan Sangh victor was twenty-eight in 1959; the independent Jatav (BLB) was only twenty-six. The political activities of the latter had been largely restricted to the Congress Seva Dal, that party's social service organization, until two years earlier. He left the Seva Dal in part because he resented what he regarded as discriminatory treatment within the Congress toward the Scheduled Castes by persons with "higher contacts" and higher social status. Equally important, he admitted, was the fact that there was little future for an ambitious young man in the local Congress. Benefits like political nominations were unlikely "since there were many men in the party who had a better claim, and even these did not get tickets."

While he had been trained as a shoemaker and started a small shoe factory of his own in 1957, much of his time was devoted to politics. Until 1957, he had been a member of a group of young men who engaged, as BLB described them, in "games" like wrestling and gambling. One of his distinctions was owning a motorcycle, which meant that at election time "people would approach me to do party work." After leaving the Seva Dal, he joined the RPI, but the leader of that party refused to give him a ticket for the corporation election in his own ward. Instead, the party's tickets were given to two older men. BLB, therefore, stood as an independent and came in second largely with the help of his friends in the Jatav community in the ward. Indeed, the Republican Party did rather badly in this ward as both of its nominees went down to resounding defeats (see table 3.2). Without a Jan Sangh Jatav in the race, those high-caste persons who cast ballots for the reserved seat apparently preferred an independent Jatav or one associated with the Congress to a nominee of the Republican Party.

Once elected, the Jatav winner returned to the RPI because, as he explained, "I only wanted to give them the lesson that they would suffer unless they ran good men rather than simply the rich." His place in the RPI and the Jatav community has been ambiguous. He ran for MLA in 1962 as a candidate of the RPI, but his relations with the local party have gone through several upheavals since then.

When all the relevant variables are drawn together, it is difficult to identify the *key* elements in the voting behavior recorded in table 3.2. The constituency provides the unusual situation of a Jatav winning the reserved seat with enough votes to have been elected outright; at the same time, if every voter who turned out had exercised the right to vote for *two* candidates, the total vote would have been 3,259 higher. (While 7,894 voters appeared at the polls, 3,259 of these voted for only one candidate.) Presumably, many of those casting only one ballot were high-caste persons who did not see fit to choose among the Scheduled Caste nominees for the reserved seat. This should, in large part, explain the 300-vote margin between the two Congress candidates; indeed, compared to some other wards, Chhatta 2 was a ward in which intra-party differences in candidate performance by the Congress were relatively small despite a high "drop-off."[13]

In summary, caste was not—by itself—a significant dimension in determining the outcome of this contest; party may have played a more important role, but this is difficult to establish. Indeed, these two factors may have served mainly as incremental values in helping voters to distinguish among candidates in a crowded field. They would have to be added to personal, ideational, and situational factors which were not quantifiable within the framework of the present study.

Kotwali 3. The Kotwali section of the city grew up around the medieval police establishment. The six wards assigned to it in the municipal elections ranged from congested bazaar areas to new housing colonies which had developed in the last two decades in an area of social and educational institutions around Agra College. Few Jatavs lived in five of the six wards; consequently, the wards with the highest literacy were in this region of the city. In Kotwali 1, such a high concentration of Banias occurred that all six candidates for the two seats were from that community. The winners were an "independent" dropped from the original Congress list and a Jan Sangh teacher who worked in a Protestant school. The weakness of party identifications may be indicated by the fact that even in this small field, the Jan Sangh victor received 2,319 votes while his running mate finished fifth with only 878.

Kotwali 3 was an especially interesting case because of the intraparty conflict evident between the two Congress candidates. Out of 7,500 eligible voters, perhaps a third were Banias with Brahmins constituting the next largest community. In 1959, the area was the home of the Seth-affiliated General Secretary of the City Congress, Roshan Lal Sutel. He was given one ticket; the other went to a businessman (BCG) inclined toward the Singhal group. Sutel had joined the Congress in 1938 after participating in several leftist political organizations including the Hindustan Socialist Republican Army which was one of the forerunners of the Communist Party of India. While working his way up through the Congress hierarchy, he was active in the trade union movement. (In 1962, he became President of the District Labor Federation of Agra.)

Singhal had originally supported a candidate for the ward other than BCG. As the latter commented, "I was attached to Singhal but was not a blind follower and so I did not get the support of that group." Like Sutel, BCG was an old member of the party, having joined it in 1934, and was prominent locally as a leader of the Congress Seva Dal. When he was denied a ticket on the first Congress list, he went directly to Lucknow and argued his case with Rawat. In the end, his candidacy was given preference by the state party. As a result, the original nominee of the Singhal group (RSS in table 3.3) ran as an independent.

In addition to the Congress, the Jan Sangh ran two candidates, both Banias. One (RK) was Vice-President of the Agra Jan Sangh. The only other party represented in this generally high-status ward was the Communist Party, which supported a Rajput active in that party.

TABLE 3.3

Kotwali 3: Candidates and Votes in Corporation Elections, 1959

Candidate	Party	Primordial Group	Vote	Percentage
1. BCG	Congress	Bania	1,397	19.4
2. HS	Independent	Muslim	1,177	16.3
3. RK	Jan Sangh	Bania	1,006	14.0
4. RL Sutel	Congress	Brahmin	909	12.6
5. RSS	Independent	Brahmin	857	11.9
6. JLL	Jan Sangh	Bania	774	10.7
7. RR	Communist	Rajput	471	6.5
8. AF	Independent	Muslim	386	5.4
9. CBS	Independent	Khatri	231	3.2
Total			7,208	100.0

Among the primordial groups in the ward, the Muslims probably had about 10 percent of the population. HS, a Muslim businessman, might have been expected to do badly. He did not live in the ward, although he did live in an adjacent ward and was known to people in the area. HS decided not to stand from his home ward because two friends were already contesting from there.

During the earlier part of the campaign, the two Congressmen worked fairly smoothly together, but charges soon arose among their workers that each man was seeking advantages for himself by cooperating with opposition candidates. Friction also developed within the Jan Sangh as allegations were advanced that HS was receiving the support of the dissident group of that party as a way of trying to embarrass the dominant faction to which RK belonged.

Factionalism necessarily helped the position of the independents. It is clear that HS received more than Muslim votes; if primordial factors had been predominant, the disparity between the two Muslim candidates would not have been so great. Estimates that only eight hundred Muslim voters reside in the ward point in the same direction. Opponents were eager to attribute the victory of HS to the expenditure of considerable money; this is impossible to prove. The candidate's own estimate suggests, however, that he did spend an amount greater than most candidates.

The results indicate that a great number of Banias and Brahmins in the ward were selective in their high-caste preferences. The left-leaning Brahmin Congressman ran considerably behind his running mate; he later attributed his defeat to "casteism and class." While he shared caste and class characteristics with the dominant communities in the ward, he argued that the Banias and Brahmins were "against me because of my work with the working class and my opposition to casteism." On the other hand, the fact that the Bania Congressman was elected may not have been due simply to the support of the upper castes; he is supposed to have received important backing from members of the backward Kori community in the ward.

Still, it does seem to be the case that many of the middle-class residents of the area did not trust Sutel, while they were willing to support the moderate businessman BCG. Persons who disliked Sutel spread their votes and may even have given some to HS. This argument is vitiated again by the indeterminate influence of the "drop off" effect in the ward. "Drop off" was substantial although lower than in Chhatta 2. In the latter case, 41 percent of the voters cast only one ballot; in Kotwali 3, the figure was about 30 percent. This still meant that over 1,260 of the 4,239 voters voted for only one man.

Thus, in Kotwali 3 (as in Chhatta 2), factors like caste may have played some threshold role—determining the nature of party candidacies and setting the boundaries for final success—but the direct impact of caste was tempered by personal and ideological differences. Nor did party act as a major determinant of electoral outcome; indeed, given the factionalism within the two major parties, not being a party candidate may have been an asset. According to some informants, party labels in many wards had a negative effect simply because certain voters were alienated by particular party labels while not being especially attracted to other parties.

Tajganj 2. As its name suggests, the Tajganj region of the city is located near the Taj Mahal—at some distance to the south of the main settled area of the city. This is an old section of the city, but it is peculiarly isolated since it grew up away from the commercial center which developed near Agra Fort during the nineteenth century.

Tajganj 2 is the larger of the two wards in the area. It is almost rural in character with large parts of the ward consisting of farming or waste land. In addition to a large Jatav population (27 percent), there is a sizable Muslim community—perhaps 15 percent of the population. On this basis alone, the ward offered little hope to Congress candidates and even less to the Jan Sangh. The former put forward a Brahmin and a Jatav (for a reserved seat); the latter party ran no candidates.

The Republican Party felt sufficiently hopeful of its chances to put up two candidates: Man Singh, the owner of a shoe factory and a prominent figure in the Agra party; and BS, a Jatav farmer. While Man Singh had helped form the RPI and was a member of the party executive, BS was simply an illiterate group follower. In the voting, however, it was Man Singh who was defeated (for the general seat), partly because of a misunderstanding on the part of BS.[14]

Because of the size and low density of the ward, the two men had hired a truck to take voters to the polls. Somehow BS believed that votes given to Man Singh would reduce his own chances, and he is said to have therefore removed the truck from circulation too early. This made it difficult for Jatav voters to get to the polling stations. Members of his own party claim that BS also feared he would be unable to overcome the votes given to both Man Singh and RP. The latter, who lived in the same area as BS, was competing directly for some of BS's voters.

A marked contrast to this political neophyte was to be found in the person of KUK. The latter had served on the old Municipal Board from July 1939 until its supersession. Neither then nor in 1959 was he affiliated with a political party. He belongs to the Meo community, which is Muslim by religion but Hindu in many of its traditions.[15] In 1959, he won support from both Muslims and from Backward Class groups in the ward.

Table 3.4 reveals a considerable gap in votes between the winner in the general contest and the winner of the reserved seat. The Congress fared badly in both instances. As we might anticipate in a reserved-seat constituency with such a large proportion of low-status groups, the "drop-off" was high with 45 percent of the voters casting only one ballot.

TABLE 3.4

Tajganj 2: Candidates and Votes in Corporation Elections, 1959

Candidate	Party	Primordial Group	Votes	Percentage
1. KUK	Independent	Meo	1,517	20.7
2. RLB	Independent	Brahmin	1,483	20.2
3. Man Singh	Republican	Jatav	1,422	19.4
4. BS (R)	Republican	Jatav	904	12.3
5. DPD	Congress	Brahmin	644	8.8
6. MSR	Independent	Backward Class*	501	6.8
7. RP (R)	Independent	Jatav	470	6.4
8. ACL (R)	Congress	Jatav	396	5.4
Totals			7,337	100.0

(R) Those contesting for the reserved seat.   * Caste not identifiable.

RESULTS OF THE ELECTIONS

Out of this mix of constituencies, candidates and parties, fifty-four winners emerged. Table 3.5 summarizes the identifications of these victors by social grouping and party at the time of their election. On the whole, both the Banias and the Jatavs are slightly overrepresented, while the Backward Classes are somewhat underrepresented. Among the latter were a Potter Congressman, a Khatik running as an independent with Republican support, and wealthy persons drawn from the Kurmi and Sonar communities who also ran as independents. The table again underlines the extent to which the Congress and Jan Sangh drew their strength from high-status communities, while the RPI was dependent on Jatav votes. The large number of independents elected included elements from almost all of the major primordial categories; especially worth noting is the presence of four out of five Muslim corporators among the independents.

Given the strong representation of independents and the fact that the Jan Sangh and the Republicans ran no candidates in some wards and only one in others, it is impossible to measure party voting on an aggregate basis in the city of Agra. Certainly, very few constituencies were "safe" for any party. Of the twenty-seven wards, only seven elected two men backed by the same political organization. The Jan Sangh captured one ward, the Congress two, and the Republicans four. In the latter instance, however, all the "safe" wards involved a reserved seat and in two of these four cases, the winner of the reserved seat did not finish among the top two

TABLE 3.5

Primordial Groups and Parties of Elected Members, Agra Corporation, 1959

Primordial Group	Party				
	Congress	Jan Sangh	RPI	Other	Total
Banias/Jains	7	4	1	4	16
Brahmins	2	1	–	4	7
Other high caste*	6	–	–	1	7
Refugees	–	2	–	–	2
Backward Class	1	–	–	3	4
Jatavs	–	–	11	2	13
Muslims	–	–	1	4†	5
	16	7	13	18	54

* Three Congress Kayasthas; two Congress and one independent Khatri; one Congress Thakur.
† One of these Muslims stood on a PSP ticket. He was the only PSP member elected to the corporation.

vote getters in the ward. These figures hardly argue for the existence of very effective local party organizations or the presence of strong party identifications among the voters.

While the results of the Agra election do not yield much data for close analysis on an aggregate basis, a few general tendencies do emerge. Since we had several independent measures like Scheduled Caste population and literacy rates available for each ward, it was possible to examine the relationship between such measures and turnout. On the whole, literacy rates are not a reliable measure of turnout, but we did find that ten of thirteen wards with many Scheduled Caste persons had low turnouts, whereas only five of thirteen constituencies with few Scheduled Caste persons had low turnouts.[16]

We also found a relationship between size of ward and turnout which was inexplicable at first. The process of delimitation has received little empirical study in India, and there is no reason to assume social bias on the part of those persons given the task of drawing corporation lines.[17] Yet, differences in ward size do appear to be related to the social composition of the wards.[18]

If the population of the city of Agra was simply divided into twenty-seven equal parts, each constituency would contain 3.7 percent of the total. In fact, Agra's wards range in size from a high of 6.3 to a low of 1.4 percent.[19] These differences are emphasized by a wide dispersion of inequalities. A 10 percent deviation from the average size of a ward would cover eight of the twenty-seven wards; only at 20 percent variance would a bare majority of wards (fourteen) be included.

In themselves, these departures from a "one man, one vote" principle need not be discriminatory, but the distributive effects are not random. As we can see from table 3.6, ten of the thirteen wards with high concentrations of Scheduled Caste residents are above average in size as compared with only four of the thirteen wards where such populations are relatively small. Whether consciously or not,

TABLE 3.6

Turnout* and Concentration of Scheduled Castes by Ward Size, Agra, 1959

	Less Than 30% Turnout		More Than 30% Turnout	
	Ward Size†		Ward Size	
Concentration of Scheduled Castes	Under 3.5%	Over 3.5%	Under 3.5%	Over 3.5%
Less than 15%	1	4	8	0
More than 15%	0	10	3	0

* Computed as a percentage of total population in the ward.
† Computed as a percentage of total population in the city.

Agra's wards were so apportioned in 1959 that members of the Scheduled Castes were somewhat underrepresented in the political system.

If we look at the *number* of candidates running in a ward in terms of turnout and size of wards, we also find some slight evidence that a larger number of candidates *increases* turnout. Controlling for size of the ward makes no difference in this case, but turnout is low in eleven of fifteen wards where there are few candidates—eight or less—whereas turnout is high in seven of eleven wards where there are more than eight candidates running. One might argue that increasing the number of candidates may mean that more people are drawn into the ambit of political participation, since each candidate adds a certain increment of voters that he has approached personally or with whom he has connections within his mohalla or primordial group.

ALDERMANIC ELECTIONS

The elections for KAVAL aldermen were held 26 November 1959. In Agra, six aldermen were to be chosen by proportional representation with a single transferable vote. Given the desire of each political actor to maximize his influence, there was an effort to reach agreements about candidates. For this reason, the loose category of "independents" began to coalesce during this time into a quasi-formal political group calling itself the Swatantra Dal (Independent Party). On 3 November 1959—less than two weeks after the municipal elections—sixteen of these independents met and decided to cooperate in the election of two aldermen.[20]

Probably the group hardest hit by the political maneuvering at this time was the Jan Sangh. We have already alluded to the divisions within that party. The leader of the dissident element, Baloji, sought his party's backing for an aldermanic seat. His opponents within the party accused him of working only for his own men in the corporation elections and withheld their support. Baloji's intense desire to become an alderman, presumably as a first step toward another effort to run for MLA, led him to approach several men elected to the corporation as independents including Ram Babu Verma, mentioned earlier as a former Jan Sangh leader. In addition to Verma, a few independents fairly sympathetic to the Jan Sangh had been elected. When Baloji sought out these men to secure promises of support for his aldermanic candidacy, the Jan Sangh responded by bringing charges against him. Rather than fight his case within the party, Baloji resigned.

As a result, not only did the Jan Sangh-inclined independents not join the party, but Baloji took with him two corporation members elected on Jan Sangh tickets (one being ACG, mentioned earlier in this chapter) as well as a considerable number of party workers. For his aldermanic candidacy he even received the support of a Jan Sangh member who had promised him backing during the election campaign and had received considerable help from Baloji's group in return. This Jan Sangh member was willing to go against his party's orders and was almost on the point of resigning from the party, but the regional organizer of the party finally gave him permission to vote for Baloji while remaining in the Jan Sangh.

The Jan Sangh itself, after some internal debate on the issue, agreed to back the President of the City Jan Sangh for alderman. The recent depletion of its forces promised to cause further embarrassment to the party if it could not elect even one alderman.

Congress members were somewhat reluctant to identify themselves as members of the two political groups when questioned in 1964, but there was general agreement in aligning five of the sixteen members elected to the corporation with Singhal and about nine with Seth. The two others were newcomers to the party in 1959 who were not strongly associated with a faction. Under the circumstances, it was relatively easy to agree that one alderman should come from each faction.

The Congress Party, therefore, entered the contest with two candidates: the President of the City Congress and a long-time Congressman who had been a member of the post-1947 Municipal Committee. The former is a Jain, the latter a Kayastha. As noted earlier, the Congress President was a close associate of Seth; the other candidate was not as directly involved in factional fights, but received the backing of the Singhal group for alderman.

The Republicans, who counted upon at least thirteen and possibly fifteen corporation members, were assured of one alderman. Skillful leadership might have enlisted enough votes for a second candidate, but defections prevented this. The party did put two men into the field. One was Khem Chand, among the most educated and socially aware members of the Jatav community. He had grown up in Agra and graduated from Agra College before joining the central government's service in Delhi. Even while in service, he became involved in community life in Delhi and was inspired by Ambedkar to convert to Buddhism and become a publicist for Ambedkar's ideas in the Jatav community.

When he was approached by some members of the Republican Party from Agra to return to his home city and run for alderman, Khem Chand saw it as an opportunity to serve the community. Therefore, he left his secure government position and entered politics.[21] Since the party was engaged in internal contention over the part being played by its rather autocratic President, some party members looked upon Khem Chand's return as an opportunity to build up a new focus of leadership.

While he participated in the decision to support Khem Chand for one aldermanic position, the President also insisted that one of his own supporters—a "renegade" Brahmin who had been active in the Scheduled Caste Federation—be put up for the party's other alderman. The party decided to assign eight members to vote for Khem Chand and six to the Brahmin. Seven votes were required to assure election on the first ballot, but transfers could elect a second alderman. Agreements with nonparty members were sought.

Along with these party-related candidates there were several independents who encouraged corporators to submit their names for alderman. One of these was Kalyan Das, a wealthy Jain iron merchant and businessman from the western part of the city. Some of the independents elected to the corporation from that area were particularly favorable toward his candidacy. (Later, these members constituted a major segment within the Swatantra Dal around Kalyan Das.)

There were four other persons who were formally entered in the contest for alderman. Two of these were Muslims supported by two different subgroups among the five Muslims in the municipality. The other two serious candidates included the editor of the second major paper of Agra, *Amar-ujala,* and a candidate originally put forward by the Seth faction. The latter refused to withdraw when the Seth group switched its support to the City Congress President.

Only fifty-three of the fifty-four corporators actually had their votes recorded in these elections; one blank ballot was submitted. Both Congress nominees were easily elected, as were the two leading independents (Baloji and Kalyan Das) and the chief nominee of the RPI, Khem Chand. All received the required votes on the first ballot. The Jan Sangh nominee had only five and the second RPI candidate three. On the basis of transfers, the Jan Sangh nominee was elected. Ten first-preference votes were scattered among the four other aldermanic candidates.

The manner in which votes were split became a matter of special controversy within the RPI. While the party had no assurance that its candidates would receive sufficient support from the men it had endorsed for the corporation elections, it did expect to hold together at least thirteen votes. Instead, only three votes went to the Brahmin nominee in addition to seven cast for Khem Chand. This discrepancy reflected the emergence of an effort to undermine the authority of the party president, as well as the "availability" of some Republicans to influence (or material benefits) from non-Republican candidates.

CONCLUSIONS

If any notion of political modernization can be associated with the sheer number and complexity of factors evident in a given political arena, political behavior in Agra may be described as highly "modernized." On the other hand, it is evident that there is a low level of *institutionalization* of political behavior.[22] Parties are fragmented; independents compete on equal terms with persons running on party tickets; the dividing line between group membership and nonmembership is vague.

In some disorganized fashion, however, the electoral process in Agra managed to produce a set of legitimated political actors who reflected most of the political forces and groups of any substance operating in the city. Factors like party and caste may have been insignificant variables in particular wards for a variety of reasons: high concentrations of certain primordial groups caused parties of different ideational shades to nominate candidates of the same primordial group; candidates nominated by the same party varied considerably in their outlooks; parties did not contest where they felt they had little public support; a large number of local "notables" recruited by parties for the particular election and individuals running as independents distorted the implications of party, primordial or ideational influences at the ward level. Thus, in many instances, "personality" emerged as the most important factor in the final results of particular local contests. Agra informants referring to the centrality of "personality" in local politics meant more, however, than personal appearance and manner of public behavior. Rather, they included under this term such matters as past services to the ward, general personal character, family reputation, and the expenditure of effort (and/or money) by a candidate in campaigning.

We shall, in the next chapter, see many of the same elements at work in Poona, although politics appeared somewhat more institutionalized in that city during the period from 1962 to 1964 than was the case in Agra in 1959.

4

THE POONA ELECTORAL PROCESS IN 1962

As in earlier years, the municipal elections in Poona in 1962 were preceded, six months earlier, by general elections. These offered an opportunity for major gains by the Congress from the debacle of 1957. The marked success of the Congress in these elections did not, however, prevent their defeat in the subsequent municipal elections.

THE GENERAL ELECTIONS

By 1962, Y. B. Chavan had regained so much political ground for the Congress in the new state of Maharashtra—now under the political dominance of non-Brahmins—that he had won not only widespread support for the Congress Party but personal adulation for himself. In the minds of many Maharashtrians, the Chief Minister was only a step or two below Shivaji in the realm of local folk heroes. He healed many of the wounds left by the Samyukta Maharashtra movement, ran an effective administration in the state, helped to organize the Congress in such a disciplined fashion as to prevent major state factionalism from flaring up, and, in the process, won the grudging admiration of many persons in the political opposition. It was clear going into the elections of 1962 that only a united opposition in contests for Parliament and the State Assembly would have the remotest chance of defeating the Congress.[1]

In Poona, where the bases of opposition to the Congress were more institutionalized than they are in much of the Maharashtrian countryside, fragmentation among political groups rather than unity confronted the Congress. Remnants of the Samiti ran a slate of candidates distinct from both the Jan Sangh and the PSP. Local notables with personal followings stood as independents. About the only substantive "issues" these parties attempted to capitalize upon was the flood disaster of 1961.

Poona normally experiences high water after the monsoons, but on 12 July 1961 a major earthen dam collapsed at Panshet due to an abnormally intense monsoon. The failure at Panshet—about twenty miles above the city—was compounded by the malfunctioning of new installations at Khadakwasla dam, which lies closer to the city. The latter dam had recently undergone extensive additions which some informants allege were placed into service prematurely in order to advertise Congress achievements prior to the elections. Under the strain of rising waters, the dam's inadequately tested restraining gates failed to function properly and added to the flood problem. The flood hit the heart of the city early in the morning, when there was not much street activity in the area; insufficient warning, however, caused an enormous loss of property. About ten thousand families were either temporarily or permanently made homeless, four to five thousand houses were destroyed, but few lives were *reported* lost.[2]

Governmental inquiries later raised a number of questions about the timing of the putting into operation of Khadakwasla dam's new facilities as well as about some of the specific decisions made by local officials at the time of the flood;[3] but the criticisms made by the inquiry commission were not available until after the elections of 1962. Still, in the period following the floods, opposition parties apparently regarded the events as "a godsent opportunity for political exploitation."[4]

Instead of providing a basis for anti-Congress sentiments, however, the flood was treated by most people as a natural disaster or as a failure on the part of the particular engineers involved, rather than anything attributable to state politicians. The personal attention given by the Chief Minister to the matter rallied the public behind him; Poona's population in 1964 recalled various anecdotes about Chavan's efforts to revive the city's spirit, including his venturing out on the remaining girders of the principal bridge in a major section of Poona which had been partially washed away. In addition to this personal involvement, a large amount of money was poured into the city for relief centers, rehabilitation, and reconstruction.[5] To administer the recovery program, Chavan sent his most trusted administrator to the city. This man, S. G. Barve, was already widely admired in Poona for his past services to the city.

Barve had served as head of the administration in Poona district during the turbulent period 1947-49. As a member of the IAS, he then assumed the position of Commissioner of Poona Municipality, which he held until 1952. He was in charge of the municipal administration during the period that no elective body existed and in the first three months of the body elected in 1952. He turned over his charge to the new government in a spirit that reflected goodwill toward him and more than a decade later he was still remembered as one of the best administrators Poona ever had. He said of this period in his career:

> Municipal administration generally was not held in much esteem amongst the services; and when I was appointed to be the Municipal Commissioner of the Poona Municipality this was generally considered in the service circles as a matter for expression of sympathy and commiseration with me rather than of congratulation. ... Municipal administration is concerned with a large number of petty, nagging, vexatious issues touching the daily life and material conveniences of thousands of persons most of whom are apt to be oblivious of any benefits they might derive and intolerant of even the most trivial shortcomings. The Municipal establishments, through whom one would have to function, were generally speaking, poorly organized, ill-paid, factious and intrigue-ridden; municipal councillors, generally speaking, were zealous of the exercise of their authority and habituated to petty interference with administrative details. ...
>
> I must confess, however, that in the sequel I have no regrets whatever. ... There is a certain directness about ad-

ministrative duties in a limited sphere like this one which is
capable of giving personal satisfaction one could seldom
achieve in other offices wherein one functions largely im-
personally as but one cog in the wheels of an enormous
machinery.[6]

After his service in Poona, Barve moved on to the Bombay Secretariat. He
was Chavan's administrative assistant in the negotiations for the creation of
Maharashtra and also served on several important national assignments. It was on
the basis of his close association with Poona and Chavan that Barve was given the
task of helping to restore Poona in 1961. By that time, too, Chavan had convinced
Barve that he could be of great service to Maharashtra by participating directly in
the state's political life. In 1961, therefore, Barve resigned from the IAS and took
the unusual course of immediately joining the Congress Party with the expectation
that he would receive an MLA ticket for the 1962 elections from a safe
constituency and ultimately be placed in a position of importance in the State
Cabinet.[7]

His prominence and general capabilities made Barve a probable winner in
many different constituencies for which the Congress could have supported him.
However, the Congress saw fit to slate Barve, a Brahmin, for the Shivajinagar
constituency in Poona, which had a large Brahmin population. V. M. Sirsikar, in his
study of this contest has written:

Shri Barve's entry into Maharashtra politics was a shrewd
game on the part of the Congress leadership. His candida-
ture from the Shivajinagar constituency was an equally strategic move. It appeared to be a concession to the disgruntled intelligentsia who were critical of the Congress rule for
the neglect of their talent.[8]

Indeed, the distribution of tickets by Congress in the city constituted a
generally skillful effort to placate and win to the party a variety of primordial and
ideational segments of the population. Aside from the Barve nomination to gain
Brahmin support, tickets were given in the other four municipally-related
constituencies in a manner reflecting group interests: B. N. Sanas, who had
narrowly lost to S. M. Joshi in 1957, was placed in a Congress-inclined non-Brahmin
constituency; R. V. Telang, a former PSP mayor who had joined the Congress in
1961, was set up in Sanas' previous constituency against his own former party
leader, S. M. Joshi;[9] and K. T. Girme, a Mali, was supported by the Congress for the
seat in the cantonment. Girme was actually a resident of the city who had served as
leader of the small Congress contingent elected to the corporation in the wake of
the 1957 debacle.[10] It should be noted that in some fashion all four of the Congress
MLA candidates in 1962 were men who had served for some portion of their
political careers in the municipal government of Poona. These four urban
constituencies (along with two rural districts) formed part of one MP unit. For the
latter seat, the Congress chose S. S. More, the former leader of the PWP.

Unlike the two-man contests of 1957, there were at least three opponents for
each of the Congress candidates. In primordial terms, the MP contest is probably
the most interesting. Part of More's early reputation had been made on the basis of
outspoken anti-Brahminism. Against him, the PSP ran N. G. Goray, the incumbent

MP. The fragments of the Samiti backed P. K. Atre, a well-known left-wing Bombay and Poona political figure and editor of a popular leftist paper. Finally, the Jan Sangh entered a relatively obscure Brahmin as its nominee. Thus, More was faced by three Brahmin opponents of varying ideological hue. Significantly, More's reputation actually may have hurt him in this contest. He received 43 percent of the vote while each of his four MLA running-mates in the urban parts of Poona won over 50 percent in contests involving three to eight opponents. The greatest difference between the Congress MP and MLA candidates, as we might expect, occurred in the Shivajinagar constituency where Barve received over 30,000 votes while More was getting only 13,220. Even in Sanas' MLA district, however, Sanas received 4,500 more votes than More out of about 52,000 cast.

Among the MLA results, Barve's victory was the most one-sided. In deference to Barve's popularity among his middle class electorate, the PSP did not put up a candidate. The Jan Sangh and Hindu Mahasabha each nominated contestants. The latter supported a man with many years of service in the corporation, while the former favored R. K. Mhalgi, a leader of the Jan Sangh in Poona. A third opponent was in the field from the tiny Lohia Socialist party. Against these three, Barve received 60 percent of the vote, while the Jan Sangh nominee came in second with less than 30 percent.

Other Congress victories were not as spectacular quantitatively, but they involved opponents with more substantial personal followings. In the Shukrawar Peth constituency, where Joshi was pitted against Telang, the Congress originally had hinted of plans to enter no candidate in deference to Joshi's stature as a leader of a major opposition group. Under pressure from the local party organization, Chavan's thinking on that score apparently changed.

Joshi was aware of the risks of running in a non-Brahmin ward; his close victory of 1957 had come principally because of the ability of the particular "cause" to ride roughshod over more permanent group attachments. Explaining the situation which had come into existence by 1962, a source close to Joshi stated:

> Joshi had good personal relations with Chavan, and even in 1961 Chavan asked Joshi which constituency he expected to contest in 1962. Joshi was tired of being in the useless opposition, but since Goray ran again for MP, he had to run in order to back him up, because Goray was General Secretary of the party. Word got around that Chavan was not going to put up a candidate against Joshi, and *Sakal* and *Kesari* maligned Joshi as a 'Yes Man' for the Congress. Chavan wanted the Shivajinagar constituency [where Joshi lives] for Barve and indicated he would not contest if Joshi ran from a different one. Joshi could have done much better in that area. Then More and others brought pressures on Chavan that Goray might win if the seat was not contested; so Congress put up Telang.

Even this change in expectations would have been acceptable to most PSP leaders had it not been accompanied by other campaign tactics. They cited, in particular, the resort to anti-Brahminism on the part of More, who was accused of having made a speech in which he charged that Joshi was in the MLA contest in a non-Brahmin area to make sure that non-Brahmins like Telang were defeated as Sanas had been in 1957. Opposition leaders also commented heatedly on the pressures which state and local Congress leaders allegedly brought to bear on non-Maharshtrian businessmen and community leaders to support Congress nominees. Despite these conditioning factors, it is unlikely that Joshi would have been elected even under a more favorable set of local circumstances. Telang was elected with 54 percent of the total vote while Joshi received only 37 percent. Four other men divided the remainder.

Sanas' victory was equally large. His chief opposition for this seat was not from the PSP or Jan Sangh but from a dissident Congressman, K. U. Pardeshi. The latter was a disgruntled leader of the Congress' youth organization who felt slighted by the Congress preference for Sanas. He regarded the latter as a latecomer to the party and an interloper in his MLA constituency (an area in which Sanas did not live). Pardeshi, a member of a small non-Brahmin caste of intermediate status, drew sufficient support to his cause from dissident Congressmen including some non-Maharashtrians to worry the Congress. But none of the other candidates in the field was a real threat. A rather weak candidate was put up by the Jan Sangh. The incumbent MLA—a member of the CPI—ran with the backing of the remnants of the Samiti. The result in this four-cornered race was overwhelmingly for Sanas—55 percent of the total to Pardeshi's 21.7 percent.[11]

The feature of special interest in the cantonment contest, where Girme won with ease (53 percent of the vote), was the presence of eight opponents. The leading opposition came from a PSP candidate and there were also Jan Sangh and Swatantra Party candidates in the field, but the curious aspect of the contest was the division in the Mahar community which produced *six* Mahars contending against the rest of the field. These included four independents and two persons affiliated with the two Republican Parties which had emerged in parts of Maharashtra after the creation of the state.[12] All six Mahars together received only 6,743 votes, which would have placed even a single candidate in a poor runner-up position. (The PSP candidate actually finished second to Girme with 6,474 votes.) In this case, it would be difficult to speak of the interests of a community *as community* being expressed through politics. Indeed, several of these Mahar contestants were not so much motivated by a desire to win as by a passion to defeat each other.

As a whole, then, the Congress won a smashing victory in Poona and Maharashtra in 1962. After the elections of 1957, the Congress had held only about 135 seats of the 262 available for the territory which is now included in the state of Maharashtra. In contrast, the new legislature of 1962 included 215 Congressmen in a total body of 264. This success was based on only 52 percent of the vote, but no other party won more than 10 percent.[13]

Such a sweeping victory for the Congress in Maharashtra and in Poona was bound to frighten some of the opposition groups into recognizing how Pyrrhic their successes of 1957 had been. One result was an effort at coalition formation for the municipal elections.

THE POONA MUNICIPAL ELECTIONS

The outcome of the general elections provided ammunition to those local leaders who wished to revive a "nonpolitical" fusion organization in the municipal elections as a counterforce to the "partisanship" associated with the Congress. The instrumentality for this effort was a new Nagri Sanghatna involving some of the same personalities as in 1952. They hoped to correct the Sanghatna's earlier mistakes by constructing an organization which did more than bring together distinct political actors. For some leaders, notably Parulekar of *Sakal*, this was to be a party closer to his ideal of removing state and national politics from the municipal arena; but given the political groups operating in Poona politics, this was an unrealizable dream. Instead, the Sanghatna was used by several political organizations to achieve ends which they hoped might eventually provide a basis for general opposition to the Congress Party.[14]

Thus, whatever the nonpartisan aura given it, the formation of the new Nagri Sanghatna involved gaining the support of groups like the PSP, the Hindu Mahasabha, the PWP, and segments of the Republican Party.[15] Since the emphasis was on a "nonpartisan" electoral alliance, however, candidates did not stand as party representatives or as party members endorsed by the alliance but as members of the Sanghatna. In addition, leaders of the Sanghatna like Parulekar sought participation by nonaffiliated notables in the city. As in 1952, however, the overriding desire to win the election led the Sanghatna leaders into association with a dissident Congress faction. The victory of B. N. Sanas over K. U. Pardeshi had left the latter and some members of his personal following without an organizational base; they were welcomed into the Sanghatna.

The formal process of candidate selection for the Sanghatna in 1962 was somewhat more routinized than it had been in 1952. In 1962, according to one spokesman for the party,

> the Nagri Sanghatna asked for applications from the people of the city and then a Selection Committee from all parts of the city containing fifteen members went through the applications. The committee included J. S. Tilak, Parulekar, S. M. Joshi, N. G. Goray, and others. There was no formal system of agreements among the parties on a division of tickets. There were some differences about the distribution, but not many. The Selection Committee went to every constituency and announced the names of the possible candidates and asked the people for their views. In a few cases, they did not give out tickets when they received complaints from the public.

On the whole, however, persons belonging to the major political organizations of Poona (other than the Congress and Jan Sangh) received representation within the framework of the Sanghatna in proportion to their political strength.

The fusion organization was much helped by the willingness of S. M. Joshi and N. G. Goray, recently MLA and MP respectively, to allow their names to be put forward as candidates on Sanghatna tickets, thereby lending considerable prestige to the party. The organization was also aided by the candidacy of B. G. Jagtap, a prominent elderly Maratha educator. Jagtap had not been involved in politics for forty years (since short-lived participation in the municipality in the 1920s) but he was highly esteemed as the head of one of the leading educational societies of Poona and as the teacher of many of the new generation of Maratha leaders, including some of the members of the local Congress hierarchy. Jagtap agreed to become a candidate for the Sanghatna because he was sincerely interested in improving the city without becoming involved in partisan activity—the characteristic public posture of the Sanghatna. While these "nonpartisan" aspects appealed to such persons as Jagtap, it is clear that the direct participation of the PSP leadership made the Sanghatna a viable organization. A prominent figure in that party cited the following differences between the 1952 and 1962 performances of the Sanghatna:

> In 1952 it was a one-man show [Parulekar], and the parties were not so deeply involved, although some rebel Congressmen and a few PSP people ran. By 1962 it was very different. We decided not to allow the leaders to stand aside and only put up junior people. That was what put teeth into the contest and made the difference in the election. It became an attractive organization to the public. People saw we were serious.

The Congress also saw the need to respond to the challenge represented by the Sanghatna. Despite the rancor within the Congress Party in the corporation during the last months of the previous body, the party might have hoped to capitalize upon their successes in the general elections by simply papering over differences and renominating most incumbents. Instead, the MPCC issued a directive ordering several of the major officeholders in the party to run for the corporation; one result was that prominent local leaders like the President of the City Congress—one of Sanas' lieutenants—and the General Secretary of the City Congress felt obliged to run in these municipal elections. The party also passed over persons from whom it had experienced some dissidence in the recent past. This followed an MPCC recommendation that no nomination should be given to a man who had served in both of the previous municipal bodies. While it did not stick entirely to this injunction, the Poona Congress employed the opportunity to perform a wholesale housecleaning. No more than four men who had served in both previous bodies were renamed by the Congress and two of these were persons who were not in Congress at the time of the 1957 elections.

Unlike the Agra Congress or the Sanghatna, the Poona Congress generally chose not to compete for the candidacies of local notables or Congress dissidents. They were willing to find places for ambitious former members of the Samiti or of opposition parties, but they particularly rewarded reliable party workers and a large number of younger men with party tickets for the corporation. Contrary to the argument advanced in Agra, this did not mean a loss in quality from previous Congress nominees. Indeed, many Sanghatna interviewees conceded that the Congress had come up with better men than in the past, but they insisted this was the result of the high quality of their own candidates. The Congress approach probably did mean a sacrifice in terms of short-term results. In the long run, the organization which emerged was composed of persons dependent on state and city party leadership for direction rather than on personal followings.

Finally, the Brahmin-dominated Jan Sangh stood forward in these municipal elections as the potential spokesman of the middle classes of Poona in a fashion that the heterogeneous Sanghatna could not. In 1957, the Jan Sangh had played a minor role in Poona politics because of its stand on the Maharashtra demand. By 1962, the party had dedicated itself to the difficult task of constructing an organization independent electorally from other local groups. More than in the general elections, the municipal elections of that year provided the party with its first real opportunity to develop local electoral support. This it tried to do by nominating candidates for twenty-three seats, but with a rather low expectancy of immediate rewards.

Party Manifestoes

In addition to the campaigns in each ward, which resembled those in Agra, the election was fought on a citywide basis by the major political organizations. Both major parties and the Jan Sangh issued manifestoes;[16] equally important, the major newspapers of Poona—*Sakal* and *Kesari*—were directly involved in the campaign as the propaganda arm of the Sanghatna; the Congress received rather weak exposure in their pages, but it had its own electoral newspapers which provided some circulation of its arguments.[17]

The real impact of this citywide activity is difficult to gauge but it is useful to see their statements for the ways in which these party organizations presented themselves to the public. Thus, the Nagri Sanghatna manifesto began with a declaration that

> the work of the corporation is connected to the development of the city. It does not involve politics and politics should not enter into the corporation. It is for this reason the Nagri Sanghatna has been established. . . . The Executive body of the organization consists mainly of people who are not connected to any party; even though there are a few party leaders, we have cooperated with them on the condition that there be no party politics in the work of the corporation.[18]

One of the major functions of the corporation members, the manifesto declared, was to educate the public in democracy. Under the previous body, "the problems of citizens are pushed aside; inefficient work is going on; groupism, favoritism, selfishness is increasing." The new body would substitute a constant interaction with the public: "Even after the elections, members will often go to the voters to let them know about the working of the corporation and to collect suggestions about the working of that body."

The general recommendations of the party were limited to promises that the rural parts of the city would be upgraded, slums cleared, and educational facilities improved. A few of the more specific pledges included building a school in a particular lower-status section of the city, the provision of certain corporation services to the employees of the central government's railways located in Poona and to the state government police forces working in the city. (Both of these groups had blocs of votes to offer and were "reachable" organizationally as other, unorganized elements were not.)

Furthermore, the party made a gesture of extending the olive branch to the Congress and Jan Sangh. All of the Sanghatna's goals could be supported by these other parties, the manifesto argued, if they would only abandon their partisanship. At the same time, the Sanghatna leaders were only too eager to point up the poor performance of the Congress in the previous body and to capitalize upon the suspension of the corporation party.

The Congress issued a rather bland manifesto which placed less emphasis on practical solutions to real problems than on appeals to history and the facts of national and state power. The general tone of the document is indicated by the following extract, which includes an apologia for the recent performance of the corporation party, an appeal to left-leaning intellectuals, and an attempt to capitalize upon the popularity of Chavan:

> Congress is contesting with a view to improving the working of the corporation by having good members who are following discipline. The Congress Party will be very strict with the members of the Congress Corporation Party to see whether they are doing good work or not. . . . In India democracy is related to socialism and for the socialistic pattern of society the working of the corporation should be the way the Congress has suggested. Only the Congress Party under the able leadership of Mr. Yeshwantrao Chavan is able to do good work with the cooperation of the citizens.

Some of the arguments in favor of the Congress were more explicitly stated by S. G. Barve, who played a part in the local Congress Selection Committee and in helping to organize the 1962 municipal campaign. In a published interview, Barve argued that the Sanghatna was no more than an anti-Congress front; on behalf of the Congress, he rather defensively supported the utility of party government, "The party is meant for the benefit of society and for the city. It is a fact that parties differ on principles, but no party seeks to hurt society." [19]

Conceding that the Congress had experienced some internal difficulties in the previous municipal body, Barve insisted the problem had been resolved through the creation of a special committee within the local Congress for "the guidance and control of the party members of the Corporation." As far as the opposition was concerned, Barve discounted the importance of independents' being associated with the Sanghatna, and pointed, instead, to the organizational solidarity that the Congress had brought about:

> I do not think that two or four respected men who do not belong to any party will be able to do good work. On the contrary, I believe that those persons who belong to any strong organization, even though they are not more respected, are able to do good work.

In contrast to the Sanghatna and Congress, which issued rather brief and general manifestoes, the Jan Sangh came forth with a long and quite specific platform. After attacking the pattern of "consolidated" parties which had gotten majorities in previous elections, it appealed to the public on the basis of its organizational discipline. In contrast to other parties, it claimed, the Jan Sangh was "a party with discipline and without selfishness." [20]

Specific suggestions were advanced by the Jan Sangh under sections dealing with house construction, industrialization, rural development, taxation policy, education, water supply, transport, and health. Under education, for example, they called for: improvement of school facilities which would bring the city into conformity with the goals of the Compulsory Free Education Act; the construction of schools under corporation auspices which would take existing schools out of private rented premises; provision of more technical education for students; and increased grants from the state government based on the number of students in the schools. Some of these proposals were not really subject to influence by the corporation, but probably the most important aspect of the manifesto was not its content but its tone. It put forward a concrete set of proposals acceptable in principle to most of the members of the Nagri Sanghatna and to most of the middle-class citizens of Poona. Nowhere did it betray the kind of chauvinism or social values sometimes attributed to the Jan Sangh. The effects of this posture were not immediately felt, but it may have had consequences for the subsequent growth of the organization in Poona.

On the whole, the Congress versus anti-Congress emphasis of the campaign was clear. A few members of the Sanghatna, particularly Jagtap, might make occasional speeches in which they called upon the Congress to come forward and work with the fusion organization in bringing under control the "improper things which are going on." [21] But probably more representative of the general leadership of the Sanghatna was an editorial which appeared in *Sakal* shortly before the corporation elections. It was precipitated by Barve's suggestion that a Congress victory would insure a "well-organized chain" from New Delhi down to the corporation. The editorial was entitled "The Chain of Power."

> We can call this Shri Barve's Five-Year Plan to capture power at all levels. If one party captures power from top to bottom, then what will happen to the people? . . . In the absence of any opposition, all sorts of undue recommendations, carelessness and bribery will grow in the country.
>
> We may say this about the people of Poona: though the Congress in Maharashtra may have gained stature in Delhi, it has deteriorated in the Poona municipality over the past twenty years.
>
> It will be especially bad if power is built up in this way because the road will be closed to independent people who lack greed and want to really do good for the people. Authority will go to those people who do things by flattery and for the sake of their own stomachs.
>
> If the Congress is defeated by the free people of Poona then the chain in Maharashtra will be broken and there will be places opened to local people. There will be a break in the chain which they wish to construct from top to bottom. The Congress people have this kind of fear in their minds. It is for this reason that they are so intent on winning the local elections. [22]

Constituencies and Candidacies

For the three corporation elections up to and including the one in 1962, Poona was divided into twenty wards varying considerably in size with sixty-five seats being apportioned among the wards in very rough correspondence to population. The range was from 14,051 people per seat in one two-man ward to 6,381 persons per seat in a seven-man area (two wards). [23]

Because the six reserved seats in Poona were spread among wards of unequal size, there is no direct way of estimating the electoral impact of the four major Scheduled Caste groups upon the political behavior of the city. While six of the "largest" wards are among the half of the municipal wards having the greatest number of members of the Scheduled Castes, the resultant picture is hardly that of a rank-order correlation; the ward second highest in Scheduled Caste population (with 13 percent) was fifteenth in size per seat.[24]

The larger size of municipal wards and the better citywide organization of the major contesting parties in Poona (than in Agra) does not mean that local factors were less evident in the selection of candidates and the outcomes of particular elections. While both the Congress and the Nagri Sanghatna attempted to maximize support across the broad electorate, their overall patterns of nomination reveal the primordial tendencies referred to in earlier chapters. The Congress gave a greater number of candidacies to the non-Brahmins, whereas the Sanghatna gave nominations to Brahmins and Marathas almost equally. The Jan Sangh based itself heavily on Brahmins in 1962.

The presence of these three parties in the field might have been expected to deter the entry of a large number of independents, but candidacies in Poona do not seem to be a function of either calculation of the prospects of victory or of expectations that the public will support only those men backed by parties. As against 210 contestants in 1952 and 199 in 1957—when Samyukta Maharashtra distorted the free run of local political forces—there were 291 candidates in 1962 or 4.5 per seat. This was slightly more than Agra's 4.2 in 1959. These figures are particularly impressive given the argument widely advanced in Poona and Agra that the rewards of municipal service are outweighed by the material and psychological costs involved. It also represents (after two earlier municipal elections) an important measure of the continued interest of a segment of the politically aware public of Poona in becoming formally involved in corporation affairs.[25] Nor was this high level of participation restricted to a few parts of the city. Every constituency save one experienced an increase in candidacies over 1957. All but three showed an increase over 1952.[26]

Because of the patterns of residence in the city, Brahmin wards differ sharply in character and political preference from non-Brahmin wards. In the Brahmin-majority wards, being a Brahmin candidate makes no difference since almost all the candidates are Brahmin. Where Brahmin voters have recently had a choice, however, they have supported those Brahmins not carrying a Congress label. In contrast to these clearly Brahmin areas of the city, there are many highly heterogeneous constituencies with the Marathas constituting only one (albeit the largest) segment of the local population. Thus, in one ward, which experienced an increase in total candidacies from ten in 1952 to twenty in 1962, only one Maratha figured in this increase. The remaining candidates came from a variety of small artisan and service castes like the Tambats (Brass-workers), Shimpis (Tailors), Bhois (Fishermen) and Weavers.

The overall pattern of candidacies resulting from discrete decisions at the party and personal level is reflected in table 4.1. The Congress and the Nagri Sanghatna put up sixty-four candidates each; the Jan Sangh nominated twenty-three. In addition, two persons ran as candidates of the Lohia Socialist Party, three

TABLE 4.1

Primordial Groups and Parties of Candidates in Poona Corporation Elections, 1962

Primordial Group	Congress		Nagri Sanghatna		Others*	
	N	%	N	%	N	%
Brahmins	10	16	18	28	30	18
Intermediate†	9	14	9	14	15	9
Marathas	24	38	17	27	36	22
Low Hindus‡	6	9	7	11	22	14
Mahars	—	—	6	9	20	12
Other Scheduled Caste§	6	9	—	—	10	6
Muslims	3	5	4	6	9	6
Non-Maharashtrians‖	6	9	2	3	11	7
Other#	—	—	1	2	10	6
Total	64	100	64	100	163	100

* The 23 Jan Sangh candidates included 13 Brahmins (57%), 4 Marathas (17%), 3 Malis (13%) and 1 member each from the Lingayats, Shimpis, and "Telugus." In addition, there were two Socialist Party candidates (a Tambat and a Maratha) and three CPI members (a Maratha, a Shimpi, and a South Indian described as a "Kanarese"). Republican factions supported five candidates outside the Nagri Sanghatna; all were Mahars.

† Mainly Malis with some CKPs, Pardeshis, Kachis, Lingayats, and Dhangars.

‡ Weavers, Shimpis, Tambats, Komati, Kasais, Kumbhar, Bhoi, Koli, Lonare, Nhavi, Gir, Joshi. The last two are members of Scheduled Tribes.

§ Mang, Chambhar, Bhangi.

‖ Gujaratis, Marwaris, and Rajasthanis from the North; Tamils, Telugus, and others from the South.

Christians, Sindhis, unidentified.

as Communists, and five (all Mahars) from that splinter of the Republican Party not affiliated with the Sanghatna. This meant that 55 percent of all candidates were associated with parties of some kind; if we were to count about twenty-five persons as directly under the aegis of the Republican Party in Agra in the 1959 municipal elections, the comparable figure would be about 49 percent—hardly a marked difference. Indeed, as compared to 1952, there were an *increasing* number of independents in the Poona race; in that earlier year, 61 percent of the candidates were organizationally affiliated. These kinds of data provide little support for a possible hypothesis that repeated experience with electoral politics tends to institutionalize political performances by driving out those nonparty contestants who have little chance of winning.

When we examine the distribution of candidatures as between 1952 (see table 2.2) and 1962, the changes are not very great. The Marathas are somewhat more entrenched in Congress candidacies than they were a decade earlier (38 percent as against 30 percent). On the other hand, the virtual parity between Brahmins and Marathas maintained by the Sanghatna in 1952 was almost ritualistically continued into 1962, although for each group the absolute *number* of seats had increased.

Representational patterns of low-status primordial groups also shifted only slightly as the Sanghatna clearly identified itself with the interests of one group within the Republican Party, while the Congress abandoned efforts to win over the Mahars by offering all its six reserved seats to persons from the three other major Scheduled Caste communities in Poona. Three seats were assigned to the Chambhars, two to the Mangs, and one to a Bhangi.

There was also a tendency for the two major parties to play down the support of non-Maharashtrians. Congress gave five tickets to members of northern trading communities (four Gujaratis, one Marwari) as opposed to nine in 1952. The Sanghatna gave only one to these same northern trading communities as compared to ten in its pre-Samyukta Maharashtra incarnation.[27]

Changes over time are most directly indicated in the "party crystallization" measure presented in table 4.2. All groups increased their total candidacies except the non-Maharashtrians, who were neither courted by the parties nor self-starting politicians in Poona. More interesting was the fact that the group now best represented in politics through party organizations was the Brahmins, with the intermediate Hindu groups running a close second and the Marathas third. In the case of the Brahmins, of course, the emergence of the Jan Sangh since 1952 represented an important organizational opportunity structure not available to them in the earlier period. At the same time, existing party organizations were well equipped to accommodate the additional "load" of Marathas, but at the price of decreasing the relative recruitment of members of other primordial groups.

Along with non-Maharashtrians, the group least "satisfied" by the existing party system was the Muslims. In contrast to the situation of the non-Maharashtrians, however, it should be recognized that an *increasing* number of Muslims were participating in municipal politics, which may indicate they were themselves less dissatisfied with the possibility of participation than were the non-Maharashtrians. Low-status Hindus were also entering politics in increasing numbers, but the larger existing parties were not in a position to recruit them to party tickets and the Jan Sangh was not inclined primordially to do so. Some of the "slack" in the system might have been taken up by groups like the Communists or the Lohia Socialists, but neither worked effectively among such low-status groups for these elections.

Case Studies

Ward 5 included the traditional *peths* of Ganj, Ghorpade and Gultekadi. It reveals Poona's non-Brahminism at its most heterogeneous. A three-member ward with a total population of 33,250, it lay on the southern boundary of the "old city" of Poona. Despite a high density, it was essentially residential in character with workshops scattered among the housing areas. Literacy rates were slightly below the 72 percent male literacy marking the central city.

The primordial character of the ward is notable not only for a lack of Brahmins but for a rather small representation of Marathas—perhaps about 15 percent of the total. There were a similar number of Muslims. If anything distinguished the ward, it was a high concentration of artisan castes. The largest caste were the Weavers, who constituted about 20 percent of the ward's population, but these were divided into two distinct communities: the Padma Salis, whose origins are in the South (from what is now Andhra and Mysore); and the Sakut Salis, who claim to be Maharashtrian in origin.

While it has probably been a net advantage to be a Weaver candidate in this

TABLE 4.2

Party Crystallization Index, Poona, 1962

Primordial Group	Total Candidates	Change from 1952	Nonparty	% Nonparty	% Change from 1952
Brahmins	58	+ 7	17	29	−20
Intermediate	33	+13	11	33	+13
Marathas	77	+23	30	39	Same
Low Hindus	35	+18	19	54	+19
Mahars	26	+11	15	48	+18
Other Scheduled Caste	16	+ 7	10	62	+ 6
Muslims	16	+ 8	9	56	+31
Non-Maharashtrians	19	− 8	9	47	+32

ward, it has been no guarantee of victory. In 1952 there were ten candidates for the three seats: three Weavers, two Muslims, two Marathas, and three others. Only one Weaver—a Sakut Sali—won a seat, while both Muslims were elected. One Muslim was backed by the Nagri Sanghatna; the other victors were both Congress members. It is noteworthy, however, that two defeated Weavers came in fourth and fifth in the field.

In 1957 the Congress Muslim stood aside, but the two other incumbents contested. Both lost to two Weavers—a Padma Sali and a Sakut Sali, one running on a Samiti ticket and the other for Congress—who won easily. In addition, a member of a small Butcher community (Kasai) was elected as a Samiti candidate. The third Samiti nominee (a Maratha) was barely defeated by an eighteen-vote margin. Even during this period of Congress weakness, either Samiti or Congress nominees dominated all six of the top places in the ward; in 1952, as well, no independent had finished higher than fifth.

Candidacies in this ward increased to twenty-four in 1962.[28] The number of Weavers increased by only one, but other communities came forward, some for the first time, like the Lingayats—a major religious sect in southern Maharashtra and Mysore—who produced three candidates.

Despite the increase in candidacies, with no increase in turnout the Kasai winner of 1957 (MKK in table 4.3) increased his vote from 3,731 to 4,395. Both he and the third-place victor were Sanghatna men; the third Sanghatna nominee, a Muslim, finished eighth. This can hardly be attributed to his being a Muslim, since a Congress Muslim came in sixth and Muslims had won seats in the past. Indeed, the presence of only three Muslims in the race might well have guaranteed one of them election if voting in such a divided ward had been simply along primordial lines.

Nor does a factor like incumbency explain much of the result. While it may have helped MKK, the incumbent Weaver elected on a Samiti ticket in 1957 (NTS) fell to tenth place when he lost party backing. A somewhat better performance was recorded by the winning Congress Padma Sali of 1957, who came in fifth in 1962. Such data point to the importance of individual reputations and past services in these elections (as in Agra). Equally striking is the appearance of party voting patterns in this ward. Despite the presence of (or maybe just because of the confusion produced by) the large number of candidates, the six nominees of the two major parties finished among the top eight, with the sequence suggesting considerable solidity in the Congress vote in particular. The exception, NSH, merits special attention because of his personal relationship to MKK.

MKK joined the Congress youth organization, the Rashtriya Seva Dal (RSD), in 1940. Like many persons in that organization in Poona, he was sympathetic to the Congress Socialists and left the Congress when the Socialists withdrew in 1948. He remained an active member of the ideational grouping which eventually became the PSP while working at a full-time job at Hindustan Antibiotics, which has a large installation in the suburbs of Poona; indeed, he was the only corporator in 1964 employed as a factory worker.[29]

In 1962, with his own slating assured, MKK tried to get a Sanghatna ticket for a Brahmin friend, but the party leaders selected a Muslim (ARL) hoping to repeat their success of 1952. The Muslim elected in that earlier period had gone over to the Congress shortly after his election, and MKK claimed that this defection

TABLE 4.3

Ward 5: Candidates and Votes in Poona Corporation Elections, 1962

Candidate	Party	Primordial Group	Votes	Percentage
1. MKK	Sanghatna	Kasai	4,395	16.5
2. NSH	Independent	Kasai	2,651	10.0
3. NMC	Sanghatna	Sakut Sali	2,624	9.9
4. NVR	Congress	Lingayat	2,265	8.5
5. DRB	Congress	Padma Sali	1,891	7.1
6. AMK	Congress	Muslim	1,808	6.8
7. VNS	Independent	Joshi	1,390	5.2
8. ARL	Sanghatna	Muslim	1,335	5.0
9. CMS	Independent	Muslim	985	3.7
10. NTS	Independent	Sakut Sali	949	3.6
11. THM	Independent	Padma Sali	916	3.4
12. VBP	Jan Sangh	Padma Sali	875	3.3
13. BPD	Independent	Brahmin	821	3.1
14. GBB	Independent	Maratha	569	2.1
15. ANK	Jan Sangh	Lingayat	483	1.8
16. BGK	Independent	Mali	441	1.7
17. NKK	Jan Sangh	Maratha	437	1.6
18. RMP	Independent	Pardeshi	356	1.3
19. BBK	Independent	Chambhar	335	1.3
20. SRV	Independent	Maratha	266	1.0
21. DKJ	Independent	Mahar	250	0.9
22. SBH	Independent	Lingayat	214	0.8
23. SSG	Independent	Mang	193	0.7
24. DDR	Republican	Mahar/Buddhist	166	0.6
Total			26,615	99.9

now caused voters in the ward to resist voting for the party candidate. More likely, with MKK's Brahmin friend running as an independent, MKK did not work very hard for ARL, although he was not very successful in getting general support for the Brahmin, who came in thirteenth—considerably behind the Sanghatna Muslim.

The third Sanghatna candidate, NMC, was a Licensed Medical Practitioner.[30] He was dedicated to his practice and to serving his neighborhood in a variety of capacities like the maintenance of neighborhood mutual-aid societies. This service and continuous "availability" clearly counted in a candidate's favor. As a corporator from this ward remarked in explaining the defeat of one incumbent, DRB, "He was known to leave his house at 8:00 A.M. and did not return until very late. His door was shut to the public. He did not work for the constituency." NMC joined the Congress in the 1930s, but left party work with Independence. During the 1950s he became involved again, this time in the PSP, and that party backed him for a ticket in the Sanghatna.

The most interesting aspect of the contests in this ward, however, was the connection between MKK and NSH. Both belonged to the small Kasai community, a butcher caste having its origins in areas which are now part of Mysore and Andhra Pradesh. The Kasai community contains no more than three hundred families in all of Poona and perhaps as few as forty families in this one ward. NSH, who had never been in politics before 1962, was active in the caste association and ran a butcher shop dealing in mutton. Before prohibition was imposed, he operated a toddy shop, and this brought him into contact with many people in the ward, especially the Southern Weavers, who shared his southern background. (NSH had come to Poona from Andhra at the age of nine to live with an older brother employed in the city.) In the corporation elections he claims to have converted his friendship with the Padma Salis into support for him as a third community choice along with two members of their own caste.

While NSH was an active leader of his primordial group, MKK's partisan activities had led him away from it until about 1960, when he began to take some interest in trying to resolve caste conflicts. One of the problems which confronted the community was a case in which a girl from another caste became pregnant by a boy belonging to their own. A caste meeting was held at which a decision was reached that the boy be forced to marry the girl (also low-caste). Most wanted to turn the boy over to the police unless he agreed to the marriage. NSH and MKK, as prominent figures in the local caste group, were called upon to go to the police to inform them of the case and have the boy arrested. There is disagreement about what happened next, but a dispute developed subsequently over whether NSH had tried to intervene personally with the police behind MKK's back for the release of the boy. The resultant conflict between the two men became so intense within the caste that NSH determined to enter the corporation elections with the sole intention of defeating MKK. During the campaign, the caste held a meeting at which NSH was asked to explain his actions with regard to the dispute, and he was excused by the community. He decided to remain in the election contest, nonetheless. Furthermore, the personal rivalries were not dissipated; he worked against MKK, and, according to the latter, spent considerable money on mutton and "liquor parties"—activities which were offensive to those members of his own caste who were pursuing higher social status.

NSH himself claims that he ran so he could be of more help to people and that he was not associated with any party because there were benefits in being an independent. "Since I am not in either party," he stated, "I have balancing power and I also do not have to follow the leadership of either party. This helps me to get playgrounds, roads, and other things for the constituency."

Interestingly, then, two of the three winners in this socially heterogeneous multicandidate contest came from a decidedly minor primordial group and drew upon different kinds of communal and partisan bases of support. Nor were persons from the larger communities in the ward able to simply turn caste or party affiliations to their electoral advantage.

Ward 11, Kasba Peth, is in the oldest part of the city. It is immediately adjacent to the Mutha river with the result that it was one of the areas hardest hit by the 1961 flood. Because of that flood and the population shifts it involved, earlier figures suggesting that Marathas constituted about one-fifth and Brahmins a little less than one-third of the population are probably no longer accurate. This change may be reflected in the municipal candidacies in 1962.

Thus, in 1952 there were ten candidates in the ward, including three Marathas, two Brahmins, and four others belonging to Maharashtrian communities. The tenth candidate was an Agarwal, whose antecedents were in northern India. Despite the general antipathy toward "Marwari" businessmen, this particular Agarwal's father had been born and brought up in Poona, and he was himself a fixture in municipal politics before Independence, although less than 2 percent of the ward's population could be counted as members of trader castes.

Unlike the situation in Ward 5, personal and primordial factors figured equally with party in the outcome in Ward 11. Agarwal was the prime example of the role of personal relations within a constituency. His grandfather had served in the Poona Municipality from 1925 to 1930; he became involved in politics himself at a very early age and was President of a local unit of the Congress in a rural section of Poona District before he was twenty. In fact, he was first elected to the municipality in 1940 at the age of seventeen but was disqualified because of his youth. In 1942, he contested again and was allowed to take office. Since then, Agarwal had been regularly elected to the city government. His explanation for his continued success was "personality"—charitableness at times of local weddings and other family occasions, provision of various services to constituents in need. Little of his success apparently had to do with his political views.

Running as a Sanghatna candidate in 1952, Agarwal collected the most votes in the ward. He was trailed by a Bhoi, who ran as an independent, and two Congress members—a Koli (like the Bhoi, low in the traditional hierarchy), and a Mali. Thus, neither Marathas nor Brahmins won seats here. At the same time, only the single "notable" Sanghatna candidate was elected; the others ran fifth, seventh, and ninth in a field of ten.

Three of the four incumbents ran again in 1957; the Congress Mali did not. Agarwal again led the poll. He was now running with Samiti support. Two Marathas and two Brahmins were in the field, but none had Samiti labels; all four finished near the bottom as the Samiti swept the constituency. In addition to Agarwal, the incumbent Bhoi was reelected along with new Tambat and Mali candidates put up by the Samiti.[31]

After being elected in 1957, Agarwal was disqualified from holding his seat as the result of a lawsuit brought by one of the losers, who claimed that Agarwal was barred from serving because he shared certain financial interests with his brother, an employee of the corporation.[32] His place was taken by the candidate with the fifth highest vote in the ward. In 1962, however, Agarwal determined to run again—this time as an independent.

Like other wards, Kasba Peth experienced a considerable jump in the number of candidates from eleven in 1957 to twenty in 1962. The results are indicated in table 4.4. Only two Brahmins and two Marathas ran in this very large field and, on the whole, primordial factors do not appear to have been determinative. Nor were party candidacies a consistent advantage. Congress candidates finished 2, 6, 13, and 18; three Nagri Sanghatna nominees came in 8, 11, and 12. The latter party virtually conceded a seat to Agarwal. In addition to Agarwal, one other incumbent was elected: D. S. Kadu, a Tambat who was elected in 1957 with the help of the Samiti, was now running as a Congress nominee. One of the other incumbents did not stand; the fourth ran for the corporation from a ward where he had settled after the floods.

None of those elected was from a large caste in the ward except the Bhoi; two victors ran as independents and one as a Socialist—a party which put up only two candidates in all of Poona. The individual careers of the three men other than Agarwal are so diverse as to provide another set of examples of how complex the

TABLE 4.4

Ward 11: Candidates and Votes in Poona Corporation Elections, 1962

Candidate	Party	Primordial Group	Votes	Percentage
1. MH Agarwal	Independent	Bania	4,793	13.8
2. DS Kadu	Congress	Tambat	2,580	7.4
3. BDK	Independent	Bhoi	2,516	7.2
4. RP Vadake	Socialist	Tambat	2,299	6.6
5. MKJ	Jan Sangh	Brahmin	2,099	6.0
6. KGS	Congress	Kumbhar	2,086	6.0
7. MJS	Independent	Muslim	2,023	5.8
8. SSU	Sanghatna	Weaver	1,726	5.0
9. TRZ	Independent	Maratha	1,632	4.7
10. GKD	Independent	Mali	1,435	4.1
11. SSS	Sanghatna	Shimpi	1,420	4.1
12. RVC	Sanghatna	Brahmin	1,350	3.9
13. BSP	Congress	Maratha	1,317	3.8
14. MRN	Jan Sangh	Shimpi	1,289	3.7
15. TRL	Jan Sangh	Mali	1,188	3.4
16. SKS	Independent	Koli	1,147	3.3
17. KSK	Communist	"Kanarese"	1,139	3.3
18. RRP	Congress	Pardeshi	1,133	3.3
19. NLK	Independent	Koli	932	2.7
20. BNG	Independent	Gir	735	2.1
Total			34,839	100.2

sources of individual political recruitment and support are at the local level in urban India.

Kadu was deeply involved in the nationalist movement. He played a leading role in the local Congress, serving twice as Vice-President of the City Congress in the late 1930s as well as on the MPCC during that time. After 1947, however, he left the Congress to join the PWP and in 1951 withdrew from politics altogether because of personal financial problems. He was drawn back to public activity by the Samyukta Maharashtra demand and elected to the corporation on a Samiti ticket; he rejoined the Congress in 1960 and was given a party ticket for the corporation elections. Kadu was treated as a man of such high personal integrity and sincerity of purpose that neither the Congress nor his constituents penalized him for his fluctuating political loyalties.[33]

The Tambat (Brassworker) caste, to which both Kadu and the Socialist winner (Ram Vadake) belong, had perhaps seven hundred voters in the constituency in 1962—their greatest concentration in any ward but hardly enough to account for the votes received by the two candidates. The Tambats have several formal organizations including a producers' union (The Tambat Mazdoor [Labor] Sangh [Association]), which negotiates with wholesalers about their products, and a temple of their own. But both corporators disclaimed an active role in community affairs. To a question about the community's involvement in partisan politics, Kadu responded: "As a man of the community, I maintain good relations with these organizations, but they do not take part in politics. A few of the young men are in the RSS and a few of the laborers in the PSP unions."

Like Kadu, Vadake comes from a family which makes and sells copper and brass vessels. He participated in the 1942 "Quit India" movement and subsequently joined the Congress Socialists. He was Joint Secretary for the Praja Socialist Party in Poona in 1952-54 and after the split within its ranks he was one of the few members in Poona to follow Lohia out of the party. He then sat on the State Executive of the Socialist Party. There were only about fifty active workers of the party in the whole of Poona in 1962, which meant that Vadake's election was largely a personal matter growing out of his reputation as a dedicated public worker and Socialist idealist.

The fourth corporator came from the Bhoi community, which may have numbered as many as a thousand voters in the ward; they have been fairly shrewd and united as a caste operating in the local political arena. In 1962 the community took the unusual step of holding a kind of primary to determine which single member of the caste should run for a corporation seat in the ward. Ten candidates entered the primary, and BDK, a wholesaler of fresh fish, received seven hundred votes to the second man's two hundred. It was an informal process, but as BDK explained: "If four candidates from the community were going to contest, then we would split the votes of the community. Only if one person was put up, then we could get a chance."[34] BDK ran as an independent but after the election joined the Nagri Sanghatna. Some of the members of his community were apparently eager to run for the municipal body because corporators do receive Rs. 100 a month, a substantial amount in the calculations of the poorer sections of the Poona population, but BDK insisted this did not influence his own entry into the contest.

The view of Kasba Peth as a heterogeneous ward where neither party nor caste plays a significant part in itself contrasts, for example, with some of the Brahmin areas of Poona like Sadashiv Peth (which was divided into two electoral units). All seven persons elected from those two districts were Brahmins in an area where Brahmins constituted more than half of the population. Congress won none of the seven seats even when it put up Brahmin candidates; indeed, the main battle in this area in 1962 was between the Jan Sangh and the Sanghatna.

Kasba Peth also contrasts with several wards which are essentially rural in character. These wards lie to the north and west of the "old"—precorporation—city. Some of the corporators from these wards properly list themselves as farmers. One such ward was *Ward 19: Greater Poona North Western.*

Parts of Ward 19 are urban fringe in character, but others are truly rural. About 22 percent of the total population is Scheduled Caste with a little more than half of these being Mahars. Another 20 percent are Marathas. As we might expect from such aspects of the ward, the literacy rate is very low—only 19 percent.

In 1952 there were ten candidates for the corporation, including five Marathas and three Mahars, the latter contesting for the reserved seat available in the ward. The six party-supported candidates (Congress and Nagri Sanghatna) all ran ahead of the four independents. The top vote went to a Kumbhar (peasant cultivator) supported by the Sanghatna. The same party also backed the winning candidate for the reserved seat. The third victor was a Maratha Congressman, who was trailed by about four hundred votes by another Congress Maratha. In 1957, only five candidates ran in the constituency, including all three incumbents. The Samiti now backed the two Sanghatna incumbents. The third Samiti candidate, a

Maratha, ran well but not well enough to win. The three incumbents were all elected. There was a marked increase in candidacies by 1962 (see table 4.5). The top vote went to the two-term Congress Maratha; the other Congress nominees ran well behind him, although the 1,028 votes won by the Congress-backed Chambhar seeking the reserved seat was not a bad showing when compared to the performance of the winning Sanghatna Mahar.[35] A third Sanghatna nominee won despite membership in the tiny Christian community (less than 7 percent of the ward population). The outcome in part reflects certain personal conflicts which an emphasis on caste and party dimensions might otherwise obscure.

TABLE 4.5

Ward 19: Candidates and Votes in Poona Corporation Elections, 1962

Candidates	Party	Primordial Group	Votes	Percentage
1. VBP	Congress	Maratha	2,461	14.5
2. AMD	Sanghatna	Christian	2,015	11.9
3. SSR	Sanghatna	Maratha	1,801	10.6
4. RTN	Independent	Kumbhar	1,751	10.3
5. TRP	RPI/Gaikwad	Mahar	1,747	10.3
6. MGG	Congress	Maratha	1,351	8.0
7. GRK	Independent	Kumbhar	1,299	7.6
8. MRB	Independent	Maratha	815	4.8
Reserved				
9. DBS	Sanghatna	Mahar	1,162	6.8
10. JSR	RPI/Gaikwad	Mahar	1,058	6.2
11. NRA	Congress	Chambhar	1,028	6.1
12. SSK	Independent	Mahar	502	3.0
Total			16,990	100.1

VBP, whose father had been headman of a village now incorporated into Poona, was not involved in politics until 1952, when he joined the Congress. Within a short time he became the President of the *mandal* Congress in his area and a representative of the party to the MPCC. As well as fulfilling his new role as a local Congress leader, he was able to call upon earlier connections within the area. Asked about the defeats of other incumbents, he asserted that they had not been sufficiently available to constituents and that they used the office for their own political gains. As he put it, "Many times they avoided seeing people even when they were at home." He and the other candidates of the Congress had not worked closely together in the election.

DBS, the reserved seat winner, was an unemployed, semiretired laborer who had been on the margins of the Mahar community's political activities for many years. He did not join the Republican Party until some time after it was founded, but like other Mahars he followed Ambedkar after the 1930s and claimed he was among the earliest converts to Buddhism in Poona. After the party's formation in Maharashtra in 1957, the RPI was under the leadership of B. C. Kamble. When the split in the RPI occurred in 1959, DBS followed Kamble while the greater part of the Mahar population in Poona followed the B. K. Gaikwad group, which put up candidates independently of the Sanghatna in 1962. DBS worked within the framework of the Sanghatna and was aided, presumably, by that vote.

The third victor, a Christian newspaperman, had an unusual amount of education for the ward. Indeed, the public called upon him to help in writing applications and filling out forms. In building a winning margin, he had some bloc support: the small Christian community, the South Indians (his native tongue is Tamil), and the Sanghatna. He also took advantage of some rivalry between VBP and RTN, claiming to be spokesman for the average citizen. Like VBP, RTN had roots in the traditional leadership of the area and owned considerable property in his home village. While VBP was successful in melding traditional and contemporary political skills, RTN did not fit into the mold of a contemporary politician and he found that traditional loyalties to him had tended to erode over time. AMD was able to campaign against RTN, who came from the same part of the ward, by appealing for support from those communities which were no longer (or never had been) bound to the traditional social system in the area.

In this brief survey, we have not considered wards where non-Maharashtrians are strongly represented or inner-city wards with large Maratha populations. In Maratha-dominant Shukrawar Peth, for example, four Marathas were elected, including the Sanghatna's B. G. Jagtap, the man who was then President of the City Congress, and Shivajirao Dhere, the last mayor of the previous body.

The Overall Results

While situational factors probably determine most electoral outcomes at the ward level, at the municipal level those behaviors translate more clearly into party and caste dimensions. Thus, table 4.6 indicates that over 85 percent of the winning candidates were affiliated with political organizations—fifty-seven out of sixty-five. Furthermore, more than half the members (55 percent) of the body belonged to either the Brahmin or Maratha communities, although these two primordial groups represented only about 40 percent of the total city population.[36]

Turnout for this election was quite high. Nearly 58 percent of the eligible voters went to the polls as compared to 64.2 percent of the urban population which voted in the 1962 elections for MP in Poona. The result of that turnout was a reinforcement of the pattern already suggested earlier: Marathas were heavily represented through the Congress—they won eleven seats (out of twenty-three held by that party)—and also captured eight under the aegis of the Nagri Sanghatna; Brahmins won only two seats as members of the Congress, but seven in the Sanghatna and five as Jan Sangh representatives.[37] Two Marathas and one Brahmin were also elected as independents.

Despite a doubling over the years in the number of candidacies from among low-status groups (17 in 1952; 20 in 1957; 35 in 1962), these groups contributed only the same number of corporators as in 1952: six. Perhaps the overall increase in candidacies hurt these smaller groups, but the data is inconclusive.

As compared to 1952 (table 2.3), Marathas increased their total representation by five, whereas groups like the Mahars—divided internally and challenged by opportunities given by the Congress to the Chambhars, Mangs, and Bhangis—went from five representatives in 1952 to only two in 1962. The Muslims also declined in

TABLE 4.6

Primordial Groups and Parties of Members Elected to Poona Corporation, 1962

Primordial Group	Congress	Sanghatna	Others	Total
Brahmins	2	7	6*	15
Intermediate†	2	6	–	8
Marathas	11	8	2	21
Low Hindus‡	1	2	3	6
Mahars	–	1	1 §	2
Other Scheduled Caste ‖	4	–	–	4
Muslims	1	–	–	1
Non-Maharashtrians#	2	2	3	7
Other**	–	1	–	1
Total	23	27	15	65

* Five of these six made up the entire group of Jan Sangh members elected to the corporation in 1962.

† The two Congressmen were a Kachi and a Mali. The six from the Sanghatna included three Malis, two CKP's, and a Pardeshi.

‡ Includes a Sanghatna Weaver and two Tambats—one in the Congress and one the lone Socialist corporator. The latter is categorized under the "Others" party classification. The other three persons were somewhat lower in traditional status: a Bhoi independent and the two Kasais mentioned in the text (one a Sanghatna member, the other an independent).

§ The Mahars belonged to different segments of the Republican Party.

‖ Two Mangs, a Chambhar, and a Bhangi.

The two Congressmen were Gujaratis; Sanghatna members included a Kirad (Merchant) and a Moodliar (from Madras). The three independents are from UP or Rajasthan and are generally referred to as "Marwaris" although two of them are Brahmins by caste and one is an Agarwal.

representational strength: from six to one. Other primordial groups were about the same as in 1952.

The patterns of turnover and incumbency successes point to several facts about participation and candidacies in corporation politics. If service in the corporation was merely a burden, as some members claim, we might expect only a small number of candidates to run again. In fact, thirty-six of those sixty-five incumbents (over 55 percent) elected in 1952 ran again in 1957. While some of these might have been motivated by their interest in the Samyukta Maharashtra movement, many ran as Congress or independent candidates. Certainly, the depolarization of politics by 1962 did not reduce their desire to run. Examination of the candidate lists for 1962 indicates that at least forty incumbents contested (62 percent).

Incumbency in itself is no guarantee of reelection. Much depends on the character of the individual candidate and the shift of circumstances in his ward. Thus, one-third of the incumbents contesting in 1957 were defeated; significantly, only one of these dozen incumbents ran on a Samiti ticket. In contrast, seventeen of those twenty-four incumbents who won were sponsored by the Samiti.[38] The importance of party continuity for incumbents is not clear after 1957. Of the forty incumbents who stood again in 1962, seventeen lost—a poorer showing than in 1957. A bare majority of incumbent winners (12 out of 23) were persons backed by the Samiti in 1957 and the Sanghatna in 1962; this pattern hardly assured success, since seven of the seventeen losers duplicated that experience. Furthermore, of five Samiti winners who ran as independents in 1962, three won and two lost.[39]

CONCLUSIONS

The electoral behavior described in this chapter contributed to Poona's municipal life a body of representatives which included a solid core of experienced political leaders along with a mixture of newer and younger members. There were few "safe" seats in Poona (and in Agra). Because of the ambiguity introduced by great competitiveness among candidates, it is likely that the winners were mostly those who worked with the widest possible number of segments represented in the populations of their wards. This was the case even where they based the solid core of their following upon communal or party voting. The result was a corporate body which broadly "represented" the configuration of group identities in Poona politics, much as the body in Agra "represented" the major politicized groups in that city.

In terms of the general level of citizen participation in municipal elections, the ease of access to political arenas by the broad range of forces operating in a given ward and an evident eagerness by persons of varying ideational, primordial, and personal dispositions to stand as candidates in these elections, Poona and Agra may be evaluated as highly successful municipal arenas for democratic political participation.[40] An advocate of coherent party government might regret the rarity with which policy differences among candidates are raised; supporters of nonpartisanship might regret the contribution (no matter how marginal) of party organizations to municipal elections. Yet, despite the emphasis on administrative routine in Indian municipalities, an important function is performed for the larger political system by these pre-governmental electoral processes: they provide a regularized means of arbitrating among conflicting local interests. Elections serve as a major occasion for conflict resolution among groups in Indian society because of the apparent status value many Indians attach to relatively symbolic payoffs like municipal office. A latent consequence of such payoffs is the institutionalization of a status-seeking group's share in the system, which encourages a sense of efficacy among those many groups and individuals who participate. Furthermore, the need to win votes from groups with varying ideational, primordial, and benefit-seeking interests favors a highly pragmatic style of behavior on the part of most candidates—even those belonging to groups with the most highly self-conscious end systems. Of course, there are certain groups which are not drawn into participation in electoral politics, but the extreme elements of the Left are not strongly represented in the life of Agra and Poona, and the Right has its spokesmen in organizations like the Jan Sangh and Hindu Mahasabha—within the party system.

Williams and Adrian suggest in their study of four American cities that the arbitrational function of municipal politics

> is not one that operates according to a fixed standard of equity or political weighting. Rather it is a government of men, each with weaknesses and preferences. It is just this

human element in government which opens up the possibility that the imbalance between the majority and the minorities may become redressed.[41]

In a highly segmented polity like that in Poona or Agra, a constant effort is necessary even to determine what a majority is. Within the structure of day-to-day municipal administration, mechanisms for conflict resolution among those groups participating in urban politics tend to be obscured. Where they are most evident in the municipal arena is in the election of corporators and municipal officers, principally the mayor and deputy mayor. In chapter 6, therefore, we shall turn from our consideration of public electoral behavior to a discussion of the group life of the two corporations as exhibited in internal elections. First, however, we shall consider some of the subtler means by which even the relatively unresponsive administrative process associated with the municipal arenas contributes to the stock of rewards available to participants in the system.

5   CORPORATOR PARTICIPATION IN AGRA AND POONA

The present chapter examines the corporators of Agra and Poona in terms of formal characteristics (age, education, occupation) and group affiliations (partisan and nonpolitical associations). The middle sections of the chapter go on to describe the kinds of "outputs" which municipal bodies can provide and some of the functions which corporation members perform in order to validate their memberships. Finally, in connection with this brief review of the structure of corporator behavior in the two cities, we look at the group life of the corporations through a rather narrow focus, presenting a series of sociometric items on esteem and friendship patterns in the two municipal arenas. One of the purposes of this last exploration is to determine the kinds of criteria which may come into play in the activation of the municipal bodies as social structures in their own right.

WHO ARE THE CORPORATORS?

Corporator Characteristics

In our description of local politics in chapter 2, we noted the generational differences in political behavior between the two cities. Here we will specify some of those differences more directly. Thus, in Agra, Congressmen elected to the corporation in 1959 tended to be older than members of other political groups; furthermore, Agra Congressmen were older on the average than members of the same party in the Poona corporation. Within the Agra corporation itself, where non-Congress members averaged 44.3 years, Congress members averaged 48.8 years.[1] This age difference reflects the nature of political opportunity structures available over the past generation: the leadership and the majority of members of the Agra Congress (both within the corporation and in the city as a whole) were persons of relatively advanced age. Younger men entering politics sought outlets through political parties other than the Congress or ran for election in 1959 as independents.[2] Some of the young people elected on Congress tickets in 1959 were recruited under the 33 percent rule, which only served to further weaken the Congress organization as a vehicle for regularized recruitment into political life and as a training ground prior to the assumption of political roles in wider arenas.

In Poona, to the contrary, Congress corporators averaged 42.1 years, and non-Congress corporators, 46.6 years. Again, this is a reflection of differential recruitment patterns as groups like the Nagri Sanghatna drew upon local notables and persons of ideational commitment who had spent many years in politics, whereas the Congress depended heavily upon the development of a new generation principally composed of non-Brahmin politicians.

In each of Agra's political groups (as we might expect in a country where education is more unusual among the older generation), there is a tendency for younger corporators to be better educated. In Poona, however, this tendency is reversed. The younger members of the Poona corporation are somewhat *less* educated than both the older members of that body and the younger members of the Agra corporation (see table 5.1). Because of the configuration of political recruitment in Poona, the young in *each* political group were actually *less* educated than the older members.[3]

TABLE 5.1

Education of Agra and Poona Corporation Members by Age, 1964*

	Agra				Poona			
	Young		Old		Young		Old	
Education	*N*	*%*	*N*	*%*	*N*	*%*	*N*	*%*
Primary	6	21	12	38	13	33	6	24
Secondary	7	25	10	31	15	37	8	32
Some college	15	54	10	31	12	30	11	44
Total	28	100	32	100	40	100	25	100

* Groups are divided according to birth before and after 1919.

Thus, aside from the Republicans who began from a very low educational base, persons recruited into Agra politics were simply younger members of the same status groups previously active in the political life of that city. Their increased educational attainment represented in large part the linear progression in their status groups' educational expectations. In Poona, not only was the generational factor at work, but the younger generation belonged to a markedly different social stratum. As Marathas, in particular, pointed out, their community never had the kind of "enthusiasm" for education evident among Brahmins and other high-status groups.

Additional evidence for this understanding of the cleavage in Poona society can be found in table 5.2, which categorizes Poona corporators by a combination of traditional status and contemporary "class" factors. Following the usage developed by Milton Gordon, we might designate these categories "ethclasses."[4] "High ethclass" here includes not only Brahmins but other wealthy and high-status groups like the non-Maharashtrian merchant communities and CKP's. The "middle" category consists of Marathas, Malis, and the several small artisan castes represented in the corporation. "Low ethclass" is composed of all the Scheduled Caste members, the one Muslim and the only *functionally* Backward Class corporator.[5] This table illustrates the argument that there are two significant components to the membership of the Poona corporation—a somewhat older group of high-status members (the relatively well-educated) and a younger element of less educated middle-status corporators.[6]

TABLE 5.2

Age, Education and "Ethclass" of Poona Corporation Members, 1964

Education	High Ethclass		Middle Ethclass		Low Ethclass	
	Young	Old	Young	Old	Young	Old
Primary	1	1	8	3	4	2
Secondary	4	3	9	5	2	–
Some college	6	10	6	1	–	–
Total	11 (44%)	14	23 (72%)	9	6 (75%)	2

A variety of occupations were represented in the two municipal bodies. Contrary to what one might expect given the association of lawyers with politics in many American cities, the representation of lawyers was very small. The Agra corporation included only five;[7] in Poona, there were six lawyers by training, but two of these became full-time party workers shortly after receiving their degrees. In some respects, the local influence of doctors was more striking.

There were five medical practitioners in the Poona corporation including two who were trained in Western-style ("allopathic") medicine and a third who had received a somewhat inferior medical degree in allopathy. The others were a homeopath and a man who had received a certificate to practice traditional (ayurvedic) medicine.[8] The last was a socially conscious leader of the PSP (later in the SSP) who took an active role not only in encouraging the development of health facilities in rural Poona but also participated in various trade unions and helped to organize several social reform groups. One of the other doctors was a Congress candidate for mayor in one municipal election and in 1967 stood for MLA in a high-status part of the city. He and the only other physician in the Congress were the only two Brahmins in that party group; the three physicians associated with the Sanghatna were all non-Brahmins.

The seven doctors in the Agra corporation were highly visible politically during the period under review. Both of the men who filled the position of deputy mayor—one from the Swatantra Dal; the other as the leader of the Republican party in the corporation—were Western-style doctors. The official spokesman of the Congress in the corporation, an unsuccessful candidate for mayor in one election, was also a doctor. Along with these three, the corporation included another allopath, two homeopaths—practitioners of a form of medicine found in some Western countries—and a *vaid*. The latter, who was a refugee from the Sind, practiced traditional medicine himself but was sending his son through training in Agra's chief medical college.[9]

Being general practitioners, as all but one of these doctors were, may be a special advantage to candidates for public office because of the prestige and built-in reputation for public service associated with the healing role. However, there was no special "group interest" served by the presence of these physicians in the two bodies. They operated either as individuals or within the frameworks of their respective political parties. Similarly, there was no evidence that variations in other occupational categories were systematically related to partisan affiliations or other modes of political behavior.

At the same time, the occupational structure of the two bodies does not reflect the composition of the two cities in any strict fashion. Aside from the thirteen professionals in Agra,[10] the bulk of the corporation membership consisted of businessmen of varying stature. About fifteen of these might best be described as "substantial merchants"—persons having interests in grain, iron and steel products, paints, movie theaters and moneylending; another fifteen might better fall within a category of "small businessmen." The former were almost entirely Banias and Jains; the latter included some Bania shopkeepers, but it would seem proper to include along with them those Jatavs who ran their own small "factories" in which they employed three to ten workers turning out whole shoes or parts of shoes by hand.

In addition to the forty-three persons included under these professional or business labels, there were another nine who might be included within a "white-collar" or semiprofessional category. Among these would be three teachers in private schools (a Muslim who taught in a Muslim primary school, a Jan Sangh Agarwal who worked in a local Protestant-founded institution, and a Brahmin employed in a Jain school) and three others who were journalists or owned their own small printing shops.

Poona's corporators also numbered about a dozen "subprofessionals" among whom were several journalists, a life insurance agent, and four educators. Unlike the situation in Agra, the four persons identifiable as educators all had retired from that activity before they ran for the corporation. There were also a substantial number of businessmen in the Poona corporation. In all, about thirty members worked at some kind of commercial or service activity. But these included only about six merchants with large businesses—mainly non-Maharashtrians. Another eight corporators of lower status were successfully engaged in one aspect or another of the vegetable, fruit, or fish markets of Poona, generally in a wholesale capacity. In a somewhat different category were about fifteen shopkeepers and small businessmen. These included three bicycle shop owners and several owners of fairly prosperous restaurants or tea shops.[11] Since Marathas as a group are not usually associated with trade, it is both economically and politically significant that the operators of many of these businesses were Marathas or equivalent-status non-Brahmins.[12]

Several corporators were not directly assignable to normal occupational categories. Either they were "social workers"—persons engaged in public service of an altruistic nature who were generally supported in their activities by their families—or rentiers. Even in the case of "social workers" of low status, however, it was essential that they need not constantly attend to family obligations. Except perhaps for the three schoolteachers, there were no real "workers" in the Agra corporation—persons whose income came essentially from employment in an establishment which required them to keep to a uniform daily schedule. Only one corporator in Poona was employed in a factory on a regular basis and he was on an early shift which permitted him to be available to constituents and for municipal meetings.

Very little convincing evidence emerged from an examination of the differences in occupational structure between the corporators and their fathers (and, where available, their sons). Transitions from the countryside to the city were occasionally involved, but it was impossible to find consistent evidence of intergenerational discontinuities which might help account for partisan affiliations or political experiences.[13]

In Poona, occupational differences were even less immediately relevant to political choices than in Agra because there was no traditional series of urbanized occupations for groups like the Marathas to follow, and business was traditionally in non-Maharashtrian hands. More important than occupational backgrounds in defining the parameters of local politics, we would argue, were the associational and partisan experiences of each corporator. We turn next to this dimension.

Corporator Affiliations

As part of our examination of each corporator's background, we were concerned with the extent to which the corporation represented a first step in politics and part of a regularized career pattern. Only eight Agra members said they had never been affiliated with politically related groups prior to their election to the municipal body in 1959; another thirteen reported that they had been party supporters but not very active in those parties (see table 5.3). Eight more referred to some past activities performed on behalf of political groups, but these consisted largely of participation in campaigns for particular candidates for public office. Thus, nearly half the members of the Agra corporation were serving something resembling their political apprenticeships in the corporation.

TABLE 5.3

Prior Political Activity of Corporation Members in Agra and Poona, 1963-64

	Agra		Poona	
Type of Activity	N	%	N	%
Never active	8	13	9	14
Member only	21	35	12	18
Local party activity	9	15	15	23
City committees	13	22	13	20
Regional activity	5	8	11	17
National and state	4	7	5	8
Total	60	100	65	100

Of the 31 members mentioning sustained past political activities, nine sat on ward *(mandal)* executive bodies—mainly in the Congress Party. At a higher level, thirteen were on their respective parties' City Committees with eight of these serving as officers. Another five had been party organizers or district workers at some period in their careers, three for the Jan Sangh. In addition, four corporators had been on state bodies. These included a former President of the Agra City Congress; a man who had served on the UPCC; and two Republicans who were involved in that minor party's state executive. Thus, most corporators either had held only secondary positions in political organizations at the time of their election or that election represented their first sustained effort in politics.[14]

The picture was only marginally different in Poona. Of the total membership, nine corporators had no past political affiliation; another dozen cited no more than party membership before their contest for municipal office; an additional fifteen laid some claim to minor partisan activity in the past. As in Agra, this generally involved little more than supporting candidates. Thus, about 36 of the 65 members—55 percent as compared to Agra's 63 percent—were not intensively involved in party work before 1962. The other 29 had held positions of varying responsibility in their respective organizations: thirteen had been on City Committees; sixteen served at regional or higher levels. The presence of members like S. M. Joshi, N. G. Goray, and several members of the City Congress Executive accounted for the slightly higher weight of political experience in Poona's corporation than in Agra's.

It is quite clear, then, that corporators in the two cities hardly approach anything resembling an institutionalized political elite. Furthermore, if connection with persons previously involved in politics might be seen as even a very weak measure of corporator political status, it is notable that 70 percent of the Agra corporators said no one in their families had *ever* been politically active before them; and among the remaining 30 percent, "family involvement" in politics ranged from a mother who participated in Gandhi's noncooperation movement of the 1930s to a grandfather who was a village headman. About the same situation prevailed in Poona: forty-seven of the members said no one in their families ever had been engaged in politics before their own activation. Generally, political participation was encouraged by school, neighborhood, or peer group contacts. Only in a very few cases did it seem to grow out of family traditions.

An examination of the nonpolitical organizations in which corporators are active not only indicates a high level of general societal involvement on their part but suggests the variety of associational affiliations available in Indian cities. Certainly, Agra and Poona do not lack associational life, but very little data was collected which indicated any *direct* relationship between voluntary association membership and political activity.

About ten corporators in both cities indicated they were not *active* in organizations other than political groups and their affiliated organs, though some of these were fairly active in these political groups. All others belonged to at least one organization, and many held official positions in these groups. Table 5.4 lists those organizations mentioned by Agra corporators. Since we are more concerned here with the scope of activities in which corporators participate than we are with individual networks of affiliation, we have not limited the number of responses for each corporator. In each instance, however, officers within organizations are distinguished from members to indicate something about the *level* of participation.

As one might expect, there were many quasi-ascriptive organizations in Agra ranging from specific caste associations to educational societies which served a particular social segment. Most of these groups were not directly involved in partisan activities; the notable exception was, of course, the Republican Party and the Buddhist associations grouped around it. Despite their nominally nonpartisan natures, caste associations do provide a possible route for a given individual's entry into public work, and it is probably fair to assume that members of a given community can be mobilized behind a man of the caste running for office under certain conditions where he is seen as especially serving community interests.

TABLE 5.4

Organizational Affiliations of Agra Corporators, 1964

Professional associations:	Officer—3
	Member—1
Business/merchant association:	Officer—7
	Member—3
Unions:	Organizer—3
Cooperative societies:	Member—7
Service organizations:	Officer—4
(Harijan Sevak Sangh,	Member—2
Bharat Sevak Samaj, etc.)	
School management:	Officer—6
	Managing committee—8
Literary groups:	Officers—2
	Member—1
Temples:	Trustee—4
Mohalla samitis:	Officers—6
	Members—8
Communal groups:	Officer—5
	Members—4

Total corporators: 50   Total activity units: 74

Memberships in such groups were not perceived as dissonant with more "modern" affiliations. Thus, the same Khatri doctor who served as the first deputy mayor of Agra and was treasurer of the local unit of the Indian Medical Association was also his caste's Agra representative to the All-India Khatri Association and a member of its national executive. The latter organization's primary concerns were internal social relations rather than politics. Since this particular caste was high in status, advanced in education and not in need of special treatment, there were few occasions for it to place demands before government. This was a different situation from that of low-status castes which sometimes seek educational and occupational benefits through the application of political pressure.[15]

Even as a unified political force, the Khatris would not have been able to mobilize numbers in Agra outside the one ward where they were heavily concentrated. Presumably a politically conscious Agarwal Association might have consolidated a large enough body of citizens to make a major impact on local politics, but most Agarwals agreed that their caste organization was moribund. However, caste-related temples and educational societies still provided some institutionalized focus for their traditional identifications as they did for other groups.[16] High-status corporators, in particular, spread their activities widely among professional and occupational associations, on the one hand, and charitable and educational institutions, on the other. A number served on boards of management for private schools or were trustees of temples.

An interesting example of indigenous organizations are the *mohalla samitis* or "neighborhood associations." These vary in function according to the needs of the local population and are normally generated within the *mohallas* themselves. They are characteristically multicaste and usually nonpartisan in Agra, but patterns of housing segregation tend to limit the range of castes involved. There were a few associations in 1964 with political origins. These were created in the early 1960s by Seth Achal Singh when his men were in the minority in the Agra City Congress. While some of his opponents charged these particular samitis with being politically inspired, Seth's supporters asserted that they were simply reflective of "Sethji's commitment to Gandhian ideals of self-help."

Whatever their origins, at least fourteen corporators mentioned activity in such organizations. Many samitis seemed to have well-defined structures with an appropriate complement of "modern" officers like presidents, treasurers, and secretaries. Some apparently met like traditional panchayats to deal with social issues or with local nuisances. This obviated the need to resort to the police or to the formal judicial system, both of which were regarded with some distrust by many citizens.

While they attempted to resolve problems among neighbors, samiti efforts at conflict resolution were not always successful. Several corporators recalled that such organizations had existed in their mohallas but they had foundered on particular local quarrels. A couple of corporators suggested, furthermore, that the creation of the corporation ended the need for the performance of some of these neighborhood functions by distinct local bodies. Since their election, they claimed, people now tended to turn to them for aid in the resolution of disputes much as they had depended traditionally on local headmen to help resolve village or community quarrels.[17]

In the undeveloped western section of Agra, some of the samitis apparently served a developmental function. One corporator identified himself as the General Secretary for a Development Association covering eight mohallas in his area. This organization included an eleven-member Executive Committee and a general membership of 155. It was multicaste in character: the President was a Brahmin; the Vice-President a Punjabi; the corporator a Jatav. In addition to pressing the corporation for improvements in the area, members of the committee settled minor disputes and sought to control local problems arising from drinking and gambling. According to the corporator, the samiti sat with some regularity and had just a few days before the interview settled a land dispute that had been lingering in the courts for some time.

As we would expect from previous data, there was an even more extensive network of social and economic organizations in Poona within which many members of the corporation were active. Those affiliated with the PSP were particularly tied into a network of party-related associations including trade unions and the *Rashtriya Seva Dal* (RSD), the youth organization of the PSP. Congress' service, and youth and women's groups seemed to exist largely on paper in Agra; they appeared to be more active in Poona.

Except for the unions, the list of ninety-eight affiliations presented in table 5.5 is largely nonpartisan in composition. Of special interest are the "gymnastic associations." Many of these groups had their origins in the nationalist movement and still have political connotations. In addition to sponsoring athletic contests, they perform the functions of social clubs for their members. While they deny any political linkage, it may not be inconsequential that the major association of Poona

TABLE 5.5

Organizational Affiliations of Poona Corporators, 1964

Professional associations:	Officer—1
	Member—1
Business/merchant association:	Officer—5
	Member—5
Unions:	Organizers—2
Cooperative societies:	Officers—4
	Member—5
Service organizations:	Officer—11
	Member—3
School management:	Officer—7
	Managing committee—7
Literary organization:	Member—1
Gali samitis and mandals:	Officer—9
	Member—7
Communal group:	Officer—16
	Member—6
Gymnastic organizations:	Officer—5
	Member—3

Total corporators: 55   Total activity units: 98

was headed in 1964 by the "boss" of the Poona Congress and had its offices in Congress House. The vice-president in 1964 was one of the boss's chief lieutenants and a member of the corporation. With sixty or more centers throughout the city, these associations provided an obvious opportunity for contacts between the politically oriented and the apolitical.[18]

Like their counterparts in Agra, *gali* (block) samitis perform many neighborhood functions. They run local libraries, maintain small medical dispensaries, provide occasional entertainment, and form the basis for festival organizations for the celebration of Ganesh *utso,* the major annual ten-day festival built around the elephant-headed god Ganesh or Ganpati. During that festival, gali samitis vie for superiority in constructing tableaux and decorating the houses of the neighborhood. As in Agra, members of the samitis may be called on occasionally to act as local decision makers or arbiters where neighborhood conflicts arise. Some samitis have partisan aspects; others do not. Much depends on which persons are involved in a given samiti. Thus, one independent corporator could speak of belonging "to all the gali samitis in my area except those belonging to the Congress."

Some of the activities undertaken by such a samiti are suggested in the remarks of a PSP corporator:

> I am the President of the *Kalpana Mandal,* which has fifty members. We run a library and are especially concerned with providing facilities for students. Most mandals last only two or three years, but ours is four years old and going well. We charge no fees, but are conducting classes in which learned people from Poona lecture to the matriculation students during the year. We have schemes to start a free dis-

pensary and a study room because there is no place in Poona for students to go now.

More in evidence than in Agra are a series of economic cooperatives in Poona. These take various forms: consumer cooperatives which sell grain or milk; producers' cooperatives like the Leather Workers' Cooperative organized among the Chambhars of Poona to obtain loans from the government; labor cooperatives for the performance of labor through *shramdan* [free labor service] or by workers' selling their labor to the government on a cooperative basis.

Neither of the major caste groups in Poona has a functioning caste association. The largest community aside from the Mahars with such a body are the Malis, who were particularly interesting in 1964 because they were represented in the corporation by corporators from three different parties. A former President of the Mali Association, a Jan Sangh member who was then Vice-President of the Vegetable Merchants Association, described the community in the following terms:

> There are nearly twenty thousand Malis in Poona. The Association gives opportunities to students through scholarships and runs cooperative wedding associations. We helped a student to study in America. There are different political views in the caste. The majority are with the Congress.

This diversity of political views was also asserted by a Mali corporator belonging to the PSP:

> The members of the Association are from all parties. It is a friendly gathering of people who eat together. They have political differences but come together at marriages and deaths and when there are problems. Politics is separate. Of course, we do tend to favor our own men.

This last statement points to the most significant aspect of the varying organizational commitments of corporators in the two cities. Even caste organizations may be treated like secondary associations where political loyalties are concerned. As a result, they contribute to the construction and preservation of an indigenous variety of political pluralism. Conceivably, as is alleged to be the case in Italy, a multiplicity of organizations might be present, but political life could be divided into distinct sectors associated systematically with one or another political or ascriptive group.[19] On the Indian scene, however, there are many groups which are never more than marginally relevant to politics; others are tangentially involved when matters arise which cause concern to members. These generally function to bring together persons of varying political stripe on apolitical grounds involving other shared interests or identifications. In the total picture of public life in Agra and Poona, such organizations add an important brake against tendencies toward societal polarization which might be accentuated by intense political activity. Instead, they provide nonpolitical arenas for the interaction of persons otherwise involved in various political groups.

SATISFACTIONS AND SERVICES

In this section, we will try to provide some insight into the activities of the corporators by examining what some of them think about their involvement in municipal government and how they approach their jobs both in terms of what they apparently perceive to be the expectations of their constituents and what their own ambitions may be.

Corporation Satisfactions

Each of the Agra corporators was asked, "Would you say that you are satisfied or dissatisfied with the working of the corporation?" While respondents varied slightly in their understanding of the question, those persons most clearly outside the mainstream of political life prior to 1959—the Republicans—were most favorably oriented toward the corporation's recent performance (see table 5.6). Indeed, several members of that group specifically remarked that previous regimes had

TABLE 5.6

Satisfaction with the Regime: Agra Corporation, 1964

Group	Satisfied	Dissatisfied
Congress	7	7
Jan Sangh	2	2
Swatantra Dal	10	3
Republicans	13	1
Independents	4	4
Total	36	17

invested municipal funds in the development of middle-class sections of the city without concern for the poorer elements of the population. Thus, one Republican corporator, speaking of his own accomplishments, stated:

> I have been able to pave some areas where the Jatavs live. To the outsider, they may look terrible still, but there is an enormous improvement. We have been able to spend more money in four years than was spent for fifteen years under the Administrator. Now our areas have drains, pavements, and lights. That is because I and the party can shout and "cut some ice."

The table also indicates that while many complaints were made by the corporators against the specific working of the municipal body, a clear majority accepted the basic terms of the regime. Equally important, with only a handful of exceptions, those persons who were dissatisfied with the structure of government merely called for giving more responsibility to the corporators. Indeed, of all the corporators interviewed in Agra, only three expressed a fundamental sense of alienation from the political order; these were the only individuals who clearly indicated their opposition to existing democratic institutions.[20] All three were high-status in background. Despite the expression of these views, two of the three actually ran for reelection to the corporation in 1968, and one was reelected.

The Agra corporators were also asked whether they would be interested in running again should an election be held in the next few months. Thirty stated they would be so inclined, eighteen thought they would not, and twelve were uncertain.

Responses in the last category lay along a continuum from general acceptability ("It depends upon what the party decides") to negativism. While members of every group found some aspect of participation unsatisfactory, many of these members eventually did choose to participate: thirty-nine of the fifty-four corporators elected in 1959 ran again in the elections of 1968. Given the personal reasons (age, health, business difficulties) which might have intervened in the nearly nine years between elections, this is a remarkably high figure.[21] Even those corporators who were most unhappy with the corporation system of municipal government were capable in 1964 of conceiving of circumstances under which they might be willing to run again. As one such member asserted:

> Some men are very interested in my activities. If these friends say I should stand, I will. I have no personal interest in the corporation. The only advantage now is to be called "member saheb" by the people in the area. I am the biggest man in this area, but I don't think there is really any use to my service.

Like members of the Agra corporation, members in Poona were asked about their political intentions.[22] Such intentions, of course, depended upon the motivations which went into running for the corporation in the first place, as well as feelings of identification gained from participation in the body. Of the fifty-three Poona corporators from whom responses were available, twenty-one were definitely committed to running again given the proper party or group support. Another nineteen expressed uncertainty about their future course of action since they were only about eighteen months into their then current terms as corporators. It was also clear in some responses that the ability of the Congress and other organized political groups to dominate electoral outcomes in Poona made corporators more cautious in stating personal plans in comparison to respondents from Agra, where career plans seemed to be less obviously a function of the willingness of established political organizations to support candidacies.

Seven of the Poona "uncertains" made a clear distinction between satisfaction with their own performances and the weaknesses which they felt were inherent in the existing local political structure. Thus, a PSP member felt his time on the body had been worthwhile personally, but went on to comment that "we need more power and the means to do work for the people."

Finally, thirteen persons doubted that they would run again; at least four of these mentioned specific reasons of age or health. A fifth man, a Scheduled Caste member of the Congress, provided a financial reason:[23]

> I am satisfied with my work because I have helped to give employment to men and women of my caste in the corporation. I have requested that the officials give them jobs and they have. I would not run again, however, due to my financial condition. To attend to all the functions of a corporator it is necessary that a man have money in his pocket.

Despite these divisions of opinion and the expression of considerable reservation about running again, Poona incumbents stood for office in 1968 in record numbers, and many of those who did not do so were affected by factors extraneous to the municipal arena.

Thus, on the basis of candidacies alone, we would have to judge that the great majority of corporation members felt favorably inclined toward their own participation in the two municipal arenas. The more perplexing question, given the frequent complaints about the narrowness of their practical influence, then becomes, "What personal or collective benefits do corporators actually derive from their participation? "

Some of these personal benefits were identified in the comments of one Mali businessman—a PSP member of the Sanghatna—in response to a question about his future plans:

> People will force me to stand again because I am a straight-forward man. They are even thinking of sending me as an MLA in the future. I am getting prestige out of the corporation and it has improved my business. Customers know that I will not cheat them because I am a PSP man.

Three kinds of ends are envisioned in this statement: *individual prestige, political ambitions,* and possible *side payments* (both legitimate and illegitimate). To these individualistic goals, we might add activities by corporators which are in the service of larger collectivities: prestige which enhances the *symbolic status of a group; material benefits* which meet group demands. Part of these performances which pursue either individual or group goals involves the desire to apply influence in cases where *intervention with the bureaucracy* is called for. In the latter case, the expectation that the corporator can be called upon to intervene in administrative matters on a particularistic basis appears to be built into the understanding held about corporation memberships by both corporators and the general public. These are only a few of the factors which influence patterns of behavior by actors in the two municipal arenas, but a brief discussion of each may illuminate certain of the values which undergird municipal political involvements.

Individual and Group Prestige

Conflicts over status take many forms in the politics of Agra and Poona. Not only are certain ascriptively based groups like the Jatavs and the Marathas anxious to validate claims to the substance of political influence, but personal and group prestige are implicated in the extensive maneuvering over largely honorific offices like mayor and deputy mayor.

Even where more significant material benefits may be at stake, as in elections for state and national office, prestige plays a significant motivating part. Otherwise, it would be difficult to understand why so many persons bolt party organizations when they are refused nominations. It is this same concern with personal prestige that lies behind much of the factionalism in a city like Agra where groups contend almost as much for sheer dominance as for any substantive benefits that such dominance might bring.

Where low-status groups are concerned, symbolic group benefits are particularly important. In India, as elsewhere, the erection of a statue or the naming of a street in honor of a particular person may carry great psychic rewards to the group whose hero is involved. Thus, the Republicans in Agra made one of their early demands in the corporation the hanging of a picture of B. R. Ambedkar in the corporation meeting hall. This set off a considerable controversy which was finally resolved only by an agreement among the various political groups that a series of portraits should be hung around the meeting hall reflecting the symbolic attachments of each of the political groups.

In Poona, not only the Mahars put forward demands for symbolic payoffs of this kind. Several middle-status non-Brahmins pressed, for example, for greater recognition of Mahatma Phule, a Mali who was at the forefront of the non-Brahmin movement in the last quarter of the nineteenth century. Furthermore, members from the Hindu Mahasabha and the Jan Sangh were eager to find occasions to champion various remembrances of B. G. Tilak. On the whole, however, group status recognition is primarily a consideration for groups which are low in the economic or traditional status hierarchies. The presence of many high-status competitors for the corporation suggests, nonetheless, that a search for individual prestige is distinct from (though not necessarily inconsistent with) a goal of group status-registration through municipal political participation.[24]

Material Group Benefits

While pressing for actions by the corporation which will recognize the interests and claims to status of a given group through symbolic "recognition," corporators of certain political groups are also anxious to represent the demands of their groups for material advantages. The Republican Party has been particularly active on this score.

In the Agra corporation, the RPI made its special business the protection of Scheduled Caste interests in the corporation. Jatav corporators tried, in particular, to hold the corporation to the fulfillment of its guarantees of employment to their brethren. They were also constantly on the alert for abuses alleged to have been committed against low-level corporation workers like sweepers and bearers. In the pursuit of these community interests, the Agra Republicans succeeded in passing a resolution in August 1962, committing the corporation to filling 18 percent of all posts with Scheduled Caste persons. On a follow-up inquiry in 1964 it was reported that 328 of 1,101 appointments made by the corporation, or 29.8 percent, had gone to the Scheduled Castes in recent years. While most of these appointments were to menial positions, such actions tended to reassure members of the Jatav community that their efforts were, indeed, paying off.

Similarly, Agra Republicans were being placated in their demands for more extensive education by the fact that some primary schooling was being provided to all males in the city's schools. In the four years of the corporation's existence there had been a notable upsurge in the number of school buildings made available for this purpose, a fact in which RPI corporators took considerable pride. The attitude of such corporators was reflected in the comments of a barely literate member of that party:

> Previously there was no school in Tal Feroz Khan [an out-lying section of the city], but since the corporation has come into being there have been two primary schools built for the children: one for boys and one for girls. I had to go far for an education; there was previously no education for

Jatavs except in Rajamandi station area [near the center of
the city]. The other schools did not give admission to
Scheduled Caste persons. Only the government schools and
one institution in Pipalmandi allowed them in.

Political Ambitions

By their participation in municipal politics, the political parties hoped to promote
their own organizational development. For groups which had not achieved much
standing in state or national politics, the corporation provided a valuable platform
for perfecting and expressing their ideas and for developing the political skills of
their membership. Viewed from the perspective of the political system as a whole,
only a small proportion of the membership of a municipal body could realistically
hope to use the municipality as a stepping stone to higher positions. Still, for the
political groups to which members belonged, the corporation was a training ground
and source of recruitment to higher office. The elections of 1962 and 1967 suggest
how political careers may be fostered through participation in the municipal
corporations.

Corporators figured prominently in the outcomes of two of the three urban
MLA contests in Agra in 1962. In the northern section of the city, the winner was
the leader of the Swatantra Dal, a man who employed that group as a vehicle to
advance his own career, although his former association with the Jan Sangh was an
obvious contributory factor in his electoral success. The Jan Sangh and Republicans
also entered prominent corporators in that contest. A Bania member of the RPI
came in second and the leader of the Jan Sangh corporation party fourth.[25] Not
only did the Republicans do quite well in that contest, but the party also won the
seat in the southern section of the city behind the incumbent Republican alderman;
another Republican corporator was elected to an MLA seat from a rural
constituency in the district. Thus, three sitting members of the Agra corporation in
1964 were MLA's, and several others had been contestants for that office. Again in
1967, many of the major candidates in Agra's MLA contests had previously been
involved in municipal politics.[26]

The linkages of the corporation to contests for MLA and MP were equally
evident in Poona in 1962. As we noted in chapter 4, every one of the victorious
Congress candidates for the Legislative Assembly, except S. G. Barve, had served in
the corporation at some time prior to his election. Subsequent to that election, as
we noted earlier, several of the defeated general election candidates, including S. M.
Joshi and N. G. Goray, ran for the corporation.

The 1967 elections resulted in sending Joshi to Parliament; obviously, this
was a case in which a person's stature in the city owed relatively little to his
presence in the corporation. For other contestants, however, corporation participation came at a formative stage of their political careers. In the main, in 1967, seats
in the state legislature were either retained by Congress incumbents or contested by
recent Congress or anti-Congress corporation members. All three of the new
Congress candidates for MLA seats were incumbent corporators. One of the three
had been a prominent local Congressman before his entry into the corporation,
while the others had been little known.[27]

Asked about their reasons for being in the corporation, only five members of the Agra corporation openly admitted political ambition as a factor. Perhaps a dozen more suggested in general terms that a concern with personal prestige might lead one to pursue a career in political life. One Agra corporator put it this way:

> Even though members do not have many powers, their desire for posts is an "inborn thing." Everyone wants to be in a superior position. People enter simply for the importance it gives them. It is also a chance to establish contacts and an opportunity to work toward higher office.

Few corporators indicated that their political ambitions were shaped by ideational concerns. More often, local activities were directed into certain practical channels. Thus, a Brahmin doctor who became an MLA candidate in 1967 for the Poona Congress, spelled out (in 1964) some of his own thinking about the corporation as a rung on the political ladder:

> Personally, corporation work has been useful, but I do not think I have contributed much to the corporation. It has given me a chance to get a little training in politics and meeting people and in debating public issues. It is a way of studying politics. My service is much needed. A person whose earnings are not dependent on his public career and who has ideas about an honest career in politics has plenty of scope whether he is a Brahmin or not, although if he is a Brahmin he begins with a minus ten handicap.

Bureaucratic Intervention

Much of the corporators' actual work involves efforts on their part to "particularize" bureaucratic performances. Pressures may be exerted on local administrators by local groups, through friendly officials or ministers in the state government or through party contacts, but the most institutionalized form of making demands on the municipal administration is through the corporators. Indeed, many corporators see such activities as the primary aspect of their role. When one Agra corporator was asked to indicate what he felt was the most important function of a member, he responded:

> The foremost duty of a member is to serve the public which means he should look after the wellbeing of the constituency which he represents, including things like sanitation. He must visit the corporation and see that the men of his locality are not harassed by the officials. He must try to help people in their social functions like helping them to get a proper amount of sugar in order to celebrate a marriage.[28]

Or, in another response to the same question:

> My constituents ask me to help them get better water supply, improved pipelines, help on house taxes and assessments, power connections, and to make recommendations for jobs or transfers.[29]

To an outside observer, many of the instances of intervention cited by members may appear relatively trivial, but they are important to the corporators and their constituents. Thus, in Agra, when a tailor built two shops extending out from a building which he owned into a narrow lane, a conflict arose with municipal officials who claimed he was obstructing the lane. Thirteen members of the corporation supported a petition submitted by the tailor to block the corporation from tearing down the structures. While some members of the municipal body privately stated that corporator support to individuals like the tailor impeded proper planning in the city, none of them stood forward to argue on behalf of the administrators.

Similarly, in Poona most members tended to regard their intervention function as crucial to their roles as members. As a result, substantial effort was directed toward a concern with the welfare of one's constituency. A study of city politics in Bombay makes the point equally well for Agra and Poona:

> With only four or five exceptions, councillors spend several hours each week, some of them several hours a day, going about the ward to meet voters. Voters greet them with ten to several hundred complaints each week. The complaints are not about city issues or decisions, but mainly about three problems: failure of water supply, choked toilets and sewers, and leaking roofs.[30]

Thus in the course of one hour, one Poona Congress corporator was approached: (1) to sign certificates for school children certifying that their parents earned less than Rs. 1,200 a year, thus qualifying them for government scholarships;[31] (2) to intervene in getting a transfer of a constituent from one workshop of the State Transport Company to another closer to the constituent's home; (3) to help prevent the corporation from tearing down a hut in which a constituent had lived for twenty-five years. In this instance the landlord apparently had the support of several corporators from his own community in bringing pressure on officials to demolish the structure.

In many such cases, personal animus is often attributed by the constituent to the actions of the bureaucrat, and it is the duty of the corporator, according to this vision, to prevent that animus from working its evil influence. Sometimes the evil motives are attributed to one's neighbors, who are accused of having entered into collusive understandings with corporation officials against the constituent. Thus, when a citizen from a refugee community wrote to the deputy mayor of Agra that the Building Department was improperly issuing fines against him for making additions to his house without submitting plans for prior approval, he couched the letter in terms of a "grudge" held by his neighbors. His letter, it should be added, was countersigned by the corporators from his ward.

While corporators from the same ward may come to the aid of constituents without regard to group differences, occasionally members from a single ward may be placed in conflicting positions. Thus, in one Agra constituency, a Congressman and a member of the Swatantra Dal disagreed about certain public improvements. As the Swatantra Dal corporator recalled the matter:

> I was approached by some people who were living near an open public latrine who wanted it taken out because their living space was nearby. I went to see it and agreed that it was bad and took others to see it. Then some of the people

in the neighborhood went to see G. [the other corporator] and drew up a petition which said they wanted to keep the latrines. G. backed them up, and there was a battle for a time. I went to Chaturvedi [the mayor] for a talk, and Chaturvedi came to see it and threw the petition back in the faces of the petitioners, saying that he would have it taken out. This was done, but G. persisted, and when I was out of the city for several months, G. went to Mehra [the second mayor], who had party ties with him, and Mehra had a new latrine dug in this narrow alley.

This same sort of thing has just come up where G. is pushing to have a drain installed which would involve infringement on temple land. Garg [the corporation official in charge of public works] sent me a letter asking what I thought of a letter gotten up by G. and various other persons. There is a certain amount of communal feeling involved because the temple originally belonged to the Arya Samaj; it was given by a Brahmin to a certain Chittaramal, who died and left it to his son, Guddarmal, who had no children. The letter claims the temple is falling apart. I am not necessarily against the proposal, but this system of double constituencies is a nuisance.

As already noted, these constituency-serving activities are bound up with a notion of social service which involves taking an interest not only in municipally relevant matters, but in other areas of concern to persons from one's ward. Representative of the latter commitment was the involvement of a Poona corporator in a tenants' association formed in his slum neighborhood. The tenants, who were mainly Mahars and Muslims, organized their own group of about seventy-five residents of the huts located on some land owned by a single landlord. The group proposed to confront the landlord with various complaints about their living conditions. Their initial action, however, was to approach the Congress Scheduled Caste corporator from the ward to complain to him about their problem. A meeting was then organized with the landlord; the latter agreed to supply materials and other aid in the making of repairs to the leaky roofs which were the particular source of the residents' complaints.

The local corporator in this situation did not assume official leadership of the tenants' group, but he did take a hand in supporting its activities and in helping to pull it together. Considering the low status of the tenants, it was interesting to witness not only the part played by the corporator but the process by which the group generated its own leadership from such persons as two Mahars, both of whom were serving as postal clerks.

Interventions take many other forms. We have already noted that corporators are sometimes called upon to act as peacemakers and arbiters within their neighborhoods. However, probably the most important formalized occasion in Agra for interventions are the assessment hearings which take place every five years when the corporation revaluates property before levying its annual 18 percent house tax and 2 percent water tax. While the process was largely administrative in Poona, in Agra important responsibility in hearing appeals against new valuations was granted to the corporators by the CEO with the right of review by the latter. As a result of this arrangement, members of the Executive Committee of the Agra corporation sat in subcommittees from October to March of 1963-64 hearing hundreds of appeals. These corporators had the authority to change valuations. In some circumstances, they sent inspectors out to examine claims anew or to demand sworn statements in connection with matters raised. Citizens who were still not satisfied were able to carry the issue to the courts, but that was an unusual course of action.

In most cases, the corporators responded to appeals with considerable sympathy. Indeed, the strain on some members occasionally erupted in outbursts against the officials, who were blamed for causing many of the difficulties in the first place. Some of the corporators also felt harrassed by other members not directly involved in the appeals process who sought to intervene with them. As one member of the Executive Committee noted irritably, "They come with their own favors to ask, and request us to take up those cases first."

Influence over administrative behavior was also exercised through the use of the powers of interrogation available to corporators. The "question hour" exists in a more institutionalized form in the general body of the Poona corporation than in Agra; such inquiries frequently permit constituent complaints to be brought before the corporation. Thus, in Poona, a member might ask why an official provided aid to a landlord in evicting a particular tenant charged with nonpayment of rent when the landlord had refused to provide basic amenities for many years; or another might draw attention to the hazards created by the presence in an exposed place of a water tank where two boys had drowned, with the expectation that this would goad the relevant administrator to action.

Along with representing the interests of their own geographical constituents, corporators frequently initiated administrative inquiries on behalf of aggrieved lower-level corporation employees. Several instances of administrative corruption were publicized in this manner. Republican corporators in Agra, for example, forced an investigation when it was discovered that some higher administrative officials were demanding "kickbacks" from sweepers.

For the most part, individuals entered the corporation not so much because they expected direct material benefits but because their participation constituted access to a visible public arena in which they could express their own significance in the order of things. In order to advance their claims to personal (or group) prestige, it was vital for them to promote the interests of their constituents. While issues of national and state importance might be a source of considerable intergroup controversy, a debate over the availability of public water taps might be more crucial to many corporators both in terms of how they perceived their jobs and how their constituents viewed their successful performance of their responsibilities.

Side Payments

Among the incentives to participation held out to corporators, specific material benefits do not appear to be very prominent, although hints of special advantages bought or sold are common in accusations made by corporators against each other. In Agra, corporators were unpaid. In Poona, members received some benefits from the work they did—Rs. 100 a month—and certain fringe benefits like bus passes, but these were minor considerations for most members compared to the sums invested in their campaigns and the time they consumed in corporation business. For a few low-status corporators, however, such material benefits may have made a difference.

It is commonly thought that some members profited from supporting contestants for mayor or deputy mayor, particularly in Agra, where rumors of large sums spent by candidates for these offices were widespread. Except for such benefits, it is difficult to be certain of the occasions for material advantage for the corporators. It is probably true that some corporators receive payments from their constituents as rewards for services rendered—intervention with an administrator, helping to lower an assessment. Even where that act is performed without placing real pressure on the relevant administrator, the constituent may feel indebted to the corporator for his supposed help.

Nor is the individual member entirely powerless to influence administrative matters in his direction. While he is not in a position of formal authority, his election places him in a position of "institutionalized pressure." As we shall see in chapter 8, this contributes to politicizing administrative behavior; at the same time it allows the corporator to seek benefits for his constituency or himself from the administration which might not flow as readily to the general public. This is probably even truer for those holding the mayor's or deputy mayor's offices. As Vajpeyi asserts in a brief survey of the corporations of Uttar Pradesh, "The working of the mayoral office has shown it to exercise more influence than its seemingly impotent nature indicates. The political following, which a Mayor must secure to win an election in the Corporation, gives him a leadership position in the shaping of policies."[32] Much depends, however, upon the personal authority of the man involved and the sources of his support. While those mayors actually observed during fieldwork did not seem to play an especially directive role in municipal administration, other mayors of the two cities or of other cities of India might well fit the description provided by Vajpeyi:

> The mayor not only interferes with the administration but also takes interest in petty matters such as appointments, contracts, assessment of property tax and the allotment of the Corporation buildings.... He might not recommend the appointment of his relatives, or get a contract for his partners but there are many whom he pleases, favors, and satisfies. He is a public man and also a party man.[33]

In the final analysis, there is no simple answer to the question, "Why do people become members of municipal corporations in India?" A corporator achieves a certain measure of prestige, not only for himself but also for his caste, community, or ward; he can influence at least the execution of some decisions as they affect his own interests and/or those of his immediate reference groups. Under some conditions he can probably benefit from controlling minor patronage and from special access to municipal servants. Still, as one might expect, many corporators—particularly those of high status—attribute to themselves a form of "civic spirit." Systematic examination of such an explanation would require an investigation of individual motivations and a confrontation with theoretical issues not possible within the framework of the present study.

INTERGROUP RELATIONS IN THE CORPORATIONS[34]

Inducements to continue participation in the two corporations might be unavailing if corporators found these bodies uncongenial. Only the ideationally most committed corporators are likely to participate in an environment which is largely hostile.

Corporators in both bodies were asked to respond to the following set of three items dealing with the nature of group life within the two municipal bodies: (1) Which three members of the corporation do you most respect (or admire)? (2) Which three members of the corporation do you regard as your closest friends? (3) Which three members of the corporation do you feel contribute little to its working? It was hypothesized that political systems that promoted a high level of intergroup tension would draw a strong response on the last item. Table 5.7 indicates that the third question clearly received the least responses.

TABLE 5.7

*Response Rates in Agra and Poona to Sociometric Items**

| City | Possible Responses | | Actual Responses | | | | | |
| | | | Q.1 | | Q.2 | | Q.3 | |
	%	N	%	N	%	N	%	N
Poona	100	195	81	157	86	167	16	31
Agra	100	180	89	159	80	143	53	95

* All the interviewees in Agra responded to the series of questions. Two members of the Poona corporation were not available for the completion of interviews. All of the computations were made on the basis of the total "possible" nominations.

On the whole, members who responded to the third item specified that those named were corrupt, selfish, or simply of low intelligence. In Poona, however, a few included on the list persons who were held in esteem but were not devoting any time to the corporation's work. Therefore, the data need to be handled gingerly. For the purposes of comparison between the two bodies, however, they are useful. It is suggestive, for example, that members of the Agra corporation—where the social distance between the upper castes and the Jatavs was greater than that between the Brahmins and non-Brahmins in Poona—were more willing to provide answers to this question, which may tap a certain element of intergroup hostility. Still, out of a possible 180 responses in Agra, only 95 responses were actually made. The rate was much lower in Poona, where 31 responses were offered. The quality of intergroup tensions in Agra is partially indicated by the distribution of the "noncontributors" in that city. The 95 responses cover 22 persons but are not randomly selected. While they constituted only 23 percent of the total membership of the corporation, Jatavs constituted 69 percent of those named on this item; 9 of the 12 persons receiving four or more mentions were Jatavs.[35]

Responses to the other items did not reveal intergroup distance as markedly, but it is notable that more responses on the question of esteem and fewer on friendship were offered in Agra than in Poona. At least five high-status interviewees in Agra who answered question 3 did not respond to the first two items. These were persons who were pessimistic about the contemporary Indian scene; three of these members (to whom we have already referred), advocated a reactionary redistribution of political authority. Pessimism of this kind about the *ultimate* wisdom of democratic politics was almost entirely absent among the Poona corporators.

The Method

Responses to each of the three questions were coded for each respondent separately on the basis of his party, status group ("ethclass"), age, and education and for each of the persons nominated on the basis of these same four dimensions. Table 5.8 summarizes the distributions in these categories.

In order to analyze the interactions among individuals belonging to these putative groups, an index of cohesion was necessary. A method previously employed in studying group behavior in American state legislatures was adopted. Theoretically, in any body of persons with no group affiliations and equivalent personal skills, one would expect a random distribution of responses to the items employed here; where group ties are completely consuming, absolute cohesion would approach unity. The "homophily" index (h) used below, therefore, varies between -1 and $+1$. A negative value occurs where persons identified as belonging to a group make their choices outside of the supposed group more often than they would do by chance.[36]

The Findings

Tables 5.9 and 5.10 present the results for both cities by ethclass and party. Table 5.9 reveals a lower level of cohesion among members of the Congress in the two cities on matters of esteem (to the extent that the question taps such a sentiment) than among members of other political groups. This score contrasts, for example, with the cohesion of the Jan Sangh. Despite the small size of the latter political group in both corporations, it is more cohesive than the larger party. One might hypothesize that the Jan Sangh, based as it is on status considerations and strong party discipline, attracts members who tend to be more sensitive to a question relating to personal prestige than are members of the more heterogeneous Congress with its constant factional difficulties. In this connection, it is notable that the Swatantra Dal and Nagri Sanghatna members demonstrate relatively high "partisan" identifications. While this might reflect certain subgroup partisan identifications within the Sanghatna, such a factor is not likely to be at work in Agra.

The "ethclass" section of the table indicates that there is a tendency for groups to indicate esteem for their equals or superiors. Thus, the Banias, who are represented in three political groups in Agra, emerge as the most cohesive group in that city. They may occasionally choose "upward" or laterally—from among the Brahmins, Thakurs or others in the "high" category—but they rarely move downward in the traditional status hierarchy in distributing responses. Presumably for the same reason, the Brahmins are the most cohesive group in Poona on this

TABLE 5.8

Categorization of Corporation Members by Ethclass, Party, Age, and Education, 1963-64

Agra	N	Poona	N
Ethclass*		Ethclass	
Banias	19	Marathas	20
Other High Status	20	Brahmins	14
Low Status	16†	Scheduled Caste	6
Muslims	5	Maharashtrians	13
		Non-Maharashtrians	12
Party		Party	
Congress	18	Congress	25
Swatantra	16	Nagri Sanghatna	28‡
Republicans	12	Jan Sangh	5
Jan Sangh	6	Independents	7
Independents	8		
Age		Age	
Old§	32	Old	25
Young	28	Young	40
Education		Education	
Little	9	Little	9
Some	12	Some	26
Secondary	16	Secondary	14
College	23	College	16

* This pattern differs from that employed in our earlier discussion of educational patterns (see table 5.2) because of the high concentration of Agra representation in the Bania group. If we had joined together all Banias and most other high-status groups in Agra there would be little basis for comparison except with the Jatavs.
† Includes two non-Jatavs: a Potter and a Khatik.
‡ Includes one member of the Socialist Party elected without Sanghatna support and the one Republican not officially backed by the Sanghatna but associated with it in the corporation.
§ Those born before 1920 are placed in the "old" category.

item. They are at the top of both the traditional and "modern" status hierarchies; given some persistence of traditional values in Indian society mixed with the respect extended to those with modern education or acknowledged political skills, it is probably difficult for them to identify lower-caste persons to whom they could extend a response on this item.

While the low cohesion of the Jatavs supports the notion that higher-caste groups tend to be more cohesive on matters of esteem, there appears to be some discontinuity between that figure and the score recorded by the Republican Party, most of whose members are Jatavs.[37] In fact, the explanation is logically consistent with our argument. We have already noted that one of the Republican Party leaders

TABLE 5.9

Esteem Patterns in the Municipal Corporations*

Agra	h	Poona	h
Party		Party	
Congress	0.22	Congress	0.25
Swatantra Dal	0.29	Nagri Sanghatna	0.31
Republicans	0.38	Jan Sangh	0.31
Jan Sangh	0.42	Independents	−1.00
Independents	0.14		
Ethclass		Ethclass	
Banias	0.31	Marathas	0.19
High	0.13	Brahmins	0.43
Low	0.02	Scheduled Caste	−0.29
Muslim	−1.00	Maharashtrian	−0.33
		Non-Maharashtrian	−0.82

* Question: Which three members of the corporation do you most respect (admire)?

in Agra was a Bania doctor during this period. The Jatav score in table 5.9 reflects the frequency of mentions of the Bania leader by members of the RPI, which yields a seemingly low index of cohesion where the Jatavs are concerned.[38]

In no case does an h exceed 0.5 on this item. When we look at table 5.10, which deals with friendship choices, the situation is rather different. We might expect ethclass to be more important in the selection of friends than in the designation of prestige figures and, in six of nine cases, there *is* a stronger association on this item than on the previous one; in two other cases, the indices remain near the same level. In one of these two instances, the Brahmins of Poona decrease by a small amount, but they still remain the most cohesive ethclass in that corporation. The greatest decline is exhibited by the Banias of Agra. In part, this decline may be understood as an extension of the high party cohesion among groups in that city. In general, the lines between the Banias and other ethclasses are blurred for friendship purposes, while party membership appears to be a more important basis for interpersonal solidarity.

Similarly, and despite the admitted fluidity of party life and the recent date of formation of political groups like the Swatantra Dal and the reconstituted Nagri Sanghatna, friendship patterns appear to be equally if not more highly influenced by these supposedly secondary affiliations than by tradition-based ethclass ties.

While the Congress is more cohesive in friendship choices than in matters of esteem, it is less cohesive than other political groups in Agra. This may be due, in part, to the factionalism which existed in that city in 1964 and the fact that a number of members of the Swatantra Dal were formerly in the Congress and continued to be friendly with members of one or the other of the Congress factions. Whereas the independents in Agra indicated some common bonds of friendship among them—friendships which were manifested in public behaviors in the corporation—the independents in Poona exhibited few of the characteristics of a real group.

TABLE 5.10

Friendship Patterns in the Municipal Corporations*

Agra	h	Poona	h
Party		Party	
Congress	0.39	Congress	0.51
Swatantra Dal	0.79	Nagri Sanghatna	0.42
Republicans	0.67	Jan Sangh	0.38
Jan Sangh	0.70	Independents	0.12
Independents	0.45		
Ethclass		Ethclass	
Banias	0.06	Marathas	0.13
High	0.27	Brahmins	0.36
Low	0.34	Scheduled Caste	0.24
Muslims	0.15	Maharashtrian	0.03
		Non-Maharashtrian	−0.03

* Question: Which three members of the corporation do you regard as your closest friends?

Friendship patterns, therefore, seem to be more highly associated with party
and caste than esteem patterns. Of the two independent variables, party seems a
more important basis of distinction in the selection of friends than is ethclass. In
matters of esteem, however, much depends on the position of the particular group
in the community. Marathas tend to defer to Brahmins and Jatavs to Banias. In
Poona, this relationship may extend to an understanding of the status of political
groups; thus, implicit in the activities of the Nagri Sanghatna as an organization is
the argument of middle-class antimachine reformers everywhere that the government is being run by a group of lower-status men lacking in the proper skills and
dedication to the "public interest." Many of the individuals associated with the
Sanghatna have been long-time opponents of the Congress Party; present Maratha
control of the Congress simply, for some groups, intensifies that distaste. Still,
Poona's partisan cohesion levels are lower than in Agra.

The implications of age and education are less apparent than for party and
ethclass. Table 5.11 might be interpreted as an indication that in a limited fashion
age confers status. Thus, the older members are more cohesive in both bodies than
the younger members on the esteem item and in comparison to their own scores on
the friendship question because they do not look to the young as objects of respect
or admiration. When friendship responses are examined, younger members in Agra

TABLE 5.11

Age, Esteem, and Friendship in the Corporations, 1963-64

Agra			Poona		
Age	Esteem	Friendship	Age	Esteem	Friendship
Old	0.20	0.14	Old	0.36	0.18
Young	0.11	0.45	Young	−0.24	0.10

are much more likely to choose from among their own, but these distinctions are very weak in Poona. Older members of the Agra corporation *do* look to younger corporators as friends.

For the most part, educational categories do not appear to be "real" sources of affiliation and identification except at the highest levels of education. In both cities, college education is associated with high-status groups. Following the logic of our status hypothesis, we find predictably that persons with college education in Agra were relatively cohesive on both the deference (+0.49) and friendship (+0.31) items; in Poona, the comparable figures were +0.40 and +0.38 for the college-educated. These were the only important positive scores recorded for the educational categories. In Poona, the college-educated alone made more than a majority of their friendship selections from among others of the same educational background. For Agra interviewees, only the least educated group—illiterates or early primary grades—did not make a majority of their friendship choices from the college-educated. Indeed, the college-educated in Agra selected others of the same category for 57 percent of their responses, whereas corporators in the two middle categories of education made 64 percent of their friendship choices from among the college-educated.

Esteem and Leadership

To this point, we have been dealing with subgroups within the corporations. We have found that group cohesion is less marked in the bestowal of esteem than in the identification of friends. The reason for this, we further suggest, may lie in the recognition within the corporations of the skills and contributions of particular individuals which go beyond quasi-ascriptive or party categories. Some evidence may be developed in support of this argument from a closer examination of the characteristics of those persons most often named on the esteem item.

Persons with the greatest prestige in the two corporations received a substantial proportion of their mentions from corporators outside both their own status and party categories. If we look at all those persons who are named six or more times (table 5.12), we find that ascriptively based identifications are even less of a consideration in selection than is party. In both cities, over 55 percent of all prestige designations come from outside the party group of the designee. In Agra, 61 percent of these choices come from non-ethclass members; in Poona, where ethclass conflict was somewhat more attenuated by partisan overlap within the Sanghatna and between it and the Jan Sangh, the figure rises to 75 percent of all those responses which cross ethclass lines.

Esteem in the two corporations is by no means randomly distributed; 61 percent of all choices include only 14 percent of the members. From the table it is also clear that the major portion of that assignment of esteem cannot be explained simply by status or partisan affiliations, although it does tend to go to persons of high socioeconomic and educational status. Indeed, if any element runs through these nominations, it is a tendency to accord esteem on the basis of affiliation with modern professions. Three of the four allopaths in the Agra corporation are on this list of top nominees; similarly, the four lawyers counted in the Agra list included a majority of lawyers in that corporation. In addition, one of the two Jatavs accorded recognition on this list ("I") was college-educated and was studying law while performing his political duties as an MLA in Lucknow.[39]

His case also points up the possibility that socioeconomic status *by itself* is not the basis for these choices. The men represented in table 5.12 are not the wealthiest in the two corporations, nor does wealth in association with high caste assure esteem unless it is also associated with certain educational and personal skills. Indeed, two of the wealthiest men in the Agra corporation—both Banias—appeared on the list of those twelve members who contributed least to the corporation. They were named to that list—and excluded from the present one—despite the fact that both had invested a good deal of money and energy in politicking in the corporation and one had been elected mayor of the corporation. Instead, both were viewed as resorting to corrupt methods to advance their personal interests and not bringing much in the way of personal character into play. Neither was well educated.

Thus, while socioeconomic status may provide a threshold opportunity for the acquisition of skills on the basis of which esteem may be accumulated, these

TABLE 5.12

Characteristics of the Most Prestigious Members in the Corporations, 1963-64

Agra

Identifi- cation Letter	Nomi- nations	Ethclass	Non- Ethclass Ratio*	Party	Non- Party Ratio	Profession
A	30	Bania	0.60	Congress	0.60	Merchant
B	25	High	0.72	Swatantra	0.56	Lawyer
C	11	Bania	1.00	Republican	0.36	Doctor
D	9	Bania	0.44	Jan Sangh	0.78	Lawyer
E	8	High	0.38	Swatantra	0.50	Doctor
F	7	Bania	0.72	Congress	0.57	Doctor
G	7	Jatav	0.14	Republican	0.00	Small Mfr.
H	6	High	0.67	Congress	0.84	Lawyer
I	6	Jatav	0.67	Republican	0.67	Party Work
J	6	High	0.33	Jan Sangh	0.67	Lawyer
Total	115	Average	0.61	Average	0.56	

Poona

K	29	Maratha	0.69	Congress	0.48	Business
L	28	Brahmin	0.64	Jan Sangh	0.86	Lawyer
M	19	Brahmin	0.79	N.S.	0.63	Lawyer
N	18	Brahmin	0.83	N.S.	0.33	Party Work
O	9	Maratha	1.00	N.S.	0.33	Small Bus.
P	6	High	1.00	N.S.	0.50	Merchant
Q	6	Maratha	0.67	N.S.	0.33	Educator
Total	115	Average	0.75	Average	0.55	

* These ratios represent the relationship between mentions from the outside and from within a man's own group. Thus in Agra, "A" received thirty mentions. Eighteen of these came from outside of the Congress or Bania groups.

interpersonal and political skills grow out of certain intellectual capacities which are admired by other corporators. Generally, too, it is skill which is not too obviously tainted with concern for personal advantage. It is true that "C" (the Bania Republican leader) was seen by some members as using his position to his own advantage, but others of like character were almost systematically excluded by the interviewees.

An interesting feature of table 5.12 is the differential sources of support for "C," "G," and "I"—all members of the Republican Party. The first received all his mentions from non-Banias; most came from Jatavs. All the choices of "G" came from fellow Republicans. Only "I" was more frequently named by persons outside both his caste and party than from within. Indeed, in mentioning him, a couple of non-RPI corporators did so explicitly because he represented to non-Jatavs a model of what Jatavs should strive to emulate in terms of education, intellect, and personal integrity.

The divisions within the Congress made it difficult to accord prestige to those persons who were deeply implicated in that party's factions. Thus, all three men from the Congress were relatively marginal to its factional disputes. "F" acted as a mediator between groups within the corporation and "H" was acceptable to both factions, although active for many years in party work.[40] "A" gained in stature by standing aloof from internal party politics altogether. In an almost Gandhian fashion, he accrued prestige by *renouncing* the use of political skills. He is a very wealthy man, but the causes he involves himself in are essentially nonpolitical. He has been active, for example, in the Congress organization for the improvement of the situation of the Scheduled Castes and in a group concerned with the construction of shelters for stray cows. Although he was a member of Congress for many years, generally he declined opportunities for higher office.[41] This political style was much admired by others, which meant that his ideas were heard with respect as coming from a disinterested source. As one might expect, his own choices on the esteem item went (in two of three cases) to non-Congressmen, whereas twelve Congressmen named him. These Congress votes came from both factions of the party. The only Congress member "A" included on the esteem question was "F."[42]

None of the persons named to the list in Poona were quite like "A," although "Q" (the Maratha educator) came closest. All the others were highly partisan in their involvements, although they received considerable respect from members of parties other than their own. Indeed, all but two had served as mayor at some period of their service in the corporation. "K," (Shivajirao Dhere), after being elected to the corporation in 1957 on a Samyukta Maharashtra ticket, was the youngest mayor in Poona history. He later joined the Congress and became the leader of that party in the corporation after 1962. Similarly, "L" and "M" have been outspoken leaders of their respective political organizations for many years. Despite the fact that "M" was in the dying Hindu Mahasabha and "L" was the leader of the tiny Jan Sangh group in the corporation, both received high praise from members of other political groups.

The characteristics of those who score highest in terms of prestige in the two corporations, therefore, do not fall neatly into demographic categories. While less than satisfactory as a form of distinguishing them from other corporators, we are forced to suggest that they display certain admirable interpersonal skills and qualities of leadership which other corporators do not. These values are not necessarily those one would associate with friendship,[43] and the attributes are not standardized to fit to a particular mold, but they clearly transcend formal party or ethclass affiliations.

Our overall findings lend some weight to the notion that memberships in a modern governmental institution like a municipal corporation may further weaken already diffuse group distinctions, despite the relative closeness of municipal bodies to those intergroup conflicts which permeate local politics. Thus, while friendship patterns are influenced to some extent by partisan affiliations, neither traditional status nor party identification dominates in the allocation of prestige. Rather, interpersonal prestige is distributed in the two corporations with due consideration for status group and partisan antagonisms, but also with considerable regard for the leadership skills and personal qualities which particular individuals have exhibited within the municipal arenas.[44]

An inquiry into a few of the dimensions of intercorporator relations which concludes on such an ambiguous note might appear negative. Instead, the very finding that obvious categories of traditional social and modern political life in India do not dominate the thinking of local political actors to the exclusion of other considerations based on universalistic standards of personal behavior is, probably, a positive comment on the viability of these municipal structures as political institutions in their own right.

6

CONTESTS FOR MUNICIPAL OFFICE

Following the election of corporators (as well as the election of aldermen in Agra), the leading political actors in each city became involved in processes of group consolidation and intergroup bargaining in anticipation of the selection of a mayor and a deputy mayor. These internal corporation elections stimulated investment of energy by local actors of a kind rarely aroused by other corporation matters. For us, therefore, they provide a major opportunity to examine the forms of cooperation developed by participants in the two municipal arenas and the capacities of these arenas to manage cleavages. It should be noted at the outset, incidentally, that there is little evidence that actors other than those previously identified as engaged in the fates of the two local political systems (including state party politicians) took any part in the process of candidate selection or in the negotiations which yielded the particular municipal officials.

Coalitions to elect officers were shaped, at least in large part, by considerations of party and social status. However, personal influence also played a part in these elections. The rather limited powers formally vested in such municipal offices as mayor and deputy mayor led many candidates to be less immediately concerned with potential material benefits or with ideological victories than with the sheer advancement of personal or group prestige. Only as that prestige had implications for state and national politics did it occasionally become encapsulated in larger struggles for political power of a kind influenced by ideological or material considerations.

AGRA'S MAYORS: 1959-66

The First Election for Mayor

The failure of any single group in Agra to attain an electoral majority necessitated the formation of a postelection agreement in December 1959 to choose a mayor. [1] Table 6.1 indicates the group alignments about the time of the first mayoral election; this table differs from table 3.5 not only in the addition of aldermen but in its inclusion of several other changes in affiliation which occurred subsequent to the corporation elections: the reentry of a former Congress member into that party; the defection of two Jan Sangh corporators to the ranks of the independents; the formation of the Swatantra Dal from among sixteen independent members of the corporation. The result was a Congress party even more pronounced in its high-caste base; a Swatantra Dal which brought together a wide variety of groups,

TABLE 6.1

Primordial Groups and Parties of Members, Agra Corporation, Late 1959

Primordial Group	Congress	Swatantra Dal	Jan Sangh	RPI	Independent
Banias/Jains	8	5	3	1	2
Brahmins	3	4	1	–	–
Other high*	7	1	–	–	–
Refugees	–	–	2	–	–
Backward Class	1	3	–	–	–
Muslim	–	3	–	1	1
Jatavs	–	–	–	13	1
Total	19	16	6	15	4

* In addition to one Swatantra Dal Khatri, there were four Kayasthas, two Khatris, and a Thakur in the Congress.

including the discontented from the Jan Sangh and the Congress; a depleted Jan Sangh; and a Republican Party composed principally of Jatavs.

In constructing a majority coalition, party leaders made several important strictures on the collaboration of particular groups. The leadership of the Congress Party in Uttar Pradesh ordered its local units in the KAVAL cities to refrain from forming alliances with opposition parties unless absolutely necessary.[2] The Jan Sangh, for its part, was reluctant to work with the low-status Republican Party or with the Swatantra Dal and its ex-Jan Sangh members. As a result, the most natural allies in late 1959 were the Congress and the Swatantra Dal, despite the inclusion in the latter group of persons who had recently defected from the Congress.

With thirty-four votes between them, the two groups were assured of victory even if a few persons nominally associated with the Dal did not support the choice. The Congress and the Dal reached an agreement by which the former was to designate the coalition candidate for mayor during the first year and the Dal would nominate their candidate for deputy mayor. It was further agreed that when the first mayor's term expired in 1961, the Dal would nominate a candidate for that office and the incumbent deputy mayor would resign in favor of the Congress nominee.[3]

Once these steps had been taken, each group proceeded to select its own candidate for office. The sitting MP for Agra, Seth Achal Singh, was widely mentioned as a possible contestant for mayor before the elections; it was apparently a position which Seth very much desired. But he was ruled out of consideration by the national Congress Party's Parliamentary Board which was opposed to the idea of contesting a by-election for a seat in Parliament if a vacancy resulted from Seth's election as mayor. Seth's factional position also exposed his candidacy to opposition at the local level. Even with his withdrawal the factional struggles within the Agra Congress were such that the party failed to reach any immediate understanding on a candidate from within the local organization. The State Congress was, therefore, called upon to supply a suitable nominee. The man chosen, S. N. Chaturvedi, was a resident of rural Agra but owned some property in Agra City. He had been active in the District Congress and was somewhat inclined toward the Singhal-Rawal element in the local party, but he was sufficiently aloof from city politics to permit his nomination without rancor.

Against Chaturvedi, the Republicans nominated their alderman as mayor. They anticipated defeat, but as one Republican Party member explained, "The party did not want the Congress to win unopposed. When we were running for the corporation, the Republicans said that we would oppose the Congress, and it would have looked bad to support Congress in the first year." There was no other candidate against Chaturvedi, for the Jan Sangh was too weak to put up a candidate of its own and preferred to support Chaturvedi rather than a Republican. The result was an easy victory for Chaturvedi by a vote of 44 to 16 with almost everyone but the Republicans supporting the Congress nominee (see table 6.2).

The Second Mayoral Contest

Although the expectation of the Congress-Dal pact was that the deputy mayor would resign his position in time for the election of a mayor in 1961, the incumbent and his Baloji-led backers in the Swatantra Dal preferred that he remain in that position. This reflected a view that the post provided the Dal with influence over decision making not available to the mayor since the deputy mayor presided over the major committees of the corporation. Within the sixteen-man Dal, however, there was disagreement of a different nature over the desirability of maintaining existing arrangements.

Two groups had emerged within the Dal in the wake of the aldermanic elections. Each was led by an alderman: Baloji, in one case; a wealthy businessman, Kalyan Das Jain, in the other. There had been a general understanding within the Dal that the exchange of positions contemplated in the pact of late 1959 would bring Kalyan Das into office as mayor in 1961. However, not only was Kalyan Das disliked by some members of the Congress—particularly persons associated with the Singhal faction—but middle-class and educated elements in the Baloji faction did not feel that as a rather traditional businessman lacking in westernized sophistication he was an appropriate choice for mayor. His candidacy was also marred by a reputation for political practices which were not beyond reproach.

As a result, a "subpact" was formed in 1961 between the Baloji faction and the Congress which insured the continuation of Baloji's associate as deputy mayor in return for group support to any Congress nominee for mayor. The union between these two groups was solidified by the nomination of B. K. Mehra, a relative of the deputy mayor, as the candidate of the Congress for mayor.[4] Chaturvedi, whose term had been a relatively smooth one, retired voluntarily to enter district politics in anticipation of the general elections of 1962; he was elected to Parliament from rural Agra in that year.

Mehra, the Congress nominee, had not been involved in party politics for very long. As a well-known lawyer in the city, he was among the "notables" solicited by the Congress for the corporation elections. His short service to the party antagonized some members with respect to his candidacy for mayor, but it had the advantage associated with the Chaturvedi nomination of not giving undue recognition to either one of the Congress party factions.[5]

TABLE 6.2

Coalitions for Mayoral Elections in Agra, 1960-65

Year	Majority Nominee	Main Support	Vote	Opposition Nominees	Support	Votes
1960	S. N. Chaturvedi (Cong.)	Cong. SD	44	Khem Chand (RPI)	RPI	16
1961 1st Ballot	B. K. Mehra (Cong.)	Cong. SD (Baloji group)	26	K. D. Jain (SD)	SD (Jain Group) JS Inds.	19
				P. N. Gupta (RPI)	RPI	14
1962	R. C. Gupta (Cong.)	Cong. SD	—	No formal opposition		
1963	K. D. Jain (SD)	SD JS RPI	26	R. C. Gupta (Cong.)	Congress	25
1964	K. D. Jain (SD)	SD JS RPI	32	K. N. Jain (Cong.)	Cong. Inds.	27
1965	K. D. Jain (SD)	SD JS RPI	33	Gopal Das (Cong.)	Cong. Inds.	22

The Jain group in the Swatantra Dal, annoyed at what they considered to be a trick, placed Jain's name in the field for mayor. Beginning from his faction's eight-vote base, Jain approached the RPI and the Jan Sangh about a possible coalition. The Jan Sangh was willing to work with Jain as a way of consolidating political opposition to the Congress; the Republicans were more reluctant to enter such an agreement and, instead, nominated P. N. Gupta, the Mathur Vaish doctor, who was rapidly emerging as the leader of the party group in the corporation. These opposition groups did agree, however, that they would share second preferences in the balloting—in effect, assuring Jain's election. Since it was expected that Mehra would not win an absolute majority on the first ballot, Gupta's nomination was to be a largely symbolic act before the Republicans delivered their support to Jain as second preference. As expected, therefore, Mehra received 26 first ballot votes, Jain 19, and Gupta 14. Instead of throwing their votes to Jain, however, a few Republicans voted for Mehra and many abstained from indicating a second preference.

The reasons for this failure to act in concert vary depending upon whose description of the situation one accepts. Personal ties may have been a factor since a couple of the Republicans had been Mehra's clients and one Republican suggested that Dr. Gupta's father was an old friend of Mehra's. Some of Gupta's supporters later asserted that the agreement with the Jain group was contingent on an understanding that Jain would make no attempt to approach Republican corporators directly; it is alleged that this understanding was violated by Jain's followers with the result that Gupta released his voters to cast blank ballots or vote for whomever they wished instead of directing that second preferences go to Jain. As a result of second preferences, Mehra was elected Agra's mayor.

The Election of R. C. Gupta

Partly because of the hostilities among opposition groups, the Congress was in a strong position to maintain itself in the mayor's office in 1962. The continuation of Mehra was unsatisfactory to some of the older members of the party who invoked a newly minted "principle" that a mayor should serve only one term. They also decided to go outside of the corporation for their nominee, despite the opposition of some party members on this point; indeed, Mehra was among the most vocal opponents of such a policy. The man chosen for mayor by the Congress was Ram Chand Gupta, a senior advocate in Agra and a relative by marriage of C. B. Gupta, then Chief Minister of Uttar Pradesh.[6] One Congressman expressed the thinking of many of the corporation members on the selection of Gupta: "Agra is not a rich city. We needed someone with some influence in government circles. The city badly needs things like more water; so we wanted someone who could get more money for the city. Gupta was the only man." Gupta was selected by the Congress caucus after consideration of several names; only one negative vote was cast in caucus, that of Mehra, who stood firmly by his belief that "outsiders" should not be elected mayor.

With the opposition in disarray, the Gupta family and members of the Congress drew heavily on personal influence to try to win votes. A leader of the Jan Sangh, for example, was approached on the basis of family ties, since his father had been an estate manager for the Gupta family; indeed, he claimed that he was consulted by the Guptas on whether Ram Chand should run. Statements were also made later by Muslim and Republican members that promises of material benefits were extended in behalf of the Congress candidate.

In the face of these activities there was an abortive effort by Kalyan Das Jain to organize support for himself. Leaders of the Congress tried to dissuade Jain from this course. A lieutenant of Jain reported having been visited by Gupta and Seth Achal Singh, who suggested at considerable length that Jain withdraw. The day before the election, when it became apparent that Jain had no chance of winning, he did so. (Allegedly, promises of support to Jain for the following election were made by some persons supporting Gupta, but these were not kept for various reasons.) Thus, Ram Chand Gupta was elected mayor of Agra in 1962 without opposition.

While his term got off to a good start, resentments soon began to mount against the mayor. Realignments were also underway in the corporation by late 1962 which brought a halt to Congress mayorships in 1963. Among the sources of the growing opposition to the mayor were the special relationship he had established with the CEO and the alleged Congress involvement in a case suspending two members of the Swatantra Dal for nonattendance; equally important, an uneasy alliance was achieved among the Republicans, the Jan Sangh and the Swatantra Dal which brought that grouping into a majority position in the corporation.

The Mayor and the CEO

When Gupta became mayor, the CEO was a man with whom several members of the corporation were unhappy. A person of aristocratic temperament, the CEO apparently offended a number of corporators who accused him of assuming a patronizing attitude toward them; on several occasions, it is alleged, he made derogatory remarks in the course of corporation meetings about the capacities of members. These feelings against the CEO were not restricted to non-Congressmen. Indeed, at a meeting held to congratulate Gupta on his victory, several Congress members asked him to use his influence either to change the CEO's manner of behavior or, if that failed, to arrange his transfer out of Agra. Gupta promised to take the matter up with the Chief Minister, if necessary.

Some time later, Gupta and the CEO visited Lucknow on municipal business. The exact nature of the events that took place there is unclear, but apparently some understanding was reached—an agreement which some members of the corporation found worse than the previous situation. Non-Congressmen subsequently claimed that the CEO became the "tool" of the Congress group in the corporation; suspicions were further aroused by the fact that Gupta's son had become a deputy minister in the state government after the general elections of 1962. Suggestions that the CEO was now clearly in the control of the Congress Party became common. Yet, even those who felt aggrieved against the CEO were restrained in their charges; they did not, as they often did with each other, accuse him of personal corruption. Indeed, the tone assumed by a Muslim corporator who had been held in prison under the Defense of India Regulations during the period under review[7] was one of definite respect for this officer who had been recruited from the army into the Indian Civil Service (ICS) shortly before the departure of the British:

> K. is a very good officer. Sometimes he used to favor Ram Chand Gupta because his son is a deputy minister, but he was a real ICS officer and had known the days when the District Magistrate and ICS officer was a real power. Sometimes he did not like the new democratic ways of doing things and he was not willing to accept the language of the corporation members and the ridiculous things that sometimes go on as well as he might have. Still, he was very good about getting me a parole when my wife was ill and in conversations he was quite attentive.

Among the more partisan members of opposition groups these virtues counted for little as weighed against the feeling that the CEO was not exhibiting sufficient impartiality. The result was a drive organized by these members to bring a vote of no confidence against the CEO. A petition to that effect was drawn up in October of 1962 and received a considerable number of signatures, including even those of a few Congress members, although the latter disavowed support when the issue later turned into a party matter.

The petition required thirty-eight signatures to carry legal force as a formal demand to the state government. It is not clear whether the motion was eventually withdrawn simply because of an inability to get enough signatures or whether, as some members claim, because the Chinese invasion of 1962 caused local people to feel that an effort to remove the CEO was inappropriate for the time being. In any event, the formal petition was withdrawn, but a letter was sent to Lucknow by some corporators requesting the CEO's removal; nothing came of it.[8] Some time later, he was moved to the position of District Magistrate for Agra district, but this was merely a routine in-service transfer.

Among the many minor matters made much of by opposition party corporators was the fact that the mayor's brother—a minor official in the corporation—was assigned to a position in the terminal toll section of the bureaucracy. That unit is responsible for collecting taxes on goods brought into the city; while it is a major source of revenue to Agra, terminal tolls are also a considerable area for corruption, and municipal officials are said to look favorably upon assignments to the department as a source of income. Another item of complaint was the decision of the CEO—in opposition to the Executive Committee—to include the area of the mayor's residence within the purview of a scheme financed by central government loans for new sewer lines even though the mayor's neighborhood was not on the list designated by the committee. The greatest number of complaints were directed against the CEO and, by inference, the mayor, for their alleged parts in the suspension of two corporators.

The Disqualification Cases

Among the signators to the petition for the CEO's removal were two members who rarely attended meetings. Their failure to attend was a technical violation of the terms of the Corporation Act, which makes absentees subject to possible disqualification. The absence of these members had been duly noted by a second-level administrator and brought to the CEO's attention; acting on his own authority,[9] the CEO wrote to the state government on the matter in late 1962. Subsequently, the government responded with a demand that the two members explain their absences.

The two corporators—one a Muslim Swatantra Dal member, the other a Backward Class member of the same political group—were charged with not having attended meetings for six consecutive months. According to the act, disqualification followed from such absence "except on account of illness or any other cause accepted by the Mahapalika."[10]

Both members argued in the court case which emerged from this episode that their absences had been due, at least in part, to illness. The Muslim explained that he had visited Pakistan in May 1962 to attend weddings of his brother and sister and became ill while there; he returned to India in June. On the advice of his doctor, he did not attend meetings during July and August, but he claimed he was present at meetings held in September. He had not attended since 20 April. Before leaving for Pakistan, he pleaded, he had written to the CEO on 11 May, "informing him that he [the corporator] was proceeding to Pakistan and requesting him to place the letter before the Mahapalika" and to explain the corporator's absence to the other members. If this request was actually made, it was never transmitted to the corporation members—a further source of conflict between the CEO and the opposition groups.[11]

The case for the other alleged absentee was handled by the same lower court and the facts were similar. After attending a meeting on 22 May, he claimed to have fallen ill of malaria in July 1962. A certificate signed by the deputy mayor in his capacity as a doctor testified to the corporator's illness through August. Like the Muslim corporator, he claimed he was present at meetings held in September and October.

Contrary to these assertions, the minutes of the September meetings showed no evidence that either of the corporators had attended. Indeed, part of the case revolved around the reliability of these records, which were finally thrown into question by internal evidence that another member listed in the minutes as having made a speech on the floor of the council at a particular meeting was not included in the official record of attendance for that same meeting. Furthermore, everyone agreed that the two corporators had attended the meeting called on 10 October 1962 to elect a new deputy mayor. If it could be established that the latter was a "regular" meeting of the corporation and not one falling outside the terms of the act, there were grounds for dismissing the government's case against the two corporators. Thus, the decision ultimately revolved not around the question of actual illness, but around the reliability of attendance records and whether the meeting of 10 October was a special election meeting or should still be considered a regular meeting of the corporation. The courts ruled in favor of the corporators on both counts. The District Judge, dealing with the word "meeting," construed it to include election sessions:

> The Mahapalika exists as a body corporate, and its constituents are its members. Any meeting of the members to transact any business connected with the Mahapalika can

be described as a meeting of the Mahapalika. It is only the members of the Mahapalika who can elect the *Upa Nagar Pramukh* [deputy mayor] and hence the meeting held on 10th October 1962 must be held to be a meeting of the Mahapalika. The mere fact that the presiding officer was the Additional District Magistrate in the meeting held on the 10th October 1962 will not make any difference.

These court maneuvers must be understood against the background of a series of political actions taken in the corporation. The election of a deputy mayor in October had brought an anti-Congress coalition to the fore and accelerated the effort behind the no-confidence motion against the CEO. Apparently, in January 1963 some corporators became aware that the CEO was attempting to work up an absenteeism case, allegedly with the encouragement of the Congress mayor. Charges were originally framed (it is claimed) against four opposition members, but the case was ultimately brought only against the two corporators mentioned above. The implicated Muslim corporator claims he wrote the following letter to the CEO on 23 January:

From a reliable source, as well as from the press report, I have learned that you have already made reference to the government regarding my removal from the Mahapalika and this letter is a farce and a make-belief for the conspiracy that has been hatched up against me. . . . I am constrained to say that the above-mentioned letter is apparently a result of the unhappy relations between me and yourself and there is ample proof in this regard.

This letter was followed on 28 January by a resolution moved in the corporation by members representing the Swatantra Dal, the Republican Party, and the Jan Sangh, excusing this corporator's absence.[12] A point of order raised by a Congress leader held that the resolution was beyond the powers of the corporation and that the question could not properly be examined locally since the matter was now before the state government. The mayor took this point of order under advisement and adjourned the meeting to 2 February, much to the consternation of the opposition party members. Indeed, according to subsequent court records, the meeting broke up in "pandemonium" created by those groups supporting the resolution.

At the meeting called for 2 February, the mayor again postponed a decision. It was not until the eighth that he ruled that the matter could not be discussed by the corporation. The three opposition groups then staged a walkout from the body in protest. On the twelfth of that month, a request for a writ was filed by one of the corporators anticipating his eventual suspension, but the District Judge ruled that the writ could not be granted against the state government until an action actually took place. And, in fact, the state government made no move until April. It was only a few days before the mayoral elections scheduled for 22 April 1963, that the government saw fit to issue orders suspending the two corporators for absenteeism and, presumably, nullifying their votes against the incumbent mayor.

Prepared for that eventuality,[13] the two corporators moved the Uttar Pradesh High Court to halt the elections on the grounds that "the decision has been deliberately communicated at this late juncture." The injunction was granted, and for the next three months the case proceeded through the court system while the mayoral election was in abeyance. During this time, Mayor Gupta remained in office. By July, however, sufficient opposition had been aroused within the corporation against any Congress nominee so that the two corporators agreed to withdraw the court order and to allow the elections to be held without demanding their own participation in the particular contest.[14]

The 1963 Mayoral Elections

When mayoral candidacies were being considered prior to the issuance of the injunction, there was little Congress enthusiasm for renominating R. C. Gupta. Gupta himself spoke of standing aside; some members of the Singhal group, in particular, encouraged him not to run, but at the last minute Gupta declared himself in the race. By this time, the UPCC was becoming increasingly wary of involving the party in these local selection processes—the party leadership felt that the reputation of the Congress was being battered in some of the other KAVAL cities where the party had endorsed mayoral candidates without success[15]—and so the UPCC washed its hands of official endorsement of any mayoral candidate for Agra. Technically, then, R. C. Gupta stood as an independent in 1963 rather than as the official candidate of the Congress; he received only twenty-five votes. Most of these came from the Congress, the small group of non-Swatantra Dal independents, and a few persons nominally aligned with opposition groups.

Against Gupta, a three-party "pact" among the Jan Sangh, the Swatantra Dal, and the RPI agreed on Kalyan Das Jain as its candidate. This choice caused considerable unhappiness among some members of these groups, and several are believed to have defected to the Congress on the mayoral vote.[16] At the same time, some members of the Congress were accused of having voted against Gupta.[17] In the balance of antipathies, Kalyan Das was narrowly elected by a margin of twenty-six to twenty-five with the others abstaining.

Despite continuous difficulties in maintaining cooperation among the three opposition groupings in the following two years, Kalyan Das managed to defeat Congress challengers in both elections. In 1964, he received thirty-two votes against twenty-seven for the Congress nominee, a Jain doctor. It was generally expected that new corporation elections would be held in 1965. Instead, the Uttar Pradesh government postponed these elections (for which the Congress was unprepared) by granting two one-year extensions. As a result, another election was held in late June 1965, which mobilized the same three groups in support of Kalyan Das, who easily defeated his Congress opponent (a wealthy Bania) by a margin of thirty-three to twenty-two. Five votes were declared invalid. Rather than grant another extension, the Uttar Pradesh government decided to supersede all of the KAVAL corporations in early 1966 and to empower the CEO's to carry on with the full powers of the corporations. New elections were not held until the spring of 1968.

THE DEPUTY MAYORSHIP IN AGRA

In 1959, as part of the pact with the Congress, the Swatantra Dal selected a well-established doctor from the Khatri community to be deputy mayor. The remaining independents and Republicans put forward a wealthy (though largely uneducated) movie theater owner and moneylender from a small Bania subcommunity, Bohrey Ram Gopal. An easy victory for the coalition candidate should have been assured, but the independent candidate badly wanted to win and doggedly sought support from all the corporators. It is suggested, for example, that he promised Dr. Gupta of the RPI that he would back him if Gupta ever ran for office; and, in fact, he did provide this personal backing when Dr. Gupta ran unsuccessfully for mayor in 1961, although this did not bring many votes to the Republican leader.

In the contest for deputy mayor, the Congress-Dal nominee received thirty-one votes to the independent's twenty-nine. In addition to the Republicans and the few independents not belonging to the Swatantra Dal, the loser received the votes of the Jan Sangh and at least three votes from persons nominally in the winning coalition. Supporters of Bohrey claimed that he took votes from Seth-inclined members of the Congress with whom he was personally friendly. (Bohrey was one of those prospective Congress candidates dropped from the 1959 candidate list submitted by the Seth group to the UPCC.) The defection of several Congress members to Bohrey was further sweetened by the fact that they saw it as a way of embarrassing the Singhal faction, which had taken the lead in negotiating the municipal alliance with the Swatantra Dal. (See table 6.3 for a summary of deputy mayor contests.)

After his defeat, Bohrey brought a suit in the High Court of Uttar Pradesh raising at least ten different counts against those involved in the pact between the Congress and the Swatantra Dal.[18] Most were trivial. These included the charge that by withdrawing its prospective candidate for mayor the Swatantra Dal offered "illegal gratification" to the Congress under the terms of the national anticorruption statutes against nonmonetary gratification; and, the claim that a party directive threatening expulsion by the Congress against those persons who did not vote for the pact's candidate was a form of improper coercion.

The court dismissed most of the charges raised by simply recognizing that intergroup bargaining and vote trading are normal features of party democracy. With regard to the matter of party directives, they argued that there was nothing improper in such a party action "against the members of a group who go against the party mandate." Where the case was most troublesome, however, was in the role played by the mayor, S. N. Chaturvedi, in his capacity as Returning Officer for the election. The suit charged the mayor with acting improperly in the guise of assisting corporators who claimed disability. On this matter, one judge pointed to lower-court testimony that several members of the corporation complained about the practice at the time of the election. In the District Court, where the case was originally tried, two corporation members had given evidence to this point and, according to the District Judge, both resorted to mistruths. One claimed he was suffering from giddiness at the time, but the Judge asserted that the same man was perfectly able to sign his name to the election register; the other, a prominent lawyer, claimed that he had left his glasses behind at the courts where he practiced. On the latter claim, the District Judge noted, "This witness admits that for signing his name he did not need the glass[es], but for marking the ballot paper, he did need the glass[es] as the mark in the ballot paper had to be made against the name of the candidate."

TABLE 6.3

Deputy Mayor Coalitions in Agra, 1960-66

Year	Majority Nominee	Main Support	Vote	Opposition Nominees	Main Support	Votes
1960 (Feb.)	L. P. Tandon (SD)	Cong. SD	31	Bohrey Ram Gopal (Ind.)	Inds. RPI JS	29
1961 (July)	Effort to bring no-confidence vote fails.					
1962 (Aug.)	Tandon resigns before vote of no-confidence scheduled for 11 September 1962.					
1962 (Oct.)	P. N. Gupta (RPI)	RPI SD JS	32	Bohrey Ram Gopal (Ind.)	Cong. Inds.	21
1964 (June)	Vote of no-confidence against Gupta raised but no action taken.					

These maneuvers at the time of election arose from an agreement between the Congress and the Dal that the mayor would serve as a check to see that the promises made by members of the two groups were actually being kept. Shying away from the possible issue of perjury, therefore, the High Court strained to allow the propriety of the procedure. The deciding judge in a split court argued that the Returning Officer had to take the word of a voter requesting assistance and, furthermore, that no evidence was presented to show that improper influence was exercised by the mayor. The only impropriety might have been a violation of secrecy, but the judge argued on this point:

> Secrecy of the vote is primarily for the protection of the voter. If an individual voter deliberately discloses in whose favour he is voting to any particular individual, it cannot be said that the result of the election is, in any way, effected by it, nor can it be said that the vote as given, is a vote not properly received.

Despite the possible danger in such a doctrine, the court felt bound to accept the two stories as true and held that it was proper for the Returning Officer to have taken the members' word for their disabilities.[19]

Even while this case was weaving its way through the Indian judicial system, the corporation was faced with another controversy over the office of deputy mayor. By 1961, as we have noted, the Congress was working with only a portion of the original Swatantra Dal. Other groups in the corporation tried to bring a vote of no-confidence against the deputy mayor since a majority of the corporation was no longer supporting the agreement.

Many weapons were used against the incumbent including the complaint that the office of deputy mayor was being employed to advance the political ambitions of his group leader, Baloji. It is difficult to see how the limited powers residing in the deputy mayor could have made much difference, especially with a Congress mayor in office. Still, a motion of no-confidence was brought against Tandon in

July 1961; it failed for a lack of votes. This was due, in large part, to the unwillingness of the Republicans to support the anti-Tandon move. Dr. Gupta had expectations that Tandon would support him for the office of deputy mayor in the future when Tandon finally did resign. However, Tandon refused to withdraw at a time when he was under fire.

The Corporation Act bars more than one vote of confidence per year against a deputy mayor. Therefore, a second vote was not filed until August 1962. This time Tandon resigned before the issue could be brought to a vote ostensibly on grounds of ill health; he had suffered a mild heart attack in July.[20]

This set the stage for a new election on 10 October 1962. We have already alluded to that election in connection with the disqualification cases. It came at a time when the Congress had been badly hurt by the local results of the general elections of early 1962 (see chapter 9). As a result, when the time came to nominate a candidate for deputy mayor, the municipal political arena was almost in a state that resembled the search for new political arrangements in late 1959. The preceding three years had witnessed a progressive decrease in the number of participants necessary to create a winning coalition. Now many of the "outs" had reached a point of vulnerability to suggestions for alliances which made them willing to work harder for agreements than was previously the case. The result was to bring together groups which had previously rejected the idea of working with each other.

The process was led off by Dr. Gupta putting himself forward as the deputy mayor candidate of the Republicans. He approached the Congress for support, claiming a quid pro quo for the support that the Republicans—faced with no reasonable alternative—had extended to the Congress mayor in 1962. A few Congress members felt they owed a debt to the RPI, but most did not.

Instead, the Congress proposed to put up its own candidate, but the party choice was split between a wealthy businessman and a professional—both of them nominally associated with the Seth group. When a vote was taken in the party caucus, the businessman received four and the professional fourteen votes. While this satisfied the Congress corporators, the selection attracted no coalition partners to the Congress side. In addition to Dr. Gupta, Bohrey was again actively seeking the office of deputy mayor, but the Congress was reluctant to make him their prime candidate. Indeed, the Congress corporators decided only a few hours before the scheduled election meeting to give all members a free vote. By the time members assembled at the polling place, however, there was some feeling in the group that they should restrict their alternatives to supporting Bohrey or casting a blank ballot. Neither move was enforced by the party. Several Congressmen freely conceded when interviewed in 1964 that they had voted for Dr. Gupta.

The *Tri-Dalir* (Three-Party Pact) among the Jan Sangh, the Republicans and the Swatantra Dal was finalized only twenty hours before the election. It emerged when the two factions within the Swatantra Dal were reconciled on the basis of an agreement that they would both work for the election of Kalyan Das as the next mayor. Then the Jan Sangh and the Republicans were brought in with the understanding that Dr. Gupta would be supported for deputy mayor and would resign after about a year in office in favor of a Jan Sangh nominee who would serve for the remaining life of the corporation. New elections, as noted earlier, were expected for 1965. The *Tri-Dalir* had 36 potential votes; 32 were cast for Dr. Gupta. He won easily as Bohrey received only 21, and 7 blank ballots were submitted.

The anti-Congress pact worked smoothly enough until early 1964 when questions began to be raised about Dr. Gupta's promised resignation. The Jan Sangh, which felt itself in danger of being cheated, tried to bring about a no-confidence vote against the deputy mayor. Given its small size, it experienced difficulty forcing a vote. This was true for several reasons. First, of all the possible combinations in the corporation, one had clearly been ruled out by both sides—an alliance between the Jan Sangh and the Congress. The growing rivalry of these two parties in the state of Uttar Pradesh precluded local cooperation. This left the Jan Sangh with little bargaining space. Equally important, many persons in the three-party alliance thought the next municipal elections were so close that there was little point in precipitating a battle for a short-lived prize. Thirdly, even if Dr. Gupta resigned there was no assurance the pact would be able to elect a Jan Sangh member to the vacated post. The Republican Party appeared to be at a crisis stage. The Swatantra Dal also threatened to come unglued: some of Baloji's supporters were expressing increasing disenchantment with his leadership and with his personal ambitions; a few of these members were trying to get into the good graces of the Congress in anticipation of future corporation nominations.

The rift within the RPI was particularly interesting because it involved a conflict between the organizational and corporation wings of the party, even though many of the same persons were active in both bodies. While Dr. Gupta was a prominent voice in the local legislative body and was exercising influence in the Uttar Pradesh Republican Party, there was resistance to his leadership in the Agra City organization. This opposition crystallized around the issue of his remaining in office past the date promised in the inter-party pact. Thus, when the Jan Sangh wrote to the Chairman of the Republican Party of Agra (a member of the corporation) asking that action be taken by the party to implement the terms of the pact, the Chairman asked Gupta to resign in order to maintain the credibility of the party's promises. Gupta refused to do so.

Indeed, in May 1964 there was an organized effort to remove Gupta which involved a no-confidence motion signed by thirty-five members. Among the signatories were a majority of Congressmen, various independents, the Jan Sangh members, and even a few Republicans. On 16 June a meeting was scheduled on the subject, but by a quick parliamentary maneuver the deputy mayor assumed the role of presiding officer in the absence of the mayor and called the meeting to order, then immediately adjourned it. Other meetings were called on the subject and failed for various reasons; on 30 June 1964, for example, several pro-Gupta members objected to the matter's being discussed because the mayor (who was presiding) had failed to read out the motion within the stipulated time period. Efforts to dislodge the deputy mayor in 1965 also failed, partly because the Swatantra Dal led by Mayor Jain rallied to his support in return for continued Republican votes for Jain as mayor.

Before attempting to extract some general propositions from the behaviors evident in these local contests for office, it should be useful to examine the contests in Poona for their variations from the Agra experience.

POONA'S MAYOR AND DEPUTY MAYOR ELECTIONS

Superficially, Poona emerged from the municipal elections of 1962 with a more clear-cut set of political groups contending for authority in the corporation than did Agra. Indeed, at least until 1965, Poona's system of party government appeared to work fairly effectively, with the Congress and the Nagri Sanghatna being the chief contestants for leadership.

While the Sanghatna had about twenty-seven members immediately after the corporation elections, two of these (a father-in-law and son-in-law representing different rural parts of the city) defected very early to the Congress, allegedly as the result of Congress promises made to them of government investments in their underdeveloped constituencies. This left the Sanghatna with twenty-five persons elected on its tickets and three other corporators upon whom it could generally rely (a Socialist, a Gaikwad Republican and an independent); the Jan Sangh had five members. There were about twenty-five supporters of the Congress (including the two newcomers). The remainder were independents. As in Agra, the Jan Sangh viewed the Congress as its chief opponent; this meant that alliances for the Jan Sangh were largely restricted to the Nagri Sanghatna. In practice, too, many of the antimachine emphases of the Sanghatna and its associated middle-class appeals were in keeping with the style of the Jan Sangh. Thus, the few independents members held the balance of power.

The selection of candidates *within* the Sanghatna proved in the long-run to be almost as complicated a process as the formation of intraparty alliances, although in the first year it was relatively simple. The choice was B. G. Jagtap, a Sanghatna member with no partisan ties and high prestige in the Maratha community as an educator; the Congress responded with a Maratha educator from its own ranks; and, the Jan Sangh sought symbolic independence by placing in nomination its leader in the corporation (a Brahmin lawyer with experience in the municipal body going back to the pre-1947 period). With close to a majority on the first ballot—on the basis of Sanghatna and independent votes alone—the Jan Sangh gave its votes to Jagtap and he was easily elected (see table 6.4).

Similarly, while the Sanghatna backed a Brahmin member of the PSP for deputy mayor and the Congress supported a Backward Class corporator, the Jan Sangh entered a token candidate in the person of their one woman corporator; a single vote was also cast for an independent corporator on that ballot. Both the Jan Sangh and the independent members ultimately switched their support to the Sanghatna candidate.

In 1963, the Sanghatna put up an important financial supporter and active member of the PSP from the tiny Kirad community as its candidate for mayor and backed a Rajasthani Brahmin independent for deputy mayor. Together with the Jan Sangh, whose leader was made Chairman of the important Standing Committee in the corporation, this alliance was unassailable even against a highly-respected Brahmin Congressman running for mayor. Significantly enough, in its attempt to win a majority, the non-Brahmin Congress found itself supporting not only one of the two Congress Brahmins in the corporation for mayor, but they backed a rather outspoken anti-Congress Brahmin independent for deputy mayor.

For the 1964 elections, the Sanghatna turned to K. U. Pardeshi, a defector

TABLE 6.4

Coalitions for Mayor and Deputy Mayor Elections, Poona, 1962-67

(a) Mayoral Elections

Year	Majority Nominees	Party of Nominee	Votes	Opposition Nominees	Party of Nominees	Votes
1962	B. G. Jagtap	NS (Ind.)	32	M. R. Karle	Cong.	25
				G. P. Bhagwat	JS	6
1963	S. M. Kirad	NS (PSP)	38	B. P. Apte	Cong.	26
1964	K. U. Pardeshi	NS (Ind.)	33	J. V. Bhosale	Cong.	24
				G. P. Bhagwat	JS	7
1965	B. D. Killedar	NS (PWP)	34	K. U. Pardeshi	Ind.	29
1966	M. R. Karle	Cong.	36	B. S. Vaidya	NS (SSP)	29
1967	N. G. Goray	NS (PSP)	45	B. P. Jog	Ind.	16

(b) Deputy Mayor Elections

Year	Majority Nominees	Party of Nominee	Votes	Opposition Nominees	Party of Nominees	Votes
1962 (First Ballot)	R. S. Paranjape	NS (PSP)	29	N. K. Kachi	Cong.	25
				S. B. Limaye	JS	5
				D. H. Sharma .	Ind.	1
1963	D. H. Sharma	Ind.	35	B. P. Jog	Ind.	30
1964	B. P. Jog	Ind.	33	P. G. Satav	Ind.	30
1965	B. P. Jog	Ind.	33	S. D. Bhide	JS	31
1966	P. G. Satav	Ind.	36	S. B. Limaye	JS	29
1967	M. K. Gaikwad	Congress		(unopposed)		

from the Congress, as its candidate for mayor. As in previous years, he was a non-Brahmin. For deputy mayor, the Sanghatna backed *the same* Brahmin independent (B. P. Jog) supported unsuccessfully by the Congress for that position in 1963. Both of these men won and the fusion party was also successful in placing a Hindu Mahasabha corporator in office as Chairman of the Standing Committee.

This time the Congress went down to defeat in the contest for mayor with a Maratha candidate who had little chance of winning. The Jan Sangh, which had cooperated with the Sanghatna in 1963 and had put up only token first-ballot candidates in 1962 for mayor and deputy mayor, found the particular candidate of the Sanghatna not to its liking; in the name of party independence, therefore, the Jan Sangh nominated its leader as mayor and managed to win two votes away from the other candidates. For deputy mayor, however, the Jan Sangh saw its only non-Brahmin, P. G. Satav, bolt the party to enter the contest with Congress support. Satav, who had maintained close personal relations with some members of the Congress, particularly the leader of the Congress group in the corporation, did not receive the support of the four remaining Jan Sangh members.[21]

Growing differences within the Sanghatna began to appear more clearly during the following year. The mayoral elections of 1965 came shortly after the Indo-Pakistani war, and Congressmen in the corporation argued that the national emergency justified the continuation of the incumbents in office. They did not reach this conclusion until after the Sanghatna had made its choice of a new candidate. The latter organization, continuing its practice of recognizing various groups within the organization, nominated a Maratha hotel-keeper—the only member of the Peasants and Workers Party in the corporation. While the PWP had virtually no following in the city, the man (B. D. Killedar) was an outstanding local personality who was active in the formation of consumer and employee cooperatives and had taken a leading role in the relief work that followed the floods. As a basis for cooperation with the Jan Sangh, the Sanghatna agreed to back a Jan Sangh member for deputy mayor.

The Congress, seeing their support of the Sanghatna incumbents as an entering wedge to win office, decided to support them despite the protests of some of the older members of the Congress corporation party. These corporators felt it would be doing a disservice to the party to back a recent defector like Pardeshi. Those who argued on Pardeshi's behalf in party circles pointed to his responsible performance during his year of tenure. Not only had he acquitted himself well during the war with Pakistan, but he was prominent in the efforts to quell the Hindu-Muslim riots in Poona which preceded that war.[22]

From the Sanghatna perspective, the actions of the Congress were pure political chicanery. A member of that party, writing in his English-language daily, expressed the feelings of the Sanghatna prior to the vote:

> For the last three years, despite all the political differences these parties comprising of eminent men like Mr. S. M. Joshi, the Chairman of the Samyukta Socialist Party, Mr. N. G. Goray, Chairman of the Praja Socialist Party, Mr. V. B. Gogate, Leader of the opposition in the State Legislative Council and above all Mr. B. G. Jagtap, eminent educationist who is respected almost throughout Maharashtra and

several independents have been getting on "extremely well" and it seemed that the sailing would be smooth for the complete term of 4 years. The Congress however has been envious of the harmony and unity with which the Nagri Sanghatna has been functioning for so many years and time and again their leaders have been trying to bring about disunity in its ranks.[23]

The incumbent mayor argued that he and other members of the Sanghatna who were not affiliated with political parties were the victims of partisanship within the Sanghatna, including demands by the SSP for their participation in antigovernment agitations. In any case, he and four other persons left the Sanghatna and formed a group which functioned during the remainder of the life of the corporation in association with the Congress. On the basis of this support, the Congress appeared to have a definite advantage going into the 1965 mayoral elections, but in the balloting held on 19 October 1965, the Sanghatna nominee won by a margin of thirty-four to twenty-nine.[24] It is widely believed that a number of Congressmen defected to assert their dissatisfaction with a man who had bolted the Congress to stand against Sanas in 1962 for MLA and against the party later in that year by joining the Sanghatna. Most of these corporators returned to the Congress for the vote on the post of deputy mayor, which explains the reelection of the incumbent deputy mayor by a margin of thirty-three to thirty-one (indicated in table 6.4).

While it was little more than a symbolic gesture, in April 1966 the Nagri Sanghatna formally expelled Pardeshi along with one of his close supporters who had also been in the Congress prior to 1962 and three nonaffiliated members of the Sanghatna who were accused of joining Pardeshi in his effort to become mayor. Despite the temporary success of the Sanghatna in the face of the defections of 1965, it was now apparent that the organization lay in splinters before the end of a full term of the municipal body. In addition to the problem of defectors from the Sanghatna, there were increasing strains within the organization as the two groups which had emerged on the national political scene as the Praja Socialist Party and the Samyukta Socialist Party began to pursue separate political lives in anticipation of the 1967 general elections.

When the Congress came forward in 1966 with a nominee for mayor who was popular within that party, he easily defeated a SSP party organizer running on a Sanghatna ticket for mayor. Satav, who had been defeated for deputy mayor in 1964, stood again in 1966 and was elected this time with a vote exactly that of the Congress candidate for mayor—thirty-six to twenty-nine. Thus, as at the end of the two previous corporations, the Congress could claim a kind of dominance in the elected council, but (as earlier) it had come at the price of working with elements of varying shades of loyalty.

Indeed, internal conflicts of a more serious sort were beginning to mark the Congress organization in Poona in late 1966 as rumblings of factionalism began to appear within the local party organization.[25] Because some of these difficulties were not smoothed out in time to prevent a rather disappointing performance in the 1967 general elections, the party was doubly concerned about reasserting local discipline and loyalty in time for the corporation elections which were due to be held either late in 1967 or early in 1968. As a gesture of goodwill and, possibly, in the expectation of driving a wider split in the Sanghatna, the Congress agreed to put up no candidate of its own for mayor in 1967. Instead, it offered to support N. G. Goray, the national chairman of the Praja Socialist Party, for mayor; publicly, this was said to be a token of nonpartisan esteem for Goray on reaching his sixtieth birthday and a recognition of the role he had played in the nationalist movement. In return, the Sanghatna agreed not to oppose a Congress candidate for deputy mayor. This idyll was only partially broken by the entry as a candidate for mayor of the former deputy mayor, P. B. Jog. He was soundly defeated.[26]

By this time, however, all the principal political groups in the corporation were looking beyond the last days of the sitting body to the election of a new corporation.

OVERVIEW

It is impossible to convey much of the excitement and interest generated by these elections for municipal office among those persons associated with the two corporations and with sections of the politically-involved public. In the course of canvassing for particular candidates for mayor or deputy mayor, individual members and group leaders are approached by representatives or by the candidates themselves. Promises are made; in Agra, many members charged that a good deal of money changed hands. With the exception of the largely symbolic candidacy of the Republican alderman in the first year of the Agra corporation, all of the nominees for mayor or deputy mayor in that city were men of considerable means. This factor was somewhat less apparent in Poona, where group support was more often a major determinant of nominations and elections than personal influence or material benefits distributed to individuals.

Among those factors we have previously identified as contributing to the character of Indian municipal politics, the primordial identification of the candidates was only important as a subtle *threshold of acceptability* in Agra. Every major contender for office in that city was from a high-status group—Vaishya or Jain in most instances; a Brahmin in the case of Chaturvedi; Tandon and Mehra were Khatris. No Muslim, Backward Class, or Jatav candidates were put forward as serious candidates. Similarly, it was evident that Dr. Gupta's leadership of the Republican Party made it much easier during this period for groups like the Jan Sangh and certain members of the Swatantra Dal to work with the Republicans. As we shall see in chapter 10, however, this mediation by a high-status leader was not a permanent prerequisite for a Jan Sangh-Republican alliance.

In one sense, candidacies probably were equally reflective of status-group relations in Poona, where the Congress and Sanghatna contended for control of majority coalitions. Sensitive to its role as a meeting ground for Brahmins and non-Brahmins, the Sanghatna did not support a single Brahmin for mayor until 1967, when N. G. Goray's election was not opposed by the Congress; at the same time, the Sanghatna regularly supported Brahmins for deputy mayor either to cement its relations with the Jan Sangh or to win the backing of Brahmin independents. On the other hand, except in 1963, the Congress nominated non-Brahmins for mayor. The party apparently saw no value in trying to outbid the Sanghatna-Jan Sangh alliance for Brahmin support since the primordial criterion was not sufficiently determinative of group identifications at election time. Instead, the Congress pursued cooperation with other groups on the basis of factors which were only marginally informed by primordial considerations.[27]

Thus, to a considerable extent, primordial self-assertions in both cities were subordinated to the interests of political groups based on other factors. Ideationally, the parameters of cooperation were largely defined by antagonisms between the Congress and all those persons who identified themselves with state or national parties having an ideational basis: the Jan Sangh, the PSP, the SSP, the Hindu Mahasabha, and other party fragments. The Republican Party was of a somewhat ambiguous ideational character, but its primordial identifications and the inheritance of Ambedkar tended to keep it in opposition to the Congress.

While ideational differences existed, the nature of the two municipal arenas made specific electoral outcomes highly dependent on the temporary loyalties of those persons not affiliated with regular political organizations. The result was to give independents a substantial voice in both cities. While many independents were personally ambitious and highly oriented to those few material benefits available in the systems, they may have contributed in a small way to the performance of one useful function. They acted as a kind of buffer, stifling cleavages of a pronounced primordial or ideational character. Had such cleavages arisen, they might have severely challenged the capacity of these rather weak local political systems to produce office holders and make other decisions which would be regarded as fully legitimate in the eyes of both the participants and the public. Indeed, one of the more remarkable accomplishments of each of the systems was its ability to reflect in its electoral outcomes almost every political group's interests at some point in the history of the body. This encouraged the pragmatic, instrumental style characteristic of political behavior, decision-making processes and interpersonal relationships in both corporations.

In Agra, the fluidity of political loyalties exhibited by members of the corporation elected in 1959 may have been merely a transitional phase in the passage from Congress hegemony at the local level (as of 1957) to regularized party competition institutionalized in a competitive party system by 1967. We shall examine that possibility in chapter 10.

After the success of the Samyukta Maharashtra movement, the foundations were laid for a new and strong Congress organization in Poona. The municipal elections of 1962 found the Congress in the throes of a thoroughgoing rebuilding and recruitment effort; the organization was simply short of the necessary capacity to win the few extra seats needed to dominate a majority coalition. In its stead, the Nagri Sanghatna brought together a broad representation of personalities, ideational groupings, and primordial elements ranging from Brahmins to Mahars. Yet, the "internal contradictions" of that fusion organization paved the way to its downfall in much the manner of its fusion predecessor of 1952 and the heterogeneous Samyukta Maharashtra Samiti of 1957. In each of these cases, the organization lost a critical number of members to the temptations of identification with the Congress political machine. While the Sanghatna continued to serve as a useful haven for certain political groups even after 1966, the activation of other forces in Poona's political life lent a different texture to the Sanghatna's role in the municipal arena by the municipal elections of mid-1968, a subject to which we will return later.

7 SOURCES OF CONFLICT IN MUNICIPAL GOVERNMENT

In view of the heat generated by municipal elections and subsequent struggles over corporation offices, one might expect the policy-making authority vested in elected members in the two cities to be quite broad. In fact, that is not the case. Municipal administrators tend to dominate the focal processes of policy formulation; many of the activities of the corporations are mandated by their respective state governments. Legal limitations on local political autonomy are complemented by rather marked financial constraints placed on the corporations partly because of their dependence on their state governments for grants-in-aid and access to sources of taxation and partly because of their own unwillingness or inability to exhaust even those potential sources of revenue available to them.

Given this situation, a central question then becomes: In what kinds of decisional matters *do* corporators become involved? In this chapter we shall explore some of the formal legislative processes in which they participate; in chapter 8 our concern will shift to an emphasis on corporator-administrator relations.

While examining policy processes in Indian municipal government, it is useful to consider whether latent cleavages in the city or among the memberships of the corporations are made manifest in the raising and resolution of local "issues." As a corollary of this concern, we may at least consider whether certain *potential* issues are frustrated or "suppressed" by the powers and style of operation of these municipal bodies.

What we find, in brief, is that some of the effort expended on internal elections of officers by corporators is carried over to attempts to control places on corporation committees, but conflict subsides when matters of policy arise. Indeed, it is striking how easy it is to achieve a consensus in favor of or against many administrative proposals. Personal differences of opinion occur with respect to given proposals for specific action either in committee or on the floor of the council, but rarely do these differences reflect consistent conflicts between political groups over municipal affairs. Where partisan affiliations are mobilized, especially in Poona, these generally involve matters over which the corporation has no control—questions of national or state political performance.

THE CORPORATION SYSTEMS

Agra's Committees

Members of Agra's two standing committees—the Executive and the Development Committees—are chosen, for the most part, from members of the corporation. The exceptions are two members coopted to the Development Committee. Each body contains twelve members; half the members are replaced each year.[1]

The Development Committee:

The Development Committee is clearly the lesser body of the two with its main responsibility being the approval of construction plans in the city. It is also responsible for maintaining a Master Plan for Agra. The two coopted members are expected to bring a certain amount of expertise to bear in these processes[2] but, as noted in chapter 1, these positions have been filled on a partisan basis. During 1964, for example, one coopted member was the father-in-law of a Swatantra Dal corporator; the other was a Jan Sangh leader.

While elections normally reflect the operative political alliances for mayor and deputy mayor, once such elections have taken place, internal organization may depend upon interpersonal relations which cut across coalition lines. Rather elaborate maneuvering went on within the committee to select the two coopted members in 1964.[3] The uneasy situation which existed in the Tri-Dalir Pact by that time made it possible for the Congress and Swatantra Dal members of the committee to support common candidates—one from each group. At the same time, the Republicans, Jan Sangh, and the one non-Swatantra Dal independent on the committee agreed among themselves to back a Jan Sangh nominee. They hoped to split the Dal-Congress understanding by this candidacy. On the day of the election, three Congressmen did not appear at the appointed hour, and those persons from the Congress present tried to delay the meeting for almost two hours beyond the scheduled time. Finally, the three nominees were put forward; but the independent in the Committee further complicated matters by offering the name of a prominent Republican as a fourth candidate.

In the absence of Congress members, the Congress candidate's name was withdrawn, on the assumption that he now had no chance of winning. Perhaps reflecting the unhappiness of some Congress members about the ad hoc agreement with the Dal, two of the three Congress absentees suddenly appeared after this withdrawal. A vote was then taken which gave nine ballots to the Swatantra Dal nominee, seven to the Jan Sangh man, and two to the Republican. Thus, a situation had arisen in which the parties to the pact wound up contending against each other, while the Congress played something of a "balancer" role in choosing among them.

In the face of the efforts which went into politicking for representation on this committee, there was very little real interest in the work of the body. As one official viewed the situation, this was not necessarily the fault of the committee members.

> Plans take a long time to implement. You draw up a plan for development of an area and then have to begin the long process of land acquisition. It is often necessary to go to the courts for remedies. As a result of the Constitution almost everything has become justiciable. In an expanding economy everything becomes more valuable than it was before, and landowners always feel that they should get more. When they are not satisfied they run to the courts.[4] After the land is finally acquired, then comes the question of development. It takes much money to put in drains,

> roads and electricity. The Mahapalika will usually not have enough money and will have to approach the state government for loans and grants. After the land is developed, it is sold. There are all sorts of additional commitments like parking stands and the development of cinemas.

After basic improvements are introduced, rights of "colonization" are sold to bidders who handle the parcelling and management of land sales. Some options are available to the Development Committee in granting colonization rights and this engendered one of the continuing disputes in the corporation after 1962. The Republican deputy mayor, P. N. Gupta, who was known to be an active colonizer, was charged by his political opponents with trying to take advantage of information and influence available from his position to advance his own financial interests. On one occasion, in particular, a dispute arose when a resolution was brought forward in the general body of the corporation directed against the general practice of private colonizing; the deputy mayor, who happened to be presiding at that particular meeting, disallowed the motion.

In defense of the deputy mayor, a Jan Sangh member—also allegedly involved in the practice of colonizing—arose to contend that such activities were protected by the Constitution of India. The proposer of the anticolonizer resolution, himself a very wealthy man but engaged in a personal vendetta with the deputy mayor, argued that the question of constitutional guarantees could not prevent the corporation from acting against individual profiteers. This dispute smoldered throughout the last years of the Agra corporation and gave rise to a court suit instituted by the state government against the deputy mayor.[5]

While the particular conflict arose out of the work of the Development Committee, it represented a minor part of an ongoing personal conflict between Deputy Mayor Gupta and some of his opponents in the corporation rather than any great concern about the general principles bearing on the problem of housing the people of Agra.

The Executive Committee

The election of six new members to the Executive Committee in 1964 reflected the general alignment of forces in the corporation, but once the committee came into being, group conflicts similar to those in the Development Committee arose. These centered on the selection of the membership and chairmen for each of the subcommittees charged with oversight of the operations of the municipal departments in such areas as Education, Public Health, and Public Works. An initial list of assignments proved unsatisfactory to most of the members of the Executive Committee with the result that the party leader of the Congress and the leader of the Swatantra Dal group in the committee got together—apparently without their respective groups entering a formal alliance for the purpose—and drew up a new list of proposed assignments. One of these two men, the Swatantra Dal leader, insisted that, at the time,

> it was not a question of a group or pact but of the city's good. Out of seven members of the Executive Committee from the Pact, not one is really capable of chairing some of the important committees. The chairman of an important

> subcommittee should be as competent in the field as the
> officer he has to deal with. K. [a Congressman] is an audi-
> tor by profession. It is only right that he be chairman of
> that committee. It would be of great value to have him
> there. At the same time, N. [a Jan Sangh member] would
> like to be in charge of the subcommittee dealing with the
> supply of stores and contractual matters, but his brothers
> supply goods and are contractors even now, and it would
> not be right for him to be in a position where he could
> influence such matters.

Despite the supposed concern for integrity reflected in this comment, many corporators not on the Executive Committee—as well as some members of the committee not associated with a particular subcommittee—asserted that special advantages were sought for persons on the list. It is impossible to estimate the extent to which there were abuses of committee assignments; primarily, access to officials was seen as being of crucial importance to corporators. A position on a subcommittee like Public Works, it was asserted, allowed a member to influence the course of work by officials so as to favor his own constituency; however, with a few exceptions, most members were unable to cite specific instances in which abuses actually occurred. Suggestions were made that members in such a position reaped personal profit from the public because they were *thought* to exercise influence, even if they did not. Of some importance, too, was the public prestige which flowed to the chairman of a subcommittee.

In the course of observing one subcommittee, that dealing with education and libraries, there was no evidence of improper use of authority. The three-man subcommittee consisted of the Jan Sangh alderman (who acted as chairman), a high-status Congressman, and a Muslim member of the Swatantra Dal. They worked in close harmony with the Superintendent of Education. According to the latter, members of the subcommittee were free to visit the schools at any time and send suggestions for improvements to him.

Among its activities, this subcommittee inspected libraries maintained on a subscriber basis by mohalla groups and private educational associations. The corporation provided small annual sums to such libraries to aid in maintaining their meager collections. Similarly, the city was involved in providing annual appropriations to privately-managed schools in Agra.[6] Distribution of these municipal grants, which might have proven a source of conflict among corporators, did not seem to arouse controversy. Indeed, the patterns of aid followed by the corporation evoked no great interest or comment among elements represented in the corporation.[7]

Among its other activities, the Executive Committee acted as a reviewing agency in contracts let by the corporation. There seemed to be only marginal latitude for the corporators to make decisions in such matters, although occasionally charges of benefits gained by particular corporators or administrators were raised by other corporation members. For the most part, contracts were let on the basis of sealed bids and there was little direct evidence of corporator manipulation of results.

The kinds of disputes which arose out of contractual matters often had a personal side to them or were tangential to the contract itself. Thus, a minor issue arose in the corporation over the soliciting of bids to build sewers in 1963-64. Such bids were originally taken in February 1963, but the winner of that bid later backed out of his commitment. New bids were solicited, but only one person entered the bidding. Acting on his own authority, Deputy Mayor Gupta reopened bidding to the second lowest bidder on the first round. Conflict then emerged in the committee, not with respect to the bids themselves, but over the authority of the deputy mayor to act in a matter of this kind. As usual, Gupta's political activities and the antipathy of his small circle of constant opponents were at the heart of the dispute, rather than the substantive issue.

The closest the Executive Committee came during this period to considering an issue on direct partisan lines involved a contract for the purchase of uniforms for Class IV employees—peons and other menial servants of the corporation. The issue here was whether the Gandhi Ashram, the local outlet of the national *khadi* (homespun) program, should be favored even though it was not the lowest bidder. Congress members insisted that the Ashram be accorded special status because of its quasi-governmental nature; on the other hand, Jan Sangh and Swatantra Dal members argued that this was not a matter of sentiment but that the low bid should determine the matter. Portions of several committee meetings were consumed in a heated debate on the subject. The Executive Committee finally decided in favor of the Ashram but on the basis of an argument that the prices of the lower bidders were made possible by the lower wages paid to workers and the use of materials of poorer quality.

Executive Committee members in Agra frequently used their special access to city officials to call certain matters to the attention of the administrators. Many meetings of the committee spent time inquiring into incidents falling within the purview of particular departments. Responsible officials were called upon to answer questions, which frequently were framed in an accusatorial tone. These matters, rather than dividing the corporators, would often cause members from all political groups to "gang up" on a particular official.

Matters raised with officials may range from a failure to install street lights in certain parts of the city, to the status of a proposed smallpox vaccination campaign, to inquiries into how many Scheduled Caste persons are filling administrative positions at various levels in the corporation. It is common to find members of the Executive Committee acting explicitly as spokesmen of their constituencies' interests in these questions. They may occasionally extend this representational role to the point of presenting cases for particular persons from their areas bidding on property or contracts. This need not indicate impropriety, however, since other corporators are usually well aware of the relationships involved.

Poona's Committees

The committees of the Poona corporation are more numerous and diversified in their activities than are those found in Agra, as we noted in chapter 1, but the Standing Committee in Poona plays much the same role as the Executive Committee in Agra. It, too, processes many of the items due to be placed on the corporation's agenda; it is empowered to make certain allocative decisions with respect to contracts and appointments involving less than a certain sum. Because of the relative party solidarity in Poona in 1963-64, there seemed to be less personal and group politicking in the selection of members of committees than was true in Agra. Chairmen of these committees are elected by members of the respective bodies, but their selection is influenced by the nature of existing intergroup agreements.

Two important committees—the Transportation Committee and the School Committee—bear a more ambiguous relationship to the corporation. Both draw the majority of their memberships from among the corporators, but they are less directly influenced by decisions of the corporation than are the other committees.

As we shall see in chapter 8, the Poona Municipal Transit Company (the PMT) operates quasi-autonomously in relation to the corporation. It has its own Transit Manager, and elections to the Transportation Committee are based on four-year terms of office (unlike the two years for the Standing Committee) with staggered retirement periods. The result is that some persons not reelected to the corporation can and do continue to sit on this committee and make policy for the PMT that does not need to be referred to the corporation for review. Of nine members of the committee in early 1964, only four had been reelected to the corporation in the municipal elections of 1962.

The School Committee has been less of a source of conflict than has the PMT. There are thirteen members on the committee. Two of these are nominated by the state government; the remaining eleven are elected by the corporation for three-year terms. The latter may include three persons who are not themselves members of the corporation. While most of the regular committees of the corporation perform in much the manner of the Agra committees, it is instructive to look at some of the procedures and problems of the School Committee.

The Administrative Officer of the School Committee in Poona in 1964 was a member of the state educational service sent to the city on the basis of a formal request. Although the corporators are technically the appointing authority in such cases, the qualifications for this official have to meet the standards set down by the state.[8] Technically, too, the committee is subordinate to the Maharashtra Primary Education Board. The finances of the committee are reviewed by the corporation, but staffing and programming are under the Administrator and the School Committee. The corporation is responsible for appropriating money for programs and for building schools; the state government provides about 25 percent of the school budget and indirectly supports other programs operated through the schools by means of grants-in-aid. In practice, policy making is left up to the committee and the Administrative Officer with only occasional questions raised during annual budget meetings of the corporation.

The selection of staff for the schools is a potential source of political patronage. When authority in such matters is available to politicians, as it used to be between 1923 and 1938, it can be an important source of political influence. Staffing in Poona, however, is fairly well dominated by supralocal officials. A Selection Committee functions under the School Committee consisting of the Administrative Officer, an Inspector of Education employed in the service of the Maharashtra government, and the elected Chairman of the School Board. Considerable pressure is brought to bear on the latter to make particular appointments, but little authority can be exercised by the Chairman alone. Thus, in 1964 the Selection Committee had to fill fifty-five new teaching positions and cope with a turnover in teachers that resulted in total vacancies of nearly one hundred positions.[9] Nearly 2,500 persons applied for these openings, and there were 420 interviews held. As the Chairman (a woman member of the PSP) noted at the time, "The financial condition of the people is low today; so it is understandable that they will try for jobs in the schools." Although some corporators tried to use their access to the Chairman to influence the selections, for the most part they simply attempted to gather information about a constituent's chances of getting the position.

The corporation occasionally becomes involved in noncurricular disputes related to the schools. For example, there has been some disagreement among members about the wisdom of programs aimed at providing lunches and free milk to school children. Charges were raised against the expense of the former; only 400 students were receiving a skimpy meal of bread and vegetables daily at a cost of Rs. 6,000 a year. Rs. 1.75 lakhs[10] were also being spent on 5,000 students—third- and fourth-graders—to receive daily supplies of milk. Complaints were raised against the alleged poor quality of the food provided by contractors and, as one might expect, especially from corporators whose own wards were not involved in the programs.

On the whole, the committee systems of Agra and Poona call upon considerable activity by members of the two corporations. They are looked upon as positions of prestige and potential influence. Particularly in Agra, there is almost a pathological distrust of the possibilities of self-aggrandizement by members of committees. Distrust does not occur to the same degree in Poona, although there are occasional indications of bitterness when a person is not assigned to a choice committee. However, the great number of committees in Poona means, in effect, that almost every ambitious member has an opportunity to get on some body. There is no tradition of advancement or seniority on these committees, but specialists in certain subject matter areas may be offered first preference by their respective political groups to serve and be rechosen for particular committees. Turnover in memberships is rapid enough to ensure that many interested and qualified corporators can sit on most committees (with the exceptions noted above) during the life of a single corporation.

In sum, most of the conflicts which arise out of the committee system tend to cross political group lines in Agra; the social and ideational bases of political groups in Poona occasionally give rise to minor conflicts which might alternately be interpreted as based either on social differences or partisan cleavages, but these tend to be restrained by the functioning of a system bent on pragmatic political behavior by its major constituent elements.

POTENTIAL AND ACTUAL SOURCES OF CONFLICT IN AGRA

The few "issues" which aroused the transient interest of the general membership of the Agra corporation did *not* directly reflect some of the more important cleavages (primordial, ideational, and partisan) represented in the municipal arena. In contrast, personal conflicts figured prominently in corporation life; these were exacerbated by a great deal of personal mistrust among corporators, which made corporation politics very volatile at the time of the original study; that this was not a permanent condition was evidenced by the tone of municipal politics by 1968 in the wake of a major restructuring of partisan alignments in the city and significant administrative reforms.[11]

Ideational and partisan distinctions made little difference in the few instances where anything approaching formalized intergroup conflict surfaced. The nature of primordial forces in Agra created an obvious potential for Hindu-Muslim and caste Hindu-Jatav cleavages to be expressed in policy terms. Of those activities that we examined, however, only one occasion arose where communal identifications were marginally tapped, and even here the system worked to alleviate or suppress the potential conflict. Another area of potential disagreement was over the manner in which municipal expenditures were disbursed, but here matters were resolved by providing a few benefits to every member. Significantly, the one "issue area" which did serve as a focus for much debate in the corporation during the period under review—the erection of a new corporation building—involved the exploitation of personal and group animosities that were quite manageable within the framework of the municipal arena. We shall consider each of these three areas of corporation activity in turn.

Communal Conflicts

Despite the strong representation of orthodox Hindus in the Agra corporation (along with five Muslims and a large contingent of Jatavs), explicit communal conflicts on the floor of the municipal body were unknown. It should be recalled that the Swatantra Dal which reflected much of the shifting nature of partisan and ideational alignments in the city contained both former Jan Sangh members and three Muslims.

One of the very rare instances of an issue which evoked communal feelings, at least on one side, involved the location of several meat shops. As early as 1954, an official of the Agra Improvement Trust had written to the Town and Village Planner of Uttar Pradesh noting the "ruined condition" of the meat market located on one of the main roads of the city. He suggested that the Administrator of Agra might wish to convert the area to other uses or upgrade the market. Years of inaction followed, but after the corporation was created plans for a new market were finally submitted and approved by the Uttar Pradesh government, and the city acquired the land necessary to reorganize and improve the condition of the meat shops.

Only at this point (in 1964) was a petition brought by a Jain corporator from the area. (The Jains as a sect believe in total nonviolence and strict vegetarianism.) The corporator suggested that a school be built on the designated spot instead of the new shops. The presence of a Jain population in the vicinity obviously influenced some of the complaints, but nonreligious arguments were also advanced with respect to the health and technical features of the plan. Jan Sangh members, while avowing their support for overall centralization (segregation?) of such markets and their protection from public view, based their public arguments upon the meat shops as possible sources of disease. One Jan Sangh corporator charged specifically that a cholera epidemic in 1961 had been the result of unhealthy conditions in the meat shops.

When a corporation meeting was held on the new proposal in April, 1964, the issue took on a communal overtone because of a particularly irate Muslim corporator—a member of a Muslim Butcher subcommunity. He attributed the sudden interest in a school to blatant communal motives. During the debate which followed, many caste Hindus went out of their way to placate the Muslims on the issue. The following comments of a respected leader of the local cow-protection organization reflected the views of many supporters of the change in plans:

> At the time that the meat market was proposed, the situation was such as would permit the meat market there. Since Partition there have been very few meat eaters in the area, and the ones that live there may go nearby for their needs. It is wrong to think that the resolution is against meat markets as such. We have established markets already elsewhere; so we are not against them or the meat sellers.

Even the Republicans supported the new proposal and tried to convince the Muslims of the public benefits involved. This Republican backing carried extra weight because the ward was represented not only by the Jain but by a Republican Jatav and both men spoke in favor of the proposal in the corporation.

While four of the five Muslims reacted rather moderately to the change in plans, even they were somewhat concerned with the motives behind the alteration. As one Swatantra Dal member among them responded:

> India is a secular state, and we must live up to that. There should be no question of any change in the situation since the plan was first made and if we want to change the meat market to a different place, we should not say that it is just because the people there do not like it or that there is some change in the spirit of the residents. Since education is a nobler act, we might change it in that respect, but we should try to place the meat sellers in a better place or they will not have any faith in us.

Over the vehement protests of the Muslim Butcher (the sole Muslim in the Republican Party), the resolution was put to a vote and passed by voice. The principal dissenter immediately proclaimed his personal bitterness to the local press and observers:

> We have seen today the rule of the majority and the massacre of the minority. This is the first step toward abolition of the minority community. The meat merchants, who are all Muslims, are being deprived of their profession and thus are financially lost.

Aside from his being a Muslim, of course, this was a case in which a butcher was literally being asked to leave his own sheep ungored.

The only other instance in 1964 where a communally related matter came before the corporation involved complaints against unauthorized living arrangements made by migrant Hindus in Muslim cemeteries and mosques abandoned since Partition. Even a Muslim corporator who deplored the practice admitted that the ability of the corporation to act in such matters was limited; the authority of the corporation extended to supervision of plans for construction and overseeing buildings as they were put up, not to systematic supervision of the homeless or squatters.

Municipal Expenditures

The presentation and passage of the municipal budget is largely an administratively guided procedure in Agra and Poona, but following British tradition budgets are carefully reviewed, and the budget debates themselves constitute an occasion for the wide-ranging expression of policy sentiments and suggestions for action by administrators.

After being drawn up by the CEO, the Agra budget is processed over many sittings by members of the Executive Committee; significant alterations are rare in major departmental allocations, but specific items are sometimes influenced by the work of the Executive Committee. The budget is then formally introduced by the deputy mayor to the general body on behalf of both the Executive Committee and the city administration.

The deputy mayor's introductory statement in 1964 evoked a good deal of criticism from corporators belonging to the Congress because of attempts on his part to take credit for certain developments in the city outside of the corporation's control like the building of a major new hotel and the laying of a cornerstone for a new bridge across the Jumna. In the course of this "State of the City" address, Deputy Mayor Gupta also pointed to some of the specific projects undertaken by the corporation. The following list is a useful index of the kinds of problems and processes with which members of the corporation are principally required to busy themselves:

> The *Nagar Mahapalika* [Municipal Corporation] has not lagged behind in its support for the betterment of the city. First, never in the past twenty-five years have so many pavements and drains been installed in the slum areas, adding to the cleanliness of the city. In various *mohallas,* the plans for slum clearance projects were advanced. Secondly, the city was confronted with an acute shortage of water supply which has been admirably resolved. Water supply has gone up one and a half times and a new treatment plant is almost ready. Thirdly, we now have more public lamps and more public taps for the good of the public, which we mean to increase in the near future. . . .
>
> In the past we were not able to use the products of our slaughterhouses. Now we have a modern carcass utilization center under construction. Fifth, at many places new buildings for schools have been constructed. This year we have a provision for over Rs. 2 lakhs for construction of a new girls' school. Sixth, even though the present sanitary conditions are not satisfactory, the city is far cleaner than it used to be in the past. There has been an increase in the sanitary staff and in the money spent in that area. . . . In the past four years there was no appreciable epidemic in the city and the number of persons vaccinated against smallpox went up. Seventh, while the cycle tax has been cut from Rs. 3 to Rs. 1, there has been no increase in other taxes.

> Still, the income has "shot up." Eighth, there has been an increase in the wages of lower-grade employees and the general staff has increased. They are now provided with medical treatment.[12]

The discussions which followed the presentation of the budget saw the Congress fulfilling the formal obligations of an opposition party by attacking the local administration. Their efforts were frequently matched, however, by members of political groups nominally associated with the majority. Indeed, the debate tended to unite the general membership together against the administrators with the deputy mayor acting as the principal defender of the municipal administration. When criticisms were aimed specifically at him, Republican members would come to his personal defense, but this backing did not extend generally to the administrative wing of the corporation.[13]

Attacks were not restricted to the administrators in 1964; some individuals also voiced disapproval of the activities of the Executive Committee. As one argued, "only the members of the Executive Committee get the favor of the officials. The other forty-eight members are hardly able to get anything done according to their wishes." Several members of that body felt called upon to defend the committee for producing a deficit budget and asserted that the weaknesses apparent in local government were the result of both faulty performance by the members and the system in which they operated. As one commented:

> It is true that the budget contains a deficit of Rs. 8½ lakhs, but it is the responsibility of the entire house and not the Executive Committee alone. . . . Our expenditures have risen . . . from 2½ to 4½ lakhs of rupees a month and the major portion of the Mahapalika's expenditures are spent on the Establishment.[14] Our collection rates are barely 35 percent of the tax on house, water, and other taxes. The installments on loans have not been collected.[15]

After the failure of an attempt to introduce a parliamentary "cut motion" of 5 percent, the budget for 1964-65 was passed. An estimated expenditure of Rs. 22,521,926 (approximately $4.74 million) was involved, but this included repayments on substantial loans taken from the state government to build capital projects.[16]

While most of the budget was mandated for salaries and basic services, a few areas were open to corporator decision. The allocation of funds for minor public works was such a case and might have been a source of controversy, but the process of disbursement developed by the members not only prevented the emergence of potential conflict over the distribution of benefits to specific constituencies, but created a positive orientation toward the corporation especially among many of the low-status corporators.

Until 1959, distributive decisions were made by city administrators on the basis of their own perceptions of where the investment of municipal funds should go; many corporators claimed these administrative decisions were inequitable. Under the system devised in the first year of the corporation, each corporator was allowed to designate approximately Rs. 4,000 worth of work to be done in his own ward. At the time this proposal was put forward by corporators, primarily independents and Republicans, there was initial opposition from members of the Jan Sangh and the Congress. Some of the latter saw the approach as undermining any effort to develop the city along planned lines. A member of the Congress asserted,

> The city must be planned as a whole. It is a sheer waste of money in some places to distribute development money evenly. In my own constituency not much needs to be done on the small drains and pavements but we could use sewers and branch lines. I opposed the policy, but there was only a general discussion and not a vote. One trouble is that I cannot use the money for other purposes because the items are under specific heads.

Thus, even a member who felt the system tended to undermine the desirable goal of city planning did not feel strongly enough about the matter to press it to a vote. Part of his dissatisfaction, apparently, lay not with the policy itself but in the narrowness of its application.

Persons who favored the arrangement tied their support to a particular conception of their roles. One Swatantra Dal member stated a commonly held attitude on the policy:

> I agree strongly with the policy. Otherwise, what use is there in being in the corporation? People come with so many problems. If we do not have some funds in hand to get their work done, what good can we do?

Indeed, for a majority of members the program proved so appealing that by the time of consideration of the third budget there was an increase from Rs. 4,000 to Rs. 5,000 per member. This system of allotments also met the desire felt by members to avoid dependence upon other members of the corporation for the achievement of certain benefits to one's own constituency. Thus, in answer to a question raised about the allotment system, a Congress corporator responded:

> The members of the Executive Committee look mainly to their own areas. The individual corporator knows the needs of his people and can go about providing them with proper amenities. Of course, there is some misuse of funds but the allotment system is good in the broader service.

Similarly, a Republican member saw the advantages which flowed from a non-conflictual approach to allocations: "No other policy is really possible. Otherwise, there would be struggles in the corporation, and only the group in power would be able to get work done."

While views on the policy varied considerably at the level of individual corporators, no political group took a stand on the matter except the Jan Sangh, which officially favored a planned approach to municipal development. Of forty-three corporation members whose opinions were identified on this matter, twenty-three were favorable and twenty tended either to oppose the principle behind such equal allotments or to be against the specific manner in which the matter had been handled. As table 7.1 reveals, the Republicans were the political group most favorable to the policy, while members of the Swatantra Dal also

TABLE 7.1

Attitudes toward Allotments by Party Group: Agra*

Group	Favor	Oppose
Congress	5	8
Republicans	7	2
Swatantra Dal	6	4
Jan Sangh	1	3
Independents	4	3
Total	23	20

* Question: What is your attitude toward the allotment policy? Do you favor it? Oppose it?

tended in that direction. Corporators from the Congress and Jan Sangh tended to be less favorable, but they did not press their opposition.

The rather high level of satisfaction with the corporation evidenced by Republican corporators, described in chapter 5, may be related to their ability in instances of this kind to control at least a small part of the annual expenditures of the corporation for public works in a way which benefits the wards which they represent.

A New Corporation Building

At the time of my first visit to Agra, the existing corporation headquarters were located in the heart of an area congested with vehicular traffic near the Jumna River. The main building was crowded, poorly lit, and otherwise ill suited to even the pretense of modern office procedures.

As far back as 1945, the idea of constructing a civic center for Agra was put forward by an American advisor to the town planning unit of the Uttar Pradesh government. Serious efforts to begin the planning process occurred only after 1955. Initially, support existed for locating the building in the heart of the city, but this idea lost ground as truck traffic and general congestion increased. Finally, in 1962 an area was selected in the predominantly residential and institutional section of the city close to the major colleges of Agra.

It was only then that plans were completed for a three-story block of office buildings and an auditorium to seat a thousand persons. Because of financial difficulties, plans for the auditorium were eventually dropped. The office building was expected to cost Rs. 15.75 lakhs. For a time, there was a hope that some of the land not employed for the corporation building might be sold to businesses attracted to the area, but the city soon discovered that very little interest existed among businessmen to relocate.

At the time the city began to contemplate the construction of the building (in 1955), the state government extended it a loan of Rs. 10 lakhs. During all the years of inaction which followed, the municipality continued to pay interest on this loan. It was only around 1961 that serious estimates were taken on the work required for the building. Delays were apparently compounded by personal emnities between officials of the Engineering and Buildings Departments, who were jointly responsible for parts of the construction process. For a time, one of the elderly engineers in charge of overseeing work on the project was shunted aside to a lesser position by the CEO as a result of these quarrels. When this CEO left Agra, however, the new CEO was prevailed upon both by administrators and corporators sympathetic to the engineer to restore him to his former position.

Plans for the corporation building were finally available in early 1963, and construction began in 1964 with the expectation that it would be completed within two years; actual construction was completed in 1967. Part of this additional delay was due to a succession of mayors from different groups who fostered alterations in the plan. Minor conflicts also arose over such matters as whose names should be on a pillar (or several pillars) commemorating the participation of the "City Fathers." Another minor quarrel arose over plans for a dedication ceremony and the decision made by Mayor R. C. Gupta to extend an invitation in early 1962 to C. B. Gupta to lay a cornerstone—long before actual work had begun but just before the general elections of that year.

A more important conflict arose over land clearance prior to actual construction. The land chosen as a site was hilly; a decision was made to remove the hill. The state government was called upon to provide an engineer to make estimates on the work required. These estimates were intended to be the basis for letting contracts. The calculations of the government's "expert" proved to be staggeringly wrong, and the corporation found itself in the embarrassing position of having to enter additional contracts to complete this early phase of the project.

Groups opposed to the Swatantra Dal element in the corporation seized upon this matter to charge that corrupt practices were behind the delays and false estimates. Accusations were leveled particularly at the Dal's deputy mayor (L. P. Tandon) and at Baloji Agarwal, who were charged (rather wildly) with various financial manipulations during the electoral campaign of 1962 when Baloji stood for MLA. Tales of this kind were further embittered by insinuations of caste favoritism on the part of the deputy mayor toward the official in charge of construction—both of whom were Khatris. Given the rather restricted authority of the deputy mayor compared to the CEO, these charges appear to have had little basis in fact.

A series of partisan debating points were also made in the letting of the second round of bids on land clearance, since the job went to the second lowest bidder—supposedly on the basis of a decision that the lowest bidder had a bad record in previous work undertaken for the corporation. As usual, charges of collusion and "kickbacks" were raised, but these matters were never pressed beyond the level of venting mutual distrust. They cut across partisan lines.

In general, then, even the few occasions for conflict over "issues" in the Agra corporation tended to gravitate around debates at the level of personalities. Fears of individual or group advantage rather than deep-seated conflicts over primordial differences, ideology, class, or even partisan attitudes marked much corporation activity. With the exception of the Republican Party, whose members regularly and persistently pursued the interests of their community in the corporation through demands for equality of treatment, the other members of the corporation were virtually indistinguishable in corporation affairs in terms of their policy attitudes. The situation was quite different in Poona, where the corporation served as a major "staging area" for debates on political issues of the day.

ISSUE POLITICS IN THE POONA CORPORATION

The style prevalent in Poona was edged with partisanship, while less interpersonal conflict was apparent than in Agra. At the same time—and sometimes in a rather sophisticated fashion—ongoing conflicts between Brahmins and non-Brahmins were occasionally tapped in municipal decision-making; as we shall see in chapter 8, these antagonisms emerged particularly in connection with the selection of and support given to corporation officials.

Pervading much of the verbal crossfire of the Poona corporation was the fervent partisanship of those members committed to all-out opposition to the Congress Party. They made the corporation an arena for political discussions and constant debate over matters with supralocal implications. At the same time, however, it was possible for Poona corporators to approach procedures related to municipal development from a group perspective which was not tinged with quite the same antagonisms of personality apparent in Agra. Occasionally development issues did take on primordial aspects, but these were not usually functionally threatening to the local political order. Given the power of the non-Brahmins in the state, it was increasingly obvious that the Brahmins were the ones on the defensive.

Political Discussions

Because of the strong identification of the local Congress organization with the MPCC and the salience of national and state politics to the constituent partisan elements of the Nagri Sanghatna and to the Jan Sangh, the Poona corporation was frequently employed as a platform for the venting of political opinions about events occurring throughout India and the world. Often enough, the matters raised were relevant to the local population but were outside the scope of the powers of the municipal government. For example, a considerable verbal barrage and public campaign was mounted when the Maharashtra government decided to assume control of the electricity company providing service to Poona.

An explosion in 1961 in a plant belonging to the private electric company led to twelve days in Poona without electricity. When service was resumed, there were frequent breakdowns; many corporators complained of the mounting inefficiency in the company even in such matters as bill collection. It was no surprise or disappointment, therefore, when the Maharashtra government decided to assume control of the system in 1963. Many opposition party corporators, however, resented the decision to place the company under a newly-created Maharashtra Electricity Board rather than municipalizing it. The proposed board was part of a scheme for statewide electricity supply which ultimately would become part of a national grid system.[17]

Corporators belonging to the Sanghatna argued that the takeover by the state government was not in the interest of the city in two respects: (1) it foreclosed the use of potential profits from the undertaking for municipal purposes; (2) it raised the likelihood that electricity rates would be increased, since the state was expected to use urban profits for investment in the electrification of rural areas.

Congressmen, for the most part, went along with the government's action, although a number of them were hesitant in their support. They became defensive, however, as Sanghatna politicians organized agitations (including public demonstrations and mass petitions) on the subject. On the floor of the corporation, Sanghatna members attempted to mount a symbolic vote of no confidence against the state government, which led to a walkout by Congress corporators.

Substantively, antigovernment corporators argued that the city needed the income from the electricity company to maintain municipal services; with respect to this point, many Sanghatna members shared the following view, stated by one:

> Electricity should be the responsibility of the corporation in the same way that water supply and drainage are. These are all the same kind of corporation services. The government favors nationalization of heavy industry. At least they should allow local utilities to remain with the local self-government units. Government should give these profits to the corporations and *gram panchayats* [rural governments]. It is government's duty to supply electricity to the rural areas, but it is not good to take the money from the pockets of the citizens of Poona in order to do it.

The note of urban parochialism was manifest among many of the high-status members of the Sanghatna, but it took its most extreme form in the remarks of a prominent Brahmin independent:

> Many taxes are absent in the villages that cities have to pay. Let the villages pay more if they want certain services. If they cannot afford them, that is no reason to make the city pay for them. You go into some of these villages—I could take you and show you some time—and the people know nothing about politics. All they know is when the sun rises and how to have babies.

Congressmen, because of their loyalty to the state government, took the ambivalent position reflected in the following statement:

> I would have liked the company to be given to the corporation, but there is something to be said for the government's position. The Nagri Sanghatna had no real ideas about how to operate the company if it was taken over. The Maharashtra government felt that since the private company was not able to deal with the problem, neither would the corporation be able to do so. All the electricity in the state will be under the board and they can manage it well.

When pressed, several Sanghatna members admitted that the city did not have the capital necessary to renovate the existing machinery, but they still insisted that the facility could be run by the corporation by obtaining loans from government and retaining the old engineers and staff.

Despite the agitations of the Sanghatna, their protests were bound to fail because of the wholehearted commitment of the state government to the decision to go ahead.[18] From the viewpoint of the political groups opposed to the Congress, the agitations were important because they provided an opportunity they needed to mobilize public opinion against the Congress. This aim was also evident on other occasions when political matters were raised for discussion in the corporation.

Thus, while many of the members of the Sanghatna pursued a generally nonpartisan stance in municipal affairs, other members made corporation meetings the occasion for regular policy pronouncements. The former, despite some distaste for the practice, did not see fit to drive the matter to the point of an internal split.[19] Viewed from the ideationally influenced perspective of certain members of the Sanghatna and the Jan Sangh, the corporation was an important outlet for participants in the local political system who were frustrated by Congress majorities at the state and national levels.

When approximately two-thirds of the corporators were questioned about their attitudes toward political debates, only thirteen out of forty respondents saw the corporation as a proper sphere for such activity. Twenty-two others were clearly opposed to the practice. (Significantly, only two of the thirteen proponents were Congressmen and one of these was a recent defector from the PSP. Seven of the remaining eleven were in the Sanghatna: four from the PSP; two from the Mahasabha.) One of the Hindu Mahasabha members favoring the practice summed up the views of most others of that opinion:

> Poona is a center for education and a city of intellectuals. Much pre-Independence political thought originated in Poona, and movements like the one for the liberation of Goa and for Samyukta Maharashtra began here. That is why political discussions come naturally here. It was a Bombay case dealing with a discussion of the Imre Nagy matter [in 1956] that was taken to the High Court [and raised the question legally]. They held that the corporation could not discuss the matter, but then the Supreme Court reversed the decision and held that any matter under the sun was a fit subject for public discussion in a local body. If the corporators were given more responsible jobs there would be less political discussion.

This was by no means the dominant view within the Sanghatna. Eight of the twenty-two opponents sampled were in that group, including five members of the PSP. Indeed, one of the nationally prominent leaders of the PSP–a person who might have been expected to favor using the corporation as a vehicle for political views–indicated his own opposition to the practice:

> Subjects should really be brought up over which the corporation has some authority. When some people argue that it is a representative body [and therefore able to discuss any subject], they forget that there are legislatures and parliaments now and that unlike British times there is no reason for local bodies to be regarded as the main forum for self-government.

Still, given the opinions of the courts, there was no attempt to stifle those few corporators who stimulated so many of the political discussions. Therefore, any corporation agenda was likely to contain a number of such items which were either outside the authority of the corporation or not directly linked to the lives of the citizens of Poona. For example, an agenda chosen at random (for 8 May 1964) included the following items:

1. An omnibus resolution calling for the merger of Goa, Dadra, and Nagar Haveli into Maharashtra; the settlement of the dispute with Mysore over Belgaum District; and the resolution of the dispute between Maharashtra and Andhra over the distribution of Krishna and Godavari river waters.

2. A request addressed to the state government to eliminate the "flood line" established after the 1961 floods which prevented construction near the river.[20]

3. A congratulatory resolution for Poona film makers who had won a national prize.

4. A resolution calling upon the central government to abolish fines levied on persons participating in communal rioting in Bihar. (Proponents of this resolution asserted these riots were a natural reaction to similar rioting in East Pakistan.)

5. Condemnation of the Maharashtra government for its announced plan to divert funds originally raised for flood relief in 1961 to other functions.

6. A general condemnation of Pakistan for its mistreatment of minorities.

7. A request to the Minister of Public Works of Maharashtra asking that his department be made subject to the same rules as the corporation departments. (This flowed from the existence of different standards set by the two governments in the matter of setback from roads.)

8. A resolution calling for the granting of relief to persons with loans still outstanding to the government since the floods. (While the government had granted homeowners some tax relief, it had demanded a rapid rate of installment repayments on the loans.)

9. A congratulatory message to a local student who had won a sports event.

10. A resolution to appropriate an additional Rs. 6 lakhs toward the construction of an outdoor "cultural center." (The corporation had already provided Rs. 2 lakhs in its regular budget for the undertaking.)

11. On behalf of the Cycle Renters and Repairers Association, but in the name of a "socialistic pattern of society," the state government was moved to bring a halt to the black-marketing of tires and bicycles.

12. A proposal that the government's plan to build two-room apartments in Poona be modified to permit the corporation to build cheaper, one-room flats.

Only one of these items (no. 10) was entirely within the authority of the corporation, although even here a government loan might have been required. Many other matters were, of course, highly relevant to the lives of Poona's citizens, but the corporation was not the decision-making body in these matters. The two congratulatory items (nos. 3 and 9) were part of the normal routine of most legislative bodies.[21]

It should also be noted that fewer than a dozen members were behind the twelve proposals. Indeed, at least half the items were the partial result of the interests of one member, an independent associated with the Nagri Sanghatna. On three items (nos. 8, 9, 10) he was joined by the single Lohia Socialist in the corporation; on two (nos. 4 and 5), he worked with the leader of the Hindu Mahasabha group; on one (no. 12), he was associated with the lone PWP member of the Sanghatna.

While the origins of these items were limited to a few members, the discussions which they provoked were sometimes heated and consumed a great part of the time of meetings of the general body. The attention lavished on such discussions certainly attested to the relatively limited concern of some municipal political actors with those areas of activity where their authority actually lay. One exceptional area, however, was that of municipal expenditures for city development. There was much disagreement about the way in which such expenditures had been handled in the past, and should be handled in the future, but this was not an issue which those corporators dissatisfied with the previous practices chose to resolve in the manner adopted in Agra.

Municipal Development

There was a rather strong feeling in Poona that differential attention had been given to the major sections of the city over the years. This view was tied to a traditional difference in treatment between the eastern and western sections of the city because of distinct patterns of caste and class settlement. Before the floods, at least, it was commonly felt that eastern Poona, where the industrial workers and most of the lower-status urbanized groups lived, was given less attention than the western section. The latter was where many Brahmins resided and where the major institutional centers of the city were located. Whether merited or not, the feeling of deprivation was quite strong among corporators from the eastern part of the city, as the following statement by a Gujarati member of the Congress from that area indicates:

> There is partiality for the west because the chairman of the committees and the officials live in the west. In this part of the city there are more business people and minority groups. The officials do not pay attention to us even though we need road widening very badly. It was only this year after many years that we got Rs. 2 lakhs for the road repairs, but this is only for a few parts of the road. In the west they reconstruct roads all the time.

Corporators from western Poona insisted that recent demographic changes had altered the face of the city. As one suggested:

> Formerly there was a communal aspect to the controversy between east and west, particularly in the 1920s, but now there is little because Scheduled Caste people have settled in large numbers in the west. Very few differences remain. It is only like any city there are new parts and old parts and better houses are in the west because of the later development of that area. In the corporation, a majority are now from the east; so proper attention is given.

Some of the heat was taken out of the earlier conflict by the territorial expansion of the city in 1951. The addition of rural areas to the corporation added a third group of corporators to the body who were highly vocal about the needs of rural Poona for development funds. Indeed, an obvious note of exasperation with these members informed the remarks of a Nagri Sanghatna member who lived in an eastern, inner-city ward and was himself quite intense on the traditional east-west dispute: "The city is trying to do its best for the rural areas, but these people want everything in a short time, and it is not possible."

Development plans for the city included a considerable outlay for the rural areas, particularly in the light of the limited income derived from these sections of the population.[22] Still, rural representatives remained dissatisfied. One of the two men who crossed over to the Congress from the Sanghatna on just this issue, spelled out some of his grievances against the latter organization:

> Nagri Sanghatna members were on the various committees in the corporation, but they reserved only a small amount for the rural areas and were more interested in the city. I differed with the Nagri Sanghatna over the amount to be spent on the villages. I wanted to develop more roads and schools for the rural areas. There is a population of seven or eight thousand in Mundhwa and a population of that size has only four latrines. If a man dies, we have to go through the mud to the burning ghats. We felt we could do something if we joined the Congress because it is a big and strong party.

To obtain more systematic data on this matter, corporators were asked whether they would favor a system of allocations to the city's wards resembling that in Agra. Table 7.2 reveals a pattern where group status tends to be associated with attitudes in a general fashion. The lone Jan Sangh member favoring this proposal was a non-Brahmin who later left that party; non-Brahmin independents from eastern Poona received the idea positively, while high-status independents from the western part of the city were opposed. The dominantly non-Brahmin Congress—most of whose members came from the more congested sections of the city or from rural Poona—favored the idea. The bimodal Sanghatna was divided on this question. When we examined this breakdown more closely, however, we noticed a rather interesting factor at work: of the eight Congressmen opposed to such a policy, four might be identified as the "top leaders" of the Poona Congress corporation party; a fifth was a wealthy newcomer to the Congress who had been very prominent in the PSP. Among those favoring the policy, only one might have been identified as a major figure in the local Congress. This suggests at least the possibility of a cosmopolitan-local orientation at work: persons leading the Congress were less interested in specific constituency benefits than were the rank and file in the corporation party.

Among members of the Nagri Sanghatna, too, group leaders tended to be opposed to the policy while corporators more closely tied toward their territorial constituencies favored the idea. These views cut across groups within the Sanghatna. In the case of the PSP, for example, four members favored the proposal while seven opposed it, but those in opposition included the leading members of the party in the corporation, while none of the latter were favorable.[23]

TABLE 7.2

Attitudes toward Hypothetical Allotments by Party Group, Poona*

Group	Favor	Oppose
Congress	15	8
Nagri Sanghatna	11	15
Jan Sangh	1	3
Independents	3	4
Total	30	30

* Question: Would you favor or oppose a system in which a certain amount of money was set aside each year to be divided evenly among wards for development as members of that ward see fit?

Although this form of "localism" might have been expected to bear a relationship to caste, such was not the case. Brahmins interviewed were evenly divided on the proposition, and non-Brahmins of middle-status (principally Marathas) *opposed* the hypothesized allocation system by a single vote: 10 to 9. A Maratha Sanghatna member from an eastern ward pinpointed the thinking of some of the other members:

> An allotment policy is not right because there is no relation between being from an area that contributes a good income to the city and requiring more attention from the city. The present system is good where the corporation asks members to submit applications and then the Commissioner and the chairman of the committee concerned think over the need for the item.

In contrast to Agra, where part of the support for the allotment policy stemmed from a desire to remove decision-making authority from the hands of *other* corporators, this did not seem to be a motivating factor in Poona. The Jan Sangh Chairman of the Standing Committee in early 1964 was held in high personal esteem; his predecessors also drew little unfavorable comment from corporators. Rather, as several Poona corporators favoring the proposition indicated, the main thrust of their unhappiness was aimed at the slowness of allocative procedures not with the substance of those decisions.

Under the system as it actually operated, however, there were occasional dissatisfactions with allocative decisions. Political pressures were sometimes applied, although they did not necessarily assume a partisan character. Thus, in the relatively low-status Bhavani Peth constituency, there was a demand advanced by all four corporators in 1964 (three Congressmen and the Sanghatna mayor). They pressured the corporation into granting money to expand an existing school in the ward, despite the low priority the project originally had on the list of school construction tasks recommended by municipal officials.

A Congressman from another ward, viewing the political maneuvers involved in this case, commented:

> Since 1957 I have been trying to get a girls' school in an
> open plot in my constituency, but it has never been done
> because I was part of the minority in the 1957 corporation
> and now also. I once got the approval of the corporation
> for the plan, but then a priority list was drawn up. My
> school was fourth on the list. Bhavani Peth has a corpora-
> tion school already, but — was mayor from the ruling
> party. His request for an additional floor for the school
> building was eleventh on the original priority list, and yet,
> since the majority party controlled the Standing Commit-
> tee, the work was sanctioned and has already started. When
> I complained, M. and S., who are Congress corporators
> from that constituency, took the position that their constit-
> uency was benefited from this action and so I had to drop
> my argument.

From the same ward, the lone Nagri Sanghatna member proposed in 1963 (in
conjunction with a Sanghatna corporator from a nearby ward) that the corporation
acquire two and one-half acres of land for housing to be constructed under corporation auspices on the basis of grants available from the state government. This
proposal received unanimous support in the Improvement Committee but ran into
difficulties when it came to the floor of the corporation. A technical exception was
raised by members of the Congress, who argued that there was no provision in the
existing budget for undertaking the required expenditure of Rs. 5 lakhs. Because
there were several Nagri Sanghatna members absent, the Congress was able to defeat
the resolution and embarrass the Sanghatna politically.

The following evening a meeting was held in the Bhavani Peth slum area
where local residents expressed their anger against the Congress for opposing the
acquisition of the vacant land for development. Another meeting was then
organized sponsored by an ongoing group active in Poona calling itself the Slum
Clearance and Development Committee, an organization in which members of the
Nagri Sanghatna—particularly some PSP activists—had taken a leading part. At that
meeting, according to a newspaper report,[24] a Congress corporator from the ward
"said he would work to correct the mistake made by the Congress Party."
Furthermore, he is reported to have said that "to attract the attention of the
corporators and the officials on this problem, we will have a *morcha* [demonstra-
tion] on the corporation and I will take an active part in that *morcha*."

Since the Congress had determined to oppose the plan as politically
motivated and fiscally illegitimate, this statement by a Congress corporator was
looked upon with considerable disfavor. The member in question was brought
before the President of the MPCC, who happened to be visiting the city, and forced
to issue a retraction in which he blamed the Sanghatna newspapers for distorting his
statements.[25] In this matter, as in others, the intervention of a state party leader did
not seem inappropriate. As the accused corporator later affirmed, "It is his duty to
solve local problems."

Other allocative decisions did not appear to stimulate as obvious partisan
ramifications. There were occasional charges that decisions were made on the basis
of illegal gratifications, but it is impossible for an outside observer to assume the
approach of a prosecuting attorney in order to isolate the truth of these charges.
Thus, a highly desirable plot of land in a rural area was designated for a school at

the beginning of the decade. A prominent local manufacturing company offered to exchange some of its own land nearby for this corporation plot. The Standing Committee agreed to this in April 1961. No further action was taken on building the school for the following three years. Then in February 1964, a representative from the ward called upon the corporation to revoke the earlier exchange. He charged that the company had not been the owner of the land it promised to exchange at the time of the earlier understanding. This corporator also alleged that the land promised for the school would be detrimental to the health of schoolchildren since the fumes from the factory were asserted to be dangerous. The CEO insisted, however, that the exchange had to stand because of the earlier commitment made by the corporation.

In June 1964 the dispute was aired in the Standing Committee with the leader of the Congress group speaking in behalf of the company. (Opponents of the company argued that it was only about this time that the latter actually acquired the plot it had promised to the corporation three years earlier.) After considerable debate, the resolution put forward by the ward's corporator was passed rescinding the deal. Votes on the matter crossed party lines with a member of the Sanghatna joining two Congress members against the proposal, while the Jan Sangh chairman voted with a Sanghatna and Congress majority. Two weeks after this resolution was passed, however, the Standing Committee reversed its earlier decision and restored the original agreement. Supporters of this decision vigorously denied suggestions of impropriety and simply maintained their desire for the corporation to live up to its agreements.[26] Since the dispute crossed party lines, there was no incentive for the party organizations to keep the issue alive and the matter ceased to arouse the corporation's interest.

Thus, while the outcomes of issues were occasionally influenced by individual or territorial considerations, decisions appeared most commonly to acquire the character of conflicts in Poona when they lent themselves to organized partisan definitions. For much the same reason, issues which might have been stimulated by primordial factors tended either to be suppressed or converted into partisan values where those did not conflict with the desire of the major party groups to draw support from the broad range of political groups present in the city.

Primordial Politics

As in Agra, the two Republicans in the Poona corporation made use of their positions to promote the interests of the Mahar community. The effectiveness of such demands as official assurances that Scheduled Caste teachers would not be restricted to Scheduled Caste sections of the city depended, however, upon the willingness of other groups like the PSP and SSP to back them.

Thus, an adjournment motion was submitted[27] in 1965 by one of the Republicans and the man who was the only Lohia Socialist in the corporation, calling for favorable action by the central government on a list of demands put forward by the Republican Party (Gaikwad group) during demonstrations staged in New Delhi in support of greater social justice for the Scheduled Castes. Corporators from the various political groups made their views known on this motion. A Jan Sangh leader was particularly opposed to such "casteist" demands, but he was partially conciliatory in certain of his comments which justified conversions to Buddhism while condemning the conversion of Indians to Christianity or Islam. However, the anti-Gaikwad Republican, who was formally affiliated with the Sanghatna, attacked the demonstrations as a stunt and spoke against the motion; it was ultimately defeated twenty-eight to twenty-four. Under the circumstances, it would be difficult to interpret the results as falling simply along primordial or ideational lines, since some conservative members of the Sanghatna supported the motion as a form of disapproval of government actions, while several Congress members otherwise sympathetic to the cause felt it their duty to defend the government.[28]

In another area, that of language, a potentiality for conflict also existed. Given the pride in Marathi reflected in the Samyukta Maharashtra movement, one might have expected some differences of opinion to exist over the practice of setting up non-Marathi schools for groups wishing to have such schools. While one or two of the Gujarati corporators were unhappy with the extent to which their demands for more Gujarati schools were being met by the school administration, this was not an issue which had much salience for the corporation. Indeed, the Congress (which drew considerable electoral support from non-Maharashtrians and from Muslims who could receive their education in non-Marathi schools) served as an organizational dike against the development of linguistic cleavages by supporting the constitutional guarantees of education in one's mother tongue.

The Muslim population in the city of Poona was obviously in too weak a position to challenge the dominant Hindu community politically. In 1965, there were severe anti-Muslim riots in Poona resulting from the desecration of an idol located in the main market by a drunken Muslim. More than a dozen mosques and more than sixty shops were burned by local Hindu mobs in "retaliation." The leading members of the corporation did what they could to quell the outbreak, but it became evident that much latent anti-Muslim feeling existed in the city as a whole which could be exploited under certain circumstances. There was little that municipal politics alone could do to rectify this situation. The one communal issue which directly involved members of the corporation operating within the municipal arena is more interesting for what it reveals about the ideational divisions within the Brahmin population of Poona than about communal relations in general.

In March, 1966, a Muslim man and a Brahmin girl working together in a corporation office expressed their desire to marry. Parents on both sides tried to dissuade them. The girl's father tried to have the man transferred from his position; her mother was particularly set against the marriage. It should be noted that the mother was an active worker in the Jan Sangh and the father head of the office in which the two young people worked. The girl approached distant relatives who were associated with reformist groups,[29] but they readily pointed out the various hazards to intermarriage. When the couple held firm to their opinions, a local organization—the *Jati Nirmulan Saunstha* (Caste Removal Association)—decided to give the story some publicity, and meetings were held at which social reform groups and leftist political organizations congratulated the couple. This publicity provoked the Hindu Mahasabha into organizing several processions and protest meetings. At one Mahasabha meeting, for example, a woman speaker resorted to a rather traditional demand that "those who violate the codes of caste and community must have no place in the community and deserve excommunication." [30]

While Brahmins were associated with the Mahasabha, many of the leaders of the reform groups were also Brahmins. Thus, the Hindu girl's chief defenders were a Brahmin couple, both of whom were active in the PSP. The wife was a corporator and chairman of the School Board during the period of my earlier field work, while the husband was active in the trade union movement and sat on the state executive of the PSP. During the 1967 general elections, the issue of the marriage was used by P. K. Atre, a Brahmin *left-wing* independent active in Bombay and Poona politics to stir up antagonism toward the PSP and possibly to win some conservative support to his side in his race for MLA in Bombay City. It was also later used against the husband, who stood for the corporation in 1968 on a Sanghatna ticket. The Jan Sangh at that time rallied the women of his Brahmin ward behind a candidate with no previous political experience. Feeling ran high enough to cause the defeat of the PSP reformer primarily on this "issue."

In the corporation itself, the matter was brought forward in 1966 as the subject for an adjournment motion. The motion was sponsored by the *Maratha* leader of the Congress corporation party, who accused the PSP organizers of congratulatory meetings of seeking Muslim political support. After a very heated discussion, a corporation vote was taken on the motion which found a majority of corporators present opposed to the actions of the reform groups. [31]

In chapter 8 we shall see some examples of Brahmin versus non-Brahmin conflicts with respect to administrative behavior in the corporation. Very few cases of direct conflict over "decisions" emerged which smacked of primordial differences of this kind. One of the rare instances which might be placed in such a light arose when the Public Works Committee, in May 1964, considered a proposal that land be provided to the Peasants' Education Society, a non-Brahmin group. While conceding the need of that organization for land to build a student hostel, a Jan Sangh member of the committee argued that a grant to one group would start claims by many others.

The land in question had been used as a site by the corporation for training health workers for many years, but the city no longer used it for that purpose. As early as 1949, the Education Society had applied to acquire the property. Despite the objections of a Jan Sangh member that the organization did not have the capacity to build and maintain a hostel, other members of the corporation favored it. In one of the few formal committee votes taken during this period, the proposal was passed three to two with three Marathas voting for it (one from the Congress; two from the Sanghatna) while two non-Marathas (a Brahmin and a non-Maharashtrian) voted against it. However, once the committee passed its recommendation on to the general body, the controversy subsided and the caste dimension was sidestepped.

OVERVIEW

In contrast to studies of American municipal government which find decision-making processes to lie at the heart of local politics, there is a qualitative difference between those few issues generated by municipal politics in the Agra and Poona corporations and the stuff of political life in the two cities. For the most part, corporation members go about their legally defined tasks with a modicum of pressure from groups or "interests" outside the corporation and without much concern for the policy-making aspects of their roles. Factors which figure in their elections and their own perceptions of their responsibilities do not seem to foster a great commitment to rule making at the municipal level, although members regularly express a desire for greater authority over administrative behavior.

Rather, the two municipal bodies are treated by these political actors principally as rule-applying, rule-manipulating, and rule-modifying agencies. Furthermore, as presently constituted, much of the actual rule application is seen as an administrative task which follows from the authority vested in state governments and relatively autonomous local administrators. The result is that attempts to *manipulate* or *modify* the rules in favor of particular groups or individuals have become the lifeblood of the work of the corporators.[32] Occasionally there is a "spillover" of this concern to substantive policy areas, but the administrative nature of local government, as perceived by the participants, tends to reduce the demand among corporators for a larger share in the framing, agitation, and resolution of "issues" to little more than a rhetorical or partisan device. Certainly, corporators verbalize a great deal of discontent with their highly restricted policy roles, but their continued willingness to participate suggests that a direct voice in policy making is not a paramount aspect of their present role expectations.

Insofar as an analysis of political styles and the substance of municipal issues—both actual and potential—does emerge from this and earlier chapters, we can characterize the two cities somewhat differently. In both places, there is a tendency for primordial differences, which figure, at least modestly, in elections, to be subordinated to the need to build majorities on rather shaky group foundations. A safe Jan Sangh majority in either city might operate quite differently, but obviously an Agra Jan Sangh which needs to work with a Republican Party and with Muslim independents cannot afford to alienate them by provoking primordial confrontations. Thus, in a fashion consistent with the instrumentalism of Indian politics generally, primordial factors do not figure prominently in the few intergroup conflicts which do emerge in either city.

Similarly, while the ideational bases of political groups are not abandoned at the municipal level, there is an aura to urban affairs which the right to make pronouncements about national policy does not entirely obscure. Even if there were Congress and Jan Sangh ways to run a city, the structure of municipal government in India would not allow much experimentation in this regard. Partisan ideational tendencies (especially in Poona) do cause differences in outlook between the Congress, on the one hand, and groups like the PSP and Jan Sangh, but these differences bear only a marginal relationship to the authority of the municipal body.

Partisanship, in its own right, does seem an important factor in explaining municipal behavior in Poona but not in Agra. In Agra, personality looms larger in the few cases which provoked heated controversy in the period under review. A resort to conflict over personalities may have been a transient phenomenon in Agra—the product of a search for personal prestige in an unstable political milieu.

Certainly, personal prestige was pursued in Agra with a zeal unknown to most (but not all) corporators in Poona; it was out of proportion to the kinds of authority attached to positions like mayor or deputy mayor, for example. The uncertainty of political alliances and the great number of independents may have contributed to this highly personalistic and self-aggrandizing political behavior and to the mutual distrust evident in the system. As we shall suggest, a sharp reduction in the number of independents and a surcease to some of the factionalism evident particularly in the Agra Congress promised to contribute a less Hobbesian tone to local politics after the elections of 1968 than was the case during the earlier period of observation.

In contrast, the style of politics evident in Poona during 1964 was highly influenced—though by no means dominated—by the attachment of individuals to political groups. These groups (principally the Congress and the Nagri Sanghatna—Jan Sangh association) contributed to a pragmatic but more consistently structured series of behaviors than was apparent in Agra. By their preservation of these structures, they sifted out some of the potential sources of conflict which might have been seriously threatening to the continued health of a rather weak municipal arena. To a limited extent, this party system helped to reshape the style of operation of those disparate elements represented in the corporation into a form which could be handled pragmatically by the municipal system. Its share of this task was probably more demanding on the Sanghatna, which had to aggregate the interests of groups which were ideationally and primordially antagonistic, than it was for the Congress, which had greater resources with which to maneuver among groups, less need to appeal to ideology, and a more narrowly-defined primordial base.

Ultimately, of course, the substantive rewards which the municipal arenas were able to feed out to active participants were rather restricted. With the exception of a few allocative decisions, corporators had to look for nonmaterial benefits like symbolic recognition through municipal offices or nominations to higher office as outlets for their ambitions. Many expressed considerable discontent with the time they wasted in these municipal arenas. Yet, as we have observed, this was no real deterrent to participation; over time, the total number of municipal candidacies (including those of 1968) increased markedly in both cities with a substantial number of incumbents and previous losers continuing to run for the municipal body.

In summary, then, the municipal arenas of the two cities provided important outlets for persons of moderate political ambition, rewarding them with local prestige, some influence over administrative performances, and occasional decision-making authority in areas affecting constituency interests. In a "politics of scarcity" this is an accomplishment of no mean proportions. Whether these benefits hold any significance for the larger political system is a matter of speculation on which we shall reserve comment until the final chapter.

8 ADMINISTRATIVE POLITICS

A full understanding of the arenas in which corporator performances take place requires that we pay some attention to two dimensions of municipal life which we have only touched tangentially: those patterns of behavior characteristic of municipal administrative personnel; and that cycle of political activities at the local level which involve municipal political actors in national and state politics. This and the following chapter take up these questions.

An insight into one aspect of municipal administration was provided by an earlier discussion of the relations which existed in Agra between a particular mayor and the CEO; in chapter 5, the importance of administrative interventions in fulfilling the role of corporator was emphasized. Here we are generally concerned with specifying certain situational factors which tend to "politicize" administration. Given legal barriers against political domination of municipal administration in Agra and Poona, our problem becomes one of identifying some of those factors which draw the two "wings" of the corporation into a working political relationship—a relationship exemplified by mutual self-interest, as well as by conflict, bargaining and occasional concern for the public interest.

A system of national and provincial administration in the form of the Indian Civil Service and attendant subordinate services preceded representative democracy at the national level in India by over seventy-five years. Democratic control of administrative performances did not fully emerge until after 1947. Until that time, the ICS—after 1947, retitled the Indian Administrative Service (IAS)[1]—and its provincial counterparts were directed largely along bureaucratic lines.[2] Even if bureaucratic norms actually operated within the elite class of civil servants, such values only partially permeated the lower echelons of these and related government services and probably were weakly felt at the level of local government.

With few exceptions, where urban governments functioned prior to 1947, the administrative staff was selected by those upper-status members who composed the "representative" wing of the municipal body. To some extent the popularization of the corporation system after 1950 in cities like Agra and Poona constituted an attempt to "depoliticize" local administration by placing at its head an official of IAS training, with considerable autonomy in decision making and the authority to staff the municipal services in keeping with rules set down by the state government and his own sense of bureaucratic proprieties.

At lower levels of the municipal hierarchy, however, commitments to bureaucratic norms are leavened by responsiveness to those personal contacts and social relations which earlier permeated municipal administration. This is not to suggest that many leading administrators in the two cities are prone to simply

180

abandon bureaucratic standards of behavior. Many idealize the situation of administrators freed from the "burden" of politicians and capable of acting according to recognized bureaucratic norms. But it is important to recognize that, at least on an informal basis, there are tendencies toward responsiveness to democratically elected politicians today which were not systematically built into the expectations previously associated with bureaucratic roles in the two cities.

Agra's municipal administrators during my earlier visit seemed to be marked by low service commitment and high social integration with community life. Charges of corruption and indications that administrators served their own personal interests were a regular feature of municipal life in that city. While many of the same charges were heard in Poona, they were presented less shrilly, and there seemed to be a greater tendency toward professionalization which was accompanied by higher morale in the local administrative services. We shall suggest that these different styles of administrative behavior reflect (at least in part) a difference in the internal lives of the two administrative systems themselves, as well as the political atmosphere in which local bureaucrats function.

An additional factor, of course, was the timing of the introduction of the corporation system of government into the two cities. Thus, the advent of the Agra corporation in 1959 after seventeen years of relative insulation of local administration from public pressures left local administrators ill prepared for democratic politics and rather antagonistic toward dealing with corporators on a basis consistent with egalitarian values. At the same time, they were rather contemptuous of public demands for actions on matters involving individual benefits, even though their actual behaviors were often highly influenced by such pressures.[3]

In the context of over a hundred years of relatively continuous municipal life, most local administrators in Poona were institutionally habituated to working with politicians as equals and with the public as an accepted feature of the administrative environment. These were sometimes still regarded as a burden, but such pressures seemed to be more readily accepted as part of the normal routine than was the case in Agra. Thus, when a controversy arose over the "aloofness" of the CEO serving in Poona in 1964, several of the longtime administrators expressed the view that the CEO had handled the matter badly because their own expectations were in consonance with those of many corporators.

In this chapter, we shall emphasize the ways in which administration is affected by politics in Agra and Poona. Specific details of urban administration will be described only where illustrative of certain features of administrative behavior.

BUREAUCRATIC FACTIONALISM IN AGRA

Administrative Politics before the Corporation

Because of the limited tour of duty of a CEO, the permanent top officials of the municipal bureaucracy in Agra have played a key role in day-to-day administrative matters.[4] Under the old Municipal Board, the chief administrators were locally selected. Thus, in 1940 the board was fully responsible for choosing an Executive Officer. A Kayastha by caste, "M" was allegedly appointed in order to block the selection of a Muslim applicant for the same position.

Although charges were occasionally raised about his honesty and efficiency, this officer managed to remain in his post continuously for nearly fourteen years. When the Board was superseded in 1942, he became Assistant Executive Officer (AEO) under the Administrator appointed by the state government to run the city. In 1954, however, the Administrator who had taken over the task of operating the municipal administration after the collapse of the nominated committee dismissed "M" without charges on the publicly stated grounds that the new regime could not afford his salary. The only auxiliary help the Administrator felt he required was that of the Municipal Secretary, "B."

The latter was a Brahmin of a younger generation than "M." Born in a princely state of Uttar Pradesh, where his father worked for a large company, "B" received a bachelor's degree in commerce and then a diploma from the All-India Local Self-Government Institute in Allahabad—an organization which trains persons in some of the more technical aspects of municipal service—before going to work for the Kanpur Development Board in 1942. This career was pursued against the current of the political events of the time, for he was not politically involved. He entered municipal service simply, as he admitted, because "it was a hard time to get a job." After six months with the Development Board in Kanpur, "B" was appointed Secretary of the Kanpur District Board. In 1948 he answered an advertisement for an opening as Secretary for the Municipal Committee in Agra; he was serving in that position when the Administrator dismissed "M" in March of 1954.

When "M" was dismissed, he took the matter to the courts and won a favorable ruling in 1955 declaring that he must be restored to his post. At first, the Administrator refused to accept the court's verdict claiming that he had some right to determine the quality of the work being done and to act accordingly. Several informants suggested that "M" then appealed to state politicians—particularly to members of his own caste who held high positions in the state government—and to friends within the state administration. As a result of these efforts he was restored to his post in 1957 and was serving as AEO at the time the corporation was created two years later. In 1964, he was within a few years of retirement and had settled rather snugly into an administrative routine generally lacking in luster.

When the senior AEO returned to his position in the municipality, "B," who had assumed some of his duties, was given the option of serving as a second-level officer in Agra or holding a more responsible post as Executive Officer for one of the smaller municipalities in Uttar Pradesh then under supersession. He chose the latter course and went to another city where he remained until 1959, when municipal elections were held there. By that time, the new Corporation Act had been promulgated. It provided for two AEO positions in Agra. "B" was asked to return and was willing to do so.

Administrative Politics under the Corporation

Relations between the two AEO's, given the prior history of conflict, were correct but cool. Feelings of distance drawn from the past were compounded by other differences in administrative behavior. Many of the corporators spoke highly of "B," although they found him personally less approachable than "M." In this connection, one member claimed to have observed a change in "B" after a visit he had made to England for six months in 1962 under a Colombo Plan fellowship:

> "B" used to have a reputation for "fierceness" although he is a very honest person. People, including both politicians and lower officials were reluctant to go to him. I even tried to explain to him that dealing openly with the public and providing explanations for his decisions would not compromise him, but he could not understand this. Only when "B" had been in England for a time and came back to Agra did he understand that officials who acted openly with the public could still do their jobs well.

Various descriptions of the factional divisions within the municipal administration were provided by corporation members and subordinate officials, but the main differences were ascribed to personal styles. As one corporation member summed these up,

> "M" works with the staff on the basis of groups. He has his own men in every department. He puts them where illegal gratifications are the greatest and shields them when they are caught. "B" 's trouble is not dishonesty, but he does not know how to be courteous. He has his own group, too, and the quarrel between them goes on. "B" is defamed because he is rude and not of an obliging nature.

It was not only at the level of AEO's that differences among officials existed. We alluded earlier to political conflicts arising over the construction of a new corporation building; that project saw jockeying for influence among the AEO's and the associated City Engineers. The man who was the last Administrator of Agra before the creation of the corporation favored a particular man as City Engineer during his term of office; the new Corporation Act provided for a second post to take over the development work previously assigned to the Agra Improvement Trust. For this position, an Executive Engineer from the Public Works Department (PWD) of Uttar Pradesh was deputed for a year: the latter was nearing retirement at the time. Once he began his service in Agra, some of the other officials encouraged this temporary appointee to stay on in the municipal service. Indeed, it is alleged that charges of incompetence were brought before the Executive Committee against the regular City Engineer; many felt that the man in question had no background to undertake major construction projects like the corporation building. Despite doubts on this point, major responsibility was firmly under the control of the latter official in 1964, while the retired PWD Engineer was responsible for the other administrative tasks associated with the Engineering Department. Since the assignment of specific duties depended upon the preferences of each CEO, these responsibilities were subject to change with every new appointee and he, in turn, might be expected to respond to maneuvering within the municipal bureaucracy.

At even lower levels in the bureaucracy, rivalry for control of an office might sometimes become bitter. For example, two men had come into conflict over the relatively minor position of Superintendent of Property for the corporation a few years earlier. The older man had drifted into corporation work after a succession of positions. Born in 1926 into a Brahmin family of some recent political prominence and educated in the nearby city of Firozabad, he went into service at the Central

Ordnance Depot in Agra in 1944 after completing high school. Shortly afterwards, he quit that position and entered the bangle business in Firozabad. Later he assumed a position in a bangle factory in Bihar. When he fell ill there, he returned to Firozabad, but being a businessman did not appeal to him. Apparently his earlier associations with business had had status overtones for this Brahmin which he found repugnant at the time. As he remarked in 1964, "I felt the work of Banias was the worst. I have a different view now and see what a mistake I made."

As a result of his dissatisfaction with "Bania" work, the man joined the Central Food and Supply Service as a clerk—a position he held until the end of 1947, when rationing (which that service administered) was ended. It was only then that he answered an advertisement for an inspector's position in the Terminal Toll Department of the municipality. After holding various posts in the Tax and Terminal Toll Sections of the corporation, in 1958 he staked a claim to the position of Superintendent of (Corporation) Property; the corporation also has a Superintendent for Nazul—property belonging to the state but managed by the municipality.

The appointment as Superintendent of Property was contested by a man three years younger than the official whose career pattern we have just described. The younger man was born in the Punjab and received a BS from Amritsar with the expectation of becoming an engineer before his family was forced to flee their home in 1947. He joined the state government's mechanical workshop in Agra as an unpaid apprentice to learn the practical aspects of engineering, but family reverses soon led him to seek paid employment. Like many others in the Agra corporation, he regarded municipal service as an expedient until another position became available. None ever did.

To some degree, he was overeducated for the position he took, and this added to a sense of frustration apparent throughout his comments. Within the corporation he had held various posts in different sections of the administration. In 1958, he was promoted to Property Superintendent, although the older man also attempted to assert a right to that post. A series of legal claims were then advanced on both sides as the latter attempted to assert his one and a half years of seniority in the corporation over the younger man.

When the matter was first raised in early 1959, the Administrator ruled in favor of the younger man, but the other claimant appealed to the Commissioner of the Division, who overruled the Administrator. The younger man then appealed this decision to the state government, but it refused to intervene. He finally turned to the courts, charging that it was not within the authority of the Commissioner of the Division to pass on seniority matters. Referring to the followup, the younger man later asserted:

> The Act says that the Commissioner may hear appeals against the punishments given by the Administrator, but it says nothing about such cases of seniority which are not really punishments but merely a declaration of the situation. My plea was upheld but the then MNA [CEO] refused to enforce it. In the meantime, the office of Superintendent of Nazul fell vacant and [the other contender] received it. The MNA, however, felt it was a matter of principle. At this point, I wrote to the MNA that I would accept the ruling

that years of service is the only measure of seniority and not quality. If the MNA would make this a general ruling, then I would not have contested it, but he refused to do so. My record was better than [the other man]. The matter came to the attention of the Executive Committee, and I had to go into a long discussion with them. There were no rules of seniority formulated for the corporation at the time. The Executive Committee upheld the MNA, but I was allowed to file a suit against this ruling.

In this instance, the courts upheld the first decision—that the younger man was entitled to the post, even if the older administrator had been in municipal service for a longer period of time. As in other cases of interpersonal conflicts within the Agra corporation (among both administrators and politicians), there was a personal antipathy associated with the conflict which made cooperation in later years difficult. A contest over the office involved here took place despite the fact that—or perhaps, just because—both men were unhappy with their career prospects.

Administrative Recruitment

Despite its unattractiveness to some employees, the municipal corporation in Agra is the largest single employer in the city. In 1964, the corporation had upwards of 4,200 employees. As in the state and national governments, the administrative hierarchy was divided into four major classes: Class I, which included only six persons—the CEO, the two AEO's, the City Auditor (who belonged to an Uttar Pradesh state service) and the two City Engineers; other major administrators were in Class II. These included eight Assistant Engineers, various supervisory posts, and the Public Health Officer, who was deputed by the state government. While a CEO received Rs. 24,684 a year in salary and allowances in 1964, some responsible officers in Class II made as little as Rs. 3,960 including a "dearness" allowance geared to a rise in the cost of living. Below these higher administrators were the ranks of Class III clerical positions and the Class IV menial staff. The latter included "chaprassis"—the ubiquitous errand boys of Indian offices—as well as the sanitation and work crews of the city.

In terms of sheer size of staff, the largest department was probably the Health Department. In addition to twenty clerks on its home staff, there was a field staff of sanitary inspectors, supervisors and assistants of over 200 persons and 2,000 scavengers. The department also employed at least another 250 people in specialized services like maintaining vital statistics and running nine male and three female dispensaries maintained by the city, as well as two maternity homes and an infectious diseases hospital. Two other major outlets for municipal employment were the Education Department, which had about 500 teachers on its staff in addition to about 40 clerical positions, and the Municipal Waterworks with about 350 employees ranging from Head Engineer through clerks, meter readers, and mechanics, down to a crew of men assigned to working on the mains and dredging the river manually.

While some of the top positions were filled by the state government—CEO; Municipal Auditor; Public Health Officer; the official in charge of the municipal slaughterhouses—other high salary appointments were made by the CEO in consultation with the State Public Service Commission. Appointments to many of the low-wage positions in the corporation—particularly the menial jobs—rested with the heads of the relevant departments. Class III positions, involving salaries below Rs. 200 per month, were filled by a Selection Committee consisting of the CEO, the City Auditor, and the head of the department. In practice, this meant that much of municipal employment—though not the most important offices—was in the hands of local officials, since the CEO was likely to accept the advice of his subordinates in recruitment matters involving their own departments.

While prospective employees were supposed to be recruited by means of lists maintained at the state-operated employment exchange in the city, some corporation members suggested the system was not as uncontrollable as it seemed. As one pointed out, "Although all employees are recruited from the employment exchange, the officials know who are on the list and can pick the men that they are interested in." Thus, it was not unusual to find members of the corporation requesting officials to hire certain persons recommended by them and the officials finding it possible to do so within the terms of the law. In some cases, the law specified requirements like educational attainment or an examination, and a post would have to be filled on that basis, although it was sometimes possible to make "temporary" appointments without reference to such rules.[5]

The rather low salary scales of the corporation has meant, as we suggested earlier, that persons recruited to municipal service generally have not succeeded in obtaining better employment elsewhere. A prominent Congressman emphasized the difficulties inherent in getting good people to work for the corporation:

> The pay scale is not good enough to get good engineers and doctors. The city has to take people on deputation from the [state] government, and even then it only gets good people when they are newly enrolled in the service. They stay only a couple of years and then the city has to begin again with new people. Many of the [present] staff are of an old and inefficient type because intelligent persons prefer state and central service.

Among the top administrators in Agra, most of whom were interviewed, only a few uniformities in career patterns were observed. None of them had participated in the nationalist movement, except for the Corporation Secretary. Significantly, he was also one of the few low-caste (Ahir) administrators in a relatively high position. Most administrators belonged to the higher castes: Brahmins, Kayasthas, Khatris, Banias. The only Jatav municipal official was the female Superintendent of Female Education, a rather obscure post in the municipal hierarchy; indeed, the woman in question rarely appeared at corporation meetings or on other public occasions.

Many of the higher-level bureaucrats interviewed came from one of two kinds of social backgrounds: families with some minor *zamindari* holdings, or families already involved in some form of government service. Representative of both of these was a Brahmin subordinate official born in a village in a nearby district who left his father's small *zamindari* in the second decade of this century to live with an uncle who was then a subinspector of police in Agra. After graduating from high school in 1933, he entered municipal service as a clerk, partly because his brother was a teacher in the corporation schools and helped him arrange for the position. In turn, two of his own sons were employed in the corporation in 1964, although one was in a temporary position awaiting possible employment in the Central Railway Service. The other had met the local requirement of a written examination and was holding a permanent position in the municipal administration.[6]

While several of these locally-recruited administrators indicated that they had come from high-status families with some claim to *zamindari* rights prior to 1947, and others had family connections to some kind of governmental service, those persons regularly involved in the Uttar Pradesh state service were almost uniformly from families with histories of government employment. The father of one CEO had served as Deputy Director of Education for Uttar Pradesh; the Public Health Officer's father was also in the service of the state; the Chief Auditor's father had been employed by a small princely state; the father of the superintendent of the slaughterhouses[7] was also a veterinarian in that section of the provincial service.

Attitudes toward the Corporation

Agra's locally recruited administrators varied widely in their appraisal of the corporation form of government and their views about their proper relationship to the corporators. Several were outspokenly hostile toward the democratization process associated with the new system; a few roundly condemned what they called "political interference" and asserted that only by their taking a strong stance would the corporators learn to act properly since they admitted corporators "appreciated straightforwardness."

A CEO might regard democratic participation with some measure of composure, possibly because his own period as a local official was a temporary one. Thus, one Agra CEO in 1964 commented,

> The main purpose of having corporators is to bring the needs of each area to a central place. These should be attended to and this is possible only through representatives of the people. The corporators are driven by certain considerations. The administrators have to look into these demands and see if the need is genuine.

Other administrators were not so sanguine. They complained particularly about the "inefficiency" introduced by the corporators into municipal business as well as the impropriety of many of the demands made by them. A senior official stressed the former in the following terms:

> In the Administrator's regime, projects were pushed, but now it is very difficult to do things speedily. It used to be possible to implement a scheme in a year and a half, but now it takes seven or eight years. The "vested interests" have increased in power with the coming of the corporation. We cannot proceed with any scheme. For ten years, we have been trying to get a market of a modern sort in the area around the present Mahapalika, but the shopkeepers have influence on the members and nothing is done.

According to the comments of other officials, "vested interests" sometimes included corporation employees. Thus, an official charged,

> Employees are no longer inclined to perform their duties as they ought to because many are connected with the corporators. They look to the corporators to influence matters in the corporation and help them.

The high-status (if not high economic) origins of many of the administrative officials may have been reflected in the particular contempt they displayed toward the low-status corporators. With great frequency, administrators referred to their negative performances and the lack of "quality" available but they took comfort in the ultimate authority they felt was vested in the CEO. As one official summed up this view of corporator-administrator relations, "They can only ask the MNA [Mukhya Nagar Adhikari] to do things; they cannot make any orders."

To a limited extent, the MNA (CEO) may on his own feel some personal responsibility in consulting with the leading politicians of the corporation, particularly the mayor. An Agra CEO remarked in this respect,

> While the entire power of the corporation is in the MNA, the mayor commands the respect of the corporation and he comes to know the feelings of the people. When the MNA takes action, he should inform the mayor. It is always better if he knows what is happening.

In this regard, CEO's may internalize democratic norms more readily than do some subordinate officials.

The mayor, of course, plays no official role in the selection of CEO's, but if the position is held by an important local political figure with connections to the state government, he may be consulted informally by state officials. Although this did not seem to have happened in Agra during the period under review, an Agra administrator suggested how the process might work:

> Sometimes mayors request the Chief Minister for a certain man and if he has been able to meet all the other qualifications, he may be appointed. This involves someone who has had senior charges in the state for perhaps fifteen or sixteen years. By this length of time in senior posts in the state, he is known to certain people even if he is not directly approached on the matter.

In an earlier chapter, we examined a case in which an Agra mayor and CEO were supposed to have operated closely, presumably as a result of the partisan influence which the mayor was able to exercise in Uttar Pradesh. Given the factionalism of Uttar Pradesh politics during the period, persons in the administrative services had to be careful in maneuvering around political minefields. Thus, a CEO who might be able to cope with the factionalism surrounding one post in the state could find himself in difficulty with key people in another.

Indeed, this was the case with one of the first CEO's in Agra. He served at the time of the transition from the Administrator regime to the corporation and was highly regarded by Agra corporators as an able administrator willing to work with the members. At the end of his term in Agra, he was transferred to another KAVAL city and there ran into intraparty conflicts within the Congress organization. Agra newspapers in 1964 carried charges made by one faction in that city that he had favored the other Congress faction within the corporation.[8] Under such circumstances, the administrator caught in the middle may seek a transfer. In the short run such events may be taken in stride, but a career can be damaged if a man gains a reputation for not being able to cope with local politicians. It is, therefore, in his own career interest to maintain a good relationship with them.[9]

Of a somewhat different character was a conflict which arose around a new Muslim CEO who came to Agra in the second part of 1964. Within about six months after his arrival he found himself in considerable difficulty with members of the Congress Corporation Party, who took the lead in accusing him of abuse of his office to his own material advantage; allegations of communal favoritism were also raised in connection with practices which the CEO allegedly followed in accepting bids for land development in Agra and in his relations with corporation employees. Several corporators, apparently with the help of certain subordinate officials of the corporation, brought these matters to the attention of state leaders.[10] As a result of these charges and others arising out of activities in which the CEO allegedly engaged while serving in a state post in Lucknow before his assignment to Agra, he was suspended, and a closed administrative trial was conducted under the direction of a senior IAS officer. Ultimately, charges against the CEO were dropped and he was restored to the service. While some administrative officials interviewed in Agra in 1968 felt the charges against the official were unjustified, corporators were more doubtful. A highly respected Congress corporator active in the raising of the charges asserted, "The bureaucracy in India is united in doing wrong, and no one can actually bring a successful action against an IAS officer. It is like a dictatorship."

Indeed, the characteristic tone of relations between corporators and administrators in Agra in 1964 (as in the case of relations among corporators) was one of mutual distrust. Some slight changes have taken place in the climate of relations since that time because of events which we shall detail in the next section, but the perspectives of the administrator cited below reflect much of the earlier sentiment:

> The officials have great troubles from the corporators. They want to interfere in administration. During the Board, there was not much intrusion. There was the Chairman and one or two strong members who had some say. Now they want to see us all the time. There are some good members, but the majority are not. A few are sober and justified, but most want to have the officers connive with their parties and want us to do anything for them. If we do not cooperate they will criticize the officials in the Executive Committee, in the Mahapalika or to our superiors. They make all sorts of charges.

Recent Events in Agra Administration

In the four years between 1964 and 1968, the administration of Agra underwent considerable change in both personnel and organization. During this period, too, the city experienced Administrator rule from February 1966 (when the corporation was superseded) through the first quarter of 1968, when elections for the new corporation were held.

Several administrators commented favorably on what they regarded as the successes of the Administrator system, including its capacity to act in building up certain upper-status sections of the city and raising house and water taxes—moves which corporators might have been reluctant to endorse. Corporators, on the other hand, generally remarked that many improprieties and considerable corruption had occurred under the Administrator regime.

For some time prior to 1964, some corporators and many of the top administrators in the municipal body had sought to "provincialize" municipal services. On the one hand, corporators felt that corruption was increased by the ability of officers to maintain permanent relationships with persons in the city. From the perspective of the administrators, there was a hope that provincialization would increase their salary ranges and bring them other benefits associated with state employment—benefits which were otherwise not available in a financially backward municipality like Agra. Resolutions on the subject were put forward at various times by the mayors of the larger cities of Uttar Pradesh, by the Executive and Assistant Executive Officers of major cities, and by other bodies of local employees.

Tentative steps toward provincialization were taken by the State Legislative Assembly in 1965 and 1966 while Charan Singh, then a member of the Congress, was Minister for Local Self-government in the Uttar Pradesh Government. When the act provincializing municipal services was passed in 1966, it was generally believed that the government would provide extra benefits to persons falling under it such as house allowances for those transferred. As it turned out, increases in income were slight and other drawbacks were soon discovered.[11] Of the hundred top posts in Agra, about twenty persons had moved between July 1966, when the new rules went into effect, and mid-1968. Interviewees, including both administrators and corporators, complained about the disruption caused in corporation business, although they conceded that many of the new men were of high quality. At the same time, local administrators subject to the act were busy attempting to prevent their own transfers—in large part because of the expense of moving their families and the upset to their regular style of life.

One administrator, who had been transferred to a nearby city to which he planned to commute, already foresaw the possibility that if he was dissatisfied with his new assignment he would have "to manipulate in the services to come back to Agra." This suggested a potential for intra-administrative confusion and self-serving in Uttar Pradesh which threatened to be as dangerous as anything under the old system.

Among the first to be transferred was the senior AEO. He was moved to Kanpur, but died shortly after taking up his new post. The junior AEO remained in Agra for another year but was then supposed to go to Lucknow. Because of serious illness in his family, he remained in Agra for a time and then was sent to Kanpur. Allegedly through the influence of friends of the recently investigated CEO, he spent the following year being shunted around among Kanpur, Lucknow and, most recently, Varanasi. It was generally believed that he was being "punished" by these IAS officers since, as one lower official stated, " 'B' is thought to have had a hand in making the corporators angry with [the former CEO] ."[12]

By 1968, increasing pressure was being applied by administrators from Agra to prevent transfers. A former corporator claimed that,

> some persons enter the municipal services only because they want to stay in their native places where their families are living. This new system upsets that arrangement, and we will find it harder to attract some good people at the lower levels. The corporation also made provisions for housing to municipal employees on cheap loans, but now the people who invested in that housing will be in some difficulty. They may have to give the places out to tenants, which people do not like to do after investing in a place, or they will try to sell the houses but new employees will not want to buy them.

The resentment of the intermediate-level employees was especially marked. They felt improperly included among those subject to transfer. At their behest, one of the first actions taken by the newly elected corporators in 1968 was to introduce resolutions calling upon the state government to cease transfers of subordinate officials. Both the Jan Sangh and the Congress introduced such resolutions in mid-1968—indicative of the ways in which administrative personnel may call upon the corporators to aid them. The two resolutions, which were somewhat at loggerheads, reflected the partisan interests of their proposers.

The Congress resolution merely called upon the Commissioner of the division to appoint an inquiry body to study the effects of provincialization upon the public and the administration. Until that study was completed, the resolution proposed that there be no additional transfers. As one Congressman expressed the concern of many corporators, "There is a fear that new officers will not take pains when they are not local people. Local problems are more personal. Now there are bottlenecks everywhere and a local man knows how to handle these things."

Like a good number of members of the Congress, many Jan Sangh corporators favored the general principle of transfer for the very top officers. A Jan Sangh corporator argued quite bluntly:

> The old employees think we can be used because they have so many personal affiliations and prejudices in favor of some of the members. The law is actually good because most of the employees are not honest and the majority who have been transferred are not poor. The top officers have been here a long time and have earned huge money illegally. They are running their own businesses and own big houses. In the interest of Agra, they should leave.

However, the Jan Sangh still put forward a resolution calling on the state government to be more selective in its transfers and recommending that all transfers be done in consultation with the CEO.[13] Up to that time, transfers had taken place without reference to that official. However, the Jan Sangh went no further in trying to restrain the operations of the system. On the whole, members of that party and other supporters of the two resolutions were quite willing to maintain a transfer system for the top municipal officers, but either supported drawing the cut-off point higher in the salary scale or were merely trying to placate the corporation employees without expecting that the government would respond favorably to their resolutions.

As we have suggested, the system was new and many members were unsure about its ultimate benefits. At the same time, the political situation was clouded in Uttar Pradesh because of the rise and fall of a non-Congress government and the assumption of state authority by administrators operating under the nominal direction of the central government in early 1968. It was generally felt that the non-Congress government which came to power in 1967 headed by the dissident Congressman, Charan Singh, did not have time to influence local matters very much. Charan Singh was himself highly admired in Agra; but most respondents felt his government had never functioned properly. About the only difference local administrators noted in their relations with the state was a greater frequency of visits by state ministers. A middle-rank official commented in the following terms about the effects of the SVD (Samyukta Vidhayak Dal) government which had ruled Uttar Pradesh throughout 1967 and the first two months of 1968:

> The Local Self-government Minister came here two or three times whereas his predecessors never came. His presence was not such a good thing because of the way in which he acted. He would bring together local people who had complaints against the officials, sit them in the corporation lounge and call the officials in to defend themselves against the public charges. It was not a procedure befitting the services. Otherwise, we had no particular reaction to the SVD government.

The experience under administrative rule in Uttar Pradesh and in the corporation received condemnation from Jan Sangh and Congress corporators alike in mid-1968. A Congress member stated a view commonly held by corporators at the time: "Administrator rule in the corporation was badly handled. That and the actions taken under Governor's rule [in the state] have raised the faith of the people in democracy." [14]

ADMINISTRATIVE BEHAVIOR IN POONA

While mutual distrust characterized many of the attitudes among administrators and corporators in Agra, the Poona situation reflected a closer working relationship. Indeed, where conflicts did arise—as they occasionally did—they were likely to be more highly exploited just because the routine expectations of amity were not being met.

On the whole, Maharashtra has had a reputation for being well administered; unlike the situation in Uttar Pradesh, of course, the Congress has not been as openly faction-ridden. [15] This does not mean that the party is above exploiting its control of administration for its own benefit, but it does mean that administrators are not paralyzed in quite the way they are in Uttar Pradesh. To a considerable extent, they are better able to function even within a politicized context because the parameters of their activities are relatively consistent.

In Poona, possibly as a result of these factors, superior and subordinate officials evidenced higher morale than in Agra and more capacity for action. They seemed to be younger, better trained, and generally more interested in their work than was the case in Agra. Given the greater education of the general population, they also operated in a milieu which was more favorable to the exercise of expertise. Members of the public were more concerned with citywide problems like slum clearance or the rehabilitation of the flood-affected areas of the city than was the public in Agra.

This does not mean that relations between corporation members and administrators were uniformly smooth; complaints about "interference" were as common as in Agra. Still, there was a depth of perspective in Poona that was frequently lacking in the other city. From the side of the administrator, one could find many comments to match the remarks of one official:

> There is a certain amount of political interference in running the department. I don't mind some complaints. That is part of the job. Corporators try to interfere in transfers. Generally I tell them that I will stick to the rules and they respect that, but sometimes if I find that their complaint is justified I will change my mind.

The corporators, in turn, tended to individualize their attitudes toward administrators. A CEO like S. G. Barve received high commendation on all sides. Others were viewed in different lights. Criticisms were pointed at qualities of personality, however, rather than at questions of partisan involvement or factional activity within the administration. This was certainly true in the case which arose in 1964 over the unwillingness of a CEO to treat the corporators with the propriety they demanded. It should be noted at the outset that his immediate successor fared much better.

A CEO Conflict in Poona

The CEO appointed in late 1963 to the Poona corporation had served during a brief period of his career as an Inspector of Prisons—a point frequently noted by members of the corporation. When appointed to the Poona corporation, it was expected that he would serve only eighteen months or long enough to complete the time before his retirement. The CEO already maintained a home in Poona, and the appointment was intended to smooth the way to that retirement.[16]

While corporators could cite no substantive issues which gave rise to the conflict with the CEO, the relationship proved difficult from the start. The major source of conflict was simply the general attitude the CEO displayed toward the members. Many of the Poona corporators are well educated, and, as a body, they are highly articulate. Furthermore, they draw upon rather good personal relations with members of the subordinate staff of the municipal bureaucracy, a source which provides them with ammunition with which they can probe into what they feel are the shortcomings of the administration. Under the corporators' frequent criticisms, the CEO in question found it difficult to maintain his own equilibrium and, after a time, he refused to attend corporation meetings or to maintain much contact with the corporators.

There is no formal requirement that the CEO in either city attend every general meeting of the corporation, but the convention of such attendance is accepted where other major matters do not call him away. In Poona, the particular CEO remained away for a period of time when he might easily have attended. In this case, some of the CEO's own higher officers expressed sympathy for the complaints lodged by the corporators. These complaints were finally brought before the Chief Minister of Maharashtra and other state Cabinet members in the course of visits they paid to Poona on other matters. Through the intervention of these state politicians,[17] a truce was provisionally arranged, but amicable relations did not last; a return to hard questioning by corporators soon provoked complaints by the CEO and renewed efforts to dislodge him by the corporators.

The persistent food crisis provided an "out" for all parties. The CEO, who had past experience in problems of rationing and food supply, was "temporarily" assigned to a position for Poona district with responsibility in that area. No CEO was immediately sent in his place, but after a few months a new appointment was made. The successor proved so popular that an effort to reassign him to a new post before his three-year term was concluded evoked a petition from the members of the corporation requesting that he be allowed to remain in the city. Indeed, he was still serving Poona in 1968. Without losing the substance of his authority, he had gained considerable personal support by consulting regularly with corporation members and listening patiently and amiably to their problems and requests.

Significantly, partisanship played little part in these matters. The Congress with its majority in the state government worked harmoniously with the Nagri Sanghatna majority in the corporation in removing the earlier CEO and retaining the second man. While some Congress members felt compelled to defend the earlier CEO as part of their regular defense of government appointees, they were not disposed to put that defense in black-and-white terms. One Congressman stated:

> The Commissioner [CEO] was a straightforward man. He did not like the foolishness in questions. He took the correct legal position that he could not be compelled to attend meetings and the option of the decision lies with the Commissioner alone. He is correct legally, but he might have followed the convention.

Indicative of the moderation of many of the Nagri Sanghatna attitudes about the same matter were the following comments:

> Even if you refuse to answer questions, there are different ways of doing it. Some members [exceeded propriety] in their questions, but the Commissioner should have been more accommodating. When answers are not to the point, the corporators have a right to demand correct answers. It is true that many of the same questions could have been asked directly of the officials with no great effort but some questions which expose inefficiency or wrongdoing should be answered. The Commissioner is due to retire and was not really taking an interest in the kind of work involved in dealing with the members and the public that a Commissioner should.

If one sampled opinion on a partisan basis, however, it was clear that at least superficially this issue had taken on partisan overtones in 1964. Of thirty-five members asked their attitudes on the conflict between the CEO and the corporators, twelve indicated various degrees of support to the CEO, particularly on legal grounds, concerning his right to behave as he had under the Municipal

Corporation Act. Fifteen were clearly of the opinion that he had acted in an undesirable manner, while the others took varying views: the quarrel was petty; both were wrong. Of the twelve defending the CEO, nine belonged to the Congress and only one to the Sanghatna; on the other hand, ten of the fifteen critics of the CEO were in the Sanghatna, while only one was a member of the Congress. This clear division reflected again the practice discussed earlier in a different context of the Sanghatna making extensive use of corporation meetings to attack state and local administrative behavior, while the Congress often found itself at least formally in the position of having to defend those performances whatever the real feelings of party members.

The Administrative Selection Process

In Poona, some authority is given to corporators in the selection of key administrators. While subordinate offices are filled by the CEO or department heads, a few of the top positions—those involving salaries of Rs. 400 or more per month—require the approval of the corporators. These include the two AEO's, the Manager of the Poona Municipal Transit (PMT) System, the Administrative Officer of the School Board, and the Municipal Secretary.

Occasionally, conflicts arise over these posts, partly because of the desire of non-Brahmin corporators to decrease the traditional domination of administrative positions by Brahmins and other high-caste groups. An element of this appeared in a dispute that began in 1964, when several posts had to be filled as the result of pending retirements, including that of an AEO.

The particular AEO who had joined the municipal service in 1935, was held in high personal esteem in the corporation. He had learned how to get along with local politicians at a time when the Municipal Board was relatively autonomous administratively. From 1945 until the creation of the corporation he served as the Executive Officer of Poona under that Board. Recalling that earlier period, he mentioned the limited authority that then lay with the Executive Officer:

> The Executive Officer could not even order a light to be fixed. The whole matter would have to be referred to the Standing Committee, and then someone from an area where there was not much electricity would object that such money was being spent on these things. The Executive Officer had no control over the staff except the peons. He could only make recommendations for suspension or punishment to a five-member Special Committee that the man was not doing his work but the matter might not be considered by the committee.

When S. G. Barve came to Poona as Administrator and then CEO, this official became his assistant. The Corporation Act for Poona originally provided for only one AEO, but Barve convinced the Bombay government of the need for a second officer to handle the financial operations of the corporation particularly in regard to maintaining contacts with state administrative agencies. The senior officer continued to oversee many of the other administrative responsibilities of the corporation. The second AEO serving in Poona in 1964 was selected by the state government from among persons in the state service.

At the time of the 1964 study, the senior man was due to retire but was expected to remain on the corporation payroll to perform certain special assignments in areas where he had already invested considerable energy. Pending the appointment of a new CEO, however, he continued to function as Acting CEO. It was expected that the other AEO would be recalled by the Maharashtra government, but a request was being made that the corporation be allowed to retain him—a request which was later granted.

With the expected vacancy in the senior AEO position, there was general agreement that the post should go to the Municipal Secretary, a Maratha. This, in itself, appeared to satisfy many non-Brahmins, since the retiring official was from a high caste (CKP). At the same time, the Municipal Secretary maintained excellent personal relations with many of the older Brahmin corporators. His service in the city had been of considerable length and was beyond the reproach of corporators interviewed. He easily fulfilled all the requirements for the AEO post, including ten years of local service and legal training.

Controversy developed, however, over his successor as Municipal Secretary. A Brahmin eligible for retirement in eighteen months was next in line in terms of seniority, but several objections were raised. Most of these were framed in terms of competence or lack of formal qualifications—he did not have a law degree—but intimations of anti-Brahminism were also widespread. At the same time, a number of corporation employees (including several non-Brahmins) actively campaigned among the members to upset the line of seniority. Rather than fight a caste-tinged battle to the finish, however, most corporators ultimately came to rest upon the seniority principle. It permitted the office to be assigned on relatively "objective" grounds. Members also argued that strict adherence to the seniority system would encourage persons in the municipal service to hope for advancement. Given the relatively short time before the Brahmin candidate's retirement, the matter was resolved in his favor.

In 1966, when the issue arose again,[18] lines were more clearly drawn. The man next in seniority was a CKP serving as Assistant Municipal Secretary. His major challenger was a Maratha who held the office of Labour Officer in the corporation. Despite the fact that the former was a very popular figure in the corporation, particularly among Nagri Sanghatna members, the latter amassed enough support from the corporators, and particularly from the Congress, to obtain the office. No formal vote was taken on the matter, however. The other man was shunted into a newly created position as Public Relations Officer for the corporation—a post which clearly carried less authority.

These events should not be taken as an indication of the systematic exploitation by the corporators of opportunities to politicize administrative positions or to depend solely upon primordial criteria for promotions. Both men were highly respected locally. Furthermore, an instance arose in 1968 when the corporators virtually abdicated their power to fill a pending vacancy for Administrator of the School Committee. The committee itself performed the task of initially sifting applications and emerged with a list of seven "eligibles." Three of these were referred to the corporation. These three included a Maratha, who was head of a leading non-Brahmin school in the city, as well as candidates of CKP and Weaver backgrounds who met the formal qualifications required by government. On the basis of qualifications alone, the Maratha was the leading candidate, but at the last minute a newspaper published a story that he had been suspended from Law School for a year for some impropriety during his younger days. While persons were prepared to testify to his subsequent uprightness, the man chose to have his name withdrawn to save himself and his supporters further embarrassment. Rather than settle for either of the other two candidates, the corporators fell back on making a request to the state government to intervene and select a person from its Educational Department to fill the position.

The most important instance of administrator-corporator relations in Poona, a case tinged with caste,[19] partisan, and personal overtones, involved the man who held the position of Manager of the PMT. It was probably the most focused-upon partisan "issue" operating in Poona during the decade and a half under review.

The PMT Controversy

Until 1950, municipal bus service in Poona was operated by a private company. In that year, the service was municipalized and the new Corporation Act formally established the position of Manager as the director of the PMT in association with a Transportation Committee. In 1954, the post of Manager fell vacant when the incumbent Manager was found lacking in some of the qualifications prescribed by the state government. An ad-hoc committee was then formed within the corporation to select a new manager. Working in collaboration with the CEO, the nine members of that committee recommended a man who had worked for twelve years in the corporation including five years as Superintendent of Taxes and was holding a subordinate position in the PMT at the time of his appointment as Manager.

This candidacy was promoted by a leading Maratha politician in the corporation, an emerging figure in the Congress, who sought representation of non-Brahmins in local administrative positions. The candidate recommended by the committee was strongly supported by all groups in the corporation and only one negative vote was cast against him—that of a corporation member then associated with the Sanghatna. Allegedly, this corporator maintained an animus against the Manager for actions taken against him while the Manager was responsible for tax administration.[20]

The Maratha Manager ran the PMT with a firm, if sometimes authoritarian, hand. Bus service, under his direction, was quite efficient, given the company's limited resources and a difficult situation with respect to spare parts. Still, the Manager made a number of political enemies. He allegedly fought the entry of a Socialist union into the PMT and looked favorably upon the Congress-affiliated union; he was often accused of favoring non-Brahmins in employment, although he insisted that the kinds of employment available in the bus repair shop or in driving buses appealed to few upper-caste Poona residents. Still, the Manager did see one of his missions as improving the economic position of the non-Brahmins:

> I am an officer who thinks of the poorer classes and works for their uplift. These are the people who cannot take higher education or have their own businesses. They can only serve others. I work to extract good qualities from my

employees. Otherwise they would pass their entire lives as coolies. Some people from the literate class claim I am for the non-Brahmins. I may be for the non-Brahmins, but I have never done an injustice to the Brahmins. I am moved by the illiteracy and poverty of the poorer classes and am trying to help them to improve themselves educationally. For example, forty conductors have passed the SSC exam[21] because of the inspiration I gave them, four or five conductors are getting a college education. Some persons addicted to vices like liquor have left those vices. I have myself visited the staff and impressed on them the need to economize.

Partly moved by his antipathy toward their union, PSP members of the Samyukta Maharashtra Samiti included among the planks of their 1957 municipal platform a demand that an investigation be launched into allegations of maladministration and favoritism in the PMT. One of the local leaders of the PSP, Mohan Dharia, was placed in charge of a committee to conduct this investigation, and when a vacancy occurred in the Transportation Committee he was also selected for the position of Chairman of that body. This effort to investigate the activities of the Manager ultimately failed for want of sufficient evidence to draw up a list of formal charges. The Samiti was unable to substantiate its public allegations against the Manager despite the efforts of the special investigative body; their task was obviously made more difficult by the refusal of the Manager to allow them access to his files.

Having failed at its immediate goal of suspension, the Samiti tried to use its representation on the Transportation Committee to bring the activities of the Manager under tighter control. Before any action could be taken, however, the Manager met with members of the Samiti and promised to act in accordance with the wishes of the Transportation Committee; the Chief Minister, Mr. Chavan, played a part in trying to reconcile the two sides. As a result of what seemed to be a general agreement, members of the Transportation Committee met and drew up a list of Fourteen Points to which the Manager subscribed in principle; Dharia agreed to drop all attempts to press charges against the Manager if the Fourteen Points were fulfilled within a few months.

While varying in their specific content, many of the Fourteen Points sought to decentralize authority in the PMT away from the Manager. They included items calling for delegation of more powers to subordinate officers, weekly meetings of the officers, and a regularized system of appointments and promotions. As one member of the Sanghatna remarked of the Manager, "He has tried to concentrate all the powers in his own hands. He controls the union and victimizes those who oppose him. He will dismiss people who oppose him without the slightest pretext." Thus, in the matter of unionism in the PMT, three "points" were raised including a demand that the Manager stay out of the work of the unions, that the two unions merge into one, and that the unified union should be recognized by the Manager whatever its political complexion. The Manager publicly agreed to fulfill these demands but privately he regarded them as an attempt to usurp his powers.

Equally important, some members of the Samiti began to waver in their desire to press the matter. Apparently under pressure from Samiti leadership,

Dharia halted efforts to pursue any further investigation or bring pressure to bear on the Manager. This caused considerable discontent among a few members of the Samiti particularly the long-time independent opponent of the Manager and a prominent noncorporator active in the PSP-affiliated trade unions. They demanded that the investigation continue, but major leaders of the PSP allegedly feared for the Samiti's stability in the face of a threat from a supporter of the Manager that he would leave the Samiti unless the investigation was dropped.

Disruption within the PSP on this issue reached a high point in February 1959, when the leader of the PSP union issued a statement attacking Dharia for not making sure the union received proper recognition in the PMT. Recalling that period of inner-party factionalism, one of those most involved on the side of the dissidents later remarked:

> The corporation members including those of the Samiti started backing out because [the Manager] obliged every-one by providing jobs for brothers and nephews. Then chaos started as the PSP came out of the Samiti [with the realization of Maharashtra]. I called a meeting of the Samiti and the Executive Council, which was composed of noncorporators like the publisher of *Prabhat,* passed a resolution that [the Manager] should not be kept. We felt that the Fourteen Point program was only an evasion of that issue.

The former Chairman of the Transportation Committee responded to the pressures for retreat with a report which spoke glowingly of the successes of the Samiti in the whole matter including the promise of bringing together the unions. In concluding that report, Dharia was quite explicit that he was responding to the charges leveled by his chief antagonist within the PSP:

> This committee has worked to make the PMT efficient and to increase the prestige of the committee. I feel bad that Mr. S.– L–, a responsible leader, has made charges that the Samiti has done nothing, that there has been no efficiency in the work, that the Chairman of the Transport Committee kept all the members in the dark as to what was going on—such are some of the false statements made by him. We have tried to follow the policy of the Samiti. We have told Mr. L– that if he does not like this policy, we will first go to the PSP and then the Samiti and we will try to change the policy, but he has not acted properly and gone through proper channels. Instead, he has made false statements and published that report.

Elements within the PSP attempted to smooth over the tough patches reflected in these statements, but the Samiti's collapse ended any serious effort to take the matter further at that time.

A new occasion for the venting of opposition to the Manager surfaced in December 1962, following the victory of the Nagri Sanghatna. At that time, an inquiry was opened by the police into the operations of the PMT on the basis of an anonymous letter sent to them charging that the Manager had been abusing import license regulations. The police turned the charges over to an arm of the central government, the CBI (Central Bureau of Investigation), which proceeded to spend over two years investigating the charges and tracking down every possible piece of evidence. Pending the outcome of that effort, the Manager was suspended in early 1964 but was kept on full pay. He continued to argue during this period that all he had done was to exchange import quotas with persons who had the necessary parts already in stock; this was done, he asserted, in order to keep the buses running. In early 1965, while a Sanghatna majority prevailed in the corporation, members voted thirty-one to fourteen to put the Manager on half-pay during his suspension. All fourteen votes in the Manager's favor came from persons associated with the Congress.[22]

In 1967 the CBI was apparently prepared to press charges against the Manager, but actual prosecution by the Central Government required permission from the "appointing authority." The CBI called upon the Government of Maharashtra to act in the matter. Instead of directing that action be taken, the state government sent a rather ambiguous letter to the corporation which was interpreted in two quite different ways. The letter stated that the Maharashtra government did not find it feasible to grant sanction to file a suit of its own. The implication drawn by members of the Sanghatna was that the corporation could still act since members felt that the corporation had been the appointing authority in the case of the Manager; however, Congress members interpreted the government letter to mean a *denial* to the corporation of any authority to act in the matter. They insisted the state was the proper and final authority in granting permission to file a suit. With a Congress majority now functioning in the corporation, the Transport Committee voted five to four in the spring of 1967 to reject the request of the CBI.[23] The Manager was restored to his post shortly thereafter and the matter was dropped from the Sanghatna agenda, although some members continued to view the whole affair in terms of partisan and primordial support—support provided to the Manager by both the Government of Maharashtra and the local Congress leadership in Poona. When asked what he thought of the operations of the PMT, one Congress member answered:

> There is no fault in its working. A few corporators wanted [the Manager] under their control, but he must look to the rules and regulations. He is a Maratha and there are a few Brahmin corporators who feel [the Manager] favors only Marathas; that is not so. He employs all persons, but mostly non-Brahmins.[24]

Administrator Attitudes toward the Corporation

Despite episodes of this kind, relations between administrators and politicians in Poona were generally cordial at a personal level. Several administrators devoted portions of their days to dealing with problems raised by the members. Most of those officials interviewed felt that the political pressures placed on them were a nuisance but could be borne with a certain exercise of restraint on both sides. A senior official later employed in Delhi reflected the attitude of many of the higher officers interviewed in Poona:

> There are many quarrels in the corporation often on smaller issues. While I was there, we planned schemes for water supply, drainage, and other things worth lakhs, and these plans were sanctioned with no objection. It is the smaller things which upset the corporators, and I realized early that it was not proper to take a very rigid attitude toward them on these smaller things.

As a correlate of this attitude, there was little expression of support in Poona either by administrators or corporators for the concept of provincializing municipal services—a sentiment that was common in Agra in 1964. Several Poona administrators commented favorably on Poona as a place to live; others stressed the need for municipal administration to be responsive to local sentiments. Thus, a senior official in the local health department stressed the benefits of localism:

> The health officer knows his own city and its problems in much the same way a private practitioner knows his own patients. It is true that if transfers are made, [political] pressures on the officials would be reduced—there is presently a certain amount of threats if we do not go along—but it is not a great fear that is involved.

Similarly, the senior Assistant Executive Officer remarked:

> Local men have more of a desire to do something for their cities than do men who come here only for a short period. Of course, if there is a bright young man, he may feel that he cannot advance too much in one place and so for him a system of transfers might be desirable. Others, however, might feel that it disrupts the education of their children and causes them additional expenses in moving all the time. I have been approached by employees of the [state] government seeking to come into the corporation service because posts here are not transferable. Pay scales may not be higher here, but it is a nice city and Poona is a good educational center.

Sentiments of this kind combined with a general tolerance for the behavior of politicians made corporator-administrator relations normally friendly if not always mutually beyond reproach.

CORRUPTION

Any survey of administrative behavior in the two cities should include some mention of the place of corruption in municipal administration. Complaints about corruption are raised against both corporators and administrators, but access to such charges is easier in the latter instance. The control of day-to-day policy means that temptations to corruption of the often ill-paid municipal workers are numerous. Certainly, the *feeling* was common in both cities that administrative corruption was rife, although comments on that score were probably more frequently volunteered in Agra than Poona. While condemning such behavior, many corporators recognized that the origins of corruption lay in forces over which they had little control; a common attitude was reflected in the following statement:

The reason for corruption is that everyone is running after the wants of life, and people feel there is a shortage of time. They regard the giving of obligations not as corruption but as reflecting the spirit of cooperation. It is an accepted habit for speeding up work. There is an exchange involved. It is not the spirit of corruption [which is involved] but a desire to push cooperation.

In a similar vein, several corporators made a distinction between "white" and "black" corruption. The former involved the payment of money to officials to perform services that they would have otherwise performed less rapidly; the second involved efforts to change probable outcomes. Those holding to such distinctions failed to recognize the tendency on the part of some officials to refrain from acting on the expectation that bribes would be forthcoming to stimulate action. Of course, inaction occasionally carried decisional consequences of its own.

Given the climate of opinion in these matters, most corporators saw wholesale efforts at cleansing administration as tilting at windmills. Some forms of undue benefactions were taken for granted (at least in Agra), like the practice of "rewarding" officials in the process of letting contracts and expediting large projects, even though such payments were ultimately underwritten by public funds through the necessity of accepting higher bids. The difficulties which lay in the way of attempts to suspend individuals or to investigate charges of corruption were felt by many corporators to be almost insurmountable. Corporators charged that administrators tended to drag their feet in such inquiries, and that the result of all of these efforts might be the dismissal or punishment of some underling rather than the person of higher rank who was ultimately responsible for the commission of such acts. Under the circumstances, as one Agra Congress member suggested, the only viable approach was "to make good use even of a bad man."

Typical of the kinds of incidents against which such comments were directed was the case related by a Congress corporator in Agra:

I was chairman of the subcommittee on health during the first year of the corporation, and certain bills for medicines for the city's dispensaries came to me for approval. These medicines had been purchased during 1959-1960, and the bills came for approval in February 1960. I examined them and found them vastly inflated. While I do not remember exact figures, a German stethoscope marketing for Rs. 14 or 15 was billed for Rs. 52 and there was a huge difference between the market price for boric acid and the amounts charged in the bills. Since I was an importer of boric acid, I knew the prices. A special committee was formed consisting of myself and two of the doctors in the corporation [corporators] and we discovered that there was a huge conspiracy going on between the doctors in the hospitals and dispensaries, the Health Officer and the people in the Health Department, and the sellers of these products. The checks were already prepared for my signature at the time, and the goods had been consumed, but I refused to go ahead. I stopped payment in March 1960. The amount of the bill was something like Rs. 18-19,000, but I got it settled for less than Rs. 10,000. I wrote the MNA of the time about it. Persons were suspended but not penalized. In fact, some of these same people were reinstated two or three years later.

For this member, the follow-up to his efforts was particularly disappointing. It reflected badly on democracy, he felt, that "some of the members prevailed on the officials to give the people a light warning but not to do anything further in punishment."

Within the two municipal administrations, the collection of taxes on goods entering the city called Octroi or Terminal Tolls were particularly prone to corruption. When one has a situation in which barriers are set up on all of the main roads leading into the city and they are staffed by underpaid officers who are supervised by equally underpaid inspectors responsible for verifying the value of goods entering the city, there is an obvious temptation to corruption. This is recognized as a danger by everyone, and, in principle, state governments and local officials oppose such levies. Still, they constitute a major source of revenue for most large Indian cities and are thought to be easier to administer and collect than alternative forms of taxation. At its worst, however, as Gyan Chand notes in his "arguments against octroi,"

> There is no other local tax which offers such scope for fraud, evasion, underassessment, nepotism and extortion. . . . The outposts are put under the charge of a [collector] who is the appraiser, assessor and collector of the tax. . . . The high standard of efficiency and probity without which octroi must either be unproductive or oppressive is rendered unattainable owing to the low scale of salaries which are paid to these officers. [25]

Indeed, a point was reached in Agra where the main effort made was to regularize the corruption rather than to hope to stop it entirely. An Agra corporator recalled recent actions in that regard:

> The city is supposed to get Rs. 30 lakhs from the Terminal Toll and Octroi. Last year a subcommittee of the Executive Committee was established to investigate collections. The public was certain that everyone in the department was a thief. I thought it would do no good to speak to the clerks involved, but I found that there were real difficulties involved which could be removed. Some of the members of the senior staff force these people lower down into malpractices. The public has the habit of tipping clerks on the posts even though they are collecting taxes. There is nothing wrong with this as long as the proper duties are collected, but the public gives one or two annas per trip. Clerks get only Rs. 60 a month and one or two annas a trip adds up to Rs. 1 or 2 a day. Some posts are not so lucrative. The persons who were assigned to worse posts complained against those who were on the good ones, hoping to get on to the good posts. We worked out an agreement by which each clerk is to get moved around every few months. It has stopped the internal bickering and increased the revenues of the department by Rs. 2 lakhs in a short time. The real

problem is to pay these clerks a living wage. If they got enough they would refuse bribes. The question of corruption is really the question of survival.

Some of the higher officials also feel themselves handicapped in any efforts to act against corruption. In one case, a local medical employee was charged with embezzling supplies from the medical department. There was some feeling that this action was the result of connivance by higher officials in the department, but there was little the corporation was able to do about it. According to one administrator,

> Regulations are such that all the corporation could do was to request that the health officer be transferred by the state government. A letter was written to the government, but someone there was looking out for their fellow government official and was not in sympathy with the local body, as is frequently the case. The government regarded it as only a small thing and the man went free. The local man involved was later reinstated but had been punished. The real reason that some of the corporators were interested in the matter was they had someone else in mind for the position.
>
> In a situation like this, it is easy to talk of corruption, but what can you do with a man who is earning Rs. 150 a month? It is very hard for him to resist temptation. If a child is ill, as they often are, there is no health insurance to protect them.

In this connection, it should also be reported that members of the municipal services had a rather inadequate retirement system. A better pension plan, which the city could not afford, would have provided some of the protection for the future needed to discourage activities of the type reported here.

CORPORATOR PERSPECTIVES ON ADMINISTRATORS

As part of the same battery of questions which asked corporators to name those members whom they most respected and with whom they had the friendliest relations, they were requested to indicate which administrators fell into these same categories, as well as to identify administrators whom they felt did not contribute positively to the operation of the corporations. Table 8.1 presents the response rates.

On the whole, there appears to be a higher level of interpersonal distance in the Agra corporation than between administrators and members in Poona.

TABLE 8.1

Pattern of Response Rates to Administrator Items, 1964

City	Possible Responses		Actual Responses					
			Q.1		Q.2		Q.3	
	%	N	%	N	%	N	%	N
Poona	100	195	83	161	42	81	14	28
Agra	100	180	75	135	15	27	31	56

Differences in response rates on the esteem item (Q.1) are rather small—8 percent. Response rates possibly reflecting variations in social distance are more evident on the friendship item (Q.2), where very few Agra corporators identify administrators as friends as compared to Poona corporators, and on the last item (Q.3), which illustrates a greater tendency among Agra corporators to name administrators they feel do not contribute to the working of the corporation than is true among Poona members. This item reveals the same tendency we saw in chapter 5 with respect to intercorporator attitudes: a greater proclivity toward "naming names" in Agra.

Table 8.2 presents a list of top nominees in the two cities on the esteem item by the administrative position held. It is notable that respect is not assigned simply on the basis of seniority or relative rank in the corporation, but from this data and from volunteered comments it was apparent that such choices were made on a quite specific personalized level.

If we analyze these listings by the ethclass, party, age, and education of those members who cited administrators, we find relatively few consistent sets of cleavages at work in the two cities. There are a few exceptions. Thus, if we look at the two AEO's in Agra, we find that the senior man was accorded more esteem by Congress and Republican corporators than by members from other parties, while

TABLE 8.2

Esteem Indicated by Corporators toward Administrators in the Agra and Poona Corporations, 1964

Agra

Symbol	Office	Nominations
A	AEO (Jr.)	32
B	Waterworks Superintendent	19
C	AEO (Sr.)	17
D	City Engineer I	12
E	City Engineer II	9
F	CEO	6
G	Education Superintendent	4
H	Public Health	4
I	Corporation Secretary	4
J	Asst. Engineer	4
Total		111

Poona

K	City Engineer	32
L	AEO (local)	21
M	Municipal Secretary	19
N	AEO (state)	17
O	Public Health	15
P	CEO	6
Q	Development Engineer	5
R	Education Officer	5
S	Collector of Taxes	5
T	Waterworks Superintendent	4
Total		129

the younger man received the heaviest proportion of his nominations from the Swatantra Dal.[26] On other dimensions, the differences between the two men were less clear. The younger man was especially popular among high-caste Hindus, while the senior AEO received nominations from all groups; on the other hand, the latter was highly regarded by older members of the corporation, but age did not seem a major distinguishing factor in according respect to the junior man.

Similarly, some of the controversy surrounding the activities of the two City Engineers in Agra was reflected in the slightly different patterns of support they received on the esteem item. The Bania City Engineer (I) recruited from the Uttar Pradesh Public Works Department was highly supported by Bania corporators, while the support for the local Khatri City Engineer (II) was scattered. There was a clearer pattern of party support with the former receiving the particular backing of Congress corporators, while the "local" man was especially popular among members of the Swatantra Dal. Age made no difference, and education was not informative except that persons of slightly higher education (with some secondary schooling) were more favorable to the former PWD officer, while those with only primary education were more likely to favor the local man.

On the whole, caste does not show up as an important source of differences among corporator choices in Poona. The Municipal Secretary (a Maratha) received variable party support, but this reflected especially *strong* scores among non-Maharashtrians and Maharashtrian Hindus *other than* Brahmins and Marathas. He also had a high score among the college-educated as well as the older corporators. Looked at from another direction, the *only* person in the Poona corporation who received a disproportionately favorable vote on this question among Brahmins was the senior AEO.[27] In contrast, Marathas were more strongly favorable to the junior AEO (a Maratha) and to the City Engineer (a Parsi), both of whom were younger men.

On the second question, only three men in the Agra corporation received three or more nominations among the twenty-seven given: the junior AEO (six), the senior AEO (four), and the Corporation Secretary (three). Such small figures make it difficult to analyze sources of support. In Poona, where eighty-one nominations were made, seven officials received four or more nominations on the friendship item. Six of the seven appeared on the previous list with the Superintendent of Octroi being the principal addition. Only one official received what might be regarded as differential group support. The Maratha Municipal Secretary was *most* favorably mentioned as a "friend" by the Brahmin corporators, by persons with either secondary or college education and by the older members of the corporation—those persons who would normally be described as "high status." On the whole, therefore, this is a clear case of blurring of potential lines of cleavage in the nominations given to officers, as was true of responses on the previous item as well.

Finally, on the question of those administrators who did not contribute to the operations of the municipal body, the small number of responses in Poona were concentrated among three persons, with two receiving three mentions each and the Manager of the PMT six. With only six nominations, analysis of support bases is not practicable. However, it was apparent that antipathy to the Manager was *not* concentrated in any particular subgroup of the membership. Of the fifty-six responses in Agra on this item, 60 percent went to six officials. Significantly, and reflective of the cleavages persistent in Agra public life, five of these six men were also on the esteem list. The top score (nine mentions) went to the Senior AEO trailed by the Public Health Officer with seven. However, partially due to the uneven pattern of responses, differences in subgroup bases of opposition were not the reciprocal of groups found to be favorable to a particular administrator on the esteem item.[28]

In the latter connection, it should be noted that the pattern of responses was itself rather unusual on this item. On the other questions there was not a large deviation between the proportion of corporators belonging to a given category and the number of responses on the item. In this case, however, there was a considerable maldistribution of responses in Agra. Republicans and Swatantra Dal members were sharply overrepresented among those who identified administrators toward whom they had negative feelings, while Congress members were generally more satisfied with the administrators—or, at least, more reluctant to provide names. Thus, while the Congress members constituted 30 percent of the total body, they provided only eight of the fifty-six mentions on the third question (14 percent).

In Agra, generally, the relationships depicted earlier in the text provide the appropriate framework for interpreting the findings reported here. Certain administrators are singled out for particular praise or blame by sections of the corporation. However, subgroup cleavages on these items are not uniform. For Poona, too, some tendencies toward group loyalties exist in particular administrative situations, but they do not show up as clearly in direct questioning about interpersonal relations. Thus, the PMT Manager who figured prominently in the conflicts of the corporation and had many defenders while under attack was *not* named on either the esteem or friendship lists in sufficient number by potential sources of support (like Maratha or Congress corporators) to appear on a list like that in table 8.2; there was enough antipathy from diverse sectors, however, to account for his being mentioned prominently on the third item among those few administrators named.

Obviously, future inquiries into interpersonal relations in municipal arenas must go more deeply into a consideration of those sources of mutual identification which can best explain the ways in which corporators and administrators respond to each other both in group terms and in terms of personal character.

CONCLUSIONS

Amendments to the Corporation Acts of both Uttar Pradesh and Maharashtra were being discussed in 1964, but most of these were minor in nature.[29] Demands for a cabinet system of urban government have gone unheard, as have recommendations for increases in authority which would allow elected members to exercise more meaningful influence over policy through direct and continuous means rather than in the sporadic and informal manner described in this volume. Yet, if our exploration of administrative matters has indicated anything, it is that formally blocking or "protecting" local administration from political involvement is no guarantee of actual noninvolvement.

No doubt a good argument could be made that introducing local politicians directly into the administrative process would simply politicize Indian municipal administration more than is already the case. Taken in context, however, it is no more to be feared than democratic participation at other levels of government. At some point, the justification for tutelage in government begins to ring hollow. Whether democracy is suitable for India at any level is open to question, depending on one's value preferences, but to allow it at some levels and to bar its effective operations in some of India's larger cities does not appear wholly consistent.

It is probably true, as certain administrators (particularly in Agra) charge, that a good number of corporators are irresponsible, self-seeking, and not capable of running the city efficiently and economically. Leaving open the question of how adequate the bureaucrats are in this respect, it is apparent that corporators who fit this bill of particulars are as readily identified by other members as they are by the administrators. The most admired members in both corporations are generally those who are known for their personal integrity or political skills. Many are highly competent individuals by any standard and are as much at home in matters bearing on national and state politics as they are in municipal affairs. Certainly, the argument grounded on competence is not entirely satisfactory given the somewhat greater powers assigned to politicians in the *zilla parishads* than to the corporators.

Even within the rather narrow framework of the powers presently available to corporators, tendencies in the direction of democratic administration seem to be developing on an informal basis. The process is clearly more advanced in Poona than Agra. Despite the occasional flareup over a CEO who does not play according to the rules, relations in that city have been regularized to the point where administrators are respected for their professionalism and are allowed to exercise considerable autonomy in their own spheres. At the same time, administrators are quick to differentiate among corporators in terms of their individual capacities and to respond to demands for particularized behavior in certain situations. In Agra these tendencies were not quite as well institutionalized in 1964. The lack of firmly based civic traditions in Uttar Pradesh has created a gulf between the older administrators and many of the corporators. In this respect, it may have been indicative of future trends that the younger Agra AEO verbalized considerably more sympathy than his senior colleague for the problems of the politician, although the latter had a reputation for "using" them more effectively to achieve his own ends while the younger man was seen as more "rigid" in his behavior. The provincialization of municipal services may have effected a change in these relationships, moving administration even further from being responsive to local influences, but that remains to be determined in the next few years.

In Poona, then, one gets a sense of a relatively high level of morale among local administrators at the same time that informal interpenetration of administration and political life proceeds on a give-and-take basis. In Agra, these processes were underway in a rather fitful fashion in 1964, but the discontinuities and conflicts were equally evident. Some of the worst sources of conflict within the administration were eliminated in the course of provincialization, although access to administrators by corporators was probably decreased. Part of the price for this short-run conflict reduction is the risk of a reassertion of bureaucratic formalism in relations between corporators and officials, which may make administration even less responsive to public demands in Agra than it has been in the past. At the same time, however, some of the new men transferred into Agra after 1966 come of a post-Independence generation increasingly habituated to seeing administrative behavior in the context of a general society which has become highly politicized. This may mean that, in the long run, administrators' own expectations about their roles will include, more and more frequently, a publicly responsive dimension not evident among an older generation of administrators imbued with the spirit of bureaucratic formalism.[30]

9

LOCAL POLITICS OUTSIDE THE MUNICIPAL ARENAS

As a step toward understanding the changes which took place in municipal politics between 1964 and 1968—the subject of chapter 10—and as a means of further observing the intersection of municipal, state, and national politics in two selected territorial units, the present chapter explores some of the organizational, group, and individual behaviors which influenced electoral outcomes for supralocal legislative bodies in the two cities.

We shall see here that despite certain broad continuities over time, a large segment of the public and an important element among the political activists in each community have exhibited a considerable capacity for shifting political allegiances, sometimes with a lack of concern for previous commitments of principle or group identification which is rather startling by comparison with many contemporary Western political systems.

INTRAPARTY FACTIONALISM IN AGRA

The Jan Sangh

The municipal elections of 1959 came upon the Jan Sangh at a time of disarray. At least in part, the factionalism present in the party leadership contributed to the loss by the Jan Sangh of several seats it otherwise might have won for the corporation. After the municipal elections were over, of course, a section of the party withdrew under the leadership of Baloji Agarwal and helped to form the Swatantra Dal in the corporation.

While there are a few claims that the differences within the party related to questions of principle—for example, the extent to which the RSS was to guide the actions of the Jan Sangh—former members of the party as well as current members insisted that much more of the conflict depended upon personal differences. Some Baloji supporters even attributed their leader's difficulties to a conscious policy followed by the state and national party. As one put it, "The policy of the Jan Sangh is not to let any man go very high. When a man gets a certain stature, they try to check him and bring in another."

Those Jan Sangh members interviewed in 1964, both inside and outside the corporation, displayed an almost chiliastic faith in the party as the wave of the future. Despite what have been described as obscurantist policies, a few tied the ultimate success of the organization to the increasing education of the nation. "Many voters do not know good from bad and will favor anyone who can make better propaganda," said one member. "Those with a little enlightenment favor the Jan Sangh."

While it was possible for party members to identify policies which they especially favored, including the need for a strong unitary state, no particular policy positions were associated with Jan Sangh membership at the municipal level. The kinds of proposals the party favored in the corporation over the years indicate something about the social bases from which they drew their support—small and medium-sized businessmen, orthodox middle-class Hindus with some education. Thus, the party put forward public demands for a cremation ground in the Tajganj area; for the removal of prostitutes from the heart of the city; for moving the Central Jail from an area with developmental possibilities and the substitution of a market.

In 1964, the Jan Sangh was essentially competing with the Congress for its high-caste constituency, particularly for the merchant communities of the city. It appeared to have a special advantage with the refugee communities and was able to gain increasing support among the younger elements of the high-status groups, especially those with a college education. Two of the party's three MLA nominees in 1962 were lawyers. Indeed, a younger generation of lawyers were beginning to make their appearance felt in Agra's Jan Sangh ranks by the early 1960s, but the occasion for them to come fully into politics was not available until the municipal elections of 1968, as we shall see in chapter 10.

While the party attempted to play down its anti-Muslim image, other parties were only too eager to make the reputation stick. Muslims, themselves, were highly suspicious of the party. A Muslim corporator put this view sharply in focus:

> The Jan Sangh is the only political organization in India that does not want Muslims to remain here. The Jan Sangh members of the corporation certainly have a dislike of Muslims, but they don't expose it to public view.

Jan Sangh efforts to gather support among the Jatavs of Agra during this period were minor, rarely extending beyond the granting of occasional symbolic positions in the party or candidacies for reserved seats. While there was some activity among the Backward Classes—the traditional artisan and service "clean" castes—few of these rose to positions of prominence in the organization, nor were many of them actively courted by the local Jan Sangh before 1967.

Rather, the party after 1960 sought to expand its hold among high-status communities and to reaffirm its internal discipline. Occasional differences did flare up within the organization, particularly between refugee and "local" elements in the party, but they did not become dysfunctional for the party.[1] These organizational efforts seemed to pay off in 1967 when the Jan Sangh took the lead in Uttar Pradesh (and much of northern India) in reaping the electoral benefits of their participation in various statewide agitations: demands for the passage of more effective legislation enforcing a ban on cow slaughter; insistence on Hindi as the national language; support to the agitations of college students, state employees, and others pressing various particularistic demands. As a result of the elections of 1967, in which the Jan Sangh established a temporary claim to being the largest opposition party in the state of Uttar Pradesh,[2] it began to seek a broadened social base. We shall look at some of the party's efforts to develop this base during our consideration of the municipal elections of 1968.

The Republican Party

While the Jan Sangh experienced internal difficulties around 1959 and 1960 which it subsequently overcame, the Republican Party had a relatively united leadership going into the municipal elections of 1959. Although a few candidacies were given to non-Jatavs, the party was clearly the voice of the Jatav community. Until 1959, too, the unchallenged leader of the party was a Jatav named Gopichand Pipal.

Pipal had been active in the political life of the Jatav community for thirty years, was the head of the Scheduled Caste Federation in Agra, and was subsequently a major figure in the state and local Republican organization. However, Pipal's tight control of the organization was increasingly resented by other persons within the Agra RPI. He was challenged on the question of aldermanic choices in 1959 and then, gradually, was displaced from power in a series of complicated maneuvers which included spreading charges against him of improper financial dealings.

While not the only claimant to Pipal's authority, one of the participants in his displacement was the Bania doctor (Dr. P. N. Gupta), who assumed a major leadership role in the corporation and in the city organization after his election to the corporation. Pipal made an intense effort to stem the growing influence of the doctor, but these attempts only discredited him further. Other opposition within the party came from several of the ambitious young Jatavs who wanted to establish themselves as political leaders in their own right.

As a consequence of these efforts stemming from diverse sources, Pipal was forced to resign as President of the five-district western zone of the party in June of 1960, but continued to cling to his position as head of the local Agra organization. Partly to divide the opposition and to divert attention from himself, he launched a counterattack against Dr. Gupta. The latter had very early established himself in the favor of the top leaders of the Uttar Pradesh Republican Party, B. P. Maurya and Cheddilal Sathi. Part of this influence stemmed from Gupta's willingness to draw upon his own substantial wealth to help finance the party. Indeed, for a period he served as Treasurer of the state organization. Because of the weakness of the Uttar Pradesh Republican Party, however, such a position may sound more exalted than it actually was.

Various major and minor accusations were exchanged between Pipal and Gupta. Some were related to the corporation, like Pipal's charge that Gupta had influenced members of the RPI to vote in corporation matters in a manner contradictory to party directives. The doctor, in response, insisted that as leader of the party group *(dal)* in the corporation, it was necessary to make agreements without constantly consulting the organization. He further asserted that *dal* members were not really accountable to the organizational wing of the party, a position which aroused intraparty debate again in 1964.

Another source of difficulty within the party was over the nature of party recruitment. Pipal was generally a protagonist of the Scheduled Caste Federation "idea"—that the RPI should appeal primarily to the ex-untouchable segment of the population. Others, however, wished to pursue multicaste support. If Pipal had had his way, of course, Dr. Gupta would have been removed from a position of leadership.

Most important, however, were charges arising out of alleged mishandling of party funds in 1959. In early 1961, the Uttar Pradesh Republican Party set up a special committee to investigate these and other charges arising out of the local conflicts in the Agra organization. It recommended that a supporter of Pipal then serving as President of the Agra organization be suspended for a year and that other members of the party be placed on probation including the doctor and the party's alderman.[3] In the face of the penalties given his supporter, Pipal launched a bitter verbal attack on the state leadership and followed it up with his resignation as local party President.[4]

The organizational wing of the RPI then came under the titular leadership of a moderate corporation member. It was the latter who felt so strongly about keeping the party's bargain with the Swatantra Dal and Jan Sangh, which permitted Gupta to serve as deputy mayor, that he was willing to insist that Gupta resign from his post. The deputy mayor refused to do this. This issue became an opportunity, however, for some of the doctor's other antagonists within the RPI to challenge him. The majority of the Agra RPI Executive Committee passed a resolution which called upon Gupta to give up the position of deputy mayor, but there was no way of enforcing it since the *dal* was controlled by persons favorable to Gupta.

The doctor's relations with the local party organization became more and more difficult in the following months. However, he was still in close personal contact with B. P. Maurya, who was General Secretary of the All-India RPI for the "Northern Zone," which included the state of Uttar Pradesh. Thus, when Maurya was jailed in 1963 for making what was described as an "antinational" speech, he sought the deputy mayor's help rather than that of the Agra organization in raising money for his legal defense.

A more serious source of divisiveness within the state party arose later in the same year. Maurya was responsible for getting his wife designated by the All-India Republican Party as the candidate of the RPI for a seat in the upper house of the Uttar Pradesh Legislature (MLC) in return for support the party promised to give to a CPI candidate for a vacancy in the Rajya Sabha. However, Mrs. Maurya's candidacy was not accepted by the leadership of the state unit then presided over by Cheddilal Sathi. Instead, seven of the nine RPI MLA's in Uttar Pradesh voted for Sathi as their candidate for MLC. It is widely alleged that, in response to this challenge to his authority, Maurya had the Uttar Pradesh organization divided into three sections and abolished the office of State President. The resultant *pradesh* ("state") organizations were created *within* Uttar Pradesh with a General Secretary as the chief connecting link among them. The latter position was filled for a time by the RPI alderman in the Agra corporation, Khem Chand, a man elected MLA from Agra in 1962. All these actions were sanctioned by the All-India party led by B. K. Gaikwad of Maharashtra, but dissident elements in the Uttar Pradesh organization refused to accept these decisions as legitimate.

As a result, Sathi joined with one of the anti-Gaikwad elements of the Maharashtra region. A separate organization of Republicans calling themselves the Republican Party (Ambedkerite), therefore, emerged after 1965. In preparation for the 1967 elections, there was a contest between the two Republican Parties over the party symbol, which was finally resolved in the courts by the awarding of the RPI's elephant symbol to the national organization led by Gaikwad. The Ambedkerites received little support in Agra except for Khem Chand who left the Gaikwad group. Much of his authority fell to another local leader, Man Singh.[5]

While the Ambedkerites spoke of backing candidates of their own in the Agra area for 1967, last-minute truce arrangements were reached by which the two groups promised to support a common slate of candidates in Uttar Pradesh. Khem Chand's association with the Ambedkerites had weakened his position in Agra, however, and he agreed to run for MP from Mainpuri, where he lost badly. When some persons did not receive tickets as a result of this accommodation, they ran as independents. The result was an overall setback for the party in the Agra area. In Agra District, as a whole, where the RPI had held three MLA seats after the 1962 elections, they retained only one in 1967.[6] As we shall see in the next chapter, events subsequent to these elections exacerbated conflicts within the RPI and made the party's position even more precarious at the time of the corporation elections of 1968.

While the Republicans proclaimed their commitment to socialism, much of their observable behavior revealed a primary concern with immediate individual and group advantage. Only a few Republicans interviewed ever volunteered comments on the ideological purposes of the party beyond a concern with "social uplift." Many simply basked in the glory and arguments of Ambedkar.

During the period of my first visit to Agra, it appeared that most Jatavs in Agra were being drawn toward the Republican Party. Some few *bare adme* ("big men") continued to associate with the Congress, but it was widely believed that they were doing so for their own personal advantage and that they were simply the last gasp of the old political style of the Jatav community.[7] With divisions compounded upon divisions within the Republican Party, however, the temptations to compete with that party for Jatav support became greater for a party like the Congress, and even the Jan Sangh began to move in the direction of the Jatavs after its successes of 1967.

The Congress Party

The Congress entered the municipal elections of 1959 deeply divided, and the party carried those divisions forward into conflicts over corporation officers. This factionalism was promoted by the man who was then President of the City Congress, a close supporter of Seth Achal Singh, and the General Secretary. They apparently were involved in raising charges against two anti-Seth leaders, one a former MLA and the other a man who had been a member of the Rajya Sabha and had held a prominent position for many years in the local Congress. Proceeding bureaucratically, these charges were sent to the UPCC and then returned to the City Congress for comment; the Seth-dominated local Congress used the occasion to pass a resolution expelling the two accused men. Some members of the local executive objected to the action since it went beyond the powers of a local body to expel a member, but the resolution was rammed through.[8]

News of the expulsions soon reached the leadership in the UPCC through friends of the Singhal group. As a result, the two Seth-aligned officers were suspended for two years allegedly on the ground that they hastily tried to expunge the record of the meeting of the Executive Committee when they found they were in difficulty with the top leadership. Both were still eligible to return to the Congress under the terms of their suspension, but they forfeited the offices they held in the party.[9] The President of the City Congress continued in his position as an alderman in the Agra corporation, however, and continued to work within the Seth group, even seeking the Congress party's nomination for MLA in 1962. The General Secretary, Roshan Lal Sutel, to whom we referred in chapter 3,[10] left the Congress for increased activity in the Agra trade union movement and eventually drifted into the small local unit of the Communist Party.

As we shall see, the Congress suffered a general setback in Agra in the 1962 MLA elections, though it held its own in the MP contest. This outcome was followed by an effort by the two factions to effect a compromise at the time of internal party elections in 1964. The two groups succeeded in settling on an agreed slate of candidates for the various lower levels of the local organization. The process of reaching accommodations and the actual elections lasted from mid-January of 1964 to well into June of that year, when a new City Congress President was to be selected. There was no general agreement, however, on the choice of an Executive Committee and a President. The Singhal group managed to control the final outcome for President and selected its own leader for that post. This only succeeded in opening a new round of battling within the local Congress.

Very little energy was left over from these internal quarrels for a serious concern with policy matters or a dedication to popular mobilization. A Congress member of the corporation summed up the picture of the City Congress in 1964 as one of "simply going on with the routine." Another member conceded the existence of "decaying tendencies" in the Congress. Uniformly, Congressmen themselves attributed internal differences to personal ambitions. Yet, many were quite prepared to take factionalism in stride almost as a necessary by-product of democracy. One Congressman said:

> Democracy means elections, and when you have places to fill, people are unhappy at not being selected. Even the humblest man in a democracy can aspire to the highest positions. Congress is a living, dynamic organization; so everyone wants a position in it because it runs the government.

By 1967, it was no longer so clear that the Congress was mandated to run the government, nor did internal factionalism necessarily reflect "dynamism." An accumulation of popular grievances was coming to the surface with which the party could not successfully cope. Thus, while many of the non-Congress members of the corporation agreed with the *principles* of the national Congress party, they strongly condemned the party for failing to live up to those principles—for allowing "bad people" to take over the operation of the party.

In Agra, there was also the feeling that the Congress was not any more congenial to minority groups like the Jatavs or the Muslims than the Jan Sangh. A Jatav leader summed up the view of many members of his community toward the Congress:

> Congress says that there should not be caste segregation or
> untouchability, but even the top leaders don't feel like
> practicing it. Even in the Congress, most of the men believe
> in class segregation. At times, Congress distributes money
> for votes, but even then they don't get them from among
> Jatavs. Their problem is that they don't pick good men. If
> they chose the right men they would get votes and not have
> to spend so much money.

Factionalism within the local Congress might have been reduced had the
statewide factions led by C. B. Gupta and Kamlapati Tripathi not generated
additional heat during the period from 1964 to 1967. Thus, one weekly took note
of the statewide implications of a contest for MLC in Agra District in April 1966;
this periodical's sentiments are clearly with the Tripathi or "dissident" faction
against the Gupta or "ministerialist" wing in the contest described below for a local
bodies constituency in Agra District (excluding the Agra corporation). The contest
is also significant because it reconfirmed Shiv Prasad Gupta's claim to a leadership
role in the political life of Agra District and City:

> The dissidents suffer from the absence of a unified
> leadership. The group consists of many factions, each with
> its own reasons for being unhappy with the ministerialist
> group. On occasions of crisis these factions pull apart. The
> present contest has also shown the weakness of the group,
> at least in . . . the Agra local bodies constituency. From this
> constituency Deputy Home Minister Shiv Prasad Gupta is
> contesting election to the Legislative Council. Gupta is a
> post-1947 Congressman and is related to the ministerialist
> boss, C. B. Gupta. He has little influence with Congressmen
> and less with the people. The dissident leaders decided to
> set up an old Congressman to contest the election against
> him. But PWD Minister Jagan Prasad Rawat, fearing that
> the success of a senior Congressman might jeopardize his
> own position, started supporting the nominee of the SSP,
> causing a wave of resentment among Congressmen. The
> only beneficiary from this wrangle was the ministerialist
> nominee, Shiv Prasad Gupta, who also has the immense
> advantage of being in power. Old Congressmen like SKD
> Paliwal . . . have issued statements in favour of Shiv Prasad
> Gupta. . . .[11]

It was apparently in the fear of making factional quarrels worse that the
Government of Uttar Pradesh decided to supersede the KAVAL corporations in
January, 1966, and to appoint Administrators for the five cities for a two-year
period rather than hold new municipal elections immediately. This would presumably prevent a worsening of inner-party relations at the local level during the period
prior to the MLA contests of 1967. The *National Herald* of Lucknow, which has
generally been associated with the left wing of the Congress, took the government
to task for its apparently politically-motivated action:

> The two-year-supersession will be understood to
> mean that the Government wants the civic affairs of [the
> KAVAL] cities to be firmly under official control till the
> general elections are over. The Government may have rea-

son to feel distressed and disturbed by the record of the elected corporations. The people have perhaps even greater reason for dissatisfaction, if not disgust. But to argue that this is enough reason for supersession or suspension is double-edged. People might like to apply it against the Government of the State as much as against the KAVAL corporations. [12]

While municipal politics fell quiet in 1966, persons from Agra continued to play roles in the battle for priority in the Uttar Pradesh Congress. By mid-1966, the bifactional conflict had grown somewhat three-sided because of the emergence of an intermediate group between C. B. Gupta and Tripathi led by Mrs. Sucheta Kripalani, the Chief Minister of the state. [13] These factional quarrels continued to dominate Uttar Pradesh politics through 1966 and into the elections of 1967, even as Mrs. Kripalani was herself shunted aside to New Delhi as an MP. After the elections, C. B. Gupta became Chief Minister of Uttar Pradesh; J. P. Rawat, who had been a supporter of the Kripalani "third force," was on the original list of ministers submitted by Gupta, but his nomination was withdrawn at the last moment, much to the embarrassment of Rawat. [14] Despite his unhappiness, Rawat did not follow Charan Singh out of the Congress a few weeks later when the latter brought down the Congress government. Rather, Rawat continued to work within the party and to try to build his own support in Agra District.

The anti-Congress coalition government which took over from the C. B. Gupta ministry announced the holding of corporation elections for October or November of 1967, but these were postponed until the spring of 1968. By the time municipal elections were actually held (in May), Charan Singh's ministry was more than three months dead, and these elections were looked to as something of a foretaste of the battle for control of the state legislature which was expected in the wake of the elections planned for late 1968 or early 1969.

THE AGRA GENERAL ELECTIONS OF 1962

The outcomes of the contests in 1962 have already been alluded to in several places. Here we will merely sketch some of the features of the four local contests (three for MLA and the one for MP) not already mentioned in connection with our earlier discussion of municipal politics.

The Congress, partly because of an inability to rise above the self-destructive status quo, nominated all of its Agra City incumbents from 1957, although two of its three MLA's were recognized to be in political difficulty. The Republicans, with hope of success at least in one seat in the city, completed an expedient electoral alliance with prominent leaders of the Muslim community. This alliance was part of a general agreement which extended to several of the districts of western Uttar Pradesh and was the handiwork of B. P. Maurya, who was running for MP from Aligarh. In Agra, the RPI enlisted the cooperation of a prominent Muslim figure who had been active in the Congress but was angry over his failure to secure a Congress ticket as its MP candidate. As a result, Muslims were encouraged to vote for RPI candidates in the five MLA districts enclosed in the MP constituency.

The Jan Sangh brought forth candidates for the three urban MLA seats who were well known in party circles, but nominated a prominent "elder statesman" of the Congress opposition in the contest for MP. Raj Nath Kunzru, a man in his eighties, had been affiliated with the Congress in his youth, but then turned to other organizations. He had served as President of the Agra branch of the Hindu Mahasabha in its heyday. Kunzru accepted the Jan Sangh ticket in 1962 though he did not see himself as a party member.

Other parties were not significantly represented in the contests in the Agra City area. Among the independents, the most important individual was clearly Baloji Agarwal, the former Jan Sangh leader who had defected from that party to take an active role in the Swatantra Dal. Baloji contested from Agra City I, where the Jan Sangh had its primary base of support in the city.

As a result of individual contestants' decisions, the pattern of party nominations, and the mix of primordial bases, each of the four contests in the city had its own flavor. In the MP contest, the major figures were Seth Achal Singh and Haider Bux, the nominee of the RPI. For Agra City I, there were four major participants: Baloji; Adiram Singhal (the Congress leader and incumbent MLA); Dr. Prakash Narayan Gupta, the Republican *dal* leader; and Rama Shanker Agarwal, a prominent figure in the Jan Sangh both in the corporation and the city. For Agra City II, there was essentially a two-man contest between the Congress incumbent and the Republican alderman, Khem Chand. The fourth urban-related contest was one that took place for Agra City (Rural)—a constituency including both urban and outlying areas. In that contest, a reserved seat was fought over principally by the Congress incumbent and a Republican Jatav.

Agra City I

All seven of the candidates for MLA in this higher-status section of Agra were Banias. The district was one in which the Congress had won easily in the past. In 1957, for example, when Baloji ran as the nominee of the Jan Sangh against Singhal for the same seat, he came in second with only 29 percent of the vote as against Singhal's 57 percent. By 1962, the Congress was internally fractionated, and previous sources of group support for the party were now diverted elsewhere by new candidates for MLA.

Baloji was in the best position in 1962 to exploit differences within the Congress. While no formal understanding was reached between him and Seth's supporters, it is generally agreed that there was no clash of interests either. As an independent, Baloji could work against Singhal at the same time that he could sound like a Seth partisan if he wished. According to some informants, Baloji voters who asked for advice on how to vote for MP were often told to vote for Seth. At the same time, Baloji was in a position to win votes from his former associates in the Jan Sangh.

Singhal was hurt politically by these tactics and also by the wholesale defection of Jatavs and a substantial withdrawal of Muslim support from the Congress. These "vote banks," which the Congress had been able to depend upon in the past, were now attracted to the RPI nominee, Dr. Gupta.

The campaign itself was pitched largely at the level of personalities. Singhal had suffered a heart attack during his term as MLA and even before that had exhibited some reluctance to interact with the public. There were widespread complaints, therefore, against a "cool attitude" that he was said to exhibit toward the public. As one Congressman suggested, "People love those who mingle and go out and live among them as one of their own kind. The aristocratic approach to contact is not good. It appears unfriendly and not sympathetic."

In contrast to this image of Singhal, Baloji had a highly favorable public personality. During his term of service in the corporation, he was very active in attending to public demands and even used an association with the corporation union to solicit the support of corporation employees. In fact, some corporation members claimed that he received campaign funds from corporation workers, although this is not clearly substantiated. It is known that some corporation employees worked hard for his election.

In terms of percentages, Baloji merely advanced his performance from 1957 by five percentage points—from 29 to 34 percent in 1962. In terms of actual voter shifts, it is probable that many of the voters who backed him in 1957 as a Jan Sangh candidate did not support him in 1962 as an independent. What seems to be more likely from evidence presented below, is that much of his support came from persons who supported the Congress candidate for MP in 1962.

Perhaps the most surprising aspect of the result is the clear weakness of the Congress candidate, evidenced by a drop from 57 percent of the vote in 1957 to only 22 percent in 1967. Not only did Baloji run well, but the second-place finisher in this contest was the Republican nominee. The latter's success in winning the support of 24 percent of the voters was a tribute to the solidarity of the Jatavs and the Muslims as well as a reflection of Dr. Gupta's own popularity in the area. The Jan Sangh nominee ran a rather weak fourth with 17 percent; three other candidates divided 2 percent of the votes among them.

Agra City II

Deokinandan Bibhab was the Congress Bania incumbent in the south and west sections of the city, an area including Agra Cantonment. He was born in Agra in 1904 and was an early Gandhian supporter. He was first elected to the Uttar Pradesh Assembly in 1952 and was chairman of the important Estimates Committee in that body after his reelection in 1957.

By 1962 there were various challenges to his following. Increasing political self-consciousness among Jatavs in a district with a high proportion of Scheduled Caste population and a disaffected Muslim section contributed to Bibhab's difficulties. Within party circles, too, he was challenged by other claimants to the nomination, including the recently rehabilitated former President of the City Congress. In order to advance his own claims to the nomination, the latter sought to exploit some questions in the public's mind about the incumbent's profits made as a private colonizer. While these charges may have been baseless, they were widely repeated. The jockeying for the Congress nomination left behind sufficient bad feeling to make the incumbent's task more difficult in the election itself.

Insofar as any "issue" was formally discussed in this contest, it was the matter of the incumbent's benefit from his private landholdings. Otherwise, campaigning for MLA was a matter of organizing group support, and the Congress simply fell short of doing this successfully. Certainly they were not exceeded in expenditures by the Republican nominee, Khem Chand. The latter ran a relatively quiet campaign in which much depended on the enthusiasm of his campaign workers. His workers, as Khem Chand proudly claimed, "said it was not my election, but theirs."

Indeed, if the figures available are to be relied upon, the relatively low literacy and socioeconomic situation of this district as compared with Agra City I did not prevent a higher turnout here. This contest drew an almost 80 percent vote, whereas Agra City I attracted only 67 percent. In a total of 49,269 votes cast, 1,164 votes separated the two top men. Khem Chand won with almost 35 percent of that vote as against the Congress nominee's 32 percent. The Jan Sangh nominee, a prominent Punjabi figure in that party, came in a distant third with 20 percent. Five other candidates were in the field with the only party nominee, a man supported by the Communist Party, receiving 3.3 percent of the vote.

Agra City (Rural)

In 1957, Bibhab's constituency had been joined to an outlying section of the city and nearby rural area to constitute a double-member constituency. In the four-man race in 1957, Bibhab and Chhatrapati Ambesh were the nominees of the Congress. The Jatav, Ambesh, received more votes than Bibhab in that contest, while the Jatav candidate of the Scheduled Caste Federation ran behind Raj Nath Kunzru, who stood as an independent for the general seat.

When double-member constituencies were abolished before the 1962 elections, a reserved constituency was created which included six corporation wards. There were five candidates for this seat, including the incumbent, Ambesh. The latter was identified with the "big men" in the Jatav community, but he was more successful than many of these in bridging the gap to the Jatav masses. Against him the RPI supported Karan Singh Ken, a Jatav leader of the RPI.

Because of the closeness of the contest between these two Jatavs, the three other candidates in the field had an influence on the outcome simply by their presence. In particular, the situation of Suraj Bhan Naagar is worthy of comment. Naagar, who was formerly associated with the Republican Party, left that organization in the wake of various internal party quarrels. Bearing a certain bitterness against the party, he determined to stand as a candidate for MLA in a way that would maximize his opposition to the RPI. Of his maneuvers, a man close to him in the corporation later explained:

> It was thought that if some other man besides the Congress-man ran for the Scheduled Caste reserved seat, this would split the vote and give the election to Congress. [Naagar] negotiated with the Congress, having left the Republican Party. They asked him what to do about their problem and he said, "I will take the backing of some other party so I can get votes away from the Republicans." The Jan Sangh thought he might win and they had no candidate of their own to enter; they had even approached him before the elections to be their candidate.

Even with Jan Sangh backing, Naagar was able to collect only 2,852 votes—5.6 percent. However, this made the differences between victory and defeat for the Congress as Ambesh drew 42.8 percent of the vote cast for MLA and Ken received 40.8 percent. Two other candidates—a Socialist and a Swatantra Party nominee—divided the remaining 11 percent.

Agra City–MP

The three MLA districts just described were included with two rural districts—one of which, Kheragarh, is the home district of J. P. Rawat—in a single MP constituency. This was an area that Seth Achal Singh had cultivated politically for well over a decade. In 1957 he had defeated the other candidates, including Paliwal, with an absolute majority of the vote.

Opposition candidates for MP were more numerous in 1962. There were four candidates running against Seth, one of whom was Haji Haider Bux. Despite the presence of Raj Nath Kunzru as the candidate of the Jan Sangh, the campaign was soon turned into a Seth-Bux conflict. The campaign was heavily charged with appeals to anti-Muslim sentiment, and rumors were common that the Jan Sangh was anxious to defeat Bux, even if it meant supporting Seth. Indeed, Republicans assert that the Jan Sangh late in the campaign began to seek votes unofficially for Seth.

Bux, himself, had been a Congressman from 1947 to 1962 after being elected to the Uttar Pradesh Assembly in 1946 as an MLA on a Muslim League ticket, though he denied he had ever been active in the League. In 1957 he ran as a Congress candidate for MLA from the Firozabad constituency, but lost that contest to an independent. As a result of the alliance of 1962, he received a sizable Jatav and Muslim vote, but he was not strongly tied personally to anti-Congress sentiment, and returned to the Congress shortly after his defeat.

This return took place despite some rather extreme charges exchanged by the Congress and the Republicans in the election contest—charges which Bux dismissed as campaign tactics. For example, Congress campaign sheets intimated that Bux was a Pakistani spy, and fabricated an elaborate series of incidents suggesting embezzlement of funds from a Rajasthani educational institution. To these accusations, the Republican campaign paper responded, "If he was working as a spy, why hasn't the Government taken any action? Now when he has joined the Republican Party [after being in the Congress], they say he is a spy."[15] Despite what appeared to be fear on the part of the Congress that a serious challenge existed, the incumbent won by a convincing margin, just falling short of an absolute majority. Indeed, Seth's overall support decreased by only 2 percent between 1957 and 1962 even while two of his Congress running-mates were losing their MLA contests.

Contrary to the usual impression that one has about the sources of support for the Congress, table 9.1 shows that Seth actually performed better in the three urbanized districts than he did in the two largely rural constituencies. In Agra City I, the highest-status city district, he received 55 percent of the total vote cast as against 49 percent in the two other urbanized districts and only 44 percent in the two rural MLA constituencies.

TABLE 9.1

Percentage of Votes Received by Major Party Candidates in Agra MP Contest, 1962

	Agra City MLA Districts			Rural Agra*	Overall†
	I	II	"Rural"		
Candidate	%	%	%	%	%
Seth Achal Singh (Congress)	55	49	49	44	48
Haider Bux (RPI)	24	35	38	22	28
Kunzru (J.S.)	16	14	7	9	11
Others	5	2	5	26	13
Totals	100	100	99	101	100

* Percentages of total votes cast in the two consolidated rural MLA constituencies.

† Based on total votes cast in the MP contest.

Seth's poor showing in the two rural constituencies was, in large part, a reflection of the support given by rural voters to his rural-based opponents rather than that provided to his main urban opponents. Thus, Bux received his greatest vote in the Agra City (Rural) constituency, and Kunzru fared best in Agra City I. Two minor candidates drew their principal backing in rural Agra. In one case this was due to the continuing influence of Paliwal. B. P. Agarwal, who ran on the Swatantra Party ticket—Paliwal was active in that party in 1962—received 20,090 votes in the two rural MLA districts compared to Seth's 45,000 and Bux's 22,659. In the MP contest as a whole, however, Agarwal received only 8.8 percent of the vote.

Looking at the three urbanized districts alone, voting patterns for Congress MLA and MP candidates are particularly lacking in cohesion as compared to votes cast for Jan Sangh and RPI nominees in each constituency. To the extent that party voting has developed in India at all, one might expect that the Congress following would be most reliable because of the long history of the party. Instead, as table 9.2 indicates, Jan Sangh and Republican voters tended to vote the party line in 1962—no matter what the primordial character of the candidates—whereas Congress voters varied substantially, even where primordial factors made no difference. The table also presents a comparison of the performances of the three major parties' candidates for MP and MLA in each of the urbanized MLA constituencies; Seth ran substantially ahead of his three Congress runningmates everywhere, with the smallest difference coming in Agra City (Rural), where he was teamed with a Jatav. In all three units, the Republican voting pattern was highly consistent; this was also the case for the Jan Sangh in two districts, though in the third slightly greater differences appeared as Jan Sangh voters cast more ballots for the dynamic Punjabi leader of the party in Agra City II than they did for Kunzru. These intraparty differences in voting are further accentuated if we compare variances within MLA districts by votes cast at each polling station (see table 9.3).[16]

Examination of these details of the vote tends to support the argument that a large part of the difference in Congress votes in Agra City I is due to a substantial

TABLE 9.2

Percentage of MP and MLA Vote Received by Major Party Candidates, in Urban MLA Units, Agra, 1962

MLA District	Congress			Republican			Jan Sangh		
	MP %	MLA %	Diff. %	MP %	MLA %	Diff. %	MP %	MLA %	Diff. %
Agra I	55	22	+33	24	24	—	16	17	−1
Agra II	49	32	+17	35	35	—	14	20	−6
Agra City (Rural)	49	43	+ 6	38	41	−3	7	6	+1
Mean Difference			+19			−1			−2

TABLE 9.3

Variation in Party Vote for MP and MLA Candidates of Major Parties, in Agra City MLA Districts, 1962

MLA District	Difference in Percentage of Total Vote in Each Contest*			Number of Stations
	High (6+ %)	Medium (4-5.9%)	Low (0-3.9%)	
Agra City I:				
Congress	28	—	—	
Republican	1	—	27	28
Jan Sangh	2	4	22	
Agra City II:				
Congress	21	2	—	
Republican	—	1	22	23
Jan Sangh	12	6	5	
Agra City Rural:				
Congress	12	12	10	
Republican	—	5	29	34
Jan Sangh	3	1	30	

* Based on difference in percentage of vote received by candidates for MLA and MP in each polling station.

transfer of votes cast for Seth for MP directly to Baloji for MLA. Indeed, the 33 percent vote difference recorded within the Congress is almost exactly reflected in Baloji's share of the MLA vote. The other major parties' consistency in public support argues in favor of this proposition, although aggregate data of the kind available here makes it impossible to be completely confident of this argument.[17]

Interestingly, the Republican Party seems *more* effective in these terms than either the Congress or the Jan Sangh. The RPI was better able to "deliver" its voters in the face of such factors as a shaky Muslim-Jatav alliance and the rather disparate primordial groupings represented by its MP and MLA candidate combinations. The Congress candidates appear to have worked independently of each other. The Jan Sangh, at least in one district, displayed some tendency toward differentiation, but on the whole revealed high group cohesion.

Still, these data make it difficult to speak of the persistence of a "party vote" in Agra between 1957 and 1962. The drop in public support given to MLA candidates put forward by the Congress was substantial in each of the three urbanized units; there is no reason to assume that Seth's vote was a "truer" index of party strength than the MLA vote in the city and its immediate environs despite its consistency over time. If anything, the vote for MLA was probably the better test of immediate public predispositions to the political parties. A rather curious rank ordering of party performances would result if we simply aggregated gross MLA vote totals across the three urbanized MLA districts. The RPI would stand *first* with about 33 percent of the total vote; the Congress a close second with 32 percent, and the Jan Sangh would trail at only 14 percent. All other MLA candidates accumulated nearly 21 percent of the ballots cast—another indication of a high level of dispersion in the local political system.

The special features of the 1962 general elections in Agra, which included a major defection from the Congress in one district and the creation of a temporary but effective Muslim-Jatav alliance, point to the evanescent character of voting behavior patterns in a city like Agra. Under the circumstances, it is particularly useful to examine the results of the 1967 elections for evidence of persistence and change in electoral behaviors over time.

THE AGRA ELECTIONS OF 1967

Constituency lines were altered in many parts of India for the general elections of 1967. New MLA constituencies emerged in Agra. They varied in different degrees from the districts of 1962 with the new Agra East closely resembling the high-status Agra I constituency of 1962 while the other two districts were altered more substantially.[18] It is impossible, therefore, to draw precise parallels between the electoral units involved in the two elections; problems of comparison are further complicated at the subconstituency level by the creation of new polling stations. Still, a trend in Agra toward increased strength for the Jan Sangh, continuing incoherence in the vote for the Congress, and the impact of the Republican Party were clear themes in the 1967 elections throughout the city. Overall, what resulted was something approximating a three-party system. We shall look at these phenomena in each of the three MLA districts and in the results of the MP election.

Agra East

Like the constituency lines, the cast of characters in the election contest for this MLA contest changed only marginally between 1962 and 1967, but with important differences in individual roles and outcomes. As it had in 1962, the Jan Sangh nominated Rama Shanker Agarwal as its candidate for MLA. Agarwal, who was an increasingly prominent figure in the local and state party organizations, had not done well in the contest of 1962, but there was no serious challenge to his candidacy within the party in 1967. To the extent that minor factionalism existed in the Jan Sangh, there was a tendency to identify Rama Shanker as active in the "local" faction (versus the "refugee" or "Punjabi" faction) but these conflicts were successfully held in check by the state organization's demand for discipline and the balancing of other candidacies among factions.

The situation for the Congress was much more difficult. Adiram Singhal was President of the City Congress; his attachment to the state factional network was through the Tripathi group. Although Tripathi was President of the UPCC in 1966, by the time that the UPCC set up an Election Committee to pass on MLA tickets, the latter decision-making body was slightly weighted in favor of C. B. Gupta's men.

The choice of candidates was further complicated for the Congress by the introduction of a new method for processing applicants for MLA tickets. Up to 1962 the UPCC's electoral body would formally consult the relevant City or

District Congress Committee in selecting candidates. This was not done in 1967. Instead, applications for tickets were invited directly by the State Election Committee with the result that local organizations were by-passed. This procedure exacerbated Congress difficulties in Agra. Not only were the candidates finally selected for the three MLA seats opposed by one wing of the local party—that was the usual situation—but two of the three received only grudging support from either local faction. This was particularly the case in Agra East, where the nominee was Dr. P. N. Gupta, former leader of the Republican Party and ex-deputy mayor of Agra.

Dr. Gupta had withdrawn from the Republican Party shortly after the Agra corporation was superseded in early 1966. None of the members of the RPI followed him out of that party, nor was his entry into the Congress organization encouraged by local Congress leaders. When the UPCC called for applications for the party's tickets, however, Gupta approached a Party Secretary in the UPCC for help. The latter (a Tripathi man) sought to defer to Singhal's preferences, since there was a possibility that Singhal would be interested in running again himself. When it became clear that Singhal was not really anxious to contest—in large part because of his age and recent illnesses—and was not able to suggest a name acceptable to the state leadership, the party turned to Dr. Gupta. According to informants, there were not a great number of claimants within the Congress for this seat. A general feeling existed that the Congress had not strengthened its position in that upper-status area of the city in the intervening five years. As a leading Congressman remarked in 1968, "We Congressmen have become passive generally and lack adequate organization to win elections." Any serious contest in this constituency would also require the investment of substantial amounts of money. Several potential nominees were not particularly anxious to commit their personal wealth in order to overcome the organizational weaknesses of the Congress. Under the circumstances, Dr. Gupta appeared to be a most reasonable candidate.[19] Although few others were anxious to take on the contest for the Congress, Gupta still received little support from Congressmen in his constituency. Indeed, it is claimed that some Congressmen supported the Jan Sangh nominee.

The incumbent, Baloji, stood again for MLA, but there was a dwindling of support for him since 1962. Several of the corporators who had been associated with him up to 1966 were being attracted increasingly to the Jan Sangh. One of these, a man who had worked with him during the 1967 election campaign but later joined the Jan Sangh, summed up some of the problems encountered by Baloji,

> Independents have no power and will have to join a party in the Vidhan Sabha. The public view was spread by the other parties that an independent is weak and not useful for democracy. The public also felt that Baloji had not done very much for them.

Despite the fact that he received support from some prominent figures in the Muslim community and from the tiny left-wing parties of Agra like the SSP and the CPI, Baloji was hurt by the loss of middle-class support from the Bania community in the wake of the increasing attractiveness of the Jan Sangh.

The last major candidate in the race was Mahipal Singh, a Sikh who had joined the Republican Party in 1962 and was Vice President of the City party at the time of his nomination. While he was expected to attract the support of non-Jatavs in the constituency, there was considerable dissatisfaction within the ranks of the RPI over his selection, both because of his wealth and his primordial background. The fractionated condition of the party further contributed to the setback for the party indicated in table 9.4.

TABLE 9.4

Outcome of MLA Contest, Agra East, 1967

Candidate	Party	1967 Vote	Percentage
R. S. Agarwal	Jan Sangh	18,667	32.6
P. N. Gupta	Congress	14,270	24.9
Baloji Agarwal	Independent	12,651	21.9
Mahipal Singh	Republican	10,005	17.5
Eight Others	Independents	1,848	3.2

Despite the presence in the contest of an assortment of eight other candidates, it was a four-man race. Aside from these four, no one received more than 450 votes. The Jan Sangh candidate won by a substantial margin. That victory is particularly impressive when it is noted that he gained 19 percent over his own performance of 1962, possibly picking much of this up from Baloji whose support among the rather different electorate fell by about 12 percent. Gupta, now standing as the Congress candidate, drew approximately the same percentage as he had in 1962, although much of it presumably consisted of persons who had not voted for him earlier.

In lieu of public opinion data, one must rely for an explanation of the great upsurge of Jan Sangh support upon factors of the kind detailed in the comments of a member of the Jan Sangh,

> The people are fed up with the Congress. They wanted an alternative. No other parties have an organization like the Jan Sangh. It is a growing party.

At a less ideational level, the dynamism and youth of the Jan Sangh organization clearly outperformed a divided and aged Congress leadership which was increasingly ineffective in attracting young people to the party except on the basis of very short-term benefits. The growing effectiveness of the Jan Sangh organization was by no means limited to Agra East but was evident throughout the city and much of Agra district; the disrepair of the Congress was similarly evident elsewhere in the area.[20]

Agra Cantonment

Despite its name, Agra Cantonment included ten of the twenty-seven corporation wards of 1959 along with the cantonment area. These covered a substantial Muslim and "clean" Hindu element from the Agra City II constituency of 1962. Many of the Scheduled Caste *mohallas* which had been included in Agra City II previously were now to be found in a third district, Agra West.

Unlike Agra East, the Congress organization in the Agra Cantonment MLA constituency appeared to be fairly united going into the elections. Harihar Nath Agarwal, the Congress MLA candidate, was in his late forties and a successful businessman. His father had been very close to Paliwal during the nationalist movement and was one of the financial backer's of Paliwal's newspaper. H. N. Agarwal was a member of the City Congress Committee until 1952 but then left the Congress to support Paliwal. He was politically inactive after that election and remained out of politics until 1962 when he was attracted back into the Congress. Despite earlier associations with Paliwal and Tripathi, he was now affiliated with C. B. Gupta and the Seth group locally. He had been the nominee of the latter faction for City Congress President in 1964 against Adiram Singhal, losing only by a vote of twenty-one to nineteen in the City Congress Committee.

The Republican Party in 1967 nominated one of the few Muslims who had been active in that organization in the hope that some of the cooperation between communities which had been so effective in 1962 would prove itself again. The third major contestant was one of the leaders of the Punjabi element in the Jan Sangh, Raj Kumar Sama, the defeated Jan Sangh candidate of 1962 in Agra City II. These three major party nominees captured nearly 93 percent of the vote in 1967. This is all the more striking given the presence, among the *nine* other candidates, of a Secretary of the Communist Party and a former corporator running on the Swatantra ticket.[21] Both of these minor candidates and one independent were Muslims and may have attracted a bit of the substantial Muslim vote of the area away from the Muslim candidate of the RPI, who drew only 28.2 percent of the vote and finished third.[22]

Given an outcome that promised to be close, a great deal of energy went into the campaign. Congress workers later claimed that the Jan Sangh poured college student campaign workers into the area, that violence had taken place on several occasions, and that it became difficult to hold Congress meetings because of stone-throwing incidents instigated by opposition workers. Candidates also conceded the expenditure of considerable sums. One of the major party candidates admitted:

> All parties have to make contributions to groups in their areas. Sometimes it was necessary when a group approached me from a temple or a mosque or a *dharamshala* [rest house] to contribute to their organizations. I had to supply five thousand bricks to one place and a shawl to a mosque.

While the Congress managed to win this seat with about the same percentage that it had in losing Agra City II in 1962 (33.1 percent), the impressive feature of this contest was the showing of the Jan Sangh nominee. Considering that the Jan Sangh drew no more than 20 percent in any Agra MLA district in 1962, capturing slightly over 31 percent of the vote in previously losing territory is an impressive comment on the upsurge of its organizational efforts and seemed to foreshadow further gains. The Congress was anxious to attribute the rise of the Jan Sangh to transient events. "Employees', students', and cow slaughter agitations hurt the Congress even though cow slaughter was banned in Uttar Pradesh in 1957," one Congressman declared. Whether favorable attitudes toward the Jan Sangh were only a passing phenomenon remained to be tested in the municipal elections of 1968.

Agra West

The Agra West constituency contained the greatest concentration of Jatav *mohallas* in the city, as well as some rural areas where politics was dominated by high-caste and middle-caste landowning Hindus. Total candidacies increased here as elsewhere in Agra, but only three of the candidates received more than 4 percent of the vote each; nine others divided the remainder.

As its candidate, the Congress nominated Bhogilal Misra, a party leader of nearly a decade earlier. In order to contest, Misra had given up his post as Government Counsel. Misra, who had played a "balancer" role in the party in the middle 1950s was not supported by either of the city factions for the MLA ticket, but received the aid of J. P. Rawat in gaining the nomination. While he had earlier engendered the opposition of Shiv Prasad Gupta by opposing the latter for President of the District Board and participating in group activity directed against C. B. Gupta prior to 1958, relations had improved sufficiently in recent years to make Misra an acceptable candidate to the Gupta wing of the party.

Within the local organization, however, there was some dissatisfaction with this nomination. The Seth group, which was stronger in that section of the city than the Singhal forces, expected the nomination to go to one of its men. While it is argued that Seth did not encourage his defection, a former President of the City Congress decided to stand for the corporation as an independent. The electoral support he received was not great, but it made a significant difference in the outcome of what turned out to be a tightly contested race.

The Jan Sangh apparently did not have a high expectation of doing well in this constituency. Its candidate, A. P. Sharma, was a relative latecomer to the party, having been associated with the Swatantra Party during the 1962 elections. Since joining the party (after being defeated for MLA in a rural constituency in Agra), he had risen rapidly to a position of some prominence in the party, but he was not an established party figure.

Both the Congress and Jan Sangh candidates were Brahmins. The third major candidate and eventual winner was Man Singh, a leader of the Republican Party. During this period, Man Singh was on the five-man State Election Committee of the RPI and had become an important leader in the organization created by Maurya for Western Uttar Pradesh under the tripartite arrangement. While the party had its basic strength in areas of Agra City now concentrated in the Agra West constituency, recent internal factionalism made its chances of winning in 1967 more difficult. Not only was Man Singh in the race, but two candidates were apparently entered by opposition parties with the intention of dividing Jatav votes. This kind of behavior was not restricted to opposition against the RPI nominee, however, since a third independent, a Kori, was allegedly entered by the Jan Sangh to divert votes away from the Congress.

Maneuvers of this kind, while weakening each of the candidates, ultimately balanced the result so delicately that a recount was required. The Republican winner was separated by fewer than 125 votes from the Congress runner-up and by about a thousand votes from the Jan Sangh nominee. They received, respectively, 28.8 percent, 28.5 percent and 26.7 percent of the total vote. Again, the Jan Sangh made a substantial advance, although its candidate came in third. The impact of the marginal candidates was great in this constituency. These nine candidates divided over 16 percent of the vote among them, but only one, the Kori independent, received over 3 percent of the total. The outcome might have been affected by the withdrawal of any one of the lowest finishers, since even the twelfth-place man, a former Secretary of the RPI who stood as an independent with some Ambedkerite backing, received 339 votes.

Agra MP

As in each of the MLA districts, the number of candidates for MP in Agra increased to an even dozen. The entry of seven candidates more than in 1962 may have contributed substantially to the decrease in the votes cast for the three principal contenders. Thus, while Seth Achal Singh managed to win his fourth term to Parliament, he did so with a greatly reduced vote—only 33.8 percent of the total as compared to 48.1 percent in 1962. His margin of victory was decreased by the inroads made by the candidate of the Jan Sangh, the wife of the owner of one of the major tourist shops of Agra, who ran a much better race than even many Jan Sangh members expected of her. In nominating her, the party hoped to gain a source of financial support for its MLA candidates and additional aid for spreading its gospel in Agra. This nomination also recognized the party's need to capitalize upon the fact that its traditionalistic appeals had special attractiveness for the Hindu women of Agra.

The importance of having a candidate for MP who had enough wealth to help finance the campaigns of some of the poorer MLA nominees was also a consideration for the Republican Party. Lachman Dass, one of the wealthiest Jatavs of Agra, was a man who had taken an interest in the problems of the Scheduled Castes in his native Punjab and in Bombay where he lived for some years. He had not been active in local party politics since coming to Agra in 1961. Indeed, having entered Agra politics in 1967 by contesting for the top office, he subsequently became a leader in the local party and helped to organize the Republicans for the corporation elections of 1968. Lachman Dass had the twin advantages lacking to other RPI candidates of *not* having been deeply implicated in recent factional quarrels within the organization and of having known Ambedkar personally. His wealth made it difficult for party members to regard him as someone seeking to take monetary or other personal advantage out of the nomination—a constant source of factional contention within the RPI.

Table 9.5 presents the result of the contest for MP for each of the three urbanized MLA districts and the two rural constituencies. Achal Singh's loss in support was uniform throughout the district. Not only did his urban vote fall by about 14 percent in the city (see table 9.1), but it fell equally sharply in the countryside, declining to 29 percent of the total rural vote. This heavy rural loss was, in part, related to Jan Sangh growth; that party won the Fatehpur Sikri MLA seat, though in large part because of the existence of divisions within that constituency's Congress party. An increase of about 10 percent in the Jan Sangh vote in rural Agra was offset by a notable decline in the Republican vote of about 8 percent. As in 1962, some differences between urban and rural performances were accounted for by the presence of two candidates who had little appeal in urban

Agra but were popular in one or both of the rural constituencies. Between them, these two men managed to capture nearly 23 percent of the rural vote, but made almost no impact in the city.

TABLE 9.5

Percentage of Votes Received by Major Party Candidates in Agra MP Contest, 1967

| Candidate | Agra City MLA Districts | | | Rural Agra* | Overall† |
	East %	Cantt. %	West %	%	%
Seth (Cong.)	38	40	31	29	34
H. Rani (J.S.)	30	27	24	19	24
L. Dass (RPI)	20	29	31	14	22
Others	12	4	14	38	20
Total	100	100	100	100	100

* Percentages of total votes cast in the two rural MLA districts.
† Based on total vote cast in the MP contest.

Thus, Seth's popular support in the Agra MP contest dropped by slightly more than 14 percent,[23] while the Jan Sangh registered a gain of nearly 13 percent with a relatively weak candidate. The Republican Party, which experienced a setback from its 27.8 percent of 1962 to 21.7 percent in 1967, could still claim a major stake in the local political arena. The likelihood remained strong, however, that the party had reached its maximum capabilities in 1962 as a primordial organization bolstered by an alliance with influential Muslims. As we shall see, subsequent events did little to strengthen the party after these elections.

Party Voting

In examining voting behavior in Agra in 1967, we can compare the votes for MP and MLA in each of the MLA constituencies as we did for 1962 (see table 9.2). Table 9.6 attests to the operation of processes we have noted above. Republican Party voters still exhibit enormous consistency in their behavior. In each of the three urbanized MLA districts, 2 percent or less of the vote separates that party's candidate for MP from the candidate for MLA; the MP nominee runs only slightly better than the MLA in each place. The correspondence of Jan Sangh nominees is not quite as marked, but here the candidate for MP ran behind in each urban constituency. Finally, there was again considerable variation in Congress performances but nothing like that observed in 1962. The great decrease in support for Achal Singh came into closer conformity with the "basic vote" received by the party's MLA candidates. At the same time that Achal Singh's urban vote fell by 14 percent, the vote for his three Congress runningmates declined by about 2 percent. The greatest disparity was in Agra East, where there was no cooperation between the two candidates; the least difference occurred in Agra West, even though Bhogilal Misra and Seth were not really working together. Indeed, Seth was personally closest to the candidate in the cantonment, but the figures presented in table 9.6 show a 7 percent difference in their public support.

TABLE 9.6

Comparison of MP and MLA Vote Received by Major Party Candidates in Urban MLA Districts, Agra, 1967

MLA District	Congress			Republican			Jan Sangh		
	MP %	MLA %	Diff. %	MP %	MLA %	Diff. %	MP %	MLA %	Diff. %
Agra East	38	25	+13	20	18	+2	30	33	−3
Cantonment	40	33	+ 7	29	28	+1	27	31	−4
Agra West	31	30	+ 1	31	30	+1	24	28	−4
Mean Difference:			+ 7			+1			−4

These rather gross figures are further refined when we look at the same results by polling stations. Table 9.7 employs the same categorical breakdowns as the comparable table for 1962 (table 9.3). As in our discussion of that earlier election, we find the greatest consistency in party voting among those who supported the Republican Party, although party unity is slightly less evident than in 1962. In contrast, there is an enormous gulf in the vote for Congress in Agra East and—more

TABLE 9.7

Variations in Party Vote for MP and MLA Candidates of Major Parties, in Agra City MLA Districts, 1967

| MLA District | Difference in Percentage of Total Vote in Each Contest* | | | |
	High (6+ %)	Medium (4-5.9%)	Low (0-3.9%)	Number of Stations
Agra East:				
Congress	35	3	3	
Republican	4	6	31	41
Jan Sangh	8	7	26	
Agra Cantonment:				
Congress	19	6	8	
Republican	1	1	31	33
Jan Sangh	12	12	9	
Agra West:				
Congress	12	7	24	
Republican	5	4	34	43
Jan Sangh	14	4	25	

* Based on difference in percentage of vote received by candidates for MLA and MP in each polling station.

important—a fairly dispersed vote in both Agra West and the cantonment. While Agra West reveals almost no difference in gross outcomes (table 9.6), our examination of voting patterns by polling stations indicates that in more than a quarter of the units there was a high variation between the two Congress candidates, and in another seven a moderate difference. This was even more the case in the cantonment constituency, where more than half of the polling stations showed a high variance in votes between Seth Achal Singh and Harihar Nath Agarwal, although the two men were not personally in conflict. Rather, each MLA candidate for Congress ran his own campaign separately from that for MP, and there was only a marginal effect of "organization."

Jan Sangh performances fell somewhere between those of the other two parties in terms of possible organizational effectiveness. The growth in its overall vote was associated with considerable interconstituency variation. Thus, in Agra East, the two Jan Sangh Bania candidates polled nearly the same vote in about 63 percent of the polling stations. The differences were more pronounced in Agra West, although approximately the same number of polling stations witnessed strong party voting for the Jan Sangh as in Agra East. In Agra Cantonment, the Jan Sangh did not receive consistent electoral support for its two candidates. The difference between the two nominees was slight in less than a third of the units. While Jan Sangh persons interviewed denied any "groupism," some elements of local-refugee differences may have crept into these results. Without public opinion data or census materials which would pinpoint the composition of populations voting in each polling station, however, we cannot be more certain of the meanings of these variations.

On the whole, we might view these temporal trends in voting behavior in urban Agra between the elections of 1962 and 1967 as a move in the direction of "tripartism." Table 9.8 summarizes the changed positions of the parties for the three urban MLA districts of Agra over time. It should be noted that while the Jan Sangh markedly increased its following and the Congress moved slightly downward, the Republican Party experienced a severe slump. Equally impressive is the apparent increase of overall party strength in the local political system. In 1962, of course, one of the three seats had been won by an independent; at that time, the three major parties received 79 percent of the vote. Despite a sizable jump in total candidacies in each of the constituencies, the three major parties had *increased* their domination of the local political system sufficiently by 1967 to draw slightly more than 85 percent of all the votes cast.

TABLE 9.8

Variations in Group Voting between 1962 and 1967 for Urban MLA Districts, Agra

Party	1962 Vote		1967 Vote	
Congress	51,127	(32%)	50,866	(30%)
Republican	52,430	(33%)	42,760	(25%)
Jan Sangh	23,140	(14%)	52,151	(30%)
Others	33,485	(21%)	25,172	(15%)
Total	160,182	(100%)	170,949	(100%)

If these elections do, in fact, represent the influence of the three parties as of 1967, we would expect rather different partisan distributions to emerge from the municipal elections held in May 1968 than occurred in 1959. The Jan Sangh promised to make gains of a substantial nature; the Republicans might recede from their influence of 1959. Given the growth of the Jan Sangh and the relative stability of the Congress, albeit at a level very different from its political domination of Agra during the period from 1947 to 1959, we might anticipate a smaller representation in the corporation of nonaffiliated members. Part of chapter 10, therefore, will relate the structure of local politics reflected in the elections of 1967 to the results of the municipal elections which followed.

POONA POLITICS IN 1967

The Poona Congress which developed after 1960 pursued its pragmatic style and machine activities while avoiding ideational confrontation with the city's variously constituted opposition groups. The latter included Socialists in their differing incarnations and the Hindu Right. Such ideational groupings, however bitterly divided they were in program and organization, drew substantial leadership from Brahmin and other high-status communities. To some extent, however, they appealed to different audiences: the Jan Sangh to middle-class and high-status Hindus of a conservative bent; the Socialists to reformist Brahmins and to working-class non-Brahmins.

In broad outline, the system of politics introduced into Poona in the 1950s and confirmed in the elections of 1962 remained fundamentally unaltered through the municipal elections of 1968. Within the framework of that system, a variety of epiphenomena occurred which contributed to the persistence of the system while modifying relations among particular sub-units. Thus, in the face of an assortment of opposition groups and individuals operating in Poona over the last twenty years, the Congress has perennially been short of attaining a *reliable* majority, no matter what its short-run successes; on their side, anti-Congress elements have regularly attained precarious majorities, generally at the cost of internal ideational homogeneity, only to fall victim to the fragile structure of their own oppositionism. The result was a carefully balanced local political order which was not tipped markedly toward one side or the other despite the Samyukta Maharashtra Samiti successes of 1957 and easy Congress victories in early 1962.

The Sampoorna Maharashtra Samiti

Up to 1964, the most important political organization to influence the course of opposition tactics in Poona was the PSP. At the time of our first visit, that organization was passing through a difficult period. A series of defections from the PSP to the Congress in the wake of the creation of Maharashtra had hurt the party. Chavan's efforts to preempt the verbiage of socialism also tended to undermine the PSP position.

Therefore, the opportunity to join together with Ram Manohar Lohia's more militant Socialist Party in a new organization in 1964 was a great temptation to an element within the Poona PSP. While certain of them expressed a personal distaste for Lohia and for the agitational methods employed by him, even these members appreciated the need to overcome a creeping lassitude in their organization. The hope existed, as a member of the PSP suggested, that "the merger will reduce some of the extremism of the Socialist Party and make the PSP a little more revolutionary." As far as he and others were concerned, "The PSP has become too respectable."

Negotiations for merger went on through much of 1964 with the first national party meeting of the new Samyukta (United) Socialist Party (SSP) scheduled for Varanasi early in 1965. There were increasing misgivings as the time of the convention drew near, particularly on the side of the more moderate elements in the PSP. A prominent intellectual in the PSP reflected on some of this discomfort in 1968:

> Lohia wanted an unconditional merger, but some of the members of the PSP had reservations about his approach. H. V. Kamath and others felt that there should be a careful discussion of ideological differences before we rushed into

such a marriage. Such a discussion was not undertaken but even in this period serious difficulties were apparent. Each group used its own methods of working. We realized that shades of opinion were bound to exist within any party but these differences went deeper than that. For example, we would never favor *Angreezi Haatao* [Quit English]. Our differences were also clear in the approach to the Nehru resolution.

The question of ending the use of English in national and state governments and in the schools of India was associated with the more militant populism of Lohia. In seeking to gain a following in the Hindi-speaking North on this issue, the Socialist Party weakened the possibility of increasing its support in non-Hindi speaking areas of the South, particularly Madras. Moderates in the PSP advocated a less populistic style of behavior on this and other issues, but some members of the 1964 PSP asserted the need to pursue such a course. As one of these leaders later argued,

> The SSP wants to be militant but not undemocratic. We do resort to demonstrations regularly, but there are many issues to be raised. We need to give shocks to society if we are to wake the people up. Indian society is static and we have to move it, particularly the poorer sections of the population. Unfortunately, there is a failing of will among the people. They tend to think in terms of *deviwar*—God's will—which lays all the responsibility for society upon fate. We want to bring the major section of the population out of this view. For this, militancy is needed.

At the Varanasi meeting itself, a major break was precipitated by the Nehru resolution referred to above. Some members of the PSP wanted to pass a condolence resolution recognizing the support Nehru had provided to the Congress Socialists in the 1930s, but the more militant elements were opposed to any such action since they blamed Nehru for the failure to live up to his earlier promises in his post-Independence performance. Lohia was one of the few leading politicians publicly to express an antipathy toward Nehru during the latter's lifetime, and his supporters were not about to compromise their earlier attacks by passing a condolence resolution. As a result no resolution was passed; instead, a moment of silence was observed. While minor in itself, this incident revealed the differences in style of the two groupings. As a member of the PSP later summed up the result, "We saw that our minds were different and decided to go our own way."

In this split, many members of the Poona PSP decided to work within the new SSP. This group was led by S. M. Joshi. Those whose style was more Fabian in character remained in the much weakened PSP now led by N. G. Goray.[24] Indeed, Joshi emerged from Varanasi as the national Chairman of the SSP, while Goray became the Chairman of the PSP.[25]

Despite the split between Joshi and Goray at the national level, their organizations continued to cooperate within the Poona corporation. The only real note of disunity between their two organizations occurred in the spring of 1966, when the independent then serving as deputy mayor became embroiled with Joshi in an unpleasant personal duel over some remarks the SSP leader had made in a corporation meeting. The deputy mayor, who was noted for his hot temper, ordered Joshi out of the meeting hall. When Joshi refused to leave, the deputy mayor attempted to have him removed bodily.[26] This incident inflamed the wrath of SSP members of the corporation; they were also antagonized by the fact that Goray's supporters did not join in the walk out from the meeting hall staged by Joshi's followers.[27]

In terms of the electoral strategies advocated for the 1967 general elections, the two parties were very different. During the period leading up to the elections of 1967, Lohia was one of the chief advocates in India of United Fronts to remove the Congress from power. This policy of "non-Congressism" was to be pursued without concern for ideological or organizational harmony. In Maharashtra, it had what seemed to be a natural rallying point in the call for "Sampoorna [Complete] Maharashtra"—a demand for redrawing the boundary with Mysore and including Belgaum District in Maharashtra on the basis of the presence of a large Marathi-speaking population in that district. With the notable exception of the new PSP, most of the same elements that had capitalized earlier on the demand for Samyukta Maharashtra joined in the new agitations. At the time they met at Kolhapur to set up the new Samiti, one SSP figure later commented, "We felt that it was an issue in which the people were getting emotionally involved."

While supporting the principle of Sampoorna Maharashtra, the PSP was not willing to enter into a United Front on the issue nor to make it the basis of major agitations. As one spokesman of the PSP viewed the issue,

> We did not feel that it was a life and death matter. We favored a system of arbitration and clear terms being laid down for a commission but we did not feel that this should be the focus of the 1967 political campaign. We feel that the Karnatak [Mysore] is not Pakistan and it is a bad business to stir up issues in the way that they have done.

The national Congress took considerable impetus out of the Samiti's agitations in 1966 by appointing a former Chief Justice of the Supreme Court, Mehrchand Mahajan, to act as a one-man commission to make a study of the boundary dispute and report back after the elections. While the Sampoorna Maharashtra Samiti continued to agitate on the issue and to complain about the failure to provide Mahajan with clear terms of reference, the influence of Chavan and Naik with the central government was expected to protect the interests of Maharashtra.[28]

For the 1967 elections, the Samiti operated as a front within which major political groups and outstanding local individuals worked out electoral adjustments. Many of its activities seemed to have had their center in Poona; it is reflective of this that the organization's Executive Committee included S. M. Joshi (SSP), Jayantrao Tilak (Editor of *Kesari*), V. B. Gogate (Hindu Mahasabha)—all from Poona—along with S. A. Dange (CPI), Datta Deshmukh (Lal Nishan) and K. N. Dhulup (PWP). The PSP ran a few candidates on its own.

Similarly, the Jan Sangh found both the Sampoorna Maharashtra demand and United Front efforts unpalatable. The party was more concerned with building cadres and spreading its influence than with immediate electoral benefits. It was working in Poona, in particular, to consolidate the Jan Sangh following in the

Brahmin community. The disruption in the Socialist groups and the final death throes of the Hindu Mahasabha contributed to their hope for growth.

Finally, sections of the Republican Party were being drawn toward closer association with the Congress during the period preceding the elections of 1967. The Gaikwad group could reach no agreement with the Congress which was mutually satisfactory. It therefore reluctantly associated with the Samiti. In Bombay, however, a non-Gaikwad element of the Republicans joined the Congress and was rewarded with a nomination for Parliament for its leader.[29] This only increased the pressure within the RPI (Gaikwad) for cooperation with the Congress after the elections.

Outside the major urban centers of Maharashtra, the Congress organization remained in fairly good form during the elections. Personality and power conflicts occurred at the state level, but none of them immediately degenerated into the electoral factionalism evident in Uttar Pradesh. In this connection, a rather disgruntled member of the Congress remarked:

> There are two groups within the Congress organization throughout Maharashtra. One likes Chavan and the other does not, but both revere him in public. They differ among themselves but they get along well enough to work together when they see something they can divide among themselves.

Whereas surface unity existed in the Congress in the state of Maharashtra, the elections came at a time when the Poona organization was undergoing some strain. The dominant figure in the City Congress, B. N. Sanas, was in bad health and his grip on the organization was loosening. Claimants for the leadership of the City Congress were beginning to maneuver for advantage in the coming battle. Under the circumstances, they were not reluctant to weaken an opponent's position even if it meant an electoral defeat for the party. As a result, the Congress entered the electoral process in early 1967 in a weaker state than its inherent following or organizational strength warranted. However, the loss of the MP seat and two of the five MLA seats in the city which followed were due to a variety of factors which are traceable to more than the Congress divisions alone.

The Poona MP Contest

As a result of the activities of the Central Election Commission, MP and MLA constituencies in Maharashtra were redrawn for the 1967 general elections. Poona's MP constituency still conformed to the prescribed Maharashtra arrangement of six MLA districts, but in place of the Kirkee Cantonment and Haveli Taluka MLA constituencies of 1962, the new MP district included the heavily rural Mulshi district along with a newly created Bhavani Peth reserved constituency in the city.[30] The four other urban seats were considerably redrawn from previous elections. As in Agra, this makes direct comparison between elections difficult, but we can examine some of the broad features of these contests.

The sharpest contrast with 1962 was probably in the election of an MP. In place of the late S. S. More, Chavan insisted that a Brahmin be nominated for the party ticket. Recognizing the alienation of the Brahmin community from the

Congress, party leaders felt obligated to put up a few Brahmin candidates in areas where they might have some chance of winning. In a city like Poona, with its large Brahmin population, the temptation to "rise above communalism," as one observer commented, appealed to the "dream" attributed to Chavan (when he came into office) of uniting the Marathas, Brahmins and Mahars. His interest in cooperation with the Republican Party, it was argued, was part of the same ambition.

While S. G. Barve would have been an obvious choice under the circumstances, he was put forward instead for the highly publicized MP race in Bombay City against Krishna Menon. The Poona Congress turned instead to V. N. Gadgil, the son of the last Brahmin MP from Poona. Except for a brief period of membership in the PSP, V. N. Gadgil had little political experience and had spent most of his time away from Poona tending to his Bombay legal practice. Despite some grumbling in the Poona Congress, Chavan's preference in the matter was accepted.

The Sampoorna Maharashtra Samiti came forward with their most prominent figure, S. M. Joshi. Neither the PSP nor the Jan Sangh saw fit to challenge Joshi. The former still had enormous respect for its exleader and the latter was hoping to arrange an understanding with the SMS in one of Poona's MLA seats. A third Brahmin candidate entered the contest but received less than four thousand votes (1 percent of the votes cast) as an independent. At least for the purposes of this particular race, Joshi succeeded in consolidating the support of all opposition parties as well as that of some dissatisfied Congress members against the newcomer to the party.

In the latter connection, Gadgil probably did not help himself with the non-Brahmins by appealing during the campaign for Brahmin votes on the basis of an alleged ability to act as a liaison to the Congress. Without a Jan Sangh candidate in the race for MP, he carefully avoided making attacks on the Jan Sangh. This was going on at the same time that the Jan Sangh was working very hard to defeat the Congress candidate for MLA in Shukrawar Peth, where much of the Brahmin population of Poona resides.

In the essentially "straight fight" between Joshi and Gadgil, the former managed to win with 52 percent of the vote against Gadgil's 47 percent. Although this represented a narrow victory for "non-Congressism," it should be noted that Gadgil actually ran with or ahead of most of his MLA runningmates and received a higher percentage of the votes than More had in 1962.

The defeat for MP can hardly be regarded as a major setback for the local Congress organization. Indeed, it tended to strengthen the hand of non-Brahmins in the party, since they could now point to the event as proof that chances were slim of another Brahmin candidate for MP winning on a Congress ticket.

Shukrawar Peth

Except for Shukrawar Peth itself, which was partially non-Brahmin in complexion, the newly-constituted Shukrawar Peth MLA constituency included a large area that was essentially Brahmin. This new character resulted from an exchange of municipal wards with the Shivajinagar MLA constituency of 1962 which had so resoundingly elected S. G. Barve against a Jan Sangh challenger, R. K. Mhalgi.[31]

With Barve removed from the scene, the Congress was forced to seek another Brahmin candidate for the district. It turned to Dr. B. P. Apte, a well-known doctor and one of the two Brahmin Congressmen in the Poona corporation. Although Dr. Apte's first preference was to contest from the new Shivajinagar constituency where he lived, the Congress organization convinced him to contest in what was expected to be Jan Sangh territory. The contest was made more difficult by the reentry of Mhalgi as the nominee of the Jan Sangh. Both on behalf of the Jan Sangh and in his own interest, Mhalgi had assiduously cultivated the Brahmin population of this area during the five-year interim between elections. His task was made all the easier by SMS indecision in naming a candidate in the constituency.

While the existence of any agreement between the SMS and the Jan Sangh in Shukrawar Peth is strenuously denied by both sides, the fact is that the SMS was very concerned about electing S. M. Joshi to Parliament; the Jan Sangh was the main obstacle to that. The entry of a serious Jan Sangh contender in the MP race would undoubtedly have permitted the election of a Congress candidate. Although the SMS finally did sponsor a candidate in Shukrawar Peth, they did so with many misgivings. That nominee was a recent Hindu Mahasabha defector from the Nagri Sanghatna who had prevailed upon certain key figures in the Samiti to enter him as the local SMS candidate despite SSP reluctance. There was little actual enthusiasm for the Samiti candidate from constituent elements of that coalition.

Along with these three candidates, Shukrawar Peth attracted three others. Two of them were corporators—one a non-Brahmin member of the PSP; the other the Brahmin ex-deputy mayor mentioned earlier. He stood as an independent. The entry of these candidates made no difference in the final outcome as Mhalgi swept the constituency with 57 percent of the vote, trailed at considerable distance by Apte, who received about 26 percent. Among the four others, the Samiti nominee received barely 7 percent of the 54,491 votes cast. This showing suggests how weakly the Samiti had committed its forces on behalf of its nominal MLA candidate since S. M. Joshi received 64 percent of the same constituency's vote for MP. The final result indicates, again, the great anti-Congress sentiment which exists among the Brahmin section of the Poona population.

Shivajinagar

In 1962, Shivajinagar was the largest municipal ward in the corporation. It elected six corporators: two Brahmins, two Marathas, a Mali, and a Mang. Four of these, including Dr. Apte, were associated with the Congress. The remainder of the constituency in the general election of that year was solidly Brahmin. As noted above, the delimitation of 1967 moved these Brahmin wards into the Shukrawar constituency. The new territory added to Shivajinagar included the Kirkee Cantonment and several relatively nonurbanized areas formally located within the boundaries of the corporation. Given the character of Poona politics, this was now an MLA constituency which demanded non-Brahmin candidacies. On balance, its population was closely divided politically with a slight tendency to favor the Congress.

For its candidate, the Samiti turned to the last Sanghatna mayor of Poona, B. D. Killedar. Having begun his political career as secretary to S. S. More when the latter was active in the PWP, Killedar remained in that party after More's withdrawal. A popular figure in his own ward at the time he was elected to the corporation in 1962 (with the highest vote in a field of twenty-five), Killedar was highly respected as an intelligent and articulate politician. He added to his local standing by serving his term as mayor from 1965 to 1966 with his future political career in mind. Many interviewees commented on his local fence-mending during this period. The fact that he was a well-educated Maratha with socialist inclinations made his appeal as the candidate of the Sampoorna Maharashtra Samiti all the greater to residents of his constituency whether Brahmin or non-Brahmin.

Against Killedar, the Congress selected Namderao Mate, a man who had served as President of the City Congress from 1959 to 1963. While Mate was an important figure in the Congress and was completing his first term in the corporation, he was closely associated with Sanas. A man then in the process of attempting to displace Sanas in the leadership of the Poona Congress was a resident of Shivajinagar and a powerful figure in that area; as a former member of the PWP from 1948 to 1959, this leader also had connections to the Samiti camp. At first, he tried to prevent the ticket from being given to Mate, but Sanas was a member of the MPCC body responsible for distributing the party's nominations and made sure that Mate was the candidate. In his comments on his *own* lack of support for Mate, the dissident leader said:

> Mate was not acceptable to the Shivajinagar area in terms of his education and his work. He was a stranger to the area. It was not my lookout to worry about Mate. I did work for [another candidate], who is one of my dearest friends, but Mate had his own followers and ranking in the party organization.

To make matters worse for the Congress nominee, a highly influential three-term corporator from a rural section of the constituency revolted from the Congress and stood as an MLA candidate under Samiti auspices in the Haveli constituency. As one Congressman noted, "Because of the absence of [B's] support behind Mate, several places in the ward did not vote up to the usual Congress expectations."

Two other candidates entered this contest. The Jan Sangh supported an Agarwal, who drew some votes from the middle class of Shivajinagar; the fourth candidate was a Mahar corporator associated with the Kamble wing of the Republican Party. Killedar, however, gained support from the more important Gaikwad Republican element in the constituency.

In the final count, Killedar was an easy victor in this contest capturing nearly 53 percent of the vote to Mate's 35 percent. The Jan Sangh nominee came in third with only 8 percent. Under the circumstances, it was likely that there was a serious organizational defection from the Congress since areas which had gone for Congress in the past—except for 1957—revealed themselves as supporters of the Samiti candidate.

Bhavani Peth

The Congress won the three other urban Poona contests with varying degrees of ease. Its lightest task was in the newly created Bhavani Peth reserved-seat constituency, which had been carved out of wards with high concentrations of middle- and low-status Hindus and the various non-Mahar Scheduled Caste communities found in Poona. Three of the 1962 corporation's six reserved seats were now to be found in this MLA constituency. Still, candidates elected to the corporation from the wards constituting this constituency were almost evenly balanced between Congress and the Nagri Sanghatna, eight to seven. None were Brahmins; six were Marathas.

As is frequently the case in reserved constituencies, a large number of candidates entered the contest—nine in all. Only three were supported by parties. These were the nominees of the Congress, the SMS (a Gaikwad Republican), and the PSP. The Congress candidate was a Bhangi corporator. He had the advantage of Congress backing in a situation where the great majority of the population had no primordial stake in the outcome of the election. Neither the RPI nor the PSP candidates were well-known in the larger constituency. In the final count, Congress support among the heterogeneous population of the constituency appeared to help bring about victory; the Congress candidate received 53 percent of the vote as against 34 percent for the nominee of RPI—probably much higher than the RPI nominee would have got if that party had entered on its own. The PSP-supported candidate finished third with only 8 percent of the vote. This was the one MLA district where the Congress MLA candidate ran well ahead of Gadgil. The personal popularity of Joshi among the working-class may have had much to do with that result.

Kasba Peth

In its primordial composition, the new Kasba constituency was the heterogeneous equal of Bhavani Peth, but there was a greater range of status groups present including Brahmin enclaves and *galis* inhabited by artisan and service communities. The district had a good number of non-Maharashtrians: Tamils, Telugus, Gujaratis. A candidate of non-Maharashtrian background was nominated by the Jan Sangh and the Congress backed the incumbent, R. V. Telang—a former mayor of Poona. Telang, who was a non-Maharashtrian by family background, was a popular figure in the area and received substantial support from one wing of the local Congress organization.

However, if part of the organization defected in Shivajinagar, it is also widely believed in Poona that the other section was not fully supporting the party nominee in Kasba Peth. A leader in the corporation was said to have tacitly supported the SMS nominee, R. P. Vadake, a two-term corporator and one of the most militant members of the SSP. Vadake, one of the Tambat corporators to whom we referred in an earlier chapter, had built up a considerable personal following in his home area during the years he was the only prominent Lohia Socialist in the corporation. With the aid of the SMS constituent groups, he promised to do well in this race. The assistance of the Congress dissidents, while largely sub rosa, was expected to provide an additional margin of support.

Still, with nearly the largest turnout in the city—75 percent as against the 76 percent in more highly educated Shukrawar Peth—the Congress managed to win comfortably. Telang captured over 48 percent of the vote to Vadake's 39 percent, with a Jan Sangh nominee attracting 12 percent. This happened at the same time that Joshi was carrying the district with 52 percent. There is some belief that a less militant figure than Vadake might have been more successful in attracting the support of business communities to the Samiti.

Poona Cantonment

Finally, the contest in the Poona Cantonment area should be briefly mentioned. As in Agra, the name belies the fact that as a result of the new delimitation of MLA constituencies it contained substantial population from the corporation. Corporators elected from three corporation wards now included in the district were heavily non-Congress in 1962: five from the Nagri Sanghatna; one from the RPI; one Congress. Of the seven, three were Malis and three Marathas. The cantonment itself included a substantial population of Muslims and non-Maharashtrians. While the latter generally voted for the Congress, there was increasing disaffection among them from the Congress organization. Thus, during 1966 it was widely reported that members of the Congress in the cantonment area were exceedingly unhappy with the practice of setting up "outsiders"—persons from elsewhere in the area—as MLA candidates in the cantonment.[32] Despite their complaints, the MPCC redesignated K. T. Girme, the incumbent, as the party's candidate.

The SMS put up a strong candidate against Girme, R. D. Tupe, who had been active in the PSP for some years and had contested for MLA in a previous election. Given the dissent of leading Congressmen including an important member of the *zilla parishad,* the entry of a strong SMS candidate and the presence of a population without a strong commitment to the Congress, the contest between the two major candidates was expected to be close.

It was complicated, however, by the presence of five additional candidates. Two of these were refugees from the Sind and were engaged in a continuing personal dispute within their community. Neither of these men ran with party support. A third minor candidate was entered by the Jan Sangh, which sought to extend its appeal into the substantial middle-class vote in the cantonment and adjacent urban territory.

While the top two nominees in each of the other four contests captured from 83 to 88 percent of the total vote between them, in the cantonment the winning Congressman and the runner-up SSP nominee shared only about 68 percent of the total. The Congress incumbent came out ahead with 36 percent of the vote. Third was one of the Sindhis with slightly over 10 percent of the votes cast.

Overview

When the elections of 1967 were completed in Maharashtra, the Congress still held over 70 percent of the seats in the Maharashtra Legislative Assembly. This was the best showing of the party in any state in India. In this light, the victories of the opposition groups in Poona were not, in themselves, reflective of major setbacks for the Congress elsewhere in the state. If anything, they merely confirmed the peculiar complexion of politics in Poona as contrasted with the rest of Maharashtra.

If we aggregate the votes cast in the five urban constituencies, as done in table 9.9, the Congress appears to be in a fairly exposed position in Poona. From what we have said here and in earlier chapters, it is probable that the substantial Congress victories of 1962 were misleading as to basic Congress strength vis-à-vis a united opposition force in Poona. It is likely that the Congress and its natural bases of opposition in the city—the various shadings of ideational groups, most Brahmin political activists, individual leaders dissatisfied with the material and psychic benefits received from the Congress—will continue to struggle for dominance in the local political system for the foreseeable future.

TABLE 9.9

Variations in Party Voting in 1967, Poona City MLA Constituencies

Constituency	Congress	SMS		Jan Sangh	Other
Kasba Peth	22,567	18,398	(SSP)	5,603	183
Bhavani Peth (R)	25,883	16,493	(RPI)	—	6,540
Shukrawar Peth	14,146	3,784	(HM)	31,265	5,296
Shivajinagar	15,747	23,509	(PWP)	3,531	1,915
Cantonment	14,924	12,972	(SSP)	4,126	8,888
	93,267	75,156		44,525	22,822
Percentage of Total Votes:	39.6	32.0		18.9	9.7

(R) Reserved for Scheduled Caste candidates.

The figures in table 9.9 suggest that the Congress has a minimum of about 40 percent of the voting strength of Poona City upon which it can call even in the face of internal dissidence. When combined, the vote for the forces associated with the Sampoorna Maharashtra Samiti constituted about a third of the electorate, although they might have come closer to equalling the Congress if the Jan Sangh had not been so strongly represented in the Shukrawar Peth constituency. It is notable that on an aggregate basis, independents did not do well. Among those listed in table 9.9 under "Other" are 6,881 votes cast for nominees of the PSP running in Bhavani Peth and Shukrawar Peth. Independents were not a major factor anywhere except the cantonment.

Along very broad lines, one might contrast the bimodal voting behavior of Poona citizens with the tripartism of Agra, but the constant threats which existed to the stability of electoral agreements like the Sampoorna Maharashtra Samiti bring such comparisons into doubt. The presence of the SMS makes it difficult to attempt to identify a pattern of party voting in Poona as we did in Agra. This difficulty is also a reflection of the discrepancy between the two-man race for MP and the variations in number and partisanship of candidacies in each MLA district.

CONCLUSIONS

Between 1957 and 1967, the political system in Agra was transmuted into a new form of partisan crystallization. Prior to 1957, the hegemony of the Congress Party in that city was not seriously challenged. In 1959, however, its own factionalism and the rise of political groups like the Jan Sangh and the Republican Party introduced a series of elements into the political order which the Congress was not capable of responding to with adaptive modes of behavior. The corporation elections of 1959 caught the system at a time when recently mobilized elements were beginning to work toward a new political order in the city. Some of these arrangements began to stabilize by the time of the general elections in 1962, with its affirmation of some Jan Sangh and RPI strength and the apparent failure of the Congress to overcome its own incapacities. In the following years, the Congress organization probably reached its nadir in Agra. It was still associated with the major national and state political force in India, but it had failed to recruit a new generation of young men; its appeals to low-caste Hindus and Scheduled Caste communities were ineffectual; its earlier following among Muslims was being dissipated.

Indicative of these difficulties in recruitment and organizational maintenance was the domination of the party in 1967 by the same people who had run the party in 1947 and who were still quarreling over matters raised by 1952. The gerontocracy heading the Congress managed to stave off possibly worse disaster in 1967 by accepting MLA candidates imposed from above who were largely tangential to the existent City Congress. The sharp drop in Seth's support and the mounting evidence of Jan Sangh strength in areas where Congress had previously prevailed finally set off the alarm needed to create a change in organizational mood. State politics also began to change as the Uttar Pradesh Congress almost halfheartedly drew back from what seemed to be its own factional undoing. The result was a somewhat chastened Congress organization that fought the corporation elections in 1968.

What happened in Poona between 1962 and 1967 was less striking in its implications for municipal politics than was the case in Agra. Despite several setbacks in the elections in the latter year, the Congress was still fundamentally strong. The appearance in late 1966 of factionalism in the Congress might have been resolved in various ways, including a permanent groupism of the kind so well known in Uttar Pradesh and elsewhere in India. That this was prevented is a tribute to the effectiveness of the MPCC in reconciling various claimants to local positions of authority.

At the same time, "non-Congressism" was having its difficulties in remaining a consolidated force in Poona. The Jan Sangh pursued its organizational goals separate from other groups, making expedient arrangements where it saw immediate gains but carefully using these arrangements to build its own organizational strength from its base in the Shukrawar Peth MLA constituency. Other opposition groups were adrift. The demand for Sampoorna Maharashtra was short-lived and could not hope to become the basis for a sustained political coalition. The SSP remained the backbone of what leftist opposition organization remained in Poona; those Mahars associated with the Gaikwad group of the RPI were already anxiously working for an understanding with the Congress.[33] The Hindu Mahasabha had collapsed. The PSP stood apart from the SMS, while the Communists—both Left and Right—gathered little political advantage in Poona from their involvements in United Fronts.

If the setbacks of 1967 finally convinced the Agra Congress of the need to begin to cope with a rusted organizational machine requiring considerable repair, the Poona Congress emerged temporarily damaged from the same elections but sufficiently "operational" to set its organization to work at a rather high level of efficiency for the 1968 municipal elections once a few adjustments had been made.

10 MUNICIPAL POLITICS IN 1968

The general elections of 1967 gave rise to a wave of changes throughout Indian politics. Opposition groupings coalesced into electoral and then governmental alliances; offshoots of the Congress appeared in many states to complicate an already confused political scene. The election results produced non-Congress governments in eight of the Indian states.

Maharashtra proved to be one of the most secure states for the Congress, but Uttar Pradesh reflected the changing character of Indian politics. Dissident Congressmen, under the leadership of Charan Singh, left the Congress government which immediately followed the elections to form a new political group, the *Bharatiya Kranti Dal* (Indian Revolutionary Party; BKD). The new party then entered a governmental coalition with the Jan Sangh, SSP and other parties—a coalition over which Charan Singh presided as Chief Minister until February 1968, when his government collapsed, in large part because of its own internal quarrels. [1]

The Congress might have succumbed to further decay as a result of its setback in Uttar Pradesh, but there was some effort by national leaders and state party loyalists to stiffen the organization's capacity for action. The organization evidenced more awareness of the need to generate a new following and to paper over some of its internal factionalism than it had for twenty years. The disputes within the United Front government and the administrative weaknesses shown by it made the task somewhat easier as it became clear that "non-Congressism," in itself, was no panacea for dealing with the problems of the people of Uttar Pradesh.

While its rural hinterland assured a strong Congress majority in Maharashtra, the urban population of that state was less reliable. Thus, the Congress organization in the city of Bombay suffered several well-publicized defeats in the elections of 1967, including the defeat of the leader of the BPCC at the hands of a Samiti candidate. [2] One of the new phenomena in the elections of 1967 was the emergence in the city of a militant political group demanding more jobs and more control of Bombay City life by Maharashtrians. This organization, the *Shiv Sena* (Shivaji's Army), aimed its attacks particularly against South Indians who had come into the city since Independence. While many of its threats (and acts) of violence were directed at slum dwellers and small businessmen from South India, the Shiv Sena also attracted a following by publicizing incidents of alleged discrimination against Maharashtrians in white-collar positions.

The Sena's paramilitary organization and disruptive tactics were brought into play for the first time in Bombay on behalf of S. G. Barve in his MP campaign against Krishna Menon, the latter being a South Indian. It is commonly believed that the Shiv Sena operated during this campaign with the tacit approval of certain figures in the Congress who might have been reluctant to have their own party assume a similar style of public behavior. Having helped to defeat Menon, the Sena stood forward in 1968 in its own right as a participant in the Bombay corporation elections. Allegedly bolstered by financial support from several major industrialists who saw the Sena as an entering wedge in weakening the political influence of leftist parties and their affiliated trade unions in Bombay, that organization was able to mount an impressive campaign against the Congress and the still active Sampoorna Maharashtra Samiti. To the surprise of many observers, the PSP, which had stood aloof from the SMS in 1967, now entered an electoral agreement with the Shiv Sena; this alliance ran contrary to much of the public rhetoric of the PSP leadership including its earlier attacks on the SSP for fostering expedient agreements.[3]

As a result of this new alliance, the PSP managed to save itself from possible electoral oblivion in Bombay; with the help of the Shiv Sena, it elected eleven corporators—a drop of only three from the showing of the unified PSP of the previous corporation election. This act in behalf of organizational maintenance took place at the same time that the combined leftist opposition, which had won thirty-seven seats in the municipal elections of 1961, elected only six corporation members. The Shiv Sena now emerged as the second largest group in the corporation with forty corporators to the Congress Party's sixty-four. With the aid of Republicans and some independents, the Congress was able to elect a mayor.

After its strong debut in Bombay, the Sena moved into that city's suburbs and captured control of an important suburban municipality. It was now threatening to expand into territory dominated by the MPCC.[4] If its appeals were to be responded to in the Poona region, it might represent the first really serious challenge to the Congress since the creation of the state. Thus, the Poona municipal elections scheduled for June 1968 took on added interest. Regional chauvinism had already gained an enormous following in Madras, where the Dravida Munnetra Kazagham had won solid control of the state government after the 1967 elections; there was increasing talk in the press of other regional groupings stirring throughout the nation which might spell the undoing of the Indian federation.

Not only did the Poona elections therefore receive national attention in mid-1968, but elections for four of the KAVAL corporations in May[5] were looked upon as a possible barometer of the political forces operative in Uttar Pradesh prior to the holding of planned mid-term elections.

At least at some places in Uttar Pradesh, the Congress regained ground lost in 1959. It was able to mount an effective campaign in Lucknow against the Jan Sangh, which had captured the corporation in the previous election. While the latter was now beset by factionalism, the Congress quieted some of its own internal differences and made a more effective appeal to population segments like the Muslims. The position of the Congress in Lucknow and elsewhere was strengthened by the failure of opposition parties to achieve any significant understanding among themselves. As a result, a total of 1,429 candidates ran for the 242 seats contested in the four Uttar Pradesh corporations.[6]

Despite the great number of candidates and the new political groups represented, both the Congress and the Jan Sangh registered gains over their performances of 1959. While losing support in Lucknow, the Jan Sangh gained a total of thirteen seats—many of them in Agra and Varanasi—and the Congress fourteen. This growth in party strength was related to a considerable decrease in the number of independents elected.[7] As a result of these outcomes, Congress mayors were elected in Lucknow and Kanpur; the Jan Sangh came to power in Varanasi. The result in Agra, as we shall see, was more ambiguous.

TOWARD "PARTISANSHIP" IN AGRA

The corporation produced in 1959 in Agra was one in which independents held an absolute majority; one of the more striking features of the outcome of the 1968 elections was their small representation. The period between the two elections had witnessed efforts at consolidation and expansion of the followings of the three major political parties: the Congress; the Jan Sangh, and the Republicans; in 1968, too, a series of new organizational claimants to the symbols of municipal political authority appeared—most notably, the SSP, the BKD, and the CPI. In the process of partisan extensions into the Agra population, the "pool" of independents dropped sharply. At the same time, however, the *meaning* of partisan identification remained as diffuse as it had been earlier.

An important dimension of these tendencies toward partisanship in Agra politics were the choices made by incumbent members of the corporation. Despite the earlier denials of interest in running again, thirty-eight of the fifty-four corporators elected in 1959 ran for the new body. Of these, seventeen campaigned under different auspices than they had in 1959. No Jan Sangh incumbent joined the Congress, while one Congressman—a doctor "notable" with only marginal past connection to the party—crossed over to the Jan Sangh. For the most part, partisan movement was at the margins of conflict: some party members were denied tickets and ran as independents; a few independent incumbents ran on the tickets of minor parties like the SSP and the CPI; one Congress incumbent refused a Congress ticket and stood as an independent. Thus of seven incumbents who stood with Jan Sangh backing in 1968, one was a former Congressman, another had defected with Baloji from the Jan Sangh after the elections of 1959, and two had been members of the Swatantra Dal. One of these two, Ram Babu Verma, was a former leader of the Jan Sangh and had maintained a personal attachment to the ideology of Jan Sangh from the time of his departure from the party nearly fifteen years earlier. The Congress, on its side, gave tickets to four independents, all of whom had been sympathetic to the cause of the Congress prior to the factional splits of 1959. On the whole, even among the incumbents, opportunities for independents to receive party designations were taken with alacrity.

The Jan Sangh

After the election of 1967, the Jan Sangh made a diligent effort to broaden its appeal among the broad range of social groups present in Agra with the possible exception of the Muslims. It actively pursued the votes of low "clean" castes like the Kurmis, Koris, and Gadariyas (Shepherds) and the marginally untouchable Khatiks.[8] A few members of these communities had been affiliated with the party as early as its formation in Agra in 1952, but the 1968 elections provided an additional impetus for identification with the party.

The Koris, who are traditionally a weaving community, numbered on the order of 15,000 persons in the city. They had elected no one to the corporation in 1959. A man active in the formation of the Kori caste association in 1948 admitted that the Jan Sangh was only now beginning to gain ground in the community. In this election, the Jan Sangh offered him and another Kori leader tickets for the corporation and they took them. As one of them remarked in a joint interview, "Only then did the Congress give a ticket to P— [a third member of the community] because they were afraid they would lose their Kori support."

In explaining the community's general dissatisfaction with the Congress, one of the Jan Sangh Kori corporators referred to a particular incident which he argued had led to the break:

> We felt that we were not being treated properly in the Congress. In particular, two years ago a fight broke out between the *goondas* belonging to the — community and the Koris. These *goondas* would come into our area and start teasing our women after they were drinking. They attacked us and tried to kidnap some of our women. We complained to the Congress leaders but they would not do anything about it. Then we went to Raj Kumar Sama [former President of the City Jan Sangh] and he helped to arrange for police protection for the community in a few hours; so the whole community's thinking about the Jan Sangh was changed. Because we were not educated we could not approach the police in the way that an educated man like Sama could.

Similarly, a member of another low-status community indicated the instrumental nature of his caste's affiliation with the Jan Sangh:

> The Backward Classes are giving more support to the Jan Sangh because the Congress made many promises over the years but did little. For the time being, the community is supporting the Jan Sangh. If we find that the Jan Sangh is not doing a suitable job, then we can change again.

The Jan Sangh also made a bid for Jatav support by working with a one-time leader of the Republican Party—a man who more recently had served as a Secretary of the City Congress. This man, who unsuccessfully sought an MP ticket from the Congress in 1967, had defected from that party when the United Front government came to power and one of his relatives (by marriage) received a ministerial post. With visions of ministerial patronage allegedly in mind, he and several of his followers joined the Jan Sangh in 1967 and ran for the corporation in 1968.

Because of its interest in extending its base, the Agra Jan Sangh nominated sixteen persons from low castes in 1968, including four Jatavs and two members of the untouchable Valmik (Sweeper) community (see table 10.1). At the same time, however, there was a surge in the representation of Brahmin candidates among the high-status nominees of the Jan Sangh. While no one in Agra drew attention to this latter development, and respondents to a question on the point insisted that it

TABLE 10.1

Primordial Groups and Parties of Candidates for Agra Corporation Elections, 1968

Primordial Group	Congress		Jan Sangh		Republican		Others*	
	N	%	N	%	N	%	N	%
Brahmins	8	16.7	14	26.9	–	–	23	14.8
Bania/Jain	12	25.0	12	23.1	1	2.9	26	16.8
Other High†	6	12.5	6	11.5	1	2.9	20	12.9
Punjabis	3	6.3	4	7.7	3	8.6	7	4.5
Low Castes‡	6	12.5	12	23.1	–	–	25	16.1
Jatavs	7	14.6	4	7.7	24	68.6	34	21.9
Muslims	4	8.3	–	–	6	17.1	19	12.3
Others§	2	4.1	–	–	–	–	1	0.6
Total	48	100.0	52	100.0	35	100.1	155	99.9

* Includes 32 SSP, 25 BKD, 16 CPI, 6 Swatantra, 2 PSP, 1 CPI (M), 1 RPI (Ambedkar). Aside from high- and low-caste categories, the various minor parties distributed their nominations as follows: SSP: 5 Banias, 4 Brahmins, 3 Jatavs, 3 Muslims, 1 Punjabi; *BKD:* 2 Banias, 9 Brahmins, 4 Jatavs, 3 Muslims, 1 Punjabi; *CPI:* 2 Banias, 3 Brahmins, 2 Jatavs, 5 Muslims, 1 Punjabi; *Swatantra:* 1 Bania, 1 Jatav; *PSP:* 1 Brahmin, 1 Muslim; *RPI (Ambedkar):* 1 Jatav.

† Includes 11 *Kayasthas* (4 SSP, 3 Congress, 2 independents, 1 Jan Sangh, 1 CPI); 11 *Thakurs* (3 Jan Sangh, 2 SSP, 2 CPI, 1 Congress, 1 BKD, 1 independent, 1 Swatantra); 4 *Bengalis* (2 BKD, 1 Jan Sangh, 1 independent); 3 *Khatris* (2 Congress, 1 independent); 3 *Jats* (1 Jan Sangh, 1 RPI, 1 BKD); 1 *Rajput* (BKD).

‡ Includes 9 *Kachis* (3 Jan Sangh, 3 SSP, 1 Congress, 1 CPI [M], 1 Swatantra); 8 *Koris* (2 Jan Sangh, 2 SSP, 2 independents, 1 Congress, 1 Swatantra); 8 *Valmiks* (2 Jan Sangh, 4 independents, 1 Congress, 1 SSP); 5 *Khatiks* (2 Congress, 1 Jan Sangh, 1 SSP, 1 independent); 2 *Kumbhars* (1 Congress, 1 SSP); 2 *Gadariyas* (1 Jan Sangh, 1 Swatantra); 2 *Ahirs* (2 independents); 1 *Kurmi* (Jan Sangh); 1 *Sonar* (Jan Sangh); 1 *Dhobi* (Jan Sangh); 1 *Darzi* (SSP); 1 *Birga* (independent); 1 *Teli* (BKD); 1 *Daii* (BKD).

§ Three Sikhs.

reflected no more than a chance pattern of nomination, it may indicate a shift away from Bania prominence in the Jan Sangh. Equally important, the same withdrawal of Banias appeared to be taking place in the Congress.

The Congress

Following the defeats of 1967 in Agra, there was interest both locally and on the part of the state Congress organization in finding a means of reconciling local factions which would help to restore the Congress to political health. In search of someone who might pull the party together, local leaders in Agra City turned to C. D. Johri, a man whose youth had been spent in the service of the nationalist movement. At 73, Johri had a long record of dedication to Gandhianism; he was even more appealing as a compromise figure because he had lived outside of Agra from 1940 to 1965. Despite ill health, Johri felt sufficient commitment to the party to agree to become City Congress President in late 1967 when other party leaders turned to him in a state of desperation over the aimlessness of the organization.

The organization experienced some difficulties in initiating the process of revitalization. Thus, the City Congress set up an Election Committee to choose candidates for the corporation which consisted of no one younger than sixty and three members in their seventies. Among its five members were Johri, Seth Achal Singh, Adiram Singhal, S. K. D. Paliwal, and D. K. Bibhab. The party had some difficulty recruiting candidates. Many politically attractive persons were approached by organizational leaders but refused to run for the Congress; this was one major reason the party was able to muster only forty-eight candidates for the fifty-four seats to be filled.

Indeed, according to one Congress leader, only two persons who were refused tickets by the Congress even bothered to complain to Lucknow about it. This was a very different situation from the internal battling of 1959 when a Congress nomination was highly prized. The only real involvement of the UPCC in the selection of candidates was to designate Shiv Prasad Gupta and J. P. Rawat as its official representatives to handle any difficulties which might arise in the elections. Rawat did not take much part in the matter, but Gupta apparently was quite active in helping to manage the party's campaign in the city.[9] A few Congressmen commented on the possibility of Gupta's moving into the leadership vacuum which some alleged now existed in the city, given the age of Seth and the infirmity of Singhal, but the overwhelming majority of Congress interviewees stressed the new-found harmony which had come into the organization and the lack of efforts by any single leader to impose himself upon the organization.

While tickets were given to a number of young men for the corporation, the Congress leadership refused to pursue a "youth movement" in the style of the Jan Sangh (or the Poona Congress).[10] According to some informants, in fact, the Congress may have given a number of tickets to younger men in 1968 simply because it was so hard pressed to find more mature candidates. A recent candidate for MLA put the matter rather baldly: "It is increasingly difficult to get good people to go into politics because people look down on politicians. To be a *netaji* [political leader] is a joke."

Partly because of this difficulty in getting candidates, the Congress did not complete the nomination process until just before names had to be filed.[11] The Jan Sangh was better primed organizationally than the Congress for the municipal elections; some of its candidates were known well in advance. Many of those recruited to Congress party tickets were not members of the party; at the same time, several of that party's best potential candidates including incumbents were hoping to contest for MLA in the mid-term elections and did not want to get involved first in corporation contests.

One method introduced by the Congress presumably to increase internal harmony was to allow incumbent Congress nominees to take a major hand in the selection of their runningmates. It was expected that such a rule would prevent the intra-ward conflicts which hurt the Congress efforts of 1959. While this move seemed to have an immediately beneficial electoral effect, it resulted in outcomes for the corporation which ultimately affected the elections for aldermen and for the first mayor under the new body.

The Republicans

Debilitated by internal battles in the period leading up to the elections of 1967, the Republicans still had managed to win one MLA seat in Agra and to hold on to a substantial part of their following among the Jatavs. Despite the dangers likely to result from further fractionation, nonetheless, quarrels within the RPI continued to divert considerable time and energy in the months that followed.

Man Singh, the MLA elected in 1967, was at the forefront of those opposed to the Ambedkerite defection in Uttar Pradesh, but in 1968 he began to quarrel with others in the Agra organization about the leadership of the local party. The origins of this conflict are rather obscure, but out of it emerged a list of officially sponsored Republican candidates backed by the Chairman and Executive of the local party and about thirty-eight persons "endorsed" by the Man Singh group, including a number who were already standing for the RPI and other parties. [12] Since the Man Singh faction did not have a symbol of its own, it is difficult to be sure of its organizational impact on the outcome of the election; for that reason, it is not included among parties listed in the various tables of this chapter. Of the twenty *independent* candidates that Man Singh backed (including eleven Jatavs), none were elected. Still, the presence of a prominent party leader in active rebellion against the already weakened local party could not help but weaken Republican efforts to mobilize the Jatav community to effect desired political outcomes.

Other Parties

Despite the dominance of the three major parties of Agra in the election results for 1967, there was obviously sufficient "slackness" in the utilization of local political resources (and in the play of party loyalties) to make the city an attractive locus for other political groups anxious to extend their influence in Uttar Pradesh. In terms of candidacies, the most important of these groups were the SSP, BKD, and CPI. None of these parties had mounted significant electoral organizations in Agra City prior to 1968.

The ex-MLA, Baloji, was seeking an organizational home after his defeat in 1967. A member of the Congress suggested, in this connection,

> People now feel that parties have a better chance of provid-
> ing facilities. It is true that most voters in these corporation
> elections do not look to the *particular* party of the candi-
> date, but they are influenced by the quality of the organiza-
> tion of a campaign and this a party can do much better
> than an independent. An independent has to spend twice or
> three times as much as a person in a party in order to
> organize meetings, processions. It makes a difference. [My
> emphasis.]

In looking for such an organizational base upon which to build his political career, Baloji turned to the SSP. Some of his old supporters followed him into the new party; many others did not. One of the two incumbent corporators who ran as SSP nominees was a Khatik originally elected as an independent with Republican backing. The caste of this man is of some moment, because the SSP in Agra—as elsewhere in Uttar Pradesh—was making a concerted effort to recruit candidates from low-status communities. Unlike the Jan Sangh, however, its following was greater in the countryside than in urbanized areas, as its victories in rural Agra District in 1967 attest. The SSP hoped to gain a foothold in Agra City in 1968, and in that connection twelve of its thirty-two nominees were from low-status communities.

If the SSP was organizationally weak, the BKD in Agra was even more of a facade for a group of independents and party dissidents who sought to differentiate themselves somehow from the large body of candidates in the city's contests. Despite Charan Singh's popularity in Agra, the party had no well-known local leadership or organizational purpose. Still, it managed to distribute twenty-five tickets. Perhaps reflective of an upper-caste bias built into the local organization, nine of these tickets went to Brahmins and six to other high-status candidates. There is no reason to assume that the one man the party elected was especially representative of the others, but his lack of organizational involvement with the BKD may suggest something of the character of that "party" in 1968.

Shiv Dutt Sharma is an ayurvedic doctor and a popular figure in his outer city ward near the Taj Mahal. He joined the Congress in 1943 and was quite active, serving as President of his mandal organization around 1960. During his period in the Congress, Sharma was attached to the Seth group. In 1968, his connection with the Congress was still close when he tried to get a ticket for a friend from the same ward. He ran into conflict with some of the Singhal people who wanted to run a candidate more in harmony with the wishes of the incumbent Congress corporator in the ward. Only after his friend was denied a ticket in the last stages of the selection process was Sharma himself approached by the President of the City BKD as a potential nominee. Having quarreled with the Congress, he was prepared to join the BKD because, as he later claimed, "its views are similar to the Congress and related to Gandhianism." Even after the election, he had some reservations about the future of the BKD.

While the CPI had a longer history in Agra, its appeal through 1967 was rather limited. There was one community, however, for which its lure was most evident: the Muslims. Largely dissatisfied with the Congress, unwelcome in the Jan Sangh, and suspicious of the viability of identification with the RPI, a number of Muslims were attracted to the secularism and "socialism" of the Communists. Some persons active in the trade union movement were also inclined toward the CPI including Roshan Lal Sutel.

Sutel had served as General Secretary of the Agra City Congress until his suspension from the party in 1960 for factional excess.[13] While he did not join any other party immediately, he withdrew from activity in the Congress to concentrate on his union work. In 1966, however, Sutel entered the CPI and soon became a leading figure in the organization. By 1968, he was Secretary of the city unit. Not much concerned with the fine theoretical distinctions that preoccupied some of the other party leaders, Sutel was an activist who occasionally came into conflict with state and district leaders of the party as he had with Congress leaders.

During the elections of 1968, the CPI managed to field sixteen candidates; five of these were Muslims. The party did not work very hard at attracting low-caste support. Among its non-Muslim candidates were three Brahmins, two Thakurs, a Kayastha, and two Banias. The CPI, like other parties, gave tickets to persons with no real commitment to the party.

In comparison to the other small parties, the PSP was not enough of a force in Agra to even put together an organization to distribute party tickets. Aside from a Muslim incumbent in the corporation, only one other person ran as a candidate from the PSP. The incumbent was actually under some pressure to join Baloji in the SSP because he had worked for him in the MLA election, but he rejected this idea, seeing no real advantage in it.

On one level, the increase in candidacies—290 as opposed to 228 for the same number of seats in 1959—suggests a continuing incoherence in the Agra political system, but the new political organizations like the SSP and BKD absorbed (or encouraged the candidacies of) many of the additional entrants so that there were actually fewer independents in the race in 1968 than in 1959. In table 10.2, we look at some of the changing patterns of behavior in Agra politics by examining

TABLE 10.2

Primordial Changes between Elections, Agra Corporation, 1959-68

Primordial Group	1959	1968*	Net Change
Brahmins	33	45	+12
Banias/Jains	59	51	− 8
Other High	22	33	+11
Punjabis/Sindhis	6	17	+11
Low Castes	35	43	+ 8
Jatavs	44	69	+25
Muslims	29	29	—
Total	228	287	+59

* Excluded from this list are three Sikhs.

primordial group involvements. The most notable feature of this table is the absolute decline in the representation of Banias and Jains. Not only were there fewer candidates from these communities in 1968 than in 1959, but there were increases among all other communities except the Muslims. As we shall see in our later comparison of occupational structure in Poona and Agra for the new corporations, this change was associated with a notable drop in the number of merchants elected to the Agra corporation. At the other end of the social hierarchy, the cleavages in the Republican party and the prize involved in winning ten reserved seats (up two from 1959) acted as an incentive to the various political groups to get Jatav and other Scheduled Caste candidates to run on party tickets.

When we aggregate party candidacies by primordial group in a fashion that distinguishes established parties from new parties and, in turn, from independent candidacies, we find a number of interesting characteristics in the materials summarized in table 10.3. If we wish to attribute "self-starting" capabilities to

TABLE 10.3

"Party Satisfaction" Index, Agra Corporation Elections, 1968

Primordial Groups	"System" Parties*	Other Parties†	Independents	Total‡
Brahmins	.49	.38	.13	45
Bania/Jains	.49	.20	.31	51
Other High	.39	.46	.15	33
Punjabi-Sindhi	.59	.18	.24	17
Low Caste	.42	.35	.23	43
Jatavs	.51	.16	.33	69
Muslims	.34	.41	.24	29
Total	133	83	71	287

* Congress; Jan Sangh; RPI.
† SSP; BKD; Swatantra; CPI; CPI (M); PSP; RPI (Ambedkar).
‡ Excludes three Sikhs, two who stood for the Congress and one an independent.

members of primordial groups with a large proportion of independents, the Banias and Jatavs, as previously seen in the 1959 data, seem the most politicized groups. On the other hand, independent candidacies do not appear to be a function of social status alone since the least represented primordial groups among the independents are the Brahmins and "other high castes." [14]

As far as the established parties are concerned, the Punjabis and Sindhis seemed to be most heavily mobilized by such political organizations with the Jatavs in second place. High-status communities like the Kayasthas and Thakurs found some places in the major parties, but apparently not in the fashion which absorbed their communities' potential for politicization; the new parties seemed to be particularly attractive to members of this high-status category. Similarly, the relative coolness of the established parties to Muslims found them reaching out for other political groups like the CPI. One might argue that there is an interaction effect operating here: certain communities are "available" for participation in politics, but the established parties do not absorb all of that enthusiasm. The generation of new parties—either by members of "available" communities or by political entrepreneurs who turn to candidates from these communities to capitalize upon existent discontent—follows from a necessary limitation on the expansion of the major parties in the number of tickets available.

CONSTITUTION OF THE NEW CORPORATION

Candidates formally submitted their names to election authorities by 19 April 1968, and the campaign began shortly thereafter. The parties brought state and national leaders into the city to speak on behalf of their nominees; it is difficult to tell if such visits had any effect on outcomes, but they did lend an air of national importance to municipal political activities. Thus, in the course of the first three days of May, when the campaign was well under way, local public meetings were addressed by Jan Sangh leaders like Atal Behari Vajpayi (the All-India Jan Sangh President); Raj Narain, a major SSP leader of Uttar Pradesh, used the platform in

Agra to attack the Jan Sangh for not helping the cause of Hindi and the BKD for being a tool of Congress leaders.[15] The BKD imported a major leader from Bihar and the national Congress dispatched Dr. Karan Singh, Central Minister for Tourism and former Governor of Kashmir, to Agra to hold up that party's prestige.

Elections for twenty-six of the twenty-seven two-man wards in the corporation were held on 5 May,[16] and turnout ran from 63.0 percent in one ward of mixed social status to 46.7 percent in a ward where a number of the Backward Class communities (not Jatavs) resided. Some of the areas of greatest Jatav strength, in fact, had turnout above the median of 56.3 percent.[17] Because of the census which followed the 1959 elections, the wards assigned reserved seats had increased from eight to ten. Insofar as supposedly weaker candidates were to be elected from these seats, it should be noted that eight of the ten would have been elected in 1968 even without the guarantee provided by reservation. This represented a considerable advancement in both the politicization of the Scheduled Castes and the willingness of "caste" Hindus to vote for them as compared to 1959.[18]

Inter-ward comparisons are made difficult between 1959 and 1968 because of readjustments in ward lines prior to the recent elections. While these readjustments were minor in many cases, in some few they placed three incumbents in competition against each other. In consequence of this redistricting, we will look only at group data here rather than examining ward behaviors over time.[19] Table 10.4 compares votes for the major and minor parties in the two municipal elections.

As the table indicates, the arrival of a set of new parties upon the Agra political scene in 1968 did not weaken the following of the three major political organizations markedly. Instead, they drew off much of the support previously

TABLE 10.4

Comparison of Votes for the Agra Corporation, 1959 and 1968

Party	1959 %	Candidates		1968 %	Candidates	Percent Differ- ence
(a) Major Parties:						
Congress	26.5	50		25.8	48	− 0.7
Jan Sangh	15.1	34		26.1	52	+11.0
Republicans	14.5	27		15.9	35	+ 1.4
Minor Parties	3.5	12	SSP	8.9	32 ⎫	
			CPI	4.6	16 ⎪	+16.3
			BKD	4.4	25 ⎬	
			Others	1.9	10 ⎭	
Independents	40.4	115		12.4	70*	−28.0

(b) Per Ticket Vote of Major Parties:		
Party	1959	1968
Congress	1,094	1,381
Jan Sangh	918	1,290
Republicans	1,111	1,166

* Includes those independents supported by the dissident Republican MLA.

given to independents. The Jan Sangh made substantial advances, but even the Congress with fewer candidates and the Republican Party just about held their own in an "electorate," which increased from 206,278 in 1959 to 257,366 in 1968.[20] Furthermore, as table 10.4 reveals, each of the three major parties improved its average per ticket vote from 1959, with the Republicans showing the smallest advance.[21] With the aid of the substantial increase in the Jan Sangh vote, the three major parties advanced their *combined* share of the vote from 56 percent in 1959 to 68 percent in 1968.

Some additional meaning can be given to these shifts in public support in another fashion. If we "weight" the performances of the various political groups in terms of their order of finish in the *different wards* by assigning a value of "4" for a first-place, "3" for second, "2" for third, and "1" for fourth place, we find in table 10.5 an enormous shift in the importance of independents and parties like the Jan Sangh over time. In 1959, as we know from our earlier discussion, the Congress was

TABLE 10.5

Aggregated Ordering of Results for Agra Elections, by Weighted Totals

Parties	1959 Total	1968 Total
Congress	89	96
Jan Sangh	36	89
Republicans	46	39
Smaller Parties	6	32
Independents	93	14

not so much challenged in the local political system by distinct political groups as by an agglomeration of independents and minor parties. In 1968, the depth of the challenge to the Congress by the Jan Sangh is much clearer, and the independents have faded into insignificance in comparison to the new political groups.[22]

In the face of this increased competition among parties, or perhaps because of it, the aggregate data reveal a decrease in the disparity between candidates of the same party running in a given ward. In 1959, many Agra wards showed little correspondence between the votes received by candidates running on the same ticket. In 1968, differences still existed but had decreased for each of the major political groups. Table 10.6 shows that the greatest differences occurred in 1959 among RPI candidates, the least between Jan Sangh nominees. Of course, many RPI candidacies in 1959 were for reserved seats. By 1968, the greatest disparity was among Congress nominees, while the Jan Sangh continued to exercise a marginally greater consistency in the total votes received by its nominees. Most notably, all the major groups experienced an aggregate increase in the *consistency* of their vote. What individual voters did, however, in casting their ballots cannot be estimated from this data.[23]

As a result of these vote distributions, the Congress and Jan Sangh emerged in a virtual tie in terms of the number of seats won on 5 May—the Jan Sangh with nineteen, the Congress with eighteen. The Republicans provided a major part of the remaining balance, but minor party winners (two Communists,[24] one PSP, one

TABLE 10.6

Difference in Percent of Vote Received by Party Candidates in Double-Member Constituencies, 1959 and 1968 Agra Corporation Elections

Party	1959 Average	Number of Two-Candidate Wards	1968 Average	Number of Two-Candidate Wards
Congress	4.88	24	3.65	22
Jan Sangh	4.03	13	2.82	25
Republican	5.04	10	3.00	15

BKD) and two independents promised to play pivotal roles in the selection of aldermen and a mayor.

Given the narrowness of the margin of difference in seats won, the contest in the ward with the postponed election was heated. The Congress and Jan Sangh threw considerable resources into this heavily Bania neighborhood. A popular Jan Sangh incumbent and one of the founders of the Jan Sangh ran against an independent incumbent recruited into the Congress for the election and the grandnephew of Seth Achal Singh. The victory went to the Jan Sangh incumbent and the Seth family member by very narrow margins.[25] With the corporation up to its full complement of elected members, therefore, the Jan Sangh still maintained a one-seat lead over the Congress.

The Aldermanic Election

The next round of activity began with the filing of applications for the six aldermanic seats. Nineteen names were formally entered, but some of these were only bargaining counters for the various political groups. From the start, the Congress committed itself to the selection of two particular Congressmen—one from the Seth group and one who was associated with the Singhal element. The Jan Sangh hoped to elect three aldermen but gave its greatest support to Raj Kumar Sama, and to Manohar Lal, a Jatav; the Republicans made their first choice the man who had contested in 1967 for MP from Agra, Lachman Das. Given the distribution of votes, these five candidates were fairly well assured of success unless major defections took place. The principal debate then revolved around who should be designated as the sixth alderman.

Events leading up to the selection of the sixth alderman to some extent preceded these contests by nine years and had major consequences for the selection of a mayor and deputy mayor in the following weeks. They also reflected the pivotal role a small segment of apartisan Jains have played in Agra politics. Among these men is the former mayor, Kalyan Das Jain. Kalyan Das is a popular figure in the Jain community which is heavily concentrated in the western section of the city. While he has been an independent in municipal politics, he generally supported Congress candidates in general elections. Thus, in 1967 he was close to the campaign of Bhogilal Misra for MLA in Agra West. In previous years, Kalyan Das had worked with members of the Seth group, especially Sohanlal Jain (former City

Congress President), who ran as a dissident candidate for MLA against Misra in 1967. While Kalyan Das did not support Sohanlal in the latter year, another wealthy businessman, Saroj Kumar Jain, did.

In 1959, one of the wards in the Lohamandi section had seen an Agarwal Congressman and Saroj Kumar running together as nominees of the Congress. A former Congress activist (Chandra Bhan Jain) ran as an independent when he did not receive a party ticket for that contest. Kalyan Das may have contributed substantially to the latter's campaign efforts. Apparently, during canvassing in 1959, the Agarwal Congressman and Saroj Kumar Jain developed a severe emnity. These differences persisted long after the election was over while the Agarwal sat in the corporation alongside Chandra Bhan. Saroj Kumar applied for a Congress ticket in 1968 but was rebuffed upon the insistence of the Agarwal incumbent. Instead, the latter exercised his personal influence to get Chandra Bhan the second ticket in the ward.

When Saroj Kumar was refused the Congress ticket in 1968, he ran as an independent for the corporation and was elected over Chandra Bhan with the support of various members of his community *excluding* Kalyan Das but including Raj Mukat—a well-educated Jain businessman related through marriage to Kalyan Das. Raj Mukat was active at the same time in supporting other candidates including both Congress and Jan Sangh nominees. While he was not a formal partisan, his father had been Treasurer of the Agra Congress for a period in the 1950s and was a close friend of Kalyan Das. Thus, when Raj Mukat's name was put forward by Saroj Kumar as a possible candidate for alderman, it not only reflected the friendship of the two men immediately involved but affected the personal interests of elements favorable to Kalyan Das, even though bad relations existed between Saroj Kumar and Kalyan Das.[26]

Once elected to the corporation, Saroj Kumar tried to pull together the seven nonparty or small party corporators into a bargaining unit, which they called the Progressive Group. In the aldermanic elections, however, they could not agree upon one candidate. Instead, the two Communists wanted to nominate Roshan Lal Sutel; another independent and the BKD corporator had nominees of their own. Only Saroj Kumar and the PSP member were willing to back Raj Mukat Jain from the start; they were eventually joined by the BKD corporator. The problem then became one of acquiring additional votes.

Bargaining began with the Congress which was certain of controlling two seats and had an anticipated excess of three votes. The latter were promised to Raj Mukat, partly in payment for past support to the party and in return for a promise that Raj Mukat would vote for Congress nominees for mayor and deputy mayor. Indeed, there was some expectation that Raj Mukat, who was quite friendly with Shiv Prasad Gupta, could be prevailed upon by the latter to join the Congress. A first-preference vote was also cast for Raj Mukat by a Jan Sangh corporator with ties of friendship to Shiv Prasad, although the vote caused some resentment among Jan Sangh members.

On the basis of the seven first-preference votes available to Raj Mukat Jain, an additional vote was cast in his behalf by the Republicans who had a small excess. The victory for Raj Mukat, no matter how narrow, seemed an auspicious token of

Congress strength and a potential index to a victory for that party in the contests for mayor and deputy mayor. Indeed, the Jan Sangh was quite bitter at the outcome.

With the election of the sixth alderman, the directly and indirectly elected membership of the general body of the corporation was complete. Table 10.7 provides a picture of corporation membership on the eve of the mayoral election. As we noted in connection with candidacies, the relative balance of Brahmins and

TABLE 10.7

Primordial Groups and Parties of Members Elected to Agra Corporation, 1968

Primordial Group	Congress	Jan Sangh	RPI	Others	Total
Brahmins	4	7	–	1 (BKD)	12
Banias/Jains	7	2	–	3	12
Other High*	2	5	–	–	7
Punjabis	–	2	–	–	2
Low Castes†	3	5	–	–	8
Jatavs	3	1	10	–	14
Muslims	2	–	–	3‡	5
Total	21	22	10	7	60

* Four Thakurs (three Jan Sangh, one Congress) and three Kayasthas (two Jan Sangh, one Congress). One Jan Sangh Kayastha is a Bengali.
† The Congress corporators include two Khatiks and one Kori. The Jan Sangh elected two Koris, one Kurmi, one Sonar and one Gadariya.
‡ Two CPI members and a PSP corporator.

Banias (including Jains) had shifted considerably from 1959. Indeed, even the twelve corporators listed under the Bania-Jain category were tilted more heavily toward the Jain side than earlier. Four of the seven Congressmen and two of the three independents in this status category were now Jains.[27]

Equally noteworthy is the inclusion in the table of three Jatavs elected from the Congress and one from the Jan Sangh. The latter was an alderman selected by the Jan Sangh to increase the appeal of that party among the Jatavs. More significant is the representation of three *bare adme* belonging to the Congress. One was the nephew of a man active in the Congress prior to Independence. The newly-elected corporator had stood for the 1959 body as an independent. This time he received a ticket from the Congress. He had insisted upon and received a *general* ticket, unlike the other Scheduled Caste candidates the Congress supported. Assessing the position of the Jatavs in 1968, he remarked, "In UP, the Republican Party has no voice. What can you do with seven, eight, or nine seats? I also wanted to do something for the good of the people as a whole, not only the Jatavs."

Table 10.7 also reveals the presence in the corporation of eight corporators from Low Hindu communities. As contrasted to the 1959 corporation when only four corporators from these non-Jatav communities were present (a Khatik, a Potter, a Kurmi, and a Sonar), there were now three representatives of the Kori community and one from the Gadariya community. The emphasis on this as a single caste dimension should not be exaggerated, however, since in practice there exists a great deal of social distance between a relatively wealthy community like the Sonars—the traditional Goldsmiths—and the Khatiks and Koris. It also should be mentioned that two of the Jan Sangh members from these low-status communities were lawyers.

The Election for Mayor

In seeking to establish a majority for the election of a mayor, almost every combination of groups was discussed. Conversations between local leaders of the Jan Sangh and the Congress advanced quite far. Some Jan Sangh corporators looked forward to the prospect of a coalition between the two rivals; according to one, "We felt that the city body had nothing to do with provincial politics and the pact would give a stable administration to Agra." While a few local Congressmen were apparently favorable to the proposed arrangement, pressure was finally exerted by the state Congress leadership on the local party to withhold cooperation from any alliance with the Jan Sangh.

The result of this breakdown in negotiations, as many members of both of the larger parties noted, was to provide considerable leverage to the Republicans and the small "Progressive Group." A coalition with the latter would still depend for final success upon one or more defections from noncoalition partners. Thus the Republicans were able to bargain a little better than the Progressive Group, or so it appeared publicly. They demanded from the Congress, for example, the mayorship, the hanging of Ambedkar's picture in corporation offices and schools, and a massive cleaning of Scheduled Caste *mohallas*. While accepting the last demand, the Congress leaders rejected the first two.

Negotiations were heavily affected by the concern of the Congress and Jan Sangh, in particular, in strengthening themselves for the coming mid-term elections. Thus, in explaining why the Jan Sangh refused to accept the terms of the Republicans, one of the top Jan Sangh leaders commented:

> We felt that people would laugh at us for allowing their man to be mayor when we were twenty-two in the corporation. We felt that we would lose in the general election if we allowed a Republican mayor to be elected.

It is notable that in all of those interviews touching on the bargaining which went on for the mayorship, no partner was immediately rejected *at the local level* because of ideology or primordial character. Rather, strategic considerations with respect to future elections seemed to be the primary conditioning factor in the process.

In the latter stages of this bargaining, each of the major elements put forward a candidate for mayor. The Republicans nominated a leather merchant, the brother of their alderman. The Congress went through a more complicated series of internal maneuvers to choose a nominee. Originally, the names of five men were mentioned in party circles, including two former mayors—R. C. Gupta and S. N. Chaturvedi. These two were eliminated by higher authorities on the ground that they had both already held the post. This left three men in the field: D. K. Bibhab, ex-MLA; Babu

Lal Singhal, a highly respected member of the previous corporation; Mahendraji, an elderly and respected Gandhian whose name had been mentioned for mayor in the past but who had never actually been a party candidate.

All of the members of the Congress corporation party came together in the presence of some of the local party leaders and a couple of UPCC officials to indicate preferences for mayor. While Singhal received the backing of several prominent leaders, he would not make a commitment to try to outspend the candidate of the Jan Sangh if that became necessary. He and Mahendraji also were good friends. After an initial round in which Mahendraji drew ten votes to five each for Singhal and Bibhab, Singhal withdrew in favor of Mahendraji and the latter became the party's candidate for mayor.[28]

Continuing negotiations with the Republicans finally led to an agreement without "riders" between the Congress and the RPI that each party would cast first-ballot votes for its own candidates, but that the Republicans would give their second preferences to the Congress nominee in return for an assurance by the Congress of support for the Republican nominee for deputy mayor and a reversal of posts in the following year. If the two parties stood firm, and especially if the Congress was able to depend upon the vote of Raj Mukat Jain, Mahendraji was assured of victory.

The Jan Sangh was anxious to block this outcome, but it could find no coalition partner willing to support a Jan Sangh candidate for mayor. Muslim corporators in the CPI and PSP were particularly hostile to such an idea. The "Progressive Group" did have an alternative candidate—Kalyan Das Jain. By whatever means achieved, the seven corporators managed to agree upon and press this demand. The role of Saroj Kumar Jain in this course of action is open to debate, but he apparently went along with it reluctantly. The way toward the pact was allegedly smoothed by an agreement by Kalyan Das that he would support the Jan Sangh choice for deputy mayor if he won. It is less certain whether, as some informants suggest, Kalyan Das also agreed to work for the Jan Sangh in the mid-term elections by providing a large sum to the Jan Sangh campaign effort. Kalyan Das was apparently made more acceptable to the Jan Sangh through the support which he received from Ram Babu Verma, a rapidly rising power in the Jan Sangh.[29] During the last years of the previous body, when Kalyan Das sat as mayor for the Swatantra Dal, Verma had gained a reputation for being the "brains" behind Kalyan Das. Some observers felt that Verma acted in 1968 in a manner which would continue that relationship under new auspices.

Thus, when corporators met on 24 June to vote for mayor, three names remained in the race: Mahendraji, the RPI nominee, and Kalyan Das Jain. No one received a majority on the first ballot. Surprisingly, when second preferences were counted, there was an absolute tie of thirty votes each for Mahendraji and Kalyan Das. Under the rules, the candidate with the greater first-preference votes was elected: Kalyan Das. The latter received twenty-eight first-preference votes as against only twenty for the Congress nominee.[30]

The outcome indicated to most observers a high probability that at least one Congress corporator and possibly Raj Mukat Jain had supported Kalyan Das Jain. Indeed, the City Congress President went out of his way to apologize immediately to the Republicans and to deflect any possible public accusations away from that party, some of whose members had been prone to respond to monetary inducements in the past. It was widely believed that in this election the Republicans were united behind the Congress nominee and that the new mayor had had to offer material benefits to his supporter (or supporters) from the Congress and Progressive Group in order to win.

The Deputy Mayorship

While Kalyan Das agreed to support a Jan Sangh nominee for deputy mayor, the Jan Sangh again found it difficult to come up with a candidate acceptable to both its party leadership and the members of the Progressive Group. Saroj Kumar was mentioned by members of the latter group as a serious possibility, but the Jan Sangh refused to go along with this. Much to Saroj's disappointment, they agreed to support Ram Narain Gupta, an elderly businessman. Gupta had served rather unobtrusively as a Congressman in the past corporation, having been recruited to that party in 1959. Although he was offered a Congress ticket again in 1968, he had decided to stand as an independent supposedly because of a disinclination to get involved in partisan activity.

The Congress, true to its promise and apologetic for the embarrassment of an apparent defection from the party in the election for mayor, agreed to support the Republican candidate for deputy mayor, Ram Prasad Sone. Sone, a Jatav, had been one of Dr. P. N. Gupta's strongest supporters while the latter was in the RPI and was probably the most outspoken Jatav in the last years of the previous corporation. Despite the antipathy of some Congress members to his nomination, the President of the City Congress made party discipline a matter of great moral weight in this contest. Indeed, he threatened to go on a fast if potential defectors did not declare themselves openly before the election.

Ram Narain was a compromise figure for the Jan Sangh, but was not wholly acceptable to the Progressive Group. It was only with some effort that a few members of the Jan Sangh had successfully balked at Saroj Kumar's removal from the race. Part of the argument advanced publicly against Saroj Kumar was that he lived in the same part of the city as Kalyan Das. Ram Narain, on the other hand, was from an area near the cantonment where the Jan Sangh alderman, Raj Kumar Sama, would be contesting for MLA again in the mid-term elections and the prestige of the deputy mayor might prove helpful.

On the other hand, some members of the Progressive Group—particularly the three Muslim members—were finding it hard to defend their support for candidates of the Jan Sangh and their association with wealthy men like Kalyan Das. The discontent of Saroj Kumar with the selection of Ram Narain removed whatever constraints remained over the Progressive Group. The nomination of a Republican Jatav for deputy mayor also provided a perfect excuse for the collapse of the agreement between the Jan Sangh and most members of the Progressive Group. When the election for deputy mayor was held, therefore, Sone won easily with thirty-five votes to Ram Narain's twenty-six.[31] While the lines held for the major parties, it is believed that both of the votes of the CPI corporators were also cast for

Sone despite a directive from the District Executive of the CPI ordering that their votes go to the candidate of the Jan Sangh. Shortly thereafter, the two corporators were placed on suspension by the District Executive of the CPI.[32]

Thus, rather ironically, all the efforts of the Congress and the Jan Sangh to capture control of the Agra corporation and to build their local images in anticipation of the statewide elections came to very little in terms of the more honorific municipal offices. The corporation was now headed by two persons who were active in the previous Swatantra Dal-Republican coalition and neither owed any long-range loyalty to the major party groups which voted them into office in 1968 nor, of course, to each other. In a real sense, then, both the public and internal electoral processes resulted in the continuation of local government by transitory majorities. However, given the weaknesses of the corporation's political representatives and the frequent nonpartisanship of the body on matters of general concern, the lack of a reliable majority was of little policy importance.

CORPORATION POLITICS IN POONA

As in Agra, the corporation elections of 1968 in Poona witnessed the entrance into municipal politics of new political groupings alongside the existent political parties. The principal actors, as in the past, were the Congress, the Nagri Sanghatna, and the Jan Sangh. The Shiv Sena made its first appearance in the city in 1968 by endorsing forty-three candidates; a variety of smaller political groups were also represented in the city, although the proportion of independents in the race was now higher than in Agra—33 to 25 percent.

The Congress

Despite the electoral setback to the Poona Congress in 1967, the party organization was basically sound going into the corporation elections. It had surmounted the conflict for the presidency of the City Congress in early 1968 by allowing the President of the MPCC to "advise" it in its choice of a successor to Sanas. While the leader of the Congress group in the corporation (Dhere) and a prominent MLC both attempted to lay claim to the position, the state organization successfully imposed its selection of the Vice-President of the City Congress, a Sanas lieutenant. The MLC was mollified in substance by the inclusion of a number of his supporters in key positions on the City Congress Executive Committee. Thus, by the time party nominations for the corporation were to be made, it was possible to put together a local Election Committee which included the new President of the City Congress, his two rivals for the leadership, the defeated Brahmin candidate for MP—who was beginning to assume a position of prominence in the state Congress—and Mohan Dharia, former General Secretary of the MPCC and still a member of the Rajya Sabha.[33]

In contrast to the Agra situation, Congress tickets for the Poona corporation were highly desired. Decisions on the party's nominations were fairly well accepted, however, since there were few accounts of major defections from the party. In addition to a sizable core of Congress incumbents, a major portion of the new candidates supported by the Congress were relatively young men of non-Brahmin caste who possessed an almost unthinking faith in the Congress organization rather than its principles. The heavy representation of non-Brahmins in the candidacies of the Congress is indicated in table 10.8, where nearly half of all Congress tickets went to Marathas and nearly 20 percent to high non-Brahmin castes like the Malis and Pardeshis.

Although the Congress was strong enough to proclaim its basically Maratha orientation with almost no deference to the Brahmins in this election, it did respond to certain pressures. In particular, the local Congress accepted the state leadership's effort to forge a working relationship with the Gaikwad Republicans. A Congress corporator commented on that effort sympathetically,

> Chavan wanted the Republicans together with the Congress in the 1967 elections, but an agreement on seats could not be reached at that time. This time we tried to come together and will try to work together in all sectors not only in elections. The Scheduled Caste communities were tortured for so many thousands of years. Before now a major section was following the Republicans but this took them away from power. In this way, they would have no power for another twenty-five years. Our leaders thought these backward communities must be brought forward with us.

Despite the view expressed by this Maratha corporator, a few members of the local Congress were not happy with the decision. For example, some non-Mahar Scheduled Caste politicians resented the attention being paid to the Mahars. The Mang community, in particular, expressed its dissatisfaction with the arrangement. Some elements within that community further encouraged the development of their own political group, the *Bharatiya Mazdoor Paksa* (Indian Workers' Party; BMP), a group first organized two years earlier elsewhere in Maharashtra. The BMP associated itself with the Nagri Sanghatna in the corporation elections of 1968, although this did not mean a wholesale defection of Mangs to that party; a large number continued to support the Congress.[34]

Negotiations conducted between the Congress and the RPI to reach an electoral agreement in Poona implicated the national leadership of both parties. The local Republican negotiators originally sought twelve seats in the corporation, whereas the Congress was willing to provide only six. When an impasse was reached, Dharia (one of the negotiators for the national Congress) consulted with Gaikwad in Delhi, and Gaikwad apparently responded that the number was not so important as the principle of the agreement. The distribution was settled, therefore, largely on Congress terms.[35]

Another force to which the Congress responded was the organized youth wing of the party. In contrast to the largely inactive Youth Congress in Agra, the Youth Congress in Poona was a meaningful organization carrying on a variety of low-level, relatively nonideological activities while providing an arena for young men with political orientations to become involved in party work. When pressed, these young men found it difficult to formulate a coherent statement of political principles which they could associate with the Congress. Typically, one young corporator who had served as General Secretary of the Youth Congress up to 1967 and was a Secretary of the regular Poona City Congress from 1965 to April 1968, merely identified socialism with welfare egalitarianism—"that all men are treated

TABLE 10.8

Primordial Groups and Parties of Candidates for Poona Corporation Elections, 1968

Primordial Group	Congress-Republican		Nagri Sanghatna		Jan Sangh		Shiv Sena-Mahasabha		Others*	
	N	%	N	%	N	%	N	%	N	%
Brahmins	5	7	11	16	21	49	6	14	39	23
Intermediate†	13	18	8	11	3	7	5	12	11	6
Marathas	33	46	27	39	9	21	20	47	38	22
Low Hindus‡	6	8	10	14	6	14	7	16	23	13
Mahars	6	8	2	3	–	–	1	2	20	12
Other Scheduled Caste§	2	3	4	6	–	–	1	2	11	6
Muslims	2	3	1	1	1	2	1	2	6	4
Non-Maharashtrians‖	4	6	5	7	3	7	2	5	19	11
Other#	1	1	2	3	–	–	–	–	5	3
	72	100	70	100	43	100	43	100	172	100

* These included 125 independents and 47 persons associated with political organizations. Among the latter were 14 persons identified with the *Nagri Seva Samiti* (7 Brahmins, 3 Marathas, and single members from Chambhar, Dhangar, Gujarati, and "Madrasi" backgrounds); 9 backed by the *Swatantra Party* (3 Mahars; others from Chambhar, Gujarati, Joshi, Laman, Maratha, and Punjabi communities); 10 running on the tickets of the *Kamble wing* of the *Republican Party* (6 Mahars; others from Koli, Mang, Muslim, and Takare castes); 14 associated with the *Janta Aghadi* or the *CPI* (5 Marathas, 2 Brahmins, 2 Mahars; others: Mang, Weaver, Shimpi, "Madrasi," and Nhavi).

† *Intermediate* includes: 18 Malis, 6 Pardeshis, 6 Dhangars, 5 CKP's, 3 Kirads, and 2 Lingayats.

‡ *Low Hindus* include: 9 Shimpis, 7 Weavers, 7 Sonars, 5 Tambats, 4 Bhois, 3 Telis; 2 each of Dhobis, Joshis, Kasaiis, Koli, Koshti, Nhavis; 1 each of Borud, Dhor, Gundra, Kumbhar, Laman, Lodhi, Pangol.

§ These *Scheduled Castes* included 11 Mangs, 4 Chambhars, and 1 each of Bhangis, Takare, and Vadar.

‖ Persons from other regions included 11 Gujaratis, 11 "Marwaris," 5 "Madrasis," 3 Sindhis, and 1 each from Mysore, Punjab, and North India.

Two Christians, 1 each of Jain, Parsi and Sikh communities, and 3 unidentified.

equally and that they are guaranteed food, shelter, clothing, and an education." This corporator, like five or six others among those interviewed who had recently had Youth Congress experience, was already a successful businessman in a modern sector of the economy. He acted as a wholesaler of crude oil products for Esso.

Leaders of the Youth Congress formulated a request to the Congress Election Committee calling upon the latter to provide twenty seats to young people. Although counts differ slightly, this demand was substantially met. Between fourteen and sixteen seats were given to young persons associated with the Youth Congress or related service groups like the Congress Seva Dal. Of sixteen candidates claimed by one Youth Congress leader, about half were elected. At this time, too, the ambitions of younger members of the Congress were complementary to the ambitions of some of the party leaders who saw personal advantage in associating themselves with the demands of a rising group of young party workers.

For the most part Maratha or "Intermediate" non-Brahmin in caste, these young men were more educated than their parents' generation. Coming generally from substantial middle-class families, they employed their status and education to good advantage in local election campaigns. Some had their own local groups within their wards growing out of common school experiences or from a shared experience in organizing a *Ganesh utso.* One of them, for example, described how he had built a reputation through the successful organization of a *Ganesh utso mandal,* which had won top prize for the past three years in a citywide contest. As a result of his work in the *utso,* he was appointed Secretary of the Congress Committee for one of the peths in 1966 and helped to organize the successful election campaign for the MLA in his area. His education—a BA in politics—helped in these activities, he felt. Added to his education and vitality, his family's influential position in the area made him the kind of candidate the Congress might have chosen even without the organizational prodding provided by the Youth Congress.

A less satisfactory series of relationships were involved in the negotiations which went on between the Congress and those members of the corporation who had defected from the Nagri Sanghatna to support the Congress in the corporation after 1965. Some of the leaders of the Congress felt that each person should have been dealt with separately in distributing tickets, but the so-called "Pardeshi group" insisted on intergroup negotiations. These negotiations encountered various snags, and only three sitting members from the group were given Congress tickets, although two others—one of them Pardeshi's brother[36]—also received electoral recognition. Of the five elected, one was the man least involved in partisan maneuvering. He was a Tamil Brahmin running in a non-Maharashtrian section of the city. Well known as a lawyer, active in behalf of a union, and popular in the local South Indian community, he was less a real choice of the Pardeshi group for a ticket than a nonpolitical "personality" whom the Congress leadership found quite acceptable as a candidate. The other man was a Bhoi incumbent elected as an independent.

Having accommodated each of these sources of potentially disruptive pressure through the selection process, the Congress went into the corporation elections a fairly united, financially comfortable, and effectively-led organization. The interests of contending factions and of local figures with national connections coincided in such a way as to maximize the performance of the Congress. As usual, of course, some defections from the Congress occurred when persons did not receive tickets, but these were individuals of minor influence in the party; their leaving had little effect upon the configuration of results, although a few were able to influence the outcomes in particular wards by their presence in contests.

The Nagri Sanghatna

While some of the pieces that had been fitted into the jigsaw puzzle of the Nagri Sanghatna in previous years were put together again in 1968, other elements were missing: there was no prominent source of defection from the Congress to build essential support in Maratha sections of the population; the Hindu Mahasabha had splintered beyond organizational meaning and what little was left now cast its lot with the Shiv Sena; the Jan Sangh was determined to "cash in" on its electoral success in Shukrawar Peth by running a substantial number of candidates in areas where it had not challenged the Sanghatna in 1962; the PSP and SSP were willing to compromise their differences locally, but the spirit of compromise did not pervade their relations at ward level; an important section of the Mahar community was now aligned with the Congress.

Still, despite the problems that lay in the path of the Sanghatna, differences were papered over and the organization was able to mount an almost complete slate of nominees. However, populist pressures from the SSP and the consolidation of support for the Jan Sangh among the Brahmins of Poona now resulted in a heavier representation of non-Brahmins among the Sanghatna's candidates than ever before. As table 10.8 indicates, Marathas constituted almost 40 percent of Sanghatna nominees as against only 16 percent for Brahmins—a clear move away from the equivalency of previous elections. In contrast to the Congress, too, more tickets were given to lower-status Hindu communities like Shimpis (Tailors) and Weavers.

Confronted as they were on one side by a strong and united Congress organization with its basic appeal to Marathas and other non-Brahmin groups and, on the other side, by the Brahmin-dominated Jan Sangh, the Nagri Sanghatna continued to make a public display of its "nonpartisanship" and "noncommunalism" at a citywide level, but its actual mode of operation was highly dependent on the specific styles of the candidates it selected. Negotiations within the organization for nominations were sometimes bitter, particularly where claims were advanced in the same ward by SSP and PSP spokesmen. The involvement of Joshi and Goray in national politics also removed them as effective personalities in helping to organize campaigns for the corporation.

Despite these many drawbacks, the Nagri Sanghatna was able to draw upon the popularity and militancy of the SSP in some of the unionized low-status wards of the city and could capitalize upon the personal influence of those independent "notables" backed by it in some of the middle-class neighborhoods. Still, the various debilitating factors cited above threatened the long-range health of the Sanghatna, whatever its immediate successes.

The Jan Sangh

Having planted itself successfully in a few places by the time of the 1962 municipal elections, the Jan Sangh worked to nurture its organizational development in the following years. By skillful organizational appeals to the alienated Brahmin community of Poona, by playing upon nationalist sentiments, and by its display of party discipline, the Jan Sangh made a considerable impact upon the Maharashtrian Brahmin population of the city. Its efforts had been rewarded in 1967 by the overwhelming victory for MLA of R. K. Mhalgi. Banking further upon its new prestige, the party now attempted to expand out of the Brahmin areas in its patterns of nomination. In contrast to 1962, when the party nominated only twenty-six candidates, it nominated forty-five in 1968.

In those Brahmin areas where it was already strong by 1968, the organization sought the support of respectable, middle-class candidates—persons with established personal reputations. They drew upon retired government servants, professionals, and successful businessmen, some of whom had not been previously active in the party. The result was the appearance of an organization with relatively mature candidates of a "solid" middle-class character. The contrast with the youthful demeanor of Congress nominees with their highly politicized behaviors was quite sharp, as was the dissimilarity with some of the militant SSP candidates whose identifications (if not origins) were in the working-class. The Poona Jan Sangh, in these terms, contrasted not only with the other local major political organizations but with its Agra counterpart.

Despite its selection of non-Brahmin candidates in parts of the city, the Jan Sangh still had not made a full commitment to the recruitment of low-status groups. It did back a number of low-status Hindus, but not a single Scheduled Caste candidate was supported by the organization. Several Jan Sangh figures spoke rather deprecatingly of the inability of the Maratha community to consider candidates of a party on the basis of "principles" rather than personality or community. Yet, few Jan Sangh Brahmins suggested, as several Nagri Sanghatna Brahmins did, that Brahmins in their own right were probably among the most communally conscious groups in Poona politics. In this case, however, communal interests coincided with an ideology which appealed to what members of the Brahmin community like to think of as "principled" behavior.

Other Parties

Aside from the three established political organizations, the main entrant in the corporation elections was the Shiv Sena. Having very little organizational meaning in Poona before the election campaign began, it came into being in the city as an association of candidates running under a common label. The handful of local people interested in the Shiv Sena were supplemented during the campaign by party workers from Bombay and the Thana suburban municipality (near Bombay), where the Shiv Sena had elected its first local government. During the campaign, the leader of the party—Bal Thakare—and his lieutenants spent a good deal of time in Poona addressing meetings and trying to whip up enthusiasm for their candidates, many of whom appeared to be newcomers to politics who would have stood as independents had they not linked themselves to the Shiv Sena propaganda machine.

While some of the electoral appeals made by the Sena were aimed at the Maharashtrian working-class in terms of the alleged encroachments of South Indians in running the state, the real audience for which the Shiv Sena appeared to exist in Poona were the middle classes. Many of Thakare's lieutenants were young. He seemed to attract both Brahmins and non-Brahmins of middle-class backgrounds to his side. Some of these were employed quite successfully in private companies in Bombay or Poona, yet they spoke rabidly about instances of discrimination allegedly perpetrated by Southerners employed in Maharashtra against their own friends or relatives which had caused them to join the Sena.

These feelings were the basis for a Sena demand that Maharashtrians be guaranteed 80 percent of all positions in private and public enterprises in the state. The demand had most meaning in Bombay, where the number of non-Maharashtrians in top positions was more obvious than in Poona. Among non-Maharashtrians, too, the Shiv Sena was careful to direct its attacks against only South Indians: as Thakare himself said, "The Gujaratis have their own businesses, and if they hire people they are always careful to hire local people."[37]

While feelings of deprivation may have been rife in Bombay, the specific demand was more symbolic than substantively meaningful in Poona. One found many non-Sena interviewees in Poona responding favorably to the issue although not to the Sena itself.[38] Except for the tone of immoderation, spokesmen from the various parties felt that a demand for equitable treatment for the Maharashtrians was justified but that this demand could or would be handled just as well through their own political organizations. The only group which was fairly outspoken against the demand itself was the Jan Sangh, which stressed the "antinational" character of the Shiv Sena during the campaign.

Although its Maharashtrian-oriented appeals were egalitarian in emphasis, the Sena seemed largely nonideological on other matters, with a strong bias against the Indian socialists. The party leader put it this way:

> The common man wants only three things: food, clothing, and something over his head. He isn't interested in ideologies. What he wants is water twenty-four hours a day or schools for his children that are not overcrowded. Now seventy-five children are crowded into one classroom. Spouting about socialism will do no good.

Although views of this kind were shared with rightist political groups like the Jan Sangh, there were areas in which the Sena differed with the Sangh. The verbalized pragmatism of the Sena showed through in its attitude on language, for example. Asserting that Southerners learned English from an early age and brought that facility to bear in job-seeking in Bombay while Maharashtrians learned English only from the eighth standard, Thakare urged:

> The teaching of English should be encouraged, so Maharashtrians can compete. This language business is on the wrong basis now and gives an unfair advantage to people who can take interviews in English since it is still used for employment in Bombay. The Shiv Sena wants English taught from the fifth standard as long as there is not a truly enforceable national language policy.[39]

A leading Poona journalist countered some of the points made by the Sena:

> To be fair, one should consider the fact that because of the importance of Bombay, Maharashtra receives 35 percent of all the central investment in industrialization. As a result,

we must expect that skilled and unskilled labor from other parts of India will come into the state. The Shiv Sena has simply been able to get support because of the existence of educated unemployment in India and the fact that it plays upon sentimentality.

The other political parties in the 1968 race are of much less interest. These included: the *Janta Aghadi* (Peoples' Front), a loose coalition of the Communist Party and some non-Communists; the Kamble wing of the Republican Party; a few Swatantra Party nominees; and a small electoral front which called itself the *Nagri Seva Samiti* (City Service Organization). The latter emerged as a largely high-status organization—seven of its fourteen candidates were Brahmins. Unlike the Nagri Sanghatna with its strong partisan substructure, the Nagri Seva Samiti came close to the original ideal of nonpartisanship proclaimed by the Sanghatna. Organized by a woman who had been active in the nationalist movement in the 1930s and had served as a Congress MP from rural Poona from 1952 to 1957, the organization tried to appeal to politicized women. From the beginning of its efforts, it became apparent that the Nagri Seva Samiti was, indeed, an innocent grouping; it had no money, few political skills among its leadership, and little in the way of an organizational basis. Its nominees were generally citizens of good reputation who could not effectively mount a threat to the principal candidates in each ward.

THE ELECTORAL PROCESS

Table 10.8 records a marked increase in the total number of candidacies in Poona from 1962 to 1968—291 to 400. In some part, this increase may have reflected the structurally induced uncertainty which followed from a new electoral system. Through 1962, Poona's municipal elections had been based on twenty multi-member electoral wards. For the 1968 elections, single-member constituencies were created. Whose interest this innovation would serve was open to debate. Many non-Congressmen claimed that smaller units permitted the Congress to capitalize upon its financial and organizational superiority and upon its popularity in the Maratha community which constituted a substantial plurality in many of the working-class wards. On the other hand, smaller units might have permitted independents and minor party candidates with strong personal appeal to overcome the limitations associated with candidacies in larger units. It can be argued, as it was by some observers of the election, however, that the new electoral units worked particularly to the disadvantage of a party like the Nagri Sanghatna, which depended upon a series of alliances among various primordial and partisan elements for its victories. In the larger wards, cooperation among candidates of divergent backgrounds contributed to overall party strength; in the smaller wards, efforts at intergroup reconciliation were more difficult. Thus, during the election campaign, several instances came to my attention of campaign workers for the SSP undermining a PSP candidate backed by the Sanghatna in a given ward. Such cases were uncommon among Congress and Jan Sangh workers during this election.

The election itself produced the usual panoply of activities. One Congress leader described the intensive efforts which had gone into organizing the campaign of that party. About twelve hundred workers were mobilized for the period.

Various leaders of the party campaigned as a team through the city, partly to avoid divisiveness through chance remarks. Mohan Dharia in his role of campaign organizer even suggested to candidates that they maintain a diary of workers in their wards sympathetic to the Congress and of voters canvassed who showed an inclination toward the party, with the hope of drawing upon a resource base of five thousand persons to help the party. In the latter connection, candidates also were asked to maintain a list of grievances they encountered in meeting voters to which the party might attend after the election.[40]

If we turn to aggregate data from the elections, we find in table 10.9 that the net increase in candidacies by primordial groups was especially marked among Marathas. Whereas Brahmin nominees increased by twenty-four, Marathas more

TABLE 10.9

Primordial Changes between Elections, Poona Corpora-
tion, 1962-1968

Primordial Group	1962	1968	Net Change
Brahmins	58	82	+ 24
Intermediate	33	40	+ 7
Marathas	77	127	+ 50
Low Hindus	35	52	+ 17
Mahars	26	29	+ 3
Other Scheduled Caste	16	18	+ 2
Muslims	16	11	− 5
Non-Maharashtrians	19	33	+ 14
Total	280*	392†	+112

* Excludes eleven other candidates who were not readily placed in these categories.
† Excludes eight other candidates who were not classifiable.

than doubled that increase. The heavily Maratha character of candidacies in the Congress and the Sanghatna, as well as the substantial representation of Marathas in the Shiv Sena accounts for a large part of this increase. A consideration of what we have been calling "party satisfaction," shows us (in table 10.10) that the Marathas were the *least* likely element in the Poona population to run without some organizational connection in 1968. Among party groups with over twenty candidates, the Brahmins were second only to the non-Maharashtrians in their tendency to be "self-starting" candidates. The latter have been reluctant to develop an organizational base since the period of the Samyukta Maharashtra movement. Nor could one expect the Shiv Sena to provide it for most of them, particularly the South Indians.

Between 1962 and 1968, only small absolute increases were recorded for Scheduled Caste candidates. Mahars and other ex-untouchable communities were poorly represented in the major parties, despite the Congress-RPI alliance; some of the excess Mahar ambition was channeled into candidacies for groups like the Kamble wing of the RPI. As a result, neither the Mahars nor other communities like

TABLE 10.10

"Party Satisfaction" Index, Poona Corporation, 1968

Primordial Groups	"System" Parties*	Other Parties†	Independents	Total
Brahmins	.45	.18	.37	82
Intermediate	.60	.15	.25	40
Marathas	.54	.23	.23	127
Low Hindus	.42	.25	.33	52
Mahars	.28	.41	.31	29
Non-Maharash.	.37	.21	.42	33
Other SC	.33	.33	.33	18
Muslims	.36	.18	.46	11
Other‡	.38	—	.62	8
Total Candidates	185	90	125	400

* Congress, Nagri Sanghatna, Jan Sangh.
† Shiv Sena, Swatantra, RPI-Kamble, Janta Aghadi (including CPI), Nagri Seva Samiti.
‡ Primordial group not identified.

the Mangs or Bhangis were especially numerous among independent candidacies. Muslims, on the other hand, were both withdrawing from political life—they were the only primordial group with fewer candidates than in 1962—and were "displaced persons" insofar as the party system was concerned. They were neither heavily "recognized" in the candidacies of the established parties nor drawn to the various marginal organizations.

Finally, the section of the population which has been identified as "Intermediate" in character—CKP's, Pardeshis, Malis, Lingayats, Dhangars—exhibited features common to its aggregate behavior in the past: a rather small number of independents; high recruitment by the established political parties. In this case, the Intermediate primordial groups were the least represented of any group among the candidates in minor political parties or electoral fronts.

In spite of the uncertainty introduced into the electoral process by the reorganization of electoral units and the marked increase in the total number of candidacies, the three established parties continued to dominate the electoral results in Poona. However, there was a major alteration in the distribution of public support among the three (see table 10.11). In the seventy-two wards where seats were filled on 16 June,[41] the Congress tightened its claim on a majority while the Nagri Sanghatna and Jan Sangh vied with each other for second place. As in the past, the Jan Sangh and Sanghatna complemented each others' strengths, the former drawing almost all of its support from the Brahmin community; indeed, all but one of the Jan Sangh's winners were Chitpavan Brahmins. On the other hand, the previous following of the Sanghatna among Brahmins had clearly been dissipated. The SSP's voters were now increasingly from among Marathas and "Low Hindus" in keeping with that party's national efforts to capture the support of low-status communities. The shift of forces in the Sanghatna was such, in fact, that not a single PSP-connected nominee was elected. The PSP, which was Brahmin-led

TABLE 10.11

Primordial Groups and Parties of Members Elected to Poona Corporation, 1968

Primordial Group	Congress	Nagri Sanghatna	Jan Sangh	Others*	Total
Brahmins	—	2	13	—	15
Intermediate†	6	4	—	—	10
Marathas	18	5	1	4	28
Low Hindus‡	3	4	—	2	9
Mahars§	2	—	—	—	2
Other SC‖	2	2	—	—	4
Muslims	1	—	—	—	1
Other#	2	—	—	1	3
Total	34	17	14	7	72

* Includes one Shiv Sena member. He is a Maratha.

† The six Congress members include three Malis, a Kirad, a Pardeshi, and a Lingayat; the four Nagri Sanghatna winners are two Malis and two CKP's.

‡ The three Congress corporators are a Weaver, a Bhoi, and a Tambat; the four Nagri Sanghatna members include a Shimpi, a Weaver, a Tambat, and a Kasai. A Sonar and a Bhoi were elected as independents.

§ Both Mahars were members of the Republican Party (Gaikwad).

‖ The Congress elected a Mang and a Chambhar; the Nagri Sanghatna supported a Mang and a Bhangi.

A Gujarati and Tamil Brahmin were affiliated with the Congress. The independent was a Sindhi.

and more middle class in its appeals in Poona than the SSP, was apparently too weak an organization for Brahmins to depend upon. Given a choice in the matter, such voters turned increasingly to the Jan Sangh.

Leaders of the SSP actually regarded the outcome of the corporation elections as a minor victory for them since nine of the seventeen Sanghatna winners were associated with the SSP. Of the remainder, one was affiliated with the PWP and one with the Mang political group. Five were persons without previous political experience. The seventeenth Sanghatna corporator was an incumbent who had been part of an organized effort to form a bridge group between the PSP and SSP; this effort had failed, but a few of the Sanghatna candidates were identified with this "unity front" rather than with either the PSP or SSP.

With respect to incumbents, it should be reiterated that a surprisingly high number ran again considering the six-year lapse in time between elections and the supposedly limited nature of the reward system associated with corporation membership. Forty-three incumbents were candidates for reelection (66 percent of the membership of the previous body); in addition, close relatives of three incumbents stood in other wards—the husband of one female incumbent, the brother and son of two others.

Reorganization of constituencies makes direct comparisons with previous years impossible. In some wards, as in Agra, as many as three incumbents ran against each other. There was some party shifting as nine incumbents ran on tickets other than those they had stood on in 1962. Aside from three of the Nagri Sanghatna nominees of 1962 who ran for the Congress in 1968—two were associated with the Pardeshi group, the other was one of the two defectors from the Sanghatna immediately after the 1962 election—there was no major direction followed in these movements. Only two of these nine "changers" were reelected: the man whose switch from the Sanghatna to the Congress came soon after the 1962 election; and, a Bhoi corporator elected as an independent, who joined the Sanghatna immediately after the 1962 election but subsequently defected to the Congress with the Pardeshi group.[42]

If we do not count the three incumbents who planned to stand against each other in the district where the election was stayed by the courts, twenty-two of forty incumbents were reelected; six were defeated by other incumbents. Some of the other fifteen losses were not to newcomers to municipal politics since several winners were persons who had contested previously for the corporation without success; in three cases the elections brought back to the corporation persons who had been members before 1962.

The results of this election provide some additional evidence of the importance of party support even for an incumbent in Poona. Of fifteen incumbents backed by the Congress, twelve were elected; in contrast, seven incumbents who stood as independents were *all* defeated. Three of the small band of Jan Sangh incumbents stood and all three won. The case of the Nagri Sanghatna was more complicated as the base of party support was shifting away from areas where the PSP had previously managed to attract a following. Only seven of the fourteen incumbents supported by the Sanghatna were reelected.

Viewed in terms of citywide support for a party as contrasted with its 1962 following (see table 10.12), very little difference occurred in the aggregate percentage of the vote received by the three major parties taken together, but the Jan Sangh made major gains (as we would expect from table 10.11), while the Congress actually lost a little or only held its own and the Nagri Sanghatna fell off by about 6 percent. On the other hand, with its large number of candidates and the help of the Hindu Mahasabha fragment, the Shiv Sena drew only 7 percent of the vote. The national media drew optimistic conclusions from the latter results.[43] Some local observers also suggested that the Sena was a passing phenomenon, but

TABLE 10.12

Percentage of Votes for Political Groups, Comparing 1962 and 1968 Elections, Poona

Parties	1962* %		1968 %		Difference
Major Parties:					
Congress	33.3 ⎫		31.5 ⎫		−1.8
Nagri Sanghatna	30.2 ⎬ 71.9		24.5 ⎬ 70.9		−5.7
Jan Sangh	8.4 ⎭		14.9 ⎭		+6.5
Shiv Sena/HM	—		7.0		—
Other Groups	3.5		5.5		+2.0
Independents	24.6		16.6		−8.0
Totals	100.0		100.0		

* Based on figures published in *Sakal*, 20 June 1968.

this may be premature in a situation where so much of the population is potentially available for the rise and legitimization of new political movements.

Under the circumstances of a major rise in candidacies and reorganization of wards, it is probably of importance that the "established" parties were able to confirm so much of their previous strength, let alone record the impressive advance made by the Jan Sangh. The data seem to support the view that the Shiv Sena's appearance hurt the Nagri Sanghatna as much or more than either the Congress or the Jan Sangh. Disruptions within the Sanghatna made public support for the candidates of that organization more "available" for incursions in a way not quite true of the Congress or Jan Sangh. The refusal of the Poona PSP to support the Shiv Sena, in particular, made that element's Bombay alliance with the Sena awkward and created embarrassment both for it and for the Sanghatna.

Control of less than a third of the Poona vote does not appear to put the Congress in a very strong position, but the variation in votes from ward to ward and the distributions of candidacies for the different parties conceal the *breadth* of Congress following in the city while suggesting the rather shallow *depth* of party support. Thus, if we analyze the parties' positions in each ward in terms of candidates who finished first, second, and third, we find that Congress nominees finished in one of these three leading positions in 66 of the 72 contests compared to 55 for the Nagri Sanghatna, only 30 for the Jan Sangh, and 17 for the Shiv Sena. Indeed, if we give a weighted figure to these performances by assigning a score of "3" to a first-place showing, "2" to a second and "1" to a third-place finish, the differences in group strength are even more evident: 158 for the Congress, 111 for the Sanghatna, 64 for the Jan Sangh, and 25 for the Shiv Sena. Independents received 56 points, and the remaining 17 were divided among the RPI (Kamble), the Janta Agadhi and the Nagri Seva Samiti.

As a result of the shifts in voter support between 1962 and 1968, the actual consequence of the election was to create as closely divided a council as in Agra. Within the confines of the corporation, the Jan Sangh and the Nagri Sanghatna shared enough antipathy to the Congress to be willing to come together again to try to form a majority; the Congress also was in a position to bargain for majority control. The electoral result with its thirty-four to thirty-one division between the major contenders ironically placed the determinative role in the hands of the few independents and the lone Shiv Sena corporator—a situation necessitating the bargaining processes characteristic of Poona in 1962 as well as Agra in 1968.

THE NEW POONA CORPORATION

Once the election results were known, the selection of a mayor and deputy mayor became a source of considerable activity. Since the vote was bound to be close, the three major groups were extremely cautious in their behavior. The Shiv Sena and independent corporators began the negotiating process by announcing that they would operate as a unit.[44] For a few days, this statement remained valid as the major groups attempted to reach decisions on candidates and strategies.

In 1968, the choice of candidates was taken out of the hands of the Congress corporation and was made by the Election Committee of the City Congress. This was done to prevent the wrangling surrounding the attempt to choose a candidate in 1967 After consideration of two other sitting members—Namderao Mate, former President of the City Congress and recently defeated as an MLA candidate; the other, a woman corporator with occasional dissident proclivities—the party turned to D. S. Kadu, a Congressman who had served the party from 1937 until he defected to the PWP when that organization was formed after Independence. Kadu was first elected to the corporation in 1957 as a member of the SMS, but he crossed back to the Congress in 1960. An important party member summed up the view of many:

> Kadu is a good selection for mayor. When we are strong enough, we should give a chance to a man who is poor but a good worker for the party. He could never afford to secure the position on the basis of his own connections or money.

Rarely asserting leadership and not normally staking a personal claim to office, he was a very modest man who lived a remarkably marginal economic existence. At the same time, it should be noted, he had not been listed high among the members most respected by other corporators in 1964.

The Nagri Sanghatna, in its turn, nominated the leader of the SSP group in the corporation, Bhau Adhav. Adhav most recently had been the unsuccessful Samiti candidate for MP in 1967 in rural Poona. The Jan Sangh backed its perennial leader, G. P. Bhagwat. In the bargaining between these two groups, however, the Jan Sangh was adamant in its refusal to withdraw its nominee, and the Sanghatna leaders agreed to Bhagwat's candidacy.

With the independents playing a decisive role, both major groups then sought to win away these members; the Shiv Sena nominee early identified his interests with those of the Sanghatna. The major bargaining counter used was the offer to independents of support for the deputy mayorship. The Congress put forward a Sindhi independent, whereas the Sanghatna nominated a Maratha independent. The latter had been associated with the Congress prior to the election and there was some hope he might win decisive votes from the Congress.

Balloting was scheduled for the afternoon of 1 July. There were predictions of an even split, in which case the outgoing mayor would cast a deciding vote. In the end, most of the independents appear to have opted for the Congress. Kadu was elected by a vote of thirty-seven to thirty-four with one vote declared invalid.[45] Election of a deputy mayor created greater difficulties. It followed immediately after the mayoral election. The two independent nominees received an equal number of votes on the first ballot; the newly elected mayor, who had just assumed the robes of office, cast the decisive vote which gave the deputy mayorship to the Congress. Despite the narrowness of these victories, this was the first time since 1937 that the Congress was able to elect both of its candidates for mayor and deputy mayor during the first year of a municipal body.[46]

THE CORPORATORS

While background data could not be collected on all the new corporators, interview materials from this trip or from our previous visit permit us to make use of some data for forty-six of the seventy-two corporators in Poona and forty-nine of the corporators and aldermen in Agra. Data on occupations is also available on a few others.[47]

In Agra, interviewees averaged 40.4 years of age as contrasted with 41.2 in Poona. Because of some underrepresentation of Jan Sangh members in the Poona interviews, the data may be distorted toward youthfulness in that city. Whereas the Poona Jan Sangh drew its candidates from prosperous local notables including retired civil servants—interviewees averaged 53.1 years as compared to 42.1 for the Sanghatna and 37.9 for the Congress—the Agra Jan Sangh membership displayed a mean of 38.7 years in a body where the Republicans averaged 39.4 and the Congress 41.9 years.

Thus, at least in generational terms, the Congress continued to be the party of youth in Poona; indeed, there was a mean of 33.7 years for the twelve newcomers to that party.[48] A Congress leader proudly noted, "The party is no longer concerned with the British." In contrast, even among the newcomers to the Nagri Sanghatna there were several men who warmly recalled their participation in the Quit India Movement.

While trying to attract a somewhat younger following, two of the youngest corporators in the Agra Congress were persons whose recruitment to politics was not exactly a function of the general attractiveness of the party to youth—the grandnephew of Seth Achal Singh and the son of Mahendraji, the Congress candidate for mayor in the 1968 elections.

As a result of the massive Jan Sangh entry into the Agra corporation, the number of lawyers in that body went up markedly. Many of these young lawyers were recruited into Jan Sangh politics directly during their law training at Agra College, a locus of much Jan Sangh activity. Five of the seven lawyers interviewed were from the Jan Sangh and among non-interviewees there were two other lawyers. As a result, the decreasing representation of Banias in the corporation and the growing strength of the Jan Sangh lent a new professional bias to the corporation. Of 52 men for whom data was available, 16 were professionals (9 lawyers; 4 doctors—including a homeopath and a vaid—an engineer, a chartered accountant and a dentist). A closely related occupation, teaching, provided employment for 5 other corporators (3 from the Jan Sangh). On the other hand, there were 23 businessmen if that term is broadly defined. Of that number, 10 were involved in the various industries normally associated with Jatav corporators. Eight Republicans ran shoe businesses, several quite profitably. Two of the small group of 6 businessmen in the Congress were also Jatav shoe factory owners. Thus, relatively few of the substantial Bania businessmen found in the corporation in 1959 were still in the body after the 1968 elections.[49]

Professionals were not so well represented in Poona as in Agra. In Poona, 7 professionals were among the corporators interviewed (3 medical practitioners; 3 lawyers; 1 engineer); at least 2 other lawyers were in the corporation, although not interviewed. Twenty of the 46 interviewees were in business; at least 9 of these "businessmen" were among that batch of young Maratha Congressmen to whom we referred earlier. They were engaged in such activities as operating gas stations, running family cooking-ware factories, or managing restaurants.

Aside from the five teachers from primary to college level represented in the

Agra corporation, few corporators in that city could be considered "employees." In Poona, only one teacher was in the corporation in 1968, but at least ten of the corporators interviewed might readily fall into an "employee-worker" general category. These included several retired persons, however, including the retired municipal accountant for the corporation. At the same time, two employees of the Kirloskar business organization were now in the corporation—one for the Jan Sangh (an assistant to the manager of a Kirloskar factory) and the other in the Shiv Sena; two other corporators were industrial workers. To some extent, the increasingly differentiated occupational structure of Poona was beginning to be "recognized" through the political system much as the traditional social structure had already been "recognized," although by no means precisely duplicated. Concomitantly, the simpler occupational structure of the Agra corporation largely reflects that city's rather narrow range of economic activities.[50]

Finally, educational backgrounds conform to what we noted earlier in this volume. On the whole, the Agra corporators were still better educated than those in Poona. However, fewer than a dozen corporators in either city now had less than a fifth-standard education. On the other hand, 29 of the 49 Agra interviewees had college educations (12 in the Congress, 11 in the Jan Sangh, 2 Republicans, 4 of the independents). This might appear to reflect the high-status of certain corporators in Agra, but a good number of the younger *low-status* members are now college-educated like the young (28) Republican corporator with an MA in social work or the Backward Class lawyers in the Jan Sangh.

Eighteen of the 46 corporators interviewed in Poona were college-educated; another 22 had at least some secondary education. This educational differential was related to the entrepreneurial interests of the Congressmen observed. Many of these men completed their secondary schooling and then entered business. As a result, 15 of the 24 Congressmen for whom data was gathered had only secondary education, while 7 were college-educated. The non-Brahmins with college education were among the youngest men. In contrast, about half of the Jan Sangh and Sanghatna members had some college education, although among the latter there were also several with only primary education.

These data are generally in keeping with the shifting organizational character earlier ascribed to the various political groups. It is difficult to believe that the Jan Sangh in Poona is quite as advanced in age as some of our present data seem to suggest. This may reflect the greater accessibility of older members of that party for interviews.

CONCLUSIONS

Despite the increasing number of participants in Agra politics by 1968, an uncertain move toward partisanship and organizational coherence seemed to be taking place. Not only was the number of independents down markedly from 1959, when the local political system was still evolving from the Congress-dominated order of 1957, but the portion of the vote controlled by the three major parties had increased by about 12 percent. At the same time, too, the candidates of these parties seemed to be working together more closely than in 1968. Nevertheless, there continued to be enormous "play" in municipal electoral politics, which made the outcomes of particular contests unpredictable. Much still depended upon the "personality" of a given candidate and his capacity to generate a following of his own aside from any favorable image his party might carry.

While the data indicate a great rise in Brahmin and Jatav activity in municipal politics and a decline in the participation of Banias, it is difficult to see these changes as part of any conscious series of conflicts within the system. The few comments made on the withdrawal of the Banias seem to argue that businessmen in Agra no longer wished to get involved in the "dirtiness of politics." The parallels to the American experience should not be overdrawn, but the Bania withdrawal is a notable repetition of the "retreat" of the business classes from politics in the United States at the turn of the century before their partial resurgence in the form of various local reform movements. In contrast, Brahmins were especially active in the Jan Sangh or associated with the legal profession, which meant, in the latter case, that their careers were tied to a quasi-governmental series of activities. They were also, apparently, attracted to an ideological movement whose appeals combined commitment to a "renewed" tradition and militant nationalism. At the same time, all four independents elected to the corporation in 1968 were members of Bania-related communities; in addition to the Jain and Mathur Vaish elected as independents after quitting the Congress, two other independent Jains were coopted—one as an alderman, the other as mayor. Although all four were successful businessmen, none evidenced the slightest ideological fervor or real dedication to a politics which would imply organizational commitment.

Changes in their own reputations, the rise of new political groups as well as the strengthening of the Jan Sangh, the differential politicization of primordial groups in the community—all contributed to a situation in which less than 40 percent of those incumbents contesting in 1968 were reelected. The numerous changes in individual party alignments seemed less significant than "personality" and the new organizational bases of politics in accounting for this result. By the late spring of 1968, the major political parties engaged in municipal politics in Uttar Pradesh were also looking forward to the mid-term elections with great anticipation.[51]

In Poona, the political game was played in 1968 with less regard for state legislative results, but even here the introduction of the Shiv Sena into the municipal arena augured a statewide, if not national, concern with the outcome of the corporation elections. A marked setback for the Congress might have been judged an index of the party's vulnerability even in a city which had not previously been one of its greatest strongholds. Instead, the arrival of the Shiv Sena seems to have hurt the Nagri Sanghatna somewhat more than it did either of the other organizationally more coherent major political groups. Despite the ideational sophistication of the city, new political strength in these elections seems to have gone to those who could play upon primordial themes (the Jan Sangh; the Shiv Sena; to some extent, the Congress) or to those who could generate populist appeals (the Congress, in part; the Shiv Sena; the SSP—rather than the PSP—in the Nagri Sanghatna).

Notwithstanding the enormous differences in primordial, partisan, and ideological factors from ward to ward, electoral contests in 1968 in both Agra and Poona seemed as particularistic in their outcomes at ward level as in past years. Yet, the two municipal political systems still yielded amazingly equilibrated popular bodies. In Agra, the Congress and the Jan Sangh contended for the small amount of authority popularly available in the system and the considerable fund of public prestige. However, neither had the ultimate secret for securing a stable majority. The Republicans, despite their debilitation, were a third major element in the situation. Pressures for developing a stable alliance between the Republicans and the Congress, of the kind perfected in Maharashtra, found less locally generated enthusiasm than at the state levels of the two organizations. Since the Jan Sangh was, at the same time, making its own efforts to mobilize support from Scheduled Caste and Backward Class communities, the political system achieved its balance by including a wide array of representatives of these groups as legitimate participants in the otherwise power-restricted municipal arenas.

The many forces thrown together in the municipal politics of Poona were quite different from those in Agra. The nature of the Congress as an organization, its appeals to youth, its following among the Marathas gives it a different character from the Agra Congress; the Jan Sangh of Poona with its Brahmin base is analogous to the Jan Sangh in Agra except that the generational basis of the Poona party makes it seem much less vital than the more broadly based party in the Uttar Pradesh city. The SSP-dominated Nagri Sanghatna, cross-cutting the working-class orientations of the SSP with a collection of middle-class independents, was a "third force" of doubtful long-run stability. Temporarily, at least, it added an important element to the special mix of citywide and ward-level political actors—personalities, political organizations, primordial groups—which produced a closely balanced corporation drawing upon most of the major elements of the population of Poona for support. Both traditional and modern sectors of the economy were represented in the corporation; the full range of status groups found in the general population of the city had a voice in municipal politics although they varied considerably in impact from the single Muslim to the twenty-eight Marathas. In the balance among these forces, however, the determinative roles were actually played by idiosyncratic independents who provided the decisive votes.

11 MUNICIPAL POLITICS AND THE INDIAN POLITICAL SYSTEM

We shall now attempt to summarize some of our findings by presenting the municipal arenas of Agra and Poona against three different backdrops: the general processes of social and political change in India; the larger political systems within which the two arenas operate; and the problems inherent in developing a more comparative approach to the study of local government and politics transcending national boundaries.

MODERNIZATION IN AGRA AND POONA

Local and regional political life in India traditionally reflected both the hierarchical and segmented nature of Indian society.[1] Political arrangements were grounded in a hierarchical social system dominated generally by land-based elites whose political authority was often legitimated by their ritually-sanctioned position in the stratification system. Even in those urban areas which served as political centers, intellectuals and wealthy mercantile groups were generally (though not universally) retainers to local princely houses. At the same time, areas of substantial intragroup autonomy existed for localistic societal segments (clans, subcastes, tribes) which allowed them to manage much of their own lives. The result was a hierarchical political society, but one limited in the kinds of activities it could legitimately pursue. Moral justifications for the hierarchical nature of the social and political order were internalized by the various strata of the population and not simply imposed from above by the most powerful local notables. Ultimately, the stability of this arrangement depended upon a low level of pressure for major alterations in the larger social structure both from those with political authority at the top and from those below. Where attempts were made to challenge the existent authority, the use of physical and moral sanctions to bring deviants into line was legitimated by Brahmanic teachings.[2] In sum, local political systems in traditional India were based on what Durkheim has characterized as "mechanical solidarity."[3]

This model of social stability based on societal segmentation can too easily be overstated. The existence of numerous empires and petty principalities allowed for considerable variation in political behavior and belief systems in the subcontinent before the political accession of the British in the late eighteenth century. Historical evidence also points to significant shifts in actual social arrangements over time in the face of changing prescriptions of the nature of deference demanded by the value system of the particular regime.[4]

The social and political changes which have occurred in India during the past 150 years—including urbanization and the propagation of nationalistic and democratic values—have helped to move political relations closer to what Durkheim termed a state of "organic solidarity."[5] The latter concept describes a system marked by a high order of social and economic differentiation of a kind which weakens solidary ties of a subsocietal nature at the same time that it underwrites a larger social order in which interdependence is more a function of individual and voluntaristic group activities than of traditional social identifications. Under a condition of organic solidarity, restraint is placed on the relatively unfettered use of repressive force by sacrally legitimated holders of power; instead, modern legal codes and a pattern of secularized political relationships are introduced.

Even the more highly "developed" of modern politics would not be as radically "organic" as Durkheim's ideal type. Thus, recent studies of local politics in the United States reveal the continued importance of primordial identifications such as ethnicity (not to speak of race) in understanding political behavior in a society supposedly characterized by a high level of "modern" economic and status differentiation.[6] On the other hand, the achievement of some degree of "political modernization" in India is reflected in the existence of a division of social labor based on the attenuation of solidary group exclusiveness in important areas of daily life: disputes are referred to formal political agencies; social bars to interaction with nonmembers of one's group of birth have been significantly reduced; socialization of the young has become a function increasingly assigned to secondary institutions;[7] the state is expected to perform certain distributive or redistributive functions previously performed by one's solidary group or the powerful landowners within the village or town, if performed at all.

The diminution of some aspects of traditional group authority over the individual does not imply the total disintegration of such groups as meaningful units for social or political action. In India, as in the United States, ascriptive ties are likely to maintain their salience for some members of the society so long as democratic structures persist. Thus, collectivities such as *jatis* ("castes" or "subcastes" depending on the particular context), continue to function in a transmuted form to the extent that they are able to adapt their traditional functions in society to the "system rules" of the new order—an order which they have participated in molding to their own political needs.[8] At the same time, the hold of traditional primordial groups and of the status system with which they were associated have appeared to loosen under the pressure of general social and economic change; the political and social relevance of the group depends increasingly upon voluntary identifications rather than on legally or ritually enforced distinctions. To some extent, identifications with ascriptive groups comes to resemble some of the same choices as memberships in secondary associations like unions, service organizations, or political parties.

Despite the numerous frictions which arise from these newer forms of intergroup relations, the presence of some freedom of choice for individuals *as individuals* or for members of previously excluded political groups in selecting the kinds of goals which they may pursue presumably provides them with a "stake" in democracy. Thus, while occasional fears have been expressed about the potentially disintegrative effects of the "politicization of caste,"[9] it may well be the case that the sense of participation associated with this politicization is actually one of the factors working for the successful maintenance and continuity of the system.

Indeed, some of the more immediate challenges to the present political system come not from the traditional elements in the society but from the "displaced" persons—the former dominant status groups, the educated unemployed and those intellectuals whose intellectual forebears first stimulated the nationalist movement and then engendered a vision of a new society emerging after Independence—a society which was to be radically different from the segmented social order upon which the British imposed a layer of administrative organization.[10]

Traditionally, these higher-status groups did not have to struggle constantly to maintain their political ascendancy, although individual personalities and factions within these groups may have been engaged in conflicts over priority within particular arenas. Their ascendancy as part of a collectivity was an extension of their economic and social status. Democratic politics tends to weaken these linkages, although many of the economic advantages which earlier accrued to high-status groups continue to provide some special advantages to them *outside* electoral politics. Still, if the social system has changed markedly in its political manifestations in recent decades because of the opportunities available to the formerly "subject" elements in society, it may have altered as radically for the previously dominant groups.

In Poona, Brahmin social and political dominance has largely been dissipated by the massive entry of non-Brahmins, particularly Marathas, into politics and government after centuries of subordination. While many intellectual and some economic resources remain in Brahmin hands, the Marathas have recently gained a dominant place in state and rural politics—less clearly in Poona City. The increasing "spill-over" of this dominance into economic activities probably foreshadows a considerable overhauling in traditional notions of status.

Change has not proceeded as dramatically in Agra. High-status communities— Banias, Brahmins, Kayasthas—continue to dominate the economic, social and political life of the city. Yet, as we have noted, the absence of primordial cohesion within these status groups has permitted the rise of a politics suffused with personalistic factors, ideational concerns, and an outright desire for political preferment and personal material benefits. The result is a series of political groupings quite distinct from traditional notions of social organization. Furthermore, in the course of their activity many of these political groups attempt to recruit low-status elements into politics since such groups constitute important resources upon which formerly elite segments of the society may draw for their own sustenance in politics.

At the same time, the rise of a caste-based group like the Jatavs acting as a self-conscious political unit signals that more than a simple quarrel within the traditional circle of elites is involved. Whether the Republican Party can persist as a viable instrument of Jatav political interests is open to some doubt, but recent efforts by both the Congress and the Jan Sangh to draw strength from already politicized elements of the Jatav community suggest that members of that community are now in a position to bargain for advantage from a fund of experience as members of an autonomous political element.

While contention among traditional status groups is a major dimension of political life in the two cities, other activities recorded in previous chapters are much more than epiphenomena arising from traditional or even contemporary status differentials. Political groups have a life of their own in the two cities and a raison d'être beyond their conformance to or identification with primordial interests. The traditions of the Congress Party, in particular, spanning now over eighty years, represent a series of personal experiences and shared history for the older members of that party in Agra and a source of substantive and symbolic state and national benefits to some of the younger generations of politicians in both cities. On the other hand, party groups like the SSP and Jan Sangh, while attracting support from the displaced status elites in Poona (more so than in Agra, where intergenerational differences and the entry of newly politicized groups into the Jan Sangh make the picture rather different), also serve ambitions and ideational strivings which cannot be met through the largely pragmatic, machine-organized Congress Party.

These political forces—primordial relations, party identifications, ideational strains—have been examined at considerable length in order to achieve some understanding of political life at the local level in urban India. This study of two municipal arenas has also required an exploration of some of the institutional dimensions of municipal government. Putting the two together, we have emerged with a set of descriptive statements with respect to political behavior in Agra and Poona. Whether such statements are appropriate to other political systems is open to question. After outlining some of these materials and placing them within the context of contemporary Indian politics, we shall briefly discuss the utility of such an approach for cross-national comparisons.

THE MUNICIPAL ARENAS AND
THE INDIAN POLITICAL SYSTEM

The rubrics adopted in the present section follow the organization of previous chapters. They should aid us in summarizing some of the materials introduced earlier as well as serving to emphasize the critical relationships which exist between local and supralocal political systems in India.

1. *Environmental Influences.* Political behavior within the municipal arenas of Agra and Poona is shaped to a great extent by sets of geohistorical circumstances peculiar to each region and by economic and ecological factors which are associated with those environments. At the level of social action, we have been particularly concerned with portraying those distinctive patterns of primordial relationships in each city which have fed into political life.

2. *The Governmental Context.* With respect to specific governmental features of Agra and Poona, we have traced the historical and contemporary forces which have helped to shape governmental activity (or lack of activity) in municipal matters. In the process, we have stressed the rather restricted range of authority permitted to these municipal arenas and the high level of involvement by other levels of the political system in municipal affairs, most notably the state governments, through district officials and state-appointed administrators within the municipal corporations, like the Chief Executive Officers. It should be noted, however, that even within those spheres of activity where the elected corporation members have some discretion, they have not always seen fit to exercise that authority. Indeed, in some matters (for example, the tearing down of unautho-

rized constructions) they have attempted to prevent administrative action from proceeding.

3. *The Political Context.* We have attempted to "place" political behavior in each of the municipal arenas within the larger framework of political forces operating in each city and in state and national politics where these are relevant. Specific political actors (whether individuals or groups) who contributed significantly to the definition of networks of interactions within the municipal arenas were considered both in relation to their participation in electoral struggles for higher office and in terms of their activities in municipal affairs.

4. *Political Groups.* In the course of identifying political actors and their goals in the two cities, we considered the contributions of at least four different types of political groups found there: primordial, ideational, personalistic, and machine groups. We have provided examples of how such political groups have functioned as aggregative—and, on occasion, as disaggregative—political structures performing sometimes as party factions, sometimes in their own right as political parties. Their aggregative qualities have been enhanced in the two municipal arenas by their predisposition to participate in agreements with other groups to create political alliances and coalitions to achieve particular political ends: sometimes little more than the prevention of Congress majorities from coming to office in the municipal bodies.

Viewed from the perspective of "party politics," both cities lack highly crystallized party "systems." The amorphous nature of Agra politics evident in 1959 had shifted in the direction of a three-party "plus" arrangement by the spring of 1968—an arrangement in which the Congress (composed of machine and personalistic factions), the Jan Sangh (containing ideational elements and appealing to a broader primordial base than earlier), and the Republicans (primordial and quasi-ideational components) interacted in an "open system" heavily marked by the participation of individual political entrepreneurs. The recent entry of nonideational elements into politics through organizationally tenuous political groupings like the BKD and SSP merely highlights the marked instability of the larger pattern of partisan activity in Agra noted earlier.

Poona's party system consists of a political machine with certain primordial overtones (the Congress), which is regularly forced to do battle with a varied mix of oppositional elements: the Brahmin-dominated Jan Sangh with its basis in appeals to a reconstructed Hindu tradition increasingly intertwined with elements of nationalistic fervor; the ideational SSP and PSP; primordial political groups like the RPI and PWP. The situation is further complicated in Poona by the presence of independents both within the framework of coalitional politics (the Samyukta Maharashtra Samiti, the Nagri Sanghatna, the Sampoorna Maharashtra Samiti) and outside it, and the electoral "availability" (as in Agra) of large segments of the local population for the efforts of new groups like the Shiv Sena.

5. *Political Actors.* Despite the importance of primary group identifications in India, part of the great fluidity of political groups in Agra and Poona is clearly due to the operation of what strangely enough may be a kind of atomistic political individualism prevalent in many spheres of Indian politics.[11] The unsteadiness of political groups at the local level is symptomatic of the same behavior at higher levels. In part, it is a function of a larger political system which seems to reward

those who seize the "main chance" either through open defection from the party which originally sponsored them for office or by operating independently from it while nominally continuing within its ranks.

Because of this political atomism, it has been important to highlight the actions of individual politicians and the interplay of personalities. What evidence we have been able to collect also appears to indicate that many municipal election contests—both within the wards and for municipal offices like mayor and deputy mayor—depend upon personal ties that particular individuals have established to relevant "publics" rather than upon party designations, special primordial connections, or policy positions. This emphasis on particularistic behaviors seems especially appropriate given the kinds of ends which actors seek through their participation in local politics. A minority of corporators mention group ends which extend beyond their immediate constituencies. Rather, much of their effort is focused on matters like administrative intervention, representation of ward interests, and the pursuit of symbolic or substantive payoffs either for themselves or for their own neighborhoods.

It is also on this individualistic plane that we find that interpersonal relations among corporators are based on a complicated mixture of partisan attachments, personal perceptions of individual performances, and, less clearly, primordial identifications. Indeed, we found party to be somewhat *more* important as a determinant of sociometric choices than primordial ties in explaining the sources of esteem within the municipal bodies.

6. *Arena Outputs.* The result of these intersections of group and personal behaviors is a series of system outputs at the local level which do not have much weight in quantitative or monetary terms. Still, such outputs serve as important validations of the meaningfulness of the two municipal political arenas for local actors:

(a) *Individual and group status rewards.* The "payoffs" of participation for certain status groups and many politicians may be either in symbolic form ("recognition")—especially where claims to equality or superiority are being sought by emerging status groups—or in small substantive form like the placement of pavements or drains in areas which received scant public attention earlier. The limited resources of the corporations make such payoffs minor; but the public, according to the corporators themselves, perceives these benefits in relative terms (comparing them to the experiences of the past) rather than placing them on an absolute scale of civic achievement. These minor benefits are important to the political system as a whole. In a spirit common to many Western politicians, one corporator (recently turned MLA) remarked, "People are more interested in sewers and paved roads than they are in what is going on in Parliament or the State Assembly."

(b) *Partisan advantage.* Political organizations with stakes in national and state politics make use of the municipal arenas as bases of strength from which to extend their influence or to strike roots nurtured elsewhere. This was certainly the case with the Jan Sangh and the Republicans after 1959 in Agra and the SSP in Poona; on the other hand, setbacks at the municipal level may weaken party groups for participation in other arenas (for example, the Congress in 1962 and 1967).

Furthermore, the jostlings for status or for the limited material benefits available through the municipal arenas appear to take on such significance that most political groups in the city—whatever their ideology—feel compelled to test themselves in the municipal arena. The resultant coalition formation, bargaining for office, day-to-day interaction and cooperation in matters of small import does not necessarily weaken ideational, primordial, or partisan distinctions among groups, but it does induce an element of instrumental behavior into the Indian political system which may be of value in its long-run persistence.

(c) *Political expertise.* Whether viewed from the individual or group perspective, the municipal arenas provide a training ground for dealing with public affairs. Both in Agra and Poona, the corporation has served as a first step for many of the men holding MLA seats. This "education in politics" is not simply the kind of civic training envisaged by those who recommended Indian participation in local government in the last decades of the nineteenth century. Rather, the politics of the corporations provides an opportunity for new groups and new personalities entering politics to assimilate to unfamiliar forms of political behavior. On the whole, this may tend to identify the interests of these new groups with those of "The System." Strongly committed ideational organizations might bring their pre-existent values into municipal bodies and proceed to employ those arenas for the purpose of spreading their antisystem propaganda more effectively. Thus far, however, ideationally more extreme parties like the Jan Sangh and the CPI (Marxist) have chosen to follow a largely electoral and agitational approach to political life.

7. *Latent Arena Functions.* If we look beyond the restricted formal outputs of the two municipal arenas—beyond the minor patronage, the struggles for largely honorific offices, the bureaucratic interventions, the symbolic (and, occasionally, material) forms of individual or group recognition—we can identify several latent functions performed for the local political system as a result of the modes of participation outlined in the foregoing chapters:

(a) *Institutional legitimacy.* By their candidacies and their electoral activity, corporators and those defeated for election contribute considerable public legitimacy to the democratic institutions introduced into the two cities and to those winning the hotly contested elections characteristic of the two municipal bodies. These elections provide an important opportunity to mobilize opinion and group identifications in support of the municipal political order. To a limited extent, they provide a basis for the exercise of sanctions by those who are thereby legitimated to hold office. Local administrators, in particular, may be forced to view these public representatives as something more than general citizens.

It is less evident, however, that corporators are viewed as having meaningful authority by district or state officials. Certainly, few instances can be cited where the corporations' preferences have been treated as directives by their respective state governments, particularly where controversial decisions are involved. Indeed, several examples have been given of the severely limited authority vested in the corporations when confronted with a determination on the part of the state governments to act to the contrary. Part of the difficulty, as we have seen, is the partisanship which is sometimes reflected on both sides.

(b) *The broker function.* Not only may elected representatives assume a governmental role carrying certain public expectations, but they may also take on a brokerage function for and within a given sector of the urban population. By representing group interests or acting as spokesmen for their wards, they may constitute a force for integrating that population element into the larger political order. Within some communities (defined either territorially or in terms of ascriptive status), the corporator may also be called upon to deal with conflicts arising out of family disputes or local quarrels; he may intercede with district or state authorities on occasion. As a result of the status acquired in the larger political system, for example, the basis of authority within the Jatav community has shifted increasingly from the local headman or caste *panchayat* (the traditional caste council) to the elected official.[12]

(c) *Administrative particularization.* In the process of interventions with administrative authority locally or at higher levels, the corporator buttresses the legitimacy of these structures by particularizing their behaviors. Institutions which were traditionally approached with some diffidence by large segments of the population have become more *openly* subject to manipulation by individual or group will. While the consequences of this for administrative behavior may not be entirely desirable (given attendant corruption or tendencies toward administrative favoritism), it may be argued that particularizing tendencies are necessary for the survival of an administrative structure otherwise noted for its inefficiency and rigidity.[13]

(d) *Intergroup conflict resolution.* The wholehearted commitment of so many corporators' energy and time to their roles and the eagerness of the public to make use of the corporations for certain public ends stimulates a constant but manageable attempt to achieve a balance among groups and individuals striving for the hallmarks of equality or ascendancy. The municipal arenas then take on an important societal function as the locus for the registration of the success or failures of these contests. Even within the range of limited benefits available, some groups achieve sufficient advantages to become defenders of the system.

8. *System Functions.* This last item, of course, points to the performance of certain functions by the corporations for the benefit of the larger political system. By contemporary models of participatory democracy or even in Gandhian terms, Indian municipalities fall considerably short of realization of full-fledged "grass roots" democracies. By comparison with the standards of actual participation in socially heterogeneous societies in the West, however, India has done an impressive job in building a representative system of local government in her cities and towns—a system which complements highly participative national and state patterns of political behavior. The ways in which the two corporations function tend to involve citizens in democratic political processes whose outcomes they are able to observe. Levels of participation both in terms of voter support of electoral processes and, even more impressively, in respect to the number of candidates involved are evidence of considerable interest in the operations of the local political system. Insofar as they have the capacity to do so, the corporations contribute to the creation of sets of ties with the political system which run from the most remote *mohalla* or *gali* to the very large and exceedingly complex national political order which is contemporary India.

Whether decentralization of certain conflict to subordinate levels relieves the state and central governments of pressures potentially disruptive to the larger system, as Myron Weiner has argued, is open to some question.[14] Battles over primordial group status may be restricted to the local level, but even in the case of such status conflicts, some inevitably carry statewide implications (as in the case of Maharashtra's conflict between Brahmins and non-Brahmins) which are not diminished by the localization of certain aspects of the battle. Certainly, the kinds of factional conflicts which have taken place in Agra over control of the Congress machinery did not relieve the Uttar Pradesh Congress of the burdens of factionalism, nor did they ultimately strengthen the state government. The interpenetration of state-level cleavages and various localized factions merely contributed further to statewide conflicts. The picture is one of constant interdependence among levels, rather than protective insulation of the center or state by diffusion of conflicts to lower levels.

This points to a major problem in political life everywhere. Political organizations—parties, political groups, interest associations—are not merely neutral structures selflessly aggregating diverse interests according to some heaven-sent functionalist rationale. Rather, they feed as political mechanisms upon conflicts which they themselves are frequently instrumental in creating. The most "success-ful" political organization may be so classified because it is successful in exploiting distinctions—sometimes distinctions without ground in objective reality—for the benefit of the organization. While pragmatic political systems with large resource capabilities learn to manage these conflicts and, in a few cases, may even be able to resolve them, systems with few resources may simply experience a greater weakening over time of their capacity for acting effectively on broader issues because of the disintegrative effects of a multiplicity of aggregated and unaggre-gated lower-order political demands. In such instances, high levels of participation may not necessarily reflect the healthy state of the polity, but rather the existence of an *agitated polity* resulting from an incapacity on the part of existing institutions to channel demands in a direction which contributes positively to the development of the economic or social potential of society. Localistic demands met either locally or at some higher level of the system may help to postpone conflicts of a more serious order, but they may also contribute to the ineffectiveness of the polity rather than to the vitality supposedly associated with democratic participation in politics.[15]

THE COMPARATIVE STUDY OF LOCAL
GOVERNMENT AND POLITICS

The summary presented in the previous section highlights the rather eclectic approach toward local government and politics taken in the present study. While various social science models have influenced my research at different stages, the formulation which finally emerged attempted to give full weight to those special factors which helped to mold political life in the two Indian cities. Clearly, such an approach militates against any thoroughgoing attempt at cross-polity comparative analysis of urban political systems.

From the start of this research, it was obvious that the activities performed at the local level and over which particular municipalities have control vary considerably from nation to nation. This situation is complicated within a political system such as that of the United States where cities hold in common certain negative structural characteristics: traditions of local autonomy in decision making; a loosely organized and decentralized national party system; varying degrees of local financial responsibility.[16] The result is great diversity in this country, both with respect to expectations about the range of local services and the kinds of units thought to be appropriate for the performance of those services.

Despite these differences, and partly because of them, it has been possible to conduct comparative studies of local decision making in the United States which test for variations in governmental behavior in terms of a city's political structure, socioeconomic status or "value" patterns.[17] Comparison in such cases is significantly aided by the presence of a national network of media emphasizing national cultural values and innovating organizations (including the national government) which serve as communications links in standardizing proposals for local adoption.

Various methods have been developed to help in analyzing local political processes in the United States. The most popular, no doubt, are those identified with the "decisional" and "reputational" approaches to community "power."[18] The former make use of certain representative decisions or "issues" as tests of the manner in which power and influence are distributed through a municipal population; the latter seek to identify those elites which dominate public life and, thereby, putatively control the outputs of government.

Outside the United States, such techniques may not be as fruitful. In nations where municipal governments are limited severely in their decision-making authority, as they are when such authority rests substantially with officials who are part of a national or regional bureaucracy, an emphasis on *local* decisions in describing municipally relevant political phenomena is likely to be misleading. Furthermore, when the material resources available to a municipality are constricted (as is the case in many of the new nations), the range of alternatives available to the decision-making apparatus may be so circumscribed as to rule out all but the most marginal innovations and severely hamper even the maintenance of minimal public amenities like water supply or an adequate sanitation system.

Still, broadly conceived, such local political systems (as we have seen in the Indian case) may produce outputs which involve other than material values. Claims to personal or group prestige, in particular, may result in system responses which are largely symbolic in character but carry great significance for the groups involved. Such "recognition" may occur in a variety of political systems; yet it is not clear what theoretical coinage might appropriately place these claims and their realization within a common framework.

At the same time, it is our view that the employment of reputational techniques to locate an urban "power structure" may be of limited utility where only a small stock of local values is in dispute and the decisional autonomy of local political actors is severely hedged about by formal political structures. If one accepts the premises on which such techniques are based, they are probably most valuable in political systems where institutionalized sectors of society (organized business and financial interests, the military, the church, labor unions) participate through given individuals in contests over influence in decision making.[19] In the Indian cities chosen for examination, such institutionalized sectors either did not exist or were only weakly articulated forces insofar as attempting to influence local political behavior. Indeed, it generally appeared to be the case that governmental actors (including party politicians) themselves encapsulated the dominant strains in the population in shaping the outcomes of local political processes.

Although the formal methodology associated with "power structure" studies was not adopted for the present research, we have been concerned with describing the manner in which power and influence are distributed in the two cities. A multiplicity of politically relevant groups based on a variety of both broadly and narrowly defined identifications did exist and did attempt to gain influence. However, the main political "game" appeared to be played through the institutions of government at various levels of the political system. Thus, a proper understanding of the operations of a municipal political arena must go beyond dealing with the behaviors of municipal and locally based political actors alone in order to identify all those actions and actors originating from outside the immediate arena who either directly or indirectly determine the character of the local political process. The present study suggests that only through a close examination of those forces which operate within the two local political systems—by identification of the kinds of persons who participate, what some of their goals are and what activities of theirs have importance for politics—can we begin to make meaningful comparative statements. Analyses which originate from models of "system functions" ultimately arrive at a dead end unless they are sensitive to the particular cultural settings and value patterns of the societies which they are investigating.[20]

This study stands, therefore, somewhat at odds with more recent developments in research on "community power structures" because of its institutional and configurational approach. While it is "comparative" in the narrow sense of involving a study of two quite different cities and occasionally drawing upon insights from the literature of American urban politics, it is probably at midstream insofar as newer methodologies and approaches to the comparative study of local politics are concerned. It has not depended upon a deductive set of behavioral propositions, nor is the focus narrow as far as political phenomena are concerned. It is hoped, nevertheless that the present rather wide-ranging study may serve at least as a useful transitional volume in the passage from comparative local politics of a historical-descriptive nature to analyses of Indian and other urban political systems more firmly grounded in systematic behavioral science.[21]

A CAUTIONARY NOTE

Out of the interactions among politicized individuals and political groups has emerged a style of Indian politics which is peculiarly incapable of overall and continuous commitment. Perhaps societal stagnation amidst political agitation is the price that must be paid for democracy in a complex society. And, perhaps, municipal arenas like those of Agra and Poona are not the most satisfactory sites for observing the application of political energy to the realization of meaningful societal goals. But they do reflect at citizen level the extent to which politics in India is defined in terms of personal and symbolic status-seeking as a substitute, at least in part, for the attainment of substantive societal benefits. How long such a politics can be a viable alternative to economic growth and more substantial social change in India remains to be seen.

The picture we have drawn—while hopeful in some respects—should make us cautious about placing India well along the road to becoming a fully successful modern and democratic nation. Functioning pluralistic democracy may operate in the presence of subsocietal insulation as well as segmentation.[22] In India, few of the political parties and no government agencies seem capable of acting as agents of societal mobilization. Instead, the most notable feature of political organization in India today is its relatively mild discommoding effect upon the Indian public. During the past twenty years of national rhetoric, a series of crises have occurred in the society but they have not had a politically traumatizing impact of the sort which might be expected in a society which was politically mobilized. What few politically directed changes have occurred in Indian society have taken place within a rather narrow range of alternatives permitted to political leadership by the insulated and segmented society within which that leadership functions.

In William Kornhauser's terms,[23] the result is probably describable as democratic pluralism: elites are responsive to demands from below; they are accessible, as the MP's and MLA's of Agra and Poona exhibit well in their constituent relations. At the same time, to follow the Kornhauser terminology a little further, the Indian "masses" are not so fragmented as to be readily "available" to the blandishments of demagogic elites, although occasionally demagogic elements have employed appeals to local or national chauvinism or to primordial sentiments in such a way as to rally support from elements otherwise highly integrated into existent social networks. If anything, the problems which stand in the way of creating a more soundly based democracy in India may be attributable to an excess of plural structures. Where both the citizen and the government have a plethora of protections from each other, the result may be to insulate the citizen from directed change and to confound the government in activity irrelevant to societal needs.

For some of the new nations which have found themselves in this situation, alternatives to democracy have been sought. In some instances, this has meant resort to military rule, which substitutes force for effective societal mobilization; in other instances, the bureaucracy has served as a focus of political change, frequently with the cooperation of the military. Military government does not appear to be a viable alternative in India, however, partly because of the very fragmentation of Indian society, which is represented within the military services themselves.

Similarly, bureaucracies in India no longer resemble the mythologized "steel frame" so highly esteemed by the British if not by the generation of Indian nationalists. Indeed, some of the less attractive features of the earlier bureaucratic regime have been retained or accommodated to India's pattern of pluralistic democracy with consequences which include heightened resistance to administrative change, a proclivity toward emphasizing formal procedures, and great self-consciousness about one's status in the organizational hierarchy. Where bureaucratic accommodations with the new political system have occurred, they have frequently been in the direction of allowing partisan interests to influence the kinds of actions taken or not taken. This might not be such an unfortunate consequence if the infusion of partisanship followed some systematic course, but the entry of persons with political influence into the administrative process is often placed on an ad hoc basis which tends to weaken the overall system for action of any kind, making it unresponsive to an interested majority of the public, let alone an effectively organized minority.

At this point, one can do little more than hope that the incapacities of her leadership and the ineffectual nature of many of her political organizations are not the necessary product of democratization in India. As much of the material in this volume indicates, the foundations for widespread participation by diverse groups and individuals have been firmly grounded in the character of the Indian population. Whether that character is strong enough to assure good government at some point in the future is a different matter. For the time being, at least, the democratic nature of the political system erected in India no more guarantees effective government in India's cities (or at other levels of the political system) than do the diverse social and political structures which shape the character of most city governments in the United States.

Appendix:
Political Identifications
in the Two Cities

In addition to the six interview items from the 1964 visit which bear on intercorporator and corporator-bureaucrat relations,[1] each corporator interview included a set of six items which asked corporators to identify persons of historical or contemporary merit outside the corporation. The purpose of these questions was twofold: first, for those items which dealt with historic personalities or personalities operating at a present-day national level, it might prove interesting to see the extent to which corporators representing rather diverse political regions shared common public symbols; second, sharp divisions in identifications among groups within a local body might affirm the existence of deep fissures of a subcultural nature within each city—fissures which appear only in a highly complex fashion in the materials reported elsewhere in this study. They might also indicate the limits of the horizons of the corporators.

Thus, in table A.1 we summarize the responses to the first of these six items: "Would you please name the three persons active in India before the twentieth century whom you most admire?" The table presents a listing of all persons receiving more than three nominations in each body. In Agra thirty-four persons were named, but only nine received more than three nominations each; the same total number were nominated in Poona, but eleven received four or more nominations.[2]

Notable among the kinds of persons included on the two lists is the heavy representation of religious figures: Buddha, Vivekananda, Ram Tirth, Tukaram, Dnaneshwar, Ramdas, and Swami Dayanand. Except for Buddha, whose supporters are almost exclusively members of the Republican Party in the two cities,[3] other choices of saint-poets or sages appear to be regionally specific. When we turn to political personages, however, we find several persons held in common: Shivaji; Laxmibai (the Rani of Jhansi), whose military forces were active in the revolt against the British in 1857; Rana Pratap, one of the few Rajputs to hold out against the absorptive efforts of the great Mughal emperor, Akbar; and Asoka, the great Buddhist emperor. The mention of these figures is not a matter of chance; they are the symbols regularly invoked by public speakers, political organizations and the educational process as ideals of wisdom, courage, and other virtues publicly esteemed by the society.[4]

While there is considerable variation in the rank order of nominees, it is striking that five of the nine persons nominated for Agra also appear in the Poona ranking. At the same time, however, certain clearly regional commitments exist for Poona like Mahatma Phule (a leader of the non-Brahmin movement) and Tukaram, the saint-poet of Maharashtra, as contrasted with the backing given to Swami

TABLE A.1

Historical Figures: Pre-Twentieth Century Agra and Poona Nominations

Agra

Poona

Rank	Name	Nomi-nations	Rank	Name	Nomi-nations
1	Shivaji	19	1	Shivaji	52
2	Rana Pratap	18	2	Phule	18
3	Swami Dayanand	11	3	Tukaram	15
4	Buddha	9	4	Dnaneshwar	10
4	Vivekananda	9	5	Laxmibai	9
4	Laxmibai	9	6	Rana Pratap	8
7	Asoka	8	7	Baji Rao Peshwa	6
7	Akbar	8	8	Vivekananda	5
9	Ram Tirth	6	8	Ramdas	5
			8	D. Naoroji	5
			11	Asoka	4
	Total	97		Total	137

Dayanand in the region around Agra where Dayanand's Arya Samaj was particularly influential after the last quarter of the nineteenth century.

The persons listed in table A.1 are not uniformly favored by all of the groups within the two municipal bodies. Certain names "belong" to particular groups; for example, Buddha's nominations are from Jatavs in Agra; in Poona, the nominations for Mahatma Phule come mainly from non-Brahmin Maharashtrians. To isolate these group-related identifications, we analyzed nominations on the four dimensions we used earlier: ethclass, party group, age, and education.[5] Employing these categories, each nominee's scores were computed as a percentage of the *total* number of responses to an item. These "actual" nominations were then compared with an "expected" value derived from the number of nominations members of the particular corporation group would have given had its members made nominations in proportion to their representation among the total number of respondents.

Thus, in table A.1, four persons on the Agra list display marked subgroup support: Shivaji, Rana Pratap, Laxmibai, and Buddha. All have certain contemporary political symbolic connections. As we would expect, Buddha's support is heavily concentrated among Republicans; Shivaji, many of whose exploits were aimed against Muslims, is particularly popular among "high ethclass" corporators (Brahmins, Kayasthas, Thakurs), especially those of Jan Sangh and Swatantra Dal affiliation. These nominators tended to be among the older members of the local body. On the other hand, Bania corporators in 1964 were more favorable to Rana Pratap and Laxmibai than were other groups, but it is notable that the former is more popular among Jan Sangh members—again the symbology of resistance to Muslim power is strong—whereas Laxmibai is more popular among Congress corporators, since her courageous actions were exemplified in opposition to the British.

To the extent that these data point to any subcultural differences, only one seems to be of some prominence: the distinction between the Republican-Jatav grouping on the one hand, and most of the other corporators on the other. The

Republicans tend to have their own folk heroes like Buddha and, to a lesser extent, Asoka, but these differences do not go very deep since the better educated Republicans also contributed to other names on the list. It should be added that the less educated Republicans had a good deal of trouble naming *anyone* beyond Buddha.

Of the eleven persons on the Poona list, only four highlight differences in bases of support: Mahatma Phule, who seems to divide the Brahmin from non-Brahmin elements in Poona society rather sharply, receives about equal support from the various parties except for the Jan Sangh; Tukaram's principal support is among non-Brahmin Congressmen; Laxmibai's nominations actually tend to come from non-Maharashtrians—indicative, perhaps, of her role as a North Indian figure, even though she was of Maratha background. Finally, Bajirao, the Brahmin Peshwa responsible for consolidating and expanding the Maratha Empire, is favored by both Brahmins and Marathas as contrasted with other primordial groups. Curiously, his votes come from the Nagri Sanghatna more than from any other partisan element; the reasons for this are difficult to see. In contrast, Shivaji is so much a part of the fabric of Poona culture that his support is spread evenly over different ethclass categories. Partisan differences are small, although there is a slight tendency toward greater support from the Congress for him.

The second item in this series asked corporators to identify three persons active in the twentieth century whom they most admired. A stipulation was made that they include only those not living. At the time the question was employed in Agra, Prime Minister Nehru was still alive. He died in 1964, when the Poona section of the study was only half done. It was thought best to ask respondents offering Nehru's name to exclude him from this particular item.

The response rate on question 2 was much higher than on question 1 because of the lack of historical knowledge apparent among some of the less educated corporators. On this item, the top nine nominees in Agra received 124 nominations or 76 percent of the total number given. The overall *response rate* in Poona was only slightly higher—94 percent to Agra's 91 percent—with eight nominees receiving more than three nominations while four others received three. Table A.2 lists the first eight for Poona; these received 78 percent of the total nominations in that city.

Table A.2 appears to portray a strong nationalization of symbolic figures for the first half of the twentieth century. Indeed, of the leading nine nominees in Agra, only three were from Uttar Pradesh—Madan Mohan Malaviya, Motilal Nehru, and Rafi Ahmed Kidwai; regionalism may be slightly more important in Maharashtra since four persons chosen in Poona are Maharashtrians, but these include two men who are also prominent on the Agra list: Tilak and Ambedkar. Indeed, except for the interchange of Agarkar and Ambedkar, the five leading persons are the same in both cities: Gandhi, Bose, Patel, and Tilak. That Gandhi's name should be so prominent on both lists is hardly surprising, but the strength exhibited by Subash Chandra Bose twenty years after his death in an abortive effort (in league with the Axis) to rid India of the British is rather striking.

For the most part, age is not a very useful category of analysis here, and education is also of doubtful assistance, but we do find some ethclass and partisan differences in the patterns of nomination. Thus, Gandhi's ethclass support is widely

TABLE A.2

Historical Figures: Twentieth Century, Agra and Poona Corporation Members

Agra			Poona		
Rank	Name	Nomi-nations	Rank	Name	Nomi-nations
1	Gandhi	44	1	Gandhi	45
2	Bose	19	2	Tilak	41
3	Ambedkar	13	3	Bose	19
3	Patel	13	4	Patel	12
5	Tilak	10	5	Agarkar*	10
6	Tagore	8	6	D. K. Karve	8
7	Malaviya	7	7	Ambedkar	4
8	Motilal Nehru	5	7	Rajendra Prasad	4
8	Kidwai	5			
	Total	124		Total	143

* Agarkar died in 1895, but his name was frequently linked with that of Tilak. This same problem occurred for Mahatma Phule, who received three nominations on question 2; these three are not counted in his total on question 1. One nomination that Agarkar received on question 1 is also excluded.

distributed in Agra, but his strongest partisan base, as one might expect, is among members of the Congress; in Poona, members of both the Congress and Nagri Sanghatna strongly support him, but there is a marked antipathy among Brahmins to his name. In contrast, the Poona Congress and Jan Sangh members are both responsible for nominating Tilak; his ethclass support is spread evenly among the major groups with Maharashtrian Hindus (other than Marathas and Brahmins) being the most favorable.

While Bose (a Bengali) is especially popular among Agra's Banias, this favorability is not concentrated in a single party group. Patel's following in that city is even greater among Banias, but it is solidified in the Congress Party. Party makes little difference for Patel's source of nominations in Poona (many of his nominations come from independents), but there is a strong tendency in his direction on the part of non-Maharashtrians, since both he and several of them are Gujaratis.

Agarkar represents a special upper-status symbol to the politicized population of Poona. This is reflected in his strong following among Brahmins and is the only case on this item of concentration of nominations among the college-educated; party makes little difference here. In Agra, where both Banias and "other high" status groups nominate Tilak disproportionately, party backing is not as striking as the concentration of support among the college-educated for this early twentieth century figure from Poona. Curiously, Tilak's nominations on the educational dimension in Poona tend to be heaviest among those of less education.

As we would expect, Ambedkar's support is heavily in the Jatav-RPI grouping in Agra—among the less-educated segment of the population. This again points to a tendency toward subcultural differentiation on the part of that group.[6] In Poona, Ambedkar's support is concentrated among the Scheduled Castes, but party made no difference in the fragmented Poona situation. Still, three Scheduled Caste corporators (all non-Mahar Congressmen) in that city did not feel it appropriate to nominate Ambedkar.

Viewed another way, if any set of political preferences can be associated with Bania choices in Agra, it is a taste for strong leadership with somewhat conservative political overtones: Tilak, Bose and Patel score high among Banias. Such tastes are not as clear among "Other Hindus" in Agra. For the Jatavs, Ambedkar—like Buddha—is a key symbol of the integration of that community. Indeed, the direct symbolic connection *between* Ambedkar and Buddha is evidenced by their pictorial joining together on the walls and hearths of many Jatav homes.

While Gandhi serves as a figure differentiating primordial elements in Poona, his importance in Agra seems to be in terms of party symbology, principally dividing the Congress from its partisan opposition. In Poona, Gandhi's symbolic "meaning" distinguishes the Congress non-Brahmins, particularly Marathas, clearly from the more militant Brahmins like those in the Jan Sangh and Hindu Mahasabha but not from the partisan groupings of Brahmins found in the PSP and SSP.

Thus, from the first two items, we find a good deal of overlapping of historical symbols among parties and ethclasses. In Agra and Poona, however, the separation of the Jatav/RPI element from the high-status/Congress and Jan Sangh element is quite apparent. In Poona, divisions between Brahmin and non-Brahmin corporators occasionally appear as in the cases of Gandhi and Phule. Because of partisan arrangements in Poona, these symbolic differences occasionally spill over into partisan forms.

Some of the same factors are operative when we turn to the third item: nomination of three persons "currently" (1964) active in the national life of India whom corporators most respected or admired.[7] Persons receiving the greatest number of nominations in both cities are listed in table A.3. Ten persons received more than 70 percent of the total responses in Agra; the leading dozen in Poona constituted 80 percent of the total nominees in that city.

TABLE A.3

Leading National Figures Nominated by Corporation Members

Agra			Poona		
Rank	Name	Nomi-nations	Rank	Name	Nomi-nations
1	Nehru	47	1	Nehru	43
2	Shastri	13	2	Y. B. Chavan	31
3	Radhakrishnan	10	3	Shastri	11
4	M. S. Golwalkar	5	4	Radhakrishnan	10
4	V. Bhave	5	5	Sarvarkar	8
4	Morarji Desai	5	6	S. M. Joshi	7
4	C. Rajagopalachari	5	7	M. S. Golwalkar	6
4	B. Gaikwad	5	7	V. Bhave	6
9	B. P. Maurya	4	9	J. P. Narayan	5
9	D. D. Upadhyaya	4	10	Kamraj	4
			10	I. Gandhi	4
			10	M. Desai	4
	Total	103		Total	139

As we might expect, the then Prime Minister scored highest in both cities. It is interesting that many of these nominations came from persons who were not simply party loyalists, nor was his support in any sense regional. The great number of nominations given to Chavan in Poona immediately directs our attention to the regional factor. By that time, Chavan was Defense Minister of India and, therefore, part of the national leadership of India. If this list is representative, Maharashtrians tended more readily to choose regional figures; direct comparison between the two regions is made more difficult, however, by the presence of Shastri prominently on both lists since he was an Uttar Pradesh man. Still, it is impressive that about half the names on the two lists correspond and that those names on the lists which do not appear on both include men who are not regionally specific to Uttar Pradesh and Maharashtra—Rajagopalachari and Kamraj of Madras, B. R. Gaikwad of Maharashtra who figures high on the Agra list, and Indira Gandhi of Uttar Pradesh who was ranked in Poona but not Agra.[8]

To provide some additional meaning to these nominations, it is useful to introduce the responses to the fourth item dealing with persons admired at the state level. Distributions on this question appear in table A.4. There is a wider dispersion of responses in Agra than for any of the other answers; the top eleven nominees (each receiving more than three nominations) include only 61 percent of the total responses. In Poona, the top ten nominees received only 68 percent of the responses.

Our reason for bracketing the discussion of these two tables is apparent from an examination of table A.4, where three persons from Uttar Pradesh and four from Maharashtra are "carry-overs" from the national list. This is not an element of importance in Agra, where Nehru and Shastri were clearly perceived more as national figures than as state-based. In Poona, however, four of the ten state nominations go to persons who also appear on the national ranking. For this reason, we will discuss these persons after reviewing the national listing.

Shastri, Radhakrishnan (then President of India), B. R. Gaikwad and D. D. Upadhyaya (a leader of the Jan Sangh)[9] represent somewhat different trends in patterns of nomination in Agra. Upadhya, like Golwalkar (the dominant figure in the RSS), receives all his support from members of the Jan Sangh. These supporters are uniformly well educated. In contrast, the RPI/Jatav group gives its nominations to Gaikwad and B. P. Maurya, the MP from Aligarh in 1964.

The support bases of nominated persons associated with the Congress Party are more highly differentiated. On the one hand, Shastri and Morarji Desai had their principal following among Congressmen and some non-Congressmen of more traditional outlook. Their partisan Congress base is clear, whereas their ethclass support is less sharp. Incidentally, Shastri was the *only* person mentioned in Agra who was distinguished on this item by the age dimension—he received remarkably great support from older members of the corporation. At the same time, neither the President nor the Prime Minister of India aroused as strong group feelings among Agra's political groups. If anything, Radhakrishnan was more frequently named by members of the Swatantra Dal than the Congress in Agra. Nehru did, however, apparently stimulate sufficiently negative attitudes among the members of the Jan Sangh to cause them to *withhold* any support.

If we restate the subcultural dimension of Agra nominations in terms of the

TABLE A.4

Leading State Figures, Agra and Poona

Agra			Poona		
Rank	Name	Nomi-nations	Rank	Name	Nomi-nations
1	C. B. Gupta	12	1	Y. B. Chavan*	35
2	Sampurnanand	8	2	S. M. Joshi*	15
2	K. Tripathi	8	3	D. S. Desai	13
4	J. Nehru*	7	4	V. Naik	10
4	S. K. D. Paliwal	7	5	V. Bhave*	9
6	B. P. Maurya*	6	6	V. Savarkar*	6
7	Mrs. S. Kripalani	5	6	D. R. Gadgil	6
8	L. B. Shastri*	4	6	N. G. Goray	6
8	J. P. Rawat	4	9	N. V. Gadgil	5
8	S. N. Chaturvedi	4	10	Babu Patil	4
8	Charan Singh	4			
	Total	69		Total	109

* Also appear on the national rankings.

findings for this item, we seem to be reaching a point at which the higher ethclasses branch off. We have already noted a difference with respect to historical personages between RPI/Jatav choices and those of the other groups; now, we also find some difference between members of the Jan Sangh and the other political groups in Agra. Obviously, the argument in terms of "subcultures" must be handled gingerly, but at least in a superficial way there are apparent differences in the kinds of affiliations which persistent political groups make with respect to a series of national figures. At the same time, it is interesting that men like Radhakrishnan and Nehru received support from wider sectors of the population than did individuals with lesser roles in the national government like Desai or even Shastri.

Of the twelve leading national figures in Poona, seven do not draw support along clearly differentiated dimensions. For four of the other five, "crystallization" of a subgroup kind does occur. There is no question that Y. B. Chavan is a galvanizing figure in the state of Maharashtra. Not only is he clearly identified with the Congress organization but he helps to impart to that organization strong non-Brahmin overtones. Thus, we find that the greatest variance in Poona occurs in scores for Chavan with Marathas strong in his support group and Brahmins correspondingly absent. The great bulk of his nominations come from members of the Congress and from the educational category with less than secondary education. At the same time, the least support for him occurs among college-educated members of the Poona corporation who systematically exclude Chavan from the list of persons they admire.

For the few Jan Sangh members in the Poona corporation, Veer Savarkar, founder of the Hindu Mahasabha, and "Guru" Golwalkar represent their strongest points of identification. Both men score well particularly among Brahmins. Golwalkar is more clearly a Jan Sangh nominee, whereas Savarkar receives some nominations from members of the Nagri Sanghatna, most notably the Hindu

Mahasabha corporators in that party. Only two men in Poona are distinguished in their nomination patterns by the age of their nominators: Chavan and Savarkar. While Chavan draws disproportionately from younger members of the corporation, Savarkar's nominators were among the older corporators. This is in keeping with the greater age of Brahmin as compared to non-Brahmin corporators in the city. The stronger representation of Jan Sangh corporators after 1968 might have highlighted partisan cleavages more clearly than was possible in the responses from this first visit.

As we have noted, the presence of the Nagri Sanghatna in 1964 tended to prevent Brahmin and non-Brahmin cleavages from neatly overlapping with partisan differences. The figure most closely associated with this "muting" process is S. M. Joshi. Joshi's own following as shown in table A.3 (and again in A.4) does not polarize ethclasses nor are significant status differences reflected in the varying educational experiences of those persons nominating him. It is true that he receives markedly partisan backing from the Sanghatna, but other antagonisms are blurred. This can be seen equally well if we were to combine Joshi's national and state rankings. In table A.4, we find Joshi receiving fifteen nominations as compared to only seven in Poona's national ranking. If we eliminate persons naming Joshi twice—"repeaters"—seventeen different nominators are involved. Still, with this slightly larger base, ethclass makes no difference in his support.

This finding for Joshi stands in contrast to the scores for Savarkar whose *combined* total of ten nonrepeater nominations on both lists is associated with marked support among Brahmins as compared to other ethclasses. For Chavan, the two lists combined produce a total of forty-six different nominators and, of necessity, a shifting away from his Maratha base of support. However, such shifts merely result in favorable mentions being distributed among Scheduled Castes, Marathas and non-Maratha Maharashtrian Hindus, while Brahmins remain determinedly nonsupportive of Chavan. At the same time, this examination of combined lists finds all three men with strong partisan bases: Joshi among Sanghatna corporators; Savarkar from the Jan Sangh, and some elements in the Sanghatna; Chavan from the Congress, although somewhat less strongly than when the national list is analyzed alone.

Of the six individuals on the Poona state list who are not on the national ranking, only two are distinguished in partisan or ethclass terms. D. S. Desai, then Home Minister of Maharashtra and a major Chavan associate, closely followed the Chavan pattern of Congress and Maratha support. Like Chavan, too, he was identified with the younger members of the corporation and the less educated half of the body. In somewhat of a contrast, Vasantrao Naik—the non-Maratha Chief Minister of Maharashtra—was strongly identified with the Congress but did not receive an especially high score among Marathas in the corporation. D. S. Desai, in fact, represents a much more polarizing figure in Maharashtra politics as an organizational activist than did the more amiable leader of the state government.

The only other persons differentiated in Poona on partisan dimensions were N. G. Goray and D. R. Gadgil. The latter was then head of the Gokhale Institute of Politics and Economics and is currently (1969) head of the National Planning Commission by appointment. Both men were nominated most heavily by members of the Sanghatna. Gadgil, who has taken an active part in public life, also received proportionately greater support from among the college-educated in the corporation than did other nominees.

No one on the Agra state list received more than twelve votes, which reflects the scattered character of organizational identifications in that city.[10] For the three persons also ranked on the national list—Nehru, Maurya and Shastri—Nehru's nominations include only one nonrepeater; Shastri increases his combined total to sixteen nominators and strengthens his following among Congressmen. Maurya's nominators increase from four to seven, but this support is simply intensified by its concentration among Jatavs and Republicans.

No one man in table A.4 represents the Jan Sangh element in the corporation. Pitamber Das, a leader of the party in Uttar Pradesh, did receive three nominations. Of the others on the state list, only one received special concentrations of support on both the ethclass and partisan dimensions—C. B. Gupta, whose principal backing comes from both Banias and Muslims and from both Congress and Swatantra Dal groupings. Other Congress figures like Sampurnanand, Rawat, and Chaturvedi have weaker support in Congress ranks, and Rawat actually received a greater following from low-status castes and Muslim corporators. These four men, in fact, reflect the wide spread of sentiments that individual Congressmen in Uttar Pradesh could draw upon in 1964. It reveals both a great variety in the social bases of the Uttar Pradesh Congress and a potential for fractionating party loyalties in a situation where no single set of leaders inspired consistent partisan identifications.

Fifth, we asked corporators in Agra and Poona whom they most admired within the two cities (see table A.5). Four persons from the state and one from the national list reappear in Poona; three from the state list are on the Agra local

TABLE A.5

Leading Local Figures Named by Agra and Poona Corporators

Agra			Poona		
Rank	Name	Nomi-nations	Rank	Name	Nomi-nations
1	Seth Achal Singh	20	1	S. M. Joshi*	21
2	S. K. D. Paliwal†	18	2	B. N. Sanas	18
3	S. N. Chaturvedi†	12	3	D. R. Gadgil†	12
4	Hari Shankar Sharma	7	4	B. G. Jagtap	11
5	R. Kunzru	6	5	D. W. Potdar	10
6	Adiram Singhal	5	6	N. V. Gadgil†	9
7	J. P. Rawat	3	6	R. P. Paranjape	9
7	Babu Lal Mital	3	8	N. G. Goray†	8
7	Shobrun Singh	3	9	B. N. Bhide	4
7	Mahendra	3	10	S. S. More	3
7	M. P. Kakkar	3	10	K. T. Girme	3
7	N. K. Sethi	3	10	R. Patil	3
7	P. N. Shiromani	3	10	S. L. Kirloskar	3
	Total	89		Total	114

* Appears on national, state and local lists.
† Appears on both state and local lists.

ranking. Aside from the usual prominent position of politicians on the two lists, several other types of people appear, for example in Agra, Hari Shanker Sharma, a poet and writer, and N. K. Seth, a former principal of Agra College. Shobrun Singh, the highly respected head of the Law Department at Agra College was also active in the RSS; M. P. Kakkar was a prominent lawyer.

Along with the politicians on the Poona list, we find a number of educators: B. G. Jagtap, who assumed a political role only in 1962 after many years as a professional educator; R. P. Paranjape, an active social reformer and former Vice-Chancellor of Poona University; D. W. Potdar, a noted Marathi scholar and Vice-Chancellor of Poona University in early 1964; D. R. Gadgil, whom we have mentioned earlier.[11] The only other nonpolitician on the list is S. L. Kirloskar, a leading Maharashtrian industrialist. Kirloskar was one of the few Maharashtrian industrial leaders of national importance and one who had been sympathetic to Maharashtrian political claims like the Samyukta Maharashtra movement. While the techniques employed here are obviously getting at phenomena of a different kind from methods utilized by those interested in identifying "community power structure," it may be of some interest that he is the only businessman appearing among the twenty-six names of persons most admired by members of the two municipal councils.[12]

Among the thirteen nominees in Agra, there are no Jatavs or Muslims. Nine are Congressmen of varying stripe, which is impressive given the relative position of the Congress. Muslims are favorable to only one person, Adiram Singhal, and that weakly. Low-status groups, most notably the Jatavs, mentioned Rawat and Chaturvedi prominently. Apparently, no local Jatav merited their admiration. Both men, it should be noted, stood slightly to the left of the Agra Congress in outlook. Neither man received favorable support from Congressmen in Agra. Seth Achal Singh's partisan support is spread over all political groups in the city, although his following is especially strong among Banias. Paliwal, on the other hand, is favored by Congressmen but with wide ethclass support.

Caste and party show up more clearly as differentiating factors in Poona. Sanas and Bhide are two purely local figures who seem to crystallize intracorporator divisions. Bhide, a Jan Sangh leader, gets his votes from Brahmins and Jan Sangh members. Sanas shows a strong similarity to the pattern observed for Chavan and D. S. Desai—a very high partisan score from the Congress and some support among the Marathas, although he is also favorably regarded by Scheduled Caste corporators.

Indeed, one might view Chavan, Desai, and Sanas as a three-man "set" serving as the embodiments of the Congress organization for members of the Poona corporation. This might be considered evidence of support, if such were required, for the high integration of the Congress organization already described for Maharashtra and Poona. The physical decline of Sanas prior to the 1968 municipal elections might have opened the party to wounds of a dangerous variety had not Chavan been able to exercise effective control of the process through his associates in the state organization. Certainly there is no equivalent in Agra for such an integrated set of loyalties. Nor does the Brahmin community in Poona share a similar set of leadership figures. While it is possible to draw together temporary coalitions between the Nagri Sanghatna and the Jan Sangh for the achievement of limited ends, it appears that this subcommunity of political interest holds few basic symbols in common. This is in marked contrast to the Congress-Maratha nexus with Chavan, Desai, and Sanas at the three levels of the political system and, in some sense, the figure of Shivaji brooding over them all.

A sixth item, which is somewhat tangential to the previous material, asked corporators to identify those persons from outside of India whom they most admired. Given the recent assassination of President Kennedy, his name was high in the politically aware public's consciousness. It is impossible to know the extent to which the interviewer's nationality influenced these responses but the great outpouring of Indian sentiment about Kennedy in late 1963 suggests that these figures were only slightly inflated. The results are as follows:

TABLE A.6

Leading Non-Indian Figures Named by Agra and Poona Corporators

Agra			Poona		
Rank	Name	Nomi-nations	Rank	Name	Nomi-nations
1	Kennedy	32	1	Kennedy	50
2	Lincoln	12	2	Khrushchev	16
3	Khrushchev	11	3	Churchill	14
3	Churchill	11	4	Hitler	11
5	Nasser	8	5	Lincoln	6
6	F. D. Roosevelt	6	6	Nasser	5
7	Napoleon	4	7	Victoria	4
7	Hitler	4	7	Attlee	4
9	Queen Victoria	3	7	Mountbatten	4
9	Attlee	3	10	Washington	3
9	G. B. Shaw	3			
	Total	97		Total	117

Comments accompanying many of these nominations indicate a very low salience of many of these persons to the respondent. Some like Napoleon, Queen Victoria or Hitler are unidimensional figures whose names were acquired in pre-Independence primary educational systems. For some of his nominators, Hitler is seen as the man who was ultimately responsible for freeing India from British rule. At the same time, some corporators—particularly high-status and educated members— admired Churchill for his personal strength and leadership in World War II and *despite* his imperialistic attitude toward India. The low salience of this item, on the whole, makes the presentation of variations in support bases of slight value beyond noting that Nasser's nominations in Agra come from Muslim corporators, Lincoln's from Jatavs and Franklin Roosevelt's from members of the Jan Sangh.

Notes

1. The most influential works here are Floyd Hunter, *Community Power Structure* (Chapel Hill: University of North Carolina Press, 1953) and Robert A. Dahl, *Who Governs?* (New Haven: Yale University Press, 1961). Also see, William V. D'Antonio and Howard J. Ehrlich (eds.), *Power and Democracy in America* (Notre Dame: University of Notre Dame Press, 1961) and Raymond E. Wolfinger, "Reputation and Reality in the Study of 'Community Power,' " *American Sociological Review* 25 (October 1960): 636-44.

2. Major examples include Oliver P. Williams and Charles R. Adrian, *Four Cities* (Philadelphia: University of Pennsylvania Press, 1963); Robert E. Agger, Daniel Goldrich, and Bert E. Swanson, *The Rulers and the Ruled* (New York: John Wiley, 1964).

3. See Delbert C. Miller's study of an English city in his "Decision-Making Cliques in Community Power Structures," *American Journal of Sociology* 63 (November 1958): 299-310; William H. Form and William V. D'Antonio, "Integration and Cleavage among Community Influentials in Two Border Cities," *American Sociological Review* 24 (December 1959): 804-14; William V. D'Antonio, William H. Form, Charles P. Loomis, and Eugene C. Erickson, "Institutional and Occupational Representations in Eleven Community Influence Systems," *American Sociological Review* 26 (June 1961): 440-46; Orrin E. Klapp and L. Vincent Padgett, "Power Structure and Decision-Making in a Mexican Border City," *American Journal of Sociology* 65 (January 1960): 400-406.

4. Terry N. Clark, *Community Structure and Decision-Making: Comparative Analyses* (San Francisco: Chandler, 1968), p. 15.

5. In this connection, see the definition of governmental decision making employed by Agger, Goldrich, and Swanson, p. 2. The present study follows *part* of their definition of "community power structure" by being concerned with the "representation of selected aspects of political power relations over a specified period of time" (Agger *et al.,* p. 51). In a related definition of "community decisions," Clark suggests such decisions are "choices made by actors within the community among alternative goals relating to the maintenance or modification of institutions or facilities that involve the majority of community residents" (Clark, pp. 21-22).

6. A tendency to ignore nonmaterial but instrumental aspects of Western politics during the early 1960s has more recently given way to an upsurge of interest in race relations and ethnic politics with their status and symbolic dimensions. For example, see James Q. Wilson and Edward C. Banfield, "Public Regardingness as a Value Premise in Voting Behavior," *American Political Science Review* 58 (December 1964): 876-87.

7. For applications of the "political culture" emphasis, see Lucian Pye and Sidney Verba (eds.), *Political Culture and Political Development* (Princeton: Princeton University Press, 1965). Also Douglas Verney, "Political Patterns within

North America," (paper presented at the 1968 Annual Meeting of the American Political Science Association, Washington, D.C., 2-7 September 1968).

8. For various empirical tests of the relationship between political structure and behavior, see the Clark volume; Robert L. Crain, Elihu Katz, and Donald B. Rosenthal, *The Politics of Community Conflict* (Indianapolis: Bobbs-Merrill, 1969); and James Q. Wilson (ed.), *City Politics and Public Policy* (New York: John Wiley, 1968).

9. It may be useful to clarify some of the terminology employed in these pages. The notion of *municipal government* is fairly straightforward in pointing to those institutions of local government and administration operating within a city over which local citizens have at least putative control. The *municipal corporation* is a particular form of government as the term is used in India, but the concept of a city as a corporate entity embodying administrative and representative elements is an established European-derived legalism. A *municipal arena* consists of all those activities which go on in a city and its environs in relation to the operation of municipal government and politics including the relevant activities of other units of government. A *local political system* consists not only of those activities associated with the municipal arena but the many other activities within a city which bear on nonmunicipal and/or supralocal political behaviors.

10. Commonly, variables like urbanization are employed at a societal level in studying "political modernization" rather than at local levels, where the comparative implications of social and political structures would be more salient. Typical of the comparative approach are Seymour Martin Lipset, "Some Social Requisites of Democracy: Economic Development and Political Legitimacy," *American Political Science Review* 53 (March 1959): 69-105; Phillips Cutright, "National Political Development," in Nelson Polsby, Robert A. Dentler and Paul A. Smith (eds.), *Political and Social Life* (Boston: Houghton-Mifflin, 1963), pp. 569-82.

11. The most ambitious effort undertaken thus far—the International Studies of Values in Politics project—involves a comparative study of local government and politics in the United States, India, Poland, and Yugoslavia. Some elements of this study have been described in Clark, pp. 465-74, et passim. The methodological and conceptual difficulties inherent in such a study are discussed in Adam Przeworski and Henry Teune, "Equivalence in Cross-National Research," *Public Opinion Quarterly* 30 (Winter 1966-67): 551-68; and Teune, "Measurement in Comparative Research," *Comparative Political Studies* 1 (April 1968): 123-38. A recent volume edited by Robert T. Daland (ed.), *Comparative Urban Research* (Beverly Hills: Sage Publications, 1969) includes a number of studies of particular dimensions of urban politics and government in a variety of national settings as well as an interesting "accounting scheme" for comparative urban analysis by Robert Alford, but it lacks a truly comparative framework of analysis.

12. Some of the more interesting works in this area are Harold Kaplan, *Urban Political Systems: A Functional Analysis of Metro Toronto* (New York: Columbia University Press, 1969); Mark Kesselman, *The Ambiguous Consensus: A Study of Local Government in France* (New York: Random House, 1967); Frank Smallwood, *Greater London: The Politics of Metropolitan Reform* (Indianapolis: Bobbs-Merrill, 1965); Kurt Steiner, *Local Government in Japan* (Stanford: Stanford University Press, 1965); Herbert Werlin, "The Nairobi City Council: A Study in Comparative Local Government," *Comparative Studies in Society and History* 8 (January 1966): 181-98 and J. David Greenstone, "Corruption and Self-Interest in Kampala and Nairobi," ibid., pp. 199-210.

13. Hugh Tinker, *The Foundations of Local Self-Government in India, Pakistan and Burma* (London: Athlone Press, 1954). Some useful historical materials are also available in works like D. E. Wacha, *Rise and Growth of Bombay Municipal Government* (Madras: G. A. Natesan, 1913) and B. K. Boman-Behram, *The Rise of Municipal Government in the City of Ahmedabad* (Bombay: B. B. Taporevala, 1937).

14. These include R. Argal, *Municipal Government in India* (Allahabad: Agarwal Press, 1960); M. P. Sharma, *Local Self-Government and Finance in Uttar Pradesh* (Allahabad: Kitab Mahal, 1954); and, Chetakar Jha, *Local Government by Committee* (Patna: Novelty, 1963).

15. A valuable overview of Indian urbanism is available in Roy C. Turner (ed.), *India's Urban Future* (Berkeley: University of California Press, 1962). Unfortunately, the articles on urban politics are among the weakest contributions. Three papers published together as a "Seminar" on urban politics in the *Journal of Asian Studies* 20 (February 1961): 267-97, are more immediately relevant to studies of Indian urban politics. They are Henry C. Hart, "Bombay Politics: Pluralism or Polarization?"; Myron Weiner, "Violence and Politics in Calcutta"; and Lloyd I. Rudolph, "Urban Life and Populist Radicalism."

16. In addition to the materials cited above, I was especially fortunate to have access to the then incomplete dissertation by Paul R. Brass, now published as *Factional Politics in an Indian State: The Congress Party in Uttar Pradesh* (Berkeley: University of California Press, 1965).

17. For a discussion of the sociometric items, see chapter 5 below, pp. 124-32; the results of the historical and personality identification items are presented in the Appendix.

18. For the city's origins, see H. M. Elliot and John Dowson, *The History of India: The Muhammadan Period* 5 (Allahabad: Kitab Mahal, 1964): 99 ff; Hameed-Ud-Din, "The Lodis," in R. C. Majumdar (ed.), *History and Culture of the Indian People: The Delhi Sultanate* 6 (Bombay: Bharatiya Vidya Bhavan, 1960): 145.

19. Elliot and Dowson, 4: 263-64.

20. *Calcutta and Agra Gazetteer,* 1839, as cited in D. S. Chauhan, *Trends of Urbanization in Agra* (Bombay: Allied Publishers, 1966), p. 8.

21. Chauhan, in his study of migration patterns into Agra, concludes that the "push" and "pull" factors for the periods 1930-40 and 1940-54 do not differ significantly for those persons included in a survey population (pp. 313-21).

22. D. D. Kosambi, *Myth and Reality* (Bombay: Popular Prakashan, 1962), pp. 110-51.

23. Shivaji's father, however, was himself in the government service of the Muslim overlords of the region.

24. W. H. Moreland and Atul Chandra Chatterjee, *A Short History of India,* 4th ed. (New York: David McKay, 1957), p. 255.

25. James C. Grant-Duff, *A History of the Mahrattas,* revised and annotated ed. by S. M. Edwards, 2 (London: H. Milford, Oxford University Press, 1921): 273.

26. Kenneth Ballhatchet, *Social Policy and Social Change in Western India: 1817-1830* (London: Oxford University Press, 1957), pp. 268-71.

27. Anil Seal, *The Emergence of Indian Nationalism: Competition and Collaboration in the Later Nineteenth Century* (Cambridge: Cambridge University Press, 1968), pp. 84-90.

28. One population estimate (attributed to a Colonel Welsh) of 600,000 in 1801 seems highly improbable. D. B. Parasnis, *Poona in Bygone Days* (Bombay: The Times Press, 1921), p. 91. The estimate for 1808 is given by Parasnis himself. Mountstuart Elphinstone in 1818 set the figure at 110,000. Ballhatchet, p. 7.

29. F. Dawtrey Drewitt (ed.), *Bombay in the Days of George IV,* 2d ed. (London: Longmans Green, 1935), p. 85.

30. This military connection has been reinforced since 1947 by the location of the National Defense Academy, India's West Point, near Poona and the development of major defense industries in the region.

31. Among the relevant works on the period are D. D. Karve, (ed.), *The New Brahmans* (Berkeley: University of California Press, 1963); Stanley Wolpert, *Tilak and Gokhale* (Berkeley: University of California Press, 1962); Dhananjay Keer, *Mahatma Jotirao Phooley* (Bombay: Popular Prakashan, 1964). The last is a study of a major non-Brahmin leader.

32. India, Census Commissioner, *Census of India, 1931.*

33. The 1961 *Census of India* includes several units in the Poona "Town Group": Poona City (597,562); Poona and Kirkee Cantonments (124,334), both bordering on the city; and the two villages of Dapodi and Chinchwad with a combined population of 15,530.

34. This table is not taken directly from the Census but is adapted from the figures in N. V. Sovani, D. P. Apte and R. G. Pendse, *Poona: A Resurvey* (Poona: Gokhale Institute of Politics and Economics, 1956), p. 2. It differs slightly from the census figures, apparently because some attention is paid to municipal boundary problems. Both Agra and Poona municipal boundaries have expanded considerably since the beginning of the century. A strict time series would have to take these changes into account in measuring population growth. The column headed "Area Population" in table 1.2 refers to the total populations of Poona, Poona Cantonment and Kirkee Cantonment over time. It excludes Dapodi and Chinchwad.

35. A. L. Srivastava, *Program for Indian Political Science Conference, Agra* (December 1963), p. 51.

36. Uttar Pradesh, Labour Department, *Annual Review of Activities, 1956.* The low level of *true* industrialization is suggested by the identification of twenty "factories" as existing at Firozabad, a city of 98,611 people in Agra district. Most of these specialized in the manufacture of bangles and glass beads. According to the *Statement of Large Industries in Agra District for 1961,* there were then sixty-three units in the city employing thirty or more workers. The largest were three quasi-public corporate structures: the Uttar Pradesh Roadways Workshop (423); the privately-owned Agra Electric Supply Company (353); and the Municipal Waterworks (270). The largest private industries were three almost moribund spinning factories and BP Oil Mills, which processes edible oils.

37. These figures are from an unpublished survey of industrial growth in the Poona area done by Richard D. Lambert. For a report on his earlier findings, see his *Workers, Factories, and Social Change in India* (Princeton: Princeton University Press, 1963).

38. In 1955-56, the per capita income in India was Rs. 255 (approximately $54). In Uttar Pradesh the figure was Rs. 178; in Maharashtra, Rs. 287. Figures were available only for the two districts in which Agra and Poona are located—districts in which the cities constitute less than half the total population. Still, Poona District had a per capita income of Rs. 286—the state average—while Agra's average income was Rs. 210. National Council of Applied Economic Research, *Inter-District and Inter-State Income Differentials, 1955-56*, Occasional Paper no. 6 (New Delhi, 1963).

39. Concerning this problem, see George Rosen, *Democracy and Economic Change in India* (Berkeley: University of California Press, 1966), esp. pp. 15-50.

40. Census of India, *Paper no. 1 of 1963: Religion* (New Delhi: Government of India Press, 1963), pp. 40-41. These figures are approximate since they are available in the Census only for the urban portions of each district. Unfortunately, there is reason to assume an uneven distribution of population components between the major city and the smaller urban centers in each district. Thus, the city of Firozabad is generally thought to have a higher proportion of Muslims than does Agra City.

41. "Scheduled Caste" has been a term applied to the untouchables since a "schedule" of communities eligible to receive governmental benefits was appended to the Government of India Act of 1935. For a recent discussion of the effects of these policies, see Lelah Dushkin, "Scheduled Caste Policy in India: History, Problems, Prospects," *Asian Survey* 7 (September 1967): 626-36. While other "castes" are not enumerated by the Census, figures are maintained on the Scheduled Castes as the basis for special benefits now guaranteed to them under the Constitution of India.

42. Next to the Agarwals, the Mathur Vaish are the most important merchant subcommunity in Agra. Neither in 1963-64 nor in 1968 did divisions

between these two *jatis* seem to play a part in the political conflicts of the city, although there was a notable *increase* in sensitivity to the distinction in discussions with local politicians in 1968. I have employed the term Bania more frequently than the *varna* term Vaishya, although the groups involved seem to prefer the more Sanskritic associations of the latter. In conversations, the two seem to be used interchangeably along with "Agarwal" and "Gupta" (Mathur Vaish). There is no need to get involved here in the theoretical debates over a proper description of the caste system. In that connection, see Adrian C. Mayer, *Caste and Kinship in Central India* (Berkeley: University of California Press, 1966).

43. Thus, an Agra Jain might also identify himself as an Agarwal or Mathur Vaish.

44. These figures are probably more reliable than those available for Agra since they are based on the Sovani *Resurvey* data as reorganized for the Lambert volume. Cf. Lambert, pp. 233-35.

45. Lambert presents a category of "Other Religions." The figures used in table 1.4 are derived from a combination of Lambert (p. 235) and the 1961 *Census of Religions*. While by one definition, Scheduled Castes constitute 12.5 percent of the Poona population, about 5.4 percent of the total population was Buddhist. An adjustment for this difference is required in table 1.4 since, as in Agra, recent converts to Buddhism are uniformly members of the Scheduled Castes.

46. One observer has described the physical situation of the Scheduled Castes in Agra thus: "From time immemorial they have occupied sites considered uninhabitable and unhealthy by other castes. Their areas are either low-lying and liable to be inundated or such sites which are pock-marked by irregular pits, mounds or nalla-lands [drainage gullies]." A. R. Tiwari, "The Urban Regions of Agra," *The Agra University Journal of Research (Letters)* 6 (1958): 101-14.

47. Maharashtra lacks a native mercantile stratum. The traditional commercial functions of the region (including moneylending) were generally performed by persons from trading communities native to Gujarat, Rajasthan (the Marwaris), and North India (Agarwals and related groups).

48. This sense of congestion in Agra is supported by the data from the Census. An average of 1,115 persons live within each of Poona's 53.6 square miles compared to 2,018 persons in Agra's 22.9 square miles of territory.

49. For a discussion of these trends in Indian society and bibliographical references, see Donald B. Rosenthal, "Deurbanization, Elite Displacement, and Political Change in India," *Comparative Politics* 2 (January 1970): 169-201.

50. See Reinhard Bendix, *Nation-Building and Citizenship* (New York: John Wiley, 1964), pp. 284-98; David C. Potter, "Bureaucratic Change in India," in Ralph Braibanti (ed.), *Asian Bureaucratic Systems Emergent from the British Imperial Tradition* (Durham: Duke University Commonwealth-Studies Center, 1966), esp. pp. 187-207; and B. Maheshwari, *Studies in Panchayati Raj* (Delhi: Metropolitan Book Company, 1963).

51. At least in Maharashtra, the *panchayati raj* system appears to be providing a basis for political recruitment and mobility within the Congress party. In 1967, the Maharashtra Congress gave MLA (Member of the [State] Legislative Assembly) and MP (Member of Parliament) tickets to many new people including thirteen persons who were holding offices in *zilla parishads* (the highest level of the three-tiered rural government system in Maharashtra) and fifteen who were presidents or vice-presidents of *taluka panchayat samitis*—the middle level of the hierarchy. *Times of India,* 9 November 1966. In this connection, see Lawrence Shrader and Ram Joshi, "Zilla Parishad Elections in Maharashtra and the District Political Elite," *Asian Survey* 3 (March 1963): 143-55; and Mary Carras, "The Dynamics of Political Factionalism: A Study of Zilla Parishads in the State of Maharashtra" (unpublished Ph.D. dissertation, Department of South Asia Regional Studies, University of Pennsylvania, 1969).

52. Not all the remainder live in villages; in both Agra and Poona districts

about 9 percent of the population live in towns or cities other than the principal urban center. Agra City has only 27 percent of the population of its district, while Poona City is located in a district of 2.47 million persons making its population only about 30 percent of the total.

53. Below the *zilla parishad* in Agra were eighteen *shetri samitis,* and below these, forming the lowest tier, *gaon sabhas* (village committees). The latter consisted of all adult members of a village. They elected a body from their members called a *panchayat,* which had certain limited powers over local administration. The president of the *gaon sabha* was automatically a member of the *shetri samiti.* The latter, in turn, elected persons who sat on the *zilla parishad.* In Maharashtra, members of the *zilla parishad* are directly elected from single-member constituencies covering the district. The district is subdivided into "blocks," each having its own *taluka panchayat samiti.* Members of the latter bodies include persons elected to the *zilla parishad* from that *taluka* and persons elected from lower-level village *panchayats.* Both in Uttar Pradesh and in Maharashtra, the various levels coopt a number of others representing certain backward sections of the community (ex-untouchables, tribals, women) as well as various functional organizations, including cooperatives and social service groups.

54. District Magistrates are appointed to their positions by a state government to which they have been assigned after having been recruited and trained by the central government as members of the elite Indian Administrative Service (IAS). The IAS officer serves in various high-echelon administrative positions including Municipal Commissioner and in positions in the state secretariat. For a recent breakdown of recruitment and assignment patterns of IAS officers, see Potter, pp. 142-69.

55. In addition to interviews with persons associated with the Agra Cantonment, these materials draw on a description of the system by H. C. Agarwal, "Working of the Agra Cantonment Board" (thesis for Master of Commerce, B. R. College, Agra, February 1964).

56. I wish to thank Mr. Philip K. Oldenburg for permitting me to draw freely upon the materials gathered for his "Indian Urban Politics with Particular Reference to the Nagpur Corporation" (unpublished MA thesis, Department of Political Science, University of Chicago, 1967).

57. As Tinker notes, "conditions in contemporary England were not so completely different" (p. 42).

58. Ibid., p. 41.

59. C. M. P. Cross, *The Development of Self-Government in India: 1858-1918* (Cambridge: Cambridge University Press, 1932), p. 89.

60. Tinker, p. 52.

61. Several cities still have nominated members in their municipal councils. Thus, the city of Nagpur has 57 council members: 42 are elected from single-member constituencies; six are nominated by various bodies like Nagpur University and the Central and Eastern Railways; and six are chosen by the elected councillors. Three others are elected by special constituencies: one by members of the Chamber of Commerce; two from trade union constituencies.

62. A very helpful account of the history of the Poona municipality is available in M. P. Mangudkar, "Municipal Government in Poona (1882-1947)" (unpublished PhD dissertation, Poona University, 1957). This figure, which appears on p. 31 in Mangudkar, includes all those persons then eligible to vote for members of the Bombay Legislative Assembly.

63. As late as 1944, only 4.5 percent of the population of Calcutta was eligible to vote. At the 1961 municipal elections the city still had a restricted franchise, which meant that, of Calcutta's 2.23 million people, only 221,838 were on the electoral rolls. Adult franchise was introduced in Calcutta for the following municipal elections. *The Directory of Municipal Corporations in India* (Bombay: All-Indian Institute of Local Self-Government, 1964), pp. 100-101. For the earlier

figures, see West Bengal Local Self-Government Department, *Report of the Corporation of Calcutta Investigation Commission: Interim Report and Final Report* (Alipore: West Bengal Government Press, 1950), p. 19. Also see, Ali Ashraf, *The City Government of Calcultta: A Study of Inertia* Calcutta Research Series, no. 9 (Bombay: Asia Publishing, 1966).

64. Ramayan Prasad, *Local Self-Government in Vindhya Pradesh* Bombay: All-India Institute of Local Self-Government, 1963), pp. 142-43.

65. The uniqueness of this dependency relationship should not be exaggerated. Many American cities and towns are equally dependent upon their state legislatures for permission to tax their citizens.

66. Argal, p. 155. Among the other charges leveled were an "utter lack of sense of duty and responsibility toward the board's financial administration, failure to discharge obligatory duty to construct and maintain public streets, to make proper sanitary arrangements . . . to maintain and develop property vested in it . . . due mainly to discord and bitterness among members of the board who were sharply divided into two mutually opposed parties almost paralyzing the smooth functioning of the board."

67. The KAVAL anagram is frequently used in Indian publications to refer to the five corporations of Uttar Pradesh: Kanpur, Allahabad, Varanasi, Agra, and Lucknow. It was a more obvious pun when Varanasi was known as Benares.

68. *Civic Affairs* 13 (November 1965): 1. A useful discussion of the corporation form of government and its problems is available in Indian Institute of Public Administration, *Improving City Government: Proceedings of a Seminar, September 13-14, 1958* (New Delhi, 1959). Also see, R. B. Das and D. P. Singh (eds.), *Deliberative and Executive Wings in Local Government* (Calcutta: Oxford and IBH Publishing, 1968).

69. *The Directory of Municipal Corporations in India* identifies twenty corporations as of 1964. Since then, at least three others have been added. Das and Singh, p. 3.

70. Mangudkar, pp. 44 ff.

71. Ibid., pp. 95 ff.

72. *The Directory of Municipal Corporations in India,* p. 260.

73. He attended only 25 percent of the meetings in 1941 and resigned from the municipality in 1942, apparently in sympathy with the noncooperation movement of the time. *Annual Administration Report of the Agra Municipality for the Year Ending 31st March 1941* (Agra: Coronation Press, 1941).

74. One of the first acts of this body was to impose Hindi as the language of administration and to announce that those employees not familiar with the language and the script by the end of a four-month period would be subject to dismissal. The target of this order is not clear but it may have been aimed at Muslim employees who were not literate in the Devanagari script. It is unlikely that anyone working in the municipality at the time would have known *only* English.

75. The French prefectural pattern is outlined in Brian Chapman, *Introduction to French Local Government* (London: George Allen and Unwin, 1953). Also see Kesselman, esp. pp. 171-84.

76. There were eight reserved seats in Agra in 1959 based on population figures from the 1951 Census. In accordance with the 1961 Census, the number of seats reserved to the Scheduled Castes was increased by two for the 1968 elections.

77. The political conflicts which surround such elections are not peculiar to India. One study of English local government describes the aldermanic office as one "which is hardly ever filled without leaving behind feelings which disturb the atmosphere of Local Government, and render it less conducive to harmonious concentration upon essential tasks." J. H. Warren, *The English Local Government System,* 3d ed. (London: George Allen and Unwin, 1953), p. 84.

78. There was a reduction from six to four reserved seats in Poona in 1968. This reflected the substantial conversion to Buddhism of former members of the Scheduled Castes, who thereby lost their claim to special representation.

79. The Bombay Provincial Municipal Corporations Act, 1949, sec. 19. The Uttar Pradesh Nagar Mahapalika Act, 1959, sec. 11 (1) is more specific on other points but makes no mention of corporation membership for a mayor.

80. Complaints about the weaknesses of the mayoral role have been the source of many resolutions passed at annual meetings of the officials of the Indian corporations. For example, a resolution passed in 1964 asked that mayors be given emergency powers, full administrative authority, and the authority to act as the conduit for all communications between the corporation and higher levels of government (as is the case in the cities of Madras and Trivandrum). Cf. *Fourth Conference of Municipal Corporations at Hyderabad* (New Delhi: Government of India, Ministry of Health, 1964), p. 1. No action was taken by Uttar Pradesh or Maharashtra to meet these demands.

81. Some opposition party members in Uttar Pradesh clearly regarded the autonomy of the CEO as a political weapon of the state government. At the time the Uttar Pradesh Act was being promulgated, a member of the Praja Socialist Party suggested that the CEO "would be in effect a spy and agent of the State Government on the Corporation. If a Corporation were to fall afoul of the Government, the CEO would play havoc with it." *National Herald,* 2 December 1958, as quoted in Ram Gautum Gupta, "Growth and Functioning of the Kanpur Municipality" (unpublished PhD dissertation, Agra University, 1961), p. 103. Opposition parties walked out of the Uttar Pradesh Assembly in protest when certain provisions of the act were being considered. For a brief consideration of the legislative history of the Uttar Pradesh (U.P.) Act, see Institute of Public Administration, *Working of Corporations in U.P.* (Lucknow: Lucknow University, 1963), pp. 1-12. The author of that section suggests that delays were due to the feeling that "Government was more happy with the Administrators who were more beneficial politically" (p. 8, n. 2).

NOTES TO CHAPTER 2

1. For a discussion of some of the more painful aspects of the Congress transition from a protest organization rivaling the British government in India to a political organization subordinate to indigenous governments, see Stanley A. Kochanek, *The Congress Party of India* (Princeton: Princeton University Press, 1968). Part of the price paid for this subordination was a weakening of the party as an instrument for national control. Instead, it became an open-ended arena for the operation of competing interests with few restrictions on entry or exit.

2. The present typology of groups and the one dealing with alliances which follows are greatly influenced by the work of Edward C. Banfield and James Q. Wilson, *City Politics* (Cambridge: Harvard-MIT Presses, 1963), pp. 128-32.

3. Ibid., p. 129.

4. Obviously, caste cohesion should not be taken for granted. It is an empirical question whether persons are acting as part of a collectivity or simply as individuals in politics having a particular caste background. Thus, there is a significant difference between being a politician of Brahmin birth and being a Brahmin "caste man." An appreciation of that difference is vital for distinguishing situations in which "caste goals" are operative from those in which other forces are at work.

5. Apter distinguishes between "instrumental" systems, which are "characterized by a large sector of intermediate ends, separate from and independent of ultimate ends," and "consummatory" systems, where there is a "close relationship between intermediate and ultimate ends." David E. Apter, *The Politics of Modernization* (Chicago: University of Chicago Press, 1965), p. 85.

6. In this connection, see Paul R. Brass, *Factional Politics in an Indian State: The Congress Party in Uttar Pradesh* (Berkeley: University of California Press, 1965) and Myron Weiner, *Party Building in a New Nation* (Chicago: University of Chicago Press, 1967).

7. When viewed from this perspective, the literature dealing with the "one-party dominant" political system in India prior to 1967 seems peculiarly unreal. Cf. Rajni Kothari, "The Congress 'System' in India," *Asian Survey* 4 (December 1964): 1161-73; W. H. Morris-Jones, "Parliament and Dominant Party: The Indian Experience," *Parliamentary Affairs* 17 (Summer 1964): 296-307. The setbacks to the Congress in 1967 suggest the special weaknesses of such a model, since it depended upon the assumption that a self-adjusting equilibrium operated within the Indian political system with the Congress as the agent of that equilibrium.

8. The fluidity of partisan loyalties in India has encouraged a search for a more helpful unit of analysis than "party" for treating the behavior of political activists. More than a decade ago, Myron Weiner made use of the notion of "faction" as such a unit in his *Party Politics in India* (Princeton: Princeton University Press, 1957), p. 37. He defined a faction as "a group with an articulated set of goals, operating within a larger organization but not created by or with the approval of the parent body." This definition raises two fundamental difficulties. First, some factions operate without an articulated set of goals. Thus, Brass describes statewide and local factions in Uttar Pradesh which depend on certain core individuals but do not have common goals. Second, neither Brass nor Weiner deals directly with the theoretical problem raised by the existence of political groups which may alternately act as factions *within* parties and *as* parties on their own. This may reflect the fact that both of their studies concentrate on intraparty rather than interparty relations.

9. *Factional Politics;* also see his "Factionalism and the Congress Party in Uttar Pradesh," *Asian Survey* 4 (September 1964): 1037-48.

10. *Sainik* has been the leading locally-published newspaper in Agra with an estimated daily circulation of fourteen thousand in 1964. After Paliwal's death there was a conflict among claimants to his estate which resulted in publication of two competing *Sainiks* in mid-1968 and the decline of the paper as a public force.

11. Some of the details of this conflict are spelled out in Weiner, *Party Politics in India,* pp. 65-97; Kochanek, pp. 27-53; and P. N. Chopra, *Rafi Ahmed Kidwai* (Agra: Shiva Lal Agarwala, 1960), pp. 142-57.

12. In Uttar Pradesh, the Kisan Mazdoor Party existed as a unit within the Congress as early as 1946. Chopra, pp. 125-26.

13. Seth received 57.6 percent of the vote to Paliwal's 25.8 percent. A Jan Sangh candidate ran third with 10.2 percent. In the same election the Congress won handily in the three MLA seats either wholly or partly located in the city. In Agra City (North), the winner received 62.3 percent of the vote against five opponents; there, the candidate of the Jan Sangh came in second with 21.9 percent. In Agra City (West), there were ten candidates but the Congress nominee received 54.8 percent of the total. The only Congress opponent to receive over 10 percent was Gopi Chand Pipil, then the Scheduled Caste Federation candidate, who received 23.9 percent. The third seat was won by Deokinandan Bibhab, a lieutenant of Seth, with 45.7 percent against a dozen opponents; the highest vote among these was for an independent who polled only 8.6 percent. India (Republic) Election Commission, *Report on the First General Elections in India 1951-52* (New Delhi, Government of India Press, 1955), 2: 476-77.

14. In primordial terms, there does not seem to be any importance attached by Hindu Banias to Seth's being a Jain. Indeed, the Jains appear to be treated as a Vaishya subgroup or "clan" *(gotra)* among the relevant communities. On this point, see Leighton W. Hazelhurst, *Entrepreneurship and Merchant Castes in a Punjabi City,* Program in Comparative Studies on Southern Asia, Monograph 1 (Durham: Duke University Commonwealth Studies Center, 1966), esp. pp. 45-49.

15. Chopra, p. 118.

16. Thus, Rawat was a central figure in the Uttar Pradesh Congress organization when tickets for the corporation elections of 1959 were being distributed.

17. Following ministerial changes in October 1963, Rawat was advanced to the major post of Minister for Public Works. By that time, he was aligned with anti-Gupta forces in the Congress.

18. Elections for such constituencies are by members of district or other local governments within a specifically delimited area. Other special constituencies are employed for filling seats in the upper house of the Uttar Pradesh Assembly. Members of such bodies are referred to by their pre-Independence designations as MLC's, Members of the Legislative Council.

19. Paliwal subsequently became an active leader of the 45 to 50 independents in the Assembly. With other members of the opposition, he entered a strong dissent to the Nagar Mahapalika Act. In 1959, he joined the Swatantra Party. For a discussion of his difficulties with that party, see Howard L. Erdman, *The Swatantra Party and Indian Conservatism* (Cambridge: Cambridge University Press, 1967). By late 1963, he had come full circle and back into the Congress.

20. In 1952, the Congress won 390 of 430 seats in the Uttar Pradesh Assembly on the basis of 48 percent of the vote; in 1957, its majority dropped dramatically to 286 seats based on 43 percent of the popular vote. Since candidates are permitted to run for a number of seats at the same time, Paliwal also stood against Seth for MP in 1957. Seth's percentage declined to 50.1 and Paliwal's increased to 36.7 from 1952. A Scheduled Caste candidate ran third with 13 percent of the total of about 221,000 votes cast.

21. The present account draws heavily on the work done by Owen M. Lynch, now published as *The Politics of Untouchability: Social Mobility and Social Change in a City of India* (New York: Columbia University Press, 1969). This process of social mobility through traditional means—what Srinivas has called "Sanskritization"—is discussed most recently in M. N. Srinivas, *Social Change in Modern India* (Berkeley: University of California Press, 1966), esp. pp. 1-45.

22. By these interventions, the British diverted the efforts of some groups from Sanskritization toward the adoption of values involving the rejection of traditional patterns of behavior ("Westernization"). Srinivas, pp. 46-74.

23. The work of Eleanor Zelliot is particularly valuable in this area. See her "Dr. Ambedkar and the Mahar Movement" (unpublished PhD. dissertation, University of Pennsylvania, 1969), and her "Buddhism and Politics in Maharashtra," in Donald E. Smith (ed.), *South Asian Politics and Religion* (Princeton: Princeton University Press, 1966), pp. 191-212.

24. The comments of one of these businessmen, whom Lynch calls *bare adme* (big men), reflects their fears and frustrations: "When we are a minority community without any power, then it is not for us to openly criticize those in power and revile them. . . . We should take advantage of the provisions for education and business which they offer us, before it is too late.

"If I carried on as some of the members of the Republican Party do, where would I be now, as a businessman? I have made much progress by not following its way. The Hindus are in power and we are too weak to stand up to them. Only when we have educated men and powerful businessmen of our own can we stand before them as equals." Lynch, p. 113.

25. Thus, in the general elections of 1957, there was a double-member constituency in Agra involving (as such constituencies did before they were abolished for the 1962 elections) the filling of a general and reserved seat. Two Congressmen (a Bania and a Jatav) contested against a well-known Brahmin independent and a Jatav nominee of the SCF. If results are computed on the basis of the total votes cast rather than the total number of voters—each voter was allowed to cast two ballots—we find that the Jatav candidate of the Congress stood first with 29 percent, the Congress Bania second with 27 percent, and the SCF nominee came in fourth with 20 percent of the total ballots cast. Considering the limited organizational resources available to the SCF in a large double-member constituency, however, this was a fairly respectable performance.

26. The importance attached to politics by the Jatav community is neatly

indicated in the statement of one Jatav politician, "The ordinary man does not understand the intricacies of politics; neither do I. But he does understand the simple things about politics and that it is a way of getting his rights." Lynch, pp. 89-90.

27. A recent study of the Arya Samaj at the turn of the century argues that it found particular favor in merchant communities. "Dayanand's [founder of the movement] claim that caste should be determined primarily by merit, not birth, opened new paths of social mobility to educated Vaishyas who were trying to achieve social status commensurate with their improving economic status." Norman G. Barrier, "The Arya Samaj and Congress Politics in the Punjab, 1894-1908," *The Journal of Asian Studies* 26 (May 1967): 364.

28. Weiner, *Party Politics in India,* pp. 171-94.

29. Interview, 8 January 1964. On the struggles within the Agra Jan Sangh, also see Angela S. Burger, *Opposition Parties in a Dominant Party System* (Berkeley and Los Angeles: University of California Press, 1969), pp. 243-45.

30. The present study will not be concerned with the differences in political traditions among Brahmin subcastes like the Chitpavans, Deshastas and Saraswats. Instead, we shall focus upon the larger political groupings: Brahmins and non-Brahmins. For the earlier period, see Anil Seal, *The Emergence of Indian Nationalism* (Cambridge: Cambridge University Press, 1968), esp. pp. 72-80 and 84-93.

31. Interview, 17 June 1964.

32. Kewal L. Panjabi, *The Indomitable Sardar* (Bombay: Bharatiya Vidya Bhavan, 1962), p. 131.

33. Ibid., p. 208, where a Patel speech is quoted which refers to the "parrot cry of socialism."

34. Saul Rosen, *Socialism in Southern Asia* (London: Oxford University Press, 1959), p. 28; Weiner, *Party Politics in India,* pp. 43-46.

35. Maureen L. P. Patterson, "A Preliminary Study of the Brahmin versus Non-Brahmin Conflict in Maharashtra" (unpublished MA thesis, University of Pennsylvania, 1952); also Maureen L. P. Patterson, "Caste and Political Leadership in Maharashtra," *Economic Weekly* 6 (1954): 1065-67.

36. Interview, 23 June 1964.

37. In addition to the work by Patterson, the present account draws upon materials which appear in Ataram Ganesh Kulkarni, "A Study of Political Parties in Maharashtra with Special Reference to the Period 1947 to 1962," unpublished PhD dissertation, Department of Politics, University of Poona, 1968.

38. Of 38 members of the MPCC Executive Committee in 1923, 26 were Brahmins and only 2 were Marathas. With membership reduced to 15 in 1936, the relative balance was 12 and 2—still clear Brahmin domination. By 1946, however, there were 17 members of the Executive Committee. Five were Brahmins and 7 Marathas, but the balance of power was held by 3 non-Maharashtrians and 1 Christian. In 1957, with 22 members, the Executive included 11 Marathas and only 5 Brahmins. The final rout of the Brahmins was yet to come, however, since by 1966 in a body of 44 members, there were 32 Marathas and not a single Brahmin.

The same process was evident in the elections of members of the AICC from Maharashtra. It is interesting that the Brahmins still held 14 out of 30 seats on the AICC as late as 1946, while the Marathas had only 6 in that year. With an enlarged representation to the AICC by 1966, there were 38 Marathas and only 3 Brahmins out of 63 representatives from Maharashtra. These data come from Kulkarni, p. 472.

39. Interview, 6 July 1964.

40. A Socialist paper declared: "The history of these leaders is inextricably connected with caste movements and actual anti-Brahmin activities. It is commendable that Jedhe and More today deny caste interests; but one can never tell when the caste outlook will come up again, therefore, one should be cautious before

joining hands with such people." The editorial from *Nava Shakti* is quoted in Patterson, "A Preliminary Study," p. 125.

41. In this contest, a PWP nominee finished third with 15 percent. In another non-Brahmin area, a Gujarati (formerly president of the City Congress), received 62 percent of the vote against Socialist and PWP challengers. The other two urban wards were more heavily populated by Brahmins and the challenge to the Congress came from the Hindu Right. In one, the Hindu Mahasabha nominee received 34 percent to the Congress victor's 52 percent; in the other, the candidate of a small right-wing party, the Ram Rajya Parishad, collected 28 percent to 52 percent for the Congress.

42. This agreement was accepted with considerable misgivings by some elements in the Nagri Sanghatna. In one heavily Brahmin ward, three Hindu Mahasabha candidates withdrew from the Sanghatna in protest over the alliance and ran as independents. Since this occurred rather late in the election campaign, the Sanghatna did not put up candidates in that ward. There is some evidence that this withdrawal was not regarded as improper by Mahasabha leaders.

43. These figures are not directly comparable to those for MP and MLA because of the multimember constituencies involved at the corporation level.

44. The data presented in table 2.2 and others similar in nature dealing with candidacies and outcome by ascriptive categories and party were collected in the following manner: (1) The names and votes of candidates in both Agra and Poona were made available by electoral officials for the corporation. Where candidates were representatives of official parties, this was indicated in the records. In Agra, however, the Republican Party was not officially recognized in 1959; this meant that its candidates ran as independents but were publicly identified by themselves or their party as being the party's nominee; as we shall see in the next chapter, this caused some difficulty in instances where candidates were endorsed by the RPI leadership but did not count that endorsement as equal to membership. In Poona the same kind of problem occurred in the 1957 elections when the Congress did not officially nominate candidates, but known Congressmen (indicated in tables 2.5 and 2.6) ran for the corporation. The analysis for Poona in 1957 probably under-estimates the number of Congressmen because of this peculiar situation. (2) Primordially-related identifications, not noted in official records, are drawn from materials gathered from interviews. This was a very tedious process, particularly in Poona, where recollections of three elections were involved. It is necessary, therefore, to treat the data gingerly. The facility with which the castes of candidates were identified, however, was astounding when one considers that it was not unusual to find ten or more candidates running in some wards. All corporation members interviewed in 1963-64 were questioned about these matters, and a certain amount of confidence in the data derives from the convergence of identifications in multimember wards. Where differences occurred, interviewees were pressed on the matter. Problems of categorization also arose where judgments had to be made; for example, while some Poona corporators speak of certain persons as Weavers, others spoke of the same group as "Madrasis," a general reference for southerners here applied to Weavers of South Indian origin.

45. One of the several difficulties with this formulation grows out of the knowledge that independents are occasionally encouraged to enter electoral contests by major candidates with the intention of diverting votes away from certain of the other principal contestants.

46. For some of the background of the linguistic issue in India, see Joan V. Bondurant, *Regionalism versus Provincialism: A Study in Problems of Indian National Unity*, Indian Press Digests: Monograph Series, no. 4 (Berkeley: University of California Press, 1958).

47. T. R. Deogirikar, *Twelve Years in Parliament* (Poona: Chitrashala Prakashan, 1964), pp. 200-201.

48. Narayan R. Deshpande, "Mr. Y. B. Chavan: A Case Study in India's New

Leadership" (paper for meetings of the International Political Science Association, Bombay, 4-10 January 1964), p. 5.

49. Even in the city of Bombay, the Samiti was a force in the general elections and was able to construct an absolute majority in the municipal body of 1957; however, the Congress did manage to win 54 seats out of 131 in the corporation elections. B. A. V. Sharma and R. T. Jangam, *The Bombay Municipal Corporation: An Election Study* (Bombay: Popular Book Depot, 1962), esp. p. 54.

50. Parulekar did not support the agitation over Maharashtra and *Sakal* found itself in considerable danger from angry citizens. The Sanghatna continued to function in a very minor fashion in 1957 by supporting five candidates. None of them won.

51. Maharashtra is one of the few areas where separate Pradesh Congress Committees (PCC's) continue to function since reorganization of the Indian states. After 1960, this meant separate units for Bombay City and the rest of Maharashtra. From 1956 to 1960, there were three PCC's—the third being for Gujarat. The continuation of a separate PCC for Bombay in 1960 was a concession to the Congress leader in that city, S. K. Patil.

52. Deshpande, p. 17.

53. Speaking to a group of the leading intellectuals of the new state in 1960, he suggested that the realization of Maharashtra would have served an important service if it succeeded in "bringing into the main stream of national progress the intellectual classes who have hithertofore, if I may say so, somewhat stood apart, isolated and self-sufficient unto themselves." *Problems of Maharashtra,* Report of a Seminar Held under the Auspices of the Indian Committee for Cultural Freedom (Bombay: Congress for Cultural Freedom, 1960), p. 7.

54. Deshpande, p. 18.

55. The office of president was not exactly a top prize in Poona at the time. A local Congress leader commented, "Because of the Samyukta Maharashtra defeats no one was really prepared to take over the post. We needed a locally influential person who could do something with the organization. Sanas was a military contractor, President of the Taalim Sangh [the major association of sports clubs in Poona], connected with the vegetable market and active in helping people."

56. Thus, one of the new Brahmin leaders (Mohan Dharia) won over from the PSP had been active in that organization for several years. By 1960, however, he became convinced that the PSP "could not deliver the goods. Only the Congress could do this, but it needed more young people." Dharia left the PSP and by 1962 was playing a major role in organizing Maharashtra for the general elections; he held the pivotal position of General Secretary of the MPCC for a time and now serves as a member of the Rajya Sabha. By 1967, he was becoming increasingly visible as a spokesman for internal party reform on the part of the national Congress. As a prominent figure in Maharashtra, he also took a minor part in the maneuvering which went on in 1967 prior to Mrs. Gandhi's reelection as Prime Minister. Michael Brecher, "Succession in India: 1967," *Asian Survey* 7 (July 1967): 429.

57. The Hindu Mahasabha, PWP, elements of the RPI, and the Communists continued to work within the framework of the Samiti until as late as 1962. In the elections of 1962, the Samiti did badly, and the ambivalent position of the CPI at the time of the Chinese invasion destroyed the front. The Republican Party also suffered internal disruption because the question of its withdrawal from the Samiti provided the immediate opportunity for existing factions within the party to do battle. In Poona, the ultimate result was the two Republican Parties mentioned earlier.

58. At the same election, the PSP candidate for deputy mayor received 35 votes to 27 for the Congress-backed candidate. In July of the following year, the winner of this contest resigned from the PSP and joined the Congress.

59. Jan Sangh national policy was opposed to the creation of linguistic states and favored a unitary political structure in India. In Poona, the demand for Maharashtra was so strong that the Jan Sangh attached itself to the Samyukta

Maharashtra movement. The party did not participate very actively in the 1957 corporation elections. Only three persons associated with it held municipal office during this period including one member elected to the corporation in a by-election.

60. This episode is recalled for the "colored pencils" conflict within the Congress. Some of the Congressmen on the Standing Committee were most unhappy because members of the City Congress Executive suggested that Congress members of the Standing Committee use differently colored pencils as a potential check on their votes.

61. For a recent survey of the effects of that flood, see Sulabha Brahme and Prakash Gole, *Deluge in Poona* (Bombay: Asia Publishing House, 1967).

62. The capacity of the Congress in Uttar Pradesh to discipline local units was more limited. Factionalism at the state level usually provided locally dissident elements with a potential ally to champion their cause.

NOTES TO CHAPTER 3

1. Cf. *Leader* (Allahabad), 8 June 1959 for one reaction to the postponement. The solicitude shown by the Congress for the CPI and Jan Sangh evoked a caustic comment from a spokesman for the Socialist Party: "It is strange that the Government should suddenly recognize these two parties as representing public opinion in the state. . . . It is only the Congress Party that is against holding elections on July 5 because the party is not prepared to face the public at a time when it is torn by group rivalries and internal dissensions." *National Herald* (Lucknow), 30 June 1959.

2. It was later publicly charged that the minister in question told Congress financial contributors to withhold support from Congress party candidates in Lucknow. *Indian Express,* 24 October 1959.

3. *Hindustan Times,* 29 October 1959.

4. The Congress was less willing to take back some other defectors. During the life of the body elected in 1959, several independents, including some former Congressmen, worked closely with the Congress in the corporation, but they were not official members of the party. In preparation for the 1968 municipal elections, however, a number of these "independents" were given Congress tickets.

5. Legal requirements of security deposits of Rs. 150 for general-seat candidates and Rs. 75 for reserved-seat candidates were intended to discourage frivolous candidacies since such deposits are forfeited if the candidate receives less than one-eighth of the votes cast. There is little evidence from the great number of candidacies in every contest that this device really discourages the marginal candidate.

6. Adrian C. Mayer, "Municipal Elections: A Central Indian Case Study," in C. H. Phillips (ed.), *Politics and Society in India* (New York: Frederick A. Praeger, 1962), p. 132.

7. Henry C. Hart, "Urban Politics in Bombay," *Economic Weekly* 12 (June 1960): 987.

8. B. A. V. Sharma and R. T. Jangam, *The Bombay Municipal Corporation: An Election Study* (Bombay: Popular Book Depot, 1962), p. 83.

9. In some instances, demands made by local clubs and temples upon candidates just fall short of open extortion.

10. The elections were further complicated by the presence of an "endorsing" agency in the person of S. K. D. Paliwal and his newspaper. Paliwal made an effort to organize a front which he called the Independent Progressive Party. Aside from his newspaper's endorsements, however, it was nonexistent as an organization. Four of the approximately twenty-three persons it endorsed won seats; one of these already had the backing of the RPI. No organizational obligations followed these endorsements.

11. Two Muslims ran on Republican tickets. In addition, one Muslim ran as a PSP candidate; the PSP had almost no organization in Agra.

12. An independent at the time of the interview, he rejoined the Jan Sangh prior to the 1968 elections and stood for the corporation on its ticket.

13. It was possible to compute "drop-off"—the number of voters who voted for only one candidate as a percentage of the total voters casting ballots—for each ward, since total votes and total voters were both enumerated in local election statistics. This measure did not correlate with other available social indicators like turnout, literacy, number of candidates, or size of ward. The only apparent tendency was for areas with high concentrations of Scheduled Caste persons to experience a higher "drop-off." Many of these wards had reserved seats. More votes are consistently cast for general seat nominees than for reserved seat candidates. Data on percent Scheduled Caste and literacy were available by ward from the 1961 Census, since census officials employed the municipal election wards as census units in gathering data for the subsequent census.

14. In 1967, Man Singh was elected MLA from Agra on a Republican ticket. See chapter 9, pp. 229-30 and chapter 10, p. 252.

15. For a description of this community, see Partap C. Agarwal, "A Muslim Sub-Caste of North India: Problems of Cultural Integration," *Economic and Political Weekly,* 10 September 1966, pp. 159-61.

16. The data for one ward—with a large combined population of Muslims and Banias—casts some doubt on the reliability of turnout figures. According to ward census data available in Lucknow, the ward contained 7,517 persons. That is a low figure, though not the lowest in the city. Officially, 4,515 persons were supposed to have cast ballots in that ward in 1959. This would yield an incredible 60 percent turnout based on *total* population. There is no evidence that there was anything special in the electoral experience of this ward to make such a turnout possible. For the purposes of analysis, therefore, this ward will be excluded, but it does point to the need to treat the present data with considerable caution.

17. Lines for general elections are drawn under the authority of a Central Election Commissioner, a position provided for in the Constitution. The Commissioner is a senior member of the IAS and is formally responsible for selecting officers from the state cadres of the IAS to oversee state procedures. For corporation elections, district electoral officials are given responsibility for bringing voter lists up to date and structuring ward boundaries. For a discussion of the formal electoral machinery, see Shriram Maheshwari, *The General Election in India* (Allahabad: Chaitanya Publishing House, 1963), pp. 37-50.

18. Despite frequent resort to litigation over election outcomes, there has been little comment in India about any bias in the apportionment of seats. An interesting recent exception is an article by Vinayak Purohit, *Hindustan Times,* 9 May 1968. Purohit argues that the 140 single-member wards for the 1968 municipal elections in Bombay and the 28 MLA districts in that city were drawn to favor the Congress. He shows at least some tendency for Congress winners to come from smaller wards than opposition victors in the corporation elections; this disparity is not as great in MLA districts. At the same time, it is clear from his data that variations in unit size are great. Bombay municipal wards range from 7,658 to 38,938 persons—a ratio of 5 to 1; MLA constituencies vary from 70,000 to 127,989. The latter is the largest MLA constituency in India and larger than a handful of MP districts.

19. Two factors other than conscious bias may be at work here. The Census was held *after* the municipal elections in Agra, which means that the 1951 Census—insofar as it was employed for the 1959 delimitation—may not have been a reliable guide to population distributions. Second, the ward with the greatest population was in the center of the city, while the ward lowest in population was on the urban fringe. Ease of movement may, therefore, have been a factor taken into consideration in assigning boundaries.

20. *Sainik,* 4 November 1959.

21. The guarantee of positions to the Scheduled Castes in governmental services has been a source of social opportunity, but it also has meant depriving the community of important political leadership.

22. In this connection, see Samuel P. Huntington, "Political Development and Political Decay," *World Politics* 17 (April 1965): 386-430.

NOTES TO CHAPTER 4

1. For a study of the 1962 general elections in Poona which includes a small survey of voters, see V. M. Sirsikar, *Political Behaviour in India* (Bombay: Manaktalas, 1965). Descriptive materials from the same study also appear in V. M. Sirsikar, "Party Loyalties versus Caste and Communal Pulls: Poona Constituency," in Myron Weiner and Rajni Kothari (eds.), *Indian Voting Behaviour* (Calcutta: Firma K. L. Mukhopadhyay, 1965), pp. 35-46.

2. Official figures on deaths are probably unreliable. Data on property damage was collected as part of the relief process. See Sulabha Brahme and Prakash Gole, *Deluge in Poona: Aftermath and Rehabilitation* (Poona: Gokhale Institute of Politics and Economics and Asia Publishing House, 1967) and Allen Grimshaw, "Social Structure, Disaster, and Re-Integration" (Paper prepared for the meetings of the Association for Asian Studies, San Francisco, March 1965).

3. Government of Maharashtra, *Report of the Commission of Inquiry for Enquiring into the Failure of the Panshet and Khadakwasla Dams*, 2 vols. (Bombay: Government Central Press, 1963). Recriminations were directed principally at the divisional and district officials responsible for maintaining law and order and, therefore, supposedly responsible for dealing with other local crises. The report is a fascinating account of bureaucratic procrastination at the time of the floods and of attempts to shift the blame during the inquiry. The tone of the bulky second volume is indicated in one brief section entitled, "What was Done by Mohite, Divisional Commissioner and Prabhakar, Collector [District Magistrate] Between 1-30 and 4 P.M. on the 11th July 1961?" The question concerns what these officials did between the time that serious warnings were relayed to them and their first efforts to organize a meeting at 4:00 P.M.—a meeting which was not actually held until 6:30 P.M. The answer was: very little. Part 2, sec. 11, p. 123.

4. *Times of India*, 13 September 1961.

5. The same *Times of India* editorial cited above comments favorably on the rapid removal of debris and the excellent organization of relief facilities. Chavan called upon the army stationed in Poona to open relief centers, distribute food, clear roads, and aid in setting up new housing. The Chief Minister also saw that subsidies, pensions and loans were arranged for victims of the flood.

6. In M. P. Mangudkar, *Poona Nagarsanstha Shatabdi Granth* (Poona: Corporation Publications, 1960), p. 953. This volume was published in celebration of Poona's centennial as a municipality.

7. He became Minister of Finance in Chavan's Cabinet in March 1962.

8. Sirsikar, *Political Behaviour in India*, p. 115. Sirsikar suggests that Barve's early reputation gained greatly from the skillful way he handled the anti-Brahmin riots of 1948 in Poona.

9. Telang was from a Weaver community and ran against Joshi in a non-Brahmin part of the city. It was the same district in which Joshi ran in 1957.

10. In contrast to Telang or Sanas, Girme had been a loyal Congressman for twenty years. His father had also been active in politics as a member of the municipality from 1938 to 1941.

11. The Jan Sangh originally nominated the Mali who was elected Chairman of the Standing Committee in the election that caused disruption of the Congress in the last years of the previous corporation. According to Sirsikar, he withdrew from fear of the loss of business which might result if the Congress chose to exercise its control over the vegetable markets. Cf. Sirsikar, *Political Behaviour in India*, p. 118. The Samiti candidate came in fourth, after the Jan Sangh nominee. This reflects

again how dependent the Samiti's candidates had been upon the Samyukta Maharashtra movement for their success in 1957.

12. The Republican Party, in its Scheduled Caste Federation guise, joined the Samiti during its major agitations. Even before the realization of Maharashtra, the RPI became internally divided. The *public* debate was over continuing support to the Samiti once Maharashtra was assured. One element, led by B. C. Kamble, withdrew from the organization and set up its own rump Republican Party. The major body, under B. K. Gaikwad of Nasik, remained with the Samiti. It split with that fusion alliance only in 1962. Gaikwad now is also leader of the major element within the national Republican Party. See Eleanor Zelliot, "Buddhism and Politics in Maharashtra," in Donald E. Smith (ed.), *South Asian Politics and Religion* (Princeton: Princeton University Press, 1966), esp. pp. 207-12.

13. Only the PWP won more than ten seats. This restored the situation of 1952, when the PWP won fifteen seats and was the major opposition party in the Maharashtra region.

14. Civic electoral alliances of varying political elements are not peculiar to Poona but have existed in other places, including: Calcutta, where it has taken the form of a left-wing coalition; Nagpur in 1952 and 1957, where a United Civic Front was largely an alliance of the Jan Sangh and the Scheduled Caste Federation; Ahmedabad, where the Mahagujarat Parishad constituted a Gujarati analogue to Poona's Samyukta Maharashtra Samiti but lived on past the resolution of that issue. Such electoral alliances have almost uniformly been conglomerates of parties and notables functioning in opposition to the Congress.

15. Parulekar refused to permit cooperation of the Sanghatna with the Communist Party. His consistent anticommunism was apparent in the pages of *Sakal.* Thus, in an editorial on 2 August 1961, dealing with the floods, he wrote, "In Poona everyone is trying to help while the Communist Party is not providing help to a single person. Communists never try to help others but always prefer to go on strike."

16. Such manifestoes may have been issued in Agra in 1959. There was some disagreement on this point. Their relevance in Poona was made evident in interviews with corporators when several volunteered references to their own or other parties' declarations in clarifying their views on party performances in the corporation. There is little evidence how much they actually influenced electoral behavior.

17. In both cities, special electoral "newspapers" have appeared during elections to provide propaganda outlets for those political organizations which do not already have a press favorable to the party.

18. Quotations from the various manifestoes and, where necessary, from newspapers are translated from the Marathi.

19. *Maharashtra Times,* 10 September 1962.

20. Jan Sangh *Manifesto,* 23 September 1962.

21. *Sakal,* 22 September 1962.

22. Ibid.

23. This system was abandoned in 1968 in favor of seventy-three single-member constituencies. In the process of designing the earlier multimember electoral wards, the traditional *peths* of the city were either combined or subdivided. In the seven-man "area," a predominantly Brahmin population was divided between two electoral districts.

24. Census units in the city were not coterminous with municipal political units. Some data is available, however, which makes use of survey material broken down by the traditional *peths.* Especially useful is N. V. Sovani, D. P. Apte, and R. G. Pendse, *Poona: A Resurvey* (Poona: Gokhale Institute of Politics and Economics, 1956), pp. 17 ff. Literacy and caste data presented here are derived from that study and from the data in Grimshaw, op. cit., which also draws on the *Resurvey.*

25. Similarly, there were 400 candidates for the 72 Poona wards contested in

1968–an average of 5.6 per seat. One contest was postponed because of alleged irregularities in the preparation of voter lists.

26. These were three wards adjoining each other; all had high concentrations of Brahmins. Nineteen of the twenty-seven candidates in the three wards in 1952 were Brahmins. Perhaps the better educated Brahmins more readily calculated their chances of winning and paid greater attention to party nominations in 1962 than did non-Brahmins.

27. The Non-Maharashtrian category in table 4.1 (as in table 2.2) includes a few persons from South India.

28. It was not the ward with the most contestants. That distinction went to a ward where there were twenty-five candidates, but there were six seats at stake in that ward.

29. While the position of corporator is not a full-time occupation, it is necessary to have sufficient free time to participate in corporation business and to devote energy to constituent problems. Only a handful of members in Agra or Poona were employed in occupations which did not allow them a good deal of freedom in controlling their own schedules. For occupational backgrounds of the Agra and Poona corporators, see chapter 6.

30. The LMP certificate is no longer granted in India, but persons with it continue to function in much the manner of medical practitioners holding currently recognized degrees.

31. A third incumbent, the Koli, finished sixth as a Congress-associated candidate.

32. This case is listed as Special C.A. Nos. 1817 and 1818 of 1958; these were cases involving complaints against the results of the 1957 elections for the Poona corporation. While the court recognized that relationship alone was not a basis for barring a person with a relative working in the corporation, it held that the brothers in this instance shared certain debts of Rs. 10,000 and that "if the debts continued to be joint it cannot be denied that on an application of the test laid down ... the respondent No. 3 [Agarwal] had a material interest in the employment of his brother" (p. 15). By the time of the 1962 election, this joint debt had been liquidated.

33. After reelection to the corporation as a Congressman in 1968, he became mayor in the new body. See chapter 10, pp. 276-77.

34. BDK, whose old home was ravaged by the floods, later moved to a new location. He contested in 1968 with Congress support and was elected. From his old area, a younger Bhoi was put up by the community–again, as the result of an intracommunity primary–and he was elected in one of the new single-member constituencies.

35. TRP, who ran fifth in the contest for the *general* seat in 1962 was the winner of the *reserved* seat in 1952 and 1957. In 1962, he decided to stand for the general seat by declaring himself a Buddhist. He lost by only three hundred votes. In 1968, he was a candidate of the Sanghatna and was elected in a ward where most of the candidates were Mahars.

36. The figure would be increased by two corporators for the Brahmins if we included among them two "non-Maharashtrians" who are Brahmin by caste, but locally identified as coming from Uttar Pradesh and Gujarat. Both of them tended to work with the Nagri Sanghatna in the corporation, although they were elected as independents.

37. One of the five Brahmins elected on a Jan Sangh ticket died in 1963. A special election was held to fill his seat. There were three candidates: a Jan Sangh Mali, a Congress Brahmin and a Sanghatna Brahmin. In this situation, the Jan Sangh Mali (see n. 11) had a primordial edge among non-Brahmins in the large ward along with the backing of a group favored by many Brahmins. He was elected.

38. There were twenty-seven *losers* from 1952 who ran again in 1957. Six of these won seats; five of the six carried Samiti endorsements. If we categorize

two-time losers between 1952 and 1957 in terms of those who gained in rank order finish and those who lost relative position over time, we find that five of six Samiti-backed candidates gained ground; the other Samiti nominee finished in the same relative position. Almost all the others lost rank or stood equal to their previous performances. This reemphasizes the importance of the Samiti label in 1957.

39. If we look at those persons who *lost* in 1957 and ran again in 1962—thirty in all—no particular partisan pattern of success is operative, but partisanship is in itself an apparently useful factor. All seven of the losers from 1957 who were elected in 1962 ran on party tickets the second time; three of them had contested as independents in 1957. Looking at rankings between the two elections for two-time losers, seven persons either gained position or held the same relative ranking; five of these seven were party nominees in 1962. On the other hand, fourteen of the sixteen two-time losers who sank in relative rank were running as independents in 1962. This would seem to point up the incremental importance of party affiliation for the outcome of municipal elections in Poona, although the specific party of affiliation may not be important.

In 1968, a large number of incumbents stood for the corporation. In all, forty-three of the sixty-five sitting members (66 percent) contested. The figure is even more impressive if one excludes the old or those involved in politics at a higher level (Joshi, Goray, and two MLAs elected in 1967) and if one includes four persons who contested in place of an incumbent. In one instance, a contestant was the husband of an incumbent; in three other cases, the son or another close relative.

40. Contrast the processes of nomination and election in Agra and Poona, for example, with the supposed "pluralism" of New Haven. Robert A. Dahl, *Who Governs?* (New Haven: Yale University, 1961), esp. pp. 104-14.

41. Oliver P. Williams and Charles R. Adrian, *Four Cities: A Study in Comparative Policy Making* (Philadelphia: University of Pennsylvania Press, 1963), p. 29. They also comment, "The most conspicuous interests that self-consciously espouse an arbiter function for government are neighborhood and welfare-oriented groups. Ethnic blocs reaching for a higher rung on the political ladder ... make claims for special representation. The psychological minorities—persons low on a socioeconomic scale—also stress the need for personal access" (pp. 28-29).

NOTES TO CHAPTER 5

1. Age is computed on the basis of the date of birth given in 1963-64.

2. Sixty percent of both the Republican and Swatantra Dal corporators were under forty-five as compared to 26 percent of the Congressmen.

3. Among the 17 Poona Congress corporators placed in the "Young" category, 2 had college educations and 7 had only some secondary education; 4 of the 6 older Congressmen had at least secondary schooling. The difference was less marked among members of the Nagri Sanghatna. Nine of the 13 older members of that political group had college educations (69 percent); this was true for 8 of 15 younger corporators—60 percent. In contrast, half of *all* Agra corporators under forty-five had college educations as against 28 percent of those over forty-five.

4. See Milton Gordon, *Assimilation in American Life* (New York: Oxford University Press, 1964), esp. pp. 34-51.

5. Several of the corporators included in the "middle" ethclass are from groups listed among those which receive government benefits, but some of these communities, at least in Poona, are relatively well off. Thus, the Malis have recently been added to the list of communities for which seats in institutions of higher education are set aside. Apparently, this action resulted from the self-interested activity of a highly placed politician and not from a demand from the community. Allegedly, the politician's son could not qualify for a particular school on the basis of merit alone.

6. If we were to consolidate the Agra corporators into ethclasses, we might include 36 in the "high," 10 (including all the Muslims) in the "middle," and 14 Jatavs in the "low" categories. Fifty-eight percent of the high ethclass corporators are "young" by our definition. In terms of education, 10 of the older group in the high ethclass category are college-educated (48 percent) as against 11 of the young high-status members (73 percent). The same tendency operates among the Jatavs, but from a much lower point of origin. All 7 of the older Jatav corporators had less than a secondary education; 3 of the 7 younger members completed more advanced levels of schooling.

7. The husband of the lone female corporator was also a lawyer. One of the features of the political changes that took place in Agra between 1959 and 1968 was the political recruitment of young lawyers through the Jan Sangh. See chapter 10, p. 278.

8. Two of the four women corporators in Poona were married to men trained in Western medicine.

9. The representation of doctors particularly in the Agra corporation is by no means peculiar to that city. According to Sharma and Jangam, Congress candidates for the Bombay elections of 1961 included 15 doctors, 13 lawyers, 3 engineers, 5 "educationists," 4 businessmen, and 15 trade unionists. Presumably, many of those identified as "social workers" (50 in all) came from business families. In Agra, the presence of businessmen was more striking, but trade unionists were almost entirely absent. See B. A. V. Sharma and R. T. Jangam, *The Bombay Municipal Corporation: An Election Study* (Bombay: Popular Book Depot, 1962), p. 15.

10. Included among the thirteen "professionals" in the Agra corporation (5 lawyers, 7 doctors and a tax accountant) were all the three Khatris and two of the three Kayasthas in the corporation. Only 4 of the 13 were Banias.

11. Such neighborhood businesses provide a useful political locus. Like the American saloon in the nineteenth century, the tea, pan (betel), or bicycle shop offers a place for politicians and would-be politicians to congregate.

12. The emergence of a business class among the young Marathas of Poona was even more apparent in the municipal body elected in 1968. In this connection, see chapter 10, pp. 278-79.

13. Despite high growth rates in urban populations in the past thirty years including substantial migrations, both municipal bodies included large majorities of persons of local origin. Out of the 60 members of the Agra corporation, 45 (75 percent) were born in areas now included in the corporation, and many of these were elected from wards where they had been either born or brought up. Of the other 15 corporators, 7 were born in Agra district or within fifty miles of the city; 5 of these took up residence in Agra before they were fifteen. Given a higher rate of recent growth in the city, it is not surprising that a slightly lower proportion of Poona's corporators were born in the city. Still, 42 (65 percent) of the members were natives of Poona, and another 6 were born within fifty miles of the city.

14. Thirty-one of Agra's corporators indicated that their first *interest* in politics had come through the Congress. Another 10 responded that they had no real interest in organized partisan activity before corporation entry; this included 3 corporators recruited by the Congress for these elections. A third group of about 9 members had been introduced to politics through Jatav-related organizations like the Scheduled Caste Federation or the Republican Party. Finally, 6 members identified the RSS or Jan Sangh as the vehicle for their initial political activation.

15. Aside from the Republicans, caste associations or "caste federations" of the sort described by the Rudolphs, Kothari and Maru or others did not appear to be *politically* active in either Agra or Poona. Lloyd I. Rudolph, "The Modernity of Tradition," *American Political Science Review* 59 (December 1965): 975-89; Rajni Kothari and Rushikesh Maru, "Caste and Secularism in India," *Journal of Asian Studies* 25 (November 1965): 33-50. See also V. K. S. Nayar, "Communal Interest Groups in Kerala," in Donald E. Smith (ed.), *South Asian Politics and Religion* (Princeton: Princeton University Press, 1966), pp. 176-90.

16. Along with such organizations of the Hindu castes, there are several associations among Muslims in Agra for the purposes of education and "cultural" affairs, but Agra Muslims have been very reluctant in recent years to become actively involved in politically-related matters on a communal basis.

17. Thus, in a recent (1968) neighborhood dispute between Jatavs and Banias set off by a fight among children, several corporators and leaders of the RPI and Congress were called upon as the appropriate figures to arbitrate matters.

18. Congressmen insisted that the organization was apolitical but that the nominal leadership of Congress politicians helped the association gain grants from the state government. It should be noted that the connection between politics and such "sports clubs" is not peculiar to Maharashtra. Atulya Ghosh, the "boss" of the Congress in Bengal, has also been the president of the local sports association in Calcutta.

19. See Joseph LaPalombara, "Italy: Fragmentation, Isolation, and Aliena-tion," in Lucian W. Pye and Sidney Verba (eds.), *Political Culture and Political Development* (Princeton: Princeton University Press, 1963), esp. pp. 283-97.

20. This attitude as it operates within the municipal arena does not rule out a ready resort to *satyagrahas, morchas,* and hunger fasts by citizens and corporators attempting to bring pressure to bear *upon* the corporation. Corporators belonging to parties other than the Congress also frequently resort to participation in agitations against the state or central governments. Thus, in March of 1964, Jan Sangh members of the Agra corporation joined fellow party members in a three-day token fast with three batches of members fasting for one day each in protest against the state government's placing a tax on urban land and buildings over and above the regular local bodies' levies on these properties. Agitations were more common in Poona than in Agra, since PSP members were particularly favorable to using such techniques. A national leader of the PSP, for example, justified resort to coercive public protest in the following terms: "The opposition to the Congress is not reflected in the legislatures. People vote according to caste, although they back the PSP in its public activities. These agitations are needed to show our feelings and the Congress does not oppose their use. When they are out of power, as in Kerala, they were very quick to use them." Considering the many stresses in Indian society, perhaps the peaceful agitations—as distinguished from the riots, which occur with unfortunate frequency in Indian cities—perform an important expressive function in a society marked by a mountainous accumulation of frustrations. For a discussion of the Gandhian sources of legitimacy for some of these activities, see David H. Bayley, "Pedagogy of Democracy: Coercive Public Protest in India," *American Political Science Review* 61 (September 1962): 663-72.

21. The figure is even higher when we recognize that about seven of the others decided not to contest because they were already heavily involved elsewhere in district or state politics.

22. The question about satisfaction with the corporation was not asked in Poona. The corporation had been in existence for over ten years by the time the elections of 1962 were held. It was therefore assumed that members knew what they were getting into when they ran for office. Unfortunately, other (comparative) uses of this item were not taken into consideration at the time.

23. Not only did this man stand again in 1968, but he rebelled against the Congress before the election and helped to organize a political group from his caste, which then associated itself with the Nagri Sanghatna.

24. In Poona, where high-status groups are losing political power, status-registration through such political organizations as the Jan Sangh may have become both an individual and group phenomenon.

25. The incumbent Congress MLA came in third in this contest. For a discussion of these and other results of the 1962 and 1967 general elections, see chapter 9.

26. In addition, the incumbent Republican MLA (the former alderman) ran for MP from another part of Uttar Pradesh.

27. All told, ten incumbent members of the Poona corporation ran for MLA or MP from the city or its environs in 1967.

28. In the case of sugar supply, intervention would have been with a district official rather than with a municipal administrator. It was noticeable in other instances, as well, that neither the corporator nor his constituents made fine distinctions among local arenas to be influenced.

29. The corporator had just been visited by an employee of the municipal health department, a constituent, who asked his help in getting a transfer to a different position in the municipal bureaucracy.

30. Henry Hart, "Urban Politics in Bombay," *Economic Weekly* 12 (June 1960): 985.

31. This policy reflected the changeover from a system of educational benefits based on caste to one based on economic situation. It was open to abuse because those empowered to verify the validity of claims might do so for a price provided by persons who should have been excluded. Authority to verify such situations was extended to many corporators, particularly those belonging to the Congress Party.

32. Dhirendra K. Vajpeyi, "Municipal Corporations in Uttar Pradesh: Elected Representatives and Executive Officers—Their Roles and Relationships," *Journal of Local Administration Overseas* 5 (October 1966): 245. R. Argal in *Municipal Government in India* (Allahabad: Agarwal Press, 1960), p. 189, suggests that members are often likely to abuse their positions especially insofar as their own assessments are concerned. He also argues that some evade the collection of taxes. Records on defaults among members of the two corporations were not made available to me, but, in an otherwise rumor-prone polity, this was not an important source of discussion even during the time the assessment process was in full bloom in Agra.

33. Vajpeyi, 245-46. The instability of coalitions in Agra and the professionalization of the Poona bureaucracy may have made it difficult for mayors of those cities to assume such behavior in any consistent fashion. We shall see one case of a mayor in the following chapter, however, where Vajpeyi's comments seem appropriate.

34. Much of the material in the following section appears in my "Deference and Friendship Patterns in Two Indian Municipal Councils," *Social Forces* 45 (December 1966): 178-92, in a somewhat different form. Ascriptive categories have been regrouped from that paper and there has been a shifting of party identifications to a different period. As a result, computations differ slightly from those in the article.

35. The 31 responses in Poona were distributed among nineteen names. The only person named more than three times was a Mali from a rural section of Poona.

36. The "homophily" index is adapted from John C. Wahlke, Heinz Eulau, William Buchanan, and Leroy C. Ferguson, *The Legislative System* (New York: John Wiley, 1962), p. 223, n. 13: "The measure varies between 0, when exactly the expected number of in-group choices occurs, and 1, when every expected member of the group choses another member of it. The formula is based on an expected value: $E = C (G - 1/N - 1)$ where G is the number of members in a group, N is the number in the chamber, and C is the number of choices made by members of the group. . . . Thus E is based on the assumption that choices will be distributed to any group in proportion to the number of persons in it who are available for choice. . . . The formula for h is $h = (O - E)/(C - E)$, where O is the observed frequency [the actual number of ingroup choices made]. If O should be less than E, then $(C - E)$ in the denominator is replaced by E to give minus values for an excess of out-group choices."

37. Patterns on the item dealing with noncontributors are not clear in Poona. In Agra, there is a positive h score among Jatavs (0.72) on question 3, which reflects a high rejection of those three Jatavs not associated with the Republican Party at the time of the interviews and the nomination of several RPI corporators

by other members of the party who felt they were not doing an effective job. In contrast, the score for Banias is -0.53, and for high-status corporators -1.00, i.e., almost no person from a high ethclass nominated another from that category. All the party groups reveal strong negative scores except the RPI for which there is a weak positive h (0.11) indicating a slight tendency for corporators from that party to cite persons from their own group as noncontributors. It is notable that Congressmen, despite their lack of congeniality toward each other, do not go so far as to name other Congress members on this item.

38. Seven of the thirty-five responses given by members of the Republican Party went to the man in question.

39. He was a man with few personal economic resources. It should be noted that neither of the other MLAs were mentioned on this item. This is rather surprising, given the supposed political influence of one of them at the time.

40. In 1968, for example, when Congress leaders were looking for someone relatively neutral in local factional struggles to head the District Congress, they turned to "H."

41. The term "renunciation" may not be quite appropriate in the case of "A" but part of his appeal did seem to rest on his refusal to get involved in day-to-day party and corporation political routine. For a discussion of this mode of behavior in Indian politics, see W. H. Morris-Jones, "India's Political Idioms," in C. H. Phillips (ed.), *Politics and Society in India* (New York: Frederick Praeger, 1962), pp. 133-54. In 1968, "A" decided not to stand for the corporation, partly to encourage younger candidates from his area. Some Congressmen supported him within the party group for mayor after the municipal elections. While his name was discussed, he ultimately threw his own backing to a Congressman with a similar public disposition—an old friend who had not served in the corporation. In mid-1968, "A" was being mentioned prominently as a possible candidate for the Congress in the mid-term elections for the Uttar Pradesh Assembly scheduled for February 1969. The prime difficulty, it appeared, was his refusal to spend money on the scale generally expected of Congress nominees and to wage the kind of "bare-knuckles" campaign associated with such a nomination. He was finally denied the ticket.

42. While seven members of the Congress cited "A" as one of their three closest friends, he refused to provide any answer to this question on the grounds that he was not particularly close to anyone in the corporation.

43. There was a marked difference between rankings on the esteem item and nominations on the friendship question. Half of the six most frequently mentioned corporators on the latter item were not even listed among the admired leaders. "A" and "K" were the most often mentioned members in each city, but there was no other correspondence between rank orderings on the two lists.

44. The impact of membership in the corporations *over time* in affecting the thinking of members about other corporators was not measured within the present study. Research on municipal politics being conducted by Roderick Church in Lucknow will get at this question through the administration of several waves of questionnaires to corporators over an eighteen-month period.

NOTES TO CHAPTER 6

1. The Uttar Pradesh Nagar Mahapalika Act, 1959, sec. 12 (3) provides for a system of proportional representation with a single transferable vote. In practice, the filling of a single post provides an incentive to construct a majority and the single transferable vote is useful as a bargaining counter. A majority system with second ballots operates in Poona, although the Bombay Act makes no specific reference to the electoral procedure in choosing a mayor.

2. The Congress was particularly cool to the idea of cooperating with the Jan Sangh in Uttar Pradesh, where the latter was a distant but potential challenger for power.

3. The Mahapalika Act makes the term of the deputy mayor coterminous with the life of the elected body. He is not removable except through a vote of no-confidence. One of the few advantages the Act provides to a mayor is the inadmissibility of a motion of no-confidence.

4. By this "subpact" the incumbent deputy mayor was assured of remaining in office since a motion of no-confidence requires a five-eighths vote and the alliance had enough votes to block such a maneuver.

5. Informants in the Congress suggested that Mehra received the nomination after Chaturvedi refused to stand again, another potential candidate was opposed by a majority of the Congress corporators, and Mehra argued that he was promised a few nonpact votes by persons with whom he had personal connections.

6. For a brief sketch of Ram Chand Gupta, see chapter 2, p. 33.

7. Early in 1963, two Muslim corporators of Agra were placed under arrest under the *Defense of India Act* which permits imprisonment without a formal court procedure. They were arrested for acting in a manner contrary to the interests of the nation, presumably on behalf of Pakistan. One of the detainees was in the business of arranging passports to Pakistan; the other had been to Pakistan only a few months earlier. Groups like the Jan Sangh, which normally support strong governmental actions in national security matters, for the sake of local partisan politics were willing to sign a petition drawn up by anti-Congress corporators in favor of the release of the two corporation members. The petition was also signed by five Congress corporators. The men were released on a writ of habeas corpus in November 1963, because of a technicality in the administrative procedures associated with the arrest.

8. Difficulties with CEO's have arisen in Poona, too. The January 1964 issue of *Civic Affairs* (11: 59) reports that the Kanpur corporation also came close to censuring its CEO on 17 December 1963 for "his alleged rudeness and haughty behavior."

9. Many Agra corporators questioned the right of the CEO to write to the state government in the disqualification case. Some argued that the CEO is the administrative subordinate of the corporation and that his communications with the government should not exceed limits determined by the members; other corporators (principally Congressmen) and most local administrators took the position that the CEO is the servant of the state government sent to work in the corporation but not subordinate to it. This issue was raised as a point of order at one of the corporation meetings, whereupon the mayor ruled that the CEO was free to write to the government under the terms of the Act.

10. Uttar Pradesh Nagar Mahapalika Act, 1959, sec. 25 (4).

11. Quoted materials are drawn from District Court and High Court records.

12. The brief filed by the two corporators charged that the CEO was proceeding in bad faith because he was reacting to the petition of no-confidence against him. This bad faith, it was suggested, was reflected in the failure of the CEO to bring the question of their absenteeism before the corporation, since the act implied the possibility of exculpation.

13. Word of the impending action was apparently relayed to the corporators by a leading anti-Gupta politician in the District Congress.

14. The injunction was lifted without prejudice to the two suspended members' cases. When the courts decided in their favor, they returned to the corporation. The government continued to threaten further legal action but pursued the matter only sporadically. The action in Agra was parallel to a case involving a Lucknow corporator at about the same time. *Civic Affairs* 10 (February 1963): 65-66.

15. Factionalism in the Congress was rampant in the four other cities, as well as in Agra. For example, in Kanpur, where the Congress was in a majority in the corporation, there was considerable battling over the behavior of the Congress mayor. As early as 1960, one corporation member in Kanpur accused the mayor of being obsessed with the "importance and dignity of his office, which, too often,

makes him oblivious of his statutory limitations." *The Hindu,* 30 November 1960. Only in Kanpur was the Congress regularly able to elect its mayoral candidates up to 1965. In that year, however, the incumbent mayor desired to run again and was endorsed by the local Congress. Kamaraj, then President of the national party, asked the incumbent to stand aside in favor of the President of the Kanpur City Congress. The mayor refused and was nominated by his own personal following in the corporation and supported by non-Congressmen. On paper the Congress held 42 of the 80 seats in the corporation, but the incumbent received 43 of the 69 votes polled. In part, the conflict grew out of the support the incumbent had given to the Gupta wing of the state Congress organization against the Tripathi wing in an earlier election.

16. Two supporters of the Baloji group refused to vote for Kalyan Das. They were flirting with the Congress at this time with the possibility that they might be given Congress tickets for the next corporation elections. The only Muslim member of the RPI also disaffiliated himself from that corporation party (but not from the city party). While his nominal objection to the opposition pact was the quality of the candidate, allegedly he was fearful of arousing Congress wrath.

17. By this time, too, former Mayor Mehra had left the Congress. He was angered by Congress willingness to renominate Gupta even though it had balked at naming him a second time.

18. The case appears as *Bohrey Ram Gopal* v. *Dr. Ladli Prasad Tandon (Allahabad Law Journal)* 61: 50-51. The decision was delivered on 17 May 1963. Initial action at the district level was taken by the District Judge of Agra, S. D. Singh, on 28 November 1960. Two separate hearings were held by the High Court. Two judges heard the first presentation, but they disagreed on some key points, which were referred to a third judge from the High Court panel.

19. The Corporation Act was subsequently amended to make the District Magistrate the Returning Officer in such elections.

20. According to *Civic Affairs* 11 (November 1963): 59, Tandon resigned in opposition to the mayor's sponsorship of a civic reception for the Governor of Uttar Pradesh. Such a reception was held during this period, but all corporators interviewed on this point denied any relationship between this reception and Tandon's resignation.

21. This election gave rise to an incident involving the alleged kidnapping of an independent corporator. He charged that he was taken by three "wrestlers" to a spot eighteen miles from Poona the day before the elections and was forced to swear that he would cast his vote for the Congress nominee for mayor. The accused kidnappers claimed the corporator had come of his own free will and, in fact, had used the story as an excuse not to participate in the elections. *Poona Herald,* 22 October 1964.

22. For a discussion of these riots, see chapter 7, p. 176.

23. *Poona Herald,* 17 October 1965.

24. The Congress made considerable effort to win this election, even bringing in a Deputy Minister from the state government to exercise influence on their own recalcitrant corporators. Despite these efforts, it is clear that several prominent Congressmen did not support Pardeshi. *Poona Herald,* 21 October 1965.

25. For a discussion of these conflicts, see chapter 9.

26. Informants suggest that the Congress had difficulty reaching an agreement on its own candidate for mayor. While a candidate put forward by one of the emerging local factions managed to receive a majority, the other faction hinted of possible defections. The latter group proposed the name of Goray, partly because the PSP had opposed participation in agitations against the Maharashtra government promoted by the SSP in connection with the demand that Belgaum district be turned over by the state of Mysore to Maharashtra. This demand for *Sampoorna Maharashtra* (Complete Maharashtra) was the symbolic rallying point for several parties opposed to the Congress in Maharashtra in the 1967 general elections.

27. All the defectors from the Sanghatna were non-Brahmins, but only one was a Maratha. In addition to two Mali corporators who joined the Congress in the first year and the Pardeshi former mayor, the others who quit the Sanghatna in 1965 were a Maratha, a Bhoi, a CKP doctor, and a member of a Tamil family which had been settled for several generations in Poona.

NOTES TO CHAPTER 7

1. Coopted members of the Development Committee are elected annually.

2. The Uttar Pradesh Nagar Mahapalika Act, sec. 54 (c) calls for the selection of coopted members "who in the opinion of the said members have experience of municipal administration of matters pertaining to development, improvement or planning."

3. Members of the two committees are elected by the general body. The two coopted members of the Development Committee are chosen by the ten members of that body alone.

4. To get around some of the problems of land acquisition, the central government passed three amendments to the Constitution. A recent decision of the Supreme Court, however, is likely to complicate the process. For comments on that decision, see *Economic and Political Weekly*, 4 March 1967, pp. 467-68, and S. Mohan Kumaramangalam, "Parliament's Power to Amend Constitution," *Link,* 26 March 1967; 2 April 1967.

5. The proposer of the resolution responded to the deputy mayor's ruling by sending a letter to the state government charging that the deputy mayor had misused his powers by presiding in a situation where he had a personal interest. The deputy mayor was then served with an order by the state government to show cause why he should not be removed from office. The matter dragged through the courts inconclusively for several years before being dropped.

6. At the primary level, there were four kinds of schools in the city: (1) ninety-seven public primary schools which came directly under the corporation; (2) sixty-nine "aided" schools run by private groups and headed by private management committees which received aid from the local and state governments; (3) six schools which were "recognized" but received no aid; (4) some convent and mission-run schools which were "unrecognized."

7. There were 16,990 students in the city's public primary schools in August 1963, as compared to 15,894 in private primary schools. Most of the private schools were associated with primordial groups; the Muslims had their own schools, the Jains ran several as did Kayasthas and Agarwals. On the whole, the public schools catered to the lower-status groups in the community. There were few open complaints about how this "double system" of education may have operated in sociological terms.

8. In 1968, the selection of a new Administrative Officer for the School Committee set off an intensive search for a possible candidate. For a discussion of this matter, see chapter 8, pp. 196-97.

9. The committee runs 122 public primary schools and seven secondary schools. Only three of the latter are corporation schools. The other four are state-financed but administered by the committee. In Agra, the corporation ran only one secondary school in 1964, but was planning others.

10. The Indian system of computations involves the use of groupings of numbers called *crores* and *lakhs.* A crore is 10,000,000; a lakh is 100,000. A rupee was worth about 23 cents in 1964; it has since been devalued to about 13 cents.

11. In this connection, see chapter 8, pp. 189-92, and chapter 10.

12. All corporators in Agra spoke in a variant of Hindi at corporation meetings. Their comments were recorded by an assistant and are reproduced here in approximation of the original. In the case of the Deputy Mayor's Budget Speech, however, a translation was made from a written version made available to me.

13. Corporators did indicate a good deal of sympathy for the plight of the lower-level administrators. As one Swatantra Dal corporator stated, "People say that our officials do not work. How can we expect a man to work honestly and efficiently when we pay him Rs. 100 or below? [less than $24 a month]."

14. Some corporators suggested, however, that this figure was not as high as it seemed because some items listed under "Establishment" (general administration) involved direct services to the public.

15. Administrators claim the rates of collection were higher than indicated by this figure. According to Jagdish Pratap Singh, "Local Finances in Urban Areas of UP" (unpublished Ph.D. dissertation, Department of Economics, Agra University, 1960), p. 194, Agra collected only 52.9 percent of assessed property taxes and 53.4 percent of water taxes assessed in 1958-59. This compared rather poorly with cities of similar character like Allahabad and Varanasi. Collection rates for property and water rates were 78.9 percent and 84.1 percent, respectively, in Allahabad and 84.7 percent and 83.5 percent in Varanasi. Agra also had the lowest per capita expenditure of any of the KAVAL cities in 1958-59 (before the elected body went into operation).

16. In 1964, the city of Agra owed on the order of Rs. 14 million toward the repayment of loans and accumulated interest on loans made by the state and central governments for various projects, including the waterworks, housing schemes, road building, and the new corporation building.

17. While recognizing the need for the takeover of the plant, a few corporators did concede that the company had had little incentive to invest in equipment in its later years because the sword of nationalization was hanging over its head.

18. The attitude of the state government was expressed in a letter to the corporation sent by the Ministry for Industries and Labour of the Maharashtra government on 5 May 1964. In part, it read: "(3) The proposal to entrust the power supply to metropolitan and urban areas to local authorities, if accepted, would result in the creation of permanent pockets of small electricity undertakings run by the local authorities, and militate against the working of an integrated grid system and the spread of benefits from electrification over the countryside. (4) Apart from this, the local authorities are not equipped, financially and technically, to undertake operation of large-sized electrical undertakings. Besides, in the context of the limited resources of technically qualified personnel as well as finance, the creation of diverse agencies for supply of power in various areas is a luxury which the country cannot afford." Opposition to this decision was not entirely silenced. The board came under attack again in 1966 for faulty billing, and the corporation passed an adjournment motion unanimously condemning the fact that many persons mistakenly were billed at high commercial rates rather than the normal residential rates. An independent, in the course of the discussion, also charged that the board's workers were extremely discourteous. Cf. *Poona Herald,* 30 March 1966.

19. Of course, the use of corporation meetings as a platform for political discussions was contrary to the self-proclaimed principles of the Sanghatna. For their part, the Congress would have welcomed the willingness of Sanghatna members to abide by their own principles.

20. The continuing importance of the floods of 1961 is apparent in these items. Item 2 grew out of a decision by a governmentally authorized body of public leaders that persons should not be permitted to build along the river banks. Despite this decision, encroachments by the poor occurred, and property owners also began to request permission to build. Some partisanship was evident on the matter as certain PSP members opposed weakening of the regulations while other Sanghatna members took the lead in opposing the continued imposition of a "flood line." Item 5 reflected a desire on the part of the Government of Maharashtra to recover some of its investment in resettlement and rehousing flood victims by reclaiming unused relief monies set aside for them in the state treasury.

21. Sayre and Kaufman estimate that from 1938 to 1956 the New York City Council passed 2,100 local laws. Of these, approximately 30 percent dealt with "naming streets, parks and playgrounds." Wallace S. Sayre and Herbert Kaufman, *Governing New York City* (New York: Norton, 1965), p. 611. A recent study of the New Haven City Council finds considerable concern with trivia, but then goes on to assert: "interlarded among these [minor or routine items] are a few more substantial items: the Equal Opportunities Ordinance, an open-spaces program, the setting up of a charter commission on an elective school board." William Lee Miller, *The Fifteenth Ward and the Great Society* (Boston: Houghton-Mifflin, 1966), p. 32.

22. Inner-city corporators resented the fact that rural people paid lower taxes than persons who resided in areas which had been part of the municipality prior to the creation of the corporation. Under the terms of the annexation plan, the value of annexed land was assessed at only one-third that of the ratable value on urbanized Poona. Taxes were to increase gradually over the years until land values were brought into equivalence but that stage had not been reached by 1964.

23. Alternately, one might hypothesize that persons in positions of authority would be less likely to favor a proposal of this kind since they are able to dominate the decision-making process. On its face this might be a plausible explanation except that the access of the Congress leadership to municipal decision-making authority was really not much greater than that of the rank and file of that party.

24. *Sakal,* 29 July 1964.

25. His statement was published in the local Congress newspaper, *Vishal Sahyadri,* on 31 July 1964. In it, the corporator gave the following account: "I explained in that meeting that the Congress Party position was not wrong and was not opposed to reserving the land for development. I explained that Congress had rejected the proposal this time because it was not possible to reserve the land at present. If we take this land we will have to invest Rs. 5 lakhs in it immediately. The same view was taken by the Municipal Commissioner. . . . The Congress Party is opposed to the resolution because it is improper. I gave the same explanation in the meeting but they published a statement against me in order to create a misunderstanding in the Congress Party."

26. In reaction to this final change of mind, one corporator-opponent of the company complained, "Many of the members of the Standing Committee seemed to be personally interested in seeing that the land was given to the Factory and some of them moved Heaven and Earth to see that they got it." *Poona Herald,* 28 June 1964.

27. Such motions provide an opportunity to bring other business to a halt and allow a debate on a topic of political timeliness.

28. *Poona Herald,* 12 January 1965.

29. This again points up the fact that persons of high-status communities in Poona could be found either on the Left or on the Right—in this case, within the same family.

30. *Poona Herald,* 21 March 1966.

31. *Poona Herald,* 23 March 1966.

32. That may be why the introduction of the allotment process in Agra was considered so exceptional a power by the corporators. It formalized their control over the local administrators in a fashion that was outside the normal range of expectations about how members bargain with administrators to achieve constituency ends.

NOTES TO CHAPTER 8

1. The small, elite cadre of the ICS was dominated by the British almost until Independence; many of the subordinate positions in national and state administration were filled by Indians. For a recent discussion of the organization and

recruitment of the IAS, see David C. Potter, "Bureaucratic Change in India," in Ralph Braibanti (ed.), *Asian Bureaucratic Systems Emergent from the British Tradition* (Durham: Duke University Press, 1966), pp. 141-208.

2. Probably the best-known characterizations of bureaucratic performance criteria are found in the works of Max Weber. See Talcott Parsons (ed.), Max Weber, *The Theory of Social and Economic Organization* (New York: The Free Press of Glencoe, paperback, 1964), pp. 329-41. For a recent discussion of the appropriateness of applying these criteria in a developmental situation, see Richard P. Taub, *Bureaucrats under Stress: Administrators and Administration in an Indian State* (Berkeley: University of California Press, 1969), pp. 194-203.

3. One might argue that an evident duality existed in the actions of Agra administrators. Their statements were replete with references to the desirability of enforcing bureaucratic norms strictly; their behaviors suggested that other values influenced their performances. This discontinuity may in itself account for some part of the dissatisfaction with their situations evident among many of Agra's administrative personnel.

4. In the brief periods that most CEO's spent in Agra, it was difficult for many of them to gain control over vital information and behavior relating to their own administrations. As a leading corporator remarked with respect to a recent CEO, who had been in the city about two months, "I talked to him recently and it is clear that he knows only a little of what is really going on in the corporation."

5. This arrangement is not unknown in the United States, where municipal civil service rules in cities like Chicago are regularly circumvented through "temporary" appointments.

6. This official was not very happy with the more bureaucratized procedures for corporation employment. Commenting on them, he said, "Now everything is through the employment exchanges, although the municipal employees have been trying to give an advantage to the dependents of employees as is done in the railways, the police, and some other services."

7. The city maintained five slaughterhouses used by butchers of the city. The city collected fees on a graduated basis for pigs, goats, buffaloes, and even camels. Cow slaughter was not included.

8. Because of political quarrels among corporators, there are always dangers to a CEO that he may become identified with a particular group in the corporation and, therefore, an object of factional attack. In a recent case, the Municipal Commissioner of Calcutta was forced to resign over a minor incident that became politicized by the corporation members. *Civic Affairs* 14 (September 1966): 38. The CEO of Hyderabad also became the object of partisan broadsides in that municipal body. *Link,* 29 September 1968, p. 17.

9. Vajpeyi, summing up the situation in Uttar Pradesh, writes: "The working of municipal corporations has showed that administrative officers try to accommodate, within reasonable limits, the mayor and other elected representatives because there are times when the officers also stand in need of favors. It is the process of mutual accommodation, understanding and convenience. Cases of corrupt practices and where undue pressure has been brought to bear come to light only when such mutual bargains are not possible or where either party is dissatisfied and the official gets interested in divulging the secret deal." Dhirendra Kumar Vajpeyi, "Municipal Corporations in Uttar Pradesh," *Journal of Local Administration Overseas* 5 (1966): 246. The last statement places matters in a more conspiratorial light than the actual relationships may warrant.

10. Local Congressmen registered these complaints with Mrs. Sucheta Kripalani, then Chief Minister of Uttar Pradesh, during a visit she paid to Agra. It was likely that they received a sympathetic hearing, since it was widely rumored, when the CEO was originally posted to Agra in 1964, that he had fallen into disfavor with the Chief Minister over some matters arising out of his previous service in the Lucknow secretariat.

11. Included under the new regulations were not only the KAVAL cities but Class I municipalities—cities like Meerut, Mathura, and Bareilly. Doubts were raised in many minds about the equivalence of posts from one city to another. As of mid-1968, matters of salary scales and allowances still remained to be standardized in certain positions. From the side of corporators, one also heard comments like the following one, "The city has a sewer system worth Rs. 4 crores, and — who was an expert in such things, was appointed only to oversee these matters but now he has been transferred to — [a much smaller city] where there is hardly a comparable need."

12. One of the few powers available to the mayor under the previous administrative system and lost in the wake of provincialization was the power to enter negative comments in an administrator's "character roll." In the case of "B," it is alleged that the mayor of Agra entered derogatory statements in his record—presumably at the instigation of the CEO—a situation which may have made his position more difficult in gaining stable reassignment.

13. The new CEO in Agra may have been a little "gun shy" on this point, having recently engaged in a rather unpleasant exchange with the member of the Jan Sangh quoted above who condemned the fact that the CEO had written to the government on behalf of a subordinate officer asking that the man be retained in Agra for a longer period.

14. Many complaints circulated by obviously self-interested politicians suggested that Governor's rule in Uttar Pradesh was now leading to a "free rein" for administrators. The police, in particular, were accused of administrative misdeeds. Cf. *Link,* 29 September 1968, p. 16; *Organiser,* 12 October 1968, p. 3.

15. This does not mean that various differences do not erupt occasionally within the Maharashtra Congress. For example, recent conflict over the location of an agricultural university in the state apparently reflected some political maneuvering in the Congress and ultimately resulted in serious riots in eastern Maharashtra and the threatened renewal of demands for a separate (Vidarbha) state. *Economic and Political Weekly* 3 (5 October 1968): 1511-12.

16. A minor source of the difficult relations which existed between the corporation and the CEO resulted from a demand by the latter that he be reimbursed for *not* making use of the official residence provided to the CEO by the city, since he was living in his own home. Under the circumstances, he felt he ought to receive an additional housing allowance. The corporators were opposed to this request.

17. We have noted, in various places, the interventions of state politicians in local matters. In Poona this behavior was enhanced by the frequent presence in the city of leading Congress Party officials and important state government members on other business. It was not unusual to find the Chief Minister, Mr. Naik, opening a wholesale produce market, or Mr. Chavan—on his frequent visits—unveiling a statue or opening a theater. While visits to Agra by Uttar Pradesh ministers were less common, they did occur, as did visits by central ministers. Prime Minister Nehru, for example, performed one of his last public acts by laying the cornerstone of a new bridge across the Jumna in Agra in 1964.

18. When it actually came time for the Brahmin Municipal Secretary to retire, his term was extended for more than two years.

19. That feelings of caste discrimination still lingered on in 1968 was indicated by several charges made by a major figure in the Congress Corporation Party that officials were treated differently by the Nagri Sanghatna depending on their caste. This corporator, a Mali, argued that the PSP and SSP were dominated by Brahmins or CKP's, with the result that when several high-status officials were nearing retirement, they were allowed four months leave before actual retirement. A Mali official, he charged, was denied this opportunity. As he asserted, "This was due to a caste spirit which was less direct than the one shown by the Jan Sangh or the Mahasabha, but it is still there."

20. The particular corporator was an independent, but was associated with the two Nagri Sanghatnas and the Samyukta Maharashtra Samiti during their periods of power in the corporation. During the events of 1958-59, described below, he was deputy mayor.

21. The SSC (Secondary School Certificate) is equivalent to a high school diploma.

22. *Poona Herald,* 9 January 1965.

23. *Times of India,* 10 May 1967. A month later (16 June), the matter came up for discussion in the Maharashtra Assembly when the Urban Development Minister asserted—in response to an inquiry—that the state's refusal to grant permission to the Center to prosecute officials of the PMT was based on confidential information which it refused to release. Opposition members including former Poona mayor, B. D. Killedar (elected MLA in 1967), asserted that the state was trying to "shield" the PMT official from central government efforts to prosecute. Killedar further asserted that copies of the CBI report and the Union government's communications with the Maharashtra government had already been given to the members of the Poona corporation. Even the Speaker did not fully support the claims of confidentiality advanced by the state, but he permitted the exchange to end with the minister's promising to consult his colleagues on the matter. *Civic Affairs* 14 (July 1967): 39-41.

24. Or, as the Congress Chairman of the Transportation Committee in 1968 remarked, "The PMT investigation has been overworked. For a while every meeting was turned by the Nagri Sanghatna into one dealing with the PMT. Someone wrote to the CBI that — was using the licenses for his personal gain, but this was not the case. If the PMT is to be considered guilty in these matters, then the same is true of the Bombay undertaking and the State Transport. The Transportation Committee members would be equally guilty with the Manager since he had merely followed their orders." Obviously, this was not the kind of interpretation the Nagri Sanghatna placed upon events.

25. Gyan Chand, *Local Finance in India,* p. 51 as quoted in A. C. Minocha, *Finances of Urban Local Bodies in Madhya Pradesh* (Bombay: All-India Institute of Local Self-Government, 1965), p. 169. R. Argal, *Municipal Government in India* (Allahabad: Agarwal Press, 1960), p. 180, cites a 1928 report on local finances which includes the following comments, "Octroi can and is easily evaded by collusion with the *Muharrir* [collector] specifically where the supervising staff is weak; in the same way fraudulent refunds can also be obtained. . . . Chief among the opportunities of peculation by the staff is the power which octroi *muharrirs* possess of holding up goods for hours at a time, if the owner is not prepared to accede to their demands."

26. The sources of mentions for each of the more frequently nominated administrators on the three items was analyzed by examining deviations from "expected" nominations. Thus, if a group as a whole constituted a certain percentage of those making nominations on a given item and exceeded this figure markedly in actual mentions of an individual, it is noted. Figures are not presented here. As the text indicates, consistencies of support were not such as to suggest that administrator selections were made *primarily* on such subgroup bases.

27. Apparently there was sufficient support among high-status corporators for this CKP official to become the object of efforts by political parties in Poona (other than the Congress) to get him to run for the corporation in 1968. He ran as a candidate of the Jan Sangh, but was defeated. On this point, see chapter 10, p. 269.

28. In only one instance do reciprocal subgroup identifications emerge with any clarity. The locally recruited City Engineer is mentioned rather often on question 3 by members of the Republican Party, while he is distinctly underrepresented among members of the Swatantra Dal—the group which most strongly supported him on the esteem item.

29. In Agra, the only changes which actually took place between 1964 and

1968 were to give the mayor authority to make certain minor appointments and to extend to corporators an allowance for transportation in order to attend meetings. *Civic Affairs* 12 (September 1964), p. 38. There were few signs in 1968 that more authority would be granted to the two corporations' "popular" bodies.

30. In this connection, see Taub, esp. chapter 7.

NOTES TO CHAPTER 9

1. Reflecting this local-refugee conflict was the battle for control of a local college run by the Arya Samaj. Apparently there were two groups in the Arya Samaj; the one based in the refugee communities demanded a greater voice in the operation of the school. Up to 1964, the group associated with the nonrefugee element tended to dominate the Management Committee of the College. In that year, the Punjabi President of the City Jan Sangh—an unsuccessful party candidate for MLA in 1962—went on a hunger strike in the compound of the college to exercise influence over the way in which the pivotal position of Manager in the college was being handled. As a result of the fast, a compromise settlement was reached which tacitly recognized the increasing influence of refugee elements in school affairs.

2. From 98 seats immediately after the 1967 general elections, the Jan Sangh fell to only 48 in the mid-term elections of 1969 for the Uttar Pradesh Assembly.

3. Materials dealing with the controversies within the Republican Party are from the private files of participants in the dispute.

4. Typical of the tone of the debate was the resolution passed by Pipal's supporters after the meeting at which his President was suspended and a man recommended by Maurya put in his place. The resolution read, in part, "Shri B. P. Maurya and Shri Cheddilal Sathi acted contrary to the energetic workers. . . . They behaved as dictators, created differences and adopted the policy of 'Divide and Rule' by demanding Shri Gopichand Pipal's resignation and imposing D — P —, their puppet—and a principleless person—as Chairman."

5. See chapter 3, pp. 72-73.

6. One of those who won in 1962 was Banwari Lal Bipra, a young Agra corporator (see chapter 3, pp. 69-70) who ran for a seat from an MLA constituency about thirty miles from Agra. His relations with the Agra unit of the party deteriorated after 1963. While he continued to associate with the RPI in the State Legislative Assembly, he dissociated himself from the Agra party. In the 1967 elections, Bipra stood for the Dayalbagh MLA constituency near Agra City as an independent and got only 515 votes.

7. This appears to be the implication of Lynch's discussion of the role of the "big men" in the Jatav community. Owen M. Lynch, *The Politics of Untouchability: Social Mobility and Social Change in a City of India* (New York: Columbia University Press, 1969).

8. *Sainik,* 16 June 1960, carried a rather bizarre story in which residents of a particular *mohalla* charged the two Singhal-associated leaders with aiding in the protection of persons selling girls into prostitution. The Congress Executive also made an effort at the time to suspend a Singhal corporator who ran for the corporation even though he was head of the Congress Seva Dal. On 31 May 1960, the Secretary of the UPCC declared that this suspension was illegal.

9. Charges were apparently framed against Seth as well, but the decision had to be made by the AICC, since a Pradesh committee cannot suspend an MP. Seth was not punished. It is generally agreed that he was only marginally involved in his lieutenants' maneuvers.

10. Chapter 3, pp. 70-72.

11. *Link,* 17 April 1966, p. 13. In 1969, Tripathi associated himself with the section of the Congress led by Indira Gandhi; C. B. Gupta joined the "organization" Congress, the rival group.

12. *National Herald,* 3 February 1966, p. 5.

13. See, for example, *Link* 21 August 1966, p. 20; *Current,* 27 August 1966, p. 2. In the split of 1969, Mrs. Kripalani emerged as an active figure in the group opposed to Mrs. Gandhi.

14. The press carried stories of Rawat's chagrin when he showed up for swearing-in ceremonies only to find that he had not received a Cabinet post. *Link,* 19 March 1967, p. 11.

15. *Himmat* (Agra), 11 February 1962.

16. In Agra City I, each of the twenty-eight polling stations recorded vote differences of over 12 percent for the two Congress nominees.

17. It should be added that there was only a tiny "drop-off effect" in the different MLA constituencies. These ranged from 951 votes in Agra City I, where 60,592 votes were cast for MP, to Agra City II, where 617 fewer persons voted for MLA than for MP.

18. Agra East had nine corporation wards in common with Agra City I of 1962 out of the twelve wards included in the latter. The Agra Cantonment constituency of 1967 and Agra City II of 1962 contained five of the same wards and part of another; four wards were new. The new Agra West shared four wards with Agra City (Rural) and three with Agra City II in addition to having a small part of rural Agra.

19. In interviews held in 1968, the question of financing campaigns was frequently raised. It was commonly asserted that Congress candidates had to spend Rs. 1 lakh in urban Agra. In the case of Gupta, it is generally believed that financial contributions to the political campaigns of several prominent state leaders were also required before he received the party ticket.

20. Of the ten MLA seats in Agra district, the Congress won only three, the Jan Sangh three, and the Republicans one. Other seats in the district were captured by one independent and two SSP candidates. At least two of the Congress defeats in rural Agra were attributed to conflicts within the Congress between the Rawat and S. P. Gupta forces. In terms of relative strength, however, it should be noted that the Congress finished second in six of the constituencies where it did not win; the Jan Sangh finished second in only one district.

21. This corporator received less than one percent of the vote. His lack of commitment to the Swatantra and the fluidity of the local political system is indicated by his decision to stand for the corporation in 1968 as a nominee of the CPI.

22. The Communist candidate received 1,501 votes (2.5 percent of the total). No others got more than 1.2 percent.

23. The continued weakness of the Congress was noticeable in the second MP seat in Agra District in 1967. In the 1962 election that contest was won by S. N. Chaturvedi, the first mayor of Agra. In that election, Chaturvedi received only 29.8 percent of the vote in a ten-man field. His nearest rivals were candidates of the RPI and the Socialist Party (who won about 23 percent each). The latter party had little following in urban Agra, but did quite well in the countryside. When MP constituencies were reorganized for the 1967 elections, the Firozabad MP constituency was made a reserved seat. Ambesh, the MLA incumbent in Agra City (Rural), was designated for the Congress nomination. The Socialists, now operating as the SSP, won the seat with 35.3 percent of the vote. Ambesh ran second with 29.6 percent. The Republicans, as elsewhere, lost considerable ground, falling to only 11.3 percent.

24. As a spokesman of current PSP philosophy argued, "We favor a rationalist basis to a party, but this kind of thing is not popular anymore. The Gandhian approach of constructive work, education, and satyagraha against injustice is still correct. Satyagraha still has a role to play, but we must do constructive work among the people and try to educate them politically. This means keeping our means and ends in close relationship. Unfortunately, the SSP has

abandoned this view and thinks only of non-Congressism at any price." By 1968, however, the PSP had become involved in an electoral alliance in Bombay with the Shiv Sena which raised many questions about its own concern with "means" and "ends."

25. For one review of these events, see Benjamin Schoenfeld, "The Birth of India's Samyukta Socialist Party," *Pacific Affairs* 38 (fall and winter 1965-66): 245-68.

26. The dispute was set off by a demonstration of slum dwellers demanding greater water supply to their area. It was the understanding of SSP corporators that a spokesman would be permitted to introduce a motion dealing with the matter. Joshi yielded to a Congress leader at one point with the expectation that the latter would talk about the water question; when the latter did not, Joshi protested vehemently. *Poona Daily News,* 20 April 1966. The deputy mayor ordered Joshi out of the hall. When Joshi refused to leave, the marshals were summoned to remove him forcibly. Other members prevented this, but Joshi was escorted out. *Poona Herald,* 20 April 1966.

27. There was an immediate effort to bring an adjournment motion condemning the actions of the deputy mayor. The motion was finally rejected twenty-four to twenty-one after a four-hour debate. The deputy mayor later offered to apologize to Joshi. *Poona Daily News,* 22 April 1966. A few days afterwards, however, he retracted any apology. *Poona Herald,* 27 April 1966.

28. There was much dissatisfaction with the final recommendations for minor alterations offered by the Mahajan Commission. When its report was finally released, however, the opposition in Maharashtra did little about it immediately except hold minor demonstrations.

29. This candidate, D. D. Bhandare, defeated P. K. Atre, an independent Brahmin backed by the SMS, by 7,000 votes out of a total of 309,000 cast for the two men in Bombay (City) Central MP constituency. B. C. Kamble, leader of a third RPI faction, came in third in that contest.

30. There is no clear evidence that the Central Election Commissioner's office was influenced by partisanship in the new delimitation. It *is* the case that the addition of Mulshi constituency to the Poona MP area increased Congress's chance of carrying the seat more than the retention of Haveli taluka would have done. Haveli voted heavily for its own Congress MP nominee in 1967, though not as heavily as did the population of Mulshi—61 percent to 73 percent.

31. The Shukrawar Peth municipal ward sent five Marathas, one Brahmin, and one CKP to the corporation in 1962, but the other traditional *peths* added to the MLA constituency in 1967 had elected eleven Brahmins and one Maratha. The strength of overall "non-Congressism" there is indicated by the partisan breakdown for the 1962 corporation: nine Nagri Sanghatna, four Jan Sangh, four Congress, two independents.

32. *Times of India,* 9 October 1966.

33. Gaikwad refrained from supporting Krishna Menon when the latter ran for MP a second time in 1967 following the sudden death of S. G. Barve. *Times of India,* 16 April 1967. Shortly thereafter, the Republicans entered an agreement with the Congress for the *panchayati raj* elections in Maharashtra, which saw this alliance win resoundingly—forty out of fifty-seven seats, for example, in Poona District's *zilla parishad.* Gaikwad publicly expressed considerable satisfaction with the results of this cooperation. *Times of India,* 2 and 6 June 1967.

NOTES TO CHAPTER 10

1. For a discussion of the rise and fall of coalition governments in Uttar Pradesh, Bihar, and the Punjab, see Paul R. Brass, "Coalition Politics in North India," *American Political Science Review* 62 (December 1968), esp. pp. 1185-87.

2. The setbacks to the Congress organization in Bombay City in 1967 should

not be exaggerated. The highly visible losses—two MP seats out of five—were those of S. K. Patil, "boss" of the BPCC, to George Fernandes of the SSP in one MP contest and the victory of S. A. Dange, one of the key leaders of the national CPI, over a Congress candidate. However, Congress won twenty-one out of thirty MLA seats available in urbanized Bombay.

3. The kinds of rationalizations provided by the members of the PSP were typified by the following comments of a prominent member of the Poona organization, "In Bombay, the SMS included the Muslim League and the CPI, and we did not want to go into an agreement with them. To defeat the CPI, we joined with the Shiv Sena with the thinking being that by cooperating with them we put them under some constraints. Because of our contact, we have been able to influence them but we condemn their violence in the Fort area [destruction of goods being sold on sidewalk stands]."

4. Suggestions have been made that the MPCC—the Congress organization outside Bombay City—was not entirely blameless in the rise of the Shiv Sena as a challenge to the BPCC. When the Shiv Sena became involved in politics outside Bombay City, however, it began to threaten the Chavan organization.

5. Municipal elections were not held in Allahabad because of severe Hindu-Muslim riots in that city earlier in the year.

6. *National Herald,* 4 and 6 May 1968.

7. In contrast to forty-nine independents elected in 1968, ninety had won seats in the same four cities in 1959.

8. The traditional status of the Khatiks is somewhat higher than that of the Jatavs. As one informant explained the matter, "The Khatiks are fruitsellers and tenders of goats and sheep and so they tried to convince the other communities that they are Backward Class and not Scheduled Caste, but they are listed as Scheduled Caste, and this election saw them running candidates as Scheduled Caste." With the benefits of being Scheduled Caste apparent to the community, claims to Backward Class status had apparently receded.

9. The factionalism which existed in Agra district was at least temporarily patched over in 1968 in a manner similar to that employed in Agra City. Shiv Prasad Gupta and J. P. Rawat agreed to support a relatively neutral figure, P. N. Shiromani, as President of the District Congress. It is interesting that both Shiromani (a former alderman) and Johri are Kayasthas.

10. As late as July 1968, only the first stirrings were visible of proposed action to revive the Youth Congress in Agra.

11. Some Congressmen suggested that the lateness of submission of the names of candidates for the Congress was also a result of the desire of the party to forestall SSP and BKD efforts to recruit dissident Congressmen to their tickets.

12. Khem Chand, the ex-MLA associated with the Ambedkerites, had the authority to distribute corporation tickets for that group but gave the Ambedkerites' symbol (a lion) to only one Agra candidate. Following the corporation elections, Khem Chand returned to the local Republican organization and ran for MLA on its ticket in 1969.

13. See chapter 9, pp. 214-15.

14. Table 3.1 reported eighty-five candidacies for the Congress and Jan Sangh in addition to about thirty RPI-backed nominees with the overwhelming remainder being independents. Sixty-one percent of all Bania candidates contesting in 1959 ran for either the Jan Sangh or the Congress; only 33 percent of the Brahmins were candidates of those two parties.

15. *Amar-Ujala,* 1 May 1968.

16. The election was postponed for several weeks in a ward where one of the candidates died just before election day.

17. It is a popular view among high-status politicians in Agra that turnout among the Scheduled Castes is high especially among women. Thus, a local paper wrote about election day: "The women outnumbered the men and especially the

numbers of women from Muslim and Scheduled Caste areas were quite high. The educated did not show any interest in the elections." *Amar-Ujala,* 6 May 1968. On the average, wards having a reserved seat (generally areas with high concentrations of Scheduled Castes) recorded a slightly *higher* turnout in this election than wards with only general seats—58.2 percent as contrasted with 56.8 percent.

18. In 1959 six of eight reserved seats were won by the RPI, two by independents. All were Jatavs. Only three would have won if there had been no reservation. By 1968, the increasingly effective politicization of the Scheduled Castes, combined with an apparent increase in the ability of party organizations other than the RPI to enlist voter support for both reserved and general seats, resulted in a situation in which five of the ten victors for reserved seats were first in their wards and three were second. Only two winners of reserved seats came in as low as third. Of the ten elected: the Republicans won six seats, the Congress four. All RPI winners were Jatavs; the Congress supported two victorious Jatavs and two Khatiks.

19. Among the factors we attempted to measure was the impact of types of incumbency. The great movement in affiliations confuses the picture. Thus, of twenty-one incumbents who stood as they had in 1959 (including independents), only eight were elected—virtually the same proportion as those who stood with new affiliations (seven of seventeen). There is little evidence of the importance of *particular* partisan designations for incumbents. In three wards, the matter was complicated by the fact that three incumbents ran against each other.

20. These figures are for the *total votes* cast in each constituency. 160,000 voters actually went to the polls, but only about 257,000 votes were cast—an average "dropoff" of 24.1 percent per ward.

21. Figures for the other party groups were 735 per ticket for the CPI, 720 for the SSP, and only 450 for the BKD in 1968.

22. The weighted votes for the minor principal parties were fifteen for the SSP, seven for the CPI (despite the two corporators that party elected), and six for the BKD.

23. "Drop-off" showed very little difference as between wards with and without reserved seats in 1968. The former exhibited drop-offs of 24.8 percent, whereas wards without reserved seats averaged 23.7 percent. The small difference adds additional weight to the point made earlier: there appeared to be a tightening of margins of difference between candidates for reserved and general seats compared with 1959.

24. The victories of the two Muslims elected on CPI tickets were due less to their party affiliations than to their personal popularity and associations in high-density Muslim constituencies. In one of the wards there was tacit cooperation between the popular Muslim incumbent and a trade unionist sponsored by the CPI despite the presence of a second CPI nominee in the contest.

25. A turnout of 70.6 percent—considerably higher than any in the regularly held elections—is indicative of the level of interest and organizational activity generated for this contest. With only seven candidates in the race, Congress nominees finished first and fourth; less than 200 votes separated them. There was a range from 22.1 to 20.6 percent of the total vote for the four top candidates.

26. The convolutions in these relationships as understood by the men themselves and by other corporators are such as to make the current "straight-forward" narrative appear less complicated than they actually were. For example, the quarrel between Saroj Kumar and Kalyan Das apparently involved some property, but the exact nature of those differences is not known; the two men were at odds politically in 1959, 1962, and 1967.

27. In 1959, sixteen Banias and only seven Brahmins were elected to the corporation. See table 3.5.

28. Seth was supporting Bibhab, whereas Shiv Prasad Gupta inclined toward Babu Lal Singhal and Adiram Singhal favored Mahendra. As a Congress newcomer

to the corporation explained, Singhal's candidacy was intended, in part, to test Bibhab's support: "If Bibhab had gotten ten votes on the first ballot, he might have been able to get the eleventh vote away from Mahendra."

29. Despite the fact that Verma had rejoined the Jan Sangh only in 1966, he was already a member of the body which chose candidates for the corporation elections and a leading spokesman of the party in the corporation.

30. Twelve first-preference votes went to the Republican nominee, presumably ten from members of the RPI and two from the Communist Muslim corporators. The latter had felt uncomfortable about supporting a Jan Sangh nominee.

31. The sixty-first vote was cast by Kalyan Das as mayor. Presumably he backed Ram Narain as did the member from the BKD.

32. The District Executive also ordered the removal of Sutel from his position as City Secretary. A corporator explained: "There were differences at the time of the deputy mayor election between Sutel and the District Secretary of the CPI. Sutel wanted to support the Republicans, while the District Secretary wanted to support Ram Narain Gupta. The two Communist members followed Sutel."

33. Dharia was not a powerful figure in the Poona Congress organization. Indeed, part of the considerable effort he expended on the 1968 municipal elections was directed toward proving to the national leaders of the Congress that he was more than an ideologue i.e., that he could contribute significantly to the electoral and organizational success of the Congress at the local level where it counts.

34. Among local non-Scheduled Caste Congressmen, there was also some resentment against the agreement. In explaining why the Republicans were able to win only two of the six corporation seats for which they were designated, a local Congress leader admitted that not enough attention had been given to "smoothing the feelings of some of the local Congress workers. Some Congress workers felt the Harijans were being thrown upon us and did not work as they should have."

35. The total number of reserved seats available in the Poona corporation in 1968 was reduced from six to four despite an increase from sixty-five to seventy-three in the number of seats contested. This decrease reflects the exclusion of Buddhists from enumeration among the Scheduled Castes counted for reserved seats.

36. Pardeshi applied for a ticket in his own right, but defects in the electoral rolls drawn up for the election meant that he could not run as a candidate. The error was discovered just before the final filing date while he was out of the city.

37. These and other quotations from Thakare are taken from an interview with him held on 15 June 1968.

38. At a National Integration Conference held at Srinagar in June 1968, N. G. Goray recommended that 75 percent of the jobs in public- and private-sector industries in every state should be reserved for the people of the state. This proposal was attacked by several other figures present at the meeting which had been called specifically to recommend a national course of action following a series of communal riots in the spring and summer of 1968. *Times of India,* 22 June 1968.

39. The "sweet reasonableness" of much of this interview may be seen, at least in part, as an attempt by Thakare to play to what he considered to be an American's prejudices. It should be balanced against the incidents of violent attacks on South Indian shops in Bombay and threats of violence held out against those who trafficked with South India, including theaters showing Tamil films. The riots of February 1969, instigated by the Shiv Sena, point away from the moderate facade of the Sena's Poona style. The results of the violence were forty deaths, thousands of injuries, and enormous property damage in Bombay City. The decision by the Sena to force a confrontation with the government may have reflected its situation after the mid-year elections of 1968. As the *Economic and Political Weekly* of 17 August 1968 noted (p. 1266), "Shiv Sena has been able to

make no impact on the conduct of civic affairs [in Bombay].... This demonstration of the futility of the Shiv Sena's election slogans has been accompanied by crushing defeats in civic polls in Poona and Nasik Road. ... As a populist movement without a close-knit party organization, Shiv Sena needs to keep itself in the public eye through flamboyant actions and statements to retain its popular appeal."

40. Interview, 12 July 1968.

41. A stay order prevented the election from being held in one ward. As in the case of K. U. Pardeshi, one of the incumbent corporators who intended to run for the corporation discovered that he was not included on the electoral roll. He insisted upon a clarification of the situation by court action.

42. His situation was further complicated by the fact that he had moved to a new area where there were few Bhois and still won.

43. Thus *Link* wrote, immediately after the elections (30 June 1968, p. 12), "The debacle has virtually silenced Sena Pramukh [chief] Bal Thakare whose immediate reaction, ironically enough, was that 'It is money and communalism' that have succeeded in Poona. His critics have pointed out that the Sena had both money and communalism more than any other group."

44. Candidates in the ward where a stay order had been imposed tried to have the election for mayor stopped on the grounds that one vote might make a difference in the outcome, but neither the courts nor the politicians in the corporation were willing to postpone the elections.

45. An independent wrote his own name next to that of Kadu on the ballot instead of simply marking Kadu's name as he apparently intended.

46. *Poona Herald,* 2 July 1968.

47. Data from Poona covers twenty-four Congressmen, seven members of the Jan Sangh, twelve Sanghatna corporators and three others including the Shiv Sena member. Some data on three other Congressmen and one Jan Sangh corporator is also used in the brief sketch that follows.

48. If three other newcomers were added from whom data was not *directly* collected, this figure would rise to 33.9 years.

49. The remaining Agra corporators interviewed included four landowners, a newspaperman, a union leader, and a man identifiable only as a "social worker."

50. As in 1962, four women were elected to the Poona corporation—two for the Congress, two for the Jan Sangh. In addition, there were about five members who could only be described as "social workers," either because they had no visible source of income, because they were unemployed or because they were supported by members of their extended families. It is commonly believed that certain corporators regularly engaged in certain illicit activities like bootlegging as a major source of income, but evidence on this is fluid.

51. Nothing we have said up to now about the course of Agra politics should lead the reader (or the author) to think he could easily have predicted the outcome of the mid-term elections in Agra in 1969. The Congress recovery proceeded with some success, and the Republicans continued their decline, but the Jan Sangh suffered a considerable setback in Agra as they did elsewhere in Uttar Praddsh.

Agra East saw a startling number of candidates (seventeen), but only three men dominated the outcome. As in 1962 and 1967, these were Dr. P. N. Gupta (Congress), Baloji Agarwal (SSP) and R. S. Agarwal (Jan Sangh). Among them, they captured 95.3 percent of the vote. Gupta was elected with 41 percent to Baloji's 30 and Rama Shanker's 24.

In the Agra Cantonment, Deokinandan Bibhab replaced the incumbent MLA as the nominee of the Congress, and Raj Kumar Sama ran again for the Jan Sangh. The Republicans supported a Muslim candidate. Again, the votes in a nine-man field were concentrated among the top three nominees. Bibhab was elected with 34.9 percent to Sama's 34, while the Republican nominee trailed with 18.

The 1967 race in Agra West, which had seen a Republican nominee barely defeating a Congress candidate, was now followed by a narrow victory of the BKD over the Congress in a field of nine candidates. The BKD winner received only 27.6 of the total vote to Bhogilal Misra's 26.8 percent for the Congress. Khem Chand, former MLA, ran third (19.7 percent) as a Republican, and the Jan Sangh nominee of 1967 was fourth with 18.1 percent.

Thus, the apparent progression from 1962 to 1967, which had seen three-party domination increase from 79 to 85 percent of the total vote cast in the three MLA contests now saw a decline to 72 percent. The Congress candidates improved their party's vote by 4.5 percent, while the Jan Sangh nominees lost about 5 percent and the Republicans declined much more precipitously, the exact amount depending on how one counts apparent nonparticipation in the Agra East contest. By whatever alchemy, the BKD, which had had no following in the city nine months earlier, managed to win one of the three seats in the city and one of the two rural seats located within Seth Achal Singh's MP constituency.

NOTES TO CHAPTER 11

1. The statements in this paragraph and the ones which follow are subject to many qualifications. "Traditionalism" in a large and complex society with a heterogeneous and ancient civilization is obviously open to a variety of readings.

2. One of the functions of the traditional ruler was to maintain the caste system. As Basham writes, "He protected the purity of class and caste by ensuring that those who broke the caste custom were excommunicated." A. L. Basham, *The Wonder That Was India* (New York: Grove Press, 1959), pp. 88-89.

3. "In societies where this type of solidarity is highly developed, the individual does not appear. . . . Individuality is something which the society possesses." Emile Durkheim, *The Division of Labor in Society* (New York: Free Press, 1964), p. 130.

4. A survey of some of the relevant literature is included in M. N. Srinivas, *Social Change in Modern India* (Berkeley: University of California Press, 1966).

5. Organic solidarity depends, to some extent, upon the recognition of individual differences. Societal cohesion is just as strong, but, as Durkheim notes, "The yoke we submit to is much less heavy than when society completely controls us, and it leaves much more place open for the free play of our initiative." Durkheim, p. 131. For a discussion of the role of the city "as essentially a liberalizing rather than radicalizing environment" in this transition, see Irving Louis Horowitz, "Electoral Politics, Urbanization and Social Development in Latin America," *Urban Affairs Quarterly* 2 (March 1967): 3-35.

6. Recent analyses of ethnic behavior in politics include Michael Parenti, "Ethnic Politics and the Persistence of Ethnic Identification," *American Political Science Review* 61 (September 1967): 717-26; and Raymond E. Wolfinger, "The Development and Persistence of Ethnic Voting," *American Political Science Review* 59 (December 1965): 896-908. Also see James Q. Wilson and Edward C. Banfield, "Public Regardingness as a Value Premise in Voting Behavior," *American Political Science Review* 58 (December 1964): 876-87.

7. I am following here a definition of "modernization" which relates it to the quality of organizations elaborated in a given society: "The share of activities controlled by spontaneous responses is reduced by increasing efficiency or productivity of activities, by increasing emphasis on calculated social relations (formal organizations), by increasingly instrumental views of human relations (universalism, performance-orientation, etc.), by increasing specialization in the scholarly development of theories or doctrines (science, legal scholarship, etc.) and by increasing control over socialization by such scholars (formal education)." Arthur Stinchcombe, "Review Symposium," *American Sociological Review* 31 (April 1966): 266.

8. These points are made in a large literature dealing with the activation of "caste" in India's democratic politics. The most important items include: Lloyd I.

Rudolph and Susanne Hoeber Rudolph, *The Modernity of Tradition: Political Development in India* (Chicago: University of Chicago Press, 1967), esp. pt. 1; Rajni Kothari and Rushikesh Maru, "Caste and Secularism in India," *Journal of Asian Studies* 25 (November 1965): 33-50; F. G. Bailey, *Politics and Social Change* (Berkeley: University of California Press, 1963), esp. pp. 122-35.

9. Selig Harrison, *India: The Most Dangerous Decades* (Princeton: Princeton University Press, 1960) includes a detailed account of the conflicts between the Reddis and the Kammas in Andhra and references to the Brahmin and non-Brahmin differences in the politics of Maharashtra and Madras.

10. The sources of these discontents were, in part, urban in character; it is also from urban areas that discontent with perceived distortions in the democratic system may be radiating out to attract support from older elites. For a discussion of these and related problems, see my "Deurbanization, Elite Displacement and Political Change in India," *Comparative Politics* 2 (January 1970). This stratum of contemporary society is very different in perspective from the Gandhians, whose political ambitions would return India to a form of societal segmentation lauded by Gandhi as "village republics."

11. The events which followed the 1967 elections in many of the Indian states simply duplicated within the political system, as a whole, much of the self-aggrandizing politics which previously was commonplace *within* the Congress. Compare, for example, the accounts of Congress politics in Uttar Pradesh (at district and state levels) in Paul R. Brass, *Factional Politics in an Indian State* (Berkeley: University of California Press, 1965) with his recent review of "Coalition Politics in North India," *American Political Science Review* 62 (December 1968): 1174-91.

12. Owen M. Lynch, *The Politics of Untouchability: Social Mobility and Social Change in a City of India* (New York: Columbia University Press, 1969).

13. Of course, this argument can be overstated. There always have been devices by which individuals and groups manipulated the operations of supposedly "rigid" bureaucracies. In India, the domination of lower-echelon positions of the bureaucracy by certain communities historically gave them control over information and resources which made those nominally their superiors dependent upon them for a definition of the "facts" involved in any given decision. For one discussion of this phenomenon during the early period of the British in India, see Robert K. Frykenberg, "Elite Groups in a South Indian District," *Journal of Asian Studies* 24 (February 1965): 261-82. There is no reason to assume these behaviors were halted under the supposedly more thoroughgoing ICS.

14. Myron Weiner, *The Politics of Scarcity* (Chicago: University of Chicago Press, 1962), esp. pp. 230-37. While Weiner does not adequately spell out the theoretical basis of this argument in any detail, it seems to assume a "zero-sum" approach to conflict in Indian society. Unfortunately, much of Indian politics seems to respond to a form of Parkinson's law: "Conflict expands to take advantage of those political arenas made available."

15. For a discussion of the effects of the "participative ethos" in several policy areas at the community level in the United States, see Robert L. Crain and Donald B. Rosenthal, "Community Status as a Dimension of Local Decision-Making," *American Sociological Review* 32 (December 1967): 970-84.

16. In this connection, see Daniel Elazar, " 'Fragmentation' and Local Organizational Response to Federal-City Programs," *Urban Affairs Quarterly* 2 (June 1967), esp. pp. 39-42.

17. Major examples of such studies are cited above in chap. 1.

18. The decisional approach is commonly identified with Robert A. Dahl, *Who Governs?* (New Haven: Yale University Press, 1961), and Edward C. Banfield, *Political Influence* (New York: Free Press, 1961). The reputational technique grows out of the work of Floyd Hunter, *Community Power Structure* (Chapel Hill: University of North Carolina Press, 1953).

19. The viability of such methods in highly institutionalized settings may account for their apparent utility in Mexico, Venezuela, and other Latin American settings. See, for example, the items cited in chap. 1, n. 3 and Gary Hoskin, "Power Structure in a Venezuelan Town: The Case of San Cristobal," *International Journal of Comparative Sociology* 9 (September and December 1968): 188-207.

20. While functional models of political systems may be suggestive at the level of comparisons among nations, they do not seem particularly relevant when dealing with subunits of those political systems. A case in point is the model developed in Gabriel A. Almond and G. Bingham Powell, Jr., *Comparative Politics: A Development Approach* (Boston: Little, Brown, 1966). The state of theory (or the lack of it) in the comparative study of local government is indicated in Robert R. Alford, "Explanatory Variables in the Comparative Study of Urban Administration and Politics," in Robert T. Daland (ed.), *Comparative Urban Research* (Beverly Hills: Sage Publications, 1969).

21. In addition to a number of Indian scholars whose recent work bears on urban political phenomena (Ram Joshi in Bombay, V. M. Sirsikar in Poona), a group of young American scholars have been engaged in studies of political subjects in various cities of India which promise to add much to our substantive and theoretical understanding of India's cities: Richard Blue (Faridabad), Roderick Church (Lucknow), Rodney Jones (Indore), Peter Mayer (Bhopal and Tiruchirapalli), Philip Oldenburg (Delhi), William Vanderbok (Agra).

22. In Italian society, as Joseph La Palombara has described it, the nation is segmented into two distinct parts: Catholic and Communist, each with its associated networks of voluntary organizations. La Palombara, "Italy: Fragmentation, Isolation and Alienation," in Lucian W. Pye and Sidney Verba (eds.), *Political Culture and Political Development* (Princeton: Princeton University Press, 1965), pp. 199-244. On the other hand, a highly segmented polity may function reasonably well under certain conditions, as Arend Lijphart suggests in his work on the Netherlands, *Politics of Accommodation: Pluralism and Democracy in the Netherlands* (Berkeley: University of California Press, 1968), and in his "Typologies of Democratic Systems," *Comparative Political Studies* 1 (April 1968): 3-44. Also see Michael W. Suleiman, *Political Parties in Lebanon: The Challenge of a Fragmented Political Culture* (Ithaca: Cornell University Press, 1967).

23. William Kornhauser, *The Politics of Mass Society* (Glencoe: The Free Press, 1957).

NOTES TO APPENDIX

1. For presentation of these data see chapter 5, pp. 124-32, and chapter 8, pp. 204-7.

2. Response rates vary with each item and from city to city. A total of 180 responses was possible in Agra and 195 in Poona. For item 1, response rates were 73 percent in Agra and 86 percent in Poona. Those receiving more than three nominations in each city constituted 74 percent of all nominations on that item in Agra, 82 percent in Poona.

3. Buddha received three nominations in Poona.

4. Thus, in Poona, portraits of Shivaji are to be found everywhere including behind the mayor's podium in the corporation hall. The completion of a new municipally funded theater in 1968 in Poona was accompanied by the placing of a large equestrian statue of Laxmibai on the theater grounds. For a discussion of political symbology in India and other new nations, see McKim Marriott, "Cultural Policy in the New States," in Clifford Geertz, *Old Societies and New States* (New York: Free Press, 1963), esp. pp. 30-41.

5. For the organization of these categories, see chapter 5, p. 126.

6. In Agra, where Gandhi's scores (on the measure developed) range up to a +4 for his Congress support, Ambedkar receives a +10 on low-ethclass support and a

+8 for Republican Party backing. No ethclass score gets above +3 in Poona for this same item.

7. Unfortunately, it was not possible to repeat these items with the new corporators in 1968.

8. In addition to these individuals, the two lists include the names of Vinoba Bhave, a Gandhian disciple who leads the *Sarvodaya* movement, and Jayaprakash Narayan, former Socialist leader who left party work to follow Bhave but has continued to play a "nonpartisan" role in national politics.

9. Like Shastri, who succeeded to the prime ministership of India and then died early in 1966, Sarvarkar and D. D. Upadhya have both died since interviews were held.

10. Except for Maurya, *all* the persons on the Agra state list were with the Congress in 1964.

11. N. V. Gadgil, who also appears on both the state and local lists for Poona, was the city's MP until 1957. He succeeded Potdar in 1964 as Vice-Chancellor of the University but died in early 1966 and was followed into that office by D. R. Gadgil. The latter was appointed to the Planning Commission by the Prime Minister in 1967.

12. While esteem may not be *directly* convertible into influence, it is presumably a resource base which can be employed by persons with skill to maximize their influence over others. The two lists do include local people who have wielded considerable influence: Seth Achal Singh, Paliwal, Adiram Singhal, and Rawat in Agra; Joshi, Sanas, and Goray in Poona. Others on the list, of course, could not properly be seen as politically influential.

Abbreviations

AEO	Assistant Executive Officer
AICC	All-India Congress Committee
BJS (or JS)	Bharatiya Jan Sangh ("Indian People's Party")
BKD	Bharatiya Kranti Dal ("Indian Revolutionary Party")
BPCC	Bombay Pradesh ("Provincial") Congress Committee
CBI	Central Bureau of Investigation
CEO	Chief Executive Officer (same as MNA)
CPI	Communist Party of India
CSP	Congress Socialist Party
DM	District Magistrate (also Deputy Commissioner or Collector)
IAS	Indian Administrative Service (so called after Independence)
ICS	Indian Civil Service (so called before Independence)
JS (or BJS)	Jan Sangh
KAVAL	Kanpur, Allahabad, Varanasi, Agra, and Lucknow.
KMPP	Kisan Mazdoor Praja Party ("Peasants', Workers', and People's Party")
MLA	Member of Legislative Assembly (now Vidhan Sabha)
MLC	Member of the Legislative Council (now Vidhan Parishad)
MNA	Mukhya Nagar Adhikari ("Chief City Officer"; same as CEO)
MP	Member of Parliament
MPCC	Maharashtra Pradesh ("Provincial") Congress Committee
NS	Nagri Sanghatna ("City Party")
PMT	Poona Municipal Transport
PSP	Praja Socialist Party
PWD	Public Works Department
PWP	Peasants and Workers Party
RPI	Republican Party of India
RSD	Rashtriya Seva Dal ("National Service Group")
RSS	Rashtriya Swayamsevak Sangh ("National Volunteers' Organization")
SCF	Scheduled Caste Federation
SD	Swatantra Dal ("Independent Group")

SMS	Samyukta Maharashtra Samiti ("United Maharashtra Committee"). After 1967, the Sampoorna ("Complete") Maharashtra Samiti.
SRC	States Reorganization Commission
SSP	Samyukta Socialist Party
SVD	Samyukta Vidhayak Dal ("United Administrative Group")
UPCC	United Provinces Congress Committee (before Independence)
	Uttar Pradesh ("Northern Province") Congress Committee (after Independence)

Glossary

ayurvedic	traditional form of Indian medicine
bharatiya	Indian
crore	10,000,000 (lit., 1,00,00,000)
dacoit	robber, robbers (usually operating in groups)
dal	party; group
gali	neighborhood of a city (Maharashtra)
gaon; gram	village
goonda	"strong arm" man
jan, jana, janta	people
jati	functional units of Indian caste system
kisan	peasant
lakh	100,000 (lit., 1,00,000)
Lok Sabha	House of the People (Lower House of Indian Parliament)
mandal	committee; also used as ward level unit of party organization in North India
mahapalika	(municipal) corporation
mazdoor	worker
mohalla	neighborhood; city ward (Uttar Pradesh)
Mukhya Nagar Adhikari	Chief Executive Officer (lit., Chief City Officer)
nagar; nagri	city
Nagar Mahapalika	municipal corporation (Uttar Pradesh)
panchayat	originally any executive or decisional body of five men; now the units of rural government
panchayati raj	the system of rural government introduced into India after 1958
peth	traditional ward or section of Poona
pradesh	state; province
praja	people
Rajya Sabha	House of the States (Upper House of Parliament)
rashtriya	national
sabha	body; association; organization
samiti	committee; body

350

sampoorna	complete; final
samyukta	united
sangh; sanghatna	organization; party; association
swatantra	independent
swayamsevak	volunteer
taalim	sports; exercise (club)
taluka; tehsil	subdistrict administrative and governmental level
utso	festival
vaid	practitioner of ayurvedic medicine
varna	broad status category associated with caste system
Vidhan Parishad	Upper House of Indian State Legislatures
Vidhan Sabha	Lower House of Indian State Legislatures
zamindar	One who has a high claim on the produce of land as the result of a land tenure system allowing for the sub-infeudation of land without cultivation. System formally abolished after 1947.
zilla	district
zilla parishad	highest unit of district government under *panchayati raj* system

Index of Persons Mentioned

Adhav, B. P. ("Bhau"), 277; "socially conscious leader of the PSP," 106
Agarwal, Bal Krishna. *See* Baloji
Agarwal, B. P., 222
Agarwal, Harihar Nath, 228, 233
Agarwal, M. H., 95-96, 336 n. 20; as independent sponsoring agenda items, 171
Agarwal, Rama Shanker, 218, 219, 225-27, 343 n. 51; as "D," 130
Ambedkar, B. R., 35, 54, 99, 116, 297-99 passim; studies of, 315 n. 23
Ambesh, Chhatrapati, 220-21, 338 n. 23
Apte, B. P., 148, 240; "a Brahmin doctor" in Congress, 119, 147
Atre, P. K., 82, 177, 339 n. 29

Baloji, 37-38, 210, 224, 254; in general elections, 38, 166, 218-19, 226-27, 252, 343 n. 51; in municipal politics, 62-63, 75-77, 135, 166
Barve, S. G., 118; as administrator, 80-81, 193, 195; in politics, 81, 82, 87, 239, 246
Bhagwat, G. P.: chairman, Standing Committee, 173; Jan Sangh candidate for mayor, 147, 148, 277; as "L," 130, 131
Bhandare, D. D., 339 n. 29
Bhonsale, "Chhatrapati" Shivaji. *See* Shivaji
Bibhab, Deokinandan: in general elections, 219-20, 314 n. 13, 343 n. 51; in municipal politics, 251, 261-62
Bipra, Banwari Lal, 337 n. 6; as "BLB," 69-70
Bohrey Ram Gopal, 143-44, 145-46
Bux, Haji Haider, 218, 221-22

Charan Singh, 190, 246, 253, 301; as Chief Minister, 192, 217
Chaturvedi, S. N., 151, 303, 338 n. 23; in municipal politics, 134-35, 143-44, 261
Chavan, Y. B., 87, 299-305 passim; interventions in Poona, 55, 80, 198, 238-39, 265, 335 n. 17; leader of Maharashtra, 29, 51, 53-55, 57, 79, 237; study of, 317 n. 48

Dange, S. A., 237, 340 n. 2
Dayanand, Swami, 295, 296, 316 n. 27
Deo, Shankarrao, 42
Desai, D. S. ("Balasaheb"), 301-5 passim
Desai, Morarji, 51, 54, 299-301 passim

Deshmukh, Datta, 237
Dharia, Mohan, 198-99, 264, 265, 318 n. 56
Dhere, Shivajirao, 55, 56, 100, 264; as "K," 130, 131
Dhulup, K. N., 237

Elphinstone, Mountstuart, 7

Fernandes, George, 340 n. 2

Gadgil, N. V., 42, 44, 50, 52, 301, 303, 347 n. 11
Gadgil, V. N., 239; as member of Election Committee, 264
Gaikwad, B. K., 299, 300; in Congress alliance, 265, 339 n. 33; leader of Republican Party, 99, 213, 322 n. 12
Gandhi, Indira, 299, 300, 337 n. 11, 338 n. 13
Gandhi, "Mahatma" M. K., 35, 37, 39, 297-99
Ghosh, Atulya, 326 n. 18
Girme, K. T., 81, 83, 243, 303
Gogate, V. B., 149, 237; as Hindu Mahasabha leader, 171; as "M," 130, 131
Gokhale, G. K., 8; study of, 308 n. 31
Golwalkar, "Gurusi" M. S., 37, 299-301 passim
Goray, N. G., 109, 118, 268, 301, 302, 342 n. 38; in general elections, 81, 82; in municipal politics, 84, 148-49, 151; as Praja Socialist Party leader, 40-41, 236-37; in Samyukta Maharashtra movement, 50, 52
Gupta, C. B., 301, 303; in Agra politics, 137, 166, 229; factional leader in Uttar Pradesh, 32-33, 216, 217, 225, 228
Gupta, Dr. Prakash Narayan, 106, 126-27, 151, 263; as "C," 130, 131; as deputy mayor, 144, 145-46, 155-57, 162-63, 331 n. 5; in general elections, 218-19, 226-27, 343 n. 51; in municipal elections, 63, 136, 137, 143; as leader of the Republican Party, 146, 212-13, 226
Gupta, Ram Chand, 33, 136, 137-39, 142, 166, 261
Gupta, Ram Narain, 263
Gupta, Shiv Prasad, 33, 229; in district and state politics, 216, 338 n. 21; in municipal politics, 138, 251, 259, 341 n. 28

Hiray, B. S. ("Bhausaheb"), 51
Hiro Rani, 230-31

Jagtap, B. G., 84-85, 88, 100, 147, 303-4; as "Q," 130-31
Jain, Chandra Bhan, 259
Jain, Kalyan Das, 135, 258-59, 263; in corporation politics, 77, 135, 146; in mayoral contests, 135-37, 138, 142, 262
Jain, Raj Mukat, 259, 262
Jain, Saroj Kumar, 259, 262, 263
Jain, Sohanlal, 258-59; in Congress organization (as "President" or "former" President), 61, 76, 214-15; in general elections, 219, 229
Jedhe, K. M., 42, 44, 50
Jog, B. P., 147-49, 151, 236-37, 240
Johri, C. D., 250-51, 262-63
Joshi, S. M., 109, 118, 149, 268, 299-304 passim; in general elections, 44, 52, 81, 82, 237, 238-39; in municipal politics, 84, 236-37; in Samyukta Maharashtra movement, 50, 52; as leader of socialist parties, 40-41, 236

Kadu, D. S., 96-97, 277
Kamaraj, K., 299, 300, 330 n. 15
Kamble, B. C., 99, 322 n. 12, 339 n. 29
Karale, B. D. ("BDK"), 98, 275, 331 n. 27
Ken, Karan Singh, 220-21
Khem Chand: in general elections, 218, 219-20, 326 n. 26, 344 n. 51; as "I," 130, 131; as mayoral candidate, 135, 136; political recruitment, 76-77; in Republican Party, 213, 214, 340 n. 12
Kher, B. G., 42
Kidwai, Rafi Ahmed, 31, 32, 297, 298
Killedar, B. D., 148, 149, 171, 240-41, 336 n. 23
Kirad, S. H., 147, 148, 173-74
Kripalani, "Acharya" J. B., 31
Kripalani, Sucheta, 217, 334 n. 10
Krishna Menon, V. K., 239, 246, 339 n. 33
Kunzru, Raj Nath, 218, 220

Lachman Das, 230-31, 258
Lohia, Ram Manohar, 41, 235-36, 237

Mahendra(ji), 262, 279
Manohar Lal, 258
Man Singh, 72-73, 214, 229-30, 252
Mate, Namderao, 241, 277; "President of the Poona Congress," 85, 100
Maurya, B. P., 212-13, 217, 299-303 passim
Mehra, B. K., 135-37, 151, 330 n. 17
Mehta, Asoka, 43
Mhalgi, R. K., 82, 239-40, 269
Misra, Bhogilal, 32, 34, 258; in general elections, 229, 231, 344 n. 51
More, S. S., 42, 43, 81-82, 238, 240, 303

Naagar, Suraj Bhan, 220-21
Naik, V. P. (Vasantrao), 194, 237, 301, 302

Narain, Raj, 255-56
Nehru, Jawaharlal, 299-301 passim, 335 n.17

Paliwal, S. K. D., 221, 222, 228, 301-4 passim; in general elections, 31, 34; in municipal politics, 251, 319 n. 10; as a political leader, 30-31, 216
Pardeshi, K. U., 83, 84, 147-50 passim, 267, 343 n. 41
Parulekar, N. B., 45, 84, 85, 318 n. 50, 322 n. 15
Patel, "Sardar" Vallabhbhai, 41, 297-99 passim, 316 n. 32
Patil, S. K., 318 n. 51, 340 n. 2
Phool Singh, 213; "President of the City Republican Party," 146; as "G," 130, 131
Phule, "Mahatma" Jyotiba, 117, 295-99 passim; study of, 308 n. 31
Pipil, Gopi Chand, 212-13, 314 n. 13; "President of the Republican Party," 63, 76-77

Rawat, Jagan Prasad, 32-33, 135, 221, 301-4 passim; in district politics, 32, 216, 338 n. 20; in municipal politics, 61, 70, 251; in state politics, 33, 61, 217, 229
Ripon, Lord, 16-17

Sama, Raj Kumar, 249, 258, 263; in general elections, 220, 228, 343 n. 51
Sanas, B. N. ("Baburao"), 150, 241, 264, 303-5; in Congress, 49, 51, 54, 112, 238; in general elections, 51-52, 81, 83; in municipal politics, 45, 46
Satav, P. G., 149, 150, 321 n. 11; "Jan Sangh Mali," 56
Sathi, Cheddilal, 212-13, 213-14
Savarkar, V. D. ("Veer"), 39, 299-302 passim
Sharma, A. P., 229-30
Sharma, Shiv Dutt, 253
Shiromani, P. N., 76, 340 n. 9; as "H," 130, 131
Shivaji, 7-8, 79, 295-97, 305
Singh, Karan, 256
Singh, Mahipal, 226-27
Singh, Seth Achal, 303, 304; as Congress leader, 31-32, 337 n. 9; in corporation politics, 61, 111, 134, 138, 251, 341 n. 28; in general elections, 31, 218, 221-22, 224, 230-31, 233; in the municipality, 21, 312 n. 73
Singhal, Adiram, 32, 135, 215, 303, 304; in general elections, 38, 218-19, 225, 228; in municipal politics, 61, 70, 251, 341 n. 28
Singhal, Babu Lal, 261-62; as "A," 130-31
Sone, Ram Prasad, 263-64
Sutel, Roshan Lal: in Communist Party, 215, 253, 259, 342 n. 32; in Congress, 70-72, 214-15

Tandon, Dr. Ladli Prasad, 151; as deputy mayor, 135, 142-43, 144-45, 166; as "E," 130; "Khatri doctor," 110

Telang, R. V., 55, 81, 82, 242-43
Thakare, Bal, 269-70
Tilak, "Lokmanya" B. G., 8, 39, 117, 297-99; study of, 308 n. 31
Tilak, J. S. (Jayantrao), 50, 52, 84, 237
Tripathi, Kamlapati, 216-17, 225, 228, 301
Tupe, R. D., 243

Upadhyaya, Deen Dayal, 37, 299, 300

Vadake, R. P. (Ram), 97, 98, 175, 242-43
Vaidya, B. S. ("Bhai"), 150; as "N," 130
Vajpayee, Atal Behari, 37, 255
Verma, Ram Babu, 37, 75, 155-56, 248, 262; as "B," 130

Subject and Author Index

Administrative Officer, Poona School Committee, 158, 196-97
Administrators: attitudes of, in Agra, 181, 187-89, 190-92; attitudes of, in Poona, 181, 192-93, 200-201; recruitment of, in Agra, 185-87, 190-92; recruitment of, in Poona, 158-59, 195-97; in two cities, compared, 24, 180-81, 208-9. *See also* Bureaucratic politics; Political conflicts
Adrian, Charles R., 102-3, 306 n. 2
Agarwal, H. C., 311 n. 55
Agarwal, Partap C., 320 n. 15
Agarwals. *See* Banias
Agger, Robert E., et al., 306 n. 2, n. 5
Agra: bureaucratic factionalism in, 181-92; character of city, 5-6, 9-13; corporation politics, 75-78, 133-46, 159-67, 258-64; governmental organization in, 19, 21-22, 23-25, 153-57; political organization in, 30-38, 59-67, 210-17, 248-55; studies of, 308 n. 18, n. 20, 309 n. 35, 310 n. 46, 312 n. 73, 315 n. 21, 332 n. 15. *See also* Elections, corporation; Elections, general
Ahmedabad, 322 n. 14
Aldermen, 23, 75, 258-61. *See also* Corporators
Alford, Robert R., 307 n. 11, 346 n. 20
Alliances, 134, 322 n. 14; electoral agreements, 217, 221-22, 247, 265; fusion organizations, 44-45, 51-52, 83-84, 235-38, 268; governmental coalitions, in Agra, 75, 133-35, 142, 143, 145-46, 261-64; governmental coalitions, in Poona, 147-51, 276-77; types of, 29-30
Almond, Gabriel A., 346 n. 20
Ambedkerites. *See* Republican Party
Apter, David E., 28
Argal, R., 308 n. 14, 327 n. 32, 336 n. 25
Arya Samaj, 36, 296, 337 n. 1; study of, 316 n. 27
Ashraf, Ali, 311 n. 63
Assistant Executive Officers (AEO's), 181-83, 195-96, 205-7. *See also* Administrators, recruitment of
Avadi resolution, 41, 43

Ballhatchet, Kenneth, 308 n. 26, n. 28
Banias, 10-11, 13; in politics, 110, 125-29, 280

Banfield, Edward C., 306 n. 6, 313 n. 2, n. 3, 344 n. 6, 345 n. 18
Bare adme ("Big men"), 35-36, 214, 220, 260. *See also* Jatavs
Barrier, Norman G., 316 n. 27
Basham, A. L., 344 n. 2
Bayley, David H., 326 n. 20
Bendix, Reinhard, 310 n. 50
Bharatiya Kranti Dal (BKD), 246, 253, 254, 343 n. 51
Bharatiya Mazdoor Paksa (BMP). *See* Mangs
Bhois, 98, 275
Blue, Richard N., 346 n. 21
Boman-Behram, B. K., 307 n. 13
Bombay City, 16, 17; corporators, 120, 325 n. 9; electoral politics in, 64-65, 239, 246-47, 320 n. 18, 339 n. 29; Samyukta Maharashtra movement, 49, 53, 318 n. 49; studies of, 308 n. 15, 318 n. 49, 319 n. 7
Bombay Pradesh Congress Committee (BPCC), 246, 318 n. 51
Bondurant, Joan V., 317 n. 46
Brahme, Sulabha, 319 n. 61, 321 n. 2
Brahmins, 11, 33. *See also* Chitpavan Brahmins; Non-Brahminism
Brass, Paul R., 30, 31, 308 n. 16, 313 n. 6, 314 n. 8, 339 n. 1, 345 n. 11
Brecher, Michael, 318 n. 56
Buddhists, 10, 109; studies of, 315 n. 21, n. 23. *See also* Jatavs; Mahars
Bureaucratic politics, 162, 182-85, 190-92. *See also* Political conflicts
Burger, Angela S., 316 n. 29

Calcutta, 311 n. 63, 322 n. 14, 334 n. 8; studies of, 308 n. 15, 311 n. 63, 313 n. 6
Candidacies. *See* Party crystallization
Cantonments, 15-16
Carras, Mary, 310 n. 51
Caste. *See* Primordial groups
Chand, Gyan, 203
Chapman, Brian, 312 n. 75
Chatterjee, Atul Chandra, 308 n. 24
Chauhan, D. S., 308 n. 20, n. 21
Chief Executive Officer (CEO), 15, 181, 185-86, 187-88; in local controversies, Agra, 138-40, 181-82, 184-85, 188-89; in local controversies, Poona, 175, 193-95; powers of, 22-23, 25, 166, 181

Chitpavan Brahmins, 7, 8, 273; studies of, 308 n. 31, 316 n. 30, n. 35. *See also* Non-Brahminism
Chopra, P. N., 314 n. 11, n. 15
Church, Roderick, 328 n. 44, 346 n. 21
Clark, Terry N., 306 n. 4
Coalitions. *See* Alliances
Collector. *See* District Magistrate
Communal riots, 340 n. 5; in Poona, 39, 45, 149, 176. *See also* Primordial groups
Communist Party of India (CPI): in Agra, 38, 215, 228, 253-54, 262-64; in Poona, 40, 55, 237, 271, 318 n. 57
Community power, studies of, 307-8
Conflicts. *See* Demonstrations; Political conflicts; Political violence
Conflict management, 102-3, 172-73; mechanisms for, 28-30, 111, 163-65, 178-79
Congress Party, 26-27, 125-29; in Agra corporation, 76-77, 133-46 passim, 172-73, 191, 261-64; in Agra politics, 22, 30-34, 60-62, 214-17, 250-52; in Maharashtra, 41-43, 54, 83, 238, 265, 310 n. 51, 335 n. 15; in Poona corporation, 56, 85-87, 147-51, 168, 197-200, 277; in Poona politics, 39, 44-46, 85, 241, 275-76; studies of, 313 n. 1, n. 6, 314 n. 7; in Uttar Pradesh, 21-22, 59-60, 225-26, 247-48, 315 n. 20. *See also* Party crystallization; Voting behavior
Congress Socialist Party (CSP), 41; study of, 314 n. 8. *See also* Praja Socialist Party; Socialist Party
Corporations, municipal: functions of, 114-23, 177-79, 285-90; organization of, 22-25, 153-59; origins of form, 16-22; studies of, 311 n. 63, 312 n. 68, 313 n. 80, n. 81, 332 n. 15. *See also* Municipal expenditures
Corporators, 23, 59, 61, 204-7; characteristics of, 104-7, 278-79; interpersonal relations among, 120-21, 124-32; interventions by, 119-22, 157, 163-65, 195-97; satisfactions and services of, 114-23, 163-65. *See also* Incumbency; Political conflicts
Corruption: in administration, 18, 122, 139, 166, 190, 201-4; among politicians, 123, 166
Crain, Robert L., et al., 307 n. 8, 345 n. 15
Cross, C. M. P., 311 n. 59
Cutright, Phillips, 307 n. 10

Dahl, Robert A., 306 n. 1, 324 n. 40, 345 n. 18
Daland, Robert T., 307 n. 11, 346 n. 20
D'Antonio, William V., 306 n. 1, n. 3
Das, R. B., 312 n. 68, n. 69
Delimitation, 320 n. 18; in Agra, 74, 225, 256; in Poona, 88-89, 238, 271
Demonstrations, 176-77, 326 n. 20, 339 n. 26. *See also* Samyukta Maharashtra
Deogirikar, T. R., 317 n. 47

Deputy Commissioner. *See* District Magistrate
Deputy Mayors: elections, in Agra, 142-46, 263-64; elections, in Poona, 147-51, 277, 318 n. 58; legal position of, 23-24, 162-63
Deshpande, Narayan R., 317 n. 38, 318 n. 52, n. 54
Development Committee (Agra), 24, 153-55
District Magistrate, 15
Disqualification cases, 139-42
Divisional Commissioner, 15, 184
Dravida Munnetra Kazagham (DMK), 247
"Drop-off," 338 n. 17; in Agra, 1959, 69-70, 72, 73; in Agra, 1968, 341 n. 20, n. 23
Durkheim, Emile, 282-83
Dushkin, Lelah, 309 n. 41

Education, 117-18; in Agra, 156, 331 n. 6, n. 7; in Poona, 20, 24, 25, 158-59, 176. *See also* Administrative Officer
Ehrlich, Howard J., 306 n. 1
Elazar, Daniel J., 345 n. 16
Elections, corporation: in Agra, 59-78, 246-61; in Poona, 45-49, 52-54, 83-100, 264-76. *See also* Alliances
Elections, general: in Agra, 31, 217-34, 315 n. 25, 343 n. 51; in Poona, 44, 51-52, 79-83, 234-44
Erdman, Howard L., 315 n. 19
Ethclass, 105-6, 125-29
Executive Committee (Agra), 24, 121-22, 153-57, 163

Factionalism, 22, 28-29, 57, 182-85, 314 n. 7, n. 8, n. 9. *See also* Political parties
Firozabad, 309 n. 36, n. 40
Flood, in Poona politics, 56, 79-80, 170; studies of, 321 n. 2, n. 3
Form, William H., 306 n. 3
Frykenberg, Robert K., 345 n. 13
Fusion organizations. *See* Alliances

Gali samitis, 112-13. See also *Mohalla samitis*
Ganesh utso, 112, 267
Gole, Prakash, 319 n. 61, 321 n. 2
Gorakhpur, 19
Gordon, Milton, 105
Greenstone, J. David, 307 n. 12
Grimshaw, Allen, 321 n. 2
Gupta, Ram Gautum, 313 n. 81

Harrison, Selig, 345 n. 9
Hart, Henry C., 64-65, 308 n. 15, 327 n. 30
Hazelhurst, Leighton W., 314 n. 14
Hindu Mahasabha, 176-77; in general elections, 50, 237; organization, 37, 57-58, 245; in Poona corporation elections, 45, 84, 268
Homophily index, 125
Horowitz, Irving Louis, 344 n. 5
Hunter, Floyd, 307 n. 1, 345 n. 18
Huntington, Samuel P., 321 n. 22
Hyderabad, 334 n. 8

Ideational groups, 27, 30, 36-41, 178. *See also* Political parties
Improvement Committee (Poona), 174
Improvement Trust (Agra), 22, 24, 160, 183
Incumbency, as electoral factor, 101-2, 114-16, 179, 248, 274-75
Indian Administrative Service (IAS), 22, 181, 311 n. 54

Jains, 11, 160, 258-59. *See also* Banias
Jangam, R. T., 318 n. 49, 319 n. 8, 325 n. 9
Jan Sangh, 30, 57, 125-29, 133, 244-45; in Agra corporation, 75-77, 141-42, 145-46, 191, 261-64, 277; in Agra politics, 37-38, 62-63, 210-12, 248-50; in Poona corporation, 147-51, 175-76; in Poona politics, 39-40, 85-86, 87-88, 237-38, 268-69, 318 n. 59; studies of, 314 n. 8, 316 n. 29
Janta Aghadi, 271
Jatavs, 34-36, 218. *See also* Republican Party
Jha, Chetakar, 308 n. 14
Jones, Rodney, 346 n. 21
Joshi, Ram, 310 n. 51, 346 n. 21
Judicial decisions. *See* Legal cases

Kanpur, 59-60, 329 n. 8, n. 15; studies of, 313 n. 81, 332 n. 15
Kaplan, Harold, 307 n. 12
Karve, D. D., 308 n. 31
Kasais, 93-95
Kaufman, Herbert, 333 n. 21
KAVAL cities, 312 n. 67; administration of, 189-90, 216-17, 332 n. 15; politics in, 59-60, 134, 142, 247-48
Keer, Dhanajay, 308 n. 31
Kesari, 50, 82, 86
Kesselman, Mark, 307 n. 12, 312 n. 75
Khatiks, 253, 340 n. 8, 341 n. 18
Kirloskar company, 279; head of, 303-4
Kisan Mazdoor Praja Party (KMPP), 31, 41; study of, 314 n. 8
Klapp, Orrin E., 306 n. 3
Kochanek, Stanley A., 313 n. 1, 314 n. 11
Koris, 248-49
Kornhauser, William, 293
Kosambi, D. D., 308 n. 22
Kothari, Rajni, 314 n. 7, 325 n. 15, 343 n. 8
Kulkarni, Ataram Ganesh, 316 n. 37, n. 38
Kumaramangalam, S. Mohan, 331 n. 4

Lambert, Richard D., 309 n. 37, 310 n. 44, n. 45
La Palombara, Joseph, 326 n. 19, 346 n. 22
Legal cases, 138-44, 182, 184-85, 323 n. 32, 331 n. 5
Lijphart, Arend, 346 n. 22
Lipset, Seymour Martin, 307 n. 10
Lohia Socialist Party. *See* Socialist Party (Lohia)
Lynch, Owen M., 315 n. 21, n. 24, n. 26, 337 n. 7, 345 n. 12

Madras, 308 n. 15
Mahajan Commission, 237
Maharashtra, political studies of, 316 n. 30, n. 35, n. 37, 317 n. 46, n. 47, n. 48
Maharashtra Pradesh Congress Committee (MPCC), 316 n. 38, 318 n. 51, 340 n. 4; relations with Poona Congress, 56, 85, 174, 243, 245, 264
Maharashtra (State) Electricity Board, 167-69
Mahars, 35, 54, 117; political activation of, 35, 43, 83. *See also* Republican Party
Maheshwari, B., 310 n. 50
Maheshwari, Shriram, 320 n. 17
Malis, 52-53, 113
Mangs, 265, 274
Mangudkar, M. P., 311 n. 62, 312 n. 70, n. 71, 321 n. 6
Marathas, 10-11. *See also* Congress Party, in Maharashtra; Congress Party, in Poona politics; Non-Brahminism
Marriott, McKim, 346 n. 4
Maru, Rushikesh, 325 n. 15, 345 n. 8
Mayer, Adrian C., 64, 309 n. 42
Mayer, Peter, 346 n. 21
Mayors: election of, in Agra, 133-42, 261-63; election of, in Poona, 147-51, 276-77; powers of, 23-24, 188
Meos, 73
Miller, Delbert C., 306 n. 3
Miller, William Lee, 333 n. 21
Minocha, A. C., 336 n. 25
Mohalla samitis, 68-69, 110-11, 156. See also *Gali samitis*
Moreland, W. H., 308 n. 24
Morris-Jones, W. H., 314 n. 7, 328 n. 41
Mukhya Nagar Adhikari (MNA). *See* Chief Executive Officer
Municipal arenas, 287-89, 307 n. 9
Municipal Commissioner. *See* Chief Executive Officer
Municipal committee, form of government, 17, 20-22; studies of, 307 n. 13, n. 14, 312 n. 64
Municipal corporations. *See* Corporations
Municipal expenditures, 18-19, 162-65, 171-74, 201-2, 204, 332 n. 16
Municipal Secretary (Poona), 195, 196, 206
Muslims, 10; in corporation elections, Agra, 66, 228, 253, 341 n. 24; in corporation politics, Agra, 138-39, 160-61, 189, 262; in general elections, Agra, 217-18, 221-25; in Poona politics, 91, 176-77, 273. *See also* Communal riots

Nagpur, 311 n. 61, 322 n. 14; study of, 311 n. 56
Nagri Sanghatna, 29, 125-29, 318 n. 50; in corporation conflicts, 167-69, 172-73, 194, 199-200; in corporation elections, 147-52, 277; organization of, 45-46, 49, 84-87, 149-51, 268

Nagri Seva Samiti, 271
Nayar, V. K. S., 325 n. 15
Nominations. *See* Party crystallization
Non-Brahminism, 39, 41-43; in Poona Congress, 45-54, 81-82, 89, 239; in Poona corporation, 177, 196-200, 335 n. 19. *See also* Primordial groups
Non-Maharashtrians, 91, 176. *See also* Primordial groups

Oldenburg, Philip K., 311 n. 56, 346 n. 21

Padgett, L. Vincent, 306 n. 3
Panchayati raj, 14; studies of, 310 n. 50, n. 51
Panjabi, Kewal L., 316 n. 32, n. 33
Parasnis, D. B., 308 n. 28
Parenti, Michael, 344 n. 6
Party crystallization, 114-16; in Agra, 66-67, 254-55; in Poona, 46-49, 52-54, 88-91, 271-73
Patterson, Maureen L. P., 316 n. 35, n. 40
Peasants and Workers Party (PWP): formation, 42-43; in Maharashtra politics, 237, 318 n. 57, 322 n. 13; in Poona politics, 84, 149; studies of, 316 n. 35, n. 37
Personal followings, 27, 30, 31, 38, 78, 96. *See also* Baloji; Singh, Seth Achal; Sanas, B. N.
Political conflicts: in Agra, 156-57, 160-63, 165-67, 189; in Poona, 159, 167-77, 193-95, 196-201
Political parties, 26-28, 169-71, 178-79, 280-81. *See also* Congress; Jan Sangh; Praja Socialist Party; Republican Party
Political violence, 228, 335 n. 15. *See also* Communal riots
Poona: administrative politics in, 192-200; character of the city, 6-7, 9, 11-13; corporation politics in, 54-56, 147-51, 197-201, 276-77; governmental organization in, 17-18, 20-21, 23-25, 157-59; political organization in, 38-44, 52-56, 81-88, 235-38, 264-71; studies of, 308 n. 25, n. 26, n. 27, n. 28, n. 31, 309 n. 34, n. 37, 311 n. 62, 321 n. 1, n. 2, n. 6. *See also* Elections, corporation; Elections, general
Poona Municipal Transport (PMT), 24, 158, 197-200
Potter, David C., 310 n. 50, 311 n. 54, 334 n. 1
Powell, G. Bingham, Jr., 346 n. 20
Praja Socialist Party (PSP): in Agra, 38, 54; formation and reorganization of, 41-43, 235-37, 338 n. 24; in Poona corporation, 55-56, 197-99; in Poona politics, 52-54, 55, 81-83, 84-85, 273-74; studies of, 314 n. 8, 316 n. 29, n. 34, 339 n. 25. *See also* Samyukta Socialist Party
Prasad, Ramayan, 312 n. 64
Primordial groups: in corporation politics, 160-62, 166, 175-77, 194-97; in elections,

67-73, 91-100; in intergroup relations, 113, 125-29; in public life, 53-54, 109-10, 177, 295-305 passim. *See also* Congress; Jan Sangh; Republican Party; Voting behavior
Progressive Group, 259, 262-63
Przeworski, Adam, 307 n. 11
Public Works Committee (Poona), 177
Purohit, Vinayak, 320 n. 18

Rashtriya Swayamsevak Sangh (RSS), 37, 40, 210
Recruitment. *See* Administrators, recruitment of; Corporators
"Refugees," 37, 67, 243, 337 n. 1
Republican Party of India (RPI), 125-29; in Agra corporation, 76-77, 116-18, 141-42, 145-46, 166-67, 261-64; in Agra politics, 63-64, 146, 212-14, 217, 252, 340 n. 12; formation of, 34-36; in Maharashtra, 58, 83, 238, 339 n. 33; in Poona, 43, 84, 116-17, 175-77; studies of, 315 n. 21, n. 23. *See also* Party crystallization; Voting behavior
Rosen, George, 309 n. 39
Rosen, Saul, 316 n. 34
Rosenthal, Donald B., 310 n. 49, 345 n. 10, n. 15
Rudolph, Lloyd I., 308 n. 15, 325 n. 15, 344 n. 8
Rudolph, Susanne Hoeber, 344 n. 8

Sainik, 30
Sakal, 45, 82, 86, 88
Sampoorna Maharashtra Samiti (SMS), 237-45, 247, 330 n. 26
Samyukta Maharashtra Samiti (SMS), 29, 235, 272; formation and dissolution, 49-52, 79-80, 82; in Poona corporation, 54-55, 197-99
Samyukta Socialist Party (SSP), 235-37, 245, 273-74; study of, 339 n. 25
Samyukta Vidhayak Dal (SVD), 192. *See also* Charan Singh
Sanghatna. *See* Nagri Sanghatna
Sarvajanik Sabha (Poona), 8
Sayre, Wallace S., 333 n. 21
Scheduled Caste Federation (SCF): in Agra, 35, 36, 314 n. 13; in Poona, 43. *See also* Republican Party
Scheduled Castes, 10, 186, 310 n. 46; demands of, 109, 175-76; policy toward, 54, 309 n. 41; politicization of, 43, 249, 256, 260, 265; in reserved seats, 241-42, 312 n. 76, n. 78. *See also* Jatavs; Khatiks; Mahars; Mangs
Schoenfeld, Benjamin, 339 n. 25
School Committee. *See* Education
Seal, Anil, 308 n. 27, 316 n. 30
Sharma, B. A. V., 318 n. 49, 319 n. 8, 325 n. 9
Sharma, M. P., 308 n. 14

Shiv Sena, 246-47, 269-71, 338 n. 24
Shrader, Lawrence, 310 n. 51
Singh, D. P., 312 n. 68, n. 69
Singh, Jagdish Pratap, 332 n. 15
Sirsikar, V. M., 81, 321 n. 1, n. 11, 346 n. 21
Smallwood, Frank, 307 n. 12
Socialist Party, 41
Socialist Party (Lohia), 41, 235-37, 319 n. 1
Sovani, N. V., et al., 309 n. 34, 310 n. 44, 322 n. 24
Srinivas, M. N., 315 n. 21, n. 22, 344 n. 4
Srivastava, A. L., 309 n. 35
Standing Committee (Poona), 24, 56, 157-58, 175
State Government, oversight by, 18-19; in Agra, 190, 192; in Poona, 158, 167-69, 194, 198, 200. *See also* Supersessions
States Reorganization Commission, 49, 317 n. 46
Steiner, Kurt, 307 n. 12
Stinchcombe, Arthur, 344 n. 7
Suleiman, Michael W., 346 n. 22
Supersessions, 19, 50; in Agra, 19, 142, 187, 189-90, 216-17
Swatantra Dal, 125-29, 218; in corporation agreements, 133-38, 141-46, 154, 155-56; organization of, 75-76, 135, 330 n. 16
Swatantra Party, 222, 228, 271; study of, 315 n. 19

Taalim Sanghs, 111-12
Tambats, 96-98
Taub, Richard P., 334 n. 2, 337 n. 30
Teune, Henry, 307 n. 11
Tinker, Hugh, 17, 311 n. 57, n. 58, n. 60
Tiwari, A. R., 310 n. 46
Transportation Committee (Poona). *See* Poona Municipal Transport
"Tri-dalir" pact, 142, 145-46, 150
Turner, Roy C., 308 n. 15

Turnout: in Agra, 74-75, 220, 256; in Poona, 100, 242

Uttar Pradesh Congress Committee (UPCC), 216, 246; and Agra politics, 59-62, 134, 142, 225-26, 251, 261
Uttar Pradesh, political studies of, 313 n. 81, n. 6, 314 n. 11, 315 n. 21, 316 n. 29, 327 n. 32, 339 n. 1

Vajpeyi, Dhirendra Kumar, 123, 334 n. 9
Vanderbok, William, 346 n. 21
Verney, Douglas, 306 n. 7
Voting behavior: corporation elections, in Agra, 67-75, 256-58; corporation elections, in Poona, 45-46, 52, 91-102, 271-76; general elections, in Agra, 31, 218-25, 225-34, 315 n. 25, 343 n. 51; general elections, in Poona, 44, 52, 81-83, 238-44; in Maharashtra, 52, 83; in Uttar Pradesh, 34, 247. *See also* "Drop-off"; Turnout

Wacha, D. E., 307 n. 13
Wahlke, John, et al., 327 n. 36
Warren, J. H., 312 n. 77
Weber, Max, 334 n. 2
Weiner, Myron, 308 n. 15, 313 n. 6, 314 n. 8, n. 11, 321 n. 1, 345 n. 14
Werlin, Herbert, 307 n. 12
Williams, Oliver P., 102-3, 306 n. 2
Wilson, James Q., 306 n. 6, 307 n. 8, 313 n. 2, n. 3, 344 n. 6
Wolfinger, Raymond E., 306 n. 1, 344 n. 6
Wolpert, Stanley, 308 n. 31

Youth Congress (Poona), 265-66

Zelliot, Eleanor M., 315 n. 23, 322 n. 12
Zilla parishads. See Panchayati raj